SYSTEMATIC THEOLOGY
Apostolic & Contemporary

Vic Reasoner

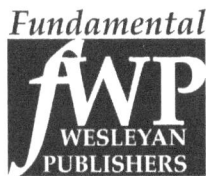

Fundamental
fWP
WESLEYAN PUBLISHERS

2120 Culverson Ave
Evansville, IN 47714-4811

Foreword

In this volume, *Systematic Theology: Apostolic and Contemporary*, Dr. Vic Reasoner has distilled his three-volume *Fundamental Wesleyan Systematic Theology* into one tome. The result is a very readable and accessible summation of the doctrines of the Christian faith. Dr. Reasoner writes as an insider, a deeply committed believer from the Wesleyan perspective. His account is a faithful rendering of "the faith that was once for all delivered to the saints" (Jude 3). I highly recommend this volume as a trustworthy introduction to the Christian faith; it will be especially valuable to believers in the Wesleyan tradition who seek to deepen their understanding of their faith.

Dr. J. Russell Frazier, Associate Professor and Dean of the School of Religion and Christian Ministry, Africa Nazarene University

TABLE of CONTENTS

The bibliography for this volume runs 39 pages. Maximum page restrictions for a one-volume edition prevented it from being included. This is an abridgement of the three-volume *Fundamental Wesleyan Systematic Theology* (2021) which contains a full bibliography.

ABBREVIATIONS

ACCS Ancient Christian Commentary on Scripture. 29 vols. Thomas C. Oden, ed. InterVarsity, 1998-2006.

BDB Brown, Francis, S. R. Driver, and Charles A. Briggs. *Hebrew and English Lexicon of the Old Testament*. Clarendon, 1907.

ACD Oden, Thomas C. ed. *Ancient Christian Doctrine*. 5 vols. InterVarsity, 2009-2010.

ANF The Ante-Nicene Fathers: The Writings of the Fathers Down to A.D. 325. 10 vols. American Reprint of the Edinburgh Edition. Edited by Alexander Roberts and James Donaldson. 1885-1896. Reprint. Eerdmans, 1979.

CF Christian Foundations. Donald G. Bloesch. 7 vols. InterVarsity, 1992-2004.

CRJ Christian Research Journal

CT Christianity Today

GRA God, Revelation and Authority. Carl F. H. Henry. 6 vols. Word, 1976-1983.

ISBE The International Standard Bible Encyclopedia. 4 vols. Geoffrey W. Bromiley, ed. Eerdmans, 1979-1995.

KJV King James Version

LXX The Septuagint - the Greek OT

NT New Testament

NICNT The New International Commentary on the New Testament. 22 vols. Joel B. Green, ed. Eerdmans, 1974-2020.

NICOT The New International Commentary on the Old Testament. 29 vols. Robert L. Hubbard Jr. and Bill T. Arnold, eds. Eerdmans, 1979-2022.

NIDNTT New International Dictionary of New Testament Theology. 4 vols. Edited by Colin Brown. Zondervan, 1975.

NIDOTTE New International Dictionary of Old Testament Theology and Exegesis. 5 Vols. Willem A. VanGemeren, ed. Grand Rapids: Zondervan, 1997.

NPNF A Select Library of the Nicene and Post-Nicene Fathers of the Christian Church. First Series. 14 vols. Edited by Philip Schaff. Second Series. 14 vols. Edited by Philip Schaff and Henry Wace. 1886-1900. Reprint. Eerdmans, 1979.

OT Old Testament

RCS Reformation Commentary on Scripture. 22 vols to date. Timothy George, ed. InterVarsity, 2011-.

TDNT Theological Dictionary of the New Testament. 10 vols. Edited by Gerhard Kittel and Gerhard Friedrich. Translated by Geoffrey W. Bromiley. Eerdmans, 1964–76.

TWOT Theological Wordbook of the Old Testament. 2 vols. R. Laird Harris, ed. Moody, 1980.

WBC Word Biblical Commentary. 61 vols to date. Nancy deClaissé-Walford, OT editor, David B. Capes, NT editor. Word/Thomas Nelson/Zondervan, 1982-.

WTJ Wesleyan Theological Journal

INTRODUCTION
The Theological Method

Our knowledge of God is based upon his self-disclosure. There is a general consciousness of God among all people. He speaks through his creation and our conscience, but his Word is our final authority. We can only have one ultimate authority. Reason, experience, and tradition all help us interpret this Word, but they cannot preempt it as the ultimate authority.

Systematic theology is the attempt to organize the doctrines of Scripture in a comprehensive, consistent, logical flow. We must approach Scripture with the assumption that it does not contradict itself and we must study it inductively. The church has always produced creedal statements of doctrine. These creedal statements unite believers across time and cultural divides. Thus, they constitute an irreducible minimum of fundamental, basic, essential or cardinal doctrines of Christianity.

Every generation faces new questions and challenges. The Bible remains our final authority because it is God's revelation. Every generation stands on the shoulders of previous generations of saints, martyrs, and scholars, but we must be "always reforming." That means we must start with the revelation of Scripture in order to address the needs of our contemporary culture. We are impotent to help our culture, however, if we adopt the prevailing assumptions and philosophy of our culture.

The Knowledge of God

"Can you fathom the mysteries of God? Can you probe the limits of the Almighty?" (Job 11:7). This question was raised in what is perhaps the oldest extant literature in the world. Paul wrote that God is immortal and lives in unapproachable light, "whom no one has seen or can see" (1 Tim 6:16). No one knows the thoughts of God except the Spirit of God. We are able to understand spiritual truth through the Spirit whom we have received from God (1 Cor 2:11-12). Spiritual realities are revealed to us by the Holy Spirit. Wisdom is the result of this knowledge of God, and through this knowledge of God comes the knowledge of self. "The fear of the Lord is the beginning of wisdom" (Ps 111:10).

Our knowledge of God is based upon his self-disclosure. He took the initiative to make himself known. All creation proclaims his existence, but the fountain of knowledge comes from his mouth. There is a God and he is not silent! He has spoken and his Word is holy. The knowledge of God was originally communicated to Adam and Eve by their Creator, who held personal conversations with them. These conversations were passed down by the human family and perpetuated from age to age. But unwritten traditions are vulnerable to distortion or extinction. Therefore, God saw fit to embody them in written revelation, appropriately authenticated and providentially preserved through every age.

The word *revelation* is based on the Greek word *apokalypsis*, an unveiling or disclosure, and *phanerosis*, an exhibition, manifestation, or expression. Therefore, we must be instructed by our Maker, not our own logic. Reason is useful to investigate the evidences of divine authority and interpret the record, but it cannot arbitrate in cases where truth is unknown. Revelation, therefore, is necessary because of the weakness and insufficiency of human reason. Reason must be enlightened by revelation.

Therefore, the holy Scriptures are the starting point in a knowledge of God. This term, *Scripture* or *Scriptures*, whether singular or plural, occurs about fifty times in the NT. Jude wrote that the faith — all the fundamental truths — was handed down as a sacred deposit once for all from the prophets and apostles to the church (v 3).

General Revelation

Every person who comes into the world encounters some degree of light (John 1:9). While sometimes described as *natural revelation*, all divine revelation is supernatural in its origin. General revelation includes nature, God's providential work in history, and the constitution of human beings — including man's religious nature. *Common grace* is God's uncovering of knowledge through means available to all mankind and is inductive.

All the Bible is true, but God has not revealed all truth in the Bible. All truth is God's truth. There are not separate categories of sacred truth and secular truth. Wherever truth is found, is God's truth. Limited reasoning about God can proceed on the basis of natural human intuition, moral insight, and philosophy. Rightly understood, divine grace has already bridged the chasm between natural and revealed theology.

God has revealed himself in nature, yet sinful man suppresses this revelation. God has made his existence plain. His eternal power and divine nature are clearly seen, so that sinful man is without excuse (Rom 1:18-20). God is not left without a witness, even among pagan cultures (Acts 14:17).

Certainly deism overemphasized natural revelation, since it rejected the supernatural revelation of Scripture, but Scripture itself affirms general revelation. We may learn of God's infinite wisdom from the animal life he created.

Ask the animals, and they will teach you, or the birds of the air, and they will tell you; or speak to the earth and it will teach you, or let the fish of the sea inform you (Job 12:7-8).

Psalm 19:1-6 explains general revelation. Pagans tended to worship the sun, moon, and stars instead of the Creator. However, in vv 7-14 the clarity of Scripture is extolled. Although mankind is fallen, he is still a moral and rational being.

In Romans 10:18 Paul quotes Psalm 19:4: "Their voice goes out into all the earth, their words to the ends of the world." This describes God's voice through nature.

In Acts 17:22-24 Paul connected with pagans through the bridge of general revelation. The ancient and modern Greek culture accepted evolution, many gods, and did not believe in sin. To them Paul was a babbler (1 Cor 1:23). Paul's approach in Acts 17 was apologetical, beginning with creation, not Scripture.

Romans 1:18-22 is the primary text on general revelation. The major premise of v 20 is that God's eternal power and deity are evident from creation. The secondary premise is that God's invisible nature can be observed through all things visible. Paul then concludes that no one has an excuse. This is the basis of Anselm's ontological argument, a purely *a priori* argument, that God cannot be conceived not to exist.

Apparently, Anselm wrote *Proslogium* as the culmination of a long mental and spiritual struggle. Suddenly, in the night, light broke through and he quickly wrote in a few pages what came to him. He wrote that God is that Being of which nothing greater can be conceived to exist. God must exist in reality and not only in man's thought. God cannot be merely a figment of our imagination, for we could never conceive of such a perfect being independent of its reality. The fact that we can conceive of his being means that his reality has a necessary existence.

Romans 2:12-16 also deals with general revelation through nature and conscience. According to this passage, even those who do not have the holy Scriptures have the moral law written on their hearts. In the opening words of *Mere Christianity*, C. S. Lewis explained, "Human beings, all over the earth, have this curious idea that they ought to behave a certain way, and cannot really get rid of it." Lewis argued that God was behind this law of nature.[1]

Acts 10:34-35 explains that Cornelius was accepted by God, although he was not regenerate. Wesley commented that Cornelius was "accepted through Christ, though he knows him not."[2]

There are four contrasts between general and special revelation.

- General revelation is made to everyone everywhere, while special revelation is made to a particular people in particular places, through Christ and the biblical authors.
- General revelation is natural because it comes through the natural order. Special revelation is supernatural, involving the incarnation of the Son and the inspiration of the Scriptures.
- General revelation is continuous, while special revelation is finished in Christ and the Scriptures.
- General revelation is creational, revealing God's glory in creation, while special revelation is saving, revealing God's grace in Christ.

Yet modernist theology has claimed that the distinction between natural and revealed theology has largely been abandoned. Natural theology in the seventeenth and eighteenth centuries was associated with deism and started with the doctrine of God and creation. Karl Barth rejected natural revelation in the strongest terms, but at the same time failed to uphold a proper view of divine revelation.

While we must affirm the consequences of sin, including a darkened mind, we must also affirm that the image of God in

---

[1]Lewis, *Mere Christianity*, 17-39.

[2]Wesley, *Notes*, 304.

man remains — including the capacity to reason. While sin is moral insanity, the preliminary grace of the Holy Spirit at least temporarily awakens the darkened mind to truth. Reason ultimately leads to God but cannot operate independent of God. We must strive to balance the fact that our intellect is darkened due to the fall, with the fact that we can still comprehend God's revelation because our rational ability has not been completely destroyed. If the effects of the fall totally destroyed our ability to think, then no rational case could be made for or against anything and the evangelistic call for the sinner to come and reason (Isa 1:18) is futile.

God gave revelation, to be grasped by reason, and since both reason and revelation come from the same source, it is impossible that one contradicts the other. However, revelation may contain truth which is above the reason of man. The Christian religion therefore is a direct revelation of God, since unaided human intellect is insufficient to find out the being, attributes, and works of God or the nature of man and God's purpose and plan for him.

God is the source of all truth and he enables the human mind to recognize truth. The inability of autonomous reason to acknowledge God is not based on an intellectual deficiency, but an unwillingness to submit to the implications of his sovereignty.

The preliminary grace of God, working through the operation of the Holy Spirit, awakens the depraved sinner and enables the darkened mind to think rationally. The faith required for salvation is not a mystical leap, but rather a rational response to the compelling evidence enabled by the Holy Spirit. God calls the sinner to come and reason with him. His Spirit awakens and strives with us.

But while general revelation discloses that God is the Creator, only Scripture reveals him as redeemer. General revelation is sufficient to condemn us but not sufficient to lead us to saving faith in Jesus Christ. While general revelation is not exhaustive, what it reveals is clear. The attempt by sinful man to suppress divine revelation is never wholly successful. Creation, providence, reason, conscience, beauty, and personal experience are all sources of theology.

Progressive Revelation

Scripture was not given in a systematic format. Rather, it was given "precept upon precept, precept upon precept, line upon line, line upon line, here a little, there a little" (Isa 28:10). God begins with the human race as though we were infants, gradually revealing more pedagogically, building upon what he previously disclosed. Early revelation was significant, but incomplete.

The concept of progressive revelation does not imply a process of Darwinian evolution, but rather of God's disclosure which brings man through the state of infancy in the Old Testament to the state of maturity in the NT. God's revelation climaxes with the death and resurrection of Jesus Christ.

According to John 1:14, God became flesh. While no one has seen God at any time, the Son declared or exegeted him (v 18). Paul wrote that he appeared in a body (1 Tim 3:16). According to Matthew 11:27, "No one knows the Father except the Son and those to whom the Son chooses to reveal him." This declaration affirms the necessity of divine revelation.

Progressive revelation is described in Hebrews 1:1-2, "God has spoken to our forefathers through the prophets at many times and in various ways, but in these last days he has spoken to us by his Son." This implies a progression and a culmination. For centuries the progress was slow, but with the advent of Jesus Christ it culminated within a generation, resulting in the closing of the canon.

Systematic Theology

Any serious reader of Scripture will eventually notice patterns and progressions of thought. To the degree that we can construct an overview of Bible doctrine that is consistent with the whole of Scripture, to that degree we can articulate and share our faith.

Where systematic theology is absent, it is replaced by a reductionist grasp of doctrine. If the whole counsel of God is not preached, the congregation will hear the same sermon every Sunday and they will be vulnerable to false doctrines. Thus, doctrine cannot be avoided. The only options are false doctrine, partial truth, or systematic theology.

Doctrine is important since it is impossible to believe what is unknown. "How can they believe in the one of whom they have not heard?" (Rom 10:9-17). Correct doctrine is a safeguard against false teaching. While it is commonly asserted that doctrine divides, it is actually *false* doctrine which divides the church. Correct doctrine equips us for service. "All Scripture is God-breathed and useful . . . so that the man of God may be thoroughly equipped for every good work" (2 Tim 3:17). In the Great Commission, Jesus charges his church to teach all nations (Matt 28:20). The greater consistency with which the church teaches truth to the world, the greater likelihood exists that the world will be convinced.

Based on Titus 3:4-8, Matt Perman explained that doctrine leads to good works and this connection is fueled by joy. Legalism may get some people to do good works, but it will never get anyone excited about doing good works. On the other hand, the gospel makes us eager to be productive.[3]

Christian theology is the systematic arrangement of the truths pertaining to the revelation of God. It is a comprehensive statement of what Scripture teaches presented in logical order. However, some theologians try to impose an overarching theme, a core axiom, or a controlling motif on the Bible, and arrange a coherent system around that assumption. Such a method always eventuates in a "Procrustean bed." Whatever does not fit the

---

[3]Perman, *What's Best Next*, 107-112.

presupposition is discarded. But we are admonished to buy truth and do not sell it (Prov 23:23).

Systematic theology must be based on solid biblical exegesis and hermeneutics. Scripture must be interpreted by utilizing the rules of grammar and the facts of history. This leads to biblical theology, and biblical theology leads to a systematic theology. Through the inductive method, Scripture is first exegeted and then connected to form more general conclusions. Every relevant passage on a particular topic must be identified and a summary statement formulated which is consistent with all of the pertinent data. This process is sometimes described as the hermeneutical spiral or circle.

The goal of systematic theology is to formulate a comprehensive, consistent statement of what Scripture teaches. Such work exemplifies the biblical concept of teaching. This should result in edification, obedience, service, and worship. Our goal must be "love, which comes from a pure heart and a good conscience and a sincere faith" (1 Tim 1:5).

Systematic theology becomes artificial whenever we approach Scripture with our own preconceived notions and attempt to deduce conclusions from isolated statements. Any theological approach which operates on this basis will have to ignore or discount passages which do not fit their presuppositions.

To the degree that our theology merely reflects our own biases, theology becomes divisive and arbitrary. Most doctrinal wars stem from a disagreement on the proper source for doctrine. We will inevitably arrive at different conclusions if we start with different sources of information. Extra-biblical sources such as the book of Mormon, the Quran, or the Apocrypha will interject concepts which distort or contradict divine revelation.

The Priority of Scripture

We cannot have more than one ultimate authority. Where the Bible is rejected as infallible, it is always replaced by another man-made authority which is then regarded as infallible. For modern man, the evolutionary process, dialectic communism, democracy (the voice of the people is the voice of God), or most likely their own reason, is assumed to be infallible.

Ultimately, either man or God determines truth. Neutrality is a myth. Since we have the Word of God, the words of the Almighty constitute our final authority. What we arrive at deductively, we then study inductively. Thus, the Bible is the foundation for our world-view.

We have the illumination of the Spirit. "He will guide you into all truth" (John 16:13). We also have the ability to reason, the God-given faculty for understanding information and developing logical thought. However, our minds have been clouded by sin. Sin is rebellion against God's authority. The tendency of autonomous man is to suppress the truth when it leads away from his desired end. Wesley was clear that reason must be "under the guidance of the Spirit of God."[4] Thus, we do not reject reason, but we do reject autonomous reason. The very idea that the cosmos, with its complex order, evolved by random chance would not be taken seriously except that rebellious men attempt to suppress truth.

> The man without the Spirit does not accept the things that come from the Spirit of God, for they are foolishness to him, and he cannot understand them, because they are spiritually discerned (1 Cor 2:14).

Although man cannot find God on his own, God provides preliminary grace. Jesus promised, "If anyone wants to do his will, he shall know concerning the doctrine, whether it is from God or whether I speak on my own authority" (John 7:17). Commenting on these words, Augustine said, "For understanding is the reward of faith. Therefore do not seek to understand in order

---

[4]Wesley, "Case of Reason Impartially Considered," Sermon #70, 2.10.

to believe, but believe that thou mayest understand."[5] Therefore, faith is the precondition of a proper understanding; submission is necessary before we can receive knowledge.

Tradition, experience, and reason cannot be the basis or starting point for an adequate theology. They do not carry any weight of authority, but have value in clarifying our interpretation of Scripture and illustrating the axioms of Scripture. They are not sources of authority, but tools with which to evaluate Scripture.

When biblical infallibility is rejected, *sola scriptura* cannot be sustained. The tendency of modernist theology is to advocate multiple sources of authority.

The valid functions of tradition, experience, and reason are to validate our interpretation of Scripture. Tradition, experience, and reason cannot establish doctrine but they can challenge our understanding of Scripture. For example, regarding the doctrine of Christian perfection, Wesley utilized the test of experience. He declared, "If I were convinced that none in England had attained what has been so clearly and strongly preached . . . I should be clearly convinced that we had all mistaken the meaning of those scriptures."[6]

Kept within their subordinate role, tradition, experience, and reason illuminate and apply scriptural truth. However, we cannot build a theology upon any of them.

We must grasp the priority and primacy of Scripture. We cannot have a dual authority or embrace theological pluralism. Unless we contend for the sufficiency of Scripture we will eventually be proving our positions on the basis of tradition, which can lead to legalism; experience, which tends toward charismaticism; or reason, which leads to a gnostic rationalism.

---

[5]Augustine, *Homilies on the Gospels*, *NPNF*1 7:184.

[6]Wesley, *BE Works*, 13:178,79.

The Use and Limitations of Reason

John Wesley declared, "It is a fundamental principle with us that to renounce reason is to renounce religion, that religion and reason go hand in hand, and that all irrational religion is false religion."[7] Yet for Wesley, *reason* meant logic which utilized inductive and deductive reasoning, not metaphysical constructions. Thus he asked, "Is it not reason (assisted by the Holy Ghost) which enables us to understand what the Holy Scriptures declare concerning the being and attributes of God?"[8]

Wesley accepted an informal confidence in the average person's ability to discern truth and goodness without sophisticated philosophic training, because we are created in the image of God and enabled by the Holy Spirit.

The ability to reason is a gift from God and a component of the image of God in man. While Paul warned against "hollow and deceptive philosophy" in Colossians 2:8, the caution is against pursuing worldly wisdom apart from God's Word — not a prohibition against thinking. Rather it is a warning against sifting God's revelation and accepting only those statements which are acceptable to human reason.

Wisdom is not inherently worldly. According to Proverbs 4:7, we are to seek wisdom and understanding. But theology must not be confounded with philosophy. Christian philosophy would probably be more devoted to general revelation, while Christian theology would restrict itself to a study of Scripture.

Philosophers tend to downplay the significance of history, while theologians see divine revelation occurring in particular events in history. Every humanistic philosophy represents the rationalization of a false worldview or religion. True theology necessarily excludes the worldview and metaphysical claims of

---

[7]Wesley, *Letter* to Thomas Rutherforth, 3.4; 28 March 1768.

[8]Wesley, "Case of Reason Impartially Considered," Sermon # 70, 1.6.

philosophy. With Blaise Pascal, we agree that the God of the philosophers is not the God of Abraham, Isaac, and Jacob.

The Hebrew word *yada* does not mean knowledge through reason; it is knowledge through direct experience. It is not contemplative or speculative knowledge, but rather relational knowledge.

Roger Olson asked, "Has God been held hostage by philosophy?"[9] Alan Padgett warned against wedding any particular philosophy to Christian theology in such a way that the philosophy is allowed to set the theological agenda.[10]

Furthermore, philosophy is always in flux. By definition, process theology must evolve into something else. But it is also possible to be always in process without ever arriving at anything conclusive (2 Tim 3:7). Dialectical theology is open-ended theology and its formulations are always tentative.

Tertullian argued in AD 203 that there should be no relationship between philosophy and theology. He asked rhetorically, "What indeed has Athens to do with Jerusalem? What concord is there between the Academy and the Church? What between heretics and Christians?"[11]

However, Augustine, writing in 397, felt that theology can be elucidated by philosophy. He stressed the priority of faith, but adopted the philosophy of Plato as a vehicle for helping us understand our theology.[12]

In the thirteenth century Thomas Aquinas took a third approach, establishing theology by means of philosophy — primarily Aristotle's arguments for the existence of God.[13] Aquinas also believed that truth also comes by divine revelation. Man's ulti-

----

[9]Olson, "God Held by Philosophy," 30-34.

[10]Padgett, "Putting Reason in Its Place," 263-278.

[11]Tertullian, *Prescription Against Heretics*, ANF 3:246.

[12]Augustine, *On Christian Doctrine*, NPNF1 2:549-554.

[13]Aquinas, *Summa contra Gentiles* (1259–1265).

mate happiness comes from the contemplation or vision of God. However, since revelation and reason both come from God they cannot be in conflict. He hoped to demonstrate from Romans 1:20 that all knowledge is based on sense experiences and the deductions made from them by reason. He failed because he tended to make reason sovereign. He also failed because of his doctrine of man as a rational creature, based on Aristotle who taught man is not a religious creature but a rational animal. Instead of opening the door to faith, philosophers eventually dismissed the validity of the Thomistic fivefold demonstration of the existence of God based on philosophic logic. The world then became secular — assuming that God's existence had been disproved.

We are exhorted to be prepared to answer everyone who asks us to give the reason for the hope that we have (1 Pet 3:15). This statement by Peter presumes that our Christian faith is reasonable. It also implies that we must have some coherent grasp of our faith. The Greek word for *reason* in this verse is *apologia*. It contains the word *logos*, which means *logic*. The logos of God describes an intelligible spoken or written word. The Gospel of John uses *logos* to describe Jesus Christ, but also as a proposition to be believed and regarded as expressive of faith in Christ. It must also be noted that Jesus Christ himself employed logic in his teachings.

Yet we cannot reduce true religion to rationalism, which is a belief in the uniformity of natural causes in a closed system. Were this the case, then nothing would be beyond human ability to discover and explain through the rational process. The rationalist declares "I believe because I understand." But we are not saved by logical deduction. For some evangelicals, conversion is merely an intellectual decision. Such theologians as B. B. Warfield, Gordon H. Clark, and Carl F. H. Henry believed a sinner can be reasoned into faith.[14] Yet true salvation is miracu-

---

[14]Bebbington, "Rating Our Theologians," 94.

lous. The demons referenced in James 2:19 are lost because they fail to believe the propositions which follow the existence of God. When we could not find God through our rational powers, God revealed himself through his Word. We believe in God, not because he is the product of our rational processes, but because he has spoken to us through his Word. Based on the statement of Augustine, in 1077 Anselm wrote, "I do not seek to understand that I may believe, but I believe that I may understand: for this I also believe, that unless I believe I will not understand."[15] This shortened phrase, "faith seeking understanding," is often regarded as the best definition of theology.

Yet there are also those who despise and vilify reason, substituting their own fanaticism. Reason is necessary in order to understand and explain the Scriptures. However, reason cannot produce faith, hope, love, or virtue.

In the early nineteenth century, Immanuel Kant substituted the human reason for the authority of Scripture. He did not directly attack scriptural authority, but he re-interpreted Scripture rationalistically. He also re-interpreted the person and work of Christ, reducing the historical Christ to the personification of the idea of the good.

Too much theology has been produced by the unregenerate who are in rebellion against God or who have appointed themselves to stand in judgment over God's revelation. Only those who have eternal life know God (John 17:3).

Perquisites for theological study include humility, reverence, patience, prayer for divine illumination, the obedience of faith, integrity, and the willingness to suffer for truth. We must approach our quest for the knowledge of God with humility. Paul warns that knowledge puffs up, but the man who loves God is known by God (1 Cor 8:1-3). "Let not the wise man boast of his wisdom or the strong man boast of his strength, but let him who

---

[15]Anselm, *Proslogion*, 6.

boasts boast about this: that he understands and knows me" (Jer 9:23).

We know only partially (1 Cor 13:12). No human has all the information necessary to understand every detail; we are fallible. Paul wrote that when he came to Corinth, "I did not come with eloquence or human wisdom as I proclaimed to you the testimony about God. For I resolved to know nothing while I was with you except Jesus Christ and him crucified" (1 Cor 2:1-2). We do not come to saving faith through logical arguments or proof texts alone.

The Use of Deductive and Inductive Logic

Deductive logic reasons from the general to the particular. It rejects experience, relying on abstract logic. The inherent danger is that deductive reasoning starts with an invalid premise. However, deductive logic is valid when the premise is Scriptural.

The premise may be based on *a priori* knowledge or empirical knowledge, which is claimed intuitively as self-evident. However, what is regarded as self-evident by one generation may be far from self-evident to earlier generations and rejected by later generations.

But if the premises in deductive reasoning are true, the conclusion *must* be true. If the premises in inductive reasoning are true, the conclusion may or may not be true.

In Acts 17:1-3 Paul reasoned with people at Thessalonica, providing evidence from the Scripture that Jesus is the Christ. The Greek verb *dialegomai* is the basis for our word *dialogue*. However, here it describes the process of supporting a conclusion by placing Scripture beside (*paratithemi*) it. According to Acts 17:17 Paul dialogued in the synagogue.

Inductive logic reasons from the particular to the general. When Paul was taken to the Areopagus and saw the inscription to an unknown God, he employed inductive logic. He even quoted their own philosophers in order to move them to a general conclusion (Acts 17:16-34).

Advocates of the inductive Bible study method sometimes reject deductive reasoning, falsely asserting that it was invented by Aristotle and calling it Western logic. However, logic has no geographic boundaries. Eastern philosophy cannot avoid the law of non-contradiction.

Advocates of the inductive method claim that we should approach the Scriptures with no prior assumptions, but this is not entirely possible. The very fact that we choose to study the Scriptures instead of some other writing implies some presuppositions as to its importance. And the very technique of immersion into the text, preferable in its original language, implies some prior assumptions.

The inherent danger in inductive reasoning is over-generalization. But inductive logic only leads to probable conclusions. It is perfectly consistent to accept the premises of a valid inductive argument but to deny that a certain conclusion follows. The degree of certainty depends on how broad was the sample which was examined. Thus, where the Bible provides only limited information, one cannot always arrive at a dogmatic conclusion.

All the observations we make inductively are viewed through our individual perspective. Only God can observe everything absolutely objectively. We must approach Scripture with an open mind, but an open mind is *not* an empty mind. In Luke 24:45 Jesus opened their minds to understand the Scriptures.

Inductive logic can employ two types of probability. *A priori* describes probability prior to experience or observed facts. It moves from cause to effect. This approach leads to abstract philosophy.

A posteriori describes probability after experience or observed facts. It moves from effect to cause. This is empirical probability, based on what is observed through the senses.

Both are valid, although the theological method is *a posteriori*, beginning with the data furnished by revelation, rather than *a priori*, beginning with meta-physical first principles.

Deductive reasoning may be used to provide specific doctrine from which doctrinal conclusions are drawn by the inductive process. In other words, conclusions deduced can become data for the inductive process. Deductive reasoning may also be used to test the reliability of the conclusions drawn from inductive reasoning.

Inductive study provides the necessary analytical knowledge of the Bible in order to deductively build Bible doctrine. Deductive study researches and builds doctrine which informs inductive Bible study. This then results in drawing out even more meaning from the text. Inductive advocates say that we should let the Bible say what it says and not attempt to impose our assumptions on the text. Certainly this is a valid concern, but we should not assume that the unregenerate mind can grasp spiritual truth unless illuminated by the Holy Spirit. Furthermore, their inductive topical studies can be subjectively chosen.

However, when we deduce conclusions which are not clearly stated in Scripture, we must allow other Christians to disagree with our conclusions or at least with our terminology. Thus, Wesley did not insist on the term *Trinity*, because it is not found in Scripture.[16] However, he was very deeply trinitarian in his theology because it can be deduced from Scripture. He believed that the explanation of the Trinity in the Athanasian Creed was the best he ever saw,[17] yet he was uncomfortable with the language in this creed which consigned those who disagreed with its language to hell.

Thus, we start with divine revelation, not autonomous human reason. However, we must use the logical processes of human reason in order to properly understand Scripture.

The Use and Limitations of Tradition

Wesley valued tradition. He wrote in his *Address to the Clergy*,

---

[16]Wesley, "On the Trinity," Sermon # 55, § 4.

[17]Wesley, "On the Trinity," § 3.

Can anyone who spends several years in those seats of learning, be excused if they do not add to that learning the reading of the Fathers? The Fathers are the most authentic commentators on Scripture, for they were nearest the fountain and were eminently endued with that Spirit by whom all Scripture was given. It will be easily perceived, I speak chiefly of those who wrote before the council of Nicaea.[18]

But he also declared, "If by *catholic* principles you mean any other than *scriptural*, they weigh nothing with *me*: I allow no other rule, whether of faith or practice, than the Holy Scriptures."[19] Adam Clarke wrote that he was not averse to consulting the Greek and Latin fathers of the church or the councils for their opinions, but "no opinions, of fathers or doctors, no decisions of popes or councils" can be authoritative for Christian doctrine. The doctrines of Protestantism rest on the Bible alone.[20]

But is the Bible our final authority or our sole authority? There is a difference between *sola scriptura* and *solo scriptura* (Scripture only). None of the magisterial Reformers held to a "Scripture only" position. "Scripture was their primary and ultimate authority, but they were committed to reading it in the light of how the church had understood it across the centuries."[21]

Wesley advised, "All the knowledge you want is comprised in one book — the Bible. When you understand this, you will know enough." He then went on in the same letter to recommend

---

[18]Wesley, "Address to Clergy," *Works*, 10:484.

[19]Wesley, *Journal*, 11 June 1739. See also his letter to James Hervey, 20 March 1739.

[20]Clarke, *Works*, 6:273; 3:132.

[21]Giles, *Eternal Generation of the Son*, 53.

commentaries and other practical books, philosophers, poets, and a historian.[22] Clarke wrote,

> No man ever taught me the doctrine I embraced; I received it singly by reading the Bible. From that alone I saw that justification by faith, the witness of the Spirit, and the sanctification of the heart were all attainable. These I saw as clearly as I do now; and from them I have never swerved. I often read the Bible on my knees. When I came to a passage I did not fully understand, I said, "Lord, here is thy book; it is given for the salvation of man; it can be no salvation to him unless he understand it; thou has the key of this text, unlock it to me;" and praying thus I generally received such light as was satisfactory to myself.[23]

When Marcion first raised the question in the second century concerning which books were canonical, church councils did not arbitrarily make that decision. Instead they made a statement recognizing which books had already been received and used as God-given. The church did not determine which books to include as Scripture. While modernists teach that the church produced the Scriptures, conservatives teach that the people of God are those who responded in faith to the Word of God.

The early ecumenical councils did not determine truth by a majority vote. Their statements were true to the degree that they were accurate summaries of biblical authority. Some council decisions actually contradicted the decisions rendered by other councils. Wesley pointed out that church councils not only "may err," but "have erred."[24] They are only true so long as they do

---

[22]Wesley, *Letter* to Philothea Briggs, 25 Jan 1771.

[23]Etheridge, *Life of Clarke*, 358.

[24]Wesley, *Journal*, 13 Sept 1736.

reflect biblical teaching. Essentially, the ecumenical consensus unraveled after the first five hundred years of the church.

Oden explained that general councils were not infallible, but the Spirit that guides the church is fully trustworthy. Consent within a council was confirmation that their decision was Spirit-led.[25] While I can accept the concept of guidance and illumination in church councils, infallibility should be restricted only to the inspiration of Scripture.

Roman Catholic theology used to say that there are two valid and authoritative sources — Scripture and tradition.[26] Today, they tend to speak of the "one source" of revelation, but claim that tradition is part of that "one source." In either case, they continue to deny the sufficiency of Scripture.

Their position is that Scripture and tradition have been deposited with the Roman Catholic Church and the responsibility for their interpretation lies with the magisterium of the church, which they define as their own organization. According to Roman dogma, when the pope speaks *ex cathedra*, he is infallible. In reality, however, they have tended to misinterpret Scripture and elevate church dogma above Scripture.

Logically, there can only be one ultimate authority, and this is addressed by the Protestant doctrine of *sola scriptura*. What Luther meant by sola scriptura is essentially what Wesley meant by *homo unius libri* (a man of one book). Martin Luther declared, "A simple layman armed with Scripture is to be believed above a Pope or a council without it."[27] When the Diet of Worms demanded that he recant, he replied

> Unless I am convinced by Scripture and clear reason —
> I do not accept the authority of popes and councils, for
> they have contradicted each other — my conscience is

---

[25]Oden, *The Living God*, 349.

[26]Wesley, "Popery Calmly Considered," *BE Works*, 14:217.

[27]Bainton, *Here I Stand*, 90.

captive to the Word of God. I cannot and will not recant anything, for to go against conscience is neither right nor safe.[28]

Ultimately, I cannot trust in ecclesiastical authority, based on tradition, to guarantee my salvation. Thus, Protestants uphold the right to private judgment and the liberty of conscience.

The Protestant doctrine of *sola scriptura* was not meant to deny the existence of general revelation, but only the infallibility of popes, councils, and extra-biblical tradition. The biblical texts that support *sola scriptura* do not view God's general revelation as a rival to his written revelation.

An over-emphasis upon tradition will lead to legalism. According to Mark 7:1-13 it is possible to zealously uphold human traditions while at the same time setting aside the commands of God's Word. Jesus indicted the Pharisees, "Thus you nullify the word of God for the sake of your tradition" (Matt 15:6). Wesley taught, "Enjoin nothing that the Bible does not clearly enjoin. Forbid nothing that it does not clearly forbid."[29]

Compliant personalities tend to submit to tradition and perpetuate the status quo. Jesus accused the Pharisees of letting go of the commands of God, while holding on to the traditions of men (Mark 7:8). The Pharisees very rarely appealed to Scripture to support their opinions. Rather, they cited rabbinical precedent. Thus, Jesus frequently rebuked them by saying, "Have you not read?"

Certainly, the teachings passed down from authoritative sources, inspired by the Holy Spirit, are valid. Such passages as 1 Corinthians 11:23 and 2 Thessalonians 2:15, 3:6 refer to apostolic tradition. But extra-biblical tradition has no authority.

---

[28]Bainton, *Here I Stand*, 144. *Clear* or *evident reason*, as Luther used the term meant a "logical inference from biblical principles" [Packer, "Sola Scriptura," 44].

[29]Wesley, *Letter* to John Dickins, 26 Dec 1789.

The Use and Limitations of Experience

True salvation is heartfelt, but we should not seek any experience the Scriptures do not command us to seek. I have no authority to preach my experience, and you are under no obligation to seek my experience. Contrary to the modern charismatic emphasis, Wesley cautioned that if a person sought after anything but more love, he was misguided.[30] John Wesley wrote: "Try all things by the written Word, and let all bow down before it. You are in danger of [fanaticism] every hour, if you depart ever so little from Scripture; yea, or from the plain, literal meaning of any text, taken in connection with the context."[31]

Wesley wrote in his *Journal* of a conversation with John Simpson. While Wesley believed him to be sincere, he said Simpson "is led into a thousand mistakes by one wrong principle, the making *inward impressions* his rule of action, and not the *written Word*."[32]

Robert Barclay, the Quaker theologian, denied that spiritual revelation had to be tested by the Scriptures.[33] Wesley responded, "The Scriptures are the touchstone whereby Christians examine all, real or supposed, revelations. In all cases they appeal to the law and to the testimony, and try every spirit thereby."[34]

Friedrich Schleiermacher (1768-1834) began his theology with personal experience, not with Scripture. But experience is valid when it comports with biblical norms (1 John 4:1). The persuasion of experience is limited to the person who had the experience.

---

[30]Wesley, *BE Works*, 13:114.

[31]Wesley, *BE Works*, 13:113. Wesley used the word *enthusiasm*.

[32]Wesley, *Journal*, 22 June 1742.

[33]Barclay, *Apology*, 13, 38.

[34]Wesley, "Letter to Person Joined with the Quakers," *BE Works*, 14:309.

Truth is objective, which means that it is open to verification. Truth is what corresponds to reality. This is all in opposition to existential, pragmatic, and subjective views of truth which are the presuppositions of modernism hermeneutics.

Old modernism was concerned with truth, but they did not see it as divinely revealed. Neoorthodoxy is concerned with revelation, but they do not see it as conveying propositional truth.

Mormons claim that we can know the book of Mormon is from God through a "burning in the bosom." Yet the book of Mormon contains anachronisms and historical inaccuracies. Therefore, our subjective experience must be confirmed through objective verification. If existential feelings have no basis in propositional truth, they cannot be valid. Experience must correspond with objective truth.

Full Assurance

In the theological methods just referenced: tradition, experience, or philosophy, the seeker is attempting to define the Almighty. On the other hand, if we start with God's Word, we are attempting to grasp what he has revealed. The difference amounts to whether we define God according to our assumptions or whether we change our assumptions based on what God has revealed.

The verb *plerophoreo* is made up of two words: *full* and *to carry*. It means fully assured. One cannot be *fully* assured and doubt simultaneously.

Plerophoreo is used as a verb in Colossians 4:12 to describe the spiritual maturity of Epaphras. It is used as a noun in Colossians 2:2 where Paul expresses his desire that they might know the freedom of mind and confidence that comes from a full understanding of the mystery of God in Christ. This full assurance of understanding includes a systematic grasp of all the truths and treasures of the faith. This full assurance of understanding is an abiding and continual affirming by the Spirit of truth which produces a life of confidence.

Scripture also speaks of the full assurance of faith in 1 Thessalonians 1:5 and Hebrews 10:22. Wesley taught this full assurance of faith is "the common privilege of Christians."[35] He wrote,

> The plerophory (or full assurance) of faith is such a divine testimony that we are reconciled to God as excludes all doubt and fear concerning it. This refers only to what is present.[36]

Scripture even promises the full assurance of hope. The full assurance of hope in Hebrews 6:11 should be understood as an objective confidence based on the promises in God's Word regarding the success of Christ's kingdom. I am suggesting that it should be defined in a corporate sense — faith in the power of the gospel and faith in the final triumph of Christ's kingdom on earth.

According to W. B. Pope, the full assurance or *pleophory* of faith, of hope, and of understanding are three various forms of the same thing — the sure conviction of the reality of the object personally trusted in, hoped for, and apprehended in knowledge.[37]

If any distinction can be made, it seems that the full assurance of understanding refers to objective truth, the full assurance of faith refers to personal salvation, and the full assurance of hope describes a hope for the future. Perfect love always hopes (1 Cor 13:7).

In contrast to those who are ever learning but never able to come to a knowledge of the truth (2 Tim 3:7), assurance describes a spiritual maturity in which the believer lives in confidence of the truth. Paul said he was persuaded (*peitho*; Rom

---

[35]Wesley, *Letter* to Dr. Rutherforth, 28 March 1768.

[36]Wesley, *Letter* to Elizabeth Ritchie, 6 Oct 1778.

[37]Pope, *Prayers of St. Paul*, 214.

8:38, 14:14; 2 Tim 1:5) or fully convinced. John uses the verb *eideo* sixteen times and the verb *ginosko* twenty-four times in 1 John. In this general letter John deals with objective knowledge and subjective assurance. The noun *parrhesia* describing boldness and confidence, also occurs four times.

We do not have to be tossed back and forth with every new theological trend (Eph 4:14). We can know what we believe, and that belief can be rooted in a reality that corresponds with Scripture and produce a transformed life. We know God exists and his Word is true. We know we are forgiven and accepted. We know that we have been born again and that we have the Holy Spirit. We know that in the end truth will conquer.[38] Such assurance is based upon the Word of God and is made personal through the indwelling Holy Spirit.

The Creeds of Christendom

Creedal statements are essentially a systematic statement of fundamental Christian theology. They originated in order to prepare believers for baptism, to guard against heresy, and to provide a means through which the corporate body of Christ can confess their faith, as instructed in Romans 10:9-10. They were not written in order to formulate doctrine, but as a defense against heresies.

New Christians were not expected to articulate complicated theology, however. Examples in Acts 8:26-30, 16:25-34 indicate that new converts were baptized quickly and were not required to attend seminary first.

While it can be legitimate to require church leaders to subscribe to a more comprehensive doctrinal statement, a strict requirement for adherence to specific philosophic and theological

---

[38]John Wyclif stated this belief [Schaff, *History of the Christian Church*, 6:320].

language not contained in Scripture itself may violate the doctrine of the sufficiency of Scripture.

According to Thomas Oden, an article of faith has three conditions: it must be based on revelation, stated in Scripture, and universally accepted within the church.[39] In Latin, the Apostles' Creed begins with the word *credo*, which means *I believe*. Everyone believes something. Often, however, we declare what we do not believe. An atheist does not believe in God. An agnostic does not know what he believes. To declare that you do not believe in creeds merely becomes your statement of what you do *not* believe.

Some denominations claim that a creed is sectarian. Some organizations assert "no creed but Christ." This, then, becomes their creed. Noncreedal churches accept members solely on a personal profession of faith — but faith in what?

> The effort to be practicing Christians without knowing what Christianity is about must always fail. The true Christian should be, indeed must be, a theologian. He must know at least something of the wealth of truth revealed in the Holy Scriptures. And he must know it with sufficient clarity to state it and defend his statement. And what can be stated and defended is a creed.[40]

According to Matthew 24:24, false Christs will appear and deceive the very elect. We must trust in the Christ who was born of the Virgin Mary, who suffered under Pontius Pilate, who was crucified, dead, buried, and rose again on the third day. Most of the Apostles' Creed focuses on the person and work of Jesus Christ.

The earliest creed was "Jesus is Lord." But over time it became necessary to explain the implications of that declaration

---

[39]Oden, *The Living God*, 344.

[40]Tozer, *That Incredible Christian*, 22-23.

more fully. The earliest summaries of Christian teaching were to prepare people for baptism. Rufinus explained that the Apostles' Creed is not written on paper or parchment, "but is retained in the hearts of the faithful, that it may be certain that no one has learnt it by reading, as is sometimes the case with unbelievers, but by tradition from the Apostles."[41]

An early Christian statement was hidden in the Greek word for *fish* — *ichthus*. This word became an acronym which declared Jesus (*I*) Christ (*ch*) God's (*th*) Son (*u*), Savior (*s*).

Orthodox creedal statements are not divisive. The great ecumenical creeds of the church, the Apostles' Creed, the Nicene Creed, and the Athanasian Creed were all formulated *before* the church divided.

The Apostles' Creed may have been an expansion of Matthew 28:19. It was known to Irenaeus and Tertullian by the latter part of the second century, with the exception of two or thee phrases.

The creeds were formulated in response to error which threatened to divide or bring schism into the church. We have always had to defend orthodoxy against legalism, mysticism, rationalism, and modernism. Peter refers to the straight way (2 Pet 2:15). He utilized the Greek word *euthus* to describe the way or road that leads to truth, salvation, and heaven. In contrast, false doctrine is a twisted, crooked road. When theologians employ their own logic in order to justify their presupposition, the result is similar to the blacksmith who advertised, "All kinds of fancy twistings and turnings done here."

As early as AD 190, Irenaeus summarized the Christian faith, which was under attack by the gnostics.[42] This presupposes

---

[41]Rufinus, *Commentary on the Apostles' Creed*, *NPNF2* 3:543.

[42]Irenaeus, *Against Heresies*, *ANF* 1:315-567; especially books 3-5. As a boy, Irenaeus sat under the ministry of Polycarp, who in turn was discipled by the Apostle John.

that there is an objective body of teaching that Christians are expected to confess as their faith.

Romans 16:17-18 warns against divisions. This word *dichostasia* means to stand apart. I want to stand with those who believe. I do not want to stand apart from the community of faith. Paul warns us to stay away from those whose teaching is contrary to that teaching which has been handed down by the apostles (see also 1 Cor 11:2; 2 Tim 2:2).

But what are the essentials or fundamentals of the faith? They are stated in the great creeds of the church. Thus, the Christian faith can be defined. It is objective and can be stated propositionally.

Some may ask, Why not just believe the Bible if it is our final authority for faith and practice? The supreme authority of the Bible was never questioned in the early church. Yet a creed is simply an attempt to summarize the main points of the Bible. There is no section in the creeds that states, "I believe in Scripture," because the creed is basically a summary of the main points of what the Scripture teaches concerning the gospel. Commenting on the Apostles' Creed in the fourth century, Rufinus Tyrannius (345-410) said the creed serves as a "short word" summarizing the whole of biblical faith.[43] Gerald Bray explained,

> Although the supreme authority of the Bible was never questioned in the early church, from very early times its teaching was summarized in short statements of belief that individual Christians were meant to learn and recite on appropriate occasions.[44]

---

[43]Rufinus, *Commentary on the Apostles' Creed, NPNF*2 3:542.

[44]Oden, *ACD* 1:xxxii.

Fundamentalism?

The term *fundamental* refers to basic, rudimentary, foundational, essential, or cardinal principles — an irreducible minimum. By the turn of the twentieth century historic Christianity was under attack by liberalism or modernism. While the term *liberal* is not necessarily a pejorative term, when used in a negative sense, however, it refers to enlightenment philosophy or modernism, which categorically closes the natural world to Almighty God.

Classic modernism rejects the possibility of miracles, and everything is explained by human reason within the parameters of natural causes. According to Jesus, modernists are badly mistaken because they reject the authority of Scripture and the prerogative of God to perform miracles (Matt 22:29). True enlightenment is the illumination of Holy Scriptures by the Holy Spirit resulting in our walking in the light. Any "enlightenment" which denies the teachings of the holy Scriptures is actually darkness.

For this kind of modernism, faith is an openness to wherever human reason takes us in our subjective journey. Truth is relative and confirmed by human experience. Truth is evaluated on the basis of what works for me. And there is a preference for whatever is new and innovative. Oden described modernism as a tradition against tradition.[45]

J. Gresham Machen described liberalism, by whatever name, as "the denial of any entrance of the creative power of God (as distinguished from the ordinary course of nature) in connection with the origin of Christianity."[46]

Fundamentalism *at its best* was a modern attempt to defend historic Christianity. With the validity of the Bible under attack, classic fundamentalism was originally a battle for the Bible. As

---

[45]Oden, *After Modernity*, 164.

[46]Machen, *Christianity and Liberalism*, 2.

I use the term, *fundamentalism* is a categoric defense of absolutes and the Bible as the final authority of absolute truth. The opposite of truth is its antithesis. Fundamentalism rejects the methodology that truth is discovered through a synthesis and thus the discovery of truth is always in process.

The Fundamentalist Movement began in America after World War I. Classic fundamentalism was an ecumenical coalition defending the inspiration and inerrancy of Scripture, the virgin birth of Christ, his substitutionary atonement, his bodily resurrection, and the historical reality of his miracles.

The classic statement, *The Fundamentals* (1910-1915), was a collection of ninety articles, written by a broad coalition of scholars, defending basic, historic Christianity — including much of what Oden assumed had been left out — the existence of God, the deity of Christ, his incarnation, his dual nature, the deity and personality of the Holy Spirit, sin, atonement, grace, justification by faith, regeneration, discipleship, consecration, the church, Satan, prayer, evangelism, preaching, and missions. It must also be noted that *The Fundamentals* contained four articles on science and they all compromised too much ground to evolution. Eventually, the movement was taken over by a much more sectarian viewpoint

In the sixteenth century the term *evangelical* had originally been a synonym for *Protestant*, which was first used in 1529. By the eighteenth century it was used to describe the Methodist revival in Britain.[47] However, as early as 1916, B. B. Warfield wrote that nobody any longer seemed to know what *evangelical* means.[48]

And so the basic question centers on the rhetorical question — what's in a name? Any term must be defined. Any term, whether *evangelical, fundamental* or even *Methodist*, can be

---

[47]Noll, *Rise of Evangelicalism*, 17.

[48]Warfield, *Person and Work of Christ*, 345.

abused. In fact, the term *methodist* itself originated as a pejorative term.[49]

Writing in 1958, J. I. Packer said the term *fundamentalism* had long been a theological swearword, but that it was just a twentieth-century name for historic evangelicalism. He concluded that the fundamentalism controversy had the potential of doing immense good in invigorating the evangelical cause.[50]

Today, Islamic terrorists are labeled *fundamentalists*. Oden called this an "amusing generalization."[51] However, we must defend Christian doctrine with a Christlike spirit.

---

[49]Packer, *"Fundamentalism" and the Word of God*, 30-31,75.

[50]Packer, *"Fundamentalism" and the Word of God*, 19, 176.

[51]Oden, *After Modernity*, 81.

CHAPTER ONE
The Doctrine of Special Revelation

God has spoken. Through the process of inspiration, the Holy Spirit insured that the human authors accurately recorded God's words. The purpose of inspiration was to insure that we receive the Word of God without error. Those who claim to be qualified to determine which parts of the Holy Scriptures are trustworthy have, in fact, established themselves as the final authority over Scripture.

The Bible is our final authority for faith and practice because it came from the ultimate authority — God who knows everything and cannot err. When considered objectively, human reason concludes that the Bible is the Word of God because it corresponds to reality, is internally consistent, has been confirmed by miracles, it is authenticated through fulfilled prophecy, and is accepted as the Word of God by Jesus Christ. God's Word is forever settled and stands eternally. It has been providentially preserved and what we have today is reliable and trustworthy. Its authority is not lost in translation, although some translations are more accurate than others are.

Modernist theories about how Scripture was written are highly speculative and provide little help in understanding the text. The biblical text should be interpreted utilizing the rules of grammar and the background of history. Since the Bible is God's Word and our final authority on every subject it addresses, it must be preached clearly. The task of the preacher is to rightly interpret the primary meaning of the text and make the contemporary application. Just as the original writers relied on divine inspiration to accurately record the message, so every preacher must reply on the illumination of the Spirit to understand the text and the anointing of the Spirit in order to proclaim it.

God's revelation is the actual starting point of theology. In fact, divine revelation is the starting point for all human knowledge. It is the infinite communicating with the finite. We cannot start with *our* concept of God because it is distorted and must be conformed to God's self-disclosure. Christian theology is based on the records of God's revelation of himself and of his will in Christ Jesus. The holy Scriptures are the divine rule of faith.

This divine revelation opens the door to an analysis of the inspiration, the inerrancy, the authority, the canon, the preservation, the translation, the interpretation, and the exposition of Scripture.

The Inspiration of Scripture

Inspiration is that supernatural influence of the Holy Spirit whereby the sacred writers were divinely supervised in their production of Scripture, being restrained from error and guided in the choice of words they used, consistently with their disparate personalities and stylistic peculiarities.[52]

How do we know that the Bible is the Word of God? The classic approach proceeds from the premise that the Bible is reliable and trustworthy. On the basis of its teachings we have sufficient evidence to believe that Jesus Christ is the Son of God. If Jesus Christ is the Son of God, his authority is infallible. He teaches that the Bible is the very Word of God. The Word of

---

[52]Henry, *Expositor's Bible Commentary*, 1:25.

God is trustworthy because God is trustworthy. Therefore, the church believes the Bible to be trustworthy and infallible.

Calvin wrote that we are assured the Bible is the Word of God by the *Testimonium Spiritus Sancti*, the testimony of the Holy Spirit. This is the full assurance (*plerophoria*) of faith. However, according to Calvin, "This singular privilege God bestows on his elect only."[53]

What Calvin taught about the testimony of the Holy Spirit is compatible with a Wesleyan theology, except the ancillary issue of whether election is conditional or unconditional. Later, I will dispute Calvin's doctrine of election, but along with Calvin, I affirm the role of the Holy Spirit in inspiration, confirmation, and illumination. Arminius also affirmed the *testi-monium Spiritus Sancti*, without the distorted view of election.[54]

After the inspiration of Scripture has been established, every doctrine we discuss going forward will be inductively drawn from Scripture — but still corroborated by experience, tradition, and reason.

The good news is that God has spoken and that he condescended to communicate truth to us using human language. God's revelation is conveyed in intelligible ideas and meaningful words. Otherwise, we could not comprehend him. Wesley wrote,

> I want to know one thing, the way to heaven — how to land safe on that happy shore. God himself has condescended to teach the way: for this very end he came from heaven. He hath written it down in a book. O give me that book! At any price give me the Book of God!

---

[53]Calvin, *Institutes of Christian Religion*, 1.6.2, 1.7.1-5, 1:68-73. According to Sproul, Calvin alternates in sections 4 and 5 between the heart and the mind. This testimony of the Spirit is essentially the subjective preparation of the heart to receive the objective evidence instinctively ["Internal Testimony of the Holy Spirit," 337-354].

[54]Arminius, *Works*, 1:382-383.

I have it. Here is knowledge enough for me. Let me be [a man of one book].[55]

James Barr wrote,

It is not very convincing if one supposes that the writers were inspired, but not the sentences and book they wrote, or that the ideas were inspired, but not the verbal form in which they are expressed. . . . What we know about the authors, the ideas, the inner theology and so on is known ultimately from the verbal form . . . of the Bible.[56]

John Oswalt summarized Barr's thought,

If our only access to "revelation" is through a fictional narrative that is the product of successive rewritings, and indeed, reconceptualizations by different communities with different, and often, competing agendas, it may be best just to discard the term "revelation" all together.[57]

Contrary to the modernist assumption that God's communication is nonverbal and noninformational because he is transcendent and cannot truly be spoken of in human language, God accommodated himself to human expression and spoke truth without even stuttering. He writes straight, even on crooked lines![58] Wesley declared,

---

[55]Wesley, "Preface" to *Sermons On Several Occasions*, § 5.

[56]Barr, *Fundamentalism*, 287.

[57]Kinlaw, *Lectures in Old Testament Theology*, 458.

[58]Küng, *Infallible?* 180.

An exact knowledge of the truth was accompanied in the inspired writers with an exactly regular series of arguments, a precise expression of their meaning, and a genuine vigor of suitable affections. . . . And the language of his messengers also is exact in the highest degree: for the words which were given them accurately answered the impression made upon their minds.[59]

God revealed truth in ways we could grasp. "Holy Scripture is the truth of God accommodated to the human mind so that the human mind can assimilate it."[60] John Calvin said in his comments on 1 Corinthians 2:7 that "He accommodates himself to our capacity in addressing us."[61] Any attempt to define God by human concepts apart from his accommodation is futile.[62]

Not only did God speak to and through common men, he used common men to write what he had spoken. Modernism tends to promote a breakdown of communication, leaving only the intellectuals to inform us of what God might have said — although that remains an ongoing academic debate among themselves. The agnostic who doubts the ability of language to convey meaning adequately usually fails to apply that same scepticism to his own writings.

Modernists imply that God not only accommodated his revelation into a form that we could grasp, but that the matter or content was adapted. They say that God spoke in the culture of Bible times even when he knew they were in error. Thus, he accommodated their superstitions, prejudices, and folklore. They imply that if God were writing today he might say the exact opposite, because we are more intelligent. While the God of truth

---

[59]Wesley, *Notes*, 5-6.

[60]Ramm, *Protestant Biblical Interpretation*, 99.

[61]Calvin, *Commentary*, 20.1.104.

[62]Dunning, *Grace, Faith, and Holiness*, 112.

condescended to man's level to communicate with him, he did not compromise truth. Their emphasis on contextualization often results in subjective Bible interpretation which is simply a reflection of different cultural situations.

God adapted his truth to limited human understanding, but he did not accommodate himself to human error. Such a view of accommodation is contrary to the pattern and character of Jesus. However, modernists treat this concept of accommodation differently. They claim that God accommodated Scripture to the prejudices and superstitions of the ancient world. They often claim that human language is inadequate to speak about God because he transcends our ability to communicate.

But the same God who transcends us is also immanent — he is with us and in his sovereignty is perfectly able to communicate with us. God was the first to speak. In fact, human language is a divine gift making it possible for the infinite mind of God to communicate with the finite mind of mankind. He used the vernacular language of the common man to convey his eternal holy message in their own historical context.

Inspiration means God superintended the human authors, using their individual personalities, so that they composed and recorded without error his revelation to man. The purpose of inspiration was to convey truth from God, the source of all truth, to humanity.

While the terms *revelation* and *inspiration* are sometimes used interchangeably, *inspiration* denotes the agency of the Holy Spirit. The Son reveals while the Spirit inspires. The function of the Holy Spirit was to insure that the words which were written accurately represented God's intention.

The word *plenary* describes the extent of inspiration. Both terms, *verbal inspiration* and *plenary inspiration*, rule out partial inspiration. Wesley quoted Martin Luther who said, "Divinity is nothing but a grammar of the language of the Holy Spirit."

Wesley then proceeded to explain that our emphasis in doing theology must rely on every word.[63]

Jesus declared that we live by *every* word that comes from the mouth of God (Matt 4:4). In Matthew 19:4-5 Jesus introduced the quotation from Genesis 2:24 with the statement, "He who made them said." Thus, Jesus regarded God as the author. John Wenham commented that in certain contexts *God* and *Scripture* become interchangeable.[64]

All Scripture is inspired, but all Scripture does not have equal value. Divine inspiration does not imply equal clearness and fullness. According to Wiley,

> By plenary inspiration, we mean that the whole and every part is divinely inspired. This does not necessarily presuppose the mechanical theory of inspiration, as some contend, or any particular method, only that the results of that inspiration give us the Holy Scriptures as the final and authoritative rule of faith in the Church.[65]

The human authors were *carried along by the Holy Spirit* (2 Pet 1:21), so that they could claim their words were the words of God. Isaiah claimed his message came directly from God forty times. Jeremiah claimed the same thing a hundred times and Ezekiel did so sixty times. In all, the phrase *thus saith the Lord* occurs in the Bible over two thousand times and the phrase "the Word of the Lord came" about 3800 times.

Both terms, *Scripture* and *Bible*, imply that something has been written. The term *Scripture* is based on a generic Greek word, *graphe*, which simply means a writing. The word *bible* is from another Greek word, *biblos*, which simply means *book*. But there is only one *holy* book or writing.

---

[63]Wesley, *Notes*, 6.

[64]Wenham, *Christ and the Bible*, 28.

[65]Wiley, *Christian Theology*, 1:183-184.

The Scriptures are holy because they come from God, because they were inspired by the Holy Spirit, and because they were given to holy men. These holy men (2 Pet 1:21) acted as secretaries for God. However, the process of inspiration was not mechanical, monolithic, or uniform.

Apparently God wrote the ten commandments himself (Exod 34:1). He also directly wrote the words contained in Daniel 5:24-25. But at Exodus 34:27-28 God commanded Moses to write. However, there is no less authority in the words which Moses wrote, since he was writing what God told him.

Sometimes the human authors took dictation. Older theologians spoke of *dictation*, referring to the fact that the authors wrote word for word what God intended, not that a particular method of stenography was necessarily used.

God dictated Exodus 17:14,24:4,34:27; Numbers 33:2; Deuteronomy 31:22,24; Joshua 24:26; 1 Samuel 10:25; 1 Chronicles 28:19; Jeremiah 1:9; and 1 Corinthians 2:13. Apparently the letters to the seven churches in Revelation 2-3 were dictated verbatim by the Lord Jesus.

In some instances someone else wrote down the words the human author received from God. This was the case with Baruch (Jer 36:4) and apparently with Mark who wrote the testimony of Peter — according to Papias, Clement of Alexandria, Irenaeus, and Origen — all apostolic fathers of the second and third centuries.

The prophets received supernatural information and spoke with prophetic utterance. According to Hebrews 1:1 revelation came at times by dreams or visions. In the case of Ezekiel, it came by symbolic action and later by verbal communication. *Thus says the Lord* was often used as the introductory decree. What the prophet said in God's name was the Word of God. The prophet also wrote God's words.

God providentially ordered the life, education, and circumstances of each writer to fit him for his task. Like an orchestra directed by the Spirit, each writer played a different part. The speech of Isaiah was florid and full, while the message of Amos was plain and abrupt.

Their writings were based on direct knowledge. They were often eyewitnesses, yet Paul did not remember how many he had baptized (1 Cor 1:16). Parts of Scripture were based on oral tradition, previous documentation, personal contacts among writers, or ordinary sources of information such as government documents. Much of the book of Numbers is based on the results of a census.[66]

Solomon and Luke both did research.[67] Yet, in other instances the message came by direct supernatural revelation. However, their own personalities were not bypassed. As we read from the original language, there are obvious differences in their writing styles. However, the final product, in every instance, was said to be *Scripture*, which was inspired by God (2 Tim 3:16). At all times the biblical writers were superintended by the Holy Spirit.

Writing in the third century, Origen articulated the doctrine of the church that Holy Scriptures are not merely "human compositions," but written by historical people, "by inspiration of the Holy Spirit," so that they are "transmitted and entrusted to us by the will of God."[68]

Modernists tend to substitute illumination for inspiration. Illumination, however, does not make the Bible into the Word of God. The Bible is objectively the Word of God, whether or not we comprehend those words. It is the ministry of the Holy Spirit to make us understand and apply God's Word to our need. But modernism maintains that the book itself is not extraordinary. They like to say that there is no inspiration in the ink, the paper, or the leather binding. No thinking conservative makes such

---

[66]See also 1 Kgs 11:41, 14:29, 15:31; 1 Chr 29:29; 2 Chr 32:32, 36:23; Ezra 1:2-4, 4:7-23, 5:6-7, 6:6-12; Dan 6:25-27.

[67]1 Kgs 4:32-33; Luke 1:1-4; 1 Pet 1:10-11.

[68]Origen, *On First Principles*, 4.1.9; *ANF* 4:357.

assertions, however. Furthermore, human beings do not always err. Sometimes even unregenerate people speak the truth. Modernists seem to imply a gnostic philosophy that anything physical is necessarily imperfect. Yet everything God created in the physical realm was perfect. According to John 5:45-47 there is no loss of authority between the words of Jesus and the writings of Moses since Moses wrote about Christ.

The Word of God in Psalm 119 has divine attributes such as righteousness, faithfulness, wonderfulness, uprightness, purity, truth, and eternity. The Word of God evokes a godly fear, awe, and joy. It produces purity, gives direction, boldness, joy, illumination, revival, strength, salvation, hope, and peace. We are to lift our hands to his commandments. Nathanael Burwash noted that the Word has the attributes of truth, immutability and eternity, and divine power and life.[69]

J. B. Phillips paraphrased the NT in sections from 1947-1957. As he handled God's Word he said he felt rather like an electrician rewiring an ancient house without being able to turn off the main service panel.[70]

In Hebrews 4:12-13 the Word of God is depicted as having a discernment which only God has. John 1:1 correlates God's Word with Jesus Christ. Thus, the Word of God should be received as from the very mouth of God.

According to Scripture, the Spirit of the Lord rests not only on the prophet who spoke but also upon his words. God declared to Isaiah, "My Spirit, who is on you, and my words that I have put in your mouth . . . will not depart" (Isa 59:21; see also Jer 1:9). If God inspired the audible words, the inspiration was not lost when those same words were written.

The most complete biblical description of the process of inspiration is found in 2 Peter 1:12-21. Yet "it is no more possi-

---

[69]Burwash, *Manual of Christian Theology*, 226-227.

[70]Phillips, *Letters to Young Churches*, xi.

ble to describe exactly how the Divine action took place than it is to explain any other miracles recorded in the Bible."[71]

Peter said that Scripture did not arise from private self-inspiration, but that the prophets of old were carried along (*phero*) by the Spirit of God as wind in the sails moves a boat along the water. It is significant that Peter always used this verb *phero* in the passive voice except in 2:11, where it is used to explain what angels do *not* do.

This same verb occurred in 1 Peter 1:13, where it describes the glorification which Christ will bring at his revelation. This verb also occurs in 2 Peter 1:17-18, where the voice of the Father *was brought* to Christ and the apostles heard this declaration *brought* from heaven. In this context, *phero* describes revelation. But in v 21, where it occurs twice, it describes the process of inspiration. The Word of God was never *revealed* by the will of man, but men spoke from God as they were *borne along* by the Holy Spirit.

Thus, in the immediate context of this chapter, where the verb occurs four times, the prophets and apostles somehow heard the voice of God declaring truth which could only be known through supernatural revelation, and they felt an obligation to somehow preserve and pass down this revelation.

Michael Green wrote, "The prophets raised their sails, so to speak (they were obedient and receptive), and the Holy Spirit filled them and carried their craft along in the direction he wished." This metaphor is similar to Paul's statement that Scripture was *theopneustos* which means God-breathed (2 Tim 3:16). The Holy Spirit is described both as wind and breath.

The root meaning of the Hebrew word *ruach* and the Greek word *pneuma* is wind and translated *Spirit* in such relevant passages as Ezekiel 37:9; John 3:8; Acts 2:2. That the Word of God was breathed out indicates that it was spoken, and this *inspiration* was not lost when the words were written.

---

[71]Vine, *Divine Inspiration of the Bible*, 10.

Packer explained that the nature of Scripture is incarnational. Just as in the person of Jesus Christ we see the Son of God having taken to himself human nature while his essential identity is his divine identity, "so in the Scriptures we see the human form which God's Word took to itself, but its essential identity is that it is God's Word."[72]

There is a divine/human interaction; but it is clear God is in control of the process. The prophets and apostles spoke *because* they heard God speak. In Acts 1:16 Peter explained that the Holy Spirit spoke by the mouth of the human writers. Pope explained that the Holy Spirit spoke through the mouth of David and the result was Scripture.[73]

Paul declared in 1 Thessalonians 2:13 that what they heard from him was the word of God, not the word of men. Men, whether prophets or apostles, were carried along by the Holy Spirit. They were elevated above their humanity and so overshadowed that they were enabled to receive and convey God's words. Their finished product provided the inerrant and authoritative Word of God for the whole world.

In contrast, the modernist view is that inspiration is not the objective revelation of truth, but the subjective dynamic which man experiences when something read or preached jumps out at him. If this is the case, the question that begs an answer is why limit inspiration to the Bible? Could not a reader experience inspiration reading any other literary classic?

The Inerrancy of Scripture

God so superintended the process of inspiration that the final product was accurate and without human error. If God had chosen to reveal his truth through an imperfect revelation of truth mingled with error, it would require an infallible human source

---

[72]Packer, "Lamp in a Dark Place," 23.

[73]Pope, *Compendium*, 1:164.

to determine which part was true. Either the Holy Scriptures are without error or the human critic must be regarded as inerrant.

God alone is the source of all truth. The God whom the Bible reveals could speak in no other way than infallibly, and the Bible in which God is revealed asserts that God alone speaks infallibly. "Whatever the holy, unerring, and faithful Father speaks is — simply by virtue of having come from him — holy, unerring, and faithful."[74] Paul Feinberg formulated a contemporary definition,

> Inerrancy means that when all facts are known, the Scriptures in their original autographs and properly interpreted will be shown to be wholly true in everything they affirm, whether that has to do with doctrine or morality or with the social, physical, or life sciences.[75]

According to deductive logic, inspiration demands inerrancy. If the Bible contains errors, its authority is limited. "If the words were not wholly God's, then their teaching would not be wholly God's." Men deny infallibility for ethical reasons, not for intellectual reasons. They are sinners against God and in rebellion against his authority.[76]

If the work of the Holy Spirit was to transmit revelation to the human authors and to superintend their writings, then divine revelation which contains error reflects negatively on the capability of the Holy Spirit.

There is a long tradition within the church that holds Scripture as being without error. Until the end of the eighteenth century, it was taken for granted that biblical statements on any subject were reliable and true. The word *inerrancy* first became

---

[74]Horton, "The Truthfulness of Scripture," 26.

[75]Feinburg, "Meaning of Inerrancy," 294.

[76]Packer, *Fundamentalism and the Word of God*, 90.

current in the English language by the middle nineteenth century. Thus, one cannot conclude that Wesley, and others who lived in the eighteenth century, did not affirm the inerrancy of Scripture merely because he did not use that specific word. He did articulate the concept, however.

Prior to the mid-nineteenth century, the term *inspiration* was synonymous with inerrancy. Then *plenary* was added to *inspiration* to preserve the same meaning. Then the Bible was said to be *infallible*. Until about 1960-1965 the word *infallible* was used interchangeably with the word *inerrant*.[77] After *infallible* was used in a weaker sense to mean that the Bible will not lead us astray in matters of faith and practice, we had to resort to using *inerrant* to convey the same meaning the church historically has believed.

The original meaning of infallibility is based on the Latin root — to lead into error, to disappoint or deceive. *Infallibility* means that Scripture is incapable of deception or leading astray. Stated in positive terms, infallibility means that Scripture unfailingly leads us into the truth. The Scriptures cannot be infallible unless they are inerrant.

The Bible itself also claims to be free from error. Using the inductive method, we discover:

- In Psalm 12:6 *flawless* (*tahor*) is used of pure gold without alloy. The emphasis here is on the product. The statement that God's Word is like silver refined seven times expresses the concept of absolute purity or total freedom from imperfection.
- The process of refining gold is also used of God's Word in Psalm 18:30, 119:140. These metaphors borrowed from the refining process and focusing on the pure product are meant to convey the concept that all Scripture is without error. Psalm 119:160 declares that the sum of God's Word is truth.

_____

[77]Grudem, *Systematic Theology*, 93.

- In 2 Samuel 22:31 and Psalm 18:30 the way of God is perfect and the Word of God is flawless. Here the word *tamim* is used of God's attributes and the word *tsaraph* is used of God's revelation. *Tamim* is used of animals without blemish.

Because of the nature of Hebrew parallelism, the two descriptive words, *tamim* and *tsaraph*, are being used as synonyms. Two verses later, in both passages, David declares that God made his way perfect *tamim*. *Tsaraph* is also used in Deuteronomy 32:4 to describe the works of God. Thus, his works and his words are pure and free from any mixture of error.

- In Psalm 18:30,119:140; Proverbs 30:5 *flawless* (*tsaraph*) means refined gold. What God says is completely reliable since it has been refined. By using this Hebrew word, the focus is on the process not the product.
- In Psalm 19:7 *perfect* means complete. *Tamim* is used of animals without blemish; "what is complete, entirely in accord with truth and fact."[78]
- A literal translation of the Masoretic text of Psalm 138:2 reads, "For you have exalted above all your name and your word." In the culture of the OT, people already understood that the *name* of God was exalted above all things. On the other hand, to say that God exalted his Word above his very name or equal to his name would be understood as an amazing claim for Scripture.
- According to Proverbs 30:5 *every* word of God is flawless. Here *tsaraph* is used in the context of refined gold. It is devoid of foreign elements. What God says is completely reliable since it has been refined. The emphasis is on the purity of God's Word, devoid of error.
- In Ecclesiastes 12:10 the author declares that what he wrote was upright and true.

---

[78]BDB, *Hebrew and English Lexicon*, 1071.

- Jesus said the smallest letter or part of a letter would not have to be altered (Matt 5:18). Thus, inspiration is verbal, since God spoke by the mouth of all his prophets. However, verbal inspiration does not necessarily connote mechanical dictation. Since the very words are inspired, interpretation involves the meaning of words and their syntactical arrangement.
- Jesus declared in Revelation 21:5 that his words are trustworthy and true. They did not lose those qualities in the process of John recording them.
- In John 10:35 Jesus declared that Scripture cannot be broken. The Greek verb *luo* means that it cannot be dissolved or contravened. Scripture cannot be annulled or its authority be defied or denied because it is the Word of God. Thus, it is infallible.
- Jesus said that the Word of God is true (John 17:17).
- Paul insists in Romans 9:1 that he was speaking the truth and not lying.
- In 3 John 12 the author insisted that "you know my testimony is true."

The tension at this point relates to the divine/human components in the process of inspiration. Because mankind is fallen, it is often assumed that nothing can pass through human hands without being tainted with error. Barth wrote that the prophets and apostles were "sinful in their action, and capable and actually guilty of error in their spoken and written word."[79] For Barth, the capacity of the Bible for error extends even to its religious or theological content.[80] Therefore he concluded, "No human word, no word of Paul is absolute truth."[81]

---

[79]Barth, *Church Dogmatics*, 1/2:529.

[80]Barth, *Church Dogmatics*, 1/2:508.

[81]Barth, *Romans*, 19.

Barth's theological motif is the sovereignty of sin. But God did not create man in this fallen condition, and his plan of redemption is to liberate us from this sinful condition. If God is sovereign, then he is able to partially or completely deliver us from the effects of sin, whether temporarily or permanently. Those who proclaim a complete deliverance from sin ought to be able to transfer this concept to the work of the Holy Spirit in inspiration, not just to sanctification.

Certainly Peter was in error when Jesus rebuked him (Matt 16:23) and when Paul rebuked him (Gal 2:11), but when he wrote his two letters, whether by his own hand or with the assistance of a secretary, he was temporarily elevated by the Holy Spirit to a position of infallibility, so that 1 and 2 Peter should be regarded as the inspired Word of God.

However, no inspired writer was gifted with complete knowledge. The dynamic of inspiration did not make Paul an infallible brain surgeon. The miracle of inspiration, however, did produce an inerrant document in human language which accurately reflected the Word of God.

Through the incarnation Jesus Christ, the living Word, became the God-man, fully God and fully man. In a similar way the written Word has a dual nature. To emphasize either the human or divine side, without maintaining the balance, is to fall into error. In both cases the Holy Spirit used fallible human agents to produce a theanthropic result — a sinless Savior and an errorless book. The same Spirit who overshadowed the Virgin Mary so that the living Word was conceived without Adam's sin also overshadowed the human authors so that their word became the inerrant Word of God. On the other hand, some evangelicals believe the direct inspiration of the Spirit can produce a manuscript without error, but not even an apostle without sin.

Modernists emphasize the human process and deny the supernatural source. Conservatives sometimes overlook the fact that God accommodated his revelation to human experience, language, culture, and literature. Inspiration does not imply any suppression or setting aside of the natural power and faculties of the human writers.

As we develop a systematic theology, we will again deal with this question when we consider the dual nature of Christ. Do we so emphasize his humanity that we regard him as a sinner? Was he even capable of sin because he was God?

And we will encounter this question again when we deal with Christian maturity. Is there any level of deliverance from sin in this life, or is sin such an integral aspect of humanity that to be human, by definition, constitutes sin?

Wesley preached, "'All Scripture is given by inspiration of God' (consequently all Scripture is infallibly true)."[82] He stated, "We know, 'All Scripture is given by inspiration of God,' and is therefore true and right concerning all things."[83] He declared, "Every part thereof is worthy of God; and all together are one entire body, wherein is no defect, no excess."[84]

For Gregory Boyd in *Inspired Imperfection* (2020) to claim that errors in Scripture actually support its trustworthiness is contradictory.

> No organism can be stronger than its weakest part, that if error be found in any one element, or in any class of statements, certainty as to any portion could rise no higher than belongs to that exercise of human reason to which it will be left to discriminate the infallible from the fallible.[85]

When we look at 2 Timothy 3:16, all Scripture is God-breathed and profitable. Even through there is no verb expressed

---

[82]Wesley, "The Means of Grace," Sermon #16, 3.8.

[83]Wesley, "On Charity," Sermon #91, Introduction.

[84]Wesley, *Notes*, 5.

[85]Hodge and Warfield, "Inspiration," 242.

in the declaration, the two predicate adjectives, *inspired* and *profitable*, indicate by their parallelism that all Scripture *is* inspired. It is said to be profitable in four areas. These four synonyms: teaching, reproof, correction, and instruction, cannot be limited to *soteriology* or salvation, because the result is that the man of God is thoroughly equipped for *every* good work. *Every* good work cannot be limited to the spiritual realm. *Every good work* would not only include loving God, but it would include loving our neighbor as ourselves — which would extend into the ethical, moral, social, political, and educational arenas of life. To restrict this Scriptural authority to personal salvation cuts Scripture off from any objective, external verification. Jesus asked, "If I speak to you concerning earthly things, and you do not believe me, how then will you believe if I speak of heavenly things?" (John 3:12).

However, the most fundamental battle over the Bible is not over inerrancy, but over authority. The ravings of a lunatic could be recorded without error, but they would provide no help in determining truth. While it is inconceivable that God's revelation would be flawed, the more basic concern is that any intellectual who purports to have discovered mistakes in the Bible is essentially establishing himself or herself above God. Sinful man has a vested interest in asserting that the Bible contains error, because it allows him to pick and choose which parts to submit to. Biblical authority was not questioned within the church, however, until the age of Enlightenment of the eighteenth century.

The Authority of Scripture

The authority of Scripture is based simply on the character of the one who inspired the book. The Bible is our rule book and final authority because it was inspired by God. This was implied by the statement by Isaiah, "To the law and to the testimony" (8:20). God's Word is called the *law* because of our obligation to believe and obey it. It is also called the *testimony* because it is a witness between God and man of God's will and of man's duty.[86]

Those who do not know the Scriptures are liable to err (Mark 12:24). The Bereans were noble-minded because they tested everything against the final authority of Scripture (Acts 17:11). *Infallibility* means it is trustworthy and reliable (1 Tim 1:15,3:1,4:9; 2 Tim 2:11; Titus 3:8). God cannot lie (Titus 1:2).

But human reason asks whether or not anyone could write a book and in it claim that it was from God? Wesley employed a deductive syllogism in answer to this question:

> I beg your leave in order to propose a short, clear, and strong argument to prove the divine inspiration of the holy Scriptures. The Bible must be the invention of either good men or angels, bad men or devils, or of God.
> 1. It could not be the invention either of good men or angels; for they neither would nor could make a book and tell lies all the time they were writing it, saying, "Thus saith the Lord," when it was their own invention.
> 2. It could not be the invention of bad men or devils; for they would not make a book which commands all duty, forbids all sin, and condemns their own souls to hell for all eternity.
> 3. Therefore, I draw this conclusion, that the Bible must be given by divine inspiration.[87]

Other books may claim divine inspiration, but they must be evaluated on two bases:

---

[86]Wesley, *Notes*, 3:1969.

[87]Wesley, "Clear and Concise Demonstration of the Divine Inspiration of Holy Scripture," *Works*, 11:484-486.

• External credibility

Do they contain factual errors, hearsay evidence, or historical inconsistencies? The books of the Bible were accepted as from God when they were written by a culture who could have easily spotted factual error. Furthermore, God confirmed his word to those who heard it through miracles.

The Bible is historically reliable, corresponds to human experience, is true to nature, confirmed by miracles, authenticated by fulfilled prophecy, and accepted by Jesus Christ.

• Internal consistency

The written Word of God came over a span of 1500 years, through forty human authors, in ten different literary genres, addressing hundreds of topics. These authors represented twenty occupations on three continents, in ten countries and in three languages. In spite of being written over such a diversity of circumstances, it contains a unified message.

Furthermore, the substance of the Bible is not trivial, confused, or irrelevant. The message of the Bible points to God and lifts the reader's thoughts to the most important issues. Scripture carries a majesty fitting of a divine author.

Biblical authority is undermined by traditionalism which puts extra-biblical tradition on a par with Scripture and by rationalism which lifts human reason above divine revelation.

We must also consider the *sufficiency* of Scripture. God has told us all we need to know. However, we forbidden to seek information outside of Scripture, so long as that information — whether it pertains to science, history, philosophy, or ethics — does not contradict divine revelation. God has communicated truly, but not exhaustively. Frame even pointed out that since Scripture contains no lessons in Hebrew or Greek grammar, we must study the Bible with a background of extra-biblical information.[88] However, "all human knowledge must be reconcilable with Scripture."[89]

The Holy Spirit had the foresight to include revelation applicable to modern questions. When the Scriptures are accurately understood, interpreted and applied, with the illumination of the Holy Spirit, as well as careful study and discernment, they are sufficient for the believer's direction in Christian living. Whatever is not contained in the Bible in either word, precept, or example is not to be taught as a test of faith or fellowship. Whatever is contained there, when properly interpreted and applied under the direction of the Holy Spirit, is the final authority for faith and practice. The Bible is of such complete sufficiency that whatever is not contained in its pages is not to be considered essential to the faith or practice of any believer. What is not a matter of revelation cannot be made a matter of creed or faith.[90] "Nothing is required of us by God that is not commanded in Scripture either explicitly or by implication."[91]

The confirmation of miracles

Craig Keener defined a miracle as "an extraordinary event with an unusual supernatural cause."[92] The Bible employs three basic words to describe a miracle: *sign*, *wonder*, and *power*. Throughout the Old Testament God repeatedly performed miraculous signs. While *semeion* does not always refer to a miracle, it often designates some notable feature that confirms the truth of

---

[88]Frame, *Doctrine of the Word of God*, 232.

[89]Frame, *Doctrine of the Word of God*, 300.

[90]Ramm, *Protestant Biblical Interpretation*, 178.

[91]Grudem, *Systematic Theology*, 133.

[92]Keener, *Miracles*, 1:110.

the message. Thus, our faith is not in the sign, but what the sign sign-ified.[93]

Often the words *sign* and *wonder* are used to describe the same event. In the NT, *terata* (wonder) never appears alone, but always with *sign*. The function of a *wonder* is to elicit a reaction.

Sometimes the third word, *dunamis* (power), is also attached. While *sign* and *wonder* refer to the effect, *power* refers to the divine cause. All three terms occur together in Acts 2:22; 2 Corinthians 12:12; 2 Thessalonians 2:9.

Thus, a miracle is an unusual event (a wonder) that confirms an unusual message (a sign) by means of unusual ability (power). Such miracles glorify God, provide evidence for belief in God, and accredit certain people to be spokesmen for God.

Yet the impact of miracles is primarily on the audience which witnessed the miracle. Once the culture accepts Scripture on the basis of faith, they do not continue to need confirming miracles. Thus, Calvinists have tended to advocate the doctrine of cessation.[94] They argue that since the canon of Scripture has been completed, miracles are either rare or no longer happen.[95] The believer experiences the supernatural only when he encounters God's Word. John Frame declared that he was a "semi-cessationist." He believes miracles, except for tongues and prophecy, continue, but are rare today.[96] However, this seems like an arbitrary distinction. Any gift of the Spirit involves divine enablement.

While modernism categorically denies the possibility of miracles, the danger is that this cessationist position relegates miracles only to the past. Wesley argued

---

[93]Morris, *John*, 610.

[94]Calvin, *Institutes of the Christian Religion*, 1:427; 2:636.

[95]MacArthur, *Charismatic Chaos*, 54-77; *Strange Fire*, 231-248.

[96]Frame, *Doctrine of God*, 262-266.

I do not recollect any Scripture wherein we are taught that miracles were to be confined within the limits either of the apostolic or the Cyprianic age — or of any period of time, longer or shorter, even till the restitution of all things. I have not observed either in the Old Testament or the New any intimation at all of this kind.[97]

It only takes one clear miracle to negate a hard cessationist position. I experienced such a miracle in 1961.[98] While my theology is based on an inductive study of what Scripture teaches and not my personal experience, this is an example of how experience, tradition, or reason can either negate or confirm doctrine — even though doctrine is not established on such secondary sources.

At the opposite end of the evangelical theological spectrum, charismatics tend to seek the miraculous as an end, instead of a means to the end — the confirmation of the gospel. Trench concluded that a true miracle can only come from God, and we know it is from God only if it confirms the good. A miracle is never a mere freak of power, performed deliberately for flamboyant display, without a compelling need. Thus, a miracle is an ethical act and it should be accepted as truly miraculous only when it seals doctrines of holiness.[99]

We must not formulate a doctrine which restricts God's sovereignty. He is free to act according to his gracious will and there remains a mystery surrounding his actions. Yet we must not become gullible. Those who seek miracles tend to find what they are seeking — whether or not there is any verification.

---

[97]Wesley, *Principles of a Methodist Farther Explained*, *BE Works*, 9:219.

[98]Yocum, *Conformed to Christ*, 134-136; "Five-year-old Victor Walks Again," 9.

[99]Trench, *Miracles*, 15-21.

However, for the purposes of this discussion, we should expect miracles to confirm the preaching of God's Word in regions where the gospel has not penetrated. After the gospel has converted a region or culture, miracles may continue as a mark of divine blessing and favor — even where such confirmation of the faith is no longer necessary.[100] The universe is open to God's intervention and he continues to work, whether or not we are aware of his influence. Everything cannot be explained naturally.

The confirmation of prophecy

For prophecy to have any confirming value, there must be evidence that the prophecy was uttered before the fulfillment, that the event could not be anticipated or staged by human ingenuity, the possibility of coincidence must be ruled out, and the occurrence must be public enough that it is undeniable.

Some 20-25% of Scripture was prophetic when given. Fulfilled prophecy functions as a standing miracle. However, the damning influence of higher criticism is to challenge the assumption that the prophecy was given *before* the fulfillment.

Old Testament prophecy converged on the person and work of the coming Messiah, who personally fulfilled 332 distinct prophecies.[101]

The Canon of Scripture

The term *canon* originated from the Greek word *kanon*, which meant a reed, cane, or straight rod which was used as a rule or measure. Thus, the word *canon* described a rule or measure. In the passive sense, it described that which was measured or determined. In this context, the *canonical books* are those

---

[100]Keener, *Miracles*, 1:260-262.

[101]Hamilton, *Basis of the Christian Faith*, 160.

which measure up. Athanasius first used the word *canon* in this sense in AD 367.[102]

The major test of canonicity is the mark of apostolic authority. Was it written by an apostle or by one closely associated with an apostle? Thus, the authority of the apostles is vested in their inspired writings and not in a church council. It was the Bible which created the church and not the church which created the Bible. Wesley wrote, "In all cases, the church is to be judged by the Scriptures, not the Scripture by the church."[103]

Roman Catholic theology holds that the church is invested with the authority to determine what books are binding on the faithful, since the Holy Spirit is continuously at work within the church. The Reformation position is that the Holy Spirit alone authorizes the canon and he leads the church to recognize and accept what he has determined. Thus, it has been often explained that the canon is not an inspired list of books, but a list of inspired books.

Brevard S. Childs proposed a canonical critical method that assumes the Old Testament as we now have it. Its authority is that it is accepted by the community of faith. Without abandoning higher criticism, he seeks to interpret the text for today, regardless of the process by which the text evolved.[104] Kaiser expressed concern that Childs would ultimately be led back to Rome for authentication of the canon.[105] The canonical critical method puts the authority in the church instead of the book. The problem is not solved by the fact that the church canonized the Scripture. By what authority did the church declare this body of literature to be authoritative? God spoke and the church simply recognized the unique quality of his revelation.

---

[102]Athanasius, *Letters, NPNF2* 4:551-552.

[103]Wesley, *BE Works*, 14:219.

[104]Childs, *Introduction to the Old Testament*, 89.

[105]Kaiser, *Toward an Exegetical Theology*, 81-82.

The OT Canon

The OT Scriptures claim to be from God and were universally accepted by Israel at the time of their writing as being from God. Although the Jews count the books differently, their Bible is the same as our OT. The Jews divided their Scripture into three parts:

- The Law of Moses – the first five books; the Pentateuch
- The Prophets – the books of history and prophecy
- The Writings – poetry and wisdom books

In Luke 24:44-45, Jesus specifies the Law of Moses, the Prophets and the Psalms, which are the three major divisions of the OT. Jesus Christ ascribed divine authority to the OT, appealing to Scripture as the final authority.[106] He attests that the entire OT is Scripture. In the synoptic Gospels, Jesus quotes from the OT over 150 times. He also declares that the OT as one unit points to him (John 5:39). According to Revelation 19:10, the purpose of prophecy is to exalt Christ.

According to Acts 1:16, the Holy Spirit spoke through the mouth of David. According to Acts 7:38, Moses received the *living oracles* or utterances from God. The term *oracle* (*logion*) comes from *logos* (word) and is used in Romans 3:2 to describe the very words of God. Paul's reference to the *oracles of God* included the entire OT.

Several NT passages use the terms *God* and *Scripture* interchangeably. This is called a *metonymy*, in which the name of one thing is used for that of another with which it is associated. Here the name of the author and the work authored are used interchangeably.

- Romans 9:17 says that the Scripture said to Pharaoh.

---

[106]See such passages as Matt 22:29; Mark 7:13.

- Galatians 3:8 says that the Scripture foresaw.
- In Matthew 19:4-5 a quote from Genesis is introduced as coming from the Creator.
- There are thirty-seven OT citations in Hebrews,[107] but the human author is never identified. Instead, seven times God spoke, Christ spoke twice, and the Holy Spirit spoke three times. The one exception is 4:7 where David is named. The same passage is cited in 3:7 and attributed to the Holy Spirit. Apparently, David is named this once to highlight the fact that he wrote these words long *after* the incident took place in the wilderness, to highlight the time between Joshua and David and to demonstrate that the warning has continual validity.

Paul also declared the OT was inspired, referencing the writings of the prophets as *Holy Scriptures* (Rom 1:2,16:26). His classic statement in 2 Timothy 3:15-16 has already been referenced.

The NT Canon

The phrase *it is written* occurs about eighty times in the New Testament as the specific formula in which OT citations are introduced. The Christian writers of the NT built on the authority of what had already been written.

The Greek verb *gegraptai* occurs in the perfect passive indicative, describing completed action which endures to the present as a permanent, unchangeable witness. It is an expression meaning that what it cited is authoritatively binding.[108]

Christopher Wordsworth deduced, "The New Testament canonizes the Old; the Incarnate Word sets His seal on the Writ-

---

[107]Guthrie, "Hebrews," 919.

[108]Shrenk, "γράφω," *TDNT* 1:747.

ten Word. The Incarnate Word is God; therefore, the inspiration of the Old Testament is authenticated by God Himself."[109]

Virtually all that we know about Jesus Christ comes through Scripture, and certainly all the words of Christ to which we have access are contained in Scripture. Without faith in those words, he cannot be our Savior and Lord. Jerome said, "Ignorance of the Scriptures is ignorance of Christ."

Yet no single verse in the NT can speak concerning the entire NT the way 2 Timothy 3:15-17 and 2 Peter 1:19-21 do about the OT. That is because the NT could not speak of itself as a completed document while the NT writers were still in the process of writing it.

However, the NT is also Scripture. It contains the words of Jesus Christ which will never pass away (Matt 24:35); and it contains the writings of the apostles, who were commanded to write just as the OT prophets were commanded to speak. The apostles were commissioned by Christ and thus represent an extension of his teaching and authority. Paul claimed to receive the gospel he preached by divine revelation (Gal 1:11-12). He also asserted that what he was writing is the Lord's command (1 Cor 14:37). John claimed that he was writing what he had heard and seen from Jesus Christ (1 John 1:1). Peter made a similar claim in 2 Peter 1:16-18.

The NT is canonical because it was inspired. Such inspiration is discernable because of its intrinsic contents. Christ is its central theme. The message has a moral and spiritual effect, and historically the literature was recognized as inspired by the Christian church. Furthermore, the literature was either written by an apostle or by one closely associated with the apostles.[110]

Wordsworth argued that the NT was received by the primitive church as the unerring Word of God. This reception is evinced by catalogs it proclaimed, by its councils; it is shown by

---

[109]Wordsworth, *On the Canon*, 55

[110]Tenney, *New Testament Survey*, 402-404.

the fury of persecutors and by the fraud of heretics, by the courage of martyrs and by the zeal of the church.[111]

According to the promise of Jesus, the apostles would be inspired (Mark 13:11; Luke 12:12). Jesus explained to them that the Holy Spirit would bring everything that he had said to their remembrance (John 14:26,16:13).

Peter equated the writings of Paul with the rest of the Scriptures (2 Pet 3:16). This word *graphe* was used in the NT some fifty times to refer to the OT. Here Peter uses *graphe* to describe the NT documents which were in existence when he wrote these words. Benson observed, "In this clause Peter expressly acknowledges Paul's epistles to be a part of the *Scriptures*, and therefore to have been written by divine inspiration."[112]

Then in 2 Peter 1:16, Peter includes his writings along with Paul and the other apostles through the plural pronoun *we*. So we conclude that the NT is also inspired, although it was not written by prophets.

The NT is the word of the prophets made more certain. It is the verification or the fulfillment of their prophecies. To paraphrase 2 Peter 1:19, Peter says, "If you don't believe what I am writing to you, go to the Old Testament prophets. What we apostles write is in agreement with the OT prophecies, and is thus confirmed by them." Thus, Peter is expressing absolute certainty. The adjective *bebaios* means *certain*, and is based on the concept of solid ground which is unshakable and will bear the full weight of our faith.

When we put the OT together with the NT, we have a more sure word. We have both the prediction of a Messiah and the fulfillment of that prediction in Jesus Christ. Amos Binney

---

[111]Wordsworth, *On the Canon*, 153.

[112]Benson, *Notes*, 5:647. See also Green, *BECNT*, 340-341.

explained that the OT prophecy concerning Christ was always sure, but it is now made more sure to us by its fulfillment.[113]

John professed to have an anointing (1 John 2:20) and also claimed to be in the Spirit when he received the revelation of Jesus Christ (Rev 1:10). In all John was commanded to write his revelation twelve times.

The NT only had eight or nine authors (depending on whether Paul wrote Hebrews) and it was completed within one generation. The great difference between the old and the new was that the OT was written over a span of approximately eight hundred years while the NT was completed between the advent of Christ and the death of his apostles. Thus, while the preparation took centuries, the fulfillment came to pass quickly.

These NT books also claimed to be from God and were accepted as coming from God because they were written by apostles or those closely associated with apostles. The apostles laid the foundation of the church and were given authority by Christ to rule on doctrine. Their writings were universally accepted by the church at the time they wrote. The contents of their writings were consistent with truth, they possessed a spiritual depth, and they glorified Christ.

It is important to understand that the church did not vote for the books they liked, but there was an overwhelming consensus that these books were from God and therefore carried authority. However, not all congregations had immediate access to all the NT books. Many books were actually letters written to specific congregations. Other churches would request copies and in time a list of books developed. However, these letters all had to be hand copied

The Roman emperor Diocletian issued an edict to destroy all religious books in 303. The Christian church was forced to recognize which books were part of their Bible and which were simply letters, sermons, and tracts. We have some of this early

---

[113]Binney, *The People's Commentary*, 650.

literature and it has value, but it was not accepted as biblical primarily because it was not written by apostles.

In AD 140 Marcion, a heretic, published a list of eleven New Testament books which he accepted. This forced the church to deal with the issue of which books belong since we have twenty-seven NT books. We have a list from AD 170 AD, the Muratorian fragment, named for the Italian librarian who discovered it in AD 1740, which cites all but four books in our NT. Those four were some of the last to be written and probably had not had enough time to circulate. In 330 Eusebius gives the same exact list as our NT.[114] Three general church councils, the Council of Laodicea meeting in 363, the Third Council of Carthage in 397, and the Council of Carthage in 419, confirmed this same list.

Roman Catholics and Protestants both accept the same NT. However, the Roman Catholic Church added fourteen additional books (depending upon how they are counted) to the OT called the *Apocrypha*, which means "hidden things."

These writings date from 300 BC to around AD 100. They do not claim inspiration from God; they contain historical, chronological, and geographical error, and they teach doctrines which contradict the rest of Scripture. While the NT cites from the OT several hundred times,[115] the NT never cites the Apocrypha. Nor did the Jews accept the Apocrypha into their Hebrew canon.

---

[114]Eusebius, *Ecclesiastical History*, *NPNF2* 1:155-157.

[115]The fourth edition of the United Bible Societies' Greek Testament (1993) lists 343 OT quotations in the New Testament, as well as no fewer than 2,309 allusions and verbal parallels. The books most used are Psalms (79 quotations, 333 allusions), and Isaiah (66 quotations, 348 allusions). In the Book of Revelation, there are no formal quotations at all, but no fewer than 620 allusions.

"The New Testament is filled with quotations from the Old Testament, and its language saturated with expressions derived from the Septuagint Greek versions" [Pfeiffer, *Introduction to the Old Testament*, 8].

While they were added by the Council of Trent in 1546, they had not been accepted for two thousand years. It reminds me of an unknown will, suddenly produced at the time of an estate settlement. Bruce Metzger concluded,

> When one compares the books of the Apocrypha with the books of the Old Testament, the impartial reader must conclude that, as a whole, the true greatness of the canonical books is clearly apparent. Though several books within the Old Testament are manifestly quite disparate and occupy varying levels, and though some readers would perhaps be willing to exchange passages in several Apocryphal books for others in the canonical books, yet it is probable that the judgment of most readers today would be in accord with that of Judaism and the earliest Church, both of which saw a profound difference between the two groups of books.[116]

The statement "all things necessary for salvation" is the Reformation argument against the Apocrypha — that it is not inspired. It has been perverted to mean that Scripture is only trustworthy in matters of salvation, not history or science.

There are also about fifty "gospels" which are falsely ascribed to an apostle. The Gospel of Thomas would be the most well-known of this fifty. It was not written by the apostle Thomas, but is dated about AD 140. Actually, the Gospel of Thomas cannot be called a "gospel" because it contains no narrative. It contains 114 parables, proverbs, and other sayings attributed to Jesus. While it contains some sayings which are also found in other gospels, it does not call Jesus *Christ*, *Lord*, or *Savior*. It does not mention his death or his resurrection. The book is considered to be gnostic literature.

---

[116]Metzger, *Introduction to the Apocrypha*, 172.

But the question must also be raised, why was this information withheld from Christians for 1800 years? And why is it now coming forth? The doctrine of progressive revelation would explain why those before Christ did not have a complete understanding of the Messiah, but since our faith under the new covenant is specifically in the person and work of Jesus Christ, why would vital information be withheld after his advent?

Not only has God acted in history; he has spoken once for all. After having spoken through dreams, visions, voices, and angels, "In these last days he has spoken [aorist active indicative] to us by his Son" (Heb 1:2). It is blasphemy to attempt to add to that final revelation of Christ. The Bible was completed when that generation of men who were with him on earth finished their writings. God leads us, but does not reveal new truth to us.

No charismatic prophecy is on a par with Scripture. Most charismatics agree that the canon is closed. Yet if their new revelations are actually God's words, how can they not be as authoritative as Scripture? The canon is closed because there are no more apostles. The office of an apostle was foundational (Eph 2:20). They had seen Christ (1 Cor 9:1, 15:8) and were given authority by Christ. Their apostleship was confirmed by miracles (2 Cor 12:12). Paul was the last apostle and he said he was born late (1 Cor 15:8). They had no direct successors, but their authority rests in their writings.

The canon is closed because Christ has come and the faith was once for all delivered (Jude 3). It is closed because Hebrews 1:1-2 explains that Jesus is the final revelation. It is closed because the final words of Revelation 22:18-19 declare that revelation has closed. God would not wait hundreds of years and then add a postscript. The concept of progressive revelation should not be misapplied to teach an open canon.

Yet God still continues to speak *through* Scripture, particularly through the preaching and teaching of his Word. We still need the Holy Spirit to illuminate God's Word, helping us to understand and apply it properly. But God has told us all we need to know — even though he has not told us all we might want to know. If we seek to know more than the Bible tells us (for example, when Christ will return) we only open ourselves up to deception.

Actually, very little literature even claims to be directly from God. Comparative religion tends to put other texts on a par with the Bible assuming that they all stem from the same source. The few "inspired" books respected by other religions would include

- **the Vedas**

Composed in Sanskrit, they are the oldest scriptures of Hinduism. They contain no predictive prophecy and offer no miracles as confirmation that they were sent by God.

- **the Zend-Avesta**

These are the writings of the Zoroastrian faith, most of which have been lost. Hundreds of years later Gathas attempted to gather what Zoroaster had supposedly said, if indeed he was a historical person.

- **the Analects**

These are the writings of Confucius which comprise an ethical code. He made no claims to supernatural authority. He was neither a prophet nor a philosopher. He simply declared that this is how it has always been done.

- **the Quran**

While accepted by Muslims, it came later than the Bible in the seventh century AD and contains no self-authenticating proofs such as fulfilled prophecy. Gleason Archer has listed three pages of historical inaccuracies found in the Quran.[117] In 644-656 Caliph Hadrat Uthman destroyed all variant copies of the Quran in order to establish an "authorized" edition. However, in 1972 an ancient Quran was discovered in Yemen which contains two extra suras or chapters.[118]

According to Ali Dashti, there were so many grammatical flaws in the Quran that Arabic grammatical rules had to be altered in order to support the claim that the Quran was flawless.[119]

- **the book of Mormon**

Joseph Smith wrote and copyrighted the book of Mormon in 1830. He had a history of defrauding people and had a criminal record in New York. Gleason Archer has listed four pages of historical inaccuracies found in the book of Mormon.[120] The book of Mormon is probably an expansion and plagiarism of a work by Solomon Spaulding, a retired minister who wrote historical fiction.

- **Science and Health with Key to the Scriptures**

Published in 1875, it has been demonstrated that Mary Baker Eddy plagiarized from other sources, but claimed God gave it to her directly. She denied practically every biblical doctrine.

---

[117]Archer, *Survey of Old Testament Introduction*, 498-500.

[118]MacMillan, "City of the Book," 10-18; Lester, "What Is the Koran?" 43-56. See also Wegner, "Has the Old Testament Text Been Hopelessly Corrupted?" 134-136 for an assessment of why it is impossible to recover the original text of the Quran, in contrast with the amazing preservation of the Hebrew text of the OT.

[119]Zacharias, *Jesus Among Other Gods*, 160.

[120]Archer, *Survey of Old Testament Introduction*, 501-504.

Some Seventh-Day Adventists also consider Ellen G. White an inspired and inerrant prophet. With the rise of the new age movement there has been a new openness to mystical writings such as these. While these writings have value for those in cultural and anthropological studies, Western civilization, at its best, was based upon the foundation of the Bible (although the Bible came from the East). It is possible to find occasional nuggets of truth even in strange sources, but the holy Scriptures are the measure of truth. Sermons, songs, tracts, books, and other religious literature will hopefully *contain* truth, but the Scripture *is* truth (John 17:17).

The Preservation of Scripture

Even if we accept the inspiration of the original text, has it been tampered with? God's Word is forever settled or stands eternally (Ps 119:89; 1 Pet 1:25). Not the smallest letter nor the least stroke of a pen will by any means disappear (Matt 5:18). What is settled in heaven need not be disputed on earth. The Waldensians in the twelfth century had a motto, "Hammer away, ye hostile hands. Your hammers break; God's anvil stands!" "'Is not my word like fire,' declares the Lord, 'and like a hammer that breaks a rock in pieces?'" (Jer 23:29).

The Reliability of the OT

We do not have the originals. The oldest copies we have are a thousand years after the books were originally written. While this might raise questions concerning the accuracy of the text, actually we have no cause for concern. We now possess some ten thousand OT manuscripts and fragments, which includes the Masoretic Text and the Dead Sea Scrolls. The task of textual criticism is to establish the original text from the evidence.

Literary criticism does not mean faultfinding; it means to evaluate. Biblical criticism does not have to be negative. It may mean an objective evaluation of the writing. It becomes negative when the Bible is approached with certain modernist presuppositions. It is legitimate to use critical inductive logic to establish which variant manuscript reading was the inspired original. It is illegitimate to use critical deductive logic to call into question whether something in the original text is true. This is the usual distinction between lower and higher criticism.

However, if "higher criticism" describes the sources, author, provenance, date, unity, circumstances, and purpose of the biblical text, it is valid and useful. Such analysis can demonstrate that apocryphal and pseudepigraphical writings have no legitimate place in the biblical canon. The issue is whether "higher criticism" assumes ontological and evolutionary naturalism.

The occupation of the scribes was to copy the texts. They had such reverence for the name of God that they would get up and wash their pen before writing God's name. After they finished with their copy of a book they would count to the middle verse, middle word, and middle letter of the book. If their copy did not correspond to their original, the copy was destroyed!

Writing was done on leather made from animal skin called *parchment*. Later writing material was made from papyrus, which were reeds woven together. Paper was not used until a little over a thousand years ago. When the old parchment copies became torn and hard to read due to smears, they would be given a funeral and buried because of their reverence for God's living Word. We do not have many old copies, but we can be assured that the copies we do have are extremely accurate.

Gleason Archer comparing the Isaiah scroll found at the Dead Sea in 1947 which were a thousand years older than the earliest OT previously extant. As a textual critic, he concluded, "They proved to be word for word identical with our standard Hebrew Bible in more than 95 per cent of the text. The 5 per cent consisted chiefly of obvious slips of the pen and variations in spelling."[121]

Bruce Waltke noted that there was no variation in 90% of the text of the most recent critical edition of the Hebrew Bible.[122] Shemaryahu Talmon, professor in the Department of Biblical Studies in the Hebrew University of Jerusalem, explained that those variations "affect the intrinsic message only in a relatively few instances."[123]

The Reliability of the NT

Those who copied the NT originals were not as careful as the Jewish scribes had been. However, we have copies that go back to within one generation or less from the originals. In 2017 there were 5856 handwritten NT Greek manuscripts available, making the NT the best textually supported book from antiquity.

Textual critics compare the texts and determine what the original words were. Thus, we have the original text in the copies, and the original autograph can be reconstructed through a comparison process to over 99% accuracy.

A textual variant includes any variation in the wording, including word order, omission or addition of words, and even spelling differences. Variants may be neither viable nor meaningful, viable but not meaningful, meaningful but not viable, both meaningful and viable. This last category — both meaningful and viable — is by far the smallest category. One-fifth of 1% of all textual variants are significant. Not one variation affects an article of faith or a precept of duty. Even Bart Ehrman conceded, "Essential Christian beliefs are not affected by textual variants in

---

[121]Archer, *Survey of Old Testament Introduction*, 25.

[122]Waltke, "Old Testament Textual Criticism," 157.

[123]Talmon, "Old Testament Text," 1:161.

the manuscript tradition of the New Testament."[124] Frederick Kenyon concluded,

> The number of manuscripts of the New Testament, of early translations from it, and of quotations from it in the oldest writers of the Church, is so large that it is practically certain that the true reading of every doubtful passage is preserved in some one or other of these ancient authorities. . . . This can be said of no other ancient book in the world.[125]

F. F. Bruce explained,

> If the great number of manuscripts increases the number of scribal errors, it increases proportionately the means of correcting such errors, so that the margin of doubt left in the process of recovering the exact original wording is . . . in truth remarkably small.[126]

More recently, Daniel Wallace also said

> The New Testament is far and away the best-attested work of Greek or Latin literature from the ancient world. Precisely because we have hundreds of thousands of variants *and* hundreds of *early manuscripts*, we are in an excellent position for recovering the wording of the original.[127]

---

[124]Ehrman, *Misquoting Jesus*, 252. Q&A section added to the 2007 paperback edition.

[125]Kenyon, *Our Bible and the Ancient Manuscripts*, 55.

[126]Bruce, *The New Testament Documents*, 19.

[127]Wallace, "Has the New Testament Text Been Corrupted?" 151.

In comparison there are only five existing copies of the writings of Aristotle. We do not have the original text, and the oldest copy is 1400 years later than when the original would have been written. We only have seven surviving copies of Plato, and they are 1200 years newer than when the original would have been written. Yet no one doubts the historicity of Aristotle or Plato!

Westcott and Hort, two early textual critics, concluded in 1881,

> The proportion of words, virtually accepted on all hands as raised above doubt, is very great; no less than seven-eights of the whole. The remaining one-eighth, formed in great part by changes of order and other comparative trivialities, constitutes the whole area of criticism. If the principles followed in this edition are sound, this area may be very greatly reduced. . . . We find that setting aside differences of orthography [spelling], the words in our opinion still subject to doubt make up about one-sixtieth of the N. T. In this second estimate the proportion of comparatively trivial variations is beyond measure larger than in the former so that the amount of what can in any sense be called substantially a variation is but a small fraction of the whole residuary variation, and can hardly form more than a thousandth part of the entire text.[128]

The doctrine of divine preservation holds that God has preserved what the Spirit has inspired. However, God has apparently used secondary sources, at times, to preserve his Word. There are four major sources from which the genuine reading can be determined: ancient manuscripts, ancient translations, scrip-

---

[128]Westcott and Hort, *New Testament in the Original Greek*, 2:2.

tural quotations found in the works of ancient writers, and parallel passages.

At the end of the first century the Roman emperor Diocletian issued an edict to destroy all religious books. Until Constantine converted in the fourth century, early copies of the Bible were destroyed. Every copy was by hand, and these copies were also subject to natural disasters and normal conditions of decomposition.

There are five textual problems in the NT. The ending of Mark is the longest at 255 words. The other four combined are 306 words.[129] Out of 138,607 words in the Greek NT, only 561 words or 0.4% are in question. Each textual question must be resolved individually.

The oldest Mark manuscript we have is P137 which dates to the third century and is only a fragment. The two oldest and most reliable manuscripts, Vaticanus AD 300 and Sinaiticus AD 350, omit Mark 16:9-20. By the end of the fourth century, scholars were aware of different endings of Mark in different manuscripts.[130]

However, these verses in question are first quoted by Irenaeus, who died in AD 202. He wrote,

Also, towards the conclusion of his Gospel, Mark says: "So then, after the Lord Jesus had spoken to them, He was received up into heaven, and sitteth on the right hand of God."[131]

---

[129]The other four references are John 7:53-8:11; Acts 8:37; 1 John 5:7; Rom 8:1.

[130]Oden, *ACCS* 2.249.

[131]Irenaeus, *Against Heresies*, ANF 1:426.

From the time frame in which Irenaeus cited these verses in question, until the oldest extant Mark copies in the fourth century, ten church fathers all cite these verses.[132]

Some have objected that textual criticism is subjective and that God gave the Textus Receptus instead of an eclectic text. This "Received Text" was actually a Greek NT first published in 1516 by Desiderius Erasmus. Prior to this period the Bible was in Latin. The new humanistic philosophers wanted the NT in its original language.

Now that many more copies of the Greek NT have been discovered, should we utilize them or must we confine ourselves to the Textus Receptus? Essentially, this is the debate over whether or not to work from an eclectic text. *Eclectic* means that each variant reading is examined or critiqued on its own merits.[133]

Some conservative critics accept the King James Version only. They teach the divine preservation or advanced revelation of the King James Version, meaning that it is inerrantly inspired, that mistakes in it are advance revelation, or that the 1611 KJV was written in eternity past and that Abraham and Moses read from it.

Some accept only the Textus Receptus, asserting the superiority of this specific Greek text. The problem with claiming the Textus Receptus is the original autograph is that there are eighteen editions of the Textus Receptus and no two of them agree.[134] Although the New King James Version of 1982 is based on this same Greek text, it is opposed by advocates of the position described in the previous paragraph. Yet the Textus Receptus normally used today was first published in 1894. There are nearly 300 differences between the KJV and the Textus Receptus. Some of the most thorough refutations of this position come

---

[132]Bock, "The Ending of Mark," 130.

[133]Earle, "Rationale For an Eclectic New Testament Text," 53-57.

[134]Custer, *Truth about the King James Version Controversy*, 10.

from within the fundamentalist camp.[135] In his translation of the NT, Wesley made 12,000 changes from the KJV. About 430 of these changes indicate that he was using a Greek text other than the Textus Receptus.[136]

Those who oppose the concept of an eclectic text advocate the Majority Text approach, which determines the correct text by the number of manuscripts which agree. This is invalid because we would expect there to be fewer of the older manuscripts and more later manuscripts. The Majority text differs from the Textus Receptus in 1838 instances.

All of these disputes could be resolved if we had a complete copy of the original autographs. According to Tertullian, the original autographs of the apostles may have existed as late at the second century.[137] Perhaps God did not see fit to preserve the original Old and New Testament manuscripts because they would have become objects of idolatry. Ultimately, the brass serpent which God instructed Moses to make had to be destroyed by Hezekiah because it was being worshiped (2 Kgs 18:4).

God does not always disclose his purposes to us. Admittedly, God *could* have assigned an angel to superintend the preservation of the original manuscript, but errors could have still been interjected by copyists. Angels *could* have been assigned to oversee each copy that was made, but errors could have been interjected into the translation.

Again, if angels preserved the truth at every level of transmission from God to man, it would have been more efficient to

---

[135]Wisdom, "Textus Receptus: Is it Fundamental to Our Faith?"; Wood, "Question of Preservation"; MacRae and Newman, *Facts on the Textus Receptus*; Panosian, *What is the "Inspired" Word of God?*; Corner, *Critique of Gail Riplinger*.

[136]Earle, "Matthew," 81.

[137]Tertullian, *The Prescription Against Heretics*, ANF 3:260. This evidence is evaluated by Wallace, "Did the Original New Testament Manuscripts still exist in the Second Century?"

assign them to preach the Word. Somehow the answer must be found in the balance between divine sovereignty and human responsibility.

When our copies agree with the original, they are just as authoritative as the original. The issue is not primarily the possession of the original autograph manuscript. Logically, it had to exist — whether or not it exists today. Through the science of textual criticism, the original *text* can be reconstructed — even if we do not possess the original document.[138]

Thus, we should handle the question of the missing autograph originals just as a secular literary scholar handling the same problem in reference to other ancient texts — by giving the benefit of the doubt to the accepted principles of textual analysis and reconstruction.

When Moses destroyed the original autograph of the Ten Commandments, his replacement copy was also authoritative. When Jeremiah's original scroll was cut into pieces and burned by Jehoiakim, the replacement copy was still authoritative (Jer 36:28). Solomon possessed a copy of the original Mosaic law (Deut 17:18), yet his copy was still considered authoritative (1 Kgs 2:3). Although the men of Hezekiah copied the proverbs of Solomon (Prov 25:1), the copies were regarded as canonical. When Ezra read from the law of God (Neh 8:8), it was a copy of the original but still regarded as authoritative. Jesus preached from a scroll copy of Isaiah located in the synagogue in Nazareth, yet he treated it as Scripture (Luke 4:16-21). Copies of the original text, as well as translations, function authoritatively proportionate to the extent they reflect the original autographs. Variations are the exception, not the rule. What has been written in the original stands or remains in the copies. While no one has seen the inerrant original manuscripts, no one has seen any errant original manuscripts either. We cannot logically assert that the

---

[138]Bahnsen, "Inerrancy of the Autographs," 160-162; Frame, *Doctrine of the Word of God*, 243.

copies of the original text are full of errors if we don't have the original to compare them with.

Thus, this academic debate is actually a debate over the nature of Scripture. Scripture is the words of men who were moved by the Holy Spirit to write the disclosure of God. Their finished product was inspired, not every copy made from the original.

The doctrine of the preservation of God's Word is based on God's providence and verified by textual criticism. Greg Bahnsen concluded,

> The paramount features and qualities of Scripture — such as inspiration, infallibility, and inerrancy — are uniformly identified with God's own original word as found in the autographic text, which alone can be identified and esteemed as God's own word to man.

The loss of the original, physical documents does not automatically entail the loss of the original words.

> We *can* believe our copies of Scripture and can be saved without having the autographic codex, for the Bible itself indicates that copies can faithfully reflect the original text and therefore function authoritatively.[139]

---

[139]Bahnsen, "Inerrancy of the Autographs," 169-170.

The Translation of Scripture

The OT was written in Hebrew and Aramaic.[140] The NT was written in Koine Greek. These original languages have priority over every translation. However, unless we can read these languages, we must rely upon a translation. There have continued to be new translations made because language is constantly changing. Every generation needs fresh translations in order to accurately convey the *same* meaning.

The dialect of the common man was Koine Greek, not classical or Attic Greek. However, until Adolf Deissman made this discovery around 1895, earlier scholars such as Hermann Cremer claimed that the Greek of the NT was a special Greek given by the Holy Spirit. If the gospel was written in the tongue of the common man in the period of its inception, modern translators reason that is should be put in the vernacular of the common man of our day.[141]

While some translations are better than others, and all are imperfect, to the degree that the translation reflects the original meaning, the power and authority of God's Word has not been lost. To the extent that any translation conveys biblical meaning, it should be received as God's words to us.

Unlike the Quran, the Bible is still the Word of God no matter which language it is translated to. Don Richardson argued, "If the Koran makes full sense only in Arabic, it is not revelation for all mankind unless Allah requires all mankind to learn

---

[140]Ezra 4:8-6:18, 7:12-26; Dan 2:4-7:28; Jer 10:11 are in Aramaic, which is a Semitic dialect, based on a corruption of Hebrew with the Chaldean dialect. The Jews in Babylonian exile forgot their mother tongue and never recovered their use of Hebrew after their return from captivity.

[141]Cairns, *Christianity Through the Centuries*, 40-41.

Arabic."[142]Timothy George compared the Bible to the Quran, which when translated is not authoritative.

> Christians believe that the Bible can be translated into any human language. Why? Because the gospel itself is culture-permeable. The Bible, as the revealed Word, has come to us in Greek and Hebrew, the privileged languages of inspiration. But we can translate and transmit it to all people groups, no matter their language, because Christianity says that the gospel we proclaim is world-embracing, as limitless as the gracious love of the Creator.[143]

While some conservatives want to fight over which translation is better, the real battle is over the inspiration of Scripture. However, it is important to understand the debate over the philosophy of translation. *Formal equivalency* advocates a word-for-word translation, while *functional equivalency* leads to more of a paraphrase or thought-for-thought. While the paraphrase may be easier to understand, the reader may not be aware that he or she is getting more of the translator's opinion than if they were reading from a word-for-word translation. More literal translation follows a functional equivalency method of translation. The more a translation attempts to smooth out or fix culturally sensitive issues, the more the reader gets the opinions of the translator, without knowing it. A formal equivalency philosophy of translation reflects a higher view of inspiration.

Starting with the *New Revised Standard Version* in 1990, *The New International Version Inclusive Language Edition* of 1996, *Today's New International Version* (2001), and the *New International Version* (2011), there have been attempts to pro-

---

[142]Richardson, *Secrets of the Koran*, 90; Morey, *The Islamic Invasion*, 209-210.

[143]George, "Is the God of Muhammad the Father of Jesus?" 30.

duce gender-inclusive translations. *Gender neutral* (the term often used by opponents) and *gender accurate* or *gender inclusive* (the term often used by proponents) means that the general idea of a passage is translated and male-oriented details of meaning are omitted.

When cultural shifts in language intersect Scripture, a high view of Scripture and the necessity for clear, accurate translation require that the absolute priority is to make the intent and message reliably plain for the reader. Since every word is inspired, it ought to be the task of Bible translators to render as accurate a translation as possible.

Hebrews 2:7-8 contains seven masculine singular pronouns in the Greek text. Six refer to Jesus Christ and one refers to God the Father. While it might be helpful to distinguish between the two objects of these pronouns, as the old NIV did by inserting the word *God*, the new gender-neutral NIV distorts the meaning by rendering the other six masculine pronouns as *them*. This translation would imply that the subject is not Jesus Christ, but humanity. Such ambiguity is too high a price to pay for political correctness.

It is the task of hermeneutics and ultimately of the pastor/teacher to interpret the text and make application. But students of the Word need to start with a reliable translation, if not the text in its original languages. While the Bible does not discriminate against women, gender inclusive translations can distort the accuracy of the translation.[144]

The Interpretation of Scripture

Where textual criticism ends, *hermeneutics* begins. Hermes was the Greek god who allegedly interpreted the message of the gods to humans. The verb *hermeneuo* is used in Luke 24:27 where Christ interprets or explains the OT. It means to verbalize,

---

[144]See Poythress and Grudem, *Gender-Neutral Bible Controversy.*

translate, and explain. This word, in various forms, is used in Matthew 1:23; Mark 5:41, 15:22,34; John 1:8,38, 9:7; Acts 4:36, 9:36, 13:8; 1 Corinthians 12: 10, 14:28; Hebrews 7:2.

The task of hermeneutics is to ascertain what God has said in Scripture; to determine the meaning of the Word of God. Walter Kaiser wrote, "The primary task of the biblical scholar is to unfold the meaning of the text of Scripture as it was originally intended to be understood by the writer of that text."[145]

Packer stated, "Biblical authority is an empty notion unless we know how to determine what the Bible means."[146] We must correctly handle the Word of truth (2 Tim 2:15). The verb *orthotomeo* means to cut a straight line. Applied to this context, the meaning is that we are commanded to guide the Word of truth along a straight line.

The authority of Scripture is nullified if its real meaning is missed. Although the Bible means what it says and generally speaks in simple terms, there are difficulties inherent in all communication. Furthermore, Christians sometimes differ regarding what Scripture teaches, therefore we need an objective standard of interpretation which avoids making the interpreter the final authority. In 1981 John Stott wrote, "It is increasingly clear to me that hermeneutics is Issue No.1 in the church today, & not least for evangelical Christians. Our differences are largely due to different ways of reading and understanding Scripture."[147]

There was no uniform method of exegesis in the early church. Some early church fathers delighted in incorporating Greek philosophy. By the third century, Asian mystics, Jewish rabbinical teachers, and the Greek and Roman philosophers came together as the Alexandrian school.

Located at the mouth of the Nile River, Alexandria was an early center of Christianity. Tradition credits Mark with founding

---

[145]Kaiser, "Literary Form of Genesis 1-11," 48.

[146]Packer, "Hermeneutics and Biblical Authority," 3.

[147]Chapman, *Godly Ambition*, 105.

the church there. Soon afterward a school started. The first leader of this seminary whose name we know was Pantaeus, a converted Stoic philosopher. He was followed by Clement of Alexandria, who adopted allegorical methods and was fascinated with pagan philosophy. He was succeeded by Origen, who also followed Philo, the Jewish philosopher who was attracted to mysticism and Greek philosophy.

By the fourth century, a school at Antioch, begun by Diodorus and Theodorus, was developed by Lucian. They opposed allegory and advocate a grammatical-historical method of interpretation, with close adherence to the plain, natural meaning according to the use of language and the condition of the writer.[148] Christopher Hall argued for the value of patristic exegesis because "the fathers lived and worked in *hermeneutical proximity* to the biblical writers."[149] As Ray Dunning wrote, when we move from Scripture to the apostolic fathers, it is like moving from a brilliantly lighted room into the twilight shadows.[150]

God's revelation is logical, following the conventional rules of grammar. Therefore, the Bible must be interpreted like any other book. This does not mean, however, that the Bible is to be read without any awareness of its spiritual sense and the fact that we must have the illumination of the Spirit of God in order to understand it. John Calvin taught that through regeneration the "spectacles of faith" vastly improve our spiritual eyesight.[151]

The rules of hermeneutics refer to the guidelines by which we interpret or exegete. The word *exegesis* refers to the process of *bringing out* the meaning of a biblical text. The Greek verb

---

[148]Schaff, *History of the Christian Church*, 2:816.

[149]Hall, *Reading Scripture with the Church Fathers*, 54.

[150]Dunning, *Grace, Faith and Holiness*, 600-606.

[151]Calvin, *Institutes of Christian Religion*, 1.6.1; 1.14.1.

eksegeomai is used in Luke 24:35; John 1:18; Acts 10:8, 15:12,14, 21:19.

Allegorical, dogmatic, or mystical hermeneutic are inadequate methods because they are subjective. These approaches tend to be rationalistic, ignoring the historical context, imposing eisegesis for exegesis, and tend to personal application rather than an overarching explanation. If we must rely on a mystic to tell us what God told him the text meant, the text itself is actually unnecessary.

Jonathan Cahn utilizes a method of biblical interpretation called Kabbalah. This is ancient Jewish mysticism or occult knowledge. The word is usually translated as "tradition." Kabbalah is a doctrine of esoteric knowledge concerning God and the universe, having come down as a revelation to the Sages from a remote past, and preserved only by a privileged few. Kabbalah is considered part of the Jewish Oral Law. Most forms of Kabbalah teach that every letter, word, number, and accent of scripture contains a hidden sense; and it teaches the methods of interpretation for ascertaining these occult meanings. These ancient mysteries are classic new age expressions which have been used for centuries by freemasonry, theosophy, and new age rabbis.

In the book of Colossians, Paul confronts a philosophy that was identified with the teachings of the Essenes. The apocalyptic tendencies of the Essenes distracted from the all-sufficiency of Christ. T. K Abbott wrote,

> The teaching of the Colossian false teachers was essentially traditional and esoteric. The Essenes, their spiritual predecessors, as well as the Gnostics, subsequently claimed to possess such a source of knowledge.[152]

---

[152]Abbott, *ICC*, 247.

Especially popular amongst the Essenes was the pesher method of scriptural interpretation in which "everything from the past was transformed and given a contemporary value and meaning," especially texts taken from the prophetic books. While Cahn uses the Kabbalist method to find hidden meaning in the numerical arrangements of the Bible, this method may be applied to almost any piece of literature and draw almost any interpretation from it.

However, in one passage Paul specifically identifies his use of an allegorical interpretation (Gal 4:21-31).[153] This is the exception instead of the rule.

Dogmatic implies the approach that a passage of Scripture means what the church says its means. This means the church alone can interpret Scripture, that the church is the official interpreter of Scripture, and no passage of Scripture can be interpreted to conflict with Roman Catholic doctrine.

In contrast, Wesley and the Reformers substituted an infallible book for an infallible church.[154] Wesley explained

> The faith of the *Protestants*, in general, embraces only those truths, as necessary to salvation, which are clearly revealed in the oracles of God. Whatever is plainly declared in the Old and New Testaments is the object of their faith. They believe neither more nor less than what is manifestly contained in, and provable by, the Holy Scriptures. . . . The written Word is the whole and sole rule of their faith, as well as practice. They believe whatsoever God has declared, and profess to do whatsoever He hath commanded. This is the proper faith of Protestants: by this they will abide, and no other.[155]

---

[153]Judg 9:7-11 is also an allegory, having a continuous second level of meaning.

[154]Baker, "John Wesley's Churchmanship," 270.

[155]Wesley, "On Faith," Sermon #106, 1.8.

It should come as no surprise that if I approach Scripture with certain presuppositions, I will find confirmation for what I assume to be in Scripture. But if every theological tradition follows suit, the result is that no one can agree on what the Bible actually says. If Scripture is our final authority and we approach Scripture with a commitment to inductive study, we may find that we have broad agreement that extends beyond our own tradition. The grammatical-historical hermeneutic is not only the most objective and inductive method, it is also the broad Reformation and Protestant hermeneutics.

Wesley wrote, "We believe the written word of God to be the *only and the sufficient* rule both of Christian faith and practice."[156] Thomas Oden wrote that Wesley followed Luther and Calvin in their method in reading Scripture texts.[157] Prior to the Reformation the Roman church determined what the Bible meant. Beginning at the time of the Protestant Reformation, theologians had to wrestle with the proper hermeneutical method. Wesley wrote,

> The general rule of interpreting Scripture is this: the literal sense of every text is to be taken, if it be not contrary to some other texts. But in that case, the obscure text is to be interpreted by those which speak more plainly.[158]

Wesley also warned,

> Try all things by the written Word, and let all bow down before it. You are in danger of [fanaticism] every hour, if you depart ever so little from Scripture; yea, or

---

[156]Wesley, *BE Works*, 9:34.

[157]Oden, *John Wesley's Teachings*, 1:71.

[158]Wesley, *Letter* to Samuel Furly, 10 May 1755.

from the plain, literal meaning of any text, taken in connection with the context.[159]

Mystical writings are not open to verification. The grammatical-historical hermeneutic, in contrast to other methods, interprets Scripture according to the natural, ordinary, usual sense of the words based on the laws of grammar and the facts of history.

The apostles had authority to pass down the teachings of Jesus Christ (2 Pet 3:2). But Peter confronted the charge that they fabricated or embellished their accounts. The apostles did not create myths. Pagans explained everything by myths. The OT, however, never employs the term *myth*.

> Mythology in the Old Testament is always depicted as a forbidden pagan environment and as a religious compromise to which the Hebrews themselves were vulnerable from time to time. This compromise occurred despite the fact that the God of Israel was known to stand in a very different relationship to nature and history than did the polytheistic divinities.[160]

The word *myth* is used five times in the NT, always in a negative connotation.[161] If a parable communicates some literal truth, it is not a myth. A myth may communicate superstition, but not valid information. Bruce Waltke wrote, "The term 'myth' in theology should be reserved for stories informed by pantheism and magic."[162]

---

[159]Wesley, *BE Works*, 13:113.

[160]Henry, *GRA* 1:47.

[161]1 Tim 1:4, 4:7; 2 Tim 4:4; Titus 1:13-14; 2 Pet 1:16.

[162]Waltke, "Myth, History, and the Bible," 559.

Many OT passages depict Yahweh guiding historical events as a warrior who overthrows and destroys nations. He destroyed Israel's foes at the exodus. He demolishes Israel's corrupt pagan neighbor nations. He stands invisibly behind Israel's destruction of corrupt, idolatrous enemy nations. He is the author of judgment and destruction of the Canaanites, Egypt, Moab, the Philistines, and Tyre. Israel faced the same doom for her disobedience and idolatry.

Christianity is inseparably tied to historical events. God is active in history, and our faith is rooted in his historic acts — not a leap of faith. Every major theme of Christian theology, whether the nature of God's relationship to the world, the meaning of Christ, the plan of salvation, or the fate of the universe, directly or indirectly involves questions about how the present relates to the past. Jesus Christ always treated the history of the OT as factual. NT authors consistently refer to historical details recorded in the OT without any indication that they considered those incidents to be unreliable or untrustworthy.

Jesus consistently treats the historical narratives in the OT as the record of fact.

> It is impossible for Scripture to be indifferent to historical events when those events are a fulfilment of prophecy. Similarly those events are also demonstrations of the faithfulness of God to his covenant commitments. Historical events demonstrate that what he has promised comes to pass. To remove the historical from the concerns of Scripture is to remove what demonstrates the faithfulness of God.[163]

Unless history is simply the chronicle of meaningless facts, the real debate is over which lens we utilize to interpret these facts. Apparently the "facts" which do not correspond with a

---

[163]Weeks, *The Sufficiency of Scripture*, 49-50.

modernist worldview must be relegated to another dimension or interpreted as myth. This is why Francis Schaeffer insisted on biblical history which occurred in space and time.[164] The world in which we live, the world which exists in space and time, has fallen under the curse of sin and the gospel promises deliverance from sin in space and time. Christian theology must address the real world, not merely some esoteric meta-physical concept. God's acts in ordinary history are themselves a revelation of himself.

The Barrenness of Historical Criticism

Since the development of the grammatical-historical herme-neutic, modernism has proposed the historical-critical hermeneu-tic. Instead of concentrating on the biblical text, the trend was to develop naturalistic theories as to how the text came into being.

While modernists ask if there is some religious meaning in the text not dependent on the literal, historical interpretation, the problem is that each interpretation will be subjective and not authoritative. The historical-critical method itself is based on modernist presuppositions. It is rationalistic. It both redefines inspiration and rejects the supernatural. It imposes evolutionary concepts upon the religion of Israel. It negates biblical authority through its assumptions about accommodation.

The 1982 Chicago Statement on Hermeneutics declared,

WE AFFIRM that legitimate critical techniques should be used in determining the canonical text and its mean-ing.

WE DENY the legitimacy of allowing any method of biblical criticism to question the truth or integrity of the

---

[164]Schaeffer, *Works*, 1:86-87.

writer's expressed meaning, or of any other scriptural teaching.[165]

The function of textual criticism or lower criticism is to recover the original text. Ancient manuscripts often have variation in the text, either by accident or design. Copyists were sometimes careless, accidently confusing similar words, transposing, repeating, or omitting letters and words. Sometimes the text contained marginal notes which got incorporated into the text. Sometimes the text was purposely amended by a scribe who thought he could improve it by exchanging a difficult word for an easier one. Rough passages were smoothed out or difficult clauses omitted. Sometimes the text was wilfully corrupted by those who sought to interject their dogmatic interpretation. As manuscripts continued to be copied, the errors would be multiplied.

It is legitimate to use critical methods to reconstruct the original text, but "higher criticism" tends to use source criticism, form criticism, and redaction criticism in order to reconstruct alleged prior sources or attempt to establish the motive of the author. Instead of concentrating on the biblical text, the trend has been to develop naturalistic theories regarding how the text came into being. Thus, a student could graduate with a PhD in biblical studies without believing the Bible is the Word of God or even being a Christian. Yet he would be an expert in all the hypothetical theories about how the Bible came into being.

Source criticism assumes that Matthew, Mark, Luke, and John did not actually write the Gospels which bear their names. Instead, eyewitness accounts were passed on orally for a generation. Some were embellished or modified over time. Then these eyewitness accounts were gathered, edited, and written down in a document called *Quelle* or Q. No one has ever seen Q, but it is

---

[165]Radmacher and Preus, *Hermeneutics, Inerrancy, and the Bible*, 885.

assumed that the editors who compiled the synoptic gospels drew from this source and altered the material to address the contemporary needs within the early church.

However, the renowned twentieth-century archaeologist, William F. Albright, concluded, "every book of the New Testament was written by a baptized Jew between the forties and the eighties of the first century A. D. (very probably sometime between about 50 and 75 A. D.)."[166]

This same "cut and paste" approach to the Scriptures produced the documentary hypothesis which explained the five books of Moses were actually written by four different sources and later pieced together into their present form a thousand years after Moses. The hypothesis was first advanced by Thomas Hobbes in the mid-seventeenth century.[167] Thus, the Pentateuch is not regarded as historically accurate, but a natural product of the Jewish religion. Oswald T. Allis, *The Five Books of Moses* (1947) dismissed the claims of this documentary hypothesis and his research has never been refuted.

Within this documentary hypothesis, their premise is their conclusion — that there was no supernatural revelation. They use selective data. They are unrealistic in their expectations, tending not to believe primitive man could express something two different ways, using synonyms. They refuse alternate explanations. They assume a temporal and cultural superiority or chauvinism. If any discrepancies between pagan documents and the Bible existed, they assumed the pagan documents to be more reliable. They assumed an evolutionary view of religion which began with animism, then polytheism (the use of the plural noun - *elohim*), then monotheism, then Israel backslid to polytheism, before monotheism became institutionalized around 700 BC.

But the higher critics do not agree on the proper evolutionary sequence. Some have said different names point to different

---

[166]Albright, "Toward a More Conservative View," 3.

[167]Harrison, *Introduction to the Old Testament*, 9-10.

authors while others have said the same name nevertheless different authors. Furthermore, there are J sections where *elohim* is used and E passages where *Yahweh* is used. David Rosenburg and Harold Bloom in *The Book of J* (1990) even attempt to reconstruct a prior J source.

Some have observed there is not much difference between the E passages and the J passages. Yet some scholars say that J comes later than E, while other scholars claim J is really earlier than E. Some say P is earlier than J, while others have argued that P must have come last instead of first. It has been argued that the E material is really older than the J material. It has been argued that the D material is actually much older than previously thought.

Then the P source was broken down into separate components such as P, Pg, P1, P2, P3. The same analysis was applied to the J source. J was broken into J1 and J2. An L source (lay) was suggested. Someone else identified an N source (nomadic). When J and E are compared there are similarities, attributed to a common G source. There was also an S source (Seir) and some advocated a K source (Kenite).[168]

Thus, while much attention is devoted to developmental theories, little attention is given to the contents and message of the book. John Barton admitted in 1984 that Biblical criticism is non-scientific despite exaggerated claims to watertight, scientific methods for elucidating the OT text.[169] He said the critics began with a hunch suggested by an imaginative guess by an informed mind and then formed a hypothesis. They formulated more precisely as they went and sometimes retraced their steps and tried a different approach. "This manner of encounter with the text is repeated at every level of the critical enterprise; and it

---

[168]Archer, *Survey of Old Testament Introduction*, 81-176.

[169]Barton, *Reading the Old Testament*, 6.

provides, perhaps, the only true sense in which criticism can be called 'scientific.'"[170]

In 1977, Bruce Vawter wrote of scholars who reject the documentary approach to the composition of Genesis which they caricature as a scissors-and-paste concept of authorship.

> Today their once thin ranks have been increasingly swelled by other distinguished scholars who . . . have cast serious doubt on the validity of the neat J, E, and P divisions of Genesis, distinct in point of time and ethos, which were finally assembled by a Redactor to make up the book as we now know it. . . . The judgments and reservations of these scholars must certainly be respected, and they do forbid us from pretending to a consensus that no longer exists.

Yet in the very next paragraph Vawter declared, "We remain convinced of the documentary hypothesis, nevertheless, despite all its shortcomings and the obvious objections against it."[171]

Gleason Archer concluded,

> Almost every pillar has been shaken and shattered by a generation of scholars who were brought up on the Graf-Wellhausen system and yet have found it inadequate to explain the date of the Pentateuch. At the same time it must be recognized that for the most part, even those scholars who have repudiated Wellhausen have shown no tendency to embrace a more conservative view of the origin of the books of Moses.[172]

---

[170]Barton, *Reading the Old Testament*, 25.

[171]Vawter, *On Genesis*, 15-16.

[172]Archer, *Survey of Old Testament Introduction*, 104.

Form criticism built upon this unproven assumption and dominated scholarship for the first half of the twentieth century, attempting to reconstruct each independent unit between the oral traditions and the Bible as we now have it. It was assumed that the church created legends, tales, myths, and parables to meet particular needs. Thus, the Bible was regarded as a piece of propaganda created by the church to serve its own interests. They emphasize the *sitz in labem* or the life situation which they think produced that particular writing.

Rudolf Bultmann, one of the most famous form critics, attempted to strip away the mythology that he claimed had developed about Jesus and ended up with only forty brief sayings that he considered genuine. Eta Linnemann, a student of Bultmann, estimates that historical-critical theology assumes upwards of 80-90% of the hypotheses without verification.[173] Thus, the historical-critical method is an *a priori* approach to locate the canon in the canon, which will produce a historical-critical interpretation as to what constitutes the canon.[174]

This places the church or the academic guild in authority over the Word since the Word of God was claimed to have been carried orally before the church wrote it down. The Bible was regarded as a piece of propaganda created by the church to serve its own interests. However, the authority is not vested in who wrote it down, but who spoke it.

The next method to gain popularity was *redaction criticism*, coined by Willi Marxsen in 1954. The focus moved to the redactors or editors who picked and chose what material would be interwoven to create the biblical accounts and what motivated these editors to select the material which we now have. How did he arrange his material and direct it toward particular themes? This becomes problematic particularly when redaction criticism

---

[173]Linnemann, *Historical Criticism of the Bible*, 96; *Biblical Criticism on Trial*, 177-188.

[174]Maier, *End of the Historical-Critical Method*, 9-11.

assumes that the biblical writers were creative, fabricating sayings and episodes to meet particular needs. All this draws the interpreter away from the text to an attempt to deduce what motivated the editor in his selection. John Barton admitted,

> If redaction criticism plays its hand too confidently, we end up with a piece of writing so coherent that no division into sources is warranted any longer; and the sources and the redactor vanish together in a puff of smoke.[175]

Redaction criticism can only be used where similar documents can be compared, however. Thus, it operates primarily in the Gospel accounts and in the OT between Samuel, Kings, and Chronicles. It is assumed that different church situations produced different accounts.[176]

There may be literary dependence, but the humble modern critic would never know that fact with complete certainty. Redaction criticism gives very little input in terms of the meaning of the final text. While there was selectivity and arrangement of events by gospel writers, there was not modification and creativity. All this offers very little help in interpretation of Scripture. David Bauer also concluded source criticism, form criticism, and redaction criticism have contributed little to the advancement of our understanding of the message.[177]

Walter Kaiser explained that good exegesis cannot be built on "hypothetical sources which have never materialized in any form. These sources are deductively 'authenticated' and then

---

[175]Barton, *Reading the Old Testament*, 57.

[176]Kantzer, "Redaction Criticism?" 1-I to 12-I; Thomas, "Redaction Criticism," 233-270.

[177]Bauer, *Structure of Matthew's Gospel*, 11-12.

inductively 'proven' from the same document in what becomes a most vicious circle."[178]

Across the twentieth century the interpretive battle was over whether to read the Bible through the lens of "original intent" or through the lens of "liberal activism." Around 1989 modernism collapsed philosophically. It seems that while modernists have recognized the barrenness of higher criticism, conservatives have finally embraced it, desiring academic respectability.

Postmodernism interprets doctrine in terms of a cultural-linguistic system, teaching people to practice the faith of a religious community. It remains liberal because it is anthropological rather than theological. But while modernism assumes that doctrine reflects religious concerns common to humanity, postmodernism sees doctrine as the structure for individual religious experience.

I accept the premise that no interpreter approaches the text with a *tabula rasa* — a blank slate. Stated in other terms, we all approach the text with presuppositions which must be identified and examined. However, the new hermeneutic is too existential and does not focus adequately on an objective understanding of God's revelation.

Postmodernism is more open to the supernatural and has less faith in science. It is relativistic. There is no overarching absolute — no meta narrative. There is no grand story. Truth does not exist in any objective sense. Postmodernism provides no hope. Even the Bible is interpreted with a hermeneutic of suspicion, which Oden defined as an attack on the integrity of the biblical writers or hearers, questioning their motives or social status.[179]

This means for the postmodern that while Paul gave his opinion of right and wrong, we must also strive to understand the point of view of his opponents. Since we all have a different frame of reference, we can never completely understand each

---

[178]Kaiser, *Toward an Exegetical Theology*, 64.

[179]Oden, *John Wesley's Teachings*, 1:76-77.

other. The result seems to be that there is no objective meaning. In the development of feminist hermeneutics, more radical feminists consider the text to be a product of a patriarchal society which must be interpreted in light of women's experience. Since it is assumed that women read the Bible with a different perspective than men, feminist hermeneutics attempts to deconstruct the text from any perceived male bias. Thus, experience becomes an interpretative category. Radical feminists have repudiated the Christian tradition entirely in order to construct a new post-Christian feminist religion.

But what a passage means is fixed by the author and not subject to change by readers. Meaning is determined by the author; it is discovered by the readers. Thomas Oden resisted "speculative fashion of redaction and form criticism and reader-response theories and socio pragmatic contextualizations that tyrannize and nonchalantly rape the text."

> The text has rights over against its interpreters, some of whom stand poised to exploit, assault, and mug the text. When contemporary readers make themselves the absolute masters of the text, then the author has lost all rights of authorship. Authorial intent becomes subservient to contemporary ideological interests.[180]

Jonathan Chaves concluded that postmodern hermeneutics, in its approach to language, is "profoundly anti-Christian" and that these deconstructionists are really Marxists who have applied their leftist analysis as an attack on religion and social mores.[181] In 2 Corinthians 4:2 Paul says that Christian ministers do not *doloo* adulterate, corrupt, or tamper with God's Word.

---

[180]Oden, *Requiem*, 133-135; 73-74.

[181]Chaves, "Soul and Reason in Literary Criticism," 828-835.

Basic Principles of Interpretation

Above all, preaching should be a faithful interpretation of the Word which is based upon its literal grammatical meaning and its intention as found in the whole of Scripture. This implied the necessity of studying the text in its original language, or by the help of commentators, and according to the laws of interpretation.

These laws pertain to the methods of interpreting figurative language, that which is common and that which is peculiar to language itself, the observance of the context of every passage and its connection with the writer's general system of teaching, recognition of the analogy of faith, and the absolute necessity of a spiritual sympathy with the sacred word under the direct influence of the Holy Spirit.

• The law of non-contradiction

A true contradiction is to both affirm and deny the same reality. For the Bible to assert genuine contradictions would mean that it could not have been inspired by the source of all truth. The Bible assumes the validity of the law of non-contradiction when it states

- No man can serve two masters (Matt 6:24).
- A good tree cannot produce bad fruit (Matt 7:18).
- He who is not with me is against me (Matt 12:30).

While the Bible is trustworthy and accurate, it should not be expected to comport with modern technical precision in matters of chronology. Variations in reporting an event do not necessarily constitute a contradiction.

Many apparent contradictions are resolved when we see them in the light of the whole of Scripture. However, the Bible does contain paradoxes. Augustine explained,

If we are perplexed by an apparent contradiction in Scripture, it is not allowable to say, The author of this book is mistaken; but either the manuscript is faulty, or the translation is wrong, or you have not understood.[182]

The task of systematic theology is not to pick portions of Scripture which support a preconceived doctrinal position, but rather to reconcile apparent contradictory statements in Scripture.

Martin Luther struggled to reconcile the theology of Paul against that of James regarding salvation by faith and works. Luther's reaction to the doctrine of salvation by works in James was to declare that it was really an epistle of straw which did not contain the gospel and casting doubt on the apostleship of James.[183]

Marcion may have been the first to depreciate the OT, but not the last. Dispensationalism tends to pit law against grace; the OT against the NT.

• **Clarity**

The perspicuity of Scripture refers to its inherent clarity. The Reformer John Knox explained, "The Word of God is plain in itself. If there appear any obscurity in one place, the Holy Ghost, which is never contrarious to Himself, explaineth the same more clearly in other places; so that there can remain no doubt, but unto such as obstinately will remain ignorant."[184]

Martin Luther responded to the claims by Erasmus that the Scripture was obscure, "If Scripture is obscure or equivocal, why need it have been brought down to us by act of God?" Luther wrote,

---

[182]Augustine, *Reply to Faustus the Manichean*, *NPNF*1 4:180.

[183]Rittgers, *RCS* 13:200-201.

[184]John Knox, *History of the Reformation in Scotland*, 280.

I certainly grant that many *passages* in the Scriptures are obscure and hard to elucidate, but that is due, not to the exalted nature of their subject, but to our own linguistic and grammatical ignorance; and it does not in any way prevent us knowing all the *contents* of Scripture.

Luther contended that if anyone finds the Bible wholly obscure, the fault is not in the Bible, but in him — he is spiritually blind, cannot discern Christ, and needs the help of the Holy Spirit to make him see.[185]

The Bible makes sense and can be understood through the application of our mind and the illumination of the Holy Spirit. Wesley explained, "We need the same Spirit to *understand* the Scripture which enabled the holy men of old to *write* it."[186] The Word of God is spiritual and therefore can only be spiritually perceived (1 Cor 2:14). Yet the Holy Spirit does not bypass our mind. This does not imply that a non-Christian is unable to understand the meaning of any Scripture. It means that without the regeneration of the Holy Spirit, the sinner will not welcome the message. Understanding is more of an issue of the will than of the intellect.

Instead of the inadequate position of soteriological inerrancy, a more adequate position is soteriological perspicuity. All Scripture is God-breathed and therefore true, but not all Scripture is equally clear. However, the way of salvation is so clear that even a fool need not go astray (Isa 35:8).

---

[185]Luther, *Bondage of the Will*, 128, 70-74.

[186]Wesley, *Letter* to the Lord Bishop of Gloucester, *BE Works*, 11:509.

- **The Analogy of Faith**

Where the Bible is not clear, obscure passages are interpreted in light of clear passages. Terry explained,

> No single statement or obscure passage of one book can be allowed to set aside a doctrine which is clearly established by many passages. The obscure texts must be interpreted in the light of those which are plain and positive. . . . No doctrine which rests upon a single passage of Scripture can belong to fundamental doctrines recognized in the analogy of faith.[187]

John Wesley commented on the *oracles of God*:

> That grand scheme of doctrine which is delivered therein, touching original sin, justification by faith, and present, inward salvation. There is a wonderful analogy between all these; and a close and intimate connection between the chief heads of that faith "which was once delivered to the saints." Every article, therefore, concerning which there is any question should be determined by this rule; every doubtful scripture interpreted according to the grand truths which run through the whole.[188]

The term *analogy of faith* is found only in Romans 12:6. There it means the proportion of faith given to each believer.[189] Theologically, *the analogy of faith* describes the method of interpreting the parts of Scripture, especially difficult and obscure ones, consistent with the whole of Scripture.

---

[187]Terry, *Biblical Hermeneutics*, 579, 581.

[188]Wesley, *Notes*, 397.

[189]Ramm, *Protestant Biblical Interpretation*, 107.

- **Genres**

It is helpful to be aware of literature types, yet the Bible is one book and we should not build walls between sections of the Bible.

> If we try to use the rules for interpreting one genre to interpret a different type, we will almost surely misinterpret the passage that we are studying. We cannot, for example, read a psalm in the same way that we read a parable. This should not be surprising. We know from our own culture that we cannot read a phone book as if it were a novel, a shopping list as if it were an advertisement, a poem as if it were a court brief.[190]

There are ten basic genres found in Scripture: law, Old Testament narrative, psalms, wisdom literature, prophecy, gospel, parables, New Testament history, epistle, and apocalyptic literature. Each type of literature may have specific parameters which need to be taken into account. Rhetoric is also associated with genre. Scripture is analyzed for the techniques used in persuasion. Adam Clarke advised,

> Never take a text which you do not fully understand; and make it a point of conscience to give the *literal* meaning of it to the people: this is a matter of great and solemn importance. To give God's words a different meaning to what he intended to convey by them, or to put a construction upon them which we have not the fullest proof he has intended, is awful indeed![191]

---

[190]Stuart, "Interpret = Understand + Explain," 12.

[191]Clarke, *Letter to a Preacher*, 101-102.

However, prophetic and apocalyptic literature frequently employ symbolism. Taking the Bible literally means interpreting the Bible according to the rules of grammar and the facts of history. It does not imply the disregard for symbolism, especially when it is apparent that the context is symbolic. Symbolism and images, however, are not a code, they do not exist in isolation, and we need biblical indication for any symbol, type, or image.[192]

- **Priority of the original language**

The original Hebrew and Greek text is the final authority in matters of translation. Every translation should start with the original text.

- **One basic meaning; many applications**

During the mediaeval period the prevalent approach to Bible interpretation held that the text had four levels of meaning. The lowest level was the historical or literal meaning. Then the spiritual or typological meaning followed. Next was the tropological or moral meaning, followed by the anagogical or future meaning. Of course, this approach had the effect of discouraging the non-professional from even reading, much less understanding the Bible.

Scripture has one basic meaning, but is capable of many applications.[193] This principle was articulated in 1643 by William Ames,

> There is only one meaning for every place in Scripture. Otherwise the meaning of Scripture would not only be unclear and uncertain, but there would be no meaning

---

[192]Jordan, *Through New Eyes*, 15-16.

[193]Terry, *Biblical Hermeneutics*, 511-513.

at all — for anything which does not mean one thing surely means nothing.[194]

Regarding prophetic passages, Milton S. Terry was emphatic that there is no double sense.

A fundamental principle in grammatico-historical exposition is that words and sentences can have but one signification in one and the same connection. The moment we neglect this principle we drift out upon a sea of uncertainty and conjecture.[195]

Terry quoted John Owen, "If the Scripture has more than one meaning, it has no meaning at all." Scripture has one specific meaning, and the object of the interpreter is to determine what the passage means and adhere rigidly to that meaning.[196] This single sense amounts to the author's intended meaning. The primary task of the interpreter is to recognize the meaning which the author intended and to exegete the implications of that meaning.

However, this principle does not negate the existence of typology in Scripture. A *type* is a person, institution, office, event, or action in the OT which has symbolic significance regarding something future in the NT.

Yet some OT passages do not always seem to be used in the NT with reference to their original context. Frame believes that in such cases the NT is making an application of the OT text.[197] The same Holy Spirit who inspired the original truth has the

---

[194]Ames, *The Marrow of Theology*, 188.

[195]Terry, *Biblical Hermeneutics*, 205.

[196]Terry, *Biblical Hermeneutics*, 493-499. For a more recent discussion, see Bloesch, *Holy Scripture*, 184-192.

[197]Frame, *Doctrine of the Word of God*, 190-193.

prerogative to assign a different meaning to the same words. We do not have that prerogative.[198]

Some theologians, however, believe that along with the literal sense, the Holy Spirit may encode a hidden meaning. This fuller sense is implied in the Latin phrase *sensus plenior*. While the author himself may not grasp the full implication of his message, *fuller sense* does not imply a different meaning. Daniel did not understand all of his vision (12:8-9). In fact, Packer stated with regard to all Scripture, "God's meaning and message through each passage, when set in its total biblical context, exceeds what the human writer had in mind."[199]

Without limiting the illumination of the Holy Spirit, the text has one basic meaning but multiple applications. Regarding application Wesley wrote,

> I apply no Scripture phrase either to myself or any other without carefully considering, both the original meaning and the secondary sense, wherein (allowing for different times and circumstances) it may be applied to ordinary Christians.[200]

• **The centrality of Christ**

Jesus Christ is the climax of God's special revelation. He is the unveiled mystery of God (Col 1:27, 2:2, 4:3). He is the divine wisdom. His coming marked the beginning of the last days. As the *logos* of God, he is the mediating agent in creation, in redemption, and in coming judgment.

---

[198]Bahnsen, "Inerrancy of the Autographa," 170-171; Nicole, "Patrick Fairbairn," 768-776. See also Beale and Carson, *Commentary on the New Testament Use of the Old Testament.*

[199]Packer, "Biblical Authority, Hermeneutics and Inerrancy," 147.

[200]Wesley, *Letter* to John Church, 2 Feb 1745, 3.5.

Augustine is famous for stating that Christ is concealed in the OT and revealed in the NT.[201] Pope defined revelation as the unfolding of the eternal counsel of God in Christ. He is the personal revelation of God. The sum and substance of truth is found in him (Eph 4:21). "His testimony is the last word of all objective revelation."[202]

Jesus began with Moses and all the prophets, explaining everything they said concerning him (Luke 24:27,44).[203] Jesus declared that the Scriptures testify concerning him (John 5:39,46). He is the key to knowledge (Luke 11:52). Yet the authority of Scripture cannot be reduced solely to its function of directing us to Christ.

Pope taught the "hydrostatic law" of exegesis, meaning that the water in the Epistles never rises above its source in the Gospels. Thus, our union with God in Christ through the Holy Spirit is the basis of the Christian's perfection.[204]

- **Context**

The best commentary on Scripture is Scripture. An obscure verse must be interpreted in its broader setting. The Bible contains quotations from pagan philosophers (Acts 17:28), from demons (Mark 5:9), from Satan (Job 1:9), as well as Job's misguided counselors. We must distinguish between what Scripture reports and what it teaches. Scripture records without error statements which are false. It is incumbent upon the interpreter to pay attention to the context.

However, Proverbs 10-31 has no context from one verse to the next; the broader context is wisdom statements.

---

[201] Augustine, *Expositions on Psalms*, NPNF1 8:531.

[202] Pope, *Compendium*, 1:38.

[203] see Hodgkin, *Christ in All the Scriptures*.

[204] Moss, *W. B. Pope*, 105.

- **Cross reference**

Use Scripture to interpret Scripture. Compare parallel passages. Look at the use of the same word in other passages. This technique used to be called *uses loquendi*, which describes the meaning of the term in current usage as employed by a particular writer or prevalent in a particular period of time.

- **Historical and cultural background**

We must avoid two opposing errors. On the one hand we live in a world of technical expertise. We may create the perception that reading the Bible is a daunting challenge best left to the experts if we over-emphasize the fact that we have cultural blinders and cannot understand the ancient world of the Bible. While the Roman Catholic church claims that only the institution can determine what the text means, in Protestant circles, too often, we are told that only the experts can determine what the text means.

Yet Scripture transcends cultural barriers. If it takes an expert to tell you what God said, then he did not communicate very clearly! Tyndale declared that if God spared his life, ere many years he would cause a boy that drove the plough to know more of the Scripture than the Pope.[205]

The 1982 Chicago Statement on Hermeneutics, formulated by the International Council on Biblical Inerrancy, stated:

> WE AFFIRM that translations of the text of Scripture can communicate knowledge of God across all temporal and cultural boundaries.
> WE DENY that the meaning of biblical texts is so tied to the culture out of which they came that understand-

---

[205]Foxe, *Foxe's Book of Martyrs*, ch 12.

ing of the same meaning in other cultures is impossible.[206]

On the other hand, we need to understand the languages and grammar, as well as the historical background in order to avoid common mistakes. Extra-biblical data does have value in clarifying what Scripture teaches and for prompting correction of faulty interpretations. However, extra-biblical views cannot be used to disprove Scripture or hold priority over it.

Problem Passages

Some biblical passages are difficult to understand. Others may be difficult to accept. Here we are dealing with statements that are difficult to reconcile.

The careful reader will occasionally discover statements in Scripture which appear to be contradictions. According to Terry, such problems are found in the genealogical tables and in various numerical, historical, doctrinal, ethical, and prophetic statements.

The interpreter should not ignore the difficulty, but should attempt to explain the apparent inconsistency by rational methods.

> It does not follow that because he is not able to solve the problem it is therefore insoluble. The lack of sufficient data has often effectually baffled the efforts of the most able and accomplished exegetes.

Terry explained that most discrepancies are the errors of copyists, the variety of names applied to the same person or place, different methods of reckoning times and seasons, differ-

---

[206]Radmacher and Preus, *Hermeneutics, Inerrancy, and the Bible*, 884.

ent local and historical standpoints, and the special scope and plan of each particular book. "Variations are not contradictions, and many essential variations arise from different methods of arranging a series of particular facts."[207]

Those who are looking for contradictions tend to find what they are looking for. However, if we approach the Scripture believing it to be rational, we can understand its meaning — sometimes with the help of a good commentary. Concerning Bible difficulties, Gleason Archer counseled,

> Be fully persuaded in your own mind that an adequate explanation exists, even though you have not yet found it. . . . Avoid the fallacy of shifting from one a priori to its opposite every time an apparent problem arises. The Bible is either the inerrant Word of God or else it is an imperfect record by fallible men. Once we have come into agreement with Jesus that the Scripture is completely trustworthy and authoritative, then it is out of the question for us to shift over to the opposite assumption, that the Bible is only the errant record of fallible men as they wrote about God. If the Bible is truly the Word of God, as Jesus said, then it must be treated with respect, trust, and complete obedience. . . . Carefully study the context and framework of the verse in which the problem arises until you gain some idea of what the verse is intended to mean within its own setting. . . . No interpretation of Scripture is valid that is not based on careful exegesis. . . . In the case of parallel passages, the only method that can be justified is harmonization. . . . Whenever historical accounts of the Bible are called into question on the basis of alleged disagreement with the finds of archaeology or the testimony of ancient non-Hebrew documents, always remember that the

---

[207]Terry, *Biblical Hermeneutics*, 514.

Bible is itself an archaeological document of the highest caliber. It is simply crass bias for critics to hold that whenever a pagan record disagrees with the biblical account, it must be the Hebrew author that was in error.[208]

Nelson Glueck declared, "No archaeological discovery has ever controverted a single properly understood Biblical statement."[209]

The Bible speaks in ordinary language. We should not expect technical precision, exhaustive detail, or complete comprehensiveness. We must distinguish between imprecision and error. Biblical history is truthful but incomplete. It does not comport with modern ideals of historiography. Yet incompleteness does not negate infallibility.

The language employed in Scripture is that of simple observation, not scientific empiricism. Thus, phenomenal language, as well as figurative and symbolic language, does not imply a woeful ignorance in ancient civilizations.

Virtually all of the criticisms of cosmographic references in the Bible can be shown to be distortions of the texts, for a proper hermeneutic recognizes the frequent use of phenomenological language and of poetic imagery, including figures of speech like metaphors, similes, hyperbole, metonymy, etc., within the overall context of straightforward narrative and didactic prose.[210]

Often the same event is recorded in two parallel accounts, with different details included. While this may present difficulty in harmonizing apparent contradictions, the variation itself does

---

[208]Archer, *Encyclopedia of Bible Difficulties*, 15-17.

[209]Glueck, *Rivers in the Desert*, 136.

[210]Hanna, *Biblical Christianity*, 151-152.

not necessitate a contradiction. "It is possible that if our knowledge were greater, all seeming difficulties could be swept away."[211]

We should approach any difficult passage with the assumption that the writers knew more about the subject than we know. Wesley acknowledged that difficulties exist in reconciling the genealogies of Matthew and Luke. He argued that both writers worked with the material to which they had access. "Nor was it needful they should correct the mistakes, if there were any."[212] But it should be noted that Wesley did not affirm that there were mistakes in the genealogies.

A different kind of issue stems from 1 Corinthians 7:6-12. In answer to the questions from Corinth, Paul speaks with apostolic authority in v 6. He is addressing a situation which had not been addressed in prior Scripture. But since all Scripture is profitable and Paul is writing Scripture, he is not simply giving an off-the-cuff opinion. However, in v 10, since Scripture has already addressed this issue, he cites precedent previously established in Matthew 5:32. Once again, however, in v 12 Paul speaks a new authoritative word.

To carry this concept to a wider application, if *all* Scripture is from God and therefore authoritative, it does not matter whether the words are printed in red. We are to live by every word, regardless of color, that proceeds from the mouth of God (Matt 4:4).

The Exposition of Scripture

Hermeneutics leads to exegesis and exegesis leads to exposition. Exegesis is like a diver bringing up pearls from the ocean bed. An expositor is like the jeweler who arrays them in orderly

---

[211]Harrison, "The Phenomena of Scripture," 250. See also Clarke, *Commentary*, 2:378 on errors by copiers.

[212]Wesley, *Notes*, 10.

fashion and in proper relation to each other. If the Bible is our final authority, then its message must be presented as God intended. According to John Stott in *Between Two Worlds* (1982), we must bridge the gap between our modern minds and the minds of the biblical writers. Packer wrote,

> The Bible being what it is, all true interpretation of it must take the form of preaching. With this goes an equally important converse: that, preaching being what it is, all true preaching must take the form of biblical interpretation.[213]

The 1982 Chicago Statement on Hermeneutics declared,

> WE AFFIRM that the only type of preaching which sufficiently conveys the divine revelation and its proper application to life is that which faithfully expounds the text of Scripture as the Word of God.
> WE DENY that the preacher has any message from God apart from the text of Scripture.[214]

A high view of the inspiration of Scripture should be transferred into expositional preaching. Martin Luther articulated the conviction of the church from the earliest times by declaring that to hear or read the Scripture is nothing else than to hear God.[215]

With such preaching, the message finds its sole source in Scripture. The message is extracted from Scripture through careful exegesis. The message preparation correctly interprets Scripture in its normal sense and its context. The message clearly explains the original God-intended meaning of Scripture. The

---

[213]Packer, "Preaching as Biblical Interpretation," 187.

[214]Radmacher and Preus, *Hermeneutics, Inerrancy, and the Bible,* 887.

[215]Packer, "Sola Scriptura," 43.

message applies the Scriptural meaning for today. Anything less than expository preaching is technically not really preaching at all, but is merely the subjective opinion or experience of the speaker.

CHAPTER TWO
The Doctrine of God

God is always greater than any description of him. Humanity knows innately that there must be a supreme being who is the sufficient cause for all that exists. This concept of a supreme being cannot be successfully dismissed. To reject the true God merely creates a vacuum which will be replaced by something else.

Furthermore, God has spoken through his Word and continues to speak through nature. Logically, there can be only one such supreme and sovereign being.

God has revealed himself to us. While the task of theology involves the collection and organization of these attributes, God is not limited to the sum total of what we know about him. He is incomprehensible and cannot be contained in any "box" we build for him. One attribute cannot be pitted against another, nor can God be reduced to merely one attribute.

The revealed attributes of God may be divided into two categories — those he shares with us and those he retains for himself. While the mature Christian is always becoming more like God, he will never become like God with regard to those attributes of God which God does not share.

God alone has the power to create and sustain his creation. Science may explain how current systems operate, but it cannot explain how creation occurred nor why God created. The term *providence* describes the wisdom and power which God continually exercises in his preservation and government of the world.

God is completely and consistently good. He has the power to prevent evil, but to do so would prevent mankind from experiencing the consequences of his sinful choices. Thus, God does not always choose to exercise his sovereign control. While he never ordains evil, he often permits it in order to provide a greater good. Thus, God permits, restrains, prevents, and overrules the free choices of mankind.

God has not locked himself out of his own creation. He retains the prerogative to intervene and even perform miracles as he sees fit. He is a covenant-keeping God who maintains a loving relationship with his covenant people who trust him, worship him, and pray to him. He also involves his people in his plans as his partners.

No people ever rise above their religion and no religion is greater than its concept of God. The essence of idolatry is to entertain unworthy thoughts about God. A. W. Tozer wrote, "Without doubt, the mightiest thought the mind can entertain is the thought of God, and the weightiest word in any language is its word for God." Our tendency is always to reduce or lower God and exalt man in God's place.

Theories about the Existence of God

A proper understanding of God is the most important doctrine of the church. Tozer warned that a loss of the majesty of God would lead to "a hundred lesser evils." He claimed that there was scarcely an error in doctrine or ethics that could not be traced to a wrong concept of God.[216] William Temple said, "If your concept of God is wrong, the more religion you get, the more dangerous you become to yourself and to everyone else."[217]

---

[216]Tozer, *Knowledge of the Holy*, 6, 9-10.

[217]Quoted by Kinlaw, *Let's Start With Jesus*, 16.

1. **Atheism** denies that there is any personal God. Throughout history all cultures have believed in some kind of god. Why is there a universal consciousness of God? It is unreasonable to reject such a widely accepted belief without considering the evidence.

The Bible never attempts to prove the existence of God. His existence is assumed. Any formal proof of God's existence is unnecessary. The first humans knew God. God appeared to the patriarchs. Evidence for God's existence has always been on display. "The heavens declare the glory of God" (Ps 19:1).

> For since the creation of the world God's invisible qualities — his eternal power and divine nature — have been clearly seen, being understood from what has been made, so that men are without excuse. For although they knew God, they neither glorified him as God nor gave thanks to him, but their thinking became futile and their foolish hearts were darkened (Rom 1:18-21).

Why would people want to reject the concept of God? The belief in someone over us means we are under some obligation to him. This means that he makes the rules and not us. But if there is a God, ignoring him does not change reality. Autonomous reason then becomes an idol. The Bible declares that godless and wicked men suppress the truth by their wickedness, even though God has made himself plain to them. Atheism is not based on intellectual doubt, but is a willful choice.

Why do atheists have to spend their time attempting to refute something that does not exist? The real question is not *whether* God is, but *who* God is. The only atheism that the Scripture admits is practical atheism. According to Psalm 14:1, "the fool has said in his heart, There is no God." The Hebrew word *nabal*, translated *fool*, describes this insensitivity to ethical and spiritual claims.

2. According to **agnosticism**, we cannot be certain whether or not God exists. This term was coined by Thomas Henry Huxley. Sometimes agnostics hope to postpone any belief in God, believing this gives them freedom to avoid the consequences of that reality. But agnosticism is a self-defeating position. How can an agnostic be sure of his doubts? In order to doubt anything, one must know something — otherwise one would not even know what he is doubting. We do not know everything about God, yet there is *sufficient* reason to believe in God.

3. **Polytheism** believes that there are many gods. While there may be angels and demons, by definition there can be only one sovereign, all-powerful being. It is this being alone who we refer to as *God*.

When Psalm 86:8-10 states that "among the gods there is none like you, O Lord,"

> God is not acknowledging pagan deities or recognizing the existence of other supernatural beings like himself; rather, he is addressing the earthly judges and administrators of his law whom he has set up to represent him.[218]

Verse 10 states "you alone are God." According to 1 Chronicles 16: 26 these *gods* are merely idols.

In Psalm 136:2-3, he is the God of gods and the Lord of lords. He is the true God over all conceived power in heaven and earth, as stated in Deuteronomy 10:17 and Revelation 19:16. If he is above all power and authority, whether real or imagined, then he alone is God.

---

[218]Kaiser, *Hard Sayings of the Bible*, 279. In John 10:34-36 Jesus referenced Ps 82:6. He rebutted the Jews by pointing out that if human magistrates imperfectly administered God's will, yet they are given an exalted title, how much more was he worthy of the title "Son of God."

When the pagans created gods in their own image, the gods were as wicked as the people who created them. Polytheism leads to immorality, idolatry, and demonism. The three monotheistic religions are: Christianity, Judaism, Islam — all of which have a historical context. In contrast, Mormon theology teaches that there is an infinite begetting of gods and that the material universe is eternal, just like the proliferation of gods.[219]

4. **Pantheism** reduces everything to a single essence. Everything is evolving and nothing is infinite. It holds that everything is god, thus denying his personality. Since everything is interrelated and one, there is no difference between God, a person, a carrot, or a rock. Pantheism asserts that truth is relative, god is impersonal, there is no death, all is one, and through a cosmic consciousness we come to the realization that we, too, are gods.

This philosophy was first stated by Zenophanes, in the sixth century BC. New age teaching has recycled this ancient heresy. C. S. Lewis explained,

> Once, before creation, it would have been true to say that everything was God. But God created: He caused things to be other than Himself that, being distinct, they might learn to love Him, and achieve union instead of mere sameness.[220]

We must distinguish between the Creator and his creation.

5. **Deism** teaches that God is transcendent and does not intervene in human affairs. Many who claim to believe in God do not put forth any effort to worship or serve him. This is the polar opposite to pantheism, which emphasizes the immanence of God.

---

[219]McConkie, *Mormon Doctrine*, 321.

[220]Lewis, *The Problem of Pain*, 150-151.

6. **Theism** affirms that there is a God. This is the most reasonable position to hold. Theism does not assume we know everything about God; but while his revelation is not exhaustive, it is sufficient. In fact, we would be certain of very little else about God unless he disclosed himself to us. What we know about God comes through his revelation to us. There is one personal God who is both immanent and transcendent. He exists as three distinct personalities: Father, Son, and Holy Spirit.

Before we argue for the existence of God, let us first define him:

> God is the source and end of all things, that than which nothing greater can be conceived; uncreated, sufficient, necessary being; infinite, unmeasurable, eternal One, Father, Son, and Spirit; all-present, all-knowing, all powerful, and all-empowering creator, redeemer, and consummator of all things; immanent without ceasing to be transcendent, Holy One present in our midst; whose way of personal being is incomparably free, self-determining, spiritual, responsive, and self-congruent; whose activity is incomparably good, holy, righteous, just, benevolent, loving, gracious, merciful, forbearing, kind; hence eternally blessed, eternally rejoicing, whose holiness is incomparable in beauty.[221]

This is the revelation of God given through Scripture. Compare this definition with Richard Dawkins's statement in *The God Delusion*.

> The God of the Old Testament is arguably the most unpleasant character in all fiction: jealous and proud of it; a petty, unjust, unforgiving control-freak; a vindictive, bloodthirsty ethnic cleanser; a misogynistic, homo-

---

[221]Oden, *The Living God*, 130.

phobic, racist, infan-ticidal, genocidal, filicidal, pesti-lential, megalomaniacal, sado-masochistic, capriciously malevolent bully.[222]

If that is God, then I am the atheist! In the words of John Wesley, "You represent God as worse than the devil — more false, more cruel, more unjust."[223] Sometimes people attempt to embrace atheism as a coping mechanism to deal with the fear and insecurity which results from such unreal gods.

Arguments for God's Existence

We know innately that God exists, even if our consciousness of him is perverted. However, his existence can also be demonstrated. It is legitimate to consider the rational evidence *for* God's existence, just as we have evaluated the evidence *against* his existence. While it is true that we cannot reason ourselves into a saving relationship with God, yet God still calls us to come and reason with him (Isa 1:18). These are *a posteriori* arguments.

1. The **cosmological** argument holds that there must be an uncaused cause which is sufficient to cause all that is. It seems unlikely that a highly ordered universe could have developed by chance. "The heavens declare the glory of God; the skies proclaim the work of his hands" (Ps 19:1).

The Greek word *cosmos* means order. It is also used to refer to the universe, since the universe reflects order and complexity, not random chance. Everything cannot be contingent. There must be a starting point. The theory of evolution does not avoid this

---

[222]Dawkins, *The God Delusion*, 51. Yet Dawkins assumes to know the nature of one he professes not to know or that he claims does not exist.

[223]Wesley, "Free Grace," Sermon #110, ¶ 26.

conclusion, but merely pushes the question further back in time. William Lane Craig explained, "Every being which begins has a cause for its beginning; now the world is a being which begins; therefore, it possesses a cause for its beginning."[224]

> What may be known about God is plain to them. For since the creation of the world God's invisible qualities — his eternal power and divine nature — have been clearly seen, being understood from what has been made, so that men are without excuse (Rom 1:19-20).

Anthony Flew, the leading atheist of his day, wrestled with such questions as: How did the laws of nature come to be? How did life originate from non-life? How did the universe come into existence? Since the early 1980s, Flew reconsidered the evidence. He came to believe that he had arrived at his conclusion regarding the nonexistence of God much too quickly, much too easily, and for the wrong reasons. It seemed to him that those who advocated the cosmological argument were providing scientific proof that the universe had a beginning. An infinite regress does not explain causation. The almost unbelievable complexity of DNA points to the fact that the universe is intricately purpose driven. Faced with the arguments of Intelligent Design, Flew adopted a new answer to the question "Who wrote the laws of nature?" He concluded that there is a Divine lawmaker.[225]

2. The **teleological** argument is an argument from design. The first two arguments overlap, and sometimes the same scriptural argument is placed under either category, depending on the author. However, the basic thrust of the cosmological argument is *how* and the basic thrust of the teleological argument is *why*.

---

[224]Craig, *Reasonable Faith*, 96.

[225]Flew, *There Is a God*, 70, 75, 109, 135.

The Greek word *telos* refers to an end or purpose. "Does he who implanted the ear not hear? Does he who formed the eye not see?" (Ps 94:9). "Lift up your eyes and look to the heavens: Who created all these?" (Isa 40:26). "For every house is built by someone, but God is the builder of everything" (Heb 3:4). "He has not left himself without testimony: He has shown kindness by giving you rain from heaven and crops in their seasons; he provides you with plenty of food and fills your hearts with joy" (Acts 14:17). There must be an intelligent designer.

The ascetic argument for the existence of God is the recognition of the unnecessary beauty which exists in all of creation. In Job 38:25-27 God describes a land where no human lives. Yet God takes pleasure in maintaining it and causing it to flourish.

Beauty cannot be reduced to utility, yet it produces admiration and pleasure. The dialectic materialism advocated by Karl Marx explained everything in terms of utilitarianism. A survival of the fittest worldview holds that nature is red in tooth and claw. Yet this worldview does not explain the beauty of nature. This beauty cannot be explained except in terms of a Creator who cares about creation enough to make it beautiful.

G. K. Chesterton wrote about the problem of pleasure. The process of human nourishment and reproduction did not require pleasure. Yet the pleasures of life point to the goodness of God. Chesterton wrote, "The worst moment for the atheist is when he is really thankful and has no one to thank."[226]

3. According to the **anthropological** argument, our ability to think and reason has been implanted by God and is a reflection of him. The Greek word *anthropos* means mankind. Anthropology can be approached socially or theologically.

Mankind is distinct from the rest of creation. Every culture in history has recognized that God exists — even if they did not have an accurate understanding of his nature. Don Richardson

---

[226]Chesterton, *St. Francis*, 78.

said that 90 percent of the world's folk religions are permeated with monotheistic presuppositions.[227]

Twentieth century communism failed to eradicate a consciousness of God. Furthermore, many people have claimed to have an experience with God. While experience can only convince the person who has the encounter, when we see a conversion or transformation in the person's life we must consider their explanation that it was through a higher power. It is legitimate to ask God to reveal himself.

4. The **moral** argument observes that everyone has a conscience — a sense of what is right and what we ought to do. Mankind speaks only in the indicative mood, not the imperative. Yet this moral imperative is innate within mankind. Immanuel Kant called it the "categorical imperative." We feel this morality so deeply that we cannot face the fact that we are breaking it, so we make excuses.

If we say there is no right and wrong, we contradict ourselves because we are saying it is *right* that there is no right or wrong. The more excuses we have, the more we believe there is a rule of right and wrong.

Our conscience reflects, sometimes imperfectly, God as the lawgiver and judge. "The wicked man flees though no one pursues" (Prov 28:1). Moral consciousness implies a spiritual world which is just as real as the physical world.

> Indeed, when Gentiles, who do not have the law, do by nature things required by the law, they are a law for themselves, even though they do not have the law, since they show that the requirements of the law are written on their hearts, their consciences also bearing witness, and their thoughts now accusing, now even defending them (Rom 2:14-15).

---

[227]Richardson, *Eternity in Their Hearts*, 44.

C. S. Lewis wrote, "It seems then, we are forced to believe in a real Right and Wrong. People may be sometimes mistaken about them, just as people sometimes get their sums wrong; but they are not a matter of mere taste and opinion any more than the multiplication table."[228]

5. The Greek word *ontos* refers to being or existence. We cannot conceive of time and space not existing. Such concepts as infinity, eternity, perfection, and absoluteness must have some basis. These concepts are incommunicable attributes of God.

The **ontological** argument is an *a priori* deductive argument, starting with the concept of a necessary being. Paul's contention that these pagan philosophers cannot escape a knowledge of their Creator utilizes a presuppositional, *a priori* apologetic. This argument moves from necessary thought to actual being. It is based on pure reason, not empirical evidence. In fact, the ability to perform such thinking sets us apart from animals.

In Ecclesiastes 3:11 Solomon wrote that God has also set eternity in our hearts. We observe the changes of time, but we cannot grasp the concept of eternity. The first eight verses of this chapter describe the rhythm of life. There is a time for everything. However, we cannot fathom or comprehend the concept of eternity because everything we observe has a start and an end. Solomon says that within our heart we have a concept of something that we cannot comprehend. And this something that we are aware of is the nature of God. God has put within our mind an awareness of himself. This is not a figment of our imagination since we can only imagine things with which we have some knowledge. C. S. Lewis explained, "If I find in myself a desire which no experience in this world can satisfy, the most probable explanation is that I was made for another world."[229]

---

[228]Lewis, *The Case for Christianity*, 6.

[229]Lewis, *Mere Christianity*, 106.

In Acts 17 we read about Paul's visit to Athens. He was intrigued to discover an altar with the inscription, "To an unknown god." The Greeks had created many gods, but somehow they were not satisfied. Adolf Deissmann wrote:

> In Greek antiquity cases were not altogether rare in which "anonymous" altars "to unknown gods" or "to the god whom it may concern" were erected when people were convinced, for example after experiencing some deliverance, that a deity had been gracious to them, but were not certain of the deity's name.[230]

These pagan Greek philosophers had an awareness of the eternal in their hearts and somehow they conceived of a God whom they did not know. The very fact that they had the concept in their mind is proof that he exists. Paul explained that God gave us life so that we would seek him, reach out for him, and find him — he is not far from each one of us since we live and move and have our being in him.

It is significant that our existence is explained in Acts 17:28 with the Greek verb *eimi*. The participle form, *on onta*, is the basis for the term from which *ontology* comes. We exist because he exists and our existence presupposes his. However, our existence is dependent upon him while his existence is independent of us. Yet somehow we reflect his image, and Paul argued that we are his *offspring*. The Greek word *genos*, found in Acts 17:28, means offspring, family, or kinship based on creation. Thus, an inanimate idol cannot represent the true God.

The fact that Paul quoted the poetry of pagan philosophers, who were pantheistic, does not mean he was invoking them as authorities. Paul was inspired; they were not. However, Paul was using them to illustrate his premise that in spite of their inade-

---

[230]Deissmann, *Paul: A Study in Social and Religious History*, 287-291.

quate views about God, they still possessed an innate awareness of God, although distorted and suppressed, which is not reflected in their idolatry. Thus, Paul calls them to repentance (v 30) since they are without excuse (Rom 1:20).

Augustine wrote, "God is more truly thought than He is uttered, and exists more truly than he is thought."[231] Anselm defined God as "something than which nothing greater can be thought" or "that than which a greater cannot be thought."[232] He argued that this being must exist in the mind, even in the mind of the person who denies the existence of God. He suggested that, if the greatest possible being exists in the mind, it must also exist in reality. We have the idea of a perfect being, and a necessary part of that perfection is that he should actually exist.

There is nothing higher or greater than this being. Did we create this idea, or do we have this thought because it is reality? Since we are not perfect, the idea could not have originated with us because we can only think about things with which we have some knowledge. Yet we cannot conceive of this being not existing. Therefore, he must exist.

In addition to these five arguments, we have divine revelation. God has spoken. Wesley wrote,

> I want to know one thing, the way to heaven — how to land safe on that happy shore. God himself has condescended to teach the way: for this very end he came from heaven. He hath written it down in a book. O give me that book! At any price give me the Book of God! I have it. Here is knowledge enough for me. Let me be a man of one book.[233]

---

[231]Augustine, *On the Trinity. NPNF*1 3:109.

[232]Logan, *Reading Anselm's Proslogium*, 33; 35.

[233]Wesley, "Preface" to *Sermons On Several Occasions*, § 5.

Those who believe in Jesus Christ have the testimony of God in their hearts (1 John 5:10). On his deathbed, Samuel Wesley told his son John, "The inward witness, son, the inward witness. That is the proof, the strongest proof, of Christianity."[234]

The Names of God

We serve a God who has disclosed himself. The names of God are his self-revelation. There is a connection between God, his name, and his word (Ps 138:2) — whether the word is given in written form, as a creative decree (Ps 33:6), or as governing decrees (Ps 147:15-18).

The patriarchs knew God as *Elohim*. This word occurs 2570 times in the OT. It corresponds to the Greek word *theos*. The root meaning is "strong and mighty one." It generally occurs as a plural noun, but normally with a singular verb. This implies God's Trinitarian nature. While Hebrew syntax has a plural of majesty, the *we* by which kings and queens referred to themselves, there is no evidence of this usage during the biblical period.[235]

In its singular form *el* is coupled with various designations:

- El Elyon – God Most High (Gen 14:18-20)
- El Roi – God who sees me (Gen 16:13)
- El Shaddai – God Almighty (Gen 17:1)
- El Olam – God Everlasting (Gen 21:33)
- El Bethel – God of Bethel (Gen 31:13)

In Exodus 3:14, God instructed and encouraged Moses by revealing his name. According to Exodus 6:3, Abraham, Isaac, and Jacob knew God as *El Shaddai*, but God did not reveal his proper name to them. *Yahweh* occurs 162 times in Genesis,

---

[234]Wesley, *Letter* to John Smith, 22 March 1748, § 6.

[235]Archer, *Encyclopedia of Biblical Difficulties*, 359.

however. The word was introduced as early as Genesis 2:4, but not its significance. Of course, since Moses was the author of Genesis and Exodus, he may have simply inserted *Yahweh* anachronistically.

However, modernists claim that every reference to Yahweh prior to Exodus 3:14 was inserted by a later redactor. The result of this hypothesis was that the unity of the Pentateuch was shredded into various literary strands. But different names were used by Moses to imply different theological distinctions. While *elohim* is a general term, used of all gods, both the true and the false, and while *adonai* is used both of God and men, *Yahweh* is used only in reference to the one true God.

Yahweh, which used to be translated *Jehovah*, comes from the Hebrew verb *hayah*. This verb, *to be*, is in the timeless present — covering past, present, and future. It is also in the third person masculine form.

In the Hebrew phrase, "I am who I am," the first verb functions as a name. It takes the masculine noun form, *Yahweh*, in Exodus 3:15. *Yahweh* is probably a contraction of the "I am who I am" phrase.[236] God does not bother to explain himself or justify his existence. He simply employs the ontological argument.

The name *Yahweh* appears 6828 times in the OT. Unlike other designations, this name does not limit God's nature to any particular characteristic. Yahweh refers to his person, his character, his authority, his power, and his reputation.[237] Yahweh is God's proper name. The other Hebrew words are actually titles.

God's disclosure was not meant to express evasion or reluctance. The phrase, "I am who I am," carries four facets of meaning:

- existence – "I am the one who is," in contrast to the false gods who are not.

---

[236]Cole, *TOTC*, 69.

[237]Kaiser, "Name," *ZPEB*, 4:360-370.

- causation – "I create whatever I create."
- explanation – "I am because I am." There is not external cause for God's existence outside himself.
- assurance of divine intervention – "I will be gracious to whom I will." Although God transcends time, he is present in time, always remembering his covenant.[238] God is now; he is present in time. God is here; he is present in space.

In nine instances, the Hebrew name *Yahweh* is made a compound noun with the addition of a verb. Thus, we are no longer simply talking about God's action but about his essence.

- **Yahweh-Jireh** (Gen 22:14) – God provides. The basic meaning of this Hebrew verb *raah* means *to see*. As used in this verse, *yireh* means God can provide because he can foresee what we will need. Thus, for him to provide is for him to see to it that our needs are supplied.
- **Yahweh-Rapha** (Exod 15:26) – God heals. Physical healing is based on the nature of God, as well as the ministry of Christ to break the curse of sin. According to Romans 8:23, we who are now saved await the redemption of our bodies. But with the coming of his kingdom, the future breaks into the present and health is often his gracious gift.
- **Yahweh-Nissi** (Exod 17:15) – the Lord my banner or standard. This Hebrew word means a standard, a flag, a signal, or a rally point. But *standard* can also mean a requirement, a rule, or the absolute by which everything is measured. There are doctrinal standards and lifestyle standards which the Bible prescribes. However, the Bible itself, and not a manmade list of rules, is our standard for faith and practice. This is what is meant by the sufficiency of Scripture.
- **Yahweh-Meqaddiskem** (Exod 31:13) – the Lord who sanctifies. This word is from *qadash*.

---

[238]Grisanti, "היה," *NIDOTTE* 1:1025.

- **Yahweh-Shalom** (Judg 6:24) – the Lord my peace.
- **Yahweh-Elyown** (Ps 7:17) – the Lord most high. Our concept of God is our highest ideal. As Tozer explained, there is scarcely an error in doctrine or ethics that could not be traced to a wrong concept of God. God is transcendent and over all.
- **Yahweh-Roi** (Ps 23:1) – the Lord my shepherd.
- Yahweh-Sabaoth (Isa 6:3) – the Lord of angelic hosts. The Hebrew word *tsaba* refers to warfare or battle.
- **Yahweh-Tsedeq** (Jer 23:6) – the Lord our righteousness. His character is the foundation of righteousness, and his law establishes what is right.

Thus, God, who is most high, acts by providing, healing, protecting, leading, sanctifying, giving peace, lifting us to a higher ideal, making righteous, guiding, ruling, judging, and saving.

A third Hebrew word, *adonai*, became popular because the Jews were reluctant to pronounce *Yahweh* lest they became guilty of taking God's name in vain. *Adonai* describes God's dominion as Lord and can be translated *Master*. Yet it first appears in Genesis 15:2 and occurs only 450 times in the OT.

In Revelation 1:8, we find the Greek equivalent for four of the Hebrew names or titles for God, as well as a reference to a non-communicable attribute — everlasting; and they are all applied to Jesus Christ. Yahweh = *ego eimi*; Adonai = *kurios*; Elohim = *theos*; Shaddai = *pantokrator*.

The Monotheistic God

Is the Yahweh of Judaism, the Allah of Islam, and the God which Jesus revealed all the same God? While all three religions affirm an Abrahamic tradition and are monotheistic, this goes deeper than a Hebrew, Arabic, and Greek synonym for the same being. There are ten contrasts between the attributes of Allah, as found in the Quran, and God as found in the Bible.

- Knowable versus unknowable
- Personal versus nonpersonal. Islam claims that if Allah had personality this would lower him to the level of a man.
- Spiritual versus non-spiritual
- Trinitarian versus Unitarian
- Limited by his own nature versus unlimited
- Trustworthy versus capricious
- Active in history versus passive. The Muslim concept of Allah is very much like the deist view of God.
- Attributes versus no attributes. While it is claimed that the Quran contains 99 attributes of Allah, they are all negative. Thus, the Quran never tells us who he is.
- Grace versus works. The Quran contains no concept of grace regarding Allah. There is no savior or intercessor. The Quran only records his works.[239]

We should reject an inclusivistic or pluralistic understanding of God which basically says that all religions are man's attempt to worship the same object, regardless of what he, she, or it is called. The scandal of the Christian faith is that there is no other way to God except through Jesus Christ.

The Revelation of God's Nature

An *attribute* is something true about God. It is a description of God's nature. *Attribute* does not imply that we are merely attributing or adding something to the concept of God. Some theologians prefer terms such as *properties*, *virtues*, or *perfections*. Older theologians tended to force a distinction between attributes and essence.

What we know about the character of God is derived essentially from his self-disclosure. This is inductive or *a posteriori*. However, the *a priori* method may also be valid. Some attributes

---

[239]Morey, *The Islamic Invasion*, 47-63.

may be inferred by reasoning from effect to cause. Thus, the revelation of Scripture corresponds to reality.

Apophatic (negative) theology asserts that God can only be defined by what he is not, because there are no adequate positive models to express God's attributes. While God is incomparable, he reveals himself in Scripture in relationship to his people. The limitations and defects that the created order experiences cannot apply to the Almighty. Sometimes it is easier to grasp what God is *not* than to grasp what he is. This is the logic of *contrast*.

Logic also ascribes the highest degree of all that we observe to God. This is the logic of *comparison*. And there are *intrinsic* qualities of God which can be inferred deductively by taking the concept of God to consistent conclusions.

Yet God is not the sum total of the attributes we discuss. Furthermore, we cannot emphasize one attribute at the expense of another without distorting his internal unity. According to Romans 11:22, God is both kind and stern. Here the word *apotomia* carries the connotation of an abrupt judgment. It corresponds to the wrath described in Romans 2:5, where v 4 also refers to his kindness.

God is not composed of elements more fundamental than himself. God cannot be divided into various parts. One attribute cannot be pitted against another attribute. He is not the sum total or the composite of his attributes. *What God is* is no different from *that God is*. This concept is referred to as divine simplicity — God's underlying unity. In affirming this doctrine, Arminius stated, "God is his own essence and his own being."[240] Ultimately, the attributes of God coalesce. The multiplicity of attributes are simply the nature of God from various perspectives.

God has numberless attributes. He is incomprehensible, yet we can compile his characteristics as revealed in Scripture.

In contrast, the new age god is unknowable. They misrepresent the concept of *transcendence*, explaining that God is beyond

---

[240]Arminius, *Works*, 2:115.

all categories, concepts, and thoughts. However, *transcendence* itself is a category or concept.

God has revealed himself because he wants us to know him and fellowship with him. Wesley emphasized that proper contemplation of God's attributes always leads to human happiness. Idolatry is what stands in the way of happiness.[241] It is helpful to divide the attributes which he has revealed concerning himself into two categories. The Westminster Confession (1646) referred to incommunicable and communicable attributes.

Absolute attributes God does not share

According to Peter, we share in the divine nature through regeneration (2 Pet 1:4). This participation is described through the use of the Greek word *koinonos*, which is used in the NT to describe sharing or fellowship.

The doctrine of *theosis* can mean a pantheistic union of God and man, or it can be used to describe a participation in the divine life. It should be understood as potential which will be realized, to some degree, at the consummation. But even then, we will not become gods. Peter said we share in God's nature (*physis*). He does not say that we share in God's essence (*ousia*).

God is self-existent. This concept of self-existence is also called *aseity*, which means of or from itself. In Exodus 3:14, *I am* means that God is self-determining. He is uncreated. His name *Yahweh* declares, "I am *because* I am." "Before me no god was formed, nor will there be one after me" (Isa 43:10). "I am the first and I am the last, apart from me there is no God" (Isa 44:6).

God is also self-disclosing. "He made known to us the mystery of his will according to his good pleasure which he purposed in Christ" (Eph 1:9).

---

[241]Oden, *John Wesley's Teachings*, 1:47-48.

God is also self-sufficient. "Before the mountains were born or you brought forth the earth and the world, from everlasting to everlasting you are God" (Ps 90:2). "Before me no god was formed, nor will there be one after me"(Isa 43:10).

God is living and active. God had no origin. He is dependent upon no one. He alone can declare, "I am because I am" (Exod 3:14). God is self-sufficient. He is "all in all" (1 Cor 15:28).

God is not under any obligations. "Who has ever given to God, that God should repay him? For from him and through him and to him are all things" (Rom 11:34-35).

> I have no need of a bull from your stall or of goats from your pens, for every animal of the forest is mine, and the cattle on a thousand hills. I know every bird in the mountains, and the creatures of the field are mine: If I were hungry I would not tell you, for the world is mine, and all that is in it (Ps 50:9-12).

God alone is independent and absolutely free. Yet even his freedom has bounds; he cannot contradict himself. He is constrained by his own nature. "For he cannot deny himself" (2 Tim 2:13).

God is one. "The Lord our God, the Lord is one" (Deut 6:4). In Isaiah 44:8, God asks, "Is there any God beside me?" and in the following chapter he answers his own question, "I am God, there is no other" (Isa 45:22). David declared, "Among the gods there is no one like you, O Lord." But lest he be misunderstood, he then says, "You alone are God" (Ps 86:8-10). "There is no God but one" (1 Cor 8:4). There is one God and Father of all (Eph 4:6).

- He is above all. This describes his transcendence and sovereignty.
- He is through all. This describes his providence and omnipotence.

- He is in all. This refers to his immanence and omnipresence.

The doctrine of God's unity does not deny that there are genuine distinctions within God, but it denies that there are internal divisions and contradictions. Deuteronomy 6:4 does not teach the numeric unity of God, but rather that Yahweh is the only God that is entitled to the name *Yahweh*.

There is only one being who possesses the attributes which constitute the Godhead. This doctrine of divine unity rejects polytheism and dualism. The symmetry and unity within the universe suggest a single creator.

The early church had to refute the dualistic view that there were two gods — one good and one bad. Irenaeus wrote that there could not be any other principality or power above God because if there was anything beyond him, he would not be God. The pagans taught that there was a certain God above the Creator of heaven and earth, and another above him, and another above him in endless succession of demigods. Irenaeus pointed out that none of these could be fully God.[242]

But thinking people often express confusion over the doctrine of the Trinity. Having established that there is one God, do we now claim that there are three Gods?

Heretics have always opposed the doctrine of the Trinity, but it should not come as a surprise that we cannot define and explain a superior and complex being through human logic or experience. The rationalist will reject what he cannot grasp, but if the Bible is God's self-disclosure, Tozer argued, "The fact that it cannot be satisfactorily explained, instead of being against it, is in its favor. Such a truth had to be revealed; no one could have imagined it."[243]

The doctrine of the Trinity is not irrational or illogical; it is above or beyond human reason. It is a revealed mystery. While

---

[242]Irenaeus, *Against Heresies*, ANF 1:359-369.

[243]Tozer, *Knowledge of the Holy*, 31.

the inductive evidence will be considered later, the law of non-contradiction leads us to conclude that God is a complex being who is essentially one. The plural *Elohim* name lays the indefinite and mysterious foundation for a plurality of persons in the Godhead, while the singular *Yahweh* forever guards the unity of God.

God is infinite. "Great is the Lord and most worthy of praise; his greatness no one can fathom" (Ps 145:3). The Hebrew language does not have a word for *infinity*, although the word is used in the King James translation of Job 22:5, Psalm 147:5; and Nahum 3:9. In these references, two Hebrew words which mean *very great* are translated *infinite*. Nor does the Greek NT use the precise term *infinite*. To declare that God is infinite is an example of philosophically ascribing the highest degree of all that we observe to God. He is infinite in his power, knowledge, wisdom, justice, righteousness, love, and kindness. Yet philosophers tend to view infinitude as an abstract concept. Aristotle's *theos* was not a living God so much as a philosophical concept.

We are finite creatures, but God has no bounds or limits. He is free from all limitations, yet he is free to limit himself. While science may still be discovering the greatness of outer space, it is ultimately finite.   Sometimes *immensity* is made a separate category. *Immense* means *unmeasured*. "The heavens, even the highest heaven, cannot contain you" (1 Kgs 8:27; 2 Chr 6:18). Yet God is fully present at every point in space. He is not divided into parts, so that part of him is present here and part of him is present there. With regard to space, God is immense or unmeasurable; with regard to time God is everlasting. Just as time is born out of eternity, so space is born out of immensity.

God is spiritual. God is spirit (John 4:24). He is immaterial and invisible. "No one has seen God at any time" (John 1:18). Jesus told his audience, "You have never heard his voice nor seen his form" (John 5:37). According to 1 Timothy 1:17, God is invisible. He is called the "Father of spirits" (Heb 12:9), but the affirmation of God's spirituality does not imply that spirit is opposed to material, as gnosticism taught. If God was located within a body, he could not be omnipresent. Contrary to pantheism, however, the universe is not his body. God transcends his creation, yet is immanently present in the world he has made.

A *theophany* is a visible manifestation of God to human beings. Almost every OT theophany was God the Son, except when God placed Moses in the cleft of the rock and showed him his glory (Exod 33:18-23). While God is everywhere, sometimes he reveals himself in holy places where his presence is intense. The question is not whether God can be seen, but whether any human can survive after seeing him.

While God is essentially invisible, God has often made himself visible so that humans may on occasion truly say that they have seen God. The word *anthropomorphism* is comprised of two Greek words, *anthropos*, which means *man*, and *morphe*, which means *form*. The term describes a picture of God in human form. Of course, the pagan depiction of false gods in human or animal form constituted idolatry. In Scripture, the true God is revealed through figures of speech which describe his eyes or hand, even though God is a spirit. Such figures of speech are *anthropomorphisms*.

The human spirit was created in God's image. Thus, human personality demands a personal God. Since man is the personal result of creation in God's image, the originating cause must also be personal. Yet because God is not confined to a body, he can be infinite, immutable, and omnipresent. If God was not a spirit, he could not be infinite.

Any aspect of the created universe becomes idolatrous if taken to represent deity. Since God does not have a body, any attempt to depict him will fall short and not do justice to his nature. Idolatry must always be resisted for this reason. Atheism is actually a form of idolatry. Since atheists are materialists, they deny his spirituality. For them, all that is real is what they can see.

God is eternal. In Genesis 21:33 and Isaiah 57:15, God is called "the everlasting God." "From everlasting to everlasting you are God" (Ps 90:2). "You remain the same, and your years will never end" (Ps 102:27). "The Lord is the everlasting God, the Creator of the ends of the earth" (Isa 40:28). He has reigned from antiquity (Ps 93:2). He rules forever (Isa 52:15). He is the Ancient of Days (Dan 7:9, 13, 22). We are temporal, but God has no beginning nor end. He is the eternal *I am*.

> In the beginning you laid the foundations of the earth, and the heavens are the work of your hands. They will perish, but you remain; they will all wear out like a garment. Like clothing you will change them and they will be discarded. But you remain the same, and your years will never end (Ps 102:25-27).

"With the Lord one day is like a thousand years and a thousand years like one day" (2 Pet 3:8). This statement is not a formula for determining the end of the world; it is a declaration that God is not affected by time. Christ declared, "I am the Alpha and the Omega, who is and who was, and who is to come" (Rev 1:8).

Is *eternity* a different category than *time*, or is eternity the sum total of all time? Is eternity the antithesis of time, or is eternity a continuum in which time runs? Does God exist above time or within time?

The absolute dichotomy between eternity and time is not found in the Bible. The limitations of human language makes it difficult to express a concept which is foreign to us. The OT does not have a single word corresponding to our word *eternity*. Instead, we find such expressions as *from generation to generation* and *from age to age*. God himself is described by the adjective *eternal*, which can mean a long duration, the past, or the future (*olam*; Gen 21:33; Isa 26:4, 40:28). The basic meaning of *olam* is farthest time or distant time. "It does not seem to mean eternity in the philosophical sense of the word," which he explains is unbounded time or eternal timelessness.[244]

In Revelation 22:2, the tree of life bears twelve crops of fruit, yielding its fruit every month. Yet according to v 5, there is no more night. There will be either no more sun or the sun will not be needed. If there is no night, there will be no more moon either. Yet there still seems to be some concept of time even in the eternal state.

It is currently popular to relegate the concept of eternity to Greek philosophy,[245] then to claim that Scripture does not teach that hell is eternal. However, before the term *eternal* or *everlasting* is stripped of any reference to duration, we must consider the implication for our concept of an eternal God, eternal heaven, eternal salvation, and an eternal kingdom — even if we struggle with the concept of an eternal hell. The duration of hell will be discussed under eschatology.

God is immutable. "I the Lord do not change" (Mal 3:6). Creation will perish, but he will remain (Ps 102:26-27; Heb 1:10-12). God is dependable, consistent, and faithful. He does not change in his being, his perfections, his purposes, or his promises.[246]

James 1:17 declares that God does not change like shifting shadows. His character, his purposes, his ways, and his truth do not change. However, the concept of *impassibility*, that God does not have any emotions, that he is unmovable and inactive, is based on Stoic philosophy, not Scripture. Plato declared that God is beyond either joy or sorrow.[247] Aristotle described God as *apatheia*, meaning imperturbability and dispassionateness.

---

[244]Tomasino, "עלום," *NIDOTTE* 3:346.

[245]For example, Ellis, "New Testament Teaching on Hell," 214.

[246]Berkhof, *Systematic Theology*, 58.

[247]Plato, *Dialogues of Plato*, 2:366.

Ignatius wrote that Christ was "impalpable" but became "passible."[248] In his view, God does not have feelings and Christ only had feelings after his incarnation.

James 1:17 does not imply remoteness, detachment, or immobility. God is relational. The statement of Christ in Mark 14:33-34 reflects intense emotional suffering.

Within the Thirty-Nine Articles of the Church of England was a statement which defined God as "without body, parts, or passions." When Wesley drafted the Twenty-Five Articles of Methodism in 1784, he deleted the word *passions*.[249]

While God cannot be governed by factors which he has created, to misunderstand this leads to the concept that God is not a person but is essentially an apathetic first cause. On the other hand, the term *passion* can suggest that God is changeable. God does have feelings and they do not change. The love of God means very little if he is apathetic.

Murphree explained that God is impassible *without consent*, but he is affectable with consent. "The nature of love is to be affected by its object. To choose to love is to consent to be affected." In his essential nature, God is impassible, transcending his creation, but in his loving nature he is voluntarily affectable.

> His tranquillity is not to be mistaken for inertia or idleness. God is not a celestial iceberg, untouched and unmoved by human beings. He is awake, not asleep; He is alert, not groggy. He is responsive, not impassive. Scripture depicts a God who has chosen to be affected by His subjects.[250]

"Jesus Christ is the same yesterday and today and forever" (Heb 13:8). However, there was a permanent change when Christ

---

[248]Ignatius, *Epistle to Polycarp*, *ANF* 1:94.

[249]Oden, *Doctrinal Standards*, 112.

[250]Murphee, *Divine Paradoxes*, 124.

took on humanity in the incarnation. Yet, his deity remained constant. He was just as much God while here on earth, in a human body, as he was at creation.

According to Numbers 23:19, "God is not a man, that he should lie, nor a son of man, that he should change his mind." First Samuel 15:29 makes a similar statement. In both cases the verb is *nacham*, which means to be sorry or console oneself. "When the word [*nacham*] is used with reference to God, there is implied an idea of change and perhaps of sorrow, but not the consciousness of wrong-doing."[251] However, there are thirteen OT passages that say God did, may, will, or is one who relents. In every instance, the word *nacham* occurs.[252] "In many cases the Lord's 'changing' of his mind is a gracious response to human factors. . . . In other places we are told or are left to infer that the change is due to feelings of compassion for a person or people."[253] Thus, *relent* is a better translation.

In Genesis 6:6-7, God is angry that he has made man, but he does not repent. In Exodus 32:12, the prayer is not that God should repent, but that he should be gracious.[254] God is unchanging in his essence, his nature, and his purposes, but as man changes, God relates to man differently. God is both loving and just. If we are unbelievers we experience his judgment, but if we repent we experience his love.

Process theology teaches that God is in the process of growing and developing. Thus, he adjusts in view of what he has learned. Instead, Oden argues for God's consistency. Immutabil-

---

[251]Girdlestone, *Synonyms*, 89.

[252]Gen 6:6-7; Exod 32:12,14; 1 Sam 15:11,35; 2 Sam 24:16; 1 Chr 21:15; Ps 106:45; Jer 18:8, 26:3,13,19, 42:10; Joel 2:13-14; Amos 7:3, 6; Jonah 3:9-10, 4:2. The verb *nacham* occurs 23 times in reference to God, including Num 23:19 and 1 Sam 15:29, and the KJV translates it every time as *repent*.

[253]Butterworth, "נחם," *NIDOTTE* 3:82.

[254]Stauffer, "θεός," *TDNT* 3:109.

ity does not mean God is rigid and unresponsive, as caricatured by process theology. "God can will a change, but this does not imply that God changes in essential nature as good."[255]

However, Islam teaches that Allah may abrogate or cancel promises made earlier. He may even contradict his own commands, since he is sovereign.

God is sovereign. There can be only one absolute ruler. "Dominion belongs to the Lord and he rules over the nations" (Ps 22:28). "The earth is the Lord's and everything in it" (Ps 24:1). "Our God is in heaven; he does whatever pleases him" (Ps 115:3). "The Lord will reign for ever and ever" (Exod 15:18). "His dominion is an eternal dominion; his kingdom endures from generation to generation. All the peoples of the earth are regarded as nothing. He does as he pleases with the powers of heaven and the peoples of the earth. No one can hold back his hand or say to him: 'What have you done?'" (Dan 4:34-35). He is the blessed and only ruler, the King of kings and Lord of lords (1 Tim 6:15). The term *dunastes*, translated *potentate* in the KJV, means to rule by force of power.

Although God is not abusive or capricious, he does rule. Yet, open theists claim that while God is powerful, he is not all-powerful. He is not in control of all that happens.

In contrast, God declares, "My purpose will stand, and I will do all that I please" (Isa 46:10). However, Calvinists tend to interpret the concept of divine sovereignty to mean that might makes right. Since God can do anything he chooses, whatever he chooses is right. However, there is a difference in stating that God is the Almighty One and reducing sovereignty to tyranny.

Calvinists tend to talk about "sovereign grace," but the emphasis is always more on sovereignty than grace. Thus, they champion unconditional election and reprobation, as well as irresistible grace. Wesley argued that "the sovereignty of God is

---

[255]Oden, *The Living God*, 110-114.

then never to be brought to supersede his justice."[256] Wesley also declared to Calvinists, "You can bring no Scripture proof that God ever did, or assertion that he ever will, act as *mere sovereign* in eternally condemning any soul that ever was or will be born into the world."[257]

Arminians also affirm God's sovereignty, but believe that God has the prerogative of not always exercising that sovereignty. In Matthew 23:37-39, God was willing to save Jerusalem, and by extension all mankind, but Jerusalem had the power to temporarily resist the will of God. Thus, we have true libertarian freedom of the will. Yet, God never surrenders the consequences of our free choices to us. He always has the last word. From the Arminian viewpoint, God is so sovereign he can allow human rebellion, yet that rebellion does not thwart his ultimate purpose. He has predestinated the *consequences* of our free choices.

Tozer said a god less than sovereign would not bestow moral freedom upon his subjects. He would be afraid to do so. Yet our freedom does not overrule God's sovereignty.[258] C. S. Lewis made a similar statement, "For to make things which are not Itself, and thus to become, in a sense, capable of being resisted by its own handiwork, is the most astonishing and unimaginable of all feats we attribute to omnipotence."[259]

The first organized rebellion against God, at the tower of Babel, was effortlessly thwarted by God (Gen 11:1-9). God laughs in derision at the futile attempt of humanism to overthrow the reign of Christ, whom he has installed as king (Ps 2:4). Yet he sustains the very same rebellious creatures who oppose his authority!

---

[256]Wesley, *BE Works*, 13:277.

[257]Wesley, *BE Works*, 13:294.

[258]Tozer, *Knowledge of the Holy*, 118.

[259]Lewis, *The Problem of Pain*, 117.

God is majestic. "O Lord, our Lord, how majestic is your name in all the earth!" (Ps 8:1,9). He is robed with majesty (Ps 93:1). When Peter recalled the transfiguration of Jesus, he wrote: "we were eye-witnesses of his majesty" (2 Pet 1:16).

God is omnipresent. God is not a local deity. "He sits enthroned above the circle of the earth, and its people are like grasshoppers. He stretches out the heavens like a canopy, and spreads them out like a tent to live in" (Isa 40:22). The whole earth is full of his glory (Isa 6:3).

God declared, "Am I only a God nearby and not a God far away? Can anyone hide in secret places so that I cannot see him? Do not I fill heaven and earth" (Jer 23:23-24). The actual presence of God is everywhere in his created universe at the same time.

The omnipresence of God means that he is able to act everywhere. God is omnipresent in both time and space. David exclaimed, "Where can I go from your Spirit? Where can I flee from your presence? If I go up to the heavens, you are there; if I make my bed in the depths, you are there. If I rise on the wings of the dawn, if I settle on the far side of the sea, even there your hand will guide me, your right hand will hold me fast" (Ps 139:7-10). While the KJV reads, "If I make my bed in hell," *hell* is the absence of God. God is not barred from hell, but voluntarily withdraws his presence from hell.

According to Ephesians 4:10, at his ascension Christ rose from earth to heaven; and when he returned to heaven he was seated upon his throne of authority, where he fills the cosmos. God is present in his cosmos. However, he is over, not trapped with, the universe. Nor is he one and the same as his creation. At the dedication of the temple, Solomon prayed, "But will God really dwell on earth? The heavens, even the highest heaven, cannot contain you. How much less this temple I have built!" (1 Kgs 8:27). "'Do not I fill heaven and earth?' declares the Lord" (Jer 23:24).

Older theologians often used the term *ubiquity* or *immensity*. Sometimes God's transcendence and his immanence are separated into two categories. He is everywhere present, yet not confined to any one location. The medieval Scholastics said, "God's center is everywhere, God's circumference nowhere."[260] Augustine said,

> He is able to be everywhere present in the entirety of His being: He cannot be confined in any place: He can come without leaving the place where He was: He can depart without forsaking the place to which He had come.[261]

Because he is everywhere, he is an ever present help in our time of need (Ps 46:1).

God is omniscient. "His understanding has no limit" (Ps 147:5). "The eyes of the Lord are everywhere, keeping watch on the wicked and the good" (Prov 15:3). In Psalm 11:4 God is depicted as squinting or narrowing his eyes so that nothing is missed.

"Who has understood the mind of the Lord, or instructed him as his counselor? Whom did the Lord consult to enlighten him, and who taught him the right way? Who was it that taught him knowledge or showed him the path of understanding?" (Isa 40:13-14).

God knows the past. Malachi describes God's book of remembrance (3:16). His history is true. He knows what is happening. "Nothing in all creation is hidden from God's sight. Everything is uncovered and laid bare before the eyes of him to whom we must give account" (Heb 4:13). John said that Jesus "knew

---

[260]Oden, *The Living God*, 59. Arminius also used it [*Works*, 1:326].

[261]Augustine, *Letters*, *NPNF*1 1:474.

all men. He did not need man's testimony about man, for he knew what was in a man" (John 2:24-25).

> O Lord, you have searched me and you know me. You know when I sit and when I rise; you perceive my thoughts from afar. You discern my going out and my lying down; you are familiar with all my ways. Before a word is on my tongue you know it completely, O Lord (Ps 139:1-4).

And he knows what will happen. "I make known the end from the beginning, from ancient times, what is still to come" (Isa 46:10). God is never surprised. Because of his foreknowledge, approximately a quarter of the whole Bible was prophetic when written.

Calvinism says that God knows the future because he has predestined the future. Boettner held that foreknowledge entails fore-ordination.[262] Since Calvinists tend to conflate foreknowledge with predestination, the concept of *foreknowledge* has been rejected by open theism. Yet knowledge is not causal. There is no causation implied in foreknowledge.

> One's knowledge of a current event does not make it true . . . nor, for that matter, does one's knowledge of past events in any way cause them to occur. Similarly, foreknowledge of a future event does not cause the occurrence of the event.[263]

Some have so reacted against Calvinism that they have denied God's foreknowledge altogether. This debate on fore-

---

[262]Boettner, *Reformed Doctrine of Predestination*, 42-46. Martin Luther advocated the same position in *Bondage of the Will* (1525). See also Frame, *Doctrine of God*, 62; 69; 139; 481-485.

[263]McCall, "Was Arminius an Unwitting Determinist?" 31-32.

knowledge centers around three issues: the nature and mode of God's foreknowledge, the implication regarding divine sovereignty, and the implications regarding human freedom.

- ## Process Theology

Process thought is a reaction against the position that there is objective, static, changeless reality. Process theology contends that God is affected by the world just as the world is affected by God. Adopting a panentheism view, the world becomes God's body. *Panentheism* is a belief system which posits that God personally exists, interpenetrates every part of nature, and timelessly extends beyond it.

Panentheism differs from *pantheism*, which holds that God is not a distinct being but is synonymous with the universe. *Panentheism* is the attempt to apply Alfred North Whitehead's process philosophy to the nature of God. Yet Whitehead himself admitted that he had never fully worked out his doctrine of God.[264] Thus, panentheism argues that God's knowledge is limited to the consciousness of finite creatures. While affirming God's immanence, it denies his transcendence. Whitehead's notion that God is a finite being is simply a finite attempt to explain God.

Applying this concept theologically, Whitehead taught the interdependence of God and the world. God is not aloof from, nor unaffected by, the world. God works in the world primarily through persuasion, not coercion. God should be thought of in terms of suffering with the world, not in terms of omnipotence. According to Cobb, "God does not know what the result will be."[265]

The result is a God who is different from us only in quantity, not quality. Process theology ends up with an immanent God

---

[264]Henry, *GRA* 6:60.

[265]Cobb and Griffin, *Process Theology*, 57.

who is actually caught in the evolutionary process. He does not superintend the world; he is a part of the world. Both God and creation are involved in an ongoing process. This process emphasis has created a new interest in the Eastern concept of perfecting grace, deification, and Eastern mystical philosophy.

Such theology denies the immutability of God. This suggests that God might not know the future of contingent events, but may himself be in process.

• Openness Theology

Freewill Theism, which is also known as openness theology or open theism, rejects the modernism of process theology but questions the immutability and foreknowledge of God.[266] They claim to be Arminian, but are actually Socinian at this point. Arminians affirm that God foreknows whatever will come to pass, but Socinians insisted that it was a contradiction of human freedom for God to foreknow the free decisions of free agents.

Open theism argues that since there are no propositions about the future to know, God can be omniscient and yet not know the future. They advocate for a God who takes risk, but if he is omniscient, there is no risk.

Open theism essentially reduces God to the attribute of love. It claims that God does not have exhaustive knowledge of the future and does not infringe upon man's free will. Thus, God reacts to our decisions, takes risks, learns, makes mistakes, and changes his mind.

Clark Pinnock has argued for open theism as a via media between classical and process theology. Yet open theism amounts to a "halfway house of conservative process theism."[267]

---

[266]Pinnock, "God Limits His Knowledge," 143-162; Olson, "Has God Been Held Hostage by Philosophy," 30-32.

[267]Gruenler, "Between Classical and Process Theism," 321,325. See Bloesch, *God the Almighty*, 254-260.

They teach that God's absolute foreknowledge is limited by human free will. Open theism believes, "The God of the Bible is with us in time and does not know the future in absolute detail."[268] David Basinger claimed, "God can never know with certainty what will happen in any context involving freedom of choice."[269] They argue that man's future free choices cannot be foreknown by God; if they were then they would no longer be free. "What God decides to do depends on what people decide to do."[270] Thus, God's promises have no absolute guarantee of success.[271]

Oden declared, "The fantasy that God is ignorant of the future is a heresy that must be rejected on scriptural grounds."[272] John Wesley explained,

> I (if one may be allowed to compare the things of men with the deep things of God) now know the sun shines. Yet the sun does not shine because I know it: but I know it because it shines. My knowledge *supposes* the sun to shine, but does not in any wise *cause* it. In like manner God knows that man sins; for he knows all things. Yet we do not sin because he knows it; but he knows it because we sin. And his knowledge *supposes* our sin, but does not in any wise *cause* it.[273]

---

[268]Olson, "Has God Been Held Hostage by Philosophy?" 30.

[269]Basinger, "Practical Implications," 163.

[270]Rice, "Biblical Support for a New Perspective," 32.

[271]Bloesch, *The Last Things*, 249.

[272]Oden, "Real Reformers are Traditionalists," 46.

[273]Wesley, "On Predestination," Sermon # 58, § 5.

John Wesley pointed out that strictly speaking there is no foreknowledge or after-knowledge with God, "but all things are known to Him as present from eternity to eternity."[274]

Another issue that must be addressed is the statements of Scripture that God does not remember our sins. According to Isaiah 43:25, "I, even I, am he who blots out your transgressions, for my own sake, and remembers your sins no more." Jeremiah 31:34 makes the same promise, which is cited in Hebrews 8:12. Apparently, God has the ability to block certain actions from his consciousness although they are still retained in his omniscience.

Does God know what will happen before it occurs? Isaiah 41:21-29 challenges idolaters by asking if their idols could tell what is going to happen. "Tell us what the future holds, so we may know that you are gods." In contrast, God alone can tell the future. How else could prophesy be given? In John 13:19 Jesus told his disciples what would happen.

According to 1 John 3:20, "God knows everything." God "calls things that are not as though they were" (Rom 4:17). There are examples where the prophets foretold the outcome of more than one choice (see Jer 38:17-18).

God through his foreknowledge knew that we would sin and need a Savior (1 Pet 1:2). Christ was chosen before creation (1 Pet 1:20). He was the Lamb that was slain from the creation of the world (Rev 13:8). The only other place the noun *prognosis* is used is Acts 2:23 and it also refers to the crucifixion of Christ.

• Calvinism

Calvinism has connected *foreknowledge, predestination,* and *election* in a way Scripture does not. Lorraine Boettner made a significant concession.

---

[274]Wesley, *Notes,* 608; see also "On Predestination," Sermon #58, § 5.

It may occasion some surprise to discover that the doctrine of Predestination was not made a matter of special study until near the end of the fourth century. . . . They of course taught that salvation was through Christ; yet they assumed that man had full power to accept or reject the gospel.[275]

It was the later Augustine who introduced the foundation for a Calvinistic understanding of predestination. Yet Vincent of Lérins rejected Augustine's doctrine of predestination, deeming it a novelty, because it was not that faith which has been believed everywhere, always, by all. He called it heresy to teach of

a certain great and special and altogether personal grace of God, so that whosoever pertain to their number, without any labor, without any industry, even though they neither ask, nor seek, nor knock, have such a dispensation from God, that, borne up by angel hands, that is, preserved by the protection of angels, it is impossible that should ever dash their feet against a stone, that is, that they should ever be offended.[276]

Calvinism teaches that God in his foreknowledge has chosen or decreed that some people are to be saved and some to be lost. Wesley objected that this was no gospel, but called this teaching "horrible decrees."[277]

If Calvinism misunderstands these words, what does the Bible mean by foreknowledge, predestination, and election?

---

[275]Boettner, *Reformed Doctrine of Predestination*, 365.

[276]Vincent, *Commonitory*, *NPNF*2 11:151; 158. Latourette, *History of Christianity*, 1:182.

[277]Wesley, "Free Grace," Sermon #110, § 26. Here Wesley referenced Calvin's own statement in his *Institutes*, 3.23.7 [2:232].

- **Foreknowledge does not determine predestination**

God calls all men everywhere to repent, but that call is not irresistible. "Many are called, but few are chosen" (Matt 20:16; 22:14). Those who respond to God's grace are the elect. Second Peter 1:10 urges us to make our calling and election sure through an obedient faith.

- **Predestination does not determine election**

God predestined the *plan* of salvation. God has not predestined who will be saved, but he has predestined that those who are born again will be holy. This is what Paul states in 2 Thessalonians 2:13, "God chose you to be saved through the sanctifying work of the Spirit." The verb *choose* does not restrict who is chosen, rather it defines what they are chosen to become.

God has predetermined that the elect would be holy. The church is the called out ones. We are called out of the world system and called to be holy. Paul reveals that God's purpose is to present us holy — if we continue in faith, not moved from the hope held out by the gospel (Col 1:22-23).

According to W. B. Pope, "It is not the Divine foreknowledge that conditions what takes place, but what takes place conditions divine foreknowledge."[278] Here Pope echoes Arminius, "A thing does not happen because it has been foreknown or predicted, but it is foreknown or predicted because it is about to be."[279] Sheldon argued that this concept should be termed the *catholic*, rather than the *Arminian* view, since it was

---

[278]Pope, *Compendium*, 1:317.

[279]Arminius, *Works*, 2:368.

held by the universal church from the apostolic age until Calvin.[280]

In 1 Samuel 23:9-13 David was told what would happen *if* he entered the town of Keilah, and so he opted not to go there. Jeremiah told King Zedekiah what would happen *if* he surrendered and what would happen if he did not (Jer 38:17-18). In Ezekiel 3:6, God told Ezekiel what would have happened *if* he had been sent to a foreign culture. But instead, God sent him to his own people.

John 6:64 teaches that Jesus had known from the beginning who they were that believed not and who would betray him. Wesley commented, "Therefore it is plain, God does foresee future contingencies."[281] Another example is found in Matthew 11:23-24. Here Jesus says that *if* the inhabitants of Tyre, Sidon, and Sodom had seen his miracles, they would have repented. But they did not see such miracles and did not have that opportunity to repent. However, according to Calvinism, because God foreknew two or more contingencies, they would *both* be predestinated!

Theologians refer to this contingent knowledge as "middle knowledge." This view holds that God not only has necessary knowledge and contingent knowledge, but a middle knowledge in between necessary and contingent knowledge. He knows what all possible created free wills would do in all possible circumstances. God, in his omniscience, has comprehensive knowledge of how free agents would behave in all possible circumstances — without predestinating their behavior. God arranges the world as he chooses based on his middle knowledge. He exercises sovereign control by creating the people he wills, knowing what choices they will make.

Samuel Wakefield made these distinctions regarding future events:

---

[280]Sheldon, *System of Christian Doctrine*, 173.

[281]Wesley, *Notes*, 232.

- There are necessary events which are fixed by God's predestination.
- There are conditional events in which the results depend upon the circumstances (see Ezek 21:19).
- There are contingent events which depend upon human choice.[282]

God in his omniscience knows what sins I will commit before I ever commit them. But we must always keep foreknowledge separate from predestination. Since he foreknew Adam's original sin, he had already predestined the atonement; but he did not predestine Adam's sin nor mine. Furthermore, God will not impute our sin to us before we commit it. According to 1 John 2:1 it is possible, by the grace of God, *not* to willfully sin. In his foreknowledge, he already knows what I will do, but he will not charge me with that sin until I commit it.

While God knows the past, present, and future simultaneously, he relates to us within the constraints of our time frame. That means God, in his magnanimous and incomprehensible love, will assure me today of my acceptance as his son, even if he knows that I will become apostate in the future.

God is omnipotent. While Psalm 139:1-6 dealt with omniscience, and vv 7-12 dealt with omnipresence, vv 13-18 deal with omnipotence.

"Is anything too hard for the Lord?" (Gen 18:14). "I know that you can do all things; no plan of yours can be thwarted" (Job 42:2). "With God all things are possible" (Matt 19:26).

In Genesis 17:1 and 35:11 God declared to Abraham, "I am God Almighty" (*El Shaddai*), which carries the meaning of all-sufficient and self-sufficient.

---

[282]Wakefield, *Christian Theology,*1:153-156; see also Oden, *The Living God*, 71-74.

The Greek word *pantokrator* occurs ten times in the NT, nine of which are in the book of Revelation. It means ruler of all. According to Revelation 19:6, the Lord God Almighty reigns. The KJV used the word *omnipotent*. The tenth reference is 2 Corinthians 6:18.

Genesis 18:14 asks, "Is anything too hard for God?" Yet God cannot contradict his own nature. "Not even Omnipotence can do what is self-contradictory."[283]

We cannot pit one attribute against another. God can do anything consistent with his nature, but he cannot deny himself (2 Tim 2:13). He cannot do anything inconsistent with his character. Thus, he cannot cease to exist since he is eternal.

Sophomoric questions such as — can God make a square into a triangle? Can God make a stone heavier than he can lift? Can God abolish the past? — all beg the question. Omnipotence cannot accomplish the impossible, since what is possible is based upon his nature.

According to Malachi 3:6, God cannot change. God cannot change for the better because he is already absolutely perfect and such perfection cannot be improved. He cannot change for the worse because then he would no longer be absolutely perfect.

According to Titus 1:2, God cannot lie. Hebrews 6:18 makes an even stronger assertion, that it is impossible for God to lie. The context refers to his oath and his covenant. In a general sense, the old and new covenants are the holy Scriptures. They cannot lie either since they are God's revelation and he is a God of truth. He cannot lie because he is light and in him is no darkness at all (1 John 1:5).

Neither can God be tempted (Jas 1:13). God cannot be corrupted. His holiness resists any invitation to sin. There is nothing sinful in his nature to which temptation can even appeal. He is unimpeachable.

---

[283]Lewis, *Miracles*, 40.

God is unlimited in his capability. He is God the Father almighty. He can do anything consistent with his nature. However, he cannot sin (2 Tim 2:13) nor lie (Heb 6:17-18; Titus 1:2).

God cannot perform contradictory actions, immoral actions, actions appropriate only to finite creatures, and actions denying his own nature as God.

God is absolute perfection. "As for God, his way is perfect" (Ps 18:30). God's creation was perfect. The first chapter of Genesis closes with the declaration that God saw all he had made and it was *very good*. That statement emphasized the perfection of his finished creation.

God's word is perfection. Psalm 18:30 declares that his word is flawless. The Hebrew word *sarap*, used here, also describes the process of refined gold. In Psalm 12:6, the word *tahor* is used to describe God's Word as flawless. This word emphasizes the product, pure gold without alloy. Psalm 19:7 declares the law of the Lord is perfect or complete. The Hebrew word *tamim* describes "what is complete, entirely in accord with truth and fact."[284]

God commands his children to become perfect. In Genesis 17:1 he told Abraham, "Walk before me and be perfect." Jesus gave the command, "Be perfect, therefore, as your heavenly Father is perfect" (Matt 5:48). Christian perfection, however, is derived from God; it is relative and not absolute, and it is imputed to those who love God with their whole heart.

We will never become like God in these noncommunicable attributes, despite the teaching of Mormonism. Lorenzo Snow, early Mormon president and prophet, taught, "As man is, God once was; as God is now, man may become."[285]

Prosperity teachers, such as Benny Hinn, claim we are now little gods on the earth. According to this teaching, all the full-

---

[284]BDB, *Lexicon*, 1071.

[285]Snow, *Biography of Lorenzo Snow*, 46-47.

ness of God dwells in *us* (Col 2:9). This is not the power to live a holy life, but power to walk in the miraculous.[286]

However, Kenneth Copeland insists, "You have the same creative faith and ability on the inside of you that God used when he created the heavens and the earth."[287]Thus, we are little gods who can create simply by speaking matter into existence. Copeland also declared, "You don't have a God in you; you are one."[288] He also taught, "All of God's attributes, all of God's authority, all of God's faith, all of God's ability was invested in that man [Adam]."[289] Morris Cerullo preached, "When we stand up here, brother, you're not looking at Morris Cerullo; you're looking at God. You're looking at Jesus."[290]

This teaching ignores the distinction between communicable and incommunicable attributes. It also implies that faith is a force. A biblical definition of faith reveals that God is the object of our faith. God does not need to have faith in himself.

Faith teachers assert that every believer is as much the incarnation of God as Jesus of Nazareth, and any born again person could have done what Jesus did in making atonement for sin.[291] Kenneth Hagin declared, "There is a real incarnation in the new birth!" He said that "every born again man is an incarnation," and that "the believer is as much an incarnation as Jesus of Nazareth."[292] Such teaching is not only heretical, it is ridiculous.

---

[286]Reeves, *Other Side of the River*, 23, 27, 30, 121.

[287]Copeland, *Inner Image of the Covenant*.

[288]Copeland, *The Force of Love*.

[289]Copeland, *Our Covenant With God*, 15.

[290]Cerullo, "The Endtime Manifestation of the Sons of God."

[291]Copeland, "Substitution and Identification."

[292]Hagin, *Zoe: The God-Kind of Life*, 42; "Walking in the Light of Life," 3; "The Virgin Birth," 8; "The Incarnation," 14.

Communicable attributes God imparts

This list of God's attributes compares with the fruit of the Spirit in Galatians 5:22-23: love, joy, peace, patience, kindness, goodness, faithfulness, gentleness, self-control. It is the work of the Holy Spirit to make us godly in these areas.

God is a person. While God is invisible, he is not an impersonal force, influence, or law. God is alive. "He is the living God" (Jer 10:10; Acts 14:15). Miley wrote, "If God is not a personal being, the result must be either atheism or pantheism. It matters little which."[293]

In Isaiah 44:6-22, God declares that apart from him there is no God. There he contrasts his existence with idols who are inanimate. God always refers to himself using personal, not impersonal, pronouns. In contrast, idols know nothing (v 18). New age teaching reduces God to energy, but Scripture promises that we can have fellowship with a personal God.

The most frequent Hebrew word for *person* is *nephesh*. The Hebrew word *panim* means face and is used as an anthropomorphism in statements such as Exodus 33:16, where God promised that his face would go with Moses. *Panim* corresponds to the Greek word *prosopa* which means face or mask. The Latin word *persona* refers to the masks worn by actors through which they spoke their words. The face or countenance reflects personality. *Person* then came to mean a role or character.

Thus, to seek his face continually, as commanded in 1 Chronicles 16:11, implies a personal relationship with a personal being. "He asks us as persons to come to Him a Person." Pope explained that the face is the expression of our individual self; the express image of our person. Pantheism makes everything God and God everything — without a personal face. Polytheism has erred in giving God a multiplicity of faces. The face of God

---

[293]Miley, *Systematic Theology*, 1:173.

is the incarnate Redeemer. God has shined in the face of Jesus (2 Cor 4:6).[294]

Christianity teaches that a person is a creation of God, made in his image and imperfectly sharing his communicable attributes, and subject to his laws. Tertullian adopted the word *persona* in his doctrine of the Trinity to refer to the three "persons."[295] Wiley wrote,

> This failure to apply the term "person" to the whole being of God gave rise to the modern controversies between philosophy and theology concerning the nature of personality; and further, to controversies within theology itself respecting the nature of the Trinity.[296]

The Greek word *hupostasis* is synonymous with the Latin word *substantia*, and should be translated *subsistence*. These words refer to underlying reality or personhood. In Hebrews 1:3 Christ is declared to be the exact reflection of the essence or *hupostasis* of God.

The early church declared that God was of one essence (*ousia*) but three persons. It is significant that this word *ousia* is the participle form of the Greek verb *eimi*.[297] Thus, forms of the same word are used to describe our being in Acts 17:28 and God's being. The difference is that God's existence is independent, while our existence is dependent upon him.

It is significant that such terms as *hupostasis*, *physis*, *ousia*, and *prosopon* come from the exegesis of the Scripture. But they were also part of the vocabulary of the Greek philosophers who

---

[294]Pope, "The Face of God," Sermon #7, *Sermons, Addresses, and Charges*, 122-129.

[295]Tertullian, *Against Praxeas*, ANF 3:598.

[296]Wiley, *Christian Theology*, 1:291.

[297]*Ousia* occurs twice in the NT, in Luke 15:12-13, where it describes property or wealth.

used these terms to define impersonal being. They were redefined by the Christian church.

Augustine himself was uneasy with utilizing the term *hupostasis*,[298] but ultimately any use of language has limitations which must be accepted in order to communicate anything. The early church modified existing language to accommodate Christian concepts. That fact alone does not necessarily mean that they capitulated to pagan philosophy.

Personality implies life, self-consciousness, intelligence, and self-determination. Aristotle held that there are three essential attributes of personality: intellect or reason; will or volition; sensibility or emotion. Scripture reveals God as conscious, self-determining, willing, and feeling — all the attributes of personality. Thus, God cannot be referenced with neuter pronouns. Without implying all of Sigmund Freud's baggage, we could say that personhood involves *ego*. The Greek word *ego* is the first person singular pronoun.

W. B. Pope insisted that the faith of the church rests upon the divine-human relationship. While revising the *First Catechism* in 1881, Pope came under criticism because he had changed the question from "What is God?" to "Who is God?" He then supplied the answer, "Our Father."[299]

In reaction to Karl Barth, who described God as "the Wholly Other," Emil Brunner emphasized the "I-Thou" concept between the individual and God.[300] For Brunner the problem in theology was that the subject and object were both made third person and impersonal. Thus God communicates truth about himself rather than communicating himself.

God is not nameless energy or an abstract idea. God is not anonymous; he has a name. While words fall short, there is no

---

[298] Augustine, *On the Trinity*, NPNF1 3:92.

[299] Lidgett, "The Theological Institution," 9-10.

[300] Brunner, *Truth as Encounter*, 24; *Christian Doctrine of God*, 139.

meaning without words. The names of God reveal his character and personality. While Adam named the animals, God must name himself.

Feminism often advocates the substitution of unisex language, calling God our Parent or Creator instead of our Father. But gender neutral translations tend to promote a concept of God that is impersonal. While God transcends sexuality, he chose to relate to us in the masculine gender. This disclosure should be interpreted metaphorically. God is neither male nor female. Carl Henry argues that God is pure spirit and that the masculine pronoun is used scripturally in reference to God to emphasize his personality, in contrast to impersonal entities.[301]

According to Ephesians 3:15, God chose to reveal himself as our Father. The concept of family is derived from the very nature of God, our Father. Paul is saying that every *patria* is named after the heavenly *pater*. The existence and concept and experience of fatherhood is derived from God. God is the universal Patriarch. Every fatherly relationship has its prototype in God. God is more truly father than any human father.

> The Fatherhood of God is not a mere metaphor drawn from human relationships. The very opposite is the case. . . . The archetype of all father-hood is seen in the God-head, and all other fatherhoods are derived from Him.[302]

Athanasius wrote, "God as Father of the Son is the only true Father; and all created paternity is a shadow of the true."[303]

---

[301]Henry, *GRA* 5:159-162.

[302]Martin, *New Bible Commentary*, 1023.

[303]Athanasius, *Four Discourses Against the Arians*, NPNF2 4:320.

According to J. I. Packer, fatherhood implies authority, affection, fellowship, and honor.[304]

It may also imply origin, as in fathering something, and nurturing. While the same could be said of a mother, the difference is that a mother births and nurtures out of her own body. "Can a mother forget the baby at her breast and have no compassion on the child she has borne?" (Isa 49:15).

We cannot change the language about God without abandoning Scripture, especially if we hold to verbal inspiration. We cannot rationalize that since human language is culturally bound, it is open to revision by other cultures. Yet there is an ongoing attempt by feminist theologians to eliminate the use of masculine third-person pronouns to refer to God.

Feminist theologians generally oppose continuing to address God exclusively as our heavenly Father. They tend to advocate changing Bible translations and adjusting liturgies. But changing the language will not necessarily change harmful behavior and abuse. And changing the language about God to feminine pronouns does not deconstruct the use of sexual language. A female deity will still require explanation. The ancient world was full of goddesses, but fertility cults and sacred prostitutes did nothing to elevate the status of women.

In the OT God customarily referred to his people corporately as his *son*.[305] Before the advent of Christ, rarely did anyone address God as father.[306] Jesus scandalized his hearers by using this as his regular address. *Abba*, the Aramaic term for father, is a term of intimacy.

Jewish slaves were never allowed to address their master as *father*. Muslims object strongly to calling God our father, considering it blasphemy to say *my father*. They also object to Jesus

---

[304]Packer, *Knowing God*, 185.

[305]Henry, *GRA* 6:309.

[306]Jeremias, *Prayers of Jesus*, 57.

being called the "Son of God." They insist that God has no children and call *themselves servants of God.*[307]

While God is not a man, he has chosen to reveal his nature by using male language. If God revealed himself using male pronouns, this assumes the complementary position that God designated male and female roles and that God's purpose in being "male" was to illustrate the male role.

In contrast to all the pagan religions of Bible times, which had both gods and goddesses, God never identifies himself with female language. The Hebrew language did not even have a word for *goddess.*[308] To recast his nature as bi-sexual is to depart from Christianity and move into idolatry. We cannot change the language without rejecting the reality behind the word, as gender-neutral translations attempt to do.[309]

In Proverbs 8, *sophia* is wisdom personified and not a literal person. The interpretative question is the relationship between wisdom and Christ. Should this wisdom be connected with the *logos* in John's Gospel? Is wisdom a personification or a hypostasis (an actual being)?

Arians interpreted Proverbs 8 as Christ, then argued on the basis of v 22 that he was a created being. But that interpretation pushes this metaphor beyond its intended meaning. God is the author of wisdom, but God did not create God. Although Augustine, Calvin, and Wesley equated Wisdom with Jesus Christ, and although modern feminism is interested in *sophia*, this is a personification.[310] On the basis of progressive revelation, humanity had to await the coming of Christ and the outpouring of the Holy

---

[307]Hansen, "Son and the Crescent." 19-23.

[308]Grider, *Wesleyan-Holiness Theology*, 130.

[309]Poythress and Grudem, *The Gender-Neutral Bible Controversy* (2000).

[310]Oden, *ACCS* 9:60-67; Wesley, *Notes*, 3:1845; Waltke, *Proverbs 1-15*, 126-133, 409; Frame, *Doctrine of God*, 382-383.

Spirit before we can formulate precise distinctions within the Godhead.

Nowhere in Scripture is God addressed as mother or with the feminine pronoun. Donald Bloesch argued that the debate over sexist language is ultimately a debate concerning the nature of God.[311] He explained in 1982,

> Patriarchy preserves the biblical principle of an above and a below, of a first and a second, of headship and servanthood. To deny or erase these distinctions between members of the Trinity or between God and man or between man and woman is to end up in a pantheistic monism in which creaturehood is swallowed up in deity.[312]

All pagan religions conceived of God in their own image. Thus, there was a multiplicity of gods and goddesses. There was no covenant relationship between god and man. Mankind evolved into godhood through cultic ritual. In the Christian view, however, Christ is male and his church is female. He completes us and we complete him.[313] Thus, we have a present covenant relationship with God through his indwelling Spirit.

We are persons in his image. If we are created in his image and we don't know who or what he is, then we have an identity crisis. If he is nothing, we are nothing.

God is free. God decides, chooses, and determines, based solely upon his character. He was under no necessity to create or

---

[311]Bloesch, *Battle for the Trinity*, xv-xvi. Bloesch argues that there is no necessary correlation between grammatical gender and actual gender [p. 33].

[312]Bloesch, *Is the Bible Sexist?* 66,78-79; see also *God the Almighty*, 25-27; *Jesus Christ*, 75-79.

[313]According to Eph 1:23.

sustain the universe. He has chosen us according to his will (Eph 1:11). Pope explained that *thelma* is the exercise of God's will; *boule* is the determination of that will, and *energeo* is the outworking of his will in his acts.[314]

However, Calvinism often makes an artificial distinction between God's secret will and his revealed will.[315] While Deuteronomy 29:29 refers to secret things and revealed things, God cannot contradict himself. This is the closest that Scripture comes to a "secret council." Psalm 25:14 does not refer to a *council* in the Hebrew text. Paul could not actually declare the *whole* will or purpose of God (Acts 20:27) if there was a secret part.

Thus, the doctrine of unconditional election entails contradictory wills of God, teaching that God commands all people to believe and simultaneously withholds the grace necessary for belief.

God is holy. *Holy* is used more often as a prefix to God's name than any other attribute. This is the only attribute of God which is repeated three times in succession (Isa 6:3; Rev 4:8). "Who is like you — majestic in holiness, awesome in glory" (Exod 15:11). Kinlaw explained, "Nothing in the Old Testament is holy in itself except Him."[316]

His intrinsic holiness is described in the phrase "whose name is holy" (Isa 57:15). "Holy and awesome is his name" (Ps 111:9). When Amos speaks of him "swearing by his holiness" (4:2), it is the same as saying "the Sovereign Lord has sworn by himself" (6:8). Thus, to say that God is holy is another way of

---

[314]Pope, *Compendium*, 1:308.

[315]See Piper, "Are There Two Wills in God?" 107-132, where he attempts to affirm that God simultaneously wills that all persons be saved and wills to elect unconditionally those who will actually be saved. Unless God is schizophrenic, it would appear that one of these wills is disingenuous.

[316]Kinlaw, *Lectures in Old Testament Theology*, 220.

saying he is God. The first petition in the model prayer which Jesus gave is that God's name be kept holy (Matt 6:9).

Some theologians argue that holiness is not simply an attribute of God, but it is his essence. However, this distinction hinges on how the word *attribute* is defined. If an attribute is defined as an essential characteristic of a person or thing, it seems to be a matter of semantics to distinguish between attribute and essence. Donald Bloesch warned that in our delineation of the attributes of God, we must guard against singling out any one of them as giving an exhaustive definition of God.[317]

Al Truesdale wrote that the Hebrew word for *holy* (*qadash*) "refers positively to what is uniquely God's, to the essential difference between God and man. He is Yahweh, and His glory He does not share with any other. Holiness distinguished him from everything else."[318]

Qadash conveys the concepts of glory, separation, and purity. The English word *holy* does not occur in the book of Genesis, but when Jacob realized that God was present where he was, he declared the place was awesome (Gen 28:17). The concept of glory corresponds to the majestic splendor of the presence of God. According to Exodus 15:11, God's holiness makes him glorious. He is awesome in his radiance and majesty.

Alfred Edersheim held that the primary meaning for *qadash* was "splendid, beautiful, pure, uncontaminated."[319] We are called to worship Yahweh in the beauty or splendor of his holiness (Ps 96:9, 29:2, 110:3, 1 Chr 16:29; 2 Chr 20:21).

The glory of God in many theophanic passages is the created light that shines from God's presence. The Hebrew word for glory (*kabod*) was often used in the Bible to describe the manifestation of God's presence with his people. In Exodus 16:10 and Ezekiel 10:3-4 it is described as a brilliant light. Exodus 19:16

---

[317]Bloesch, *God the Almighty*, 42.

[318]Truesdale, "Theism," 1:117.

[319]Edersheim, *Bible History: Old Testament*, 2:110.

describes a glory cloud, as does 1 Kings 8:10-11. In Exodus 33:18 Moses desired to see this glory or beauty of the Lord.

The glory of God the creator is seen even in the phenomena of nature. This glory was the visible resplendence of Yahweh's own presence and person. The Hebrew word *shekinah* does not appear in the Bible. It first occurs in the Jewish Targums and was borrowed by Christians to express the visible majesty of God's presence. The word was derived from *shakan* (to dwell).

To say that God dwelt in any place was to say that his glory was there. The *shekinah* was the visible presence of the glory of God. This *shekinah* glory became incarnate in Jesus Christ (John 1:14). It was called by the later Jewish writers the *Shekinah*.

The Hebrew word *kabod* is related to the Greek word *doxa* in John 1:14, Hebrews 1:3, and Revelation 21:23, 22:5. This glorious brilliance also conveys the concept of beauty. In 2 Corinthians 4:17 Paul uses the phrase "weight of glory," based on the root meaning of *kabod* as heavy. This weighty glory was lovely, radiant, and protective. In Exodus 19:16 it is described as thick.

Jon Huntzinger wrote that Israel lived in the world of holiness. The Sabbath and special festival were set apart as holy times. Space was also viewed as holy. Specific areas were designated as more or less holy; as places where people could experience God's presence and participate in his purpose. The holy of holies in the tabernacle, and later in the temple, was the center of God's creation.[320] Here the divine and the human could meet without the divine destroying the human or the human polluting the divine.

God met with the children of Israel at the door of the tabernacle and the place was sanctified by his glory (Exod 29:43; Lev 10:3). The pillar of cloud by day and the pillar of fire by night represented the protection of God's glory. This glory was manifested as a consuming fire on top of Mount Sinai (Exod 24:17).

---

[320]Huntzinger, "Goodness and Worship," 36.

Moses asked to see God (Exod 33:18-20). He was not allowed to see God in his holiness because he could not survive the trauma. We cannot know God unless he accommodates himself to our human frailty and manifests himself in some form of incarnation.[321]

Yet Moses saw his glory, the manifestation of his activity in the world, and that revelation made his face radiant (Exod 33:32, 34:30, see Ps 34:5). At the dedication of Solomon's temple this glory so filled the house that the priests could not stand to minister (1 Kgs 8:10-11). Jehoshaphat appointed men to sing to the Lord and praise him for the splendor of his holiness (2 Chr 20:21). When Isaiah had his revelation of God, he saw the glory of God filling the whole earth (Isa 6:5). Under the new covenant, every person can now behold this glory and, as a result, experience transformation (2 Cor 3:18).

God's holiness also separates him from sin. He is set apart and transcendent. He cannot look with favor upon sin. God's holiness is absolute purity. "Your eyes are too pure to look on evil; you cannot tolerate wrong" (Hab 1:13). "Who can stand in the presence of the Lord, this holy God?" (1 Sam 6:20). James wrote that God cannot be tempted by evil (1:13).

The first specific reference to holiness occurs when Moses encountered the burning bush and found himself on holy ground. The ground was holy because God was there. Moses was warned not to come closer. He removed his sandals as an act of worship and hid his face (Exod 3:2-6).

Qadash also means that God is pure. "For to say that God is holy is nothing other than to say that God is perfect in goodness."[322] The LXX used the word *hosios*, which conveys the idea of holiness as devoutness or piety, undefiled by sin, free from

---

[321]Greathouse, *Wholeness in Christ*, 18.

[322]Oden, *The Living God*, 99.

wickedness, observing every moral obligation, pure, pious.[323] God is said to be *hosios* in Acts 2:27, 13:35; Revelation 15:4, 16:5.

God's law is an expression of his holiness. According to Romans 7:12, the law is holy, and the commandment is holy, righteous, and good. Wesley taught that the moral law is eternal. It is a copy of the eternal mind, a transcript of the divine nature.[324] And conversely, the source of a culture's law is its god.[325] Thus, culture is an external expression of religion.

God's anger is an expression of his holiness. "It is the legal, just, holy, and good answer of God to wilful sin."[326] There are over 580 references to the wrath of God in the OT. Over twenty Hebrew words are used to express this wrath. This wrath is not an impersonal force. Numbers 11:33; 2 Kings 22:13; John 3:36; Romans 1:18; Ephesians 5:6; Colossians 3:6; Hebrews 3:11, 4:3; Revelation 6:16, 14:10,19, 15:1,7, 16:1, 19:15 all attribute wrath directly to God.

"God cannot dismiss His wrath without trivializing His love."[327] Why, then, is the wrath of God not an attribute? According to Micah 7:18, he does not retain his anger forever, but his love is steadfast (see also Ps 103:8-11; Isa 54:7-8; Hos 14:4).

The command, "Be holy because I, the Lord your God, am holy" (Lev 11:45), is impossible without his enabling grace. Only God is absolutely holy. Our holiness is all derived from him and constantly dependent upon him.

Jealousy is the result of God's holiness (Exod 34:14). Actually, the word *jealous* is used as a proper name for God in Exo-

---

[323]Thayer, *Greek Lexicon*, 456; Seebass, "Holy," *NIDNTT* 2:236.

[324]Wesley, "Original, Nature, Properties, and Use of the Law," Sermon #34, 2.1-6.

[325]Rushdoony, *Politics of Guilt and Pity*, 141.

[326]Deschner, *Wesley's Christology*, 150.

[327]Truesdale, "Theism," 1:127.

dus 34:14 and the Hebrew word *qanna*, which occurs six times,[328] is used only of God. This jealous nature is a passionate concern for the covenant relationship. Hebrews 12:29 reminds us that God is a consuming fire. These words were originally stated in Deuteronomy 4:24, where Moses added that God is a jealous God. God will not share his glory with anyone else. When the sons of Aaron were careless with the holy fire and in its place offered strange fire, God consumed them with his fire explaining, "I will show myself holy" (Lev 10:3).

God's hatred of sin is also an expression of his holiness. God detests or abhors pagan customs which are unclean (Lev 20:23). He also hates the lawless practice of the Nicolaitans infiltrating his church (Rev 2:6, 15).

God's love is also an expression of his holiness. "Wherever holiness is spoken of in Scripture, love is nearby. Wherever God's love is manifested, it does not cease to be holy."[329] Yet love may become permissive without the balance of holiness. God's holiness is not unloving and God's love is not unholy. "God is not holy because He loves, but loves because He is holy."[330]

God is truth. "Let God be true and every man a liar" (Rom 3:4). God is trustworthy. His truth endures to all generations (Ps 100:5). God is true even if he contradicts all the teachings of men. However, God wants us also to speak the truth in love. It is inconsistent to affirm that God is true, but his revelation of himself contains error. He has exalted his name and his Word above all things (Ps 138:2).

God is love. "God is love" (1 John 4:8,16). "He is good; his love endures forever" (Ps 106:1). 1 John 4 is actually the love

---

[328]Exod 20:5, 34:14 twice, Deut 4:24, 5:9, 6:15.

[329]Oden, *The Living God*, 124.

[330]Wiley, *Christian Theology*, 1:383.

chapter of the Bible. Here John tells us about God's love toward us and then shows us how to love as God loves. The word *love* is used twenty-seven times in this chapter — more than in 1 Corinthians 13. As either a noun or verb, *love* occurs forty-six times in 1 John.

However, we cannot say love is God because God is more than this one attribute. We cannot exalt his love to the exclusion of his other attributes. Typically, the Scriptures speak of God's attributes in pairs or clusters.

Tozer warned that equating love with God is a major mistake which has produced much unsound religious philosophy. If God and love are identical, we destroy the concept of personality in God and deny all his attributes save one, and that one we substitute for God. But the God we have left is not the God of Scripture.[331]

Because God is self-existent, his love has no beginning. Because he is eternal, his love has no end. Because he is infinite, his love has no limit. Because he is immense, his love is measureless. Because he is holy, his love is pure. Because he is unchanging, his love never fails. Martin Luther described God as "an abyss of eternal love."[332]

This attribute of love implies affection, good will, and understanding. God does have feelings; he is not stoic. God's love pursues us. He takes the initiative and even enables us to respond. "This is love: not that we loved God, but that he loves us" (1 John 4:10).

For those who receive his love, God is our friend. We are the objects of his affection. He takes delight in us. Tozer wrote,

Modesty may demur at so rash a thought, but audacious faith dares to believe the Word and claim friendship with God. We do God more honor by believing what

[331]Tozer, *Knowledge of the Holy*, 104.
[332]Luther, *Works*, 5:288.

He has said about Himself and having the courage to come boldly to the throne of grace than by hiding in self-conscious humility among the trees of the garden.[333]

Because he loved the world, he gave his only Son (John 3:16). God's love is demonstrated foremost through his Son. "This is love: not that we loved God, but that he loved us and sent his Son as an atoning sacrifice for our sins" (1 John 4:10).

God's love is unconditional in its scope. God's love pursues everyone, yet his love is conditional in its degree. He does not love everything equally. Oden wrote,

> All things are loved by God, but all things are not loved in the same way by God, since there are degrees of capacity, receptivity, and willingness among varied creatures to receive God's love.[334]

God's love is conditional in its impartation. It can only be received through faith in his Son. Those who reject his Son spurn the Father's love. God's love is also conditional in its duration, for his Spirit will not strive with us forever (Gen 6:3).

God is righteous. "Righteousness and justice are the foundation of his throne" (Ps 97:2). "The Lord is our judge, the Lord is our lawgiver, the Lord is our king; it is he who will save us" (Isa 33:22). "Will not the Judge of all the earth do right?" (Gen 18:25). "True and just are your judgments" (Rev 16:7). "All his ways are just; a faithful God who does no wrong, upright and just is he" (Deut 32:4). His righteousness is reflected in his law. In Psalm 119, the law is pronounced righteous six times. The law of God is a reflection of his moral character. The ten commandments define true justice.

---

[333]Tozer, *Knowledge of the Holy*, 106-107.

[334]Oden, *The Living God*, 118.

Originally, the English word was *rightwiseness*. To be righteous means that God is upright or morally right. This disposition to put things right is essentially the same as God's justice. His justice obligates him to punish sin. Although such punishment may result in reformation or as a further deterrent, his primary purpose is to maintain righteousness and justice.

The world's moral order is grounded in God's own righteousness. His righteousness is reflected in his administration of divine law in human history. "The Lord reigns, let the earth be glad; let the distant shores rejoice. Clouds and thick darkness surround him; righteousness and justice are the foundation of his throne" (Ps 98:1-2; see also Ps 89:14). Psalm 36:5-6 declares, "Your love, O Lord, reaches to the heavens, your faithfulness to the skies. Your righteousness is like the mighty mountains, your justice like the great deep."

God is good. "No one is good — except God alone" (Luke 18:19). "How great is your goodness" (Ps 31:19). The earth is full of his goodness (Psalm 33:5). "No good thing does he withhold from those whose walk is blameless" (Ps 84:11). "The Lord is good to all" (Ps 145:9).

God is goodness personified. God wills the happiness of his creatures. But if God decrees and predestines that some people will perish eternally, God's goodness is called into question at the most fundamental level. Is an act good merely because God wills it, or does he will it because it is good? Wesley dismissed this whole debate:

> It seems, then, that the whole difficulty arises from considering God's will as distinct from God. Otherwise it [the debate] vanishes away. For none can doubt but God is the cause of the law of God. But the will of God is God himself. It is God considered as willing thus or thus. Consequently, to say that the will of God, or that

God Himself, is the cause of the law, is one and the same thing.[335]

The most common meaning of *goodness* in Scripture is *benevolence*. Thomas Aquinas described God as *summum bonum* (the highest good) who alone can satisfy our deepest need. All that God does, whether in creation or salvation, is oriented toward the communication of his goodness. His creation was *very good* (Gen 1:31).

Oden explained, "Divine goodness is that attribute through which God wills the happiness of creatures and desires to impart to creatures all the goodness they are capable of receiving."[336]

God's goodness is manifested in creation, in redemption, and in providence. A. W. Tozer wrote,

> The goodness of God is what disposes Him to be kind, cordial, benevolent, and full of good will toward men. He is tender-hearted and of quick sympathy, and His unfailing attitude toward all moral beings is open, frank, and friendly. . . . The whole outlook of mankind might be changed if we could all believe that we dwell under a friendly sky and that the God of heaven is eager to be friends with us. But sin has made us timid and self-conscious, as well it might. Years of rebellion against God have bred in us a fear that cannot be overcome in a day.[337]

The pagan gods were not good. The Greek gods were immoral and capricious. But the Lord is good and upright (Ps 25:8).

---

[335]Wesley, "Original, Nature, Properties, and Use of the Law," Sermon #34, 3.6-7.

[336]Oden, *The Living God*, 116.

[337]Tozer, *Knowledge of the Holy*, 88-89.

"How great is your goodness, which you have stored up for those who fear you" (Ps 32:19).

We must also deal with the existence of evil. This topic is termed *theodicy* — the attempt to assert God's goodness and justice despite apparent contradictions in history and experience. The book of Job is the classic theodicy.

We are emotional, volitional, and intellectual beings. Without dismissing an emotional response to tragedy, our emotions must be informed by our intellect. The God who made us in his image gave us an intellect. He is not offended when we ask questions — even questions about him.

It is argued that if God is all powerful, he must be able to prevent evil. If he is all good, he must want to prevent evil. But evil exists. Therefore, God is either not all powerful or not all good.

We cannot embrace a pantheism which denies evil and teaches that evil is really good disguised. According to an evolutionary worldview, evil is simply a hindrance or lag that can, in principle, be transformed into good. Marxism also rejects good and evil as absolute distinctions. Evil cannot be dismissed as an illusion, as Christian Science and Hinduism teach. Joseph Campbell regarded evil as the shadow side of good and the devil as a god who has not yet been recognized.[338]

Nor can the providence of God be denied as though he was oblivious to mundane human affairs, as deism teaches. Evil cannot be explained by affirming that it has an equal footing with God, as dualism teaches.

Nor can we embrace Calvinism, which teaches that God permitted evil for his own glory. According to the Calvinist theologian John Frame, God planned sin for a holy and good purpose.[339] Here Frame echoes Jonathan Edwards, who taught

---

[338]Campbell, *An Open Life*, 28-29.

[339]Frame, *Salvation Belongs to the Lord*, 102; *Doctrine of God*, 65, 160-182.

that God "disposes" all events in such a way that sin "will most certainly and infallibly follow," but he does so for his own "wise, holy and most excellent ends and purposes."[340] Gordon Clark wrote that Scripture "explicitly teaches that God creates sin."[341] Louis Berkhof wrote that "God's decretive will also includes the sinful deeds of man."[342] R. C. Sproul Jr. even declared,

> Every Bible-believing Christian must conclude at least that God in some sense desired that man would fall into sin. God wills all things that come to pass. It is within His omniscience to imagine every possible turn of events and to choose that chain of events which most pleases Him. . . . But wait a minute. Isn't it impossible for God to do evil? He can't sin. I am not accusing God of sinning; I am suggesting that he created sin.[343]

James Daane explained this Calvinistic position — that all things are ontologically necessary — flows from the essence of God. Therefore, God is fully responsible for sin and evil.[344] However, if God predestined sin, then it would cease to be sin and God would no longer be the ultimate good. Yet, in order to allow humanity a bona fide freedom of choice, there is a sense in which God permitted sin. But Calvin denied that there is any "mere permission" in God.[345] Calvin also wrote that Adam's fall was "not without God's knowledge and ordination."[346] Frame

---

[340]Edwards, *Freedom of the Will*, 399.

[341]Clark, *Predestination*, 12.

[342]Berkhof, *Systematic Theology*, 79.

[343]Sproul, *Almighty Over All*, 53-54. Palmer made a similar statement in *Five Points of Calvinism*, 25.

[344]Daane, *Freedom of God*, 79-80.

[345]Calvin, *Concerning the Eternal Predestination of God*, 176.

[346]Calvin, *Concerning the Eternal Predestination of God*, 121.

concluded that "we should not assume, as Arminians do, that divine permission is anything less than sovereign ordination. . . . Permission, then, is a form of ordination, a form of causation."[347] In contrast, Alvin Plantinga stated that the problem of evil can only be explained by the angels who fell and libertarian human freedom.[348]

According to process theology, evil is the lack of harmony in the cosmic process of evolution. God is doing his very best to deal with evil, but we cannot be assured of any final outcomes.[349]

Scripture reveals that God did not create evil and that he will deal with it. The original creation was *very good*. Because God is omnipotent, evil will be ultimately defeated. "When we despair over our inevitable human condition we lay an implicit charge against the justice of God."[350] The ruler of all the earth will do right (Gen 18:25).

In the KJV, Isaiah 45:7 declares that God creates evil.[351] *Calamity* is a better translation in this context. God brings about judgment, but he does not create moral evil.

God, in his omniscience, has comprehensive knowledge of how free agents would behave in all possible circumstances — without predestinating their behavior. God administrates the world as he chooses, based on his middle knowledge. He exercises sovereign control by creating the people he wills, knowing what choices they will make. All good choices are the efficacious will of God, while all evil choices are permitted for the sake of some greater good. This concept utilizes a libertarian freedom of the will, yet upholds God's sovereignty. It affirms meticulous

---

[347]Frame, *Doctrine of God*, 178.

[348]Plantinga, *God, Freedom, and Evil.*

[349]Griffin, *God, Power, and Evil*, 201, 313.

[350]Oden, *The Living God*, 107.

[351]This is the same Hebrew word *ra*.

providence while avoiding the error of making God the author of sin.

By faith in the nature of God's goodness, we accept that God permits evil in order to allow true human freedom. However, he does not relinquish control. There is no gratuitous evil which occurs by chance. Arminius declared that nothing happens by chance or accidentally. Every instance of evil serves a greater good. God does not permit any temporary evil that does not make way for a greater good. God is working all things together for the greatest good, although this conviction is known only to those who love him (Rom 8:28).

We may never know in this life what greater good was accomplished through a particular tragedy or holocaust. That is part of the reason why there will be a general judgment at the end of time. An old Methodist theologian, Benjamin Field, wrote, "The day of judgment is not to make God Himself better acquainted with the character of men, but to make both men and angels better acquainted with the character of God."[352]

God is faithful. "The faithfulness of the Lord endures forever" (Ps 117:2). According to Deuteronomy 7:9, "He is the faithful God, keeping his covenant of love to a thousand generations of those who love him and keep his commands." For the Lord is good and his mercy endures forever; his faithfulness continues through all generations (Ps 100:5). "For the word of the Lord is right and true; he is faithful in all he does. The Lord loves righteousness and justice; the earth is full of his unfailing love [*hesed*]" (Ps 33:4-5).

He is a covenant-keeping God. He is truthful, dependable, and consistent. Psalm 89:34 declares, "I will not violate my covenant or alter what my lips have uttered." "The one who calls you is faithful" (1 Thess 5:24). "He is faithful and just and will

---

[352]Field, *Student's Handbook of Christian Theology*, 397.

forgive our sins and purify us from all unrighteousness" (1 John 1:9).

The church at Corinth was not strong, but Paul used this attribute of faithfulness to build them up. God's message is consistent. "As surely as God is faithful, our message to you is not Yes and No" (2 Cor 1:17-20). God promises to protect us in temptation. "God is faithful; he will not let you be tempted beyond what you can bear." (1 Cor 10:13). God is faithful to keep us to the end. "God, who has called you into fellowship with his son Jesus Christ our Lord, is faithful" (1 Cor 1:9). He will keep us strong to the end, so that we will be blameless on the day of our Lord Jesus Christ (v 8). Our hope rests on his faithfulness.

God is wise. God alone is wise (Rom 16:27). The wisdom of God appears in creation. This is illustrated in Job 38:1-42:6. "By wisdom the Lord laid the earth's foundations" (Prov 3:19). "But God made the earth by his power; he founded the world by his wisdom and stretched out the heavens by his understanding" (Jer 10:12). "How many are your works, O Lord! In wisdom you made them all; the earth is full of your creatures. There is the sea, vast and spacious, teaming with creatures beyond number — living things both large and small" (Ps 104:24). "Wisdom and power are his" (Dan 2:20). All the treasures of wisdom and knowledge are hidden in Christ (Col 2:3).

The wisdom of God is revealed in his government. His law defines, restrains, convicts, and overrules. His wisdom is seen in redemption. He is both just and the justifier of sinners (Rom 3:26). In his wisdom he subdued Satan, provided deliverance for the human race, restoration for all creation, and did not violate his own character. "Oh the depth of the riches of the wisdom and knowledge of God" (Rom 11:33).

"The fear of the Lord is the beginning of wisdom" (Ps 111:10). "For the Lord gives wisdom; and from his mouth come knowledge and understanding" (Prov 2:6). When Daniel faced a mystery too great to solve, he prayed and God revealed the answer to him. Daniel exclaimed,

> Praise be to the name of God for ever and ever; wisdom and power are his; He gives wisdom to the wise and knowledge to the discerning, He reveals deep and hidden things; he knows what lies in the darkness and light dwells with him. I thank and praise you, O God of my fathers; You have given me wisdom and power (Dan 2:20-23).

"If any of you lacks wisdom, he should ask God" (Jas 1:5).

God is gracious. *Grace* means unmerited favor and enabling power. The Greek word for grace is *charis*. The word for gift is *charisma*. A gift is free and undeserved. It cannot be earned by our own efforts.

The whole of the Christian life is dependent upon the grace of God. Grace is not simply undeserved favor toward sinful men, in which we remain sinners and he remains gracious. Grace is God's love in action empowering those whom God regards with favor. Where sin increased, grace increased all the more (Rom 5:20).

Grace is first mentioned in the Bible when Noah found grace in the eyes of the Lord (Gen 6:8). In Exodus 33:13 Moses prayed, "If I have found grace in your sight, teach me your ways so I may know you and continue to find grace in your sight." His prayer was answered in Exodus 34:6-7. God passed in front of Moses and proclaimed, "Yahweh, Yahweh is the compassionate and gracious God, slow to anger, abounding in love and faithfulness, maintaining love to thousands, and forgiving wickedness, rebellion and sin."

God is patient, abounding in love and faithfulness, forgiving sin. God sends rain on the just and the unjust; he causes the sun to shine on the good and bad (Matt 5:45). All of God's creation dwells under this common or general grace. However, John

Murray defined common grace as "every favor of whatever kind of degree, falling short of salvation, which this undeserving and sin-cursed world enjoys at the hand of God."[353] This definition implies that "effectual grace" is available only to the elect, but the Bible does not make this distinction.

Wesley taught that unless we have quenched the Spirit, no one is wholly void of the grace of God.[354] "For the grace of God that brings salvation has appeared to all men" (Titus 2:11). Those who respond in saving faith experience his justifying grace, and every Christian may experience his perfecting grace.

Christ is full of grace and truth (John 1:14) and he gives grace to the humble (Jas 4:6; 1 Pet 5:5).

God is merciful. "God is abounding in mercy" (Exod 34:6). According to Psalm 145:8, God is rich in mercy. This statement is repeated in Ephesians 2:4. James 5:11 declares, "The Lord is full of compassion and mercy." He is the Father of compassion and the God of all comfort (2 Cor 1:3).

The earth is full of God's mercy (Ps 119:64). David said that goodness and mercy will follow us all the days of our lives (Ps 23:6). Jeremiah wrote that his mercy was fresh every morning (Lam 3:22-23).

His mercy is exhibited in his patience. "But you, O Lord, are a compassionate and gracious God, slow to anger, abounding in love and faithfulness" (Ps 86:15).

Some people believe that the God of the OT was harsh and judgmental, while the God of the NT is full of mercy and grace. But the same God initiated both covenants. Actually the OT has four times as much to say about mercy as the NT. In the Psalms we are told thirty-four times that his mercy endures forever.

There is even a statement of God's mercy within the Ten Commandments. God punishes sin to the third and fourth genera-

---

[353]Murray, *Writings*, 2:96.

[354]Wesley, "Working Out Our Own Salvation," Sermon #85, 3.4.

tion, but shows mercy to a thousand generations (Exod 20:6). This word *hesed* means that God is faithful to his covenant even when we have not been faithful. This *hesed* commitment is vividly illustrated in the book of Hosea. Snaith wrote, "This steady, persistent refusal of God to wash his hands of wayward Israel is the essential meaning of this Hebrew word which is translated loving-kindness."[355]

Hesed occurs 246 times in the OT and it has no cognate in any other Semitic language.[356] It is translated *mercy, lovingkindness, steadfast love,* and *goodness. Loyalty* is a good translation. *Hesed* occurs more frequently in the Psalms than any other book. Kinlaw explained that was because the Psalms are about worship, prayer, and communion with Yahweh. It is repeated in every verse of Psalm 136. The twenty-six verses of this psalm review creation, the Exodus, and the conquest. Both the world and Israel exist for one reason — the eternal *hesed* of God.[357]

Thomas Torrance called *hesed* the great sacramental word of the OT.[358] Oswalt concluded,

> If the giving of the covenant demonstrated that God's holiness is gracious, and if the content of the covenant demonstrated that it is ethical, then the outworking of the covenant demonstrated that holiness is faithful and kind.[359]

Thomas Oden wrote divine mercy is the disposition of God to receive sinners. God's mercy is not cheap, but it is the means

---

[355]Snaith, "חסד," *TWB* 136-137.

[356]Baer and Gordon, "חסד," *NIDOTTE* 2:211-218.

[357]Kinlaw, *Lectures in Old Testament Theology*, 187.

[358]Torrance, "Doctrine of Grace in the Old Testament," 55-65.

[359]Oswalt, *Called to Be Holy*, 34-35.

taken by divine love when sin has blocked off other avenues. Nowhere is God's almighty power manifested more clearly than in showing mercy to sinners. No power is greater than that beheld on the cross, reaching out to redeem sin.[360]

We cannot distinguish between the God of the OT, often portrayed as harsh, and the loving, compassionate God spoken of by Jesus. Attempts to make this distinction go back at least as far as Marcion, who was born around AD 100. While God occasionally commanded certain persons at a particular time to utterly destroy wicked cultures, God's ultimate purpose is to bless the world. He did not command genocide or inspire jihad.[361] By employing a moral argument to dismiss the concept of God because he is a moral monster, we are essentially proving the existence of God who has established that moral framework. The reality of evil does not disprove God's existence, since evil exists only if an absolute moral law exists.

Grace means we get what do not deserve. *Mercy* means we do not get what we do deserve. "Let us then approach the throne of grace with confidence, so that we may receive mercy and find grace to help us in our time of need" (Heb 4:16).

But mercy can only be granted when repentance has occurred. The parable of the prodigal illustrates this. When he was willing to accept justice, then he received mercy (Luke 15:17-24). Like the tax collector, we must pray, "God, have mercy on me, a sinner" (Luke 18:13).

To keep this concept of God's mercy before the people of Israel, God directed that the ark of the covenant be built. On the lid, which was covered with gold, were carved two cherubs. Their wings touched in the middle of the ark and it was at that location that God said he met with his people (Exod 25:22).

---

[360]Oden, *The Living God*, 126-127.

[361]Copan and Flannagan, *Did God Really Command Genocide?* (2014)

This *mercy seat* represented the throne of God, undergirded by divine law. Every year on the Day of Atonement, the high priest entered the Most Holy Place and brought in blood to sprinkle on the lid. The sprinkled blood turned away the wrath of God and satisfied divine justice. Mercy can be extended only because the penalty of sin was paid. Thus, David wrote, "Mercy and truth meet together; righteousness and peace kiss each other" (Ps 85:10).

Mercy can never operate apart from truth. Mercy and peace can only be granted on the basis of truth and righteousness.

God is patient. "The Lord is slow to anger" (Nah 1:3). "The Lord is gracious, and full of compassion, slow to anger and great in mercy. The Lord is good to all, and his tender mercies are over all his works" (Ps 145:8-9). His patience is depicted by Isaiah 65:2, "I have stretched out my hands all day long to a rebellious people who walk in a way that is not good." "He is patient with you, not wanting anyone to perish, but everyone to come to repentance" (2 Pet 3:9). However, we are warned not to despise the riches of his goodness, forbearance, and long-suffering since the goodness of God was meant to lead us to repentance (Rom 2:4). "A man who remains stiff-necked after many rebukes will suddenly be destroyed — without remedy (Prov 29:1).

The Work of God
•   **Creation**

"In the beginning God created the heavens and the earth" (Gen 1:1). In order to properly interpret this declaration, it is important to determine the genre of the book of Genesis. We will either re-interpret the biblical account of creation to accommodate modern scientific theory or we will evaluate scientific theories in light of God's revealed truth. Is our ultimate authority God's revelation or human reason? If we claim God's revelation as our ultimate authority, we need not adopt any agenda which applies an inadequate hermeneutic or shoddy interpretations of the Bible in an attempt to make it fit with evolutionary theory. Creationists

> are tired of the "dialogue" always being a monologue in which theologians must constantly adjust to what scientists claim and, eventually, give tacit approval to weak scientism by the constant employment of this complementarity approach.[362]

The Genesis account of creation has been treated as a myth, figurative poetry, or a nonliteral parable. Scholars who reject the category of myth seem to inconsistently employ it with regard to the creation account. Unless the Genesis account is interpreted at face value as a literal, chronological account, we are left with three options.

- Critical scholars regard it as basically myth with little or no historicity. Instead it is based on pagan near Eastern traditions.
- The second option is the *essentially nonliteral view* which does not see any detailed attempt to harmonize the biblical account with scientific theories.
- The third view, the *essentially literal view*, allows for figurative nonliteral descriptions which can then be harmonized with scientific descriptions.

The standard Hebrew lexicons all define *yom*, as used in the creation days of Genesis 1, as ordinary days as defined by evening and morning.[363] Essentially, the modernist scholars state

---

[362]Moreland and Reynolds, "Introduction," 14.

[363]BDB, *Lexicon*, 398; Jeni and Westermann, *Theological Lexicon,* 2:527-528; Koehler and Baumgartner, *Lexicon*, 2:399; Saebø, *TDOT* 6:7-31; Verhoef, *NIDOTTE* 2:419-420; Clines, *Dictionary of Classical*

what the Bible meant by *yom*, but then declare that the Bible was wrong. On the other hand, the more conservative scholars hold that the Bible is right, but try to interpret it in light of current scientific theory.

James Barr criticized conservative evangelicals who insist on a literal interpretation of Scripture except when it comes to the creation story in Genesis.

> As the scientific approach came to have more and more assent from fundamentalists themselves, they shifted their interpretation of the Bible passage from literal to non-literal in order to save that which for them was always paramount, namely the inerrancy of the Bible.[364]

Thus, science is viewed as an autonomous authority which determines how the Bible should be interpreted.

The symbolism in Revelation can only be interpreted on the basis of the prototype established in Genesis. Noel Weeks concluded that there is no question the book of Revelation uses symbols because it tells us that it is using symbols. "If Genesis had similar indications, then there would be no argument!" While acknowledging that symbolism exists in Scripture and that not all Scripture should be interpreted literally, we must also grasp the fact that symbols are possible only because they build upon some prior concrete historical phenomenon.

> In Genesis 1-3 we face not just the problem of no context which interprets the "parable." Biblical symbolism relies heavily upon the preceding history. We have only to note the use of Old Testament types in the presentation of Christ to realize the importance of images derived from past history. Genesis 1-3 has no past history

---

Hebrew, 4:166.

[364]Barr, *Fundamentalism*, 42.

upon which to build. It has no store of persons and events to produce images. Its presence in Scripture is the beginning of the store from which future Biblical writers will draw.[365]

It is popular for evangelical scholars to claim that Genesis 1-11 are prehistoric, therefore they constitute a different genre. However, such a conclusion cannot be supported inductively. Chapter 12 begins with the *waw* consecutive verb *wayomer* (and he said). This indicates a continuation of chapter 11. *Wayomer* had been previously utilized forty-one times in the first eleven chapters and 258 times after Genesis 12:1. No interpreter would suggest that it meant anything other than a continuation in any of its 299 usages in the book of Genesis. Therefore, that is the meaning it conveys in its three-hundredth usage.

How can the first eleven chapters of Genesis be arbitrarily separated into a different genre? Genesis 5 and 10-11 contain genealogies. How would such a section be interpreted other than historically? It is widely agreed that the structure of Genesis is based on the phrase *these are the generations of*. Each time this phrase occurs, it narrows the focus to something already discussed. This phrase occurs six times in Genesis 1-11 (2:4, 5:1, 6:9, 10:1, 11:10,27) and five times in Genesis 12-50 (25:12, 19, 36:1,9, 37:2). Thus, there is no precedent set for treating the first eleven chapters as a different genre.

Francis Schaeffer asked, "How should these early chapters of Genesis be read?" He argued for their historicity in time and space. The first three chapters of Genesis teach divine creation and human sin. They explain how we got here and what went wrong. "Christianity says man is now abnormal . . . as a result of a moral, historic, space-time Fall. . . . Take away the first three

---

[365]Weeks, *The Sufficiency of Scripture*, 116; 104.

chapters of Genesis, and you cannot maintain a true Christian position nor give Christianity's answers.[366]

Genesis covers creation, the fall, the flood, and the tower in the first eleven chapters. Chapters 12-50 cover Abraham, Isaac, Jacob, and Joseph. It is all history.

The Bible does contain poetic accounts of creation in Job 38:4-11; Psalm 8, 19:1-6, 102:25,104. These accounts should be compared to the Genesis account. The figurative use of language as found in the poetic literature is not present in Genesis. Nor does the narrative have any of the characteristics of a parable.[367] Walter Kaiser wrote,

> There are 64 geographical terms, 88 personal names, 48 generic names and at least 21 identifiable cultural items (such as gold, bdellium, onyx, brass, iron, gopher wood, bitumen, mortar, brick, stone, harp, pipe, cities, towers) in those opening chapters. The significance of this list may be seen by comparing it, for example, with "the paucity of references in the Koran. The single tenth chapter of Genesis has five times more geographical data of importance than the whole of the Koran." Every one of these items presents us with the possibility of establishing the reliability of our author. The content runs head on into a description of the real world rather than recounting events belonging to another world or level of reality.[368]

According to Psalm 33:6, God created by the decree of his word and the breath of his mouth. In the prophetic literature Isaiah 44:24 declares, "I am the Lord, who has made all things,

---

[366]Schaeffer, *Works*, 1:114.

[367]Young, *In the Beginning*, 13,18-19; Currid, "Cosmology of History," 44-45.

[368]Kaiser, "Literary Form of Genesis 1-11," 59.

who alone stretched out the heavens, who spread out the earth by myself." "I am the first and I am the last. My own hand laid the foundations of the earth, and my right hand spread out the heavens; when I summon them, they all stand up together" (Isa 48:12-13).

Jeremiah declared, "He made the earth by his power; he founded the world by his wisdom and stretched out the heavens by his understanding" (10:12, 51:15). "With my great power and outstretched arm I made the earth and its people and the animals that are on it" (Jer 27:5).

In the epistles we are told that God created all things (Eph 3:9). "By faith we understand that the universe was formed at God's command, so that what is seen was not made out of what was visible" (Heb 11:3). God's creation was a divine fiat or decree and he created *ex nihilo*.

The final book calls us to worship the Creator (Rev 4:11, 14:7). In Revelation 4:8 nature is depicted as continually and instinctively glorifying him. Moses Stuart reminded us that the Scriptures represent the heavens, the earth, seas, mountains, hills, forests, vapor, rain, snow, and hail as all praising God.[369] "Day and night they never stopped" praising him. There is a beauty in every season; a majesty in every location; a wonder in every specie of animal. Eugene Peterson wrote, "Worship does not divide the spiritual from the natural, it coordinates them. Nature and supernature, creation and covenant, elders and animals are all gathered."[370] "All Thy works shall praise Thy name in earth, and sky, and sea."[371] The whole earth is full of his glory. In v 8 he is worshiped by nature for his attributes. He is almighty and eternal. In v 11, God is worshiped by the church for what he has done. He created all things.

---

[369]Stuart, *Commentary*, 2:118.

[370]Peterson, *Reversed Thunder*, 62.

[371]Reginald Heber, "Holy, Holy, Holy, Lord God Almighty." (1826)

First he willed the creation, then he spoke it into being. The creation was created on account of God's will (*thelema*). The KJV reads, *for thy pleasure*. As a verb *thelo* is used in 1 Corinthians 12:18 to say that God has arranged every part of the body, *as it has pleased him* (KJV). The concept that God takes pleasure in creation is valid biblically and is to be preferred above the nonbiblical idea that God created out of loneliness.

Because of his will, creation came into being and continues to exist (Col 1:16-17). This speaks both of the creation and the preservation of that creation. Therefore, the church elders lay aside their crowns. This is a higher form of worship than instinct; it is deliberate. In Revelation 14:7 we are called to worship him who made the heavens, the earth, the sea, and fountains of water.

God created the material of the physical universe out of nothing. The Latin phrase *ex nihilo* is commonly used to express this concept. This *ex nihilo* creation reveals the infinite power of God who "calls things that are not as though they were" (Rom 4:17). According to John 1:3, creation or matter is not eternal since it was brought into being through the Logos out of non-existence. Wesley declared that the Lord God "called out of nothing by his all-powerful word the whole universe, all that is."[372]

John Oswalt quoted Alan J. Torrance, who declared, "The Christian faith knows no doctrine of creation that is not a doctrine of *creation ex nihilo*." Then Oswalt concluded,

If this doctrine is not to be found as the preunderstanding of Gen 1, then it is hard to sustain the doctrine as anything other than a theological inference, something that is hardly the essential to creation faith, as Torrance has framed it.[373]

---

[372]Wesley, "On Divine Providence," Sermon #67, § 8.

[373]Oswalt, "Creation Ex Nihilo," 180.

Without something or someone being self-existent, nothing could possibly exist. And nothing evolves unless it already exists. Natural selection cannot create. If it is a valid concept at all, it only functions within that which has been created. *Ex nihilo, nihil fit* means "out of nothing, nothing comes." If there ever was a moment when there was absolutely nothing, there would always be nothing. Thus, something or someone has to be eternal. Thus, Carl Sagan declared, "The cosmos is all that is or ever was or ever will be."[374]

Evolutionary theory holds that all organisms are related by common ancestry and implies that there are virtually no limits to the morphological change that can occur in organisms over time. While micro-evolution occurs within species, macro-evolution is an article of faith and not the conclusion of empirical evidence.

Evolution is also commonly referred to as the cause which produces biological change. Through natural selection, evolution has the creative power to produce innovation in the history of life. However, an appeal to accident, coincidence, and repetition cannot explain how something started from nothing. As a theory of origins, evolution fails to explain how things originated.

The pagans held that matter was eternal, as did Aristotle.[375] C. S. Lewis observed that many years prior to any scientific defense of evolution, there were imaginative statements of an evolutionary view of origins. His conclusion is that the popular concept of evolution is essentially mythical rather than scientific.[376]

Scripture teaches that God is eternal. "The Lord is the everlasting God, the Creator of the ends of the earth" (Isa 40:28). He

---

[374]Sagan, *Cosmos*, 4.

[375]Watson, *Theological Institutes*, 1:273.

[376]Lewis, *Christian Reflections*, 83.

is the uncaused cause. Either option — eternal matter or an eternal God — is a matter of faith, not science.[377]

Genesis 1:1 describes the absolute beginning of time, space, and matter. Edward Young paraphrased the meaning of this verse, "The beginning was by means of a creative act." He explained that Moses asserted, "Heaven and earth had a beginning and that this beginning is to be found in the fact that God had created them."[378] Pope wrote, "The Scripture precludes any other doctrine than that of an absolute creation of all things by the direct act of the Divine will."[379] He also declared, "No theory of evolution or development that seems to trace a regular succession of forms through which organic existence has passed . . . can be made consistent with Scripture."[380]

In Hebrew there are three major verbs for creation. The verb yasar describes forming or shaping something that is already present, except in Genesis 2:4 and Proverbs 16:4. The first occurrence of yasar, one of the verbs for creation, is in Genesis 2:7, but this does not imply a gradual process of creation. Instead, this verse provides additional information about the creation which was recorded in Genesis 1:27. Nothing in the text suggests that there could be millions of years between these two verses. The waw consecutive

> does not indicate the order of time, or of thought; so that the meaning is not that God planted the garden in Eden after He had created Adam, nor that He caused the trees to grow after He had planted the garden and placed the man there. . . . The process of man's creation

---

[377]Johnson, *Darwin on Trial*, 9-10.

[378]Young, "Relation of the First Verse of Genesis One," 138-139.

[379]Pope, *Compendium*, 1:366.

[380]Pope, *Compendium*, 1:398.

is described minutely here, because it serves to explain his relation to God and to the surrounding world.[381]

The verb *yalad* also implies secondary creation, except in Psalm 90:2. It often describes giving birth.

The verb *bara* literally means to cut according to pattern. It is used in Genesis 1:1,21,27 (three times), 2:3,4. *Bara*, when not in the qal stem, can be used of secondary creation. However, in the Qal stem *bara* always refers to absolute creation.[382] God created from nothing, creating everything by the word of his power (Heb 11:3). God alone creates. Satan does not have the ability to create, but is instead the destroyer (Rev 9:11).

Bara is always used with the explicit mention of the material created. The use of this verb never specifies creation from pre-existing materials.

Progressive revelation indicates that God the Son was involved in creation (Col 1:16), as was God the Holy Spirit (Gen 1:2; Ps 104:30).

Nowhere does the Bible record that God was lonely. Creation was not inevitable or necessary for God. The purpose of creation was to declare God's glory. "You are worthy, our Lord and God, to receive glory and honor and power, for you created all things, and by your will they were created and have their being" (Rev 4:11; see also Ps 148; Isa 43:7).

In contrast, evolution is process theology. Alfred Whitehead, who popularized process philosophy, said, "It is as true to say that God creates the world as that the world creates God."[383] Thus, for process theology, God and the world are interdependent.

---

[381]Keil and Delitzsch, *Commentary*, 1:78.

[382]McComiskey, "ברא" *TWOT* 1:127; BDB, *Lexicon*, 134; Young, *Studies in Genesis One*, 6-7.

[383]Whitehead, "God and the World," 93.

A proper theology of creation implies the sovereignty of God in his ability to create from nothing. It also reveals the nature of God. Everything that he created was originally good. The doctrine of creation also implies God's providence. He sustains what he created.

The doctrine of creation affirms the Creator-creature distinction. God is both transcendent and immanent. He has disclosed himself to us. Mankind is subordinate to God, not autonomous, and yet we have a mandate to have dominion over nature. Thus, we are stewards in covenant with the Creator. Although that covenant relationship was broken in the fall, God has launched a plan of restoration. Over time, redeemed humanity will not only be restored to their original position, but their final glory will exceed their original glory.

The role of science

In Job 12:7 we are challenged to ask the animals and they will teach us, the birds and they will tell us, the fish of the sea will inform us. Job 38-41 is a mandate for science. God pointed out his creation to Job, the ocean, the clouds, frost, hail, lightning, rain, snow, wind, the stars, the animal kingdom: lions, mountain goats, deer, donkeys, the ox, ostrich, the horse, the hawk, and dinosaurs. In the process, God asks Job seventy-seven questions. Science studies general revelation. After a course in God's creation and providence, Job concluded, "I know that you can do all things and that no purpose of yours can be thwarted" (42:2).

Robert Jastrow, the founder and director of NASA's Goddard Institute for Space Studies, said he was an agnostic in religious matters. However, he wrote,

At this moment it seems as though science will never be able to raise the curtain on the mystery of creation. For the scientist who has lived by his faith in the power of reason, the story ends like a bad dream. He has

scaled the mountains of ignorance; he is about to conquer the highest peak; as he pulls himself over the final
rock, he is greeted by a band of theologians who have
been sitting there for centuries.[384]

The scientific method began in the 16th century among men
who were Christians.[385] Francis Bacon wrote in the early 17th
century that God had spoken in two books, the book of nature
and the Bible. These two books are complementary and not in
conflict.

The modern era of science was based on this concept of the
divine unity of the Creator. The scientific revolution came *after*
the Protestant reformation.[386] Alfred North Whitehead wrote that
science originated with Christianity's "insistence on the rational-
ity of God."[387] If God is a rational being and humanity created in
his image is also rational, then it is legitimate for humanity to
employ rational processes to investigate the world in which they
live. Without discounting the genius of the ancient world, they
were stymied by fatalism, pantheism, polytheism, and superstition. For example, Hindu philosophy has traditionally regarded
history, as well as human life itself, as an illusion. Thus, the
observation necessary to the scientific endeavor is rejected.

The scientific method operates from empirical evidence and
applies inductive logic, generalizing a hypothesis from particular
observations and then testing that hypothesis. The facts of the
hypothesis must be observable, repeatable, and testable.

Paul Little wrote, "If we limit ourselves to what the Bible
actually says and to what the scientific facts actually are, we

---

[384]Jastrow, *God and the Astronomers*, 116.

[385]Morris, *Men of Science — Men of God* (1988).

[386]Morris, *Long War Against God*, 304-306; Lawson, *Introduction
to Christian Theology*, 15.

[387]Whitehead, *Science and the Modern World*, 18.

shrink the area of controversy enormously."[388] Not all statements by scientists are scientific statements nor are all conjectures by theologians based on biblical authority.

> Faith is no detriment to the apprehension of reality. In fact, science itself rests on presuppositions which must be accepted by faith before research is possible. One such assumption is that the universe is orderly, that it operates according to a pattern, and that therefore one can predict its behavior. . . . Another unprovable presupposition that must be accepted by faith is the reliability of our sense perceptions. One must believe that our senses are trustworthy enough to get a true picture of the universe and enable us to understand the orderliness we observe.[389]

Science cannot operate from *a priori* assumptions. Yet Karl Popper claimed that we must start with some *a priori* assumptions in order to discover new knowledge. Popper argued that many scientific theories were accepted, they were not true science because they were not open to falsification. There was no way to test the hypothesis. This, for Popper, amounted to pseudoscience.[390]

Scientism holds that science is the only path to knowledge, and the only true knowledge is that which is scientifically verified. However, much that passes for science in one generation is eventually refuted in another generation.

While science can explain *how* something works, it cannot tell us *why*. Therefore, science without Scripture is inadequate, since only the Scripture reveals the purpose for which the universe was created. Science is basically analytical, but human

---

[388]Little, *Know Why You Believe*, 103.

[389]Little, *Know Why You Believe*, 104-105.

[390]Popper, *Conjectures and Refutations*, 49,54.

understanding cannot be satisfied unless analysis is also integrated with our inner, personal lives and the transcendence of ultimate reality.

The fundamental issue is whether the Bible will be reinterpreted to conform to current scientific theory or whether current scientific theory will be evaluated in light of biblical authority.

Francis Schaeffer wrote that the Bible is not a scientific textbook, but it does establish boundaries for scientific theories. Science is free to consider questions that the Scripture does not deal with directly, provided they are within the circle defined by Scripture.[391] If my original interpretation of Scripture is correct, after examination, and that interpretation still conflicts with the apparent results of science, I must follow Scripture.[392]

Christians must never allow theology to be wedded to a secular system of thought. From the first century AD, when the Jewish writer Philo lived, there has been a tendency to accommodate Genesis to whatever the dominant philosophy was. In the late Medieval period the cosmology of Aristotle was also accepted by the church. If Christianity is based upon infallible revelation from God, it does not need to attach itself to a scientific or philosophical system.

Genesis 1 records that God made material objects. Therefore, it seems logical to assume that the account is describing material origins. If Scripture provides a God-centered worldview, there is no need to exclude science from Scripture. While Genesis 1 is theological, why cannot it also be scientific? It is describing the origin *and* function of the material world.

The phrase *after its kind* is used ten times in Genesis 1. This refers to a category of plants or animals which breed true. The Hebrew word *min* may mean *species*.[393] Science would use the term *families* in their modern classification system. The state-

---

[391]Schaeffer, *Works*, 2:129-148.

[392]Frame, *Doctrine of the Knowledge of God*, 136.

[393]Erickson, *Christian Theology*, 480.

ment in vv 21,24 is of particular interest. There is evolution within species but not between species.

In 2004 *National Geographic* declared that Darwin was not wrong. The author declared that evidence for evolution is overwhelming. He wrote, "No one needs to, and no one should, accept evolution merely as a matter of faith." Yet in that same article the author admitted that "the fossil record is like a film of evolution from which 999 of every 1,000 frames have been lost on the cutting room floor."[394]

Since Darwinian evolution is based on the premise of agnosticism, there are really only four options for a Christian theology of divine creation.

• Intelligent Design

The Intelligent Design movement can be traced to *The Mystery of Life's Origin* (1984) by Charles B. Thaxton, Walter L. Bradley, and Roger L. Olsen, and to Phillip E. Johnson's *Darwin on Trial* (1991). Other prominent names include Michael Behe and William Dembski.

Intelligent Design is an application of the basic teleological argument. It does not attempt to define God, but argues for an intelligent designer on the basis of scientific evidence. Thus, it is broader than Christianity and yet rejected by theistic evolutionists who are Christian.

The teleological argument, as stated by William Paley (1743-1805), used the watchmaker analogy. Since every watch has a maker, and since the universe is exceedingly more complex in its operation than a watch, it follows that there must be a Universe Maker. It seems unlikely that a highly ordered universe could have developed by chance. The cosmos did not evolve out of chaos. There must be an intelligent designer.

---

[394]Quammen, "Was Darwin Wrong?" 2-35.

All design implies a designer. There is a great design in the universe. Therefore, there must have been a Great Designer of the universe.

Intelligent Design demonstrates the irreducible complexity of creation. The gradual process of evolution cannot explain the simultaneous complexity. In other words, every component of a mouse trap: a catch, a spring, a hammer, a holding bar, and a foundation, must evolve simultaneously in order for it to work.[395]

- **Theistic evolution**

Theistic evolution is essentially deism. They believe that billions of years ago God initiated creation, but then withdrew and let the natural behavior of matter run its course until all living things evolved through natural selection and random mutations. BioLogos prefers the term *evolutionary creationism.* They hold to *methodological naturalism*, which says that divine causation, which constitutes the miraculous, must not be invoked when doing science. If we assert that God created, they say that real science is thwarted. Thus, whether or not it is true, science must not invoke the supernatural. In so doing, the motive is not truth, but the protection of prior naturalistic assumptions.[396] Thus, Deborah Haarsma, president of BioLogos, presented very little Scripture in her presentation of evolutionary creation.[397]

They claim the composition of Genesis was influenced by pagan creation myths. Adam and Eve were not the first humans. God did not directly form Adam from dust and Eve from Adam's rib. Adam and Eve were not the first sinners. Thus, any doctrine of original sin cannot start with them. However, there is no mention in the Genesis account of mankind evolving from previously existing beings. Mankind is the direct creation of God.

---

[395]Behe, *Darwin's Black Box*, 66.

[396]Behe, *Darwin's Black Box*, 238-239.

[397]Ham, "Response," 155.

- **Old earth creationists**

This position usually agree with the mainstream scientific estimates of the age of the universe, humanity, and earth itself, while at the same time rejecting the claims of modern evolutionary theorists with respect to biological evolution. Historically, old earth creationists have attempted to reconcile science and Scripture in three areas: theistic evolution, the day/age theory, and the gap theory.

The day/age theory distorts the words of 2 Peter 3:8. They interpret this verse as a formula which means the days of creation were not 24-hour days, but indeterminate eons of time. Another variation holds that the days were twenty-four-hour periods of time which occurred intermittently.

Theologians have also attempted to insert a gap between Genesis 1:1-2 to accommodate their theology concerning past events. They also insert a gap between the 69th and 70th week of Daniel in 9:24-27 in order to accommodate their theology about the future. Neither gap could be inductively found in the biblical text, however. In either instance, the gap is a presupposition formed onto the text.

The first proposed gap, originally suggested by Thomas Chalmers in 1814, was an attempt to reconcile the Genesis account with scientific claims by Charles Lyell that creation could not have possibly occurred in six literal days.[398] This theory was popularized in the *Scofield Reference Bible*.[399] It is significant that Richard Watson pushed back against Chalmers, among

---

[398]Fields, *Unformed and Unfilled*, 40-41. Chalmers attributed the concept to the 17th century Dutch Arminian theologian Simon Episcopius.

[399]*The Scofield Reference Bible* (1917) stated, "Relegate fossils to the primitive creation, and no conflict of science with the Genesis cosmogony remains" [p. 4]. Henry Morris felt Scofield's notes hurt the creationist cause [*History of Modern Creationism*, 58-59].

others, by objecting to a defense of Moses that appealed to a remote interpretation beyond the ability of general readers to grasp.[400]

Genesis 1:2 simply says that the earth *was* without form and void. This Hebrew word *hayah* is used 3600 times in the OT, and its normal usage is simply *was*, not *became* or *had become*. The natural flow of thought from verse 1 to verse 2 is that God first created the original building blocks or elements and then began to put them together over six days. The LXX translators interpreted Genesis 1:2 according to its normal usage, using *was* and not *became*.

However, the gap theory also postulates that *without form and void* refers to a situation of chaos. God did not create evil; and it is unnecessary to read chaos, evil, or catastrophic judgment into the phrase *without form and void*. God's creation was good and perfect. Chaos is not required in the expression *without form and void*.

The earth at this point is not in its final form, however. It is like a fetus in the womb or a diamond in the rough. The rest of the chapter describes the process by which God shaped and formed his creation. The world in Genesis 1:1 is not imperfect; it is incomplete. It is unformed, not deformed.

This same phrase, *without form and void*, also occurs in Isaiah 34:11; Jeremiah 4:23. These references describe a formless and unpopulated empty condition, but not necessarily chaos. While these two references do describe the details of judgment, the context of Genesis 1:2 does not. According to Isaiah 45:18, God did *not* create the world that it should remain in an unformed state.

Genesis 1:2 is a continuation of what God began in verse 1. Verse 2 begins with *and*. In Hebrew syntax this is a *waw-disjunctive*. Proponents of the gap theory argue that this *waw* con-

---

[400]Watson, *Theological Institutes*, 1:249-251.

junction should be translated *but*. The context would demand this in Genesis 2:17, but not necessarily so here.

Verse 2 describes the conditions present in verse 1. It simply continues to tell us that the matter which God created was at first unformed and uninhabited.

The appeal to *darkness* does not necessarily denote evil. Darkness can be just an absence of light, which would be created on the first day. And the admonition in 1:28 to *fill* the earth cannot be used to suggest a *re-filling*.

If the gap theory is correct, we have only one verse in the Bible dealing with original creation. Yet Genesis 2:3-4 does not speak of a re-creation. The gap theory is basically an argument from silence. Into this silence the fall of Satan or the existence of a pre-Adamic race which died and left fossils is interjected. They assert that this may have taken millions of years, but according to Romans 5:12 and 1 Corinthians 15:21-22 death entered through the sin of Adam. If the gap theory is correct, humanity was subject to death long before Adam and Eve. Did Jesus make atonement for their sins or only the descendants of Adam? If death came after sin, the fossil record had to come after the fall.

> If death came into the world only with Adam, then all evolutionary reconstructions of the development of animals would be excluded. Obviously without animal death there is no animal evolution. Furthermore the periods represented by fossils must occur after man's sin.[401]

More recent attempts include the explanation that the six days of creation are a literary framework, with long periods of time separating each day.[402] In *The Lost World of Genesis One*

---

[401]Weeks, *The Sufficiency of Scripture*, 109.

[402]The framework hypothesis was developed by Arie Noordtzij in 1924 and popularized by N. H. Ridderbos and Meredith Kline. This

(2009) John Walton claims that Genesis 1 does not deal with material origins but with functional origins. Thus, Genesis 1 is not a narrative of how the world was created, but more of a theology dealing with why it was created. His conclusion is that nowhere in the Bible do we have an account of how creation occurred. And therefore we could dialog with science about the account of material origins without abandoning biblical authority. Walton defends Scripture by removing any scientific implications from Genesis 1, but his defense amounts to compartmentalized truth. We are left with a theology that God made it, but that theology is removed from time and space.

The first draft of the human genome project was completed in 2000. This was the first attempt to map the DNA sequence in the entire human genome. As a result of the complexity which was discovered, Anthony Flew conceded the existence of a master designer. Francis Collins, the project manager, called the results, "the language of God."[403]

However, since human genome analysis suggested that the human race today is so diverse that we could not have descended from just two individuals, it has become a popular option among "evangelical" scholars to deny that Adam and Eve were actual historical people.[404] Today, the debate is whether Adam and Eve ever existed historically, whether they existed historically but may have not been the first human, or whether humanity is one family originating from one pair — Adam and Eve.

This leads to three approaches to Genesis 2-3. One rejects the implications of recent genetic code research, affirms that the Genesis account is accurate, and that Adam and Eve were historical individuals.

---

hypothesis is refuted by Gentry, *As It Is Written* (2016).

[403]Collins, *The Language of God* (2006).

[404]Ostling, "Search for the Historical Adam," 23-27; Lamoureux, "No Historical Adam," 58; Enns, *The Evolution of Adam*, xvi; 124; Gauger, "Adam and Eve Redux," 26-29.

The second option is to say that Adam and Eve were chosen to represent the entire human race in the early development of our race. Thus, humanity is older than Adam and Eve.

The third option is that the creation account drew upon common ancient near east accounts. Thus, the Genesis account should be regarded as parabolic, not historical.

Writing in 1967, Paul Little allowed for various interpretations of the *days* of Genesis 1, but declared that if someone does not accept the clear teaching of Scripture, such as a historic Adam as in Romans 5, that he has crossed the line of biblical orthodoxy.[405]

Apparently, the denial of a historical Adam and Eve is now an accepted "evangelical" option. Some "evangelical" scholars are willing to discard the doctrine of original sin if it implies a historical Adam as the biological father of the human race in order to accommodate modern evolutionary biology.

This assumption then leads to the conclusion that there was no fall of humanity, at a point in time, from innocence into sin. Thus, Scot McKnight denied a historical Adam *and* the historic Christian doctrine of original sin.[406] This amounts to Pelagianism.

Dennis Lamoureux declared, "My central conclusion in this book is clear: Adam never existed, and this fact has no impact whatsoever on the foundational beliefs of Christianity."[407]

Peter Enns conceded, "The problem is self-evident. Evolution demands that the special creation of the first Adam as described in the Bible is not literally historical; Paul, however,

---

[405]Little, *Know Why You Believe*, 103.

[406]McKnight and Venema, *Adam and the Genome*, 93; 100,145-146.

[407]Lamoureux, *Evolutionary Creation*, 367.

seems to require it."[408] Enns concluded that "evolution requires us to revisit how the Bible thinks of human origins."[409]

But William Barrack argues that without a historical Adam, and a consequent historical fall into sin, there is no need for a historical second Adam — Jesus Christ.[410]

Garrett DeWeese concluded that if Adam is not the progenitor of the human race, "then the doctrine of the fall as it has been understood in Christian theology for two thousand years is false, and the entrance of sin into humanity remains a mystery." It is next to impossible to reconcile the evolution of the human specie with the theology Paul develops in Romans 5. DeWeese also observed that those who accept theistic evolution tend to reject substitutionary atonement. If sin is just an intrinsic part of evolved human nature, then moral influence or Christus Victor would be more acceptable.[411]

Paul explained that the God who made the world made every nation from one man (Acts 17:24-26). Sin entered the world through one man (Rom 5:12-19). "For as in Adam all die, so in Christ will all be made alive" (1 Cor 15:22; see also vv 42-49). Paul then refers to the first man, Adam, in v 45. Paul also based church practice on a historical Adam and Eve in 1 Timothy 2:13-14.

If Adam was not a historical person, what about the genealogy of Jesus in Luke 3 which traces him all the way back to Adam? What about the theology of Romans, which teaches that sin entered the world through Adam? There are at least twenty-

---

[408]Enns, *The Evolution of Adam*, xvi.

[409]Enns, *The Evolution of Adam*, 82.

[410]Barrack, "A Historical Adam," 197-227.

[411]DeWeese, "Paul, Second Adam, and Theistic Evolution," 21-23.

five NT passages that refer to Genesis 1-11 and all of them take the account literally.[412] Douglas Moo concluded,

> It is difficult to see how Paul's argument in Rom. 5:12-21 hangs together if we regard Adam as mythical. For Adam and Christ are too closely compared in this passage to think that one could be "mythical" and the other "historical." We must be honest and admit that if Adam's sin is not "real," then any argument based on the presumption that it is must fall to the ground.[413]

James Dunn also rejected the theory that *Adam* is "some universal mythical Man" because of the connection Paul makes between "one man" and "all men."[414]

- **Young earth creationism**

Creation science rejects any gaps in the Genesis account of creation. It advocates literal twenty-four-hour days, the concept of apparent age, a young earth, based on the genealogies in Scripture, and a universal flood in Noah's day.

Those who push back claim that none of this is science but simply an attempt to impose a certain set of presuppositions on the biblical text and justify that interpretation by appealing to science. However, it would be more fair to recognize that every attempt to explain creation is beyond the empirical scientific method. The basic question is whether our final authority is divine revelation or human philosophy. However, both sides should strive for a mutual understanding, not mutual denuncia-

---

[412]For example, see the words of Jesus Christ in Mark 10:6, 13:19-20; Luke 11:50-51. See also Luke 3:38; Acts 17:26; Rom 5:12-21; 1 Cor 11:8-9, 15:20-21,44-49; 2 Cor 11:3; 1 Tim 2:11-14; Jude 14.

[413]Moo, *Romans*, 325.

[414]Dunn, *WBC* 38A:272. See also Murray, *Romans*, 1:181.

tion. Compartmentalized thinking is not a valid option. We must attempt to reconcile special revelation and natural revelation.

With the publication of *The Genesis Flood* in 1961, by John Whitcomb and Henry Morris, creationists have argued for a young earth which would be only several thousand years old. This date is established from the biblical geneologies.[415]

While the world was created in six days without any gaps, the new world had the appearance of maturity. Adam was a full-grown man the first hour he was created. However, Geisler claimed that apparent age would make God guilty of deception since he allegedly made the world look older than it actually was.[416] But who would God actually be deceiving? When Jesus fed the five thousand, he created food that had the appearance of wheat which had been sown, grown, harvested, ground, and baked into bread. He created fish which had the appearance of being caught and cooked. The wine he created for a wedding feast had the appearance of grapes which had been tended, picked, crushed, fermented, and bottled. Yet none of these processes occurred. Each creation was a miracle in which the natural processes were accelerated. God reserves the right to create a mature world in which some components appear to be older than they actually are, so that they can sustain the new life which would go through the natural cycle.

Based upon 2 Peter 3:8, some have assumed these days could each be ages of the earth of aeons of time. The word for *day* in Hebrew is *yom*. It can be used figuratively, but whenever it is qualified by a number, it always means a twenty-four-hour period. *Yom* occurs 2304 times in the OT, and most of its uses refer to the normal cycle of daily earth time, unless the context compels otherwise.

In the Pentateuch, in 119 cases where *yom* is used with a numerical adjective, it always means a literal day. This is also

---

[415]Jordan, "The Biblical Chronology Question," 9.

[416]Geisler, *Systematic Theology*, 2:646.

true of 357 instances outside the Pentateuch. All 608 uses of the plural *days* are literal, as in Exodus 20:11.

It is true that the sun was not created until the fourth day, but apparently the first three days were of the same length in anticipation of the first solar day. The phrase *evening and morning* occurs over a hundred times in the OT, always with reference to a twenty-four hour day.

The fourth commandment is based on the presupposition that the six days are all twenty-four-hour periods (Exod 20:11). While God is still resting, the point is that we have a Sabbath, one day in seven, which is based on his creative week.

God did not need 144 clock hours any more than he needed 13.5 billion years to create the cosmos. Nor did he need to take off 24 hours to rest from his exhaustion. Instead, he was establishing a pattern for us, which is explained in Exodus 20:8-11.

Those who accept a young-earth creation do not reject the geologic column, but believe that the fossil record testifies to the universal flood in the days of Noah. Thus, the Bible teaches catastrophism and not uniformitarianism.[417] Ten generations had elapsed since creation. The population of the world had grown to over a billion people. Then about eight thousand years ago God sent judgment on the world that then was. Water covered the earth, and that entire civilization was destroyed.

Psalm 104:9 declares that never again will water cover the earth. This language corresponds to Genesis 9:11-15. Second Peter 3:6 declares the *world* was destroyed by water. It was not a local flood. Recent research has discovered hundreds of flood legends.[418] The abundance of such myths can only be explained by a real event, recorded inerrantly in Scripture and distorted in pagan legends. Yet the Genesis account is older than the Gilgamesh Epic, which contains a Sumerian account of the flood.

---

[417]Ham, "Young Earth Creationism," 28-41; 69.

[418]Nelson, *Deluge Story in Stone*, 169-190; Rehwinkel, *The Flood*, 127-167; Cahill, *Gifts of the Jews*, 37-38.

The Epic account is filled with capricious gods who are in conflict with each other in contrast to the monotheism of the Genesis account.[419] Thus, truth did not evolve from myth but myth is a distortion of truth.

In *The Origin of Heathendom*, Ben Adam pointed out that there was a time when the entire human race knew God. But in spite of the revelation of God's awesome judgment through the flood, the generations after the flood eventually suppressed that knowledge. Paganism developed as the result of man's repudiation of God and God's repudiation of them.

> They came to be in the awful state of corruption set forth in Romans 1:18-32. . . . The heathen world, then, according to the Scriptures, owes its origin to the apostasy of the race and their dispersion resulting therefrom as set forth in Genesis xi. 1-9 and Romans 1.18-32.[420]

There have been many local floods but only one universal flood. If the Noahic flood was merely a local flood, the covenant which God made with Noah after the flood would be meaningless (Gen 9:15).

Christ said that everyone, except the eight souls specified by Peter (1 Pet 3:20), was destroyed by the flood (Luke 17:26-27). The depth of the flood, the duration of the flood, and the need for an ark all imply a universal flood. The fact that Peter refers to *the earth that then was* (2 Pet 3:6) implies a world catastrophe.[421]

Ironically, this great catastrophe is omitted in world history. The flood was the worst disaster in world history, and yet there is a conspiracy to ignore it! There is a willing ignorance about this flood. It has been deliberately forgotten (2 Pet 3:5) because it serves as a constant reminder that *the day of the Lord* will

---

[419]Osanai, "Comparative Study of the Flood Accounts."

[420]Adam, *The Origin of Heathendom*, 46; 60-61.

[421]Whitcomb and Morris, *The Genesis Flood*, 1-35.

bring total destruction. It is this flood which left the geologic evidence which has been misinterpreted to arrive at an old earth date.

In reference to the standard geologic column, the layers of rocks and fossils, John Whitcomb and Henry Morris explained,

> For if the Bible record is true, most of the strata could not have been deposited over long ages of time under uniformitarian conditions but were laid down in the course of a single year under catastrophic conditions.[422]

- **Providence**

While God has ceased his work of creation, Jesus taught that the heavenly Father is always working (John 5:17). Providence describes the wisdom and power which God continually exercises in his preservation and government of the world. Roger Olson gave this definition, "Providence is the exercise of God's sovereignty over nature and history; it is God's governance over the affairs of his creation."[423]

Albert Outler wrote, "Belief in the providence of God as the ultimate environment of human existence" is "the linchpin of traditional Christian doctrine." He defined providence as, "God's active 'presence' in this world — personal and gracious — in the continuance of creation, in the vicissitudes of history, as the divine love in which we live and move and have our being."[424]

Divine providence includes *conservation*, which describes God's faithfulness to his creation. God has sustained and maintained what he created. "You made the heavens, even the highest heavens, and all their starry host, the earth and all that is on it, the seas and all that is in them. You give life to everything, and

---

[422]Whitcomb and Morris, *The Genesis Flood*, 451.

[423]Olson, *Westminster Handbook to Evangelical Theology*, 244.

[424]Outler, *Who Trusts in God*, 6,17.

the multitudes of heaven worship you" (Neh 9:6). God preserves both man and beast (Ps 36:6). "You care for the land and water it; you enrich it abundantly" (Ps 65:9). "The eyes of all look to you, and you give them their food at the proper time. You open your hand and satisfy the desires of every living thing" (Ps 145:15-16). "He provides food for the cattle and for the young ravens when they call" (Ps 147:9).

But God exercises greater care over mankind. Job described God as a *watcher of men* (7:20). Job further declared, "You gave me life and showed me kindness, and in your providence watched over my spirit" (10:12). This Hebrew word *pequddah* occurs only in Job 10:12 and is translated *providence* in the NIV. It carries the meaning of oversight in directing the course of events that we experience.

According to Psalm 16:5-6, he is our inheritance. In the OT, when Israel entered the promised land, each tribe had its territory assigned. God has assigned us to Christ as his inheritance, not simply an arbitrary allotment. Thus, the meaning of the word *lot* transitioned from the idea of a portion to that of inheritance. God appoints or allows our circumstances. He also assigns our portion and cup, our sustenance and our daily bread (Matt 6:9; 1 Cor 3:5, 7:17). He is our security, bestowing covenant blessings to future generations. God does not abandon his own to work things out the best they can. He does have a plan for our lives. The security of this concept of predestination is not inconsistent with our rejection of the fatalistic doctrine of God's arbitrary predestination of election and reprobation.   As our Father, he knows what we need (Luke 12:30). "As a father has compassion on his children, so the Lord has compassion on those who fear him; for he knows how we are formed, he remembers that we are dust" (Ps 103:13-14).

"In him we live and move and have our being" (Acts 17:28). In Christ "all things hold together" (Col 1:17). Christ sustains all things by his powerful word (Heb 1:3).

Providence also includes *concurrence*, in which God works through secondary causes, such as the laws of nature. This is symbolized by Ezekiel's wheel within the wheel (Ezek 1:16; 10:9-10).[425]

Arminius explained that divine concurrence does not mean that God is necessarily causing an action, although nothing can happen without his permission. However, God may be acting in the effect which results from the action. Thus, he acts, assists, or concurs with contingent human acts which are good. And he permits human acts which are evil.[426] Concurrence does not imply approval. However, God is sovereign over the causes that come together to produce an effect.

Exodus 21:13 explains the policy that should be followed if a person is accidentally injured, but God let it happen. The Hebrew text literally says that God brought it or caused it to come into his hand. While God is sovereign, the injury was not his will. However, he permitted it. Keil explained that such acts are generally called accidents because they are above our comprehension.[427]

Providence also includes *divine government*. Psalm 127:1 implies that God has created and watches over his creation. He has compassion on all that he has made (Ps 145:9) and provides for the righteous (Ps 37:25). According to Psalm 124:1-3 God provides protection and help to his own people. He upholds the cause of the oppressed and gives food to the hungry (Ps 146:7). He provides for nature and controls the weather (Ps 147:8-18). Thus, we reject the pagan notion of fate. Jesus taught in Matthew 6:25-34 that his disciples need not worry about life because of the providence of God.

In Zechariah 1:7-11 and 6:1-8 the governance of God is depicted as four horsemen patrolling the earth. It would be another five hundred years before John describes the four horsemen riding again in Revelation 6, but their function remains the same.

---

[425]Wesley, *Notes*, 3:2284; Sutcliffe, *Commentary*, 1D:1183.

[426]Arminius, *Works*, 2:183.

[427]Keil and Delitzsch, *Commentary*, 2:132.

They symbolize God's watchful control of history and his judgment upon the enemies of Christ's kingdom. This judgment of the four horsemen came as war, famine, pestilence, and earthquake, just as Jesus declared in Matthew 24:6-7.

McClintock and Strong summarized over five hundred biblical passages under ten categories: his preserving power in general, his control of the regular operations of nature, his sovereignty over birth, his government of chance and accident, his use of noxious animals for the purposes of his government, his righteous retributions, deliverance, his supreme authority over men, his dominion over national prosperity and adversity, he sends bad laws and base rulers, stirs up adversaries, and sends adversity.[428]

The order and harmony in the course of nature also imply divine providence. This word *providence* means *foresight*. The concept of providence is taught in Romans 8:28, "God works together all things for our good." The debate is *how* God governs. We reject luck, fatalism, or that everything is predestinated. Wesley preached, "Nothing comes by chance: that is a silly word: there is no such thing as chance."[429]

However, Luke 10:31 says that *by chance* a priest was going down the road where a man who had been robbed lay. Wesley protested that this translation was a gross impropriety. "For if we speak strictly, there is no such thing in the universe as either chance or fortune."[430] The Greek word *sugkuria* occurs only here in the NT. Most English translations say *by chance*, but the Greek word actually means "a meeting together." In this instance, it was God's providential arrangement of two circumstances — the priest passing by the victim in his plight. A better translation would be *by concurrence*. God had not predestined

---

[428]McClintick and Strong, *Cyclopedia*, 8:708.

[429]Wesley, "The Education of Children," Sermon #95, § 14; "Imperfection of Human Knowledge," Sermon #69, 2.1.

[430]Wesley, *Notes*, 168.

that the victim should be robbed, nor was the priest forced to provide assistance, although Deuteronomy 22:4 commands that an animal found to be fallen in the road was to be helped.

The issue here is not one of chance, but of libertarian free will. Both the robber and the priest chose to act contrary to God's will, but their paths intersected at the point of the victim. This concurrence was not random chance. In fact, Jesus may have been emphasizing the fact that this was *not* merely a chance encounter. God's intended providence, through his priest, was thwarted because the minister chose not to minister.

Ruth 2:3 records that Ruth *happened* to work in the field of Boaz. While she did not understand the full significance of her location, this was God's providence. Wesley explained,

> It was a chance in reference to second causes, but ordered by God's providence. God wisely orders small events, even those that seem altogether contingent. Many a great affair is brought about by a little turn, fortuitous as to men, but designed by God.[431]

In the book of Ecclesiastes *fate* is mentioned seven times. This Hebrew word *miqreh* simply means an unplanned event. In 9:11 *pega* carries much the same meaning.

"The lot is cast into the lap, but its every decision is from the Lord" (Prov 16:33). "The king's heart is in the hand of the Lord; He directs it like a watercourse wherever he pleases" (Prov 21:1). "There is no wisdom, no insight, no plan that can succeed against the Lord" (Prov 21:30). "Are not two sparrows sold for a penny? Yet not one of them will fall to the ground apart from the will of your Father" (Matt 10:29).

Because we believe in providence, not chance, we reject gambling.[432] The god of the gambler is blind chance. *Gambling*

---

[431]Wesley, *Notes*, 2:883.

[432]Wakefield, *Christian Theology*, 2:521.

is playing a game for money, or some other consideration, which involves the risk of loss as well as the chance to win someone else's consideration with no honest exchange of goods or services. But the true God teaches a work ethic and stewardship. He forbids stealing and covetousness. Since we do not know the outcome of many contingencies, some have argued that life itself is a gamble. But we live by faith in God's providence and make every effort to minimize our risks through insurance.

Certainly there is a risk in farming, but there is also a trust in the God who controls the weather. Investment is a legitimate means of income, but speculation may not be. However, gambling is based on an artificial risk that lacks the dignity of wages earned or the honor of a gift. The only factor which separates gambling from stealing is that the gambler has consented to be robbed if he loses.

Process theology allows for divine action on particular entities, but it excludes the possibility of miracles. In their view, God cannot unilaterally cause anything to occur without human cooperation, he can only exercise his influence. Open theism holds that human decisions can be freely made only if God neither determines nor even knows what they will be. Thus, humanity and nature are relatively autonomous.

The polar opposite position on divine providence is that of Calvinism, which holds that God *causes* all things to be. Calvinism conflates providence with determinism and sovereign control. The result is that there is no true human freedom. They tend to view responsibility as liability, not ability. Somehow Calvinism must uphold the goodness of God and yet explain how he has ordained our evil acts. In contrast, Arminius held that God's knowledge of evil does not imply that he is its cause.

Wesley taught that there is nothing too small or too great for God's providence.[433] Particular providence is also described as *meticulous* providence. This term was introduced by Michael L.

---

[433]Wesley, "On Divine Providence," Sermon #67, ¶ 18.

Peterson in his 1982 book, *Evil and the Christian God*. This position, as held by Arminius, denies gratuitous or pointless evil. Peterson explained, "an omnipotent, omniscient, wholly good God would not allow gratuitous or pointless evil."[434] Thus, we believe that God is giving us what we would ask for if we could see things from his perspective.

God is sovereign, but he does not decree evil. A proper understanding affirms both divine sovereignty and human responsibility while rejecting both divine determinism and open theism.

In his providence, God *permits* certain acts. "My people would not listen to me . . . so I gave them over to their stubborn hearts to follow their own devices" (Ps 81:11-12). "The Israelites are stubborn, like a stubborn heifer. . . . Ephraim is joined to idols; leave him alone!" (Hos 4:16-17). "In the past, he let all nations go their own way" (Acts 14:16). In 1 Samuel 16-19, five times the account records that an evil (*ra*) spirit from the Lord came upon Saul. This evil spirit should be understood as coming by God's permission, not by his decree.[435]

In such cases, the action permitted was not necessarily God's will, since he is unalterably opposed to sin. Yet true freedom, also known as *libertarian* freedom, involves more than one option. Freedom has no meaning if it does not provide any options. Yet he allows our freedom to play itself out. Augustine wrote that even those things done against his will are not done without his permission.[436]

By faith in the nature of God's goodness, we accept that God permits evil in order to allow true human freedom. However, he does not relinquish control. Instead he works toward a greater good. Thus, there is no gratuitous evil which occurs by chance. Arminius declared that nothing happens by chance or acciden-

---

[434]Peterson, "The Inductive Problem of Evil," 85.

[435]Wesley, *Notes*, 2:945.

[436]Augustine, *Enchiridion*, NPNF1 3:269.

tally.[437] Every instance of evil ultimately serves a greater good. God does not permit any temporary evil that does not make way for a greater good. "Judgment is usually mixed with mercy, in order that sinners may be awakened and not destroyed."[438] God is working all things together for the greatest good, although this conviction is comprehended only by those who love him (Rom 8:28).

Arminius affirmed the statement of Augustine, "The good God would never permit evil, if He could not by His omnipotence produce good out of evil."[439] Wesley also taught that God does not permit any temporal evil that does not "clear the way for a greater good."[440]

God either directly or indirectly actualizes every event in the world except evil. God governs the world in such a way that nothing happens without his direct action or specific permission. Thus, if God is in control of all things, including the realm of science and history, it is inconceivable that his revelation of truth in these realms would not be trustworthy or that in his oversight he would fail to adequately communicate such truth to his prophets and apostles. His providence also extends to the preservation of his inerrant Word.

In his providence, God *permits* certain acts which are not his will. However, the consequences are predestined. Wakefield explained that God does not consent nor approve of sinful acts, but he does not always exert his power to prevent them.[441] In the desert Israel gave in to their cravings, so God gave them what

---

[437]Arminius, *Works*, 1:657.

[438]Wesley, *Letter* to Hester Ann Roe-Rogers, 29 Feb 1789.

[439]Arminius, *Works*, 3:447. The statement by Augustine is found in his *Enchiridion*, *NPNF*1 3:240.

[440]Wesley, "On Guardian Angels," Sermon #135, 5.

[441]Wakefield, *Christian Theology*, 1:266.

they asked for, but sent a wasting disease upon them (Ps 106:14-15).

In the case of Balaam, God permitted him to go to Balak (Num 22:20), even though he had forbidden Balaam in v 12. Thus, God was angry with him (v 22). Balaam's error was his presumption (Jude 11).

In his providence, God also *restrains* certain acts. "I have kept you from sinning against me" (Gen 20:6). "Keep your servant also from willful sins; may they not rule over me" (Ps 19:13). "Therefore I will block her path with thornbushes; I will wall her in so that she cannot find her way" (Hos 2:6). In 2 Thessalonians 2:7, God restrains lawlessness.

In his providence, God *prevents* certain acts. He establishes the extent or boundaries of temptation, as in the case of Job in 1:12, 2:6. "God will not let you be tempted beyond what you can bear" (1 Cor 10:13).

In his providence, God *overrules* certain acts. "You intended to harm me, but God intended it for good to accomplish what is now being done" (Gen 50:20). He causes the wrath of men to praise him (Ps 76:10). Robert Picirilli observed,

> We can only read the hand of providence after the fact. Those who use philosophical terminology would say that we must read providence a posteriori — after the event, in other words. We do not know a priori — in advance of history — what God's providence will look like.[442]

Miracles and Providence

Miracles are considered special providence. God works miracles in order to direct attention to himself, to authenticate truth, and as a divine credential for his messenger. We must be

---

[442]Picirilli, "Non-Deterministic Theology of Divine Providence," 52.

careful about explaining everything as miraculous to cover our ignorance and about denying miracles to cover our prejudices. On the other hand deism asks, "If God set in motion nature, why should he interfere with it?" God performs miracles to show that he is alive and willing to intervene in human history. God is able to transcend the very order he created. He did not lock himself out of his own creation.

Enlightenment philosophy led to the deism of the eighteenth century, which denied that God intervenes in nature by working miracles. The unitarianism of the Enlightenment became the atheism of the twentieth century. Bultmann represented twentieth-century modernism. He wrote,

> It is impossible to use electric light and the wireless and to avail ourselves of modern medical and surgical discoveries, and at the same time to believe in the New Testament world of spirits and miracles.[443]

But scientific research and supernatural miracles are not exclusive categories. Deists usually allowed for *general* providence, God's transcendent supervision over the world through the laws of nature, but they denied that God intervened in the lives of individuals. Wesley responded,

> You say "You allow a *general* providence, but deny a *particular* one." And what is a general (of whatever kind it be) that includes no particulars? Is not every general necessarily made up of its several particulars? Can you instance in any general that is not? Tell me any genus, if you can, that contains no species? What is it that constitutes a genus, but so many species added

---

[443]Bultmann, "New Testament and Mythology," 5.

together? What, I pray, is a "whole that contains no parts?" Mere nonsense and contradiction![444]

George Whitefield wrote,

But to suppose a general, without holding a particular Providence, is as absurd as to imagine there can be a chain without being composed of links. Search the Scriptures, and we shall find, that not a sparrow can fall to the ground without our heavenly Father; and that even the very hairs of our head are all numbered.[445]

Thus, God orders our steps (Ps 37:23). "In his heart a man plans his course, but the Lord determines his steps" (Prov 16:23). Miracles are God's extraordinary actions and his *ordinary* actions are called providence. In Psalm 136:4, God is thanked for his great wonders, but in v 25 he "gives food to every creature."

God's providence is manifested in the course of history. "He changes times and seasons; he sets up kings and deposes them" (Dan 2:21). History began at the point of creation and continues until the consummation.

Tom Cahill wrote that Israel invented history.[446] Augustine's *City of God* (AD 426) expressed a Christian philosophy of history. In contrast to a pagan view that history was cyclical, Augustine wrote that history was linear. With the passing of the Roman Empire, Augustine held that it was to be replaced by a superior order. While the city of man had existed since man's first rebellion, this city must fade as the heavenly city grows. Augustine expressed confidence in the divine superintendence of earthly affairs. Although "the city of this world" in every age is arrayed against God, "the city of God" does not depend on power.

---

[444]Wesley, "On Divine Providence," § 23.

[445]Whitefield, *Journal*, 264.

[446]Cahill, *Gifts of the Jews*, 58,126-128.

Augustine understood that the *millennium* began with Christ's first advent and that history is moving towards a goal. The God who guides the course of history, although opposed, will surely bring the process to a triumphant conclusion. Without this faith, we cannot determine whether all things work together, much less whether they work for good or for evil.

In contrast, humanism assumes human determinism. Marxism teaches economic determinism. Latourette described communism as a secularized version of the Christian understanding of history. Yet the climax of Marxist history is not realized under the power and direction of God, but in a classless society. This amounts to a demonic perversion of Christianity.[447]

Modernism assumes elite determinism. Those who embrace conspiracy theories assume an evil determinism. Existentialism assumes chance determinism, meaning that events occur randomly with no meaning.

Christians, however, "make known among the nations what he has done" (1 Chr 16:8). He is our help in ages past, our hope for years to come (Ps 90:1). Because God is in control, he can write history before it occurs. But he also works through human agency. "Both God and man are agents of history."[448]

C. S. Lewis wrote, "The central miracle asserted by Christians is the Incarnation. They say that God became Man. Every other miracle prepares the way for this, or results from this."[449] Miracles also confirm the gospel (Heb 2:4).

Providence and Prayer

Anyone who comes to God must believe that he exists and that he rewards those who earnestly seek him (Heb 11:6). Reason may ask, If God will give us whatever is fit without prayer and

---

[447]Latourette, *History of Christianity*, 2:1353,1481.

[448]Bebbington, *Patterns in History*, 166.

[449]Lewis, *Miracles*, 112.

if anything not fit cannot be obtained by prayer, then why pray? Why do we pray if God already knows our needs? Fatalism undercuts the need to pray if everything has already been predestined. And open theism undermines prayer by teaching that God is not sovereign over human activity.

But prayer is commanded. We should always pray (Luke 18:1). "Pray continually" (1 Thess 5:17). Wesley taught that the soul cannot subsist one moment without prayer any more than the body can without air. But he also explained, "All that a Christian does, even in eating and sleeping, is prayer when it is done in simplicity, according to the order of God."[450]

Prayer reminds men of God's providence in the world and of our dependence upon him. "Prayer excites in us a vivid sense of our unworthiness, of our entire dependence upon God, and of our absolute need of an interest in the merits of Christ."[451]

John Wesley declared, "God does nothing but in answer to prayer."[452] According to James 4:2, "You do not have because you do not ask God." When Daniel determined from Jeremiah 29:10 that the time of Jewish captivity was almost over (Dan 9:2), instead of presuming God would act sovereignly without any need for human prayer, Daniel turned to the Lord God and pleaded with him in prayer and petition, in fasting, and in sackcloth and ashes. His prayer runs from Daniel 9:4-19.

Matthew Henry observed, "When God intends great mercy for his people the first thing he does is to set them a praying."[453] Jonathan Edwards also wrote,

So is God's will, that the prayers of his saints should be one great means of carrying on the designs of Christ's

---

[450]Wesley, *BE Works*, 13:127.

[451]Wakefield, *Christian Theology*, 2:500.

[452]Wesley, *BE Works*, 13:127.

[453]Henry, *Commentary*, 4:1462.

kingdom in the world. When God has something very great to accomplish for his Church, it is his will that there should precede the extraordinary prayers of his people; as is manifest by Ezekiel 36:37, "I will yet, for this, be enquired of by the house of Israel, to do it for them."And when God is about to accomplish great things for his Church he will begin by remarkably pouring out the Spirit of grace and supplication (Zech. 12:10). If we are not to expect that the Devil should go out of a particular person, without extraordinary prayer, or "prayer and fasting;" how much less should we expect to have him cast out of the land, and the world, without it?[454]

Thus, God moves us through his Spirit to petition him to do what he has determined to do. William Temple replied to his critics who regarded answered prayer as no more than coincidence, "When I pray, coincidences happen; when I don't, they don't."[455]

---

[454]Wesley, *Christian Library*, 30:250; Edwards, *Present Revival of Religion*, Part 5.

[455]Watson, *Called and Committed*, 83.

CHAPTER THREE
The Doctrine of Christ

Jesus Christ existed eternally before his birth into this world. He was involved in creation, but his unique mission was the salvation of mankind.

At his conception in the womb of the virgin Mary, the eternal God also became a man. Through the incarnation he became completely man as well as remaining completely God. The phrase *eternally begotten of the Father* describes an eternal relationship he has always had with God the Father. Nor does the term first-born imply a beginning. Instead, it refers to his position or rank. The church has always had to refute heresies which reject his humanity or his deity — or the union of these two natures within one person.

Jesus Christ is the perfect revelation and exact representation of God. The fullness of God dwelt in him. Yet he had to humble himself in order to identify with the human race. He had to become completely human in order to become our substitute, taking the penalty of our sins upon himself.

This involved infinite suffering, as well as death. But his suffering and humiliation ended when he had completed his atonement for our sins and declared triumphantly, "It is finished."

He descended into the realm of death to announce his victory. Then he rose from the dead and ascended back to heaven where he rules as king, intercedes for his church, and prepares a place for us. He ministers today as our final prophet, our high priest, and our king. He will come again to reveal his glory, complete salvation, overthrow the world system, establish a new heaven and earth, raise the dead, and judge the world.

The gospel is the good news that God came to earth in the person of Jesus Christ to complete the work of redemption. The person and work of Jesus Christ comprises 64% of the Apostles' Creed. First Corinthians 1:30 declares that Christ Jesus has become for us wisdom, righteousness, holiness, and redemption.

The Person of Christ
The pre-incarnate existence of Jesus Christ

Did Christ have a beginning? If he is a created being he had to have a beginning point. If he is the Creator, he did not have a beginning. John 1:1-2 teaches that Christ was not a created being: "In the beginning was the Word, and the Word was with God, and the Word was God. He was with God in the beginning."

Christ alone existed before he was born. Christ was active before his birth and after his death! "Before Abraham was born, I am!" (John 8:58). Abraham lived around two thousand years before the incarnation. In John 6:51 Jesus declared that he had come down from heaven. According to John 17:5, Christ existed with the Father before the creation of the world. According to Colossians 1:16-17, Christ created all things.

The declaration, "You are my Son; today I have become your Father" (Heb 1:5) does not this imply a beginning? According to Acts 13:33 this refers to the resurrection of Jesus, not his creation. Theologians use the phrase, *the eternal generation of the Son*. This phrase describes an eternal Father/Son relationship, not a beginning point in time.

The term *only begotten*, a translation of *monogenes*, occurs in Luke 7:12, 8:42, 9:38; John 1:14,18, 3:16,18; Hebrews 11:17, and 1 John 4:9.[456] It is a title which describes the relationship of Christ to the Father, without implying that Christ had a beginning point — since he is before all things (Col 1:16). There can be only one *Only Begotten*. A. T. Robertson explained that *monogenes* refers to the eternal relationship of the Son to the Father rather than to his birth in the incarnation.[457]

The Council of Nicea in AD 325 clarified the biblical doctrine that the Son of God is eternally begotten of the Father.[458] While the word *begotten* cannot be understood in terms of human reproduction, the early church fathers used the term because they found it repeatedly in Scripture. The clause *eternally begotten of the Father* was added at Nicea to counter the false teaching of Arianism.[459] While there is no biblical text that says the Son is eternally generated or begotten, there is much in Scripture that suggests the concept and nothing that excludes it.[460] It is a valid deduction based on the biblical revelation that the one God is Father and Son as well as Spirit. This one God, with the correlate names, *Father* and *Son*, is eternal. The terms *begotten* and *generation* refer to the relationship which the two names express. An eternal Father logically requires an eternal Son.

The title *Son of God* occurs over fifty times in the NT. Yet while Jesus taught us to pray *Our Father*, he addressed the first person of the Trinity as *my* Father. There are over forty passages in which Christ speaks of God as *his* Father.

---

[456]1 John 5:18 probably refers to Jesus as "the one who was born of God." But in this instance the term is not "only begotten," it is *gennao*, without the *mono* prefix. Thus, the eternal Son of God guards and preserves the adopted sons and daughters of God.

[457]Robertson, *Word Pictures*, 5:13-14.

[458]Oden, *ACD* 2:29-42; Hall, *Learning Theology with the Church Fathers*, 35-51.

[459]Kelly, *Early Christian Creeds*, 235.

[460]Giles, *Eternal Generation of the Son*, 42, 63-90.

Bible passages referring to Jesus as God's Son have always been problematic in Muslim culture. Translators have struggled to convey a relationship without implying a sexual or biological connotation. In 2011-2013 Wycliffe Bible Translators was involved in a controversy which questioned their Muslim Idiom Translation (MIT) policy as having syncretistic tendencies. This policy held that it was more effective to use terms that Muslims were more familiar with and to avoid more theological language.

The MIT paradigm also held that divine familial terminology was metaphorical and the terms *Father* and *Son* are simply an analogy which is based in human relationships. In fact, Ephesians 3:14-15 teaches that the human family is a reflection of Trinity, which is not a metaphor. This MIT controversy was resolved by adopting the policy that the words *Father* and *Son* must "always be translated with the most directly equivalent familial words within the given linguistic and cultural context of the recipients."[461]

The biblical teaching that Jesus is also God is a concept that many Muslims find hard to accept, but there are doctrinal distinctives within Christianity which are not negotiable. There is no way to avoid teaching that Jesus is the Son of God without distorting the gospel message.

J. I. Packer observed that even in the first century, the term *Son of God* was confused in Greek mythology, describing supermen born of a union between God and human women. But John did not reject the terms *Father* and *Son*, instead he clarified them in John 1:1-18. John explained the divine sonship of Jesus by declaring that he had no beginning, he had personality, he was deity, he was creator, he is animating, he is revealing, and he became incarnate.[462]

---

[461]Moon, "Guidelines Solve Controversy?" In an appendix, Douglas Kelly also explains the details of this issue [*Systematic Theology*, 2:111-137].

[462]Packer, *Knowing God*, 47-50.

Nor does the term *firstborn*, as used of Jesus in Colossians 1:15, imply a beginning. Although this term can mean firstborn chronologically, it refers primarily to position or rank. William Martin explained that the *prime* minister is not the first minister England has ever had; he is the most preeminent. Thus, *firstborn* does not denote priority in time but preeminence in rank. The Bible never describes Christ as "first-created."[463] In Exodus 4:22 Israel is God's firstborn son. In Psalm 89:27 David was appointed as God's firstborn. Thus, the term has more to do with election than with birth order.

Christ is first over all creation. This describes his status, not his birth order. In the Greek and Jewish culture, the firstborn was the son who had the right of inheritance, not necessarily the first one born chronologically. Through his resurrection Jesus inherits the whole creation. This is the implication of Colossians 1:18; that he might have the supremacy in everything.

Over fifty times in the OT we find the term *angel of the Lord*. The word *angel* in both Hebrew and Greek can have the simple definition of messenger or representative. However, the *angel of the Lord* is represented as a divine person. The interpretative question is whether this was a pre-incarnate appearance of Christ or whether this angel was typical of Christ. According to Pope, the NT does not provide any interpretative help. "No question has occupied more attention and none been more variously decided than this."[464] "The early church taught that in all of the Old Testament theophanies, it was the pre-incarnate Son of God who appeared, not the Father."[465]

In Genesis 16:10-13, the angel of the Lord appeared to Hagar. Verse 13 explained she addressed Yahweh as *God*. Since she was addressing the angel who had spoken to her, the logical deduction is that the angel *was* God.

---

[463]Martin, *The Deity of Christ*, 34-35.

[464]Pope, *Person of Christ*, 283.

[465]Bercot, *Dictionary of Early Christian Beliefs*, 643, 20-21.

In Genesis 18:1-2,22, three men appeared to Abraham and one was Yahweh. In the conversation which followed, Abraham called him *the Judge of all the earth*. In fact, the word *Yahweh* occurs ten times in Genesis 18.

In Genesis 22 the angel of the Lord stopped Abraham from sacrificing his son, swearing by himself (v 16).

Terry wrote that "interpreters have gone wild over the mysterious character of Melchizedek, yielding to all manner of speculation."[466] He cites Whedon who concluded that "Melchizedek was nobody but himself."[467] Thus, Melchizedek is not the pre-incarnate Christ, but a type of Christ. Melchezedek thus had a geneology, it was just not recorded as would be the case with a Levitical priest. According to Hebrews 7:3, Melchizedek was *aphomoioo*, made *like* the Son of God.

Jacob awoke and declared, "Surely Yahweh is in this place" (Gen 28:16). After Jacob wrestled with a man all night, he declared, "I saw God [*elohim*] face to face" (Gen 32:30). Hosea wrote that Jacob struggled with God [*elohim*], that he struggled with the angel and overcame him (12:3-4).

The angel of the Lord appeared to Moses at the burning bush, and he hid his face because he was afraid to look at God [*elohim*] (Exod 3:2,6). As God commissioned Moses, he revealed himself to Moses as *I am who I am*. This is the basis of the noun *Yahweh*.

In Exodus 23:20-21, God explained that his name was in the angel who led Israel. Yet God has declared that he would not share his glory with another (Isa 42:8). However, Jesus shared the glory of God (John 17:1,5).

Joshua encountered a man who was his commander and Joshua called him *Lord* (*adonai* - 5:13-15). The angel of the Lord appeared to the parents of Samson and they declared that they had seen God (*elohim* - Judg 13:21-22).

---

[466]Terry, *Hermeneutics*, 342.

[467]Whedon, *Commentary*, 5:85.

Watson argued that this divine person was not God the Father, since no one has ever seen God (John 1:18). John Frame wrote that John 1:18 meant no one had ever seen God apart from his voluntary theophanic-incarnational revelation.[468] Therefore, this divine person, often called the angel of the Lord in the OT, was the promised Christ.[469] However, Jehovah's Witness theology teaches that Jesus Christ was the archangel Michael prior to divesting himself of his angelic nature and coming to this world as a perfect man.[470]

The Incarnation

There are ancient sources outside the NT which mention Jesus, but such Jewish, Roman, and Christian sources are inferior to the information provided in the Gospels.[471]

If Christ was alive and active prior to his incarnation, then the incarnation does not mark the beginning of his existence, but it describes the beginning of his salvation mission. The incarnation required a humbling and a limitation of Christ.

Job complained, "If only there were someone to arbitrate between us, to lay his hand upon us both" (9:33). "The man Christ Jesus" is our only mediator (1 Tim 2:5). As mediator, his one task was to save mankind from their fallen condition. Thus, he became incarnate. C. S. Lewis wrote, "It is an absurdity to celebrate the nativity at all if you don't believe in the Incarnation."[472]

The word *incarnation* is from Latin meaning *in flesh*. At a point in time the second person of the Godhead took on a human

---

[468]Frame, *Doctrine of God*, 590.

[469]Watson, *Theological Institutes*, 1:485-504.

[470]Martin, *Kingdom of the Cults*, 379.

[471]Yamauchi, "Jesus Outside the New Testament," 208-229.

[472]Hooper, *Collected Letters of C. S. Lewis*, 2:307.

body. This was not a metamorphosis. He is said to be the same because he has always been deity. But he has not always been humanity. "What He was He continued to be; what He was not He took to Himself. . . . In His Human nature He had no Father, but also in His Divine Nature no Mother."[473]

Athanasius explained, "The Word made himself 'bearer of the flesh' in order that human beings might become 'bearers of the Spirit.'" He also said that God became man that man might become God.[474] This has been interpreted to mean that he taught a doctrine of theosis. However, the doctrine of theosis can mean several different things. We are called by grace to participate in the divine nature. We do not become God in the sense that we become equal with God or assume his incommunicable attributes.

"The Word became flesh and made his dwelling among us" (John 1:14). God sent "his own Son in the likeness of sinful man to be a sin offering" (Rom 8:3). He "who being in very nature God" became "made in human likeness and being found in appearance as a man" (Phil 2:6-8). "For in Christ all the fullness of the Deity lives in bodily form" (Col 2:9). "He had to be made like his brothers in every way" (Heb 2:17). "Therefore, when Christ came into the world, he said: Sacrifice and offering you did not desire, but a body you prepared for me" (Heb 10:5). Therefore, he appeared in a body (1 Tim 3:16).

Although no one has ever seen God, Christ made him known by becoming flesh and living with us. "We have seen his glory, the glory of the Only Begotten, who came from the Father, full of grace and truth" (John 1:14,18). The incarnation revealed God to humanity. Thus, we see the glory of God in the *face* of Jesus Christ" (2 Cor 4:6). The Greek word for *face* (*prosopon*) thus means *personality*. Kinlaw explained that the word *person* came

---

[473]Gregory of Naziansen, *NPNF*2 7:308.

[474]Clément, *Roots of Christian Mysticism*, 56; Athanasius, *On the Incarnation*, *NPNF*2 4:65,159.

into Western language in the third and fourth centuries through the discussion of who Jesus was in relation to the other members of the Trinity.[475]

This incarnation was not only necessary for revelation, but for reconciliation. It provided us with a high priest who could sympathize with human weakness (Heb 4:14-16). It provided a substitutionary sacrifice which was adequate for the sins of the entire race (Heb 10:1-10). Through the incarnation Christ provided us an example (1 Pet 2:21). The incarnation provided us a judge (John 5:22-27). The incarnation is a test of true doctrine (1 John 4:1-3; 2 John 7).

Athanasius wrote *On the Incarnation of the Word of God* in the fourth century.

> Since the Savior has come among us, idolatry not only has no longer increased, but what there was is diminishing and gradually coming to an end: and not only does the wisdom of the Greeks no longer advance, but what there is is now fading away: And demons, so far from cheating any more by illusions and prophecies and magical arts, if they so much as dare to make the attempt, are put to shame by the sign of the Cross. And to sum the matter up: behold how the Savior's doctrine is everywhere increasing, while all idolatry and everything opposed to the faith of Christ is daily dwindling, and losing power, and falling. And thus beholding, worship the Savior "Who is above all" and mighty, even God the Word; and condemn those who are being worsted and done away by Him. For as, when the sun is come, darkness no longer prevails, but if any be still left anywhere it is driven away; so, now that the divine Appearing of the Word of God is come, the darkness of the

---

[475]Kinlaw, *Lectures in Old Testament Theology*, 108.

idols prevails no more, and all parts of the world in every direction are illuminated by His teaching.[476]

In the eleventh century Anselm wrote *Why the God-Man?* According to John Wesley, Christ came in the flesh because God decreed it from all eternity. Although God did not predestine the fall of mankind, he foreknew it. According to Romans 3:26, the justice of God requires that sinners must be punished, but the mercy of God desires to restore mankind. His creation was powerless to restore itself, therefore the remedy must come from God alone. God saved us and called us to a holy life, not because of anything we have done, but because of his own purpose and grace (2 Tim 1:9).

Although this union of God and man in Jesus Christ is unique, in process theology the entire universe is the incarnation.[477] Roman Catholicism tends to speak of the church as the continuing incarnation of Christ.[478] This position elevates the church to the position of deity. In truth, the church is not an extension of the living Word of God, but the divinely ordained channel of the Word and temple of the Holy Spirit. Neither the church nor the state can usurp the hypostatic union, although both were instituted by God.

The Virgin Birth – the Means of the Incarnation

Although Genesis 3:15 promised the seed of a woman would deliver, Isaiah 7:14 is the first use of *virgin*. The Hebrew word

---

[476]Athanasius, *Incarnation of the Word*, NPNF2 4:66. John of Damascus recorded a similar statement in the eighth century [*On the Orthodox Faith*, NPNF2 9:75].

[477]Moltmann, *God in Creation*, 150.

[478]Kärkkäinen, *Pneumatology*, 73; Bloesch, *The Church*, 29. Grider is misguided at this point [*Wesleyan-Holiness Theology*, 480-481]. Oden qualifies this concept [*Life in the Spirit*, 293].

almah is not precise, although never used of married women. The LXX uses *parthenos*, which is not ambiguous; it can only mean *virgin*. When Matthew quotes this verse in 1:23, it is *parthenos*. This word is also used by Luke the physician in 1:27, 34.

The Revised Standard Version in 1952 was unwarranted in their deletion of the virgin birth in Isaiah 7:14. It was supposed to be an update of the American Standard Version of 1901, which had it right. Based on the concept of progressive revelation, the more general word *almah* is defined by Scripture itself to have a more specific meaning. For the New Revised Standard Version in 1989 to maintain their same error in translation appears to be an act of defiance.

According to Luke 3:23, Joseph was thought to be the father of Jesus (see also Matt 13:55; Luke 4:22; John 6:42). According to Matthew 1:16, he was the husband of Mary. Joseph was called the *father* of Jesus by doubters or he was commonly accepted as the father. Joseph was the legal guardian (Luke 2:33,48).

Whenever Paul speaks of the birth of Christ, he uses the verb *ginomai*, which means *come to be* instead of the usual word for procreation, *gennao*, which means *to father*. Apparently, Paul used this more general term so that he would not be mistaken as saying that Jesus had a normal conception. Perhaps Paul implied a virgin birth in Galatians 4:4 where he says that God sent his Son, born of a woman. Normally the Scriptures refer to the father, not the mother.

The early church accepted this doctrine. Ignatius wrote about the virgin birth around 105. Taking its acceptance for granted, he felt no need to defend it. Aristides described the virgin birth as a fact of Christianity in 140. Justin Martyr also defended the doctrine around 160, as did Irenaeus around 180, and Clement of Alexandria around 195.

It is more precise to speak of the virgin conception, however. It was the conception, not the birth of Jesus, which was miraculous. Skeptics dismiss this stupendous miracle either on the basis that it is scientifically impossible *or* with the claim that virgin births are common in ancient mythology. But while pagan mythology is full of legends of a superhuman hero born of intercourse between a god and a human woman, this is scarcely a *virgin* birth.[479] It is inconsistent to argue that a virgin conception is impossible scientifically, but then argue that ancient literature is full of such accounts.

Parthenogenesis describes conception without insemination by a father. This happens within some species, but not naturally among humans. With the modern discovery of DNA, a child can now be cloned without a father; but cloning technology does not explain the virgin conception of Jesus Christ.

The virgin birth confirms the biblical prophecy of Isaiah 7:14. It identifies Jesus as the Christ. It completes the picture of his whole supernatural life. It indicates the deity of Christ. Christ existed eternally, but entered this world through the womb, the way all other humans come into the world. It also assures the humanity of Christ since Mary carried him full term. "There was no moment of time from the moment of conception when the forming child in Mary's womb was not God incarnate and yet truly human."[480]

There is no controversy that Scripture teaches Jesus was conceived by the Holy Spirit and born of the virgin Mary. J. Gresham Machen explained that the only question is whether Scripture is true or false. If the doctrine of the virgin birth is rejected, then biblical infallibility and authority is gone.

The doctrine of the virgin birth is important because it fixes the time of the incarnation. It also explains how Jesus Christ could enter the human race without being under the curse of sin.[481]

The Roman Catholic dogma of *immaculate conception* refers to Mary, not Jesus. However, Thomas Aquinas did not accept it.

---

[479]Richardson, "Virgin Birth," 357.

[480]Wright, "The Virgin Birth," 3:663.

[481]Machen, *The Virgin Birth*, 382-295.

He said it was proper to venerate Mary, but he did not believe she was miraculously conceived. There is no biblical support for this teaching, but it was declared by the Pope *ex cathedra* in 1854.

According to Matthew 1:25 Joseph consummated their marriage after Jesus was born. According to Mark 6:3, there were four sons and at least two daughters born to Joseph and Mary. Augustine explained that if both sexes are to be honored and blessed in the incarnation, and if the one giving birth must be female, then the one born must be male.[482]

The Humanity of Christ

"The Son of God became the Son of Man in order that we the sons of men should become the sons of God."[483] "History is crowded with many men who would be God but only one God who would become man."[484]

John's Gospel proves the deity of Christ and assumes his humanity. It was written that we might believe that Jesus is the Christ, the Son of God (John 20:31). John's epistles prove the humanity of Christ and assume his deity. John identifies the spirit of antichrist as anyone who denies the incarnation (1 John 2:22, 4:3; 2 John 7).

John wrote his epistles to combat that spirit of antichrist. In 1 John 1:1, John asserted that he had touched him; and what he touched was no phantom. Jesus had to have a body to identify fully with us. He had to have a body to bear the sins of the world. How could he be wounded, bruised, chastised, and whipped if he did not have a real body?

The controversy regarding the humanity of Christ was the result of gnostic influence. While the gnostics flourished in the

---

[482]Oden, *Life in the Spirit*, 8.

[483]Lewis, *Mere Christianity*, 178.

[484]MacArthur, "The King Who Would Be Man."

second century, their basic beliefs stretched a long way back. Gnosticism taught that the mind was more important than the body. Matter was evil and the mind was sacred. However, the emphasis was on mystical knowledge and intuition, not knowledge through divine revelation. And since the Bible emphatically teaches that Jesus was without sin, the gnostics at the end of the first century were teaching that Jesus did not really have a physical body, since everything physical or material was sinful. Therefore, Jesus could not have had a human body. He only *appeared* to be human. The Greek word for appearance, *dokein*, was the basis for the label *Docetism*.

But Jesus was not a phantom. In Luke 24:39 he invited his disciples to touch him, and John later records that they did so (1 John 1:1). He was not partially or occasionally human. He was fully human, yet without defect or sin. He was the second man and the last Adam (1 Cor 15:45-47). Pilate declared, "Behold the man" (John 19:5). It is very necessary to establish his humanity, because "he had to be made like his brothers in every way" (Heb 2:17) in order to qualify as our substitute.

Both Matthew 1:1-17 and Luke 3:23-38 provide a genealogy of Jesus. Skeptics have always pointed out the apparent inconsistencies between them. However, the best explanation is that Matthew provided his legal status which verified that he was lawfully the son of David, while Luke gave his natural lineage going clear back to Adam.[485]

Jesus shared in our humanity (Heb 2:14-18, 4:15-16, 10:5). His birth was normal. He grew normally, experiencing the same human limitations. He experienced the normal range of human emotions, such as love, joy, grief, pain, sorrow, pity, disappointment, compassion, misunderstanding, and anger.

Isaiah 53:2-3 tells us that Jesus was not attractive. Instead he was despised and rejected by people. According to this passage, he experienced pain and illness, people hid their faces from him,

---

[485]Kelly, *Systematic Theology*, 2:101-109.

he was despised, and considered insignificant. This connects with 52:14-15 which says that he was so disfigured that he no longer looked like a man, nor even human. Some commentators speculate that he looked more like fifty than thirty, but that does not explain Isaiah's description. Apparently, Isaiah is describing his appearance *after* his passion. Chrysostom explained that Isaiah was not describing a deformity in Christ, but that he was an object of scorn.[486] Furthermore, as the lamb of God he had to be without blemish. Yet he was ordinary enough that Judas had to identify him for the soldiers.

According to the Scriptures, he grew in stature (Luke 2:52). He got tired (John 4:6). He felt hunger (Matt 4:2). He became thirsty (John 19:28). He was a man of sorrows, and familiar with suffering (Isa 53:3). He felt the natural fear of separation at death (John 12:27). The most decisive proof of his humanity, however, is that he died. Death came through a man, and the resurrection of the dead comes also through a man (1 Cor 15:21).

Humanity was honored in the incarnation. Martin Luther preached that,

> The devil came close to us; but he did not come so close as to assume our nature. For although he fell through pride and thereupon persuaded man also to fall away from God, he nevertheless did not become man and did not come so close to us as did God's Son, who became our flesh and blood.[487]

Cults emphasize passages which speak of his humanity. They also emphasize passages which tend to deal with his voluntary submission, not his nature. Christ willingly took a subordinate position on earth, then at his ascension he was given all authority; but ultimately he will give it back, according to 1

---

[486]Oden, *ACCS* 7:345.

[487]Quoted by Oden, *The Word of Life*, 130.

Corinthians 15:28. This has reference to the *economic Trinity* or administration within the Godhead, not essence.

In the nineteenth century, when modernism emphasized the humanity of Jesus, they declared that they had rediscovered the Jesus of history. Their "quest for the historical Jesus" assumed that the Gospels are historically unreliable. It was also the attempt to deconstruct the two-nature doctrine of Christ as the God/man and replace it with an evolutionary view that we can become what we are not through the inspiration of his example. His teachings and his example became a primary source for moral instruction and enlightenment. Thus, the emphasis is on his perfect life rather than his substitutionary death. Modernist theology differs only in degree from Mormonism, which holds that Jesus was a preexistent spirit who was a spirit brother of the devil. At Cana of Galilee he was married to Mary and Martha, as well as other women.[488]

The "quest for the historical Jesus" began with Hermann Reimarus in 1774-1778. Writing from Enlightenment presuppositions, he supposed that the Gospel accounts were not reliable; and he attempted to construct a life of Christ based on rational research. This attempt was made popular by Albert Schweitzer. The moralistic Christ that emerged has long been rejected academically, "but still plays sentimentally in the churches of liberal Christianity."[489] In reply to this emphasis, Philip Schaff wrote in 1866,

> And yet the Jesus of Nazareth, without money and arms, conquered more millions than Alexander, Caesar, Mohammed, and Napoleon; without science and learning, he shed more light on things human and divine than all philosophers and scholars combined; without the eloquence of schools, he spoke such words of life as

---

[488]Martin, *Kingdom of the Cults*, 219.

[489]Oden, *The Word of Life*, 201.

were never spoken before or since, and produced effects which lie beyond the reach of any orator or poet; without writing a single line, he set more pens in motion, and furnished themes for more sermons, orations, discussions, learned volumes, works of art, and sweet songs of praise, than the whole army of great men of ancient and modern times. Born in a manger, and crucified as a malefactor, he now control the destinies of the civilized world, and rules a spiritual empire which embraces one-third of the inhabitants of the globe. There never was in this world a life so unpretending, modest, and lowly in its outward form and condition, and yet producing such extraordinary effects upon all ages, nations, and classes of men. The annals of history produce no other example of such complete and astounding success, in spite of the absence of those material, social, literary, and artistic powers and influences which are indispensable to success for a mere man. Christ stands, in this respect also, solitary and alone among all the heroes of history, and presents to us an insolvable problem, unless we admit him to be more than man, even the eternal Son of God.[490]

The second phase of historical Jesus studies included such writers as Ernst Kasemann, Edward Schillebeeckx, and the notorious Jesus Seminar, which was willing to consider any idea about Jesus so long as it was unorthodox.

The Jesus Seminar produced their *Five Gospels: What Did Jesus Really Say? The Search for the Authentic Words of Jesus*, edited by Robert Funk in 1996. In it words in red means Jesus said it, words in pink means it's close to what he said, words in gray means he didn't say it but there are echoes of his teachings in it, words in black means the saying did not come from him at

---

[490]Schaff, *Person of Christ*, 48-50.

all. Only 20% of all the words of Jesus are either red or pink; and many of those "authentic" words came from the Gospel of Thomas, the "fifth gospel." But the Gospel of Thomas was written by someone using the name of Thomas. This is called *pseudepigraphal* literature. Of course, such books were never accepted by the church because they are based on deception.[491]

Bart Ehrman asked if such pseudepigraphal accounts are any less believable then the traditional four Gospels. He attempted to raise doubt by referring to the fact we do not know the actual date of the birth of Jesus, the type of animals in the stable, nor the number of wise men. That is all true. But he projects from those questions the conclusion that the Gospels are not histories. Technically he is right, but here we are only dealing with the gcnre. The assumption is that because Matthew, Mark, Luke, and John have an agenda — essentially they are preaching a sermon that we should believe on Jesus Christ — that they are not objective accounts. But why is it reasonable to assume that the author of The Gospel of Thomas was objective when he assumed a false identity?[492]

The third phase in studies on the historical Jesus includes such writers as E. P. Sanders, Ben Witherington, and N. T. Wright who are more orthodox and deal with the Jewishness of Jesus.

The Deity of Christ

In "A Catalogue of Cults" Gary Wall surveyed 77 cults, from the Ahmadiyya Movement to Zoroastrianism. The common denominator among them all was their denial of the deity of Christ.[493] Yet the deity of Christ is essential for revelation and for reconciliation.

---

[491]Blomberg, "The Seventy-Four 'Scholars,'" 32-38.

[492]Ehrman, "What Do We Really Know about Jesus?" 24-28.

[493]Wall, "A Catalogue of Cults," 20-25.

According to 1 Corinthians 12:3, "No one can say, 'Jesus is Lord,' except by the Holy Spirit." Thus, every denial of the deity of Christ is inspired by false spirits. The Holy Spirit can reveal truth and confirm truth. Yet he will never lead us contrary to the revealed truth of the Word of God. His revelation comes through the Scriptures, which he confirms. He does not bypass our mind. Rather, he illuminates our mind.

- **Divine titles ascribed to Jesus Christ**

If the divine titles ascribed to Christ can only designate a divine being, then Jesus is deity. Isaiah called him "Mighty God" (9:6). Thomas exclaimed, "My Lord and my God!" (John 20:28).

Jesus calls himself "I am" in John 8:58. This is based on Exodus 3:14, "I am because I am." The name *Yahweh* (or Jehovah) is based upon the verb *to be*.

Jesus is called *Lord* (*kurios*) in Acts 2:36, 10:36. The LXX translated the Hebrew word *Yahweh* as *kurios* over six thousand times. In the NT *kurios* was used interchangeably with *theos*.[494] In 1 Corinthians 2:8 he is the "Lord of glory." *Lord* is the covenant name for God in Greek. It means that he is in control and speaks with absolute authority.

Jesus is identified as the *Word* (*logos*) in John 1:14 and he is called *God* in John 1:1, "The Word was God." The *Word* is a person, not merely an attribute. This *Word* became flesh, which means that he became human at the incarnation. And if this *Word* is a person, he is also God. In Romans 9:5, Christ is identified as "God over all."

Titus 2:13 refers to "our great God and Savior, Jesus Christ." Granville Sharp observed that when there are two nouns, which are not proper names, describing a person, and the two nouns are connected by the word *and*, and the first noun has the article *the* while the second does not, both nouns are referring to

---

[494]Foerster, "κύριος," *TDNT* 3:1062,1086-1094.

the same person. The same construction appears in 2 Peter 1:1, "our God and Savior Jesus Christ."

The correct textual reading of 1 Peter 3:15 should be "Christ as Lord." The Greek word *lord* (*kurios*) corresponds to *Yahweh*, the Hebrew word used in the OT for God. Therefore, it could also be translated "Christ as God." "Peter's application of that term to Christ is another indication of his identification of Jesus Christ with the Yahweh of the Old Testament."[495]

1 John 5:20 declares that Jesus Christ is the true God. And in Revelation 1:8, the nearest antecedent to "'I am the Alpha and the Omega,' says the Lord God, 'who is, and who was, and who is to come, the Almighty'"is Jesus Christ. Christ is also described as Alpha and Omega in Revelation 21:6,22:13.

- **OT passages appropriated to describe Jesus Christ**

There are also OT passages which refer to Yahweh, which are quoted in the NT and applied to Christ. The term *Emmanuel*, ascribed to Jesus in Matthew 1:23, means "God with us." Here Matthew cited Isaiah 7:14. *Emmanuel* does not refer to a child belonging to Ahaz because God would not share this name. Furthermore, the sign was not given to Ahaz but to us. In Isaiah 7:14, *you* is plural.

The ministry of John the Baptist was to prepare the way of the Lord (Matt 3:3; Luke 1:16). This prophecy was first made in Isaiah 40:3, where the Hebrew word for *lord* was *Yahweh*. In Malachi 4:5-6, the final chapter of the OT, John was referred to symbolically as Elijah. His ministry was to bring Israel back to the Lord their God, which was Jesus, according to Luke 1:16-17.

According to Isaiah 8:13-14, The Lord Almighty (*Yahweh-Sabaoth*) will be a stone that causes men to stumble and a rock

---

[495]Hiebert, *1 Peter*, 236.

that makes them fall. In 1 Peter 2:7-9 this passage is cited as fulfilled in Jesus Christ.

Isaiah 6:5-10 describes the glory of Yahweh-Sabaoth, but according to John 12:40-41 Isaiah saw the glory of Jesus.

Romans 10:9 specifies that saving faith is a belief that God raised Jesus from the dead and that he is Lord. Verse 13 promises that "everyone who calls on the name of the Lord will be saved." Here Paul cites Joel 2:32, where the Hebrew word is *Yahweh*. In Hebrews 1:8, the writer quotes from Psalm 45:6-7, "Your throne, O God, will last for ever," specifying that this statement is in reference to the Son.

God the Father is called "the first and the last" three times by Isaiah (41:6, 44:6, 48:12). There is no God other than Yahweh (Isa 44:6), yet Jesus is also called "the first and the last" in Revelation 1:11,2:8,22:13.

According to Isaiah 40:8, the Word of God stands forever. Jesus also declared that his words will never pass away (Matt 24:35).

Jeremiah 23:5-6, 33:15-16 prophesy that a righteous Branch will be raised up from the root of David. He will be called the Lord Our Righteousness (*Yahweh-Tsedeq*). Jesus is the branch of David in Isaiah 11:1. In Revelation 5:5 Jesus is the *offspring* (*rhiza*) of David. This Greek word can mean either *root* or *shoot*. However, in the last chapter of the Bible, where this concept reaches its final development, in Revelation 22:16, he is both the *rhiza* and the *genos* of David. He is both David's son and David's Lord (Matt 22:45). In his deity he is David's root and in his humanity he is David's branch.

In the OT, Yahweh is frequently described as Savior or the Author of Salvation (Isa 43:3,20-22; Ezek 34:22). In the NT Jesus Christ is our Lord and Savior. The name *Jesus*, from the Hebrew *Yeshua*, means *Yahweh is salvation*. Joel 2:32 declares that everyone who calls on the name of Yahweh shall be saved, and according to Romans 10:13 that name is Jesus. In fact, there is no other name under heaven given to men by which we must be saved (Acts 4:12).

In Isaiah 45:22-25 the whole world is called to look unto Yahweh and be saved. Then God decreed that every knee will bow and every tongue will confess his deity. In Romans 14:10-12 this passage is appropriated to describe the authority of Christ.

- ## Divine actions ascribed to Jesus Christ

In Luke 5:20-26, Jesus forgave sins, which was clearly understood to be the prerogative of God alone. Thus, Jesus performed the work of God. Jesus Christ forgives sin (Matt 9:2-6). Yet who can forgive sins but God alone? (Mark 2:7).

In Psalm 119, we are told eleven times that God has the power to make alive. In John 5:21 and 11:25 Christ also claims the power to give life.

Jesus Christ was involved in the work of creation (Col 1:16-17). According to Hebrews 1:2, God created *through* Christ.

In Psalm 102:25-27 God laid the foundations of the earth and the heavens are the work of his hands. This passage is appropriated to Jesus Christ in Hebrews 1:10-12. According to John 1:3, "Through him all things were made, without him nothing was made that has been made." Verse 10 adds, "The world was made by him."

The preservation of the world is the work of Jesus Christ. In him all things stand together (Col 1:17). According to Hebrews 1:3 he sustains all things by his powerful word. The verb *phero* means that he bears or upholds the universe. And in Revelation 3:14, Jesus Christ is described as the ruler of God's creation. The Greek word *arche* means that Christ is the origin or source of creation. In no way can it be misconstrued to mean that Christ was a created being.

Jesus Christ will raise the dead (John 5:28-29) and judge the world (2 Cor 5:10). Yet Psalm 9:7-8 declares that Yahweh will judge the world.

In Revelation 1:12-16, John describes the risen Christ. Jesus is the "faithful witness." Anyone who has seen him has seen the Father. Each aspect of his description corresponds to an OT depiction of God the Father. In each of the seven church letters of Revelation 2-3, one aspect of this portrait is emphasized as being the quality each congregation needs most to be reminded of.

And Christ makes demands that only God could rightfully make. He requires absolute faith and obedience. He demands our supreme love; he demands first place in our priorities.[496] Yet Watson pointed out that since we are to love the Lord our God with all our heart and with all our soul and with all our strength, if Christ himself is not God we would be breaking the command of Deuteronomy 6:5.[497]

- **Divine attributes ascribed to Jesus Christ**

There are also divine attributes ascribed to Jesus Christ, which are noncommunicable attributes. According to Alan Gomes, the early fathers distinguished between communicable and incommunicable attributes.[498] While they did hold that God does impart such communicable attributes as holiness and immortality to his creatures, he does not impart incommunicable attributes such as aseity or self-existence. I will not cite attributes such as wisdom, holiness, goodness, or justice, which are properly attributes of God which he shares, in measure, with man and which are also attributed to Christ.

Jesus Christ is eternal (Heb 7:3; Rev 1:8, 17-18). He is the source of life (John 1:4,5:26). Jesus is "the first and the last" (Rev 1:11,2:8, 22:13), the Alpha and Omega (Rev 1:6, 21:6, 22:13). He is forever the same (Heb 13:8). Isaiah 9:6 describes him as the "father of eternity." It is a way of saying that he has always existed. To say that George Washington was the father of

---

[496]Matt 10:37-38; Luke 14:26; John 12:26; 1 Cor 16:22; 2 Cor 5:14-15; Eph 6:24.

[497]Watson, *Theological Institutes*, 1:460.

[498]Gomes, "Value of Historical Theology," 5-6.

the United States does not mean that every American citizen is his flesh and blood. Instead it means that he existed before the United States was created and that he was involved in the formation of our nation. To say that Jesus is the father of eternity implies that he is older than time.

Jesus Christ is immutable. Just as Yahweh does not change (Mal 3:6), so Jesus Christ is the same yesterday and today and forever (Heb 13:8).

Jesus Christ is omnipresent (Matt 18:20,28:20). Many manuscripts add "who is in heaven" at the end of John 3:13.

Jesus Christ is omnipotent (Matt 28:18; Rev 1:8). According to Colossians 3:21 he has the power to bring everything under his control.

Jesus Christ is omniscient (John 16:30, 21:17).[499] In him all the treasures of wisdom and knowledge are hidden (Col 1:23).

Jesus declared his equality with God the Father (John 5:18). The Scriptures also ascribe works to Christ which are only the prerogative of God.

- **Jesus Christ receives worship**

Furthermore, Jesus Christ received worship from mankind although Deuteronomy 6:13 declares that God alone should be worshiped, and he reiterated that command (Matt 4:10). In a letter written to Pliny the Elder (in AD 112), the younger Pliny reported to his uncle that the Christians he was persecuting

---

[499]Matt 9:4, 12:25, 16:8; Mark 2:8; Luke 5:22,6:8, 9:47, 11:17; John 1:42,48, 2:23-25, 4:17-18,29, 6:64,70, 11:11,14 are all frequently cited as proof of the omniscience of Christ. While each of these references demonstrate supernatural knowledge, they do not necessarily demonstrate omniscience. However, the declaration in John 14:6 that he is "the truth" does imply omniscience.

would gather in the woods and sing hymns to Christ as to God."[500]

The angels in heaven also worship Christ. According to Hebrews 1 the angels are the highest created order, and the angels worshiped Christ at his incarnation. Twice in the book of Revelation, at 19:9 and at 22:8-9, John mistakenly attempted to worship an angel and was stopped. In both cases his motive to worship was right, but it was misdirected. God alone is to be the object of our worship; and since Christ is consistently portrayed in this book as equal with God, Christ, but not angels, is also worthy of our worship. In Revelation 5:6-14 he is worshiped in heaven. If Christ was a created being this would amount to idolatry.

- **Jesus Christ reveals God**

Finally, Colossians 1:15 declares that Jesus is the image (*eikon*) of the invisible God. Christ could not reveal God if he were not the replication of God. Christ not only represents God, he is the manifestation of God. While all humanity is in the image of God, that image is greatly marred. Christ is the perfect image of God.

Colossians 2:9 declares that all the fullness of God indwells him bodily. The term *theotetos*, used only here, refers to the Godhead. According to Philippians 2:6, he was in very nature God before the incarnation. The Greek word *morphe* denotes form or shape, not in terms of external features by which something is recognized, but by means of those characteristics that are essential to it.[501] Thus, the reality of what is meant by *form of God* belongs as much to the Son as to the Father.

And Hebrews 1:3 teaches that he is the exact representation of God. Here the Greek word *charakter* means an exact impres-

---

[500]Schaff, *History of the Christian Church*, 2:222.

[501]Silva, *Philippians*, 100-102.

sion of God's nature. It was used for the impression left by a seal. There is an exact correspondence between the impression and the seal. Thus, Jesus Christ is the perfect imprint of God.

However, early in the fourth century Arius asked how the Logos could be eternal if he came from God the Father. Arius concluded that "there was a time when he was not." Based on human reason, Arius held that Christ was a created being, that he was not eternally existent, and that he was not of the same essence with the Father. William Martin explained,

> Arius tried to force a literal meaning on the analogy of father and son, where priority must exist. From this, he argued it was clear that the Son must have had a beginning; so that once, there was no Son. As a created being, He must also be limited in power, wisdom, and knowledge. The Son was, therefore, the creation of the Father and was called into existence out of nothing. Arius did not or could not see that the very title "Eternal Father" implied the existence of an eternal Son.[502]

The position of Arius was later adopted by Lelio and Fausto Sozzini, who lived in the sixteenth century. The early Methodists strongly opposed the influence of the Socinians in the eighteenth century. More recently the Jehovah's Witnesses have revived this ancient Arian heresy.

Athanasius took the opposite position, based on divine revelation, "there was *never* a time when he was not." The Council of Nicea, the first ecumenical council, met in AD 325 to settle this issue from Scripture. Although the council was convened by Constantine, this was no conspiracy to pervert the church. The views of Arius were an objection to the prevalent view, not a correction of heresy. If Christians had denied the deity of Christ, the opposition of Arius would have been meaningless. Therefore,

---

[502]Martin, *Deity of Christ*, 7.

the council was convened to defend scriptural doctrine. The church did not create Christ. Rather, Christ created the church.

The orthodox insisted that Christ has existed from all eternity, that he was begotten, not made, and was of the same essence (*ousia*). They employed the term *homoousios* to explain that the Logos shares the same nature or being with the Father. While Christ was subordinate in his role to the Father, his work does not define his being.

The Arians advocated *homoiousios*, which meant of like essence. While wags observe that there is only one letter different in the two words, that fails to explain that the very nature of Christ was debated. We could just as well argue that since there is only one letter's difference between *dead* and *head*, there are really no essential differences. C. S. Lewis explained the importance of understanding the nature of Jesus Christ:

> I am trying here to prevent anyone saying the really foolish thing that people often say about Him: "I'm ready to accept Jesus as a great moral teacher, but I don't accept His claim to be God." This is the one thing we must not say. A man who was merely a man and said the sort of things Jesus said would not be a great moral teacher. He would either be a lunatic — on the level with a man who says he is a poached egg — or else he would be the Devil of Hell. You must make a choice. Either this man was, and is, the son of God: or else a madman or something worse. You can shut him up for a fool, you can spit at him and kill him as a demon or you can fall at his feet and call him Lord and God, but let us not come with any patronizing nonsense about his being a great human teacher. He has not left that open to us.[503]

---

[503]Lewis, *Mere Christianity*, 54–56.

The Two Natures of Christ

Christ had to be both man and God *at the same time* in order to reveal God to man and to reconcile man with God. The same two books, the Gospel of John and Hebrews, which emphasize the deity of Christ also contain the fullest evidence of his humanity. John Frame explained, "Everything that is true of God's nature is true of Jesus, and everything true of human nature is true of Jesus."[504]

Romans 1:3-4 defines the two natures of Christ. Through his incarnation he became or was born the seed of David. God promised David that his seed would reign forever (2 Sam 7:11-16). Therefore, the kingdom of Christ was a continuation of that covenant made with David. Jesus Christ came to occupy the throne of David and rule over us.

But Christ is not only the Son of David, he is the Son of God. Paul refers to the two natures of Christ — the hypostatic union of divine and human natures. Jesus Christ was "very [or truly] God and very man." The term *hypostatic* refers to his essence, nature, or being. Thus, the hypostatic union is the union of two natures within one person. However, all analogies are inadequate in their attempt to explain the God/man. We must avoid any notion that he was a *hybrid*.

In Romans 1:3-4, his human nature is mentioned first because his divine nature was not fully manifested until after his resurrection. The resurrection declared, delineated, and powerfully confirmed his divine nature. James Denney wrote that the resurrection

> only declared Him to be what He truly was…. The sonship, which was declared by the resurrection, an-

---

[504]Frame, *Salvation Belongs to the Lord*, 130.

swered to the spirit of holiness which was the inmost and deepest reality in the Person and life of Jesus."[505]

The term S*on of God* refers to the deity of Christ, while the term *Son of man* refers to his humanity. Jesus used this title, *Son of Man*, 81 times in the Gospels. No one else in the NT called him by that title, and after his death and resurrection it no longer occurs, except in four texts. In Acts 7:56 Stephen verifies that the authority of Christ has been established. Hebrews 2:6 cites Psalm 8:4. Revelation 1:13, 14:14 both allude to Daniel 7:13.

In utilizing this term, Jesus is identifying himself with the *son of man* described in Daniel 7. Thus, his kingdom succeeds the four previous world dominions.

Christ is fully God and fully man. He is one person with two natures. Colossians 2:9 teaches that the divine nature penetrates every aspect of the human nature, and the human nature is pervaded by the divine nature. The Greek term *perichoresis* is employed to describe this concept. But the two natures must be kept separate, while at the same time joined together in one person. However, this inner penetration within the person of Christ, as well as the Trinity, can be stretched beyond orthodoxy when it is used to describe a God-human relationship. And it becomes pantheism when it is used to describe a God-creation relationship.

In Christ, it was his humanity which became obedient to the death of the cross (Phil 2:9). God cannot die. Christ died the death of a man, but not as God. According to Isaiah 53:10 he was assigned a grave, but he was not abandoned to the grave (Acts 2:23-27). Since the concept of death carries the idea of separation, not cessation, there was apparently a separation of his human nature and divine nature, resulting in the person of Christ experiencing death.

---

[505]Denny, *Expositor's Greek Testament*, 2:586.

This union of two natures is implied in John 14:1-3 where the incarnate Son of God commanded us to trust in him just as we trust in God. While on earth, he refers to the glory of his deity which was veiled, but which he previously shared with the Father (John 17:5, 24). Romans 6:9 declares that he died once, but that death no longer has mastery over him. He who died was raised from the dead and seated at God's right hand (Eph 1:20-23). According to Revelation 1:5, he is the firstborn from the dead and the ruler of the world, even holding the keys of death (v 18). He had to be truly human in order to die, but he is clearly much more than human. In Revelation 5:13, 7:17, 14:10, 21:22, 22:1 this same concept is taught through the metaphor of the Lamb who died as our atonement, but who is the center of worship and authority in heaven.

The dual nature of Christ has been confused by several heretical teachings which either tend to separate Christ into two persons or unite his two natures into one. Jesus always refers to himself as *I*, not *we*.

Irenaeus wrote around AD 175-185 that the church dispersed throughout the world spoke of Christ as "our Lord, and God, and Savior, and King."[506] In 195 Clement of Alexandria described Christ as "both God and man."[507]

In general the Alexandrian school emphasized his deity, while the Antiochian school emphasized his humanity. The Council of Chalcedon in AD 451 resolved the dispute over the two natures of Christ. Greek philosophy saw all existence as one, with the human and divine aspects as a continuum. Thus, salvation was the process of self-deification.

In contrast, orthodox Christianity understood that there was an infinite gulf between the uncreated being of God and the created nature of mankind. This gulf can only be bridged by the grace extended through Jesus Christ. If his deity is denied, then

---

[506]Irenaeus, *Against Heresies*, *ANF* 1:330.

[507]Clement, *Exhortation to the Heathen*; *ANF* 2:174.

his power to save is nullified. If his humanity is denied, his substitutionary atonement is also nullified. If his humanity and deity were not in true union, then the incarnation was not real and the gulf between God and man remained as great as ever. The Chalcedon Creed separated the Christian faith from Greek and pagan philosophy.

It has been asserted that the Council of Chalcedon represented the triumph of Greek philosophy over the biblical witness. However, Greek philosophy tended to affirm that matter was eternal, thus contradicting the biblical distinction between the Creator and the creation. The fathers at Chalcedon did not embrace this pagan worldview, but were determined to speak according to Scripture. While they utilized the Greek language, and were at times limited in their vocabulary, they had to work within this limited vocabulary by redefining existing words. In the evaluation of Latourette, the early Christian creeds utilized technical philosophical terms, but never perverted the faith into a pagan philosophy.[508]

Greek philosophy knew nothing of the concept of God as a trinity. Their god was a philosophical concept, not a personal being. In contrast, the God defended at Chalcedon exists in a communion of three persons in one substance who created the world out of nothing. In fact, the attempt to interject Greek philosophy into Christian theology was not through the early ecumenical councils but through gnosticism.

Orthodox Christianity rejects three types of heresy. These options are often associated with the historical figures who first espoused them.

- **Heresies that reject the humanity of Christ**

  - Docetism teaches that Christ was not human, but only appeared to be incarnate. The Greek word *dokein* was

---

[508]Latourette, *History of Christianity*, 1:260-261.

used to teach that Christ only seemed to be human, but that it was an illusion.

- Apollinarianism (AD 362-381) was taught by Apollinaris, who believed that the divine nature or logos replaced the human soul of Jesus. Thus, Christ had a human body but not a human spirit. This emphasized deity at the expense of full humanity.

If Apollinarianism was correct, only our body would be redeemed. Our personality, including our fallen minds, would not be saved. Gregory Nazianzus argued, "For that which He has not assumed He has not healed."[509] Since the whole of our humanity fell in Adam, so the whole of our humanity needs salvation. If Christ had only taken part of our humanity, then only that part of our humanity could be saved. If any aspect of our humanity was not assumed by Christ in the incarnation, it could not be healed by him. If Christ had only assumed a body, and had not taken to himself a true human soul with a true human mind and emotions, then only the human body would be saved and there would be no salvation for our souls. But he has assumed full humanity so that we may know full salvation.

- Eutychianism (AD 449) originated with Eutyches who taught that the two natures fused into one — the divine. Monophysitism means one nature and is a closely related error. Monothelitism held that Christ had only one will and is also closely related.

If Christ had two natures, he had two wills. Thus, in his human will he struggled to avoid the suffering of the cross (Matt 26:36-46).[510] While Jesus was of the same essential nature as the

---

[509]Gregory Nazianzus, *NPNF*2 7:440.

[510]Calvin, *Commentary*, 17.3:233.

Father, this error stripped him of the same essential nature as mankind.

- **Heresies that reject the deity of Christ**

  - Eutychianism would logically also be placed under this heading.
  - The Ebionites were a first century Jewish-Christian sect that emphasized Jewish law and rejected the teachings of the Apostle Paul. Most of them considered Jesus to be a man, not God. He might be a Spirit-filled man or a super-human, but not God.
  - Arians (AD 318-381) followed Arius, who taught that Jesus Christ was a created being, not eternal. This error was revived in 1546 as Socinianism, perpetuated under Unitarianism, and currently promoted by the Jehovah's Witnesses.
  - Kenoticism is a more modern heresy, based on a misinterpretation of Philippians 2:6-7 and 2 Corinthians 8:9. It teaches that Christ emptied himself of the noncommunicable attributes of deity. Thus, he exchanged part of the divine nature for human characteristics. More radical versions hold that Christ emptied himself of all divine attributes.

- **Heresies that reject the union of humanity and deity in Christ**

  - Nestorianism (AD 428-431) followed Nestorius emphasizing a radical distinction between two natures of Jesus Christ. Nestorius held that Christ was a perfect man linked to deity, a God-bearer, not the God-man.

At the end of the eighth century Nestorianism was revived as Adoptionism, which taught that Christ was merely a man who was made the Son of God by adoption and that his humanity was gradually adopted into his deity. This concept lends itself to process philosophy.

Modernist theology tends to emphasize the humanity of Christ while rejecting his deity. But if we deny his deity we also lose his humanity, because it renders the historical documents unreliable when they represent him as both God and man. How, then, can we study them as authoritative, in search of his humanity, when we reject what they say about his deity?

Berkhof described the modernism of the early twentieth century as teaching, "Essentially all men are divine, since they all have a divine element in them; and they are all sons of God, differing from Christ only in degree."[511] At the end of the twentieth century, Donald Bloesch declared, "The soundness of any particular theological position is finally measured by how it stands on Jesus Christ. Needless to say, the Christ of Chalcedonian orthodoxy is in palpable eclipse in most circles."[512]

Orthodox Christianity stands for a true incarnation in which God is not converted into a man nor a conversion of man into God. The result of the incarnation is the God-Man. The motive of the incarnation is the love of God and the result is a fallen race reconciled with God.

The early ecumenical councils made a precise distinction between *nature* and *person*. *Nature* refers to all of the essential qualities that comprise a subject, making it what it is. In this case, it would refer to qualities that all humanity has in common. In contrast, *person* refers to the intellect, emotion, and will, as well as self-consciousness, which every human has individually. Thus, the *hypostatic union* is the divine and human natures of Christ combined in one person. At the point in time of his virgin conception, Jesus took on a human nature, but his personhood remained constant.

---

[511]Berkhof, *Systematic Theology*, 311.

[512]Bloesch, *Jesus Christ*, 234.

In Colossians 2:2 the mystery of God is Christ. Christ is fully God and God is fully in Christ (vv 9-10). Colossians 4:3 speaks of the *mystery of Christ* which connects with 2:2.

Pope explained that *mystery* has two meanings. First, it is the unfolding of what had long been promised. In this sense, Christ is an OT mystery revealed in the NT.

Second, it is what is believed on divine authority although it is incomprehensible. In this sense, the person of Christ, the God-man, will forever be a mystery.[513] This may be what is implied in Revelation 19:12, where it is declared that he has a name written on him that no one but he himself knows. Pope warned that theology has suffered repeatedly from those who attempt to speculate as they sound the depths of the hypostatic union.[514]

The orthodox doctrine is that Christ is one person with two natures, without confusion, without change, without division, and without separation. This language, formulated in AD 451 at Chalcedon, does not attempt to explain the mystery of Christ's nature, but it does attempt to guard the truth as revealed in Scripture. The phrases *without confusion*, *without change* guard against the false view that Christ had only one nature. The phrases *without division*, *without separation* guard against the false view that Christ was two persons.

The Sinlessness of Christ

The language of Paul is precise. God sent "his own Son in the likeness of sinful man to be a sin offering" (Rom 8:3). Yet sin was not an integral part of humanity. The phrase "in the likeness of sinful flesh" implies both the sinlessness and the humanity of Christ. Christ did not come in sinful flesh, but he did come in the flesh (John 1:14).

---

[513]Pope, *Person of Christ*, 30-32.

[514]Pope, *Person of Christ*, 35-36.

Jesus "committed no sin" (1 Pet 2:22). According to Wiley, He was not only free from sin, but from the possibility of sin.[515]

The Work of Christ

The work of Jesus Christ in creation has already been discussed, as well as his role in preservation. However, he plays a unique role in revelation and salvation. The agnostic claims we cannot know what God is like, yet Christ came to reveal God. According to 1 Corinthians 1:24 Christ reveals the wisdom and power of God. In him all the treasures of wisdom and knowledge are hidden (Col 1:23). Fallen man is restored to spiritual wisdom and spiritual life only through the objective reality of Christ's wisdom, righteousness, sanctification, and redemption.

Christ has made God known (John 1:18). "When a man believes in me, he does not believe in me only, but in the one who sent me. When he looks at me, he sees the one who sent me" (John 12:44-45). "Anyone who has seen me has seen the Father" (John 14:8-11). "He is the image of the invisible God" (Col 1:15). The Son is the exact representation of God (Heb 1:3).

He also came to save his people from their sins (Matt 1:21). He is the Lamb of God who takes away the sin of the world (John 1:29). Christ is the great teacher, example, and philosopher, but we would be unable to follow his example or obey his teachings if it were not for his salvation. He came to die that we might have spiritual life. Paul declares that the death, burial, and resurrection of Christ are "of first importance" (1 Cor 15:3).

The Two Estates of Christ
His humiliation

Philippians 2:5-8 describes the cost of the incarnation. It involved condescension and humiliation. He did not consider his

---

[515]Wiley, *Christian Theology*, 2:177.

equality with God something that had to be clutched tightly. In v 7 "made himself nothing" literally is *he emptied himself.* Here the Greek verb *kenoo* provides the basis for the term *kenosis*.

Of what did he empty himself? In the great hymn "And Can It Be" Charles Wesley overstates the point by saying, "emptied himself of all but love." More accurately, Christ left behind his heavenly glory but not his deity (John 17:5). He gave up status and privilege. His majesty was hidden and his noncommunicable attributes, such as omnipotence, omni-science, and omnipresence, were not fully exercised. Perhaps this is why he claimed not to know the day nor the hour of his return (Matt 24:36).

There was a change in form; his appearance was like a man. There was a change in position; he became a servant. But there was no change in nature; he was still God. "Though he was rich, yet for your sakes he became poor, so that you through his poverty might become rich" (2 Cor 8:9).

Thus, his humiliation began with the incarnation, continuing in the virgin birth, a life in poverty, and his passion, which included his betrayal, his arrest, his trial, his scourging, his crucifixion, and burial.

Christ is still the God/man. The incarnation was not terminated when Christ ascended. He is forever the God/man. He has become a priest forever (Heb 6:20). He is a priest forever (Heb 5:6). He has permanently identified with us — otherwise his ability to mediate if forfeited.

• **His substitutionary death**

"The Lord has laid on him the iniquity of us all" (Isa 53:4-6). He "gave his life as a ransom for many" (Matt 20:28). "One died for all" (1 Cor 5:14). "God made him who had no sin to be a sin offering for us" (1 Cor 5:21). The word *vicar* means substitute. It is blasphemy for the pope to claim he is the vicar of Christ. However, the word is used correctly when we speak of the vicarious atonement of Christ.

Did the Father forsake him? Psalm 22:1 begins with the cry, "My God, my God, why have you forsaken me?" For Jesus to quote the first line was to recall the entire psalm, much like the Hebrew word *shema* references the entire passage of Deuteronomy 6:4-12. This psalm is the most detailed description of his psychological suffering. But was Christ abandoned? How could God withdraw from God? If the Father forsook the Son, did the Holy Spirit also abandon him? The simple declaration "my God" is itself a statement of faith.

While Psalm 22 opens with the haunting words in question, it moves to affirmations of hope and faith. The petition of vv 19-21 does not indicate despair. By v 24 we find a strong affirmation that God has *not* despised the suffering of the afflicted one. It ends in a note of consolation, triumph, and praise. "Jesus may have had in mind the entire psalm and found strength in it in the long hours of pain."[516] God has heard his cry for help. He was not abandoned by God, nor did he suffer under Satan. According to Acts 2:25, Jesus always saw the Lord before him. Thus, God is continually present with Jesus.

Jesus coped with the agony of the cross by focusing on the joy that was set before him (Heb 12:2). All the ends of the earth will remember and turn to the Lord (Ps 22:27-31). If the Father broke fellowship with the Son, how do we explain the trinity? Thomas Oden wrote, "His cry from the cross did not imply a literal abandonment of the Son by the Father."[517] A diversity of theologians have agreed.

Gregory of Nazianzus, in the fourth century, taught that the Son "was not forsaken by the Father in terms of deity, as though deity were forsaking deity, splitting God into parts as it were."[518] Since the Father is Father in the sense that he eternally generates the Son, if the Father rejected the Son he would no longer be the

---

[516]Latourette, *History of Christianity*, 1:56.

[517]Oden, *The Word of Life*, 333.

[518]Hall, *Reading Scripture with the Church Fathers*, 73-74.

Father. John of Damascus wrote in the eighth century, "For neither as God nor as man was He ever forsaken by the Father, nor did He become sin or a curse."[519]

There can never be a division in the Godhead. Adam Clarke wrote, "Nor could *he* be *forsaken* of God, *in whom dwelt all the fullness of the Godhead bodily*."[520] Richard Watson denied that the Father and the Son were in any way separated. It is not as if one divine person is against guilty sinners while the other is for them.[521]

G. C. Berkouwer asked, "How can *God* be forsaken of God?"[522] Roger Nicole said, "There can never be a division in the Godhead."[523] McCall declared, "If we understand the doctrine of the Trinity properly, we will be in a position to see that saying 'the Trinity is broken' amounts to saying 'God does not exist.'"[524]

R.T. France notes that when we read "into these few tortured words an exegesis of the whole psalm,"transforming these words into an expression of confidence, we "turn upside down the effect which Mark has created by this powerful and enigmatic cry of agony."[525]

Tom McCall raised appropriate questions about the "broken Trinity" interpretation of Matthew 27:45-46 and Mark 15:34. While this is a popular contemporary interpretation, McCall demonstrates that this was not the traditional interpretation. Jesus was not cursed, nor did he become sin. If Christ were a sinner,

---

[519]John of Damascus, *Exposition of the Orthodox Faith*, NPNF2 9:91.

[520]Clarke, *Commentary*, 5:277.

[521]McCall and Stanglin, *After Arminius*, 192.

[522]Berkouwer, *The Triumph of Grace*, 312.

[523]Boice, *The Christ of Christmas*, 122.

[524]McCall, *Forsaken*, 44.

[525]France, *Gospel of Mark*, 653.

then he himself would need salvation. Despite the popular claim that Jesus was the greatest sinner, in him was no sin at all. The correct interpretation of 2 Corinthians 5:21, however, is that Christ became a sin offering.[526]

The union of Christ with humanity was unbroken, and his relationship with the Father was also unbroken. McCall argues that the Son's relationship to the Father matters for our hope in the gospel. The unbroken work of the triune God is the hope for the brokenness of humanity.[527]

> In the light of this cry, no believer is in a position to say that one's own hour of darkness is darker than that of God the Son. In whatever anguish, the believer can recall that he or she is crying out in companionship with One who also experienced abandonment and who continued nonetheless to pray to the Father.[528]

- **His burial**

His burial confirms the fact that he was really dead. However, his body did not experience decay (Acts 2:27, 13:37). Death could not hold him (Acts 2:24).

His exaltation

His suffering and humiliation ended with the exclamation "It is finished" (John 19:30). This one word *tetelestai* meant *paid in full* in extra-biblical sources.[529] What was finished? — the obedience of the last Adam to the will of God. He fulfilled the law and

---

[526]Clarke, *Commentary*, 338-339.

[527]McCall, *Forsaken*, 22-47; 110-112.

[528]Oden, *The Word of Life*, 334.

[529]Moulton and Milligan, *Vocabulary of the Greek New Testament*, 630.

the Messianic prophecies of Scripture. He satisfied our sin debt and propitiated the wrath of God as our substitute, thus providing the means for our reconciliation, as well as destroying the works of the devil.

This is the divine reversal. God exalted him to the highest place and gave him a name above every name (Phil 2:9). The exaltation began with descent into the realm of death, continuing in his resurrection, ascension, session, and his second advent.

• **His descent into the realm of death**

While the Apostles' Creed stated that Jesus *descended into hell*, Christ did not go to hell to suffer for us; but he did visit the realm of death in triumph. The Hebrew *sheol* and the Greek *hades* both refer to the realm of death. "Who will descend into the deep? (that is, to bring Christ up from the dead)" (Rom 10:7). "What does 'he ascended' mean except that he also descended to the lower, earthly regions?" (Eph 4:9). "And having disarmed the powers and authorities, he made a public spectacle of them, triumphing over them by the cross" (Col. 2:15). "He went and preached to the spirits in prison" (1 Pet 3:19). His purpose was to break down the gates of hell, bind up the demonic powers, declare his lordship, and to bring up the souls of the righteous dead to the kingdom of heaven. Martin Luther said:

> I believe that He descended into hell to overthrow and take captive the devil and all his power, guile and wick-edness, for me and for all who believe in Him, so that henceforth the devil cannot harm me.[530]

Bloesch concluded, "Christ's descent into Hades after his crucifixion and death has a solid foundation in both Scripture

---

[530]Quoted by Oden, *The Word of Life*, 440.

and the early church."[531] When we look at Acts 2:25-35, Romans 10:7, Philippians 2:8-10, and 1 Peter 3:19-22, "Paul seems to say here, Christ descended from heaven not merely to earth but to Hades and from Hades He has ascended again 'far above all the heavens.'"[532] The most natural way to read the Greek text is a reference to the subterranean regions.[533] Schaff felt that the word *hell* had been inadvertently substituted for the word *hades*.[534]

Rufinus of Aquileia included *he descended into hell* in his commentary on the Apostles' Creed written around AD 307-309.[535] According to Chrysostom, Christ preached condemnation to imprisoned evil spirits and subjected angels, authorities, and powers to himself before taking his seat at God's right hand. "He took the tyrant captive, the devil, I mean, and death, and the curse, and sin. Behold His spoils and His trophies."[536] Writing in the fourth century, Ambrosiaster said,

> First of all he first descended to the earth where he was born a man. Later he died and descended to hell, from which he rose again on the third day. . . .
> He robbed hell when he stole the captives who were imprisoned there, either because of the sin of Adam or because of their own sins, and who accepted him. He ascended into heaven and took them with him. Some of them rose from the dead and appeared in their bodies as a witness to the defeat of death, so that those who would probably not have believed in the resurrection of Christ would be convinced by the resurrection of the

---

[531]Bloesch, "Descent into Hell," 313-314.

[532]Bruce, *Ephesians*, 83-84.

[533]Muddiman, *Ephesians*, 192-193.

[534]Schaff, *Creeds of Christendom*, 2:45-46.

[535]Rufinus, *NPNF*2 3:553-554.

[536]Chrysostom, *Homilies on Ephesians*, *NPNF*1 13:104.

people who they knew were dead, for they saw people whom they knew had once been alive.[537]

He also ascended into heaven with his own blood to obtain eternal redemption (Heb 9:11-28). The question is one of timing. Did he ascend to heaven at the time of his resurrection or forty days later? The statement of Jesus in John 20:17 seems to mean, "There is no need for you to cling to me; I am not going yet."

• **His resurrection**

"If Christ has not been raised, our preaching is useless and so is your faith. . . . And if Christ has not been raised, your faith is futile; you are still in your sins. Then those also who have fallen asleep in Christ are lost" (1 Cor 15:12-19).

We accept the fact of the resurrection based on the authority of God's Word (Acts 1:3). "The Gospels do not explain the resurrection. The resurrection alone is what can explain the Gospels."[538] The success of the early church is evidence of the fact that the resurrection was immediately believed.[539]

At the incarnation a body was prepared for Jesus (Heb 10:5). That body really died and was raised on the third day by the Holy Spirit. If he did not physically rise again, we will not either. "We believe that Jesus died and rose again and so we believe that God will bring with Jesus those who have fallen asleep in him" (1 Thess 4:14). Oden declared,

The key test for Christianity is the resurrection. If one begins by assuming that a resurrection cannot be an event in history, then one may confidently conclude that

---

[537]Ambrosiaster, *ACT*, 48.

[538]Oden, *The Word of Life*, 451.

[539]McDowell, *Evidence that Demands a Verdict*, 241-270.

Jesus did not rise from the dead even before hearing the evidence.[540]

Classic modernism rejects the resurrection as a non-event. Modern theologians tend to reinterpret the resurrection as mythical, mental, or a leap of faith. Thus, they can affirm the resurrection, but assign a mystical or symbolic meaning to the term. They claim the resurrection was a real event, but it was not historically in space and time. By removing the resurrection from the material world they are trying to avoid conflict with science. In doing so they create two types of truth: scientific truth and religious truth. In the process they end up denying the Christian faith.[541]

Bultmann said the resurrection is an inner spiritual experience of being lifted which the hearer experiences when the resurrection is preached.[542]

Barth could not say that the resurrection was a historic actuality. In his dialectic approach he appears to affirm the resurrection, then deny it. Barth claimed that the resurrection of Jesus Christ was bodily, corporeal, and real, then claimed that it cannot be explained in historical terms. In 1962 Carl Henry asked Barth, in the presence of several reporters, whether anything that happened the first Easter morning would have warranted a news item by the reporters. After listening to Barth's circumlocutory reply, the United Press religion editor told Henry, "We got the message; it was No."[543] While Barth said we must accept it by faith anyway, Paul wrote that if Christ has not been raised, your faith is futile (1 Cor 15:17).

---

[540]Oden, *After Modernity*, 124.

[541]Van Til, *Christianity and Barthianism*, 92-113.

[542]Bultmann, "New Testament and Mythology," 42.

[543]Henry, *Confessions of a Theologian*, 211.

Tillich said the resurrection was a spiritual presence which occurred in the minds of the disciples.[544] Hans Küng taught that his resurrection consisted of a different mode of existence. The resurrection of Jesus consisted of the memories his disciples retain about him or the message they preached about him or the life of his spiritual body, the church.[545] The Jehovah's Witnesses teach that Christ was raised from the dead as an immortal spirit person.[546] Thus, there is not much difference between the cults and modernist theology, except that the modernists hold more academic clout.

The resurrected body of Christ had flesh and bone (Luke 24:39). It retained the same physical scars (John 20:25). It is recorded on four occasions that Jesus ate food after his resurrection. Twice it is recorded that someone touched him. He encouraged his disciples to touch his wounds (Luke 24:39; John 20:27).

The resurrection is not only celebrated at Easter, but each Sunday service provides a continuing testimony of the resurrection. The phrase *the first day of the week* was not found until utilized by the Gospel writers (Matt 28:1; Mark 16:2,9; Luke 24:1; John 20:1,19; Acts 20:7; 1 Cor 16:2).

The resurrection was accepted as the firstfruits of the general resurrection (1 Cor 15:20; Col 1:18). As the first eschatological act, the sting of death has been removed and the grave has been robbed of its finality (1 Cor 15:55). The resurrection of Christ means:

• His deity is demonstrated. He was "declared with power to be the Son of God by his resurrection from the dead" (Rom 1:4).

---

[544]Tillich, *Systematic Theology*, 2:157.

[545]Küng, *On Being a Christian*, 349-350; *Eternal Life?*, 105.

[546]See Gruss, *Apostles of Denial*, 87-89; Martin, *Kingdom of the Cults*, 58-59; 97-98.

- The OT prophecies, such as Psalm 16:10, 30:3, 41:10, 118:17; Hosea 6:2, concerning his resurrection were fulfilled. Thus, his Messianic Sonship is ratified.
- The Davidic promise is fulfilled (Acts 2:29-31).
- His prophetic teaching is ratified (Mark 8:31).
- As our high priest, his resurrection sealed and confirmed the salvation purchased at the cross.
- As our king, his authority over death and the grave was demonstrated. He holds the keys of death and hades (Rev 1:18).
- His suffering is vindicated.
- God accepts his sacrificial offering.
- His victory over sin is demonstrated. He destroyed the devil's work (1 John 3:8).
- His authority is made clear (Matt 28:28).
- His resurrection gives us life. The Spirit of him who raised Jesus from the dead is living in us (Rom 8:11). The new birth is our spiritual resurrection (John 5:24-25).
- He became the firstfruits of the general resurrection. "So in Christ will all be made alive" (1 Cor 15:20-23).
- His resurrection gives us a preview of God's eternal purpose. The fulfillment of the ages has come to us (1 Cor 10:11). The future has invaded the present. The resurrection marks the turning point of the ages. We are now at the end of the ages (Heb 9:26).

Athanasius wrote,

Or how, if He be not risen but is dead, does He drive away, and pursue, and cast down those false gods said by the unbelievers to be alive, and the demons they worship? For where Christ is named, and His faith, there all idolatry is deposed and all imposture of evil spirits is exposed, and any spirit is unable to endure even the name, nay even on barely hearing it flies and disappears. But this work is not that of one dead, but of one that lives — and especially of God.[547]

• His ascension and session

Jesus appeared on earth for forty days after his resurrection. Then he ascended back to heaven with the same body in which he suffered death (Acts 1:9-11). "He who descended is the very one who ascended higher than all the heavens" (Eph 4:10).

The descent of the Spirit was the result of the ascent of Christ. He had promised to send the Holy Spirit (John 14:16-18, 16:7). "Exalted to the right hand of God, he has received from the Father the promised Holy Spirit and has poured out what you now see and hear" (Acts 2:33).

King David wrote of the resurrection and session of Christ in Psalm 2. The nations rage and Satan roars, but God laughs at all humanistic schemes. Their rebellion against God is specifically directed against his Anointed One. The Hebrew word for *anointed* is (*mashiach* - Messiah); the Greek equivalent is (*christos* - Christ).

No name is any more hated by the world than Lord Jesus Christ. But God was undaunted. He has installed Christ as King. The inauguration of Christ's kingdom occurred after his resurrection. Although the text, "You are my Son; today I have become your Father" is often misused by false teachers to prove Jesus was a created being, this is not a description of his creation, but his resurrection (see Acts 13:33). The writer of Hebrews puts the verse into its correct context. "After he had provided purification for sins, he sat down at the right hand of the Majesty in heaven." He became superior to the angels, for "to which of the angels did God ever say, 'You are my Son; today I have become your Father?'" (Heb 1:3-5). Verse 8 pinpoints the resurrection of Christ as the time he became king.

---

[547]Athanasius, *Incarnation of the Word*, NPNF2 4:452.

His kingdom was not postponed until his second advent, as John Darby first began to teach in 1830. Peter Craigie commented, "'Today' points to the fact that the words were announced on the coronation day, the day on which the divine decree became effective."[548] Acts 13:33 clearly connects that day with the resurrection of Christ.

At the coronation of Christ, at the Father's right hand, the Father gave his Son an inaugural gift. He decreed, "Ask of me, and I will make the nations your inheritance, the ends of the earth your possession. You will rule them with an iron scepter; you will dash them to pieces like pottery" (Ps 2:7-9). The Father has given the Son the nations for his inheritance and the ends of the earth for his possession. He was promised this at his resurrection (Acts 13:33) and he took possession of it at his session. His commission is to make the domain of Yahweh visible on earth. As we go into all the world and preach the gospel we declare the crown rights of King Jesus. Christ is sovereign, and all who reject his lordship live in confusion. All conspiracies will fail because God has predestined his own plan.

The OT verse most frequently quoted in the NT is Psalm 110:1, "The Lord says to my Lord: 'Sit at my right hand until I make your enemies a footstool for your feet.'" Jesus claimed this was as a reference to him in Luke 22:69.

In Acts 2 Peter explained the significance of Pentecost was that Jesus had been resurrected, he had ascended to the right hand of God where he was made Lord, and he had poured out the Holy Spirit as proof of his lordship. In the context (v 34) Peter cites Psalm 110:1.

This, then, describes the present work of Jesus Christ. He is seated upon the throne of universal authority and has been since his resurrection and session. By faith we accept the teaching of Scripture that everything will someday be brought under the lordship of Christ. "In putting everything under him, God left

---

[548]Craigie, *WBC* 19:67.

nothing that is not subject to him. Yet at present we do not see everything subject to him" (Heb 2:8). Paul said, "He must reign until he has put all his enemies under his feet. The last enemy to be destroyed is death." He will hand the kingdom over to the Father after he "has destroyed all dominion, authority and power" (1 Cor 15:24-26). Therefore, Christ will not return to rescue a defeated church. He sits on his throne until the battle is won. However, since Christ is omnipresent, his physical location is relatively unimportant. Christ rules from the heavenly Zion (Ps 110:2).

The extent of his authority is what is crucial. John Jefferson Davis grasped this concept when he wrote, "Christ remains in heaven while his foes are being subdued and until that process is complete. . . . Christ does not need to be physically present on earth to subdue his spiritual foes; this he does while still at the Father's right hand in heaven."[549] The right hand of God is the right hand of power according to Matthew 26:64; Mark 14:62; Luke 22:69. This is the inheritance of Christ (Acts 2:36).

Daniel 7:9-14 describes the ascension and session of Jesus Christ. In Matthew 26:64 Jesus identified himself as the Son of Man in Daniel 7:13. Daniel 7:13-14 describes the ascension of Jesus as he returns to heaven. Christ approached the Ancient of Days and was given authority, glory, and sovereign power; all peoples, nations, and men of every language worshiped him. His dominion is an everlasting dominion that will not pass away, and his kingdom is one that will never be destroyed.

The Ancient of Days ruled in favor of Christ and against the claims of Satan. During the first century Satan tried to stop the church; but he was bound, and the kingdoms of the world were handed over to the saints. Since the kingdom of God was established, there will be no revived Roman empire. Ephesians 1:20-22 tells us that the seat of Christ is the center of universal authority.

---

[549]Davis, *Christ's Victorious Kingdom*, 33.

- **His second advent**

Christ will return in power and glory at the end of the age to conclude history, raise the dead, judge the world, and restore all things. This doctrine will be discussed under eschatology.

The present work of Christ
- **His work of intercession**

"Christ Jesus . . . is at the right hand of God and is also interceding for us" (Rom 8:34). "He always lives to intercede for them" (Heb 7:25). "We have one who speaks to the Father in our defense — Jesus Christ, the Righteous One" (1 John 2:1).

Wesley wrote, "All our blessings, temporal, spiritual, and eternal, depend on his intercession for us, which is one branch of his priestly office, whereof therefore we have always equal need."[550]

- **His work of preparation**

"I am going there to prepare a place for you" (John 14:2). Heaven is more than a state of mind. It is a place (*topos*).

- **His work of administration**

"God has made this Jesus, whom you crucified, both Lord and Christ" (Acts 2:36). "That power is like the working of his mighty strength, which he exerted in Christ when he raised him from the dead and seated him at his right hand in the heavenly realms, far above all rule and authority, power and dominion, and every title that can be given, not only in the present age but also in the one to come. And God placed all things under his feet and appointed him to be head over everything for the church" (Eph

---

[550]Wesley, *BE Works*, 13:169.

1:19-22). Thus, he is the head of the new covenant. He is the fulfillment of the old covenant promises. "In him we have both continuity with the old forms of the covenant, and an open door to the fullness of what God is doing in the future of redemption."[551]

Jesus Christ is the only physician who can cure his patients by taking on their disease. Wesley described Jesus as a healer of the soul. He preached, "Know your disease! Know your cure! Ye were born in sin; therefore 'ye must be born again', 'born of God.' Now 'go on' 'from faith to faith', until your whole sickness be healed."[552]

"To the only God our Savior be glory, majesty, power, and authority, through Jesus Christ our Lord, before all ages, now and forevermore!" (Jude 25).

The Future Work of Christ

His second advent will accomplish six things:
- The second advent of Christ will reveal his glory.

"Look, he is coming with the clouds, and every eye will see him, even those who pierced him; and all the peoples of the earth will mourn because of him" (Rev 1:7). "At the name of Jesus every knee should bow, in heaven and on earth and under the earth, and every tongue confess that Jesus Christ is Lord, to the glory of God the Father" (Phil 2:10-11).

The second coming of Christ will mean nothing less than the disclosure to the world of the sovereignty and lordship which is already his. He is now the Lord; he is now reigning at the right hand of God. However, his present reign is seen only by the eye of faith. It is un-

---

[551]Kelly, *Systematic Theology*, 2:61.

[552]Wesley, "Original Sin," Sermon #44, 3.5.

seen and unrecognized by the world. His second advent will mean the unveiling — the revelation — the disclosure of the lordship which is already his. It will mean "the appearing of the glory of our great God and Savior Jesus Christ" (Titus 2:13).[553]

- The second advent of Christ will complete salvation.

"He will appear a second time, not to bear sin, but to bring salvation to those who are waiting for him" (Heb 9:28).

- The second advent of Christ will overthrow the world system.

"And then the lawless one will be revealed, whom the Lord Jesus will overthrow with the breath of his mouth and destroy by the splendor of his coming" (2 Thess 2:8).

- The second advent of Christ will establish a new heaven and earth.

"But in keeping with his promise we are looking forward to a new heaven and a new earth, the home of righteousness" (2 Pet 3:13).

- The second advent of Christ will raise the dead.

"A time is coming when all who are in their graves will hear his voice and come out — those who have done good will rise to live, and those who have done evil will rise to be condemned" (John 5:28-29). "For the Lord himself will come down from heaven, with a loud command, with the voice of the archangel and with the trumpet call of God, and the dead in Christ will rise first" (1 Thess 4:16).

- The second advent of Christ will judge the world.

"For the Son of Man is going to come in his Father's glory with his angels, and then he will reward each person according to what he has done" (Matt 16:27; see also 25:31-46). "Moreover, the Father judges no one, but has entrusted all judgment to the Son" (John 5:22). "For he has set a day when he will judge the world with justice by the man he has appointed. He has given

---

[553]Ladd, "Historic Premillennialism," 32.

proof of this to all men by raising him from the dead" (Acts 17:31). "For we must all appear before the judgment seat of Christ, that each one may receive what is due him for the things done while in the body, whether good or bad" (2 Cor 5:10).

The Three Offices of Christ

Isaiah 33:22 describes God as our judge, lawgiver, and king. Eusebius, in the fourth century, first elucidated Christ as prophet, priest, and king. Thus, as we seek to become all that God has purposed for us, our focus should not be upon ourselves but upon Christ in all his offices. If we focus on our performance, the emphasis will be upon sanctification by works.

- **Christ is our Prophet**

Christ is the fulfillment of OT prophecy. In his incarnation, Christ appeared first as a teacher in his prophetic office. A prophet reveals God to man. He speaks for God. Christ is the final prophet, revealing to us the whole will of God. Scripture declares that he was a prophet. "He was a prophet, powerful in word and deed before God and the people" (Luke 24:19). "Surely this is the Prophet who is to come into the world" (John 6:14). "In the past God spoke to our forefathers through the prophets at many times and in various ways, but in these last days he has spoken to us by his Son" (Heb 1:1-2).

Thus, Christ is the final revelation of God. On the Emmaus Road Jesus began with Moses and all the prophets, explaining everything they said concerning him (Luke 24:27, 44). Jesus declared that the Scriptures testify concerning him (John 5:39,46). He is the "key to knowledge" (Luke 11:52). Martin Luther referred to Christ as the "star and kernel" of Scripture, "the center part of the circle" about which everything else re-volves.[554]

Christ has not been superceded by Mohammed. Christ was the last prophet and the first preacher of the gospel. Christ is our Moses who enlightens us through his teaching concerning the law of God (Acts 7:37). He did not abolish the moral law, but clarified it. According to John 4:25, he explained everything to us. He reveals truth through his words and his deeds. He himself is truth.

His prophetic office continues in the church through the work of the Spirit. Yet the living, active, revealing Christ does not contradict Scripture. It is misleading to distinguish between the Jesus portrayed in Scripture and the Jesus who is Lord of Scripture.

According to 2 Corinthians 11:4 there are other Jesuses. We dare not separate the living Word from the written Word. His teaching was confirmed by his miracles.

In healing the blind, Jesus demonstrated that he is the Light of the World. In feeding the multitudes, he demonstrated that he is the Bread of Life. In turning the water into wine, he demonstrated that he is the True Vine. In raising the dead, he demonstrated that he is the Resurrection and the Life. In his general healing ministry, he demonstrated that he is the Messiah who would heal Israel's backslidings.[555]

- **Christ is our Priest**

As Christ moved into Passion Week, he assumed his role as our priest. He is the Lamb of God who takes away the sins of the world, and he is a priest forever. He gave himself a sacrifice for sin and still makes intercession for transgressors. Even on the

---

[554]Olsen, "The Christ Alone," 6.

[555]Gregg, *All the King's Men*, 104.

cross, he continued his ministry of pardon and reconciliation (Luke 23:39-43).

In Luke 22:32 Jesus prayed for Peter. But in John 17:20, "My prayer is not for them alone [his original disciples]. I pray also for those who will believe in me through their message." In 1 John 2:1 we are told, "My dear children, I write this to you so that you will not sin. But if anybody does sin, we have one who speaks to the Father in our defense — Jesus Christ, the Righteous One." He is our advocate (*parakletos*) — our attorney. In John 14-16, Jesus uses this same term four times to describe the Holy Spirit. "The Lord has sworn and will not change his mind: You are a priest forever" (Heb 7:21; see also v 17).

A priest represents man to God and makes atonement for the sins of the people. The two main responsibilities associated with the priesthood of Christ — reconciling men to God by his blood and making living intercession for us. The book of Hebrews teaches in four passages that Jesus is the mediator of a new covenant (8:8-13, 9:15, 10:20, 12:24).

The atoning work of Christ involved both his deity and his humanity. As God, he became our great High Priest offering satisfaction for our sins. This is his active obedience. As the God-man, he also became our substitutionary sacrifice. This is his passive obedience.

It is significant that Christ was not a priest under the order of Levi, but of Melchizedek (Heb 5:6,10, 6:20, 7:1,10-11,15,17). Melchizedek was a priest in his own right and not by virtue of his relationships with others. He was a priest forever, without substitution or succession. He was not anointed with oil, but with the Holy Spirit. He did not offer animal sacrifices, but bread and wine, symbols of the Supper which Christ later instituted. And he joined together the office of king and priest.

The claim of the Church of Jesus Christ of Latter-Day Saints as the only true church on the earth today rests on its declaration that it alone is the custodian of the "Melchizedek priesthood," a priestly order that God supposedly withdrew from the world sometime after the passing of the NT apostles. Mormons believe this priesthood is something the early church had and that has now been "restored" through Joseph Smith. Yet there is no emphasis on Jesus Christ as our heavenly high priest. Instead, the Mormon view of priesthood emphasizes its religious ordinances and offices, promoting the Mormon Church hierarchy as a system for magnifying one's own spiritual worthiness.[556]

It is also a function of the priest to bless the people. The prototype was the Aaronic benediction in Numbers 6:22-27. As our high priest, Christ has blessed us in the heavenly realms with every spiritual blessing (Eph 1:3).

- **Christ is our King**

A king rules over the people. At his resurrection Christ assumed his role as king. He has conquered Satan, sin, and death. "Rabbi, you are the Son of God; you are the King of Israel" (John 1:49). "King of Kings and Lord of Lords" (Rev 19:16).

Christ won the victory in principle through his atonement. His ultimate victory at the last day is certain. Christ is a king, who has all power in heaven and earth and will reign till he has subdued all things to himself. The kingdoms of this world have legally become and are increasingly becoming the kingdoms of our God and of his Christ (Rev 11:15).

The Coalition on Revival attempted to draft a statement in 1989 on the kingdom of God and the nature of God's reign. However, they could not agree over whether Christ or Satan is the ruler of this world! What could cause conservative Bible scholars to arrive at such different conclusions? "At the center of the dispute was the issue of whether Christ is reigning over the whole world today, or if his reign is limited to the church."[557]

---

[556]See *Gospel Principles*, chapter 13-14.

[557]Frame, "Is Christ or Satan Ruler of This World?" 42-44.

The reign of Christ began at his ascension. "In putting every-thing under him, God left nothing that is not subject to him. Yet at present we do not see everything subject to him" (Heb 2:8).

"Why was not the Holy Ghost given till Jesus Christ was glorified? Because," answered Whitefield, "till then, he was himself on the earth, and had not taken on him the kingly office, nor pleaded the merits of his death before his heavenly Father, by which he purchased that invaluable blessing for us."[558]

Jesus Christ *is* king and will reign until he has subdued all things to himself. David's fallen tent was restored at the first advent (Amos 9:11).

Modernism emphasizes his teaching, but not his atonement. The social gospel has reduced his kingship to social justice, while holding that he erred in his teaching. Conservatives have emphasized salvation at the expense of his kingdom.

---

[558]Fletcher, *Works*, 2:560.

CHAPTER FOUR
The Doctrine of the Holy Spirit

The Holy Spirit is a divine person, distinct from the Father and the Son. He was involved in creation and inspired the human authors who wrote Holy Scripture. Before Pentecost he came upon special people at special times for special purposes.

Today he is the administrator of redemption. He awakens the sinner and draws him to Christ. He enables the sinner to repent and believe on the Lord Jesus Christ for salvation. He regenerates the believer, giving new life. He brings assurance of our forgiveness and adoption in the family of God. He baptizes us into the body of Christ and gives us spiritual gifts through which we are equipped to minister. He teaches the new Christian and leads him into all truth. He also preserves truth within the catholic church and frequently brings revival. He is always present to anoint the Word of God when it is preached. He helps us when we are weak and helps us pray. He produces spiritual fruit in our lives. He leads us on to Christian perfection. When Christ returns he will raise us from the dead. Therefore, we are warned not to grieve or quench his work. We are also warned not to blaspheme his ministry since he is God's only agent of salvation.

- **The Holy Spirit is given divine titles**

The Holy Spirit is a divine person, distinct from the Father and the Son. He is called *God* (Acts 5:3-4). By definition, only

God can be blasphemed. Since we are warned against blaspheming the Holy Spirit (Matt 12:31; Mark 3:29; Luke 12:10), he must be God. A comparison of 1 Corinthians 3:16-17 with 6:19-20 reveals that to be indwelt by the Holy Spirit is to be indwelt by God. In 2 Corinthians 3:17-18 he is called *Lord* (*kurios*) three times. According to Judges 15:14 "the Spirit of the Lord" is the Spirit of Yahweh. As we have also seen, the LXX translated the Hebrew word *Yahweh* as *kurios* over six thousand times. In the NT *kurios* was used interchangeably with *theos*.[559]

- **OT passages referring to God are appropriated to refer to the Holy Spirit.**

There are also OT passages which refer to Yahweh, quoted in the NT and applied to the Holy Spirit. Isaiah 6:9 cites the voice of the Lord (*adonai*). His statement is quoted in Acts 28:25 as coming from the Holy Spirit.

The word declared by the Lord (*Yahweh*) in Jeremiah 31:33-34 is quoted in Hebrews 10:15-17 as the testimony of the Holy Spirit.

- **The Holy Spirit is described with divine attributes**

The Holy Spirit is described as having attributes which are non-communicable. He is *omnipresent*. "Where can I go from your Spirit? Where can I flee from your presence?" (Ps 139:7-10).

The Holy Spirit is *omniscient*. "The Spirit searches all things, even the deep things of God" (1 Cor 2:10-11). Jesus acknowledged his foreknowledge in John 16:13, "He will tell you what is to come."

Zechariah 4:6 declares, "Not by might, nor by power, but by my Spirit, says the Lord Almighty." If the Holy Spirit is the Spirit of Yahweh-Sabaoth, then the Holy Spirit is *omnipotent*.

---

[559]Foerster, "κύριος," *TDNT* 3:1062, 1086-1094.

Several verses promise the power of the Spirit to believers without specifically stating that he has *all* power. But the omnipotence of the Spirit is a logical inference if he has power to give away to untold millions of believers.

The Holy Spirit is called the *eternal* Spirit (Heb 9:14). Four times in Revelation he is described as the sevenfold Spirit (1:4, 3:1, 4:5, 5:6). The one Holy Spirit is described in his completeness in Isaiah 11:2-3 as the Spirit of the Lord, the Spirit of wisdom and of understanding, the Spirit of counsel and of power, the Spirit of knowledge and of the fear of the Lord. It is sometimes objected that the Hebrew text only contains a sixfold description. It is the LXX that adds the seventh word — *godliness*.

- **The Holy Spirit performs divine actions**

The Spirit also performs divine works. In *creation* "the Spirit of God was hovering over the waters" (Gen 1:2). The Hebrew word for spirit is *ruach*. It can mean breath or air. A related Hebrew word, *neshamah*, also can mean *breath*. In Genesis 2:7, God breathed into man the *neshamah* of life. "The Spirit of God has made me; the breath *neshamah* of the Almighty gives me life" (Job 33:4). According to Psalm 33:6 the heavens were made by the word of the Lord, "their starry host by the breath (*ruach*) of his mouth." According to Psalm 104:30 the Holy Spirit creates and renews.

His presence pervades the OT, yet in the NT he is revealed more fully. He inspired the prophets and apostles. "Men spoke from God as they were carried along by the Holy Spirit" (2 Pet 1:21). This *inspiration*, according to 2 Timothy 3:16, means *God-breathed*.

Hebrews 3:7 cites Psalm 95:7-11, which was written by David, as spoken by the Spirit. The book of Hebrews never credits any citation to its human author except 4:7, in order to point out the time lapse from exodus to David.

Christ was made alive by the Spirit (1 Pet 3:18). In the *general resurrection*, the Spirit who raised Jesus from the dead will also give life to our mortal bodies.

The Holy Spirit is the administrator of redemption. In *regeneration* we are born of the Spirit (John 3:5-6). This renewal is by the Holy Spirit (Titus 3:5).

As confirmation of his ascension and session, Jesus Christ sent the Spirit on the day of Pentecost. After the Son ascended to the Father, the Spirit descended to the disciples. Pope explained, "The Pentecostal gift of the Holy Ghost was at once the immediate proof of the verity of the ascension, and the demonstration of the authority to which it led."[560]

The Eastern church contends that the Holy Spirit proceeds from the Father alone and that the phrase *and the Son* in the Nicene Creed is without ecumenical consensus. In their theology the Spirit is sent from the Father through the Son. They contend for the sole rule of the Father.

Galatians 4:6 teaches that God sends the Spirit of his Son into our hearts. According to John 14:16 Jesus would ask the Father and he would give another Comforter, the Spirit of truth. In John 14:26 the Father would send the Holy Spirit in the name of Jesus. In John 15:26, Jesus would send the Spirit who proceeds from the Father. The Latin word *filioque* means *and the Son*. This *filioque* controversy was the result of the words *and the Son* added to the Nicene Creed in 589 and was a factor in the great schism between the East and West in 1054.[561] The Greeks were not averse to saying that the Holy Spirit proceeded from the Father *through* the Son, but objected to saying that he proceeds from the Father *and the Son*.

However, the Western church, beginning with Augustine, teaches that the Spirit proceeds from both the Father and the Son. In John 16:15 Jesus declared that everything that belongs to the

---

[560]Pope, *Compendium*, 2:182.

[561]Oden, *ACD* 4:217-234.

Father is also his. In John 20:22 Jesus gave the Holy Spirit to his disciples. According to Acts 2:33, Christ received the promised Holy Spirit from the Father and poured him out.

Schaff pointed out that the *double* procession, from the Father and the Son, is the inevitable consequence from the Father and Son being of the same essence and from the identity of the Spirit of God and the Spirit of Christ. It connects the Trinity and Christology, also connecting Christ and mankind by bringing the Holy Spirit and his work into more immediate connection with Christ, and through Christ with the church and the believer. It was opposed, however, by the Arians, who wanted to keep Christ subordinate to the Father.[562]

The Personhood of the Holy Spirit

The Holy Spirit is referred to by personal pronouns. The Greek word for *Spirit* is *pneuma*, which is a neuter noun. Yet the masculine pronoun is used of the Spirit in John 14:26, 15:26, 16:7. In other references the pronoun *it* is used because in those cases the rules of grammar demand that the noun and pronoun agree.

Jesus describes the Holy Spirit as the *parakletos* four times: John 14:16,26, 15:26, 16:7. In 1 John 2:1 Jesus is himself called *parakletos*. This Greek word means *one called alongside to help*, and is translated *advocate, intercessor, encourager, helper, counselor, comforter, guide*, or even *defense attorney*.

In John 14:16-18 Jesus promises another *parakletos*, the Holy Spirit. In Greek there are two words for *another*. The first word, *hetros*, is another of a different kind and the second is *allos*, another of the same kind. This second word is used in John 14. Jesus promises another paraclete just like himself. If Jesus is a person, so the Holy Spirit must also be a person.

---

[562]Schaff, *History of the Christian Church*, 3:684-689.

With the Paschal Discourse in our heart and mind, we know that it was He, not It, who "brooded" over the primeval deep. He, not It, "strove with man," or "ruled in man" of old. He, not It, was in Joseph in Egypt, and upon Moses in the wilderness of wandering, and upon judges and kings of after-days. He, not It, "spake by the prophets," "moving" those holy men of God. He, not It, drew the plan of the ancient Tabernacle and of the first Temple. He, not It, lifted Ezekiel to his feet in the hour of vision. He, not It, came upon the Virgin, and anointed her Son at Jordan and led Him to the desert of temptation, and gave utterance to the saints at Pentecost, and caught Philip away from the road to Gaza, and guided Paul through Asia Minor to the nearest port for Europe. He, not It, effects the new birth of regenerate man, and is the Breath of his new life, and the Earnest of his coming glory. By him, not by It, the believer walks, and mortifies the deeds of the body, filled not with It, but Him. He, not It, is the Spirit of faith, by whom it is "given unto us to believe on Christ." He, not It, speaks to the Churches. He, not It, says from heaven that they who die in the Lord are blessed, and calls in this life upon the wandering soul of man to come to the living water.[563]

Therefore, the Holy Spirit should not be referred to as *it*. Modernist unitarians believe the Spirit of God is simply the power, influence, or activity of God. Unitarian Pentecostals teach that Jesus is the Holy Spirit. Jehovah's Witnesses define the Holy Spirit as "the invisible active force of Almighty God which moves His servants to do His will."[564] Throughout their *New World Translation* the word *spirit* is not capitalized when refer-

---

[563]Moule, *Veni Creator*, 8-11.

[564]Gruss, *Apostles of Denial*, 121.

ring to the Holy Spirit. Christian Scientists also deny the personality and deity of the Spirit.

The Holy Spirit exhibits personal attributes and actions. He can speak, be vexed, grieved, pleased, teach, guide, console, intercede, testify, be tempted, lied against, and blasphemed.

The Holy Spirit Before Pentecost

Much as Jesus Christ was concealed in the old covenant yet was at work, so the Holy Spirit was also at work before Pentecost. Oden wrote,

> The Spirit has never altogether left fallen human history, but the ministry of the Spirit glimpsed through law and prophets was proleptic, occasional, special, and anticipatory of full indwelling of the Spirit to be clarified through future events. The Holy Spirit is the coordinator and economizer of the gift of redemption both before and after the resurrection. The indwelling of the Spirit becomes a historical event only after the ascension of the Son.[565]

The OT references to the Holy Spirit may be divided into three categories. *First*, there are references to the Spirit's general activity in the world, such as his creative work depicted in Genesis 1:2, where he *hovered* or *brooded* over the waters.

Second are references which speak of God acting through specific people. Frequently the Holy Spirit came upon a leader and gave him supernatural power. George Lyons observed that the experience of the Spirit was "an intermittent and temporary endowment of a few specially favored individuals given to them

---

[565]Oden, *Life in the Spirit*, 50.

to deal with a specific crisis."[566] The Spirit came upon chosen people, enduing them with special spiritual, intellectual, and physical gifts. Such men as Balaam, Saul, Samson, and Cyrus had a special anointing of the Spirit, but their lives did not necessarily demonstrate ethical holiness.

There are around a hundred direct references to the Spirit in the OT. Approximately seventy-five, or about three-fourths, of the total references to the Spirit in the OT describe him as influencing men externally, and in some cases at least, using them instrumentally. On the other hand, only approximately one-fourth of the references to the Spirit in the OT represent him as in some manner inhabiting man internally, though not necessarily permanently.[567]

Under the old covenant, the Holy Spirit came upon special people at special times for special purposes. However, in the last days he is poured out on *all* people (Joel 2:28). "Not many people in the Old Testament are said to have actually known the Lord. In those days it was rather an aspiration . . . the new covenant would . . . bring all God's people into a personal knowledge of him."[568]

Robert Tuttle concluded,

In effect, there were no Christians prior to Pentecost. Oh, there were people in right relationship with God, but there were no Christians, as such, since to be a Christian is not only to be a descendant of Abraham; but, once again, to be baptized by the Holy Spirit into

---

[566]Lyons, "The Spirit in the Gospels," 34. Dunning made a very similar statement in *Grace, Faith, and Holiness*, 401-402.

[567]Carter, *Person and Ministry*, 83; 60.

[568]Morris, *The Atonement*, 29.

the body of Jesus Christ, *his Church*, and empowered to bear fruit.[569]

The *third* category of references to the Holy Spirit in the OT relates to the prophecies of a new age of the Spirit.[570] The OT prophets predicted the outpouring of the Spirit, although they did not witness that outpouring.[571] In the NT the metaphor changes from *outpouring* to *baptism*. Prior to John the Baptist, *baptism* was never used in this context.

During the transitional period in the life of Christ, the Holy Spirit had a unique role in the life of Christ. He was instrumental in the conception of Christ (Luke 1:35). He anointed Christ at baptism (Luke 3:22). He led and empowered Christ (Luke 4:1-19). Jesus cast out demons by the Spirit of God (Matt 12:28). The Spirit raised Jesus from the dead (Rom 8:11). According to John 3:34, Jesus had the Holy Spirit without limits, unlike the prophets before him.

Yet in his special role under the Christian economy, the Holy Spirit was not given until Pentecost. Along with the writer of Hebrews, Wesley understood that NT experience was better than the religious experience described in the OT.[572] He felt the "wide difference there is between the Jewish and the Christian dispensation was important to notice."[573] He asked,

Has there not been *a larger measure* of the Holy Spirit given under the gospel than under the Jewish dispensa-

---

[569]Tuttle, *Sanctity without Starch*, 111.

[570]Greathouse, *Fullness of the Spirit*, 41-46.

[571]For example, see Isa 32:15,44:3; Ezek 39:25-29; Joel 2:28-29.

[572]Wesley, *Notes*, 583.

[573]Wesley, "Christian Perfection," Sermon #40, 2.11.

tion? If not, in what sense was "the Spirit not given before Christ was glorified?"[574]

The least person in the kingdom of heaven has greater privilege than John the Baptist (Matt 11:11). The significance of Pentecost is the inauguration of the new covenant. To be filled with the Spirit was not the common privilege of OT saints.

The contrast between the old and the new is stated by Jesus, "He lives with you and will be in you" (John 14:17). In Psalm 51:11, David's prayer for God not to take away his Holy Spirit from David meant that David did not want to lose his crown. According to 1 Samuel 16:13, when David was anointed as king the Spirit came upon him. This was the normal operation of the Holy Spirit in the OT. There was a special anointing of the Spirit for leaders. As the "anointed one," David was a type of the coming King, the Messiah. It is significant that 1 Samuel 16:14 records the Spirit had departed from Saul. If David was anointed because Saul was rejected (16:1), then for David to lose the anointing would mean that he, too, was rejected as king.

In 2 Corinthians 3:6-11 Paul explains the differences before and after Pentecost. The old administration was of the letter, based on the fact that God literally wrote it on the two tables of stone. The Mosaic dispensation resulted in condemnation and death. Thus, the people of God lived in anticipation of a Savior. The new administration is the gospel, administered through the Spirit, based on life and righteousness.

The Ministry of the Spirit in the New Covenant

In John 14-16 Jesus explained that after his departure the Holy Spirit would represent him. According to John 7:39, the Holy Spirit would not be given until Jesus was glorified. "Here

[574]Wesley, *BE Works*, 13:181,147.

we see a clear reference to Pentecost as the time when those who would follow Christ are born of water and the Spirit."[575]

In the prophetic office of Christ as teacher, the Holy Spirit would function as the Spirit of truth. He would interpret the mystery of the person of Christ, reminding, expounding, and enlarging upon Christ's teachings. Thus, he bears witness to the truth, convicting the sinner, awakening the desire for salvation, revealing the promises of grace to the penitent, assuring the believer of his acceptance, and progressively unfolding the knowledge of Christ.

Daniel Steele called the Holy Spirit "the conservator of orthodoxy." After listing fundamental Christian doctrines, he argued that doctrine is not conserved merely by requiring sub-scription to an orthodox statement of doctrine. According to 1 John 2:20-27, the anointing of the Holy Spirit is our safeguard. The Greek word translated *anointing* or *unction* (*chrisma*) occurs three times in the NT, in 1 John 2:20 and twice in v 27. In the OT, only the prophets, priests, and kings were anointed. In the NT, every believer is a priest. Therefore, we *all* have an anointing. The Holy Spirit in the believer preserves, vitalizes, and makes real to the consciousness all the essential truths of the gospel.[576]

Latourette analyzed church history through the paradigm of 2 Corinthians 4:7. The institutional church is an imperfect earthen vessel or clay jar, but it contains the power of God. Latourette reported the good, the bad, and the ugly. Even on her best days, the church has been imperfect; but even on her worst days the power of God was still at work.

The Holy Spirit has been described as the executive of the Godhead.[577] He also has a unique role in our salvation. Salvation

---

[575]Bloesch, *Holy Spirit*, 305.

[576]Steele, *Gospel of the Comforter*, 272-274.

[577]Apparently the term was coined by Charles Hodge, for which he was congratulated by Daniel Steele [*Gospel of the Comforter*, 31; *Mile-*

was planned by the Father and purchased by the Son, but it is administered through the Spirit. When Jesus declared "It is finished," his work of atonement was accomplished; but the application of the benefit remains the administration of the Holy Spirit. Thus, the Holy Spirit perpetuates the priestly office of Christ in his ministry of reconciliation. "God chose you to be saved through the sanctifying work of the Spirit" (2 Thess 2:13).

- The Spirit awakens and convicts us. "When he comes, he will convict the world of guilt in regard to sin and righteousness and judgment" (John 16:8-11). Thus, the Holy Spirit represents Christ to the world.
- No one can come to Christ unless the Father draws and enables him (John 6:44, 65).

The Father draws and enables by the Holy Spirit. The Holy Spirit calls out the universal church of Jesus Christ. This church is united through the grace of the Lord Jesus Christ, and the love of God, and the fellowship of the Holy Spirit (2 Cor 13:14). This benediction, along with the Matthew 28:19 baptismal formula, puts the Holy Spirit on an equal basis with the Father and the Son, implying his deity.

- The Spirit enables us to repent. "God granted even the Gentiles repentance unto life" (Acts 11:18; see also 5:31). "God will grant them repentance" (2 Tim 2:25).
- The Spirit enables us to believe (Phil 1:29). The Spirit draws us to God (John 6:44,65). Faith comes from hearing the Word (Rom 10:17). Faith is the gift of God (Eph 2:8).
- The Spirit creates new life. "I will give you a new heart and put a new spirit in you . . . And I will put my spirit in you and move you to follow my decrees and be careful to keep my laws" (Ezek 36:26-27). The new birth is the birth of the

---

stone Papers, 116].

Spirit (John 3:5-8). This new life is the cleansing of all acquired pollution and renewal by the Holy Spirit (Titus 3:5). Everyone who is born again has the Holy Spirit (Rom 8:9).

- The Spirit brings assurance. "The Spirit himself testifies with our spirit that we are God's children" (Rom 8:16). "Because you are sons, God sent the Spirit of his Son into our hearts, the Spirit who calls out, Abba, Father" (Gal 4:6). "Having believed, you were marked in him with a seal, the promised Holy Spirit, who is a deposit guaranteeing our inheritance" (Eph 1:13-14; see also 4:30).
- The Spirit teaches us and leads us. "When he, the Spirit of truth, comes, he will guide you into all truth" (John 16:13). Those who live in the Spirit are to walk in the Spirit (Gal 5:25). "Those who are led by the Spirit of God are the sons of God" (Rom 8:14).

Martin Wells Knapp wrote that impressions should be tested by four criteria: Scripture, Rightness, Providence, and Reason. In a sense he utilized a quadrilateral. Divine leadership never contradicts the general principles of Scripture. God's will should not violate our conscience. His leadership is confirmed providentially. Divine impressions are always in harmony with spiritually enlightened judgment. God does not insist that we act irrationally.[578] Wesley counseled,

Beware of that daughter of pride, *enthusiasm*! O keep at the utmost distance from it. Give no place to an heated imagination. Do not hastily ascribe things to God. Do not easily suppose dreams, voices, impressions, visions, or revelations to be from God. They may be from him. They may be from nature. They may be from the devil. Therefore "believe not every spirit, but

---

[578]Knapp, *Impressions*, 52-63.

try the spirits whether they be of God." Try all things by the written Word, and let all bow down before it.[579]

- The Spirit helps us in our weaknesses (Rom 8:26). He strengthens and encourages us (Acts 9:31).
- The Spirit produces the fruit of Galatians 5:19-23
  - toward God – love, joy, peace
  - toward others – patience, kindness, goodness
  - in ourselves – faithfulness, gentleness, self-control

Wesley emphasized the fruit of the Spirit, rather than the gifts of the Spirit.[580] While Wesley was not a cessationist, he emphasized fruit over gifts, holiness over power, and character over charisma. Bloesch concluded, "It is not extraordinary gifts of the Spirit but the fruits of the Spirit that constitute the evidence of whether our conversion is genuine."[581]

Those who do not bear the fruit of the Spirit will be cut off (John 15:2). Every Christian is already clean or initially sanctified, but every branch abiding in Christ through saving faith will also be purged so that he will become more fruitful. This purging which results in more fruit is entire sanctification.

- The Spirit leads us on unto Christian perfection. A literal translation of Hebrews 6:1 reads, "Let us be led on unto perfection." Christ loved the church and gave himself for her to make her holy, cleansing her by the washing with water through the word, and to present her to himself as a radiant church, without stain or wrinkle or any other blemish, but holy and blameless" (Eph 5:25-27). This perfecting of the church was provided for by Christ, but is facilitated by the Spirit.

---

[579]Wesley, *BE Works*, 13: 112-113.

[580]Maddox, *Responsible Grace,* 136.

[581]Bloesch, *Holy Spirit*, 300.

- The Holy Spirit is the representative of Christ to his people until the second advent of Christ. Until Christ's return, the Holy Spirit is the real presence of the redeemer in his church.

Wherever the people of God assemble, the Holy Spirit is present (Matt 18:20). Wherever the Word is preached, he is there. He is present in Christian fellowship, as Christ was present in the midst of his disciples. Revelation 22:17 describes the Spirit and the church uniting as one voice to spread the kingdom of heaven upon earth.

Symbols of the Spirit

- **Water**. The Spirit is symbolized by water which cleansing, refreshing, satisfying, and is indispensable to life (Isa 44:3; John 4:14, 7:38-39).

The OT prophets predicted an early and latter rain of the Spirit. James describes the patient farmer, who waits for the early and latter rain, as an example to all Christians (5:7). Hosea promised, "As surely as the sun rises, he will appear; he will come to us like the winter [latter] rains, like the spring [former] rains that water the earth" (6:3).

Joel exclaimed, "Be glad, O people of Zion, rejoice in the Lord your God, for he has given you the autumn rains in righteousness. He sends you abundant showers, both autumn and spring rains, as before" (2:23). Joel's reference to these rains comes in the context of his great pentecostal prophecy (2:28-32). Zechariah encourages us to "ask for rain" (10:1).

The early autumn rain was needed so that the planted seed would germinate. The latter spring rain was necessary for the plant to fill out and produce fruit. The purpose of the latter rain is to guarantee an abundant harvest.

Pentecost was the early rain. Peter declared in Acts 3:19 that "times of refreshing may come from the Lord." Between the early and latter rain, there may be many times when God chooses to send revival.

If Pentecost was the early rain, we have strong basis for hope that the Holy Spirit will bring the latter rain. In fact, Hosea said this hope is as sure as the sunrise (6:3). Habakkuk declared, "The earth will be filled with the knowledge of the glory of the Lord, as the waters cover the sea" (2:14).

Just as Pentecost was the early rain which established the kingdom, the latter rain, for which we are to pray, will produce a great end time harvest of souls. "In that day the mountains will drip with new wine, and the hills will flow with milk; all the ravines of Judah will run with water. A fountain will flow out of the Lord's house and will water the valley of acacias" (Joel 3:18).

Ezekiel saw this coming kingdom as a river flowing from the temple (47:1-12). After the crucifixion of Christ and the giving of the Holy Spirit at Pentecost, God's Spirit would flow as a stream of living water from within (John 7:37-39). This prediction was made by Jesus Christ while in the old temple. A generation later that temple was destroyed. Paul taught that we are now God's temple and that God's Spirit lives in us (1 Cor 3:16-17). Therefore, we are not seeking a literal interpretation of Ezekiel 40-42, which gives the exact measurements of a temple.

Today the river of the water of life flows from the throne of God and of the Lamb (Rev 22:1). The Spirit could not be given until Christ came and made atonement. The river of the Spirit flows from the cross. We have drunk of that living water (John 4:10).

According to Ezekiel, the fresh water will flow into the Dead Sea, transforming it to fresh water and bringing it back to life. This symbolizes the transforming affect the kingdom of God will have upon the entire world. God will flood this world with his Spirit and bring healing to the nations (Ezek 37:12; Rev 22:2).

- **Wind**. Wind is unseen, yet powerful. It is the root meaning of the Hebrew word *ruah* and the Greek word *pneuma* (John 3:8; Acts 2:2). The Holy Spirit is the breath of life (Gen 2:7).

Ezekiel 37 describes breath entering the dry bones so that "they came to life." In the LXX this is exactly the same word *zoe* (life) as found in Revelation 20:4. While the regeneration of the earth, mentioned in Matthew 19:28, refers to the new heavens and earth, this new life or life from the dead is received by the church of Christ when all Israel shall be saved and the fullness of the gentiles shall flow into them.

- **Fire**. Fire is a symbol of the Holy Spirit because it illuminates, refines, purifies, and warms (Matt 3:11; Acts 2:3). The warning in 1 Thessalonians 5:19 is not to quench or put out the fire of the Spirit.

- **Oil**. Oil soothes, heals, quiets, beautifies, and consecrates. Anointing was done with oil. The Greek word *Christ* means the anointed one. Under the old covenant, the anointed ones were prophets, priests, and kings. All the OT offices converge on him. As Christ began his public ministry he quoted from Isaiah 61, "The Spirit of the Lord is on me, because he has anointed me to preach good news to the poor" (Luke 4:18). As Christians, we also have an anointing from the Holy One (1 John 2:20-27).

According to James 5:14, if a Christian is sick and calls for prayer the elders are instructed to anoint this person with oil and pray for their healing. There are three major interpretations concerning the role of oil in this situation. In Roman Catholic practice this is the sacrament of extreme unction which prepares a person for death. However, the context is healing, not death.

Some interpreters, in reaction to the first view, suggest that oil represents the use of medicine, because oil was one of the most common medicines in biblical times (see Luke 10:34).

Taken literally, this would mean that oil is prescribed for every ailment. Thus, an additional assumption is required — that oil symbolizes the best and most appropriate medicine available.

However, the elders of the church are in no position to prescribe the best medicine. Since this oil, which they are to administer, is applied in the name of the Lord Jesus Christ, along with prayer, this procedure sounds more like a spiritual ritual of the church than a medical procedure. Therefore, the third view is that oil is symbolic of the Holy Spirit, the Spirit of life, who administers divine healing. Spirit, oil, and anointing are tied together in Luke 4:18, 2 Corinthians 1:21-22, Hebrews 1:9. Thus, the oil does not itself heal, but it is a tangible reminder of the ministry of the Holy Spirit without constituting a sacrament.

• **Dove**. A dove is innocent, gentle, loving, and faithful. After the catastrophic flood, it was a dove, with an olive leaf in her mouth, which brought Noah God's overture of peace. All four Gospels record that the Holy Spirit came upon Jesus at his baptism in the form of a dove.

Gifts of the Spirit

The gifts are listed in Romans 12:6-8 and 1 Corinthians 12:7-11, 28-31. However, there is an overlap between spiritual gifts and offices in the church. Ephesians 4:11 lists four or five offices. Some theologians claim that the Bible also mentions or implies the gifts of celibacy (1 Cor 7:7), voluntary poverty (1 Cor 13:3), martyrdom (1 Cor 13:3), hospitality (1 Pet 4:9), music, intercession, and exorcism.

Every believer has a spiritual gift (1 Cor 12:7; 1 Pet 4:10). The Greek word for *gift* (*charisma*) occurs five times in 1 Corinthians 12. These gifts are a synergism of supernatural ability and God-given natural talent awakened by the Holy Spirit.

The Wesleyan way is a middle ground between rationalism and fanaticism. We believe in both the form and the power; in both a clear mind and the warm heart. All too often, however, teaching on spiritual warfare has become the domain of extremists.

Wesley neither sought nor denied supernatural manifestations. Nor did Wesley regard all supernatural phenomenon as necessarily from God. He warned against regarding extraordinary circumstances as essential to the inward work and against condemning them altogether as if they were a hindrance to God's work. While God worked many miracles through Wesley's ministry, yet Wesley did not claim to have supernatural, apostolic-like gifts. His emphasis was upon preaching the Word and all things were to be tried by the written Word. Thus, Wesley was neither a cessationist nor a charismatic.

The Holy Spirit divides the gifts of the Spirit according to the needs of the church (1 Pet 4:10). Thus, there is a division of labor, and a healthy congregation needs every member to participate. The gifts of the Spirit are best understood in clusters or gift-mixes. Bloesch wrote,

> The priesthood of believers, as the New Testament understands this, cannot be adequately understood apart from the gifts of the Holy Spirit. All Christians are called to exercise their priesthood but in different ways, depending on the gifts that have been allotted to them.[582]

Communication gifts involve speaking. *Prophecy* (*propheteia*) means *to speak forth*. Prophecy is not limited to the prediction of future events. Essentially, it is anointed preaching. Biblical prophets were social and political commentators. They did not simply read and expound upon the law, as the priests did, but they received direct messages from God. Pope explained that when Christ came, "the ancient order of the prophets ceased" because God made all of his people prophets and put his Spirit

---

[582]Bloesch, *Essentials of Evangelical Theology*, 2:107.

upon them all.[583] While the office of a prophet has ceased (Matt 11:13), the gift has not. Prophetic speech denounces sin and calls people back to God. According to 1 Corinthians 14:3, everyone who prophesies speaks to men for their strengthening, encouragement, and comfort.

Teaching (*didaskalia*) involves the interpretation and application of Scripture. There is an element of teaching in all preaching. All pastors must be apt to teach (1 Tim 3:2).

Evangelism involves sharing the gospel in cooperation with the awakening of the Holy Spirit, so that sinners are brought to a point of repentance and faith. The mind must first be convinced of the truth of the gospel. The will must then be brought to a point of decision. The emotions must accompany this resolution. The church will ultimately fulfill the great commission and will see the world converted to Christ to the level of every political nation, every language, and every culture. Daniel refers to this six times and the book of Revelation seven times.

A missionary is one who shares the gospel across cultural, linguistic, or geographic barriers. The word *apostolos* simply means one sent forth. All missionaries have an apostolic ministry in the sense that they are sent out by the church. Therefore, the *Living Bible* frequently translated the word *apostle* as *missionary*. But missionaries do not fill the apostolic office. Therefore, Stott concluded that *apostle* cannot be a generic term for missionaries, church planters, bishops, or other church leaders. Instead, it must denote that small and special group which Jesus chose, called, and authorized to teach in his name, who were eyewitnesses of his resurrection.[584] Not all Christians are missionaries, but we all share the responsibility for the mission of the church to make disciples of all nations.

Because of linguistic barriers, the gift of *languages* (*glossolalia*) enables unbelievers to hear the gospel in their own lan-

---

[583]Pope, *Compendium*, 1:76-78.

[584]Stott, *God's New Society*, 106-107.

guage. The gift of *interpretation* also helps congregations who are bilingual to hear the truth.

Counseling gifts include the gift of *exhortation*. This can be exhortation, encouragement, consolation, or counseling. The Greek word *paraklesis* is the same word for *comforter*. Thus, a counselor is a temporary assistant to the Holy Spirit. The Methodist Church used to issue a license for exhorters. This person was not ordained, but they functioned as an evangelist who exhorted people to give their lives to Christ.

The *word of knowledge* is the ability to understand the meaning of God's Word. The *word of wisdom* is the practical application of knowledge to specific situations. *Discernment of spirits* is the ability to determine whether certain teaching or behavior comes from God, Satan, or humanity. In a general sense, all Christians must do this (1 John 4:1).

Confirmation gifts include the gift of *faith*. This gift of faith does not refer to the gift of faith in salvation, but faith for specific situations. The *gifts of healing* is plural. Each instance of divine healing is a gift. The gift of *miracles* is given to confirm the Word.

Coordination gifts include *leadership* (*proistemi*). This word means to preside or rule, literally to stand in front. This is the ability to set goals in accordance with God's purpose and to communicate those goals in such a way that the church works together to accomplish these goals for the glory of God.

The gift of *administration* is the ability to follow through on established goals. In 1 Corinthians 12:28 the Greek word *kubernesis* is used. It means to guide, steer, or pilot.

Caring gifts including *giving*. The Greek word *metadidomi* means to impart or share with others. Giving is to be done with simplicity of motive. The gift of *helps* (*antilepsis*) describes the exchange of taking the burden off someone else in order to carry it for them. The gift of *mercy* (*eleeo*) means to have pity or compassion. This gift is to be given with cheerfulness. The gift of *service* (*diakonia*) overlaps with the office of deacon (*diakonia*). But the gift of service is broader than the office of deacon.

Sinning against the Spirit

Matthew 12:31; Mark 3:29; Luke 12:10 are parallel passages which all warn against blaspheming the Spirit. If we understand that salvation is the ongoing work of the Spirit, not simply a one-time decision on our part to accept Christ, then this warning becomes much more serious and relevant. We begin moving in this dangerous direction when we grieve the Spirit (Eph 4:30), quench the Spirit (1 Thess 5:19), resist the Spirit (Acts 7:51), vex the Spirit (Isa 63:10), or insult the Spirit (Heb 10:29).

Arminius explained that this sin is the rejection and refusing of Christ in opposition to conscience. This rejection of the person and work of Christ, through the testimony and power of the Holy Spirit, does not stem from ignorance, weakness, or infirmity, but from malice and hatred, so that the sinner may satisfy his own desires. This sin progresses from a general rejection of Christ and the truth of the gospel, to blaspheming Christ and the truth of the gospel, to persecuting Christ or his followers, to claiming the miraculous operations of the Holy Spirit are diabolical.[585]

This blasphemy is unpardonable because the Spirit is the agent of salvation. He is our only lifeline. Suppose we have only one exit from a building. However, suppose we change the exit sign to say *danger*. A fire breaks out and lives are lost because they refuse to exit through the door which has been mislabeled. This is what happens when the works of the Spirit are attributed to Satan. Thomas Oden wrote,

> For those who obstinately leave behind the help of the Spirit, there is nothing more left. There is no further help to be given beyond the help God offers for salva-

---

[585]Arminius, *Works*, 2:731-754.

tion. It is possible for persons to pass beyond that limit and become so hardened to God's saving action that no further recourse is to be expected. Those who absolutely turn from the work of the spirit are left by their own choice without hope and without God in the world.[586]

God's Spirit will not always strive with man (Gen 6:3). This blasphemy is usually a culmination of many rejections. It is a deliberate sin against light and results in indifference and insensibility. That state is normally arrived at through a process of disobedience and rejection of the Holy Spirit in his restorative ministry. In his comments on 1 John 5:16 Pope defined the sin unto death as "the actual rejection of the Son of God in whom life is, and whose rejection has been the supreme sin aimed at throughout the Epistle."[587]

W. T. Hogue explained,

The blasphemy against the Holy Ghost does not consist in some isolated and independent act of transgression, nor in some awful and irrevocable deed the nature of which is involved in obscurity, and which men whose consciences are awakened sometimes fear they have unwittingly committed. . . . Nor does the sin in question consist in some atrocious deed committed under a strong and sudden impulse of temptation, and which the memory of the awakened sinner recalls from the long list of his past transgressions. . . . The sin which our Lord has characterized as the blasphemy against the Holy Ghost, is rather the culminating act in a series of deliberate transgressions, rashly persisted in, against the light, convictions, and the gracious influences of the

----

[586]Oden, *Life in the Spirit*, 22.

[587]Pope, *PCNT*, 320.

Spirit of God. It is the final link in a long chain of malignant and rebellious acts against the Holy Spirit.[588]

Hogue also clarified that this state is manifested by indifference and insensibility. Those who are distressed and have a godly sorrow over sin are not beyond hope because this conviction itself is the drawing of the Holy Spirit.

---

[588]Hogue, *The Holy Spirit*, 385-386.

CHAPTER FIVE
The Doctrine of the Trinity

The one God consists of three persons — the Father, the Son, and the Holy Spirit. While the Trinity is incomprehensible, it is a contradiction only if it affirms that God is both one and three in the same sense. God is complex and unlike humanity. We should not expect to comprehend him. However, he has condescended to reveal himself to us. The revelation of Scripture is unintelligible, however, unless we accept the doctrine of the Trinity. Thus, it is foolishness for mere mortals to reject what they cannot grasp. The God which our minds can grasp will reflect our likeness and thus will always fall far short of the Almighty. Heretics have always opposed the doctrine of the Trinity, but when we reject his revelation of himself at some point we move beyond Christianity into our own man-made religion. Rather than being an impractical doctrine, the doctrine of the Trinity informs our worship and enriches our prayers.

The Trinity is involved in our salvation, and each member of the Trinity has his own unique function. However, we cannot divide the Trinity in such a way that we receive Christ at one moment and receive the Holy Spirit at a different point in time.

Marriage is the best illustration of the Trinity, and the inter-dynamics within the Trinity illustrate the relationship within a healthy marriage.

The Trinitarian concept of the one and the many also provides the basis for our concept of individuality and community within society.

Trinitarian Theology

We have seen that Father, Son, and Spirit are all regarded as God in Scripture. At the close of his inductive study of Scripture, Bickersteth concluded that the Bible teaches the Father, the Son, and the Holy Spirit are each eternal, each created all things, are each omnipresent, are each incomprehensible and omniscient, are each true, holy, and good, are each the fountain of life, they each strengthen, comfort, and sanctify us, they each fill the soul with divine love, they each gave the divine law, they each dwell in the hearts of believers, are each called the supreme Jehovah and God.[589] "In the fullness of time, God did not give us facts about himself, but gave us himself in the person of the Father who sent, the Son who was sent, and the Holy Spirit who was poured out."[590]

Yet we have also read that God is one in singularity, integrity, essence, and mutuality. "The Lord our God, the Lord is one" (Deut 6:4). There is none other (Deut 4:39). "There is no god besides me" (Deut 32:39). "I am the Lord, and there is no other; apart from me there is no God" (Isa 45:5). Thus, Christianity rejects dualism and polytheism. There can be only one absolute being who is our ultimate authority. However, the whole undivided essence of God belongs equally to each of the three persons of the Trinity.

The Eastern church, following the Cappadocians, Basil, Gregory of Nazianzus, and Gregory of Nyssa, begins with the three persons of the Godhead, then attempts to explain their unity. The Western church, following Augustine, begins with the unity of God and then attempts to explain how one God can be three persons.

When we are attempting to describe *what* God is, we see God as a unity. When we are attempting to describe *who* God is,

---

[589]Bickersteth, *The Trinity*, 150-155.

[590]Sanders, *The Triune God*, 40.

we see God as three persons. It was Tertullian who first used the word *trinity* in his tract *Against Praxeas*, written around 213. Praxeas contended that the Father, the Son, and the Holy Spirit were one and the same. While the word *trinity* is not contained in Scripture, the concept is biblical, and Tertullian utilized the word *trinity* in order to explain the biblical concept. Athanasius taught that the Trinity was a logical necessity of the doctrines of the eternal generation of the Son and procession of the Spirit.[591]

There is an *exegetical necessity* for the doctrine of the Trinity because

> there is an organic continuity between the biblical testimony and the early creeds, and that the creeds can serve as hermeneutical guidelines to reading the Bible because it is in fact the biblical text itself that necessitated the creedal formulations.[592]

Bloesch warned that a denial of the Trinity is a potent indication that a religious movement is probably a cult or an aberrant sect rather than a branch of the one holy, catholic, and apostolic church.[593]

Pope wrote, "The doctrine of the ever-blessed Trinity is essential to Christianity." While he acknowledged that no human language can adequately explain this mystery, we must attempt to accurately articulate scriptural concepts in order to guard the truth against error. "Nowhere is precision more necessary than in the ordering of the phraseology of worship."[594] Samuel Powell

---

[591]Giles, *Eternal Generation of the Son*, 20.

[592]Rowe, "Luke and the Trinity," 4.

[593]Bloesch, *God the Almighty*, 199.

[594]Pope, *Compendium*, 1:284-286.

claimed that every Christian doctrine has a Trinitarian pattern.[595] Miner Raymond wrote,

> The Trinity is the chief cornerstone of the Christian system. Eliminate that, with what logically follows it, and nothing is left but what is common to all theistic systems of religion known among men.[596]

While the doctrine of the Trinity is incomprehensible, it is a contradiction only if it is affirming that God is one and three in the same sense. Instead, the Christian faith affirms both the unity and diversity of God. This separates Christianity from all other religious philosophies. Our knowledge of God is based upon his revelation, not human reason. This means that where there is an inadequate view of biblical inspiration, the doctrine of the Trinity will become more a matter of logic and philosophy than of inductive Bible study.

God is a complex being. He is one committee consisting of three members. God has never existed as a single, solitary individual, but rather as a rich personal diversity within the Godhead.

> Christian monotheism must include more than one divine thinker, doer, actor, lover. For if God the Father and the Son of God are "one," they are not one person. Their unity is more like a marriage in which two persons become one flesh, or like persons bound together in a single community.[597]

Because of the nature of love, more than one person is required so that love may be shared. Without a plurality of persons, it is impossible for there to be love. A solitary individual

---

[595]Powell, *Teacher's Guide to Understanding the Trinity*, 42.

[596]Raymond, *Systematic Theology*, 1:392.

[597]Plantinga, "The Perfect Family," 26.

cannot express love. Love always exists between two persons. So when John says God is love (1 John 4:8,16), he is representing relationship embedded in the nature of Godhead. Augustine taught that the Holy Spirit was the bond of love that unites the Father and Son and proceeds from both of them.[598] If the Spirit proceeds from both the Father and the Son, he cannot be either, but is a third person of the Trinity.

Jesus gives us an insight into this mutual love in John 17:23-24. The Godhead desires to share their love with the whole world. The Cappadocian theologians described the *perichoresis* or mutual indwelling of the persons within the Godhead, primarily stated in John 10:38, 14:10-20, and 17:21.The interpersonal relationship between the Father and the Son, the Son and the Spirit, and the Spirit and the Father will have application in a relational understanding of human personhood.

The interpersonal relationship between the Father and the Son is described in the Gospels. Moule wrote, "Nothing shines more radiantly in the New Testament than the eternal love of the Father for the Son."[599]

"Out of Egypt I called my son" (Matt 2:15). "This is my Son, whom I love" (Matt 3:17). Jesus refers to his relationship with his Father often employing the intimate term *Abba*. Jesus coordinated his work with that of the Father, and his prayers to the Father reflect the deep *I-Thou* relationship. Again, at his transfiguration the voice of the Father declares, "This is my Son, whom I love" (Mark 9:7). In John 17:5 Jesus prays to the Father. If *father* and *son* are nothing more than titles, Jesus is simply talking to himself.

The life of Christ ends on the cross with his cry to his Father (Luke 23:46), and after the resurrection he ascends to his Father. According to Hebrews 1:5-13 the Father is talking to the Son.

---

[598]Augustine, *On the Trinity*, NPNF1 3:215; see also Lewis, *Mere Christianity*, 152-153.

[599]Moule, *Outlines of Christian Doctrine*, 39.

This session of Christ is also described in Daniel 7:9 where the Son of man approaches the Ancient of Days. In Acts 7:55 Stephen saw Jesus at the right hand of God. Thus, he saw two distinct persons.

The interpersonal relationship between the Father and the Spirit is described as the Holy Spirit comes at Pentecost, as promised by the Father (Luke 24:48-49). Paul refers to the relationship between the Father and the Spirit, without confusing them. In Romans 5:5 God gave us the Holy Spirit. In Romans 8:14-16 the sons of God are led by the Spirit of God. In 1 Corinthians 2:4-5,10-14 Paul preached with the power of the Spirit so that his hearers would have the power of God rest on them. The Spirit also reveals the deep things of God. In 1 Corinthians 3:16, God's Spirit lives in us, making us the temple of God. In 1 Corinthians 6:19, we have received the Holy Spirit from God. In 2 Corinthians 5:5 God has given us the Spirit. In Ephesians 6:17 the sword of the Spirit is the Word of God. And in 1 Thessalonians 4:8 God gives us his Holy Spirit.

The interpersonal relationship between the Son and the Spirit is also described. The virgin conception of Jesus is through the agency of the Holy Spirit. The Spirit is present at his baptism. He leads Jesus into the wilderness and sustains him. Jesus teaches and ministers in the power of the Spirit. Jesus promises the Spirit, another Paraclete, whom he will send from the Father. Paul also closely relates the Son and the Holy Spirit, without confusing them,[600] in Romans 8:2 which teaches that the Spirit of life sets me free from sin and death through Christ Jesus. In Romans 9:1 Paul speaks the truth in Christ and his conscience is confirmed by the Holy Spirit. In 2 Corinthians 3:17-18 the Spirit is called *Lord*. He transforms us to reflect the Lord's glory. According to v 16 the Lord is Christ. Thus, both the Son and the Spirit are called *kurios* (lord), but the function of the Spirit is to transform the believer into the likeness of Christ.

---

[600]McCall, "Relational Trinity: Creedal Perspective," 117-118.

Galatians 3:14 teaches that the blessing given to Abraham comes to the Gentiles through the redemption of Christ Jesus, so that by faith we might receive the promise of the Spirit. Galatians 5:5-6,22-24 explains that those in Christ Jesus eagerly await the righteousness that comes through the Spirit. Those who belong to Christ Jesus exhibit the fruit of the Spirit.

In Ephesians 1:13-14 we are told that those who believed in Christ were sealed by the Holy Spirit. In Ephesians 3:5-6 the promise in Christ Jesus for both Jew and Gentile has been revealed by the Spirit. And in 1 Peter 1:11 the Spirit of Christ in the prophets predicted the sufferings and glories of Christ.

Thus, the Bible describes a relationship between the Father and the Son, between the Father and the Spirit, and between the Son and the Spirit. Such descriptions are incomprehensible unless we understand the Trinitarian nature of God.

The rationalist will reject what he cannot understand, but it should not come as a surprise that God is beyond our ability to understand. If the Bible is his self-disclosure, we must not reject his description of himself simply because he is different from us. The doctrine of the Trinity is not irrational or illogical; it is above or beyond human reason. "All explanations of the Trinity are inadequate. We are talking about a revealed mystery, something that by its very nature, and by our very nature, cannot be figured out by our rational processes."[601] While the created order reflects a Trinitarian pattern, as Nathan Wood demonstrated in *The Trinity in the Universe* (1932), examples do not *prove* the doctrine and all attempts to illustrate the doctrine from natural revelation fall short.

An often-repeated statement says that anyone who denies the Trinity is in danger of losing his salvation, but anyone who tries to understand the Trinity is in danger of losing his mind. Yet this is an argument in its favor. Such a truth had to be revealed by God. All of the pagan gods resemble the men who created them.

---

[601]Grider, *Wesleyan-Holiness Theology*, 123.

The God of the Bible could have never been conceived by humanity because he is a compound being. God exists as a community. Tozer argued, "The fact that it cannot be satisfactorily explained, instead of being against it, is in its favor. Such a truth had to be revealed; no one could have imagined it."[602]

Paul usually uses the term *mystery* to describe the incorporation of the Gentiles into the plan of God. This word *musterion* occurs 27 times in the NT. Paul himself used it 21 times. There is not a multiplicity of mysteries, but one mystery which is presented from different aspects. "But because Paul considered this salvation-historical phenomenon as something planned long ago by the Father and carried out in the work of the Son and the Spirit, he is also speaking indirectly about the doctrine of God."[603]

Mystery does not refer to something mysterious or hard to understand, but something which can only be known through revelation. Pagan religions used this word to describe occult or esoteric knowledge to which only the initiated few had access. In contrast the Scriptures use the word to refer to something which was known through revelation. This *open secret* is the salvation purpose of God revealed in Christ and includes his incarnation, death, resurrection, and universal call to Jew and Gentile.

Indications of the Trinitarian Nature of God

Elohim, a common Hebrew name for God which is used 2555 times in the OT, is plural, but always used with a singular verb. Hebrew nouns have singular, dual (pair), and plural forms. The plural form may be an intensification (God of gods) or plural of majesty, but the pronouns are plural. As far back as the second century Justin Martyr used this argument in his dialog with the

---

[602]Tozer, *Knowledge of the Holy*, 31.

[603]Sanders, *The Triune God*, 43.

Jewish scholar, Trypho.[604] The church fathers, medieval Christian scholars, and the later Reformers understood that the plural *elohim* with the singular verb implies the Trinity.

For example, Genesis 1:26 contains the plural subject with the singular verb and three plural pronouns. Other than the angels, who else would God be talking with — since nothing else was created at this time?

Deuteronomy 6:4 declares, "The Lord our God, the Lord is one." Yet the Hebrew word for *Lord* is *Yahweh* and the Hebrew word for *God* is *elohim*, which is plural. Thus, within this foundational statement declaring monotheism there is also an unavoidable suggestion of his plurality as well.

In Isaiah 63:7-10 God saved the house of Israel through the angel of his face, but they rebelled against his Holy Spirit. While the phrase, *the angel of his face*, occurs nowhere else in Scripture, Christ was the angel of the Lord in the OT. According to 2 Corinthians 4:6, the glory of God is seen in the *face* of Jesus Christ."

Yet the doctrine of the Trinity is concealed in the OT. In the NT we encounter the baptism of Jesus Christ. The Spirit descended on him like a dove and a voice from heaven said, "This is my Son, whom I love; with him I am well pleased" (Matt 3:16-17). Augustine explained,

> The Trinity together wrought both the voice of the Father, and the flesh of the Son, and the dove of the Holy Spirit, while each of these things is referred severally to each person.[605]

The baptismal formula given in Matthew 28:19 includes the name of the Father, and the Son, and the Holy Spirit. Christian baptism is administered "into the Name." While the Name is

---

[604]Justin Martyr, *Dialogue with Trypho*, ANF 1:228.

[605]Augustine, *On the Trinity*, NPNF1 3:86.

one, not many, yet *and of* implies a distinction in the Godhead. Oneness Pentecostals misunderstand the singular *name* as that of Jesus, and claim on the basis of Acts 2:38 that believers should be baptized in Jesus' name only. Because they also hold to baptismal regeneration, they conclude that only those who are baptized in just Jesus' name are truly saved.

However, the *Didache*, written around AD 100, utilizes the Trinitarian baptismal formula.[606] Athanasius argued that if Arianism was correct, baptism would have been administered in the name of one God and two creatures.[607] Yet in his discourse on the Holy Spirit, Jesus explained that he would ask the Father for another *paraklete* like himself (John 14:16-17).

The benediction in 2 Corinthians 13:14 prays that the grace of the Lord Jesus Christ, the love of God, and the fellowship of the Holy Spirit be with us.

Ephesians 4:4-6 teaches **there is one God** and Father of all believers, whether Jew or Gentile. He is above all, transcendent and sovereign. He is through all. This describes his providence and omnipotence. He is in all. This refers to his immanent and omnipresence.

There is one Lord. *Lord* was the title for *Yahweh* in the OT. In the book of Acts Jesus Christ is called our Lord 110 times. Paul is a prisoner in the Lord (Eph 4:1). There is only one Mediator. There is only one Savior. He is the revelation of God the Father. It is this faith in Jesus Christ which unified us and defines us.

There is one Spirit who incorporates us into the body of Christ. The reason that the Holy Spirit is mentioned first by Paul in this declaration is that the Spirit was mentioned in v 3 and Paul carries that same thought of unity within the body and the Holy Spirit into v 4.

---

[606]Also known as *The Teaching of the Twelve* Apostles, *ANF* 7:379.

[607]Athanasius, *Four Discourses Against Arians*, *NPNF*2 4:370.

Without a Trinitarian understanding of God, 2 Thessalonians 2:13-14 would be unintelligible. This passage refers twice to God, Lord, Lord Jesus Christ, and Spirit as all involved in our salvation. However, Paul is teaching that the sanctification of the Christian comes through the Father, Son, and Holy Spirit together.

In 1 Peter 1:2 the foreknowledge of God the Father, the blood of Jesus Christ, and the sanctifying work of the Spirit are all part of the plan of salvation. This implies a division of administration, often described as the economic Trinity.

In Jude 20-21 we are commanded to keep ourselves in the love of God, as we wait for the mercy of our Lord Jesus Christ, and we are to pray in the Holy Spirit.

In the salutation of Revelation 1:4-5, grace and peace come from the throne of God *and* from the Holy Spirit *and* from Jesus Christ. Thus, all three members of the Trinity are named.

The Apostles' Creed is also Trinitarian in its structure. We believe in God the Father, we believe in Jesus Christ, and we believe in the Holy Spirit.

Trinitarian Heresies

Heretics have always opposed this doctrine. They have taught that the Father, Son, and Spirit are one person, that they are simply three modes, or that the Father was the sole ruler of the three.

Oden explained that in early church history the first question the church had to answer was, "Must the Son be eternally God?" The second question to arise was, "Are the Father and Son distinguishable?" The most fundamental question was, "Is the Son less than God?"[608]

Yet when we begin tinkering with the nature of God, we basically move away from Christianity into another religion. To

---

[608]Oden, *The Living God*, 212-215.

deny or erase these distinctions between members of the Trinity, between God and man, or between man and woman is to end up in a pantheistic paganism.

- ## Monarchianism

In the third century, those who attempted to maintain monotheism and the unity of the Godhead by opposing the doctrine of the Trinity were commonly termed *Monarchians*. Tertullian first gave them this label around 213 to describe their concept of the one principle of God's being, and sole rule by God, which excludes a Son or Spirit.[609]

In the fourth century, Arius taught that Christ was a created being and that the Holy Spirit was created by the Son. These ancient heresies continue to be recycled by Unitarians and Jehovah's Witnesses.

- ## Sabellianism

Sabellius applied anti-Trinitarianism to the Holy Spirit. He taught that the Father revealed himself in the law, the Son revealed himself in the incarnation, and the Holy Spirit revealed himself in inspiration. However, there is only one God who transitions into another mode. Each person functions in a temporary mission. Since the Son was the same person as the Father, they taught that the Father suffered on the cross. Therefore, they were also called *Patripassians*.

Hegel's dialectic philosophy taught that God makes himself the object of his own thought, and then identifies subject and object. Thus, the thesis is the Father, the antithesis is the Son,

---

[609]Tertullian, *Against Praxeas*, ANF 3:599.

and the synthesis is the Holy Spirit. This modern concept lends itself to process theology.[610]

Marcellus also developed a similar modal concept, teaching that before the incarnation there was a Logos, but no Son of God. The Logos was an impersonal power of reason inherent within God. After the Son of God completed the work of redemption, he was absorbed back into the Father. Thus, the Son was only a temporary manifestation. Pope explained, "Its philosophical principle was Pantheistic; the same God who is the Father is evolving Himself in the Son and Spirit."[611]

Oneness Pentecostalism advocates a unique form of modalism. While Unitarians historically have believed in a father without a son, oneness theology postulates a son with no father. They embrace the deity of Christ, but deny any plurality within the Godhead.

About a fifth of all Pentecostals in the United States practice baptism in Jesus' name only.[612] To add to the confusion there are Trinitarian groups which baptize in Jesus' name only and non-Trinitarian groups which use the formula given in Matthew 28:19.

In 1913 at a camp meeting at Arroyo Seco, California, a Canadian evangelist, Robert McAclister, preached that the apostles understood that they were commanded to baptize in the name of Jesus. Frank Ewart and Glenn Cook began to preach this and re-baptize in Jesus' name only. G. T. Haywood also advanced the doctrine of Oneness Pentecostalism.[613] In 1916 the Assemblies of God rejected this teaching and lost a quarter of its membership.

---

[610]Powell, *Trinity in German Thought*, 7-9; Wiley, *Christian Theology*, 1:426-427; Curtis, *The Christian Faith*, 486.

[611]Pope, *Compendium*, 1:273.

[612]Synan, *Holiness-Pentecostal Tradition*, 165.

[613]Alexander, "G. T. Haywood," 275-283.

Typically, Oneness Pentecostals cite proof texts which they claim identify Jesus as the Father. These verses include Isaiah 9:6; John 8:19, 10:30, 12:45, 14:7-11. These passages indicate the Father and the Son are both deity, but do not blur their distinct personalities. However, the unitarians deny that Jesus is eternal, claiming that his existence began at his birth around 6 BC.

Secondly, they cite cross references which say that both the Father and the Son perform certain divine functions. Again, this indicates their common nature but does not necessarily exclude their distinct personalities.

Then Oneness Pentecostalism does the same thing with Jesus and the Holy Spirit. They cite 2 Corinthians 3:17, which says the Lord is the Spirit, as proof that Jesus and the Holy Spirit are one. However, in vv 3-6 Paul has distinguished between them. They also cite Romans 8:9 which refers to the Spirit of Christ.

They also try to dismiss the concept of the Trinity as both pagan and illogical, claiming that the early church soon plunged into apostasy by adopting what they caricature as tritheism.

While *Dake's Annotated Reference Bible* denied the Trinity in some notes, Dake also declared that there are

> three separate and distinct persons in the Godhead, each one having His own personal body, personal soul, and personal spirit in the same sense each human being, angel, or any other being has his own body, soul, and spirit.[614]

This bizarre doctrine was perpetuated by Benny Hinn.[615]

---

[614]Dake, *Dake's Annotated Reference Bible*, NT, 280.

[615]Fisher and Goedelman, *Confusing World of Benny Hinn*, 95, 186.

- **Tritheism**

The opposite error arose in the middle of the sixth century, advocating three gods. John Philoponus and John Ascusnages made no distinction between nature and personhood.

The Economic Trinity

Each person of the Trinity was involved in creation and in providence. Each person is also involved in the work of redemption. Yet each person has a unique role. God is the speaker, Jesus is the word, and the Spirit is the breath. Thus, in salvation history we have creation, incarnation, and Pentecost.

There is an ontological or immanent Trinity which cooperates in a structural order. The term *ontological* here means the eternal being or existence of God, his inherent nature, and the term *immanent* here means internal to itself.

But there is also an *economic* Trinity. Not only is there a division of labor, but there is a subordination administratively in which God sends God. The Father loves the Son and sent him to earth. The Son prayed to the Father and was enabled by the Holy Spirit. When the Son returned to the Father, he sent the Spirit; however, Scripture never speaks of the Son commanding the Father or the Spirit sending the Father or Son. In John 5:26-27 the Father has granted life and authority to the Son. In John 14:28, Jesus taught that the Father was greater than himself. "This can refer only to the self-imposed limitations of the Son in His incarnation. He has already claimed equality with God (John 5:18) and oneness with Him (John 10:30)."[616]

Jesus disclosed in Matthew 24:36; Mark 13:32 that only the Father knew when the end of the world would be. Apparently, this was a voluntary and temporary submission to human limita-

---

[616]Martin, *The Deity of Christ*, 43.

tions which cannot be extrapolated to support the claim of openness theology that God does not know the future.

The administrative priority of the Father is indicated in 1 Corinthians 8:6, where Paul teaches that there is one God, the Father. All things came *from* (*ek*, out of) him, he is the source, and we live *for* (*eis*, unto) him. But Paul continues, there is one Lord, Jesus Christ — equally the object of Divine worship — *through* (*dia*, because of) whom all things came and *through* (*dia*) whom we live. While we originate from God, we live through the means of Christ as creator and redeemer.

In 1 Corinthians 11:3 Paul writes that the head of Christ is God. The dynamics in 1 Corinthians 15:24-28 can only be explained in terms of function, not essence. While Christ, along with his people, will reign eternally, Paul explained that at the end of time the final enemy, death, will be destroyed. Then Christ *paradidomi*, presents, delivers, or hands over the kingdom to the Father. According to John 13:3 the Father delegated everything to him. However, after Christ completes his work as mediator and everything is under his feet, Christ will present a perfect world back to the Father.

Yet Paul is very precise in his explanation that *everything* does not include the Father. The Father is not subsumed into the Son. The essential distinctions within the Trinity remain. Yet there are obviously functional distinctions which change after the great plan of redemption has been completed. Christ himself will subject himself to God, so that God may be all in all. First Timothy 6:15-16 also indicates the Father's priority. Yet Christ will not diminish in his essential nature. In fact, he will reign eternally with the Father.

Arians and their theological descendants have distorted all of these texts. However, the proper theological method, based on the law of non-contradiction, must be to harmonize these passages with passages which claim equality between the members of the Trinity. Thus, we are forced to distinguish between the essential Trinity and the economic Trinity. While the nature of God is a mystery, it can be understood to the extent that it has been revealed. Wiley explained that the economic Trinity becomes false only when it is held to be mere aspects of one God and not eternal distinctions in the divine essence itself."[617]

The Father is the planner. This is the originating cause of our salvation. God in his foreknowledge saw our sinful plight, and motivated by his holy love, before the foundation of the world chose Christ to be the Lamb of God (1 Pet 1:19-20) who would take away the sin of the world.

The Son is the purchaser. This is the procuring cause of our salvation. The blood of Christ is called *precious* in v 19. The Greek word *timios* means costly, honored, or valuable. God taught Israel in Leviticus 17:11, "The life of a creature is its blood and I have given it to you to make atonement for yourselves on the altar; it is the blood that makes atonement for one's life." Christ is the face of God (2 Cor 4:6) and the Holy Spirit is the finger of God, as we will see.

The Spirit is the provider. This is the efficient cause of our salvation. We are initiated into the church through the baptism with the Holy Spirit. It is a washing which purifies us. "He saved us through the washing of rebirth and renewal by the Holy Spirit, whom he poured out on us generously through Jesus Christ our Savior" (Titus 3:5-6). Thus, the Holy Spirit is the executive of the Godhead. He is the "finger of God" (Luke 11:20; see Exod 8:19). When Matthew quotes Exodus 8:19 in 12:28, he substitutes the word *Spirit* for *finger*.[618] The Spirit even raised Jesus from the dead (Rom 8:11).

Perhaps the key in distinguishing between speaking against the Son of Man and speaking against the Holy Spirit (Matt 12:31; Mark 3:29; Luke 12:10) is the specific function of each person. No one can come to Christ unless he is drawn by the

---

[617]Wiley, *Christian Theology*, 1:422.

[618]In contrast, the Pharisees would not lift a finger to help people with their burdens (Luke 11:46). Legalism is always impotent. The Holy Spirit is the helper (*paraklete*).

Holy Spirit. If this drawing is regarded as diabolical, the only hope of salvation is regarded as evil.

Without an understanding of the Trinity some passages make no sense. With whom is God speaking in Psalm 2:7-9? Does Jesus pray to himself in John 17? How can he simultaneously undergo baptism, speak from heaven, and descend upon himself in the form of a dove? How does he send himself?

If God were only one person, Oden asked how he both sends and is sent, how he could be both lawgiver and obedient to law, how he could both make atonement and receive it, how he could both reject sin and offer sacrifice for it, how he could both govern all things and empty himself in serving love.[619]

Implications of Trinitarian Theology

Immanuel Kant stated that doctrines like the Trinity have no use for the practical life. Yet C. S. Lewis declared that the doctrine of the Trinity matters more than anything else in the world.[620]

• A Trinitarian Concept of Worship

If Jesus is not God, then to worship him constitutes idolatry. If he is God, he is worthy of our worship. The Gloria Patri is the earliest example of an ancient Christian prayer which is still in use today. No one knows when or where it originated. While it is not found in Scripture, it is based upon the teaching of Scripture and the worship of the early church.

Glory to the Father, and to the Son, and to the Holy Ghost! As it was in the beginning, is now, and ever shall be, world without end.

---

[619]Oden, *The Word of Life*, 77.

[620]Lewis, *Mere Christianity*, 137.

• A Trinitarian Concept of Prayer

According to Ephesians 2:18, through Christ both Jew and Gentile have access to the Father by one Spirit. To pray in *the name* (Phil 2:9) means not only the person himself, but his titles, his word, his properties and qualities, his dignity, and his glory. It is not only petition and thanksgiving, but doxology. The better we know the one to whom we are praying, the more confident we can be. Prayer should be directed to the Father through the Son and in the power of the Spirit.

> Our invocations and benedictions should always include this name [Father, Son, and Spirit] (or at least one of the names within this name), but in the prayer conversation itself we should use the freedom God has given to us to call upon him in ways that speak to our deepest needs and concerns.[621]

Jude 20 describes *praying in the Spirit* as praying by the aid of the Holy Spirit. He is our guide in prayer and is sent to be our Helper. All prayer by God's children should be in the Spirit.

According to Romans 8:26-27 the Spirit will take part with, assist in supporting, lend a hand, come to the aid of and help us in our weakness. Our weakness is that we do not properly grasp the will of God. The Spirit helps our weakness in prayer by making intercession. The verb *make intercession* has the prefix *huper* (on behalf of) added and is used nowhere else in the NT. The Spirit makes intercession on our behalf. The Spirit prays for us in intercession. The Spirit prays instead of us when we cannot pray but merely groan.

---

[621]Bloesch, *God the Almighty*, 194.

- **A Trinitarian Concept of Evangelism**

If Jesus in not fully God, then our hope of salvation is based on the example of a mere human. Thus, we save ourselves by following his example.

But if we are completely unable to save ourselves by following his example, then God provides himself as our substitute. The Father who sent the Son actually does the forgiving while still remaining just (Rom 3:23-26) since Christ died on our behalf. It is the function of the Holy Spirit to convict, enable to repent and believe, give new life and assurance.

- **A Trinitarian Concept of Sanctification**

A proper doctrine of the Trinity helps us understand sanctification. We do not receive the Son in initial salvation and the Holy Spirit in sanctification. The Spirit proceeds from the Son, both to assure us of the Father's forgiveness and adoption and impart the benefits of salvation provided through the Son. The Spirit produces within the believer the character of Christ, which is also the character of the Father.

- **A Trinitarian Illumination of Marriage**

The magisterial theologians have used the analogy of marriage as a starting point in order to understand the dynamics within the Trinity. According to 1 Corinthians 11:3, the Father has authority over the Son in the Trinity, just as the husband has authority over the wife in marriage. Both the Father and the Son are equally God from an ontological, or state of being, perspective. Yet in the economic Trinity, the Son submits to the Father. In marriage both husband and wife are equally created in the image of God ontologically, but the wife submits to her husband administratively. Chrysostom warned,

If both had the very same roles, there would be no peace. The house is not rightly governed when all have precisely the same roles. There must be a differentiation of roles under a single head.[622]

Marriage is not only an analogy of the relationship within the Godhead, but marriage is also an analogy of the relationship between Christ and his church, the community of faith. If one of the primary purposes of marriage is to symbolize the union of Christ and the church, then an egalitarian marriage destroys the symbolism.

Marriage is perhaps the best illustration of the Trinity, although marriage is a double unity while the Trinity is a triple unity. If two persons become one without losing their individuality, then why cannot three persons be one without losing their personality?

But marriage not only illustrates the Trinity, the eternal conversation of the Trinity reveals the dynamic of a healthy marriage. "We come closest to understanding God's inner life by attending to the intra-Trinitarian communicative action in the economy, particularly the dialogical interaction between the Father and the Son that is on conspicuous display in the Fourth Gospel."[623] The three main topics in John's Gospel are: mutual glorification, the giving of life, and the sharing of love.

However, unlike the bonds of love within the Trinity, Genesis 3:16 explains that tension and conflict in the marriage come from our sinful nature.

- **A Trinitarian Illumination of Social Order**

All non-Christian philosophy holds to the ultimacy of either the one or the many. Is unity or plurality the basic fact of life? If

---

[622]Oden, *ACCS* 8:200.

[623]Vanhoozer, *Remythologizing Theology*, 261.

unity is the reality, and the basic nature of reality, then oneness and unity must gain priority over individualism, particulars, or the many.

If the many, or plurality, best describes ultimate reality, then the unit cannot gain priority over the many; then state, church, and society are subordinate to the will of the citizen, the believer, and of man in particular. If the one is ultimate, then individuals are sacrificed to the group. If the many is ultimate, then unity is sacrificed to the will of the many, and anarchy prevails.

Only in the Godhead is this dilemma resolved. Only in the Trinity does there reside an equal ultimacy of unity and plurality. Only within the Christian faith is there a distinction between one and many which form a self-complete unity. Thus, God is three persons with one essence. Christ is one person with two natures. In contrast, Islam says God is simply one, with one prophet superseding all previous prophets. This leads to dictatorship and tyranny.

The Eastern church teaches that the Father begets the Son and unilaterally breathes forth the Spirit. Thus, the Son does not work with the Father and has no immediate relationship with the Spirit. The result is that the one swallows up the many. This concept lends itself to a top-down system of government.

Western civilization is the product of a Trinitarian doctrine that emphasizes true communion, coordinated authority, individual freedom and responsibility.

Father

is not   is God   is not

is not

Jesus   Holy Spirit

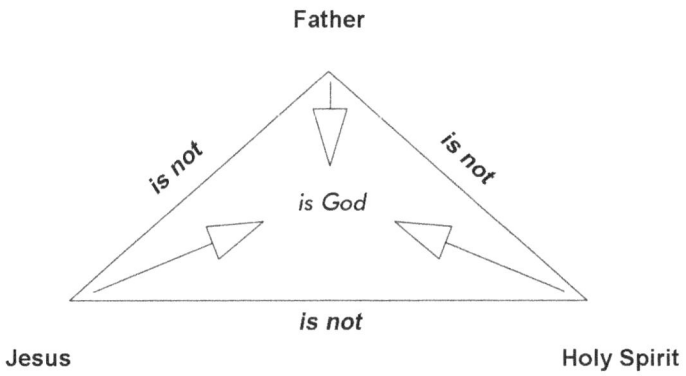

Trinity Triangle

CHAPTER SIX
The Doctrine of Angels — Holy and Apostate

Angels were created to worship God and to assist him in his government of the universe, especially his providence over the saints. After their creation, some angels fell with Satan and became demonic spirits. The destiny of fallen angels is sealed because God did not make provision for their redemption.

Apparently there are orders of angels and demons. Satan himself is a fallen angel and should never be regarded as a coequal with God. Satan is an accuser and a deceiver. But the Holy Spirit within the true believer is greater than the power of Satan, and he cannot harm us unless we allow him a foothold.

Biblical References to Angels

There are three hundred references in the Bible to angels. The Hebrew word *malak* and the Greek word *angelos* both mean *messenger*. The context alone determines whether they are human messengers or angelic beings. According to James Strong, angels, in the widest sense, are agents of God's providence, natural and supernatural.

Hebrews 1:7 describes angels was ministers. The term is applied to ordinary messengers in Job 1:14 and 1 Samuel 11:3. It is applied to prophets in Isaiah 43:19, Haggai 1:13, Malachi

3:1 and to ministers of the NT (Rev 1:20).[624] In Ecclesiastes 5:6 the temple messenger or angel was the priest (see also Mal 2:7). John the Baptist is called an *angelos* in Matthew 11:10.

Angelic beings were created by God. "Praise him, all his angels, praise him, all his heavenly host. . . . Let them praise the name of the Lord, for he commanded and they were created" (Ps 148:2,5). "For by him all things were created: things in heaven and on earth, visible and invisible, whether thrones or powers or rulers or authorities" (Col 1:16). "In speaking of the angels he says, He makes his angels winds, his servants flames of fire" (Heb 1:7). They are *ministering spirits* who serve redeemed humanity (Heb 1:14). Angels have no higher vocation than to wait upon God. They minister in God's general government of the universe, in the economy of redemption, and in God's providence over the saints.[625] Angels protect the vulnerable and the elect; they are present in worship and at death.

These *sons of God* sang at the creation of the world (Job 38:4-7). Thus, they were created before the creation of the world. However, they were not spirits of a pre-Adamic race which supposedly existed in the "gap" between Genesis 1:1-2, as taught by Finis J. Dake.[626]

Nor are demons the spirits of the *giants* produced by the cohabitation of "the sons of God" and the "daughters of men," described in Genesis 6. The Hebrew word *nephilim* was mistranslated *giants* in the LXX. The word literally means *the fallen ones* or those who fall upon others. This word occurs only here and in Numbers 13:33. In the Genesis reference these *nephilim* were on the earth *before* the sons of God united with the daugh-

---

[624]McClintock and Strong, *Cyclopedia*, 1:225-227.

[625]Pope, *Compendium*, 1:412.

[626]*Dake Annotated Reference Bible*, 54. See also, Dake, *Another Time, Another Place, Another Man* (1997). This teaching was also promoted by Clarence Larkin [*Dispensational Truth*, 7; 111], as well as the Scofield Reference Bible.

ters of men. If demonic spirits did cohabit with humanity, would those demons be designated as *sons of God*?

What we have with this terminology of *the sons of God* and *the daughters of men* (Gen 6:2) is the disconnect between what God created us to be and our fallen nature. It is the tension between nature and grace. The Spirit of God was striving with mankind (v 3), but the human race was turning from the image of God and embracing their fallen nature.

In the Numbers reference the ten spies encountered the sons of Anak, who were obviously sons of human parents. The report of the spies that they were gigantic was an exaggeration. There is no implication that they were angelic beings.

While this myth of giants, as the offspring of angels and women, is substantiated in Enoch 15:8, this is apocryphal literature, and as such has no authority. Nor was there a consensus on the interpretation of this passage in the early church.[627] The "sons of God" in this reference describes the people of God collectively. If demons cohabited with the "daughters of men," they would not be called "sons of God."

All angels were originally created in righteousness. God could have not created them other than in holiness without being charged with creating evil. Apparently each angel was created individually, since they do not reproduce (Mark 12:25). Therefore, there is a fixed number of angels. There is no basis for the folk theology that children who die become angels.

Mankind is a race; angels are a company or host. The term *host* implies a military organization. The Hebrew word *tsaba* refers to armies, warfare, or battle. When the Hebrew word for *host* is singular, it refers to the sun, moon, and stars. When it is plural, *tsabath*, it refers to an earthly army, a celestial army, or an angelic army.

Psalm 33:6 refers to the starry host and Isaiah 40:26 refers to the hosts of heaven. Judges 5:20 refers metaphorically to the

---

[627]Oden, *ACCS* 1:123-126.

stars fighting from heaven on God's behalf. Throughout Scripture, stars also symbolize angels. Yahweh-Sabaoth is the Lord of angelic hosts. Therefore, angels not only serve as messengers, but as warriors. In Luke 2:13, the heavenly host is an army (*stratia*).

Pope noted that angels were present at creation, the giving of the law at Mount Sinai,[628] and in the incarnation of Jesus Christ, but not at Pentecost. "They are comparatively lost in His higher dispensation, and their absence on that day preludes their absence now. Not that they are wholly absent: they still and ever are *ministers for them who shall be heirs of salvation*."[629] Grider cautioned that Scripture does not announce the cessation of the ministry of angels, but he also explained that we put more confidence in the ministry of the Holy Spirit.[630]

Orders of Angels

Michael and Gabriel are named in Scripture. Michael is mentioned three times in the OT, Daniel 10:13,21, 12:1. Michael was also involved in a dispute over the body of Moses. There is no record of this dispute in the OT. Deuteronomy 34:6 simply records that God buried his servant Moses. However, Jude 9 provides additional information.

Jude calls Michael an archangel (Jude 9). The Greek word *arche* literally means beginnings. Thayer suggested, "Hence the term is transferred by Paul to angels and demons holding dominions entrusted to them in the order of things."[631] The Bible never calls Gabriel an archangel. However, he is named in Daniel 8:16, 9:21; Luke 1:19,26.

---

[628]Acts 7:38,53; Heb 2:2.

[629]Pope, *Compendium*, 1:413-414.

[630]Grider, *Wesleyan-Holiness Theology*, 169.

[631]Thayer, *Lexicon*, 77.

The Bible also refers to *cherubim* and *seraphim*. There are also guardian angels (Ps 91:11; Acts 12:15; Heb 1:14). The elect are borne up lest they strike their foot against a stone.

"See that you do not look down on one of these little ones. For I tell you that their angels in heaven always see the face of my Father in heaven" (Matt 18:10). However, guardianship may be a function of angels in general, rather than a special class of angels. Likewise there is not necessarily a "death angel" or a grim reaper. In 2 Kings 19:35 and Revelation 6:8 an angel was given the power to cause death, but that function does not necessarily constitute a special order of angels. In Exodus 12:12,29-30 God himself brought death, although he could have executed the death warrant through secondary means. See also 1 Chronicles 21:14-15.

In his sermon on good angels, Wesley declared, "The angels of God have great power, in particular over the human body; power either to cause or remove pain and diseases; either to kill or to heal."[632]

He also explained that God does not need to work through any secondary causes. He does not need either angels or men to fulfill his will, but he never has bypassed the employment of instrumental agency and we may suppose he never will. "Whatever help therefore we have, either by angels or men, is as much the work of God as if he were to put forth his almighty arm and work without any means at all."[633]

Angels were created to worship God and to assist in his providential purposes — including judgment. "Praise the Lord, you his angels, you mighty ones who do his bidding, who obey his word. Praise the Lord, all his heavenly hosts, you his servants who do his will" (Ps 103:20-21; Heb 13:2). "The angel of the Lord encamps around those who fear him, and he delivers them" (Ps 34:7; see also 91:11-12). Angels are present when Christians

---

[632]Wesley, "Of Good Angels," Sermon #71, 1.7.

[633]Wesley, "Of Good Angels," Sermon #71, 2.9.

gather for worship (1 Cor 11:10). Angels carried Lazarus to Abraham's side (Luke 16:22). Presumably angels also carry away the souls of all believers (see Job 33:22).

John Calvin said, "Angels are the ministers and dispensers of divine bounty toward us. Accordingly, we are told how they watch for our safety, how they undertake our defense, direct our path, and take heed that no evil befall us."[634]

The old modernism dismissed angels and demons as outdated ideas which were nothing more than poetic metaphors for the concept of evil. Neither Karl Barth nor Paul Tillich does justice to the personal character of demons. In 1952 Gordon Rupp wrote *Principalities and Powers*, transferring "principalities and powers" to economic, social, and political forces. The motive was to demythologize Satan as a personal being in order to make the biblical teaching more acceptable to modernism. While Christianity has corrected pagan superstition stemming from an animistic worldview, this "victory" is not the result of Enlightenment philosophy, which categorically denies anything supernatural. Superstition is defeated by the preaching of God's Word.

This modern interpretation also provides a basis for liberation theology. However, it is possible to understand these powers as the structures, worldviews, and institutions that shape our world without necessarily denying the existence of Satan or embracing liberation theology.

There was a time when the secular media would not mention anything supernatural, but today there is a new postmodern openness to spirituality — both legitimate and counterfeit. While angels do exist, the Bible teaches that there are both good and bad angels. We must beware of instruction which encourages the use of occult techniques such as divination, channeling, visualization, and Eastern meditation to bring you into contact with your angel. We are not to worship or pray to angels (Col 2:18;

---

[634]Calvin, *Institutes*, 1.14.6; 1:145.

Rev 19:10, 22:8-9). We must avoid superstition and demigods. And we must also reject liberal rationalism and unbelief in anything supernatural, which goes all the way back to the Sadducees (Acts 23:8).

Among evangelicals, the Wesleyan position is a moderating position. On one hand, Calvinists hold that every specific action of the devil and demons is divinely ordained. Thus, Greg Bahnsen wrote, "While Satan may be prince of the demons, he nevertheless receives his power from God alone; the demonic host is in the final analysis at God's command, doing His sovereign bidding, and serving His divine ends."[635] While the understanding that God uses the devil is legitimate, we cannot say that God ordains and commands the actions of Satan without impugning the holiness of God.

In 2 Samuel 24:1-4 God incited David to take a census, but according to 1 Chronicles 21:1-2 *Satan* incited David. The same Hebrew verb occurs in both passages. Apparently God allowed Satan to tempt David because of David's pride. Wesley explained that the pronoun *he* in 2 Samuel 24:1 was Satan. David was not directed by God, but moved by his own curiosity, pride, and vain glory.

Archer listed four other instances of God's permissive will:

- Allowing Satan to test Job
- Allowing Judas to betray Christ
- Allowing Satan to sift Peter (Luke 22:31-32)
- In 1 Peter 4:19 God strengthens our faith by allowing Satan to test us (5:8).[636]

---

[635]Bahnsen, "Person, Work and Present Status of Satan," 18, 31; Erickson, *Christian Theology*, 398.

[636]Archer, *Encyclopedia of Bible Difficulties,* 186-188.

On the other hand, charismatic deliverance ministries often teach that demons are the cause of all disease.[637] However, such a worldview is reductionistic. People get sick because they are part of the human race, which is under the curse of sin. They may be sick because they have violated the laws of nature. Physical illness can be the result of psychological issues, physiological issues, or spiritual issues. Sickness may be chastisement from God. Sometimes God allows sickness in order to show his power in healing (John 9:2-3). In other circumstances God wants to show his grace in our suffering (2 Cor 9:12). In other instances, such as Matthew 9:32, a man was demon possessed and mute. Jesus cast out the demon and he could talk. But in Matthew 12:22, a man was blind and mute *and* demon-possessed. Yet, Jesus healed him.

In Mark 1:32 there is a distinction made between disease and demon possession. In v 34 Mark wrote that Jesus healed the sick *and* drove out demons. This statement is also made in Mark 6:13.

Although Jesus cast out demons wherever he encountered them, he did not do so when he encountered the leper in Mark 1:39-40. In the case of the paralytic in Mark 2:1-12 Jesus forgave his sin and healed his body. In the context of James 5:14-16 healing and forgiveness are also connected. Yet some disease is not the result of sin nor demonic activity. Jesus was clear in John 9:3 that the disability of the blind man was *not* the result of sin. The failure of Job's counselors was their attempt to pin a false accusation of sin on Job.

Peter Wagner has popularized the concept of spiritual mapping in order to identify territorial spirits.[638] Clinton Arnold concluded that the Bible affirms demonic activity and specific geographic locations, but that it nowhere instructs us to engage

---

[637]See Kunhiyop, *African Christian Theology*, 57-58.

[638]Wagner, *Confronting the Powers*, 72-73.

these high-ranking territorial spirits. Daniel prayed to God, but did not engage such evil spirits.[639]

Daniel 10 describes a twenty-one-day spiritual conflict between an angel who is rescued by Michael, who protects Israel, and the prince of Persia, who will be followed by the prince of Greece. This passage is often cited as proof that there are angels and demons assigned to territories. Whether or not the prince of Persia is the human ruler under demonic influence or a demon, which Ephesians 6:12 describes as a world ruler, the limited evidence suggests a political, not a territorial, conflict. Rather than attempting to identify territorial spirits, our emphasis should be on the omnipresence of the Almighty and the dominion of King Jesus.

Grudem argued that the preaching of the gospel itself breaks the chains of sin and that the apostles did not first have to break demonic strongholds. We must renounce the world, we must mortify the flesh, and we must resist the devil. "We need to accept our own responsibility to obey the Lord and not to shift blame for our own misdeeds onto some demonic force."[640]

The emphasis of the church is not on evil spirits, but that our names are written in heaven (Luke 10:20). Romans 6:18 teaches that we have already been freed from sin when we are saved. Regeneration is deliverance. Yet in some theological systems a mere consciousness and concern over sin is considered sufficient evidence that a person is born again. Such doctrine is the basis for the belief that "Christians" can be demon-possessed. According to 1 John 3:19 a true Christian is delivered from the bondage of sin.

---

[639]Arnold, *Three Crucial Questions About Spiritual Warfare*, 161.

[640]Grudem, *Systematic Theology*, 421.

Satan and fallen angels

God cannot be the creator of evil. Yet if God did not create these fallen angels then we have a dualism. Dunning explained that if Satan is perceived as having an independent existence, the doctrine of *creatio ex nihilo* is compromised.[641] Therefore, God created good angels, but some of them fell.

There are comparatively few references in the OT to demons and evil spirits. Satan tended to control indirectly through idolatry. Only four people in the OT had a direct encounter with Satan: Eve, Job, David (1 Chr 21:1), and Joshua, the high priest in Zechariah 3:1-5.

Pentecostal evangelist William Branham taught that Eve had sex with Satan and this was the original sin. This illicit sex was the forbidden fruit and the result was Cain.[642] This is more pagan and gnostic than Christian. Eve was deceived, not seduced.[643] White supremacists claim that Cain was cursed and that curse was marked by his black skin. But Genesis 4:15 does not teach this racism.

Another variation is that the fruit of that union was Cain, the father of the Jews. Building on British-Israelism, first popularized by John Wilson, *Lectures on Our Israelitish Origins* (1840), that Europeans constituted the "ten lost tribes," this view is called the Serpent Seed theory and has been perpetuated by the Christian Identity Movement.[644] Furthermore, the Christian

---

[641]Dunning, *Grace, Faith, and Holiness*, 243.

[642]Branham, "The Original Sin." See also Liardon, *God's Generals*, 339-340. See also Kunhiyop, *African Christian Theology*, 34, 58-59. The irony is that this false teaching, part of African Traditional Religion, was "revealed" to an illiterate Kentucky Pentecostal evangelist.

[643]For a refutation of Branham, see Velarde, "Did Eve Have Sex with Satan?"

[644]Abanes, *American Militias*, 162.

Identity Movement believes that other races descended from human beings created before Adam. Thus, only Whites are the true Israel and the true descendants of Adam. This provides a pseudo-biblical basis for racism. In many ways it is the polar opposite of the Zionist movement. All of these false teachings attempt to misuse Scripture to teach nonscriptural prejudice.

Despite the limited personal encounter with Satan in the Old Testament, the cosmic conflict between good and evil is a common theme. There was a dramatic increase in demonic activity associated with the incarnation and coming of Christ. This phenomenon is explained as Satan's futile attempt to thwart the coming of Christ. This increase in demonic activity may have also been permitted by God to signal Christ's authority over them.[645] According to Mark 1:22-27, demons were the first beings in Christ's ministry to recognize that he was the Son of God.

Revelation 12:3 describes a red dragon. That dragon is clearly identified in 12:9, and also 20:2, as the ancient serpent who lied to Eve in the beginning. He is also called the devil, meaning slanderer, and Satan, meaning adversary or accuser.

According to Revelation 12:4 a third of the stars of heaven were swept by Satan's influence and cast to the earth. Stars represent angels according to Revelation 1:20,9:1. While we do not know the total number of angels, Daniel 7:10 describes "ten thousand times ten thousand." According to Hebrews 12:22 and Jude 14 there are a myriad of angels. This Greek word *murias* literally means ten thousand, but Revelation 5:11 says there are myriads of myriads and thousands (*chilias*) of thousands. Obviously, John is conveying the concept of an innumerable host. Psalm 68:17 also describes the heavenly host with their chariots, which protected Elisha (2 Kgs 6:17).

---

[645]Miley, *Systematic Theology*, 2:501.

If this one-third in Revelation 12:4 can be taken literally, we could conclude that there are twice as many good angels as bad ones. There is one devil; there are many demons or fallen angels.

Apparently this fall occurred prior to Genesis 3 because at that time we see the serpent deceiving Adam and Eve. Satan fell because he rejected truth and became the father of lies (John 8:44). Regarding the phrase, "Not holding to the truth," Ralston observed that this implies he was once in it.[646]

The destiny of fallen angels is sealed. God did not make provision to redeem them. Origen's teaching that the restoration of all things, spoken of in Acts 3:21, extends even to Satan, is wrong. His statement regarding creation, that "after a time to bring back the whole to Himself," is also ambiguous.[647]

Gregory of Nyssa was more clear in his declaration that the great deceiver himself will also experience the benefit of the incarnation. "He as well as humanity, will be purged."[648] However, this belief is misguided. If Satan will be cast into the lake of fire forever, according to Revelation 20:20, he apparently was not part of the "all things" in Acts 3:21. Peter is apparently referring to the consummation of everything that has been prophesied.

Pride brought the devil under judgment (1 Tim 3:6). God did not spare angels when they sinned (2 Pet 2:4). Angels which did not keep their original position of authority are bound until the day of judgment (Jude 6). "One thing is certain; the angels who fell must have been in a state of *probation*; capable of either

---

[646]Ralston, *Elements of Divinity*, 70.

[647]Origen, *Against Celsus*, 4.99; *ANF* 4:541. See Origen's statement in Oden, *ACCS* 5:45 where he says God will ultimately heal everything. "The consummation of all things is the destruction of evil, although as to the question whether it shall be so destroyed that it can never anywhere arise again, it is beyond our present purpose to say."

[648]Gregory of Nyssa, *The Great Catechism*, *NPNF*2 5:472.

standing or falling, as Adam was in paradise."[649] Although there was no evil in the universe, Ralston explained that the possibility of sinning is essential to a state of accountability.[650] This reflects the concept of libertarian free will.

Isaiah 14:12-15 and Ezekiel 28:12-19 are also often used, but it is debatable whether or not these are descriptions of Satan. John Oswalt wrote of Isaiah 14,

> Some of the church fathers, linking this passage to Luke 10:18 and Rev.12:8,9, took it to refer to the fall of Satan described in those places. However, the great expositors of the Reformation were unanimous in arguing that the context here does not support such an interpretation (see v 16). This passage is discussing human pride, which, while monumental to be sure, is still human and not angelic.[651]

Commenting on the Ezekiel passage, Ralph H. Alexander explained,

> Tyre's king is best understood as the literal human contemporary king of that city in Ezekiel's day. Each characteristic given about him in these verses can be explained in light of the cultural and religious context of that day. Contrarily, the identification of the king as Satan must be done to a large extent on a presupposition that the descriptions here refer to Satan. Most of these descriptions — if they do in fact relate to Satan — are revealed nowhere else in Scripture. In light of the logical flow of the context and the explanations of the

---

[649]Clarke, *Commentary*, 6:951.

[650]Ralston, *Elements of Divinity*, 71.

[651]Oswalt, *Isaiah 1-39*, 320.

king's character given above, it is concluded that a human king is described herein.[652]

Many dispensationalists take the pronoun *he* in Daniel 9:27 to refer to antichrist. However, the devil does not make covenants. Wesley's comment was that "Christ confirmed the new covenant."[653]

Names for Satan

Satan is called *Beliar* (2 Cor 6:15), a variant of *Belial*, which means worthless and lawless. The Hebrew name *Abaddon* and the Greek name *Apollyon* both mean destroyer (Rev 9:11). *Beelzebul* means the dung god or lord of the flies (Matt 10:25,12:24,27; Mark 3:22; Luke 11:15,18-19). These terms are used by Jesus in contempt of Satan's status and power.[654]

It is debatable whether *Lucifer*, used only in Isaiah 14:12, refers to Satan. The Hebrew word *helel* means *to shine*. *Lucifer* means light bearer in Latin. It was the Latin name for the planet Venus, the morning star. According to Revelation 22:16 Jesus is the bright morning star. Satan, on the other hand, is the prince of darkness. According to D. H. Wheaton, the title of *morning star* or *Lucifer* (KJV) is used to taunt the king of Babylon, who had set himself among the gods. While some have applied this title to Satan, "The true claimant to the title is shown in Rev. 22:16 to be the Lord Jesus Christ in his ascended glory."[655] If Lucifer became Satan, it is not legitimate to call him *Lucifer* now.

---

[652]Alexander, *Expositor's Bible Commentary*, 6:882-885.

[653]Wesley, *Notes*, 3:2456.

[654]Bahnsen, "Person, Work, and Present Status of Satan," 27; McClintock & Strong, *Cyclopedia*, 1:722.

[655]Wheaton, "Lucifer," *New Bible Dictionary*, 713.

The application of this passage to Satan, and to the fall of the apostate angels, is one of those gross perversions of Sacred Writ which so extensively obtain, and which are to be traced to a proneness to seek for more in any given passage than it really contains, a disposition to be influenced by sound rather than sense, and an implicit faith in received interpretations.[656]

Demonic Orders

Ephesians 6:12 teaches there is an organized hierarchy in the spiritual world. These levels may be hard to distinguish because they work through human structures. Furthermore, Paul used different combinations of terms in Colossians 1:16; Ephesians 1:21, 6:12. However, there may be an evil hierarchy which corresponds to archangel, cherubs, seraphs, and angels.

- Arch (*arche*) – demons are first in order and rank.
- *Authorities* – (*exousias*) are demons under the arch-demons.
- "World rulers (*kosmokratores*) of this dark world" describes the function of demons and indicates they have infiltrated political systems of government (for example, see Dan 10:20), as well as all systems and structures not under the lordship of Christ. This is a similar phrase to "the rulers of this age" used in 1 Corinthians 2:6,8.

Satan does not rule this world, but he and his demons rule in the realm of darkness. He is the prince of this world system (John 14:30) and the god of this age (2 Cor 4:4). The whole world system is under the control of the evil one (1 John 5:19). Satan rules over a culture of rebellion, not over God's world (Col 1:13). His rule is an ethical realm, not a physical location. The earth is the Lord's and everything in it (Ps 24:1).

---

[656]Henderson, *Commentary on Isaiah*, 127.

- "Spiritual hosts of evil in the heavenlies" (not *high places* as rendered in the KJV) may be a general term for all evil spirits under the prince of the power of the air (Eph 2:2).

We are empowered by the Lord with his might and strength. God has provided protection, but the Christian has the responsibility of putting it on. We must appropriate what God has provided.

The kingdom of Satan is based on fear, guilt, greed, lust, and deception. Irenaeus wrote,

> The devil, however, as he is the apostate angel, can only go to this length, as he did at the beginning — to deceive and lead astray the mind of man into disobeying the commandments of God, and gradually to darken the hearts of those who would endeavor to serve him, to the forgetting of the true God, but to the adoration of himself as God.[657]

Satan masquerades as an angel of light (2 Cor 11:14). Paul's language, "Satan *himself* masquerades," implies the personality of Satan. Evil is more than an abstract concept. Jesus taught us to pray, "Deliver us from the evil *one*" (Matt 6:13).[658]

Satan prowls around *like* a roaring lion (1 Pet 5:8). He may roar *like* a lion, but he is not a lion. Jesus Christ is the lion of the tribe of Judah.

Richard Watson argued that the miraculous power of Christ and the apostolic church could not be duplicated by Satan or evil

---

[657]Irenaeus, *Against Heresies*, ANF 1:552-553.

[658]While the Greek syntax can be either the evil one or the evil thing (masculine or neuter), in 1 John 5:18 the adjective is masculine, as it is in 1 John 2:13. Thus, 1 John 5:19, which could be either masculine or neuter, is masculine since it refers to the same subject as v 18 [Robertson, *Word Pictures*, 6:244].

spirits. Watson also included a certain knowledge of the future along with miracles as belonging only to the kingdom of God.

Thus, Watson did not believe that Pharaoh's magicians performed miracles.[659] "If something or someone other than God can perform miracles, then the value of miracles for attesting to Christ's divinity is negated."[660] Watson wrote that evil spirits cannot create, because this is constantly attributed to God.

> "To whom will you compare me? Or who is my equal?" says the Holy One. Lift your eyes and look to the heavens: Who created all these? He who brings out the starry host one by one, and calls them each by name. Because of his great power and mighty strength, not one of them is missing (Isa 40:25-26).

Watson argued that this claim cuts off every other being from the power to create. He then said that life and death are out of the power of evil spirits. "I put to death and I bring to life" (Deut 32:39).

Watson also explained that the knowledge of future events, especially those which depend on free or contingent causes, is not attainable by evil spirits. "Declare to us the things to come, tell us what the future holds, so we may know that you are gods" (Isa 41:23).

Evil spirits do not always know the thoughts and character of men. The knowledge of the heart is attributed exclusively to God alone.[661]

Satan is successful, not because he overpowers people externally, but because he appeals to their sinful nature internally. Watson said that the history of Job reveals that evil spirits cannot

---

[659]Watson, *Theological Institutes*, 1:156-165; 171-174.

[660]Kole and MacGregor, *Mind Games*, 79.

[661]Watson, *Theological Institutes*, 1:156-175.

employ their power against a good man without God's permission.[662]

First John 5:18 promises that Jesus Christ keeps safe those who are born of God and the evil one cannot harm him. However, God can use Satan to discipline sin within the church. In 1 Corinthians 5:5 a wicked man was excommunicated and handed over to Satan for redemptive purposes. In 1 Timothy 1:20 two men in the congregation at Ephesus were also handed over to Satan until they learned not to blaspheme. In 2 Corinthians 12:7 Paul was tormented by a messenger of Satan.

Primarily, Satan is an accuser or slanderer, which is what his name means, and a deceiver. It is wrong to apply the attributes of God to Satan. We are cautioned not to be ignorant of his devices (2 Cor 2:11) and schemes (Eph 4:14, 6:11). Therefore, we must take every thought captive (2 Cor 10:5). When he offered Christ the kingdoms of the world (Matt 4:8), he deceptively offered what he did not own. His objectives are to:

- raise doubt concerning the Word of God
- distract us from spiritual priorities
- disable us from Christian ministry
- destroy us, as an attempt to strike back at God

Although we are warned in Revelation 2:24 not to learn "Satan's so-called deep secrets" there is an unhealthy curiosity and a sensationalism of the subject within some Christian novels. Eve was tempted to know that which God had not told her.

The Occult

The word *occult* means to cover over or conceal. It refers to the hidden world of darkness. Occult practices surface at the end of civilizations. Os Guinness wrote that early hunters on an

---

[662]Watson, *Theological Institutes*, 1:166.

African safari used to build their fires high at night in order to keep the animals in the bush. But when the fires burned low in the early hours of the morning, they would see the approaching shapes of animals all around them and a ring of encircling eyes in the darkness.

> When the fire was high they were far off, but when the fire was low they approached again. As we have witnessed the erosion and breakdown of the Christian culture of the West, so we have seen the vacuum filled by an upsurge of ideas that would have been unthinkable when the fires of the Christian culture were high.[663]

In Deuteronomy 18:9-14 the Word of God specifically forbids these occult practices. There is some overlap between these words.

- Human sacrifice (see 2 Kgs 23:10)
- Fire walking
- Divination. The use of divination or magic to get information from the supernatural. Pagans used arrows, livers, or images (Ezek 21:21). More modern forms include casting lots, tarot cards, Ouija boards.
- Interpretation of omens (see also Jer 10:2).
- Witchcraft or sorcery involves the use of magic and incantations. The LXX uses the Greek word *pharmakos*, which describes inducing magical effects or casting spells through drugs (see also Isa 47:9-12). *Pharmakos* is also found in Galatians 5:20; Revelation 9:21, 18:23, 21:8, 22:15.
- Spiritism or necromancy; a medium or new age channeling to consult the dead.
- False prophecy (Deut 13:1-3, 18:20-22).

---

[663]Guinness, *The Dust of Death*, 277.

In addition, Isaiah 47:13-14 forbids horoscopes and astrology — predicting the future from aspects of the planets and stars.

These practices are wrong because they are forbidden by God. The basis of witchcraft is rebellion (1 Sam 15:23). They are also wrong because they seek information God did not see fit to reveal in Scripture. They seek that information from the wrong source — the father of lies. These practices are attempts to gain not only knowledge but power without surrender to God.

It has become popular to warn Christian parents against the evils of Halloween and suggest that it is based on pagan customs. Actually, All Saints' Day celebrates the victory of the saints who are with Christ. Its history can be traced back to the late 300s. Since biblical days begin on the previous evening, the eve of All Saints' Day was All Hallows' Eve. The word *hallow* means *saint* or *holy one*, as in the Lord's Prayer — "hallowed by thy name." The defeat of evil and of demonic powers has been associated with Halloween. Thus, Martin Luther posted his 95 challenges to the wicked practices of the Roman Catholic Church on Halloween.

When Christian children are dressed up like ghosts, goblins, witches, and even the devil, they are mocking Satan who was defeated at the cross. No one really believes that a fallen archangel really wears a red suit. We dress like that on Halloween to ridicule him because he has lost the battle and no longer has power over us.[664]

Can A True Christian Be Demon-possessed?

In thirteen references, the Gospels describe those who are demonized (*daimonizomai*), whose body and soul are under the

---

[664]Jordan, "Concerning Halloween," 1. However, Luther went too far by employing scatological language [Oberman, *Luther*, 106-110].

special influence of demons. This implies that the demons are acting upon the mind and body of a subject from within.[665]

If the reality of evil spirits is denied, then their expulsion by Christ is no longer miraculous. The Gospels do not record Jesus casting out demons as an accommodation of first century superstition. However, passages such as Mark 1:32-34 distinguish between physical disease and spiritual possession. Again in Mark 6:13 the disciples anointed the sick and cast out demons.

However, all true Christians have the Holy Spirit (Rom 8:9) and "The one who is in you is greater than the one who is in the world" (1 John 4:4). Answers to this question get muddled because of the false premise of salvation through decisional regeneration, coupled with the false conclusion of unconditional eternal security. It is also confused by artificial attempts to distinguish between the human soul and the spirit, assigning one to the control of Satan while simultaneously the other faculty is under the control of the Holy Spirit.

We must renounce all former occult practices and connections. Historically, this was done at the time of baptism, the outward testimony of our deliverance from sin. However, demons may oppress believers who have given the devil a foothold (Eph 4:27).

Satan's Defeat at the Cross and Future Punishment

According to Revelation 12:7-9 the first phase of the cosmic battle takes place in heaven between Michael, the guardian of God's people, and the dragon, who is Satan. His attempted coup failed sometime before Genesis 3. Revelation 8:10,9:1 also describe his fall.

According to Revelation 12:4, a third of the stars of heaven were swept by Satan's influence and cast to the earth. God did

---

[665]Miley, *Systematic Theology*, 2:498.

not spare the angels who sinned (2 Pet 2:4). These angels who did not keep their original position of authority are bound until the day of judgment (Jude 6). Their sentence is sure and they will not escape, but they still have some limited activity on earth. They are under restraint and limits. Wesley explained, "Though still those chains do not hinder their often walking up and down, seeking whom they may devour."[666]

Satan had lost his position in heaven, yet apparently still had access to heaven (Rev 12:10). In Job we find Satan presenting himself before the Lord to accuse Job (1:6,2:1; see also 1 Kgs 22:21-22; 1 Chr 21:1; Zech 3:1). At that time Job complained that he had no advocate to argue his case. But after the atonement was completed, we now have an advocate (1 John 2:1). Satan was barred from heaven (Luke 10:18; Rev 12:7) and he no longer has authority to accuse us before God.

Revelation 12:9 tells us twice that the great dragon was cast down. Verses 7-9 seem to be out of sequence. These verses recall an earlier struggle which was alluded to in v 4. Alfred Plummer explained at v 4,

> The seer does not here interrupt his narrative to explain the point, but returns to it after ver. 6, and there describes briefly the origin and cause of the enmity of the devil toward God.

Plummer later identified the section describing the origin of the hostility of Satan towards God as vv 7-12.[667]

However, vv 10-12 seem to identify a second defeat at the time salvation and the kingdom of God came. This second demotion corresponds to Luke 10:28, where Jesus, in anticipation, said, "I saw Satan fall like lightning from heaven." It also corre-

---

[666]Wesley, *Notes,* 624.

[667]Plummer, *Pulpit Commentary*, 22:311, 315.

sponds to John 12:31, "Now is the time for judgment on this world; now the prince of this world will be driven out."

Adam and Eve had been given dominion on earth (Gen 1:26-28), and so Satan attempted to gain control of the earth by holding the human race hostage. When Adam sinned, a curse came upon the world. But God announced in Genesis 3:15 that he was at war with Satan. This was the first promise of redemption. The woman's seed would crush Satan's head. And so the dragon stood in front of the woman who was about to give birth, so that he might devour her child the moment it was born (Rev 12:4).

However, Satan does not share God's foreknowledge. Not knowing by whom or when the deliverance would come, he inspired Cain to kill his brother Abel. By the tenth generation, only Noah was righteous. Back and forth through the OT the battle was waged. Abraham did not have an heir until he was a hundred. Two nations struggled in Rebekah's womb. All the male children except Moses were aborted in Egypt. Five hundred years later a demon-possessed king tried to kill David, through whom the Messiah was promised. Later the royal line was completely destroyed except for Joash. Haman tried to annihilate the entire Jewish race. But all satanic attempts failed to thwart God's plan.

Satan tried to mislead Joseph into divorcing Mary. Herod slaughtered all the infants in Bethlehem, and baby Jesus had to be evacuated to Egypt. As Jesus began his public ministry, he confronted Satan in the wilderness during forty days of intense battle. Jesus encountered demonic opposition during his whole public ministry. Yet he explained that his ability to cast out demons was proof that the kingdom of God had finally come (Matt 12:28). There is not a clear instance in the Old Testament where demons were cast out.[668]

---

[668]Grudem, *Systematic Theology*, 417.

Satan infiltrated the disciples of Jesus and influenced Judas to betray Jesus. But at the cross, he made a public spectacle of evil powers and authorities, triumphing over them (Col 2:15).

Revelation 12:7-9 describes the second phase of this cosmic war. This description cannot be the primordial battle when Satan initially fell, because such a view conflicts with the consequences of vv 10-12. Satan, who had already lost his position in heaven, was now cast out of heaven. Satan fell at the beginning of the first creation and falls again at the start of the new creation.

In anticipation of the cross, Jesus said, "Now is the time for judgment on this world; now the prince of this world will be driven out" (John 12:31, 16:11; 1 John 3:8; Heb 2:14). "I saw Satan fall like lightning from heaven" (Luke 10:18). According to v 17, "The success of seventy-two over the demons was taken as evidence of his impending demise."[669]

According to Revelation 12:10, "Now the accuser, who accused night and day is cast down." *Now* is *arti*, a temporal adverb. Along with the aorist verb, *became*, John clearly records that salvation has been provided and the kingdom has been established at the time of his vision in the first century. Thus, the victory of the cross includes the fact that Satan can no longer accuse believers before God.

Daniel 7:21-27 describes the ascension and session of Christ. At the resurrection and ascension of Christ back to heaven the Father told him, "Sit at my right hand until I make your enemies a footstool for your feet" (Ps 110:1). The legal case has already been decided against Satan. Christ has regained control and we are seated with him (Eph 2:6). "In the mighty works of Jesus the power of the Kingdom has broken into the world; Satan has met his match; the cosmic end-struggle has begun."[670]

In Matthew 12:29 and Mark 3:27 Jesus described his conquest of Satan as binding the master of the house and robbing

---

[669]Oden, *Life in the Spirit*, 457.

[670]Bright, *The Kingdom of God*, 218.

him of his possessions. Satan's possessions are the people he holds in bondage. Yet they were created by God and for his glory. Thus, God through Christ is simply taking back what is rightfully his.

The verb for *bind* is *deo* and it is used three times in the NT to describe the bonds of marriage (Rom 7:2; 1 Cor 7:27, 39). Thus, interpreters are misled in Revelation 20:2, where the same verb is used, if they conclude that Satan is rendered completely inoperative. At the cross Satan received a mortal wound to his head. He is terminally ill, but not yet dead. He is alive, but not well, on planet earth.[671] His time is short (Rev 12:12). Demonic activity has been limited. His power has been broken. According to 2 Thessalonians 2:6-7 Satan is held back or restrained (*katecho*) through the preaching of the gospel.

The one whom Paul calls "the man of sin," John simply calls Satan. The beast and the false prophet were previously thrown alive into the lake of fire (Rev 19:20). Finally, after all Satan's puppets have been eliminated, it seems that the man of sin himself will be revealed at the last stage of world history.

This *man of sin* will be revealed *after* the millennium during the apostasy or falling away. This falling away is also described in Revelation 20:7-10. But first there must be a general drawing unto Christ. After the "thousand years" Satan will be loosed. Apparently *he* is the *man of sin* because he is the one who will be cast into the lake of fire where the beast and false prophet had already been thrown (Rev 20:7-10). This is the final appearance of the spirit of antichrist which precedes the coming of the Lord.

Preterists commonly identify "the man of sin" with Nero. Historicists tended to equate him with the Pope. Futurists identify him as a future Antichrist. But if Christ comes at the end of the millennial period, this must be describing a future enemy. And if the beast and false prophet, who were identified with

---

[671]Contrary to Hal Lindsey, *Satan is Alive and Well on Planet Earth* (1972); see Grider, *Wesleyan-Holiness Theology*, 170.

antichrist in Revelation 13, have already been cast into the lake of fire, the man of sin must be someone else. On the basis of 2 Thessalonians 2:9 some commentators identify the *man of sin* as the final incarnation of Satan.

Either his actions will be in accordance with Satan's work, or he is Satan, the man of sin, the coming of whom is in accordance with his previous activity. One argument in favor of this second option is that Satan himself is called *Beliar* in 2 Corinthians 6:15. This name means *lawless one.* In the OT a son of Belial was a lawless person. Thus Belial, the lawless one is the man of sin, the lawless one, in 2 Thessalonians 2. Whether the *man of sin* is Satan or one of his puppets, the work of Satan is restrained between the first advent and the second advent.

The victory of the cross is the *decisive* victory of Christ over Satan. The victory of the Christian church, through the atonement of Christ and enforced through our testimony, amounts to the *progressive* victory of Christ until his return. We live between those two great events. Satan has been in check mate since the cross.

Oscar Cullman developed the analogy of D-Day and V-Day to explain the decisive and the *final* victory of Christ. Based on World War 2 history, D-Day was the victory of the cross. However, the battle was not over at D-Day. Yet the second world war turned at D-Day from a defensive battle to an offensive battle — which culminated at V-Day.[672]

The third and final defeat of Satan is described in Revelation 20:10. Thus, according to Revelation 20:1-2, Satan was bound at the cross and is bound for a *thousand years.* While the concept of the millennium will be discussed under eschatology, I will explain under that heading that the millennium is the indefinite period of time between the first and second advent of Christ. During this time Satan's influence is greatly restrained and the reign of Christ from his heavenly throne will eventually prevail

---

[672]Ladd, *The Last Things*, 47.

on earth. Before Christ returns, every enemy will be defeated (1 Cor 15:24). Yet, according to Revelation 20:7 Satan will briefly be loosed (*luo*) at the end of time. This implies that he is bound now. The result is that he is no longer able to deceive the nations as he did prior to Christ's advent (Rev 20:3).

In the meantime the church must resist and stand (Eph 6:11,13). We are able to withstand, and when the battle is over we can still be standing. The believer has authority over Satan and his kingdom, since we are seated with Christ (Eph 2:6). However, this concept is often expressed in flippant terms such as "kicking the devil." But Jude 9 reminds us that Michael, in his dispute with the devil, said "The Lord rebuke you!"

> In Matthew 16:19 and 18:18 Jesus speaks of believers having authority to bind which affects both heaven and earth. In 18:19 church discipline (dealing with professing Christians) is the subject of binding and loosing, not spiritual warfare (dealing with the demonic realm). In verse 20 this is done by agreeing in prayer to God, not talking to Satan.[673]

We have been given authority over Satan, and God uses him to provide combat training for us. Judges 3:1-2 explain that God left enemies in the land of Canaan in order to train Israel for warfare.

Samuel Rutherford explained that "the devil is but God's master fencer, to teach us to handle our weapons."[674] We cannot learn to resist if there is no opposition. God will not allow more on us than we are able to bear, but resistance develops strength. As we resist Satan, we are making Satan a liar, we are bringing glory to God, we are developing strength, we learn to sympathize

---

[673]Villanueva, "Territorial Spirits," 39.

[674]Rutherford, *Letters of Samuel Rutherford*, 290. Letter #157 to John Fullerton, 14 March 1637.

with those who are suffering, and we are in training for future leadership.

The heathen still rage (Ps 2:1) and the devil still roars (1 Pet 5:8), and we do not yet see everything subject to Christ (Heb 2:8), but no weapon forged against us will prevail (Isa 54:17). If we resist the devil, he will flee (Jas 4:7). C. S. Lewis warned,

> There are two equal and opposite errors into which our race can fall about devils. One is to disbelieve in their existence. The other is to believe, and to feel an excessive and unhealthy interest in them. They themselves are equally pleased by both errors and hail a materialist or a magician with the same delight.[675]

At the second coming the devil will be thrown into the lake of fire and brimstone and be tormented day and night forever and ever (Rev 20:10). This is the final victory. Martin Luther wrote sometime between 1527-1529,

> And though this world, with devils filled,
> Should threaten to undo us,
> We will not fear, for God hath willed
> His truth to triumph through us.
> The Prince of Darkness grim,—
> We tremble not for him;
> His rage we can endure,
> For lo! His doom is sure,—
> One little word shall fell him.

That one little word is the name of Jesus. It is the name above all earthly powers, and his kingdom is forever.

---

[675]Lewis, *Screwtape Letters*, 3.

CHAPTER SEVEN
The Doctrine of Mankind

God created Adam and Eve at the beginning of human history. God created mankind, both male and female, in his image and likeness. Since the human race originated with a historical Adam and Eve, there is only one race.

While each gender has some specific role responsibilities, both genders reflect God's image. The ability to procreate, which was intended to be confined within marriage, is dependent upon both a male husband and a female wife. Human life begins at conception, and every life has intrinsic worth because it reflects the image of God.

We are embodied spirits. Nothing else in creation reflects his image. That image and likeness includes personhood, self-consciousness and self-expression, righteousness and the capacity to love, and the responsibility of libertarian free will. It also includes our dominion over the rest of creation.

That image has been greatly marred due to our fall, but not completely lost. However, we lost physical immortality and original righteousness. Even in our fallen state we still reflect a distorted and inconsistent shadow of what we were meant to be.

Biblical Anthropology

Anthropology is from the Greek word *anthropos*, the generic word for mankind, including male and female. The fact that God created male *and* female, rather than just one gender, reflects the plurality of persons within the Trinity since we are created in the image of God.

Humanity was made a little lower than the angels (Ps 8:5; Heb 2:7). We are God's offspring (Acts 17:28). The Greek word for *offspring* is *genos*. This word describes kinship based on creation. Thus, he is our Father.

Scripture speaks of the fatherhood of God metaphorically (Job 38:28). The doctrine of creation, that humanity has descended from one original pair, means that we are all related. Yet the doctrine of sin also explains that we are estranged from God and from each other. Only those who trust in Christ are given the right to become sons of God (John 1:12).

Irenaeus wrote, "The glory of God is a living man [or man fully alive]."[676] According to the Westminster Shorter Catechism (1646-1647), the chief end of man is to "glorify him and enjoy him forever."[677] C. S. Lewis explained,

> Nature is mortal; we shall outlive her. When all the suns and nebulae have passed away, each one of you will still be alive. Nature is only the image, the symbol; but it is the symbol Scripture invited me to use. We are summoned to pass in through Nature, beyond her, into the splendor which she fitfully reflects.[678]

However, most theories about man are either too optimistic or too pessimistic. Enlightenment optimism concerning human reason led to humanistic pessimism which taught that homo sapiens were nothing more than an evolution from lower species. Man is neither a zero nor a machine.[679]

---

[676]Irenaeus, *Against Heresies, ANF* 1:490.

[677]Wesley, *BE Works*, 12:93.

[678]Lewis, *The Weight of Glory*, 44.

[679]Schaeffer, *Works*, 1:268.

Bloesch observed that liberal theology is fundamentally anthropology.[680] Thus, Schleiermacher and Tillich both begin with anthropology.

The Creation of Man

According to Genesis 2:7, God formed the man from the dust of the ground and breathed into his nostrils the breath of life and man *became* a living soul. Purkiser explained, "Dust plus breath equals flesh; flesh plus spirit equals soul."[681] Thus, mankind is best described as embodied souls.

Became is from the Hebrew verb *hayah* (*to be*). Man did not evolve; he *became* by a direct act of God. The Hebrew word *adam* is a generic word for mankind, but it also is the proper name, *Adam*, when *adam* is prefaced with the definite article.[682] Thus, the notion of preadamic mankind is actually a contradiction, since *adam* is a generic term for original humanity.

God created two genders. Both male (*zakar*) and female (*neqebah*) are *adam*. Eve did not evolve. She was formed from Adam by God (Gen 2:21-23; 1 Cor 11:8).

The Hebrew word for *earth* (*adamah*) in Genesis 2:7 refers to the ground from which mankind was formed. Thus, *adam* and *adamah* are related words and *Adam* symbolizes the earthly man.

God also breathed life into *adam*, making him a living soul. He breathed into us the Spirit of life. The word for *breath* and *spirit* is the same word in both Hebrew (*ruach*) and in Greek (*pneuma*).

Other creatures also have soul or life (*nephesh*). Leviticus 17:11-14 declares that life (*nephesh*) is in the blood. Although *nephesh* occurs over seven hundred times in the OT, it seldom denotes a *soul*. It literally means *breath*, whether animals or

---

[680]Bloesch, *Word & Spirit*, 117.

[681]Purkiser, *God, Man, and Salvation*, 72.

[682]The exceptions are Gen 1:26, 2:5, 2:20.

humans. Since breath is tantamount to life itself, *nephesh* essentially means *life*.[683] Thus, it carries the connotation of the whole self.[684]

Mankind (*adam*) is composed of flesh (*basar*) and spirit (*ruach*), both of which are dependent upon God. Mankind is distinct from animal life because we alone are the image of God. We also have *lebab*. This word is rarely used in the OT of any subject other than mankind.[685] It describes the inner life of a person, including conscience, will, memory, moral character, and intellect.

Humanity alone is made in God's image (Gen 1:26). In Genesis 1:24-25 the creation is "each according to its kind." In v 26 man "rules over nature." Thus, no suitable wife could be found for Adam from among creation (Gen 2:20; 1 Cor 15:39).

Mankind did not begin as primal barbarians. In *The Origin of Heathendom*, Ben Adam pointed out that there was a time when the entire human race knew God. But in spite of the revelation of God's awesome judgment through the flood, the generations after the flood eventually suppressed that knowledge. Paganism developed as the result of man's repudiation of God and God's repudiation of them:

> and they came to be in the awful state of corruption set forth in Romans 1:18-32. . . . The heathen world, then, according to the Scriptures, owes its origin to the apostasy of the race and their dispersion resulting therefrom as set forth in Genesis 11:1-9 and Romans 1:18-32.[686]

---

[683]Fredericks, "נפשׁ," *NIDOTTE* 3:133.

[684]BDB, *Lexicon*, 659-661.

[685]It occurs in its noun form 851 times. Only 14 times is the subject something other than mankind. These 14 poetic references never have an animate object as their subject.

[686]Adam, *The Origin of Heathendom,* 46; 60-61.

What is the *Image of God*?

Wesley did not distinguish between image and likeness. Here he followed the Reformed interpretation that this was Hebrew parallelism.[687] According to Wiley, Protestants generally reject any distinction between image and likeness.[688]

The terms *image* and *likeness* occur together only in Genesis 1:26. However, in v 27, which deals with the actual work of creation, only *image* is used. In Genesis 5:1 only the word *likeness* is used. The Hebrew word for *likeness* is not translated in the LXX by the usual Greek word *homoiosis*, but by *eikon*, which means *image*. Genesis 9:6 contains only the word *image*. However, in Genesis 5:3 both terms are used. In the NT both terms occur only in 1 Corinthians 11:7. *Image* alone is used in Colossians 3:10 and *likeness* alone occurs in James 3:9.

This image is not to be conceived as something in us. It is what we are. Wesley described the image of God as a mind that could distinguish truth from error (unerring understanding), a will that loved God (uncorrupted will), freedom (perfect freedom).[689]

The image of God in man has been greatly marred but not completely lost. It may be distorted beyond recognition, but it is not destroyed. According to Genesis 9:6, murder is still forbidden even though man has fallen. In light of Genesis 9:6, 1 Corinthians 11:7, and James 3:9, we cannot conclude that man has completely lost the image of God.

Our fall is *total* in the sense that we are affected in every area, yet mankind still has dignity and worth. The basis for human dignity and destiny is dependent upon God's glory. It is a sin to murder or take human life (Exod 20:13) because man is in the image of God. Murder, then, is an attack on the image of

---

[687]Oden, *ACCS* 1:40.

[688]Wiley, *Christian Theology*, 2:31.

[689]Wesley, "The Image of God," Sermon #141.

God. In contrast, it is not necessarily wrong, nor is it considered murder, to kill an animal.

In Mark 12:13-17 Jesus essentially taught that we pay taxes to Caesar because money has his image on it. That image resembled Caesar and represented him. We should also give ourselves to God because we bear *his* image.

The *image of God* has been interpreted substantively, referring to something inherent within humanity, such as reason, the intellect, or innate holiness. According to Mormon theology, God has a body, so the human body is the image of God.

It has also been understood relationally, referring to how humanity relates to each other and to God. The image of God involves a fourfold relationship: with God, with others, with self, and a responsibility to nature. Murphree contends that being social is one of the ways we are created in God's image.[690] William Ury argued that human personhood is primarily understood in the context of interrelatedness within the Trinity.[691]

Dennis Kinlaw wrote that Jesus reveals the nature of personhood. Jesus had a clear consciousness of his own identity. But while we are distinct individuals, we are never alone. We exist in webs of relationships. Relationships are reciprocal. We both give and receive. And personhood implies freedom, freedom to give and not just receive. Personhood also means we have the capacity to make moral judgments. We have the ability to stand outside ourselves and to relate to something beyond ourselves. We find completeness in relating to others through a trusting love. Thus, Kinlaw concludes that no person is self-originating, no person is ever self-sustaining, and no person is self-explanatory.[692]

The capacity to love is part of the divine image. Wesley explained, "But love is the very image of God: it is the bright-

---

[690]Murphree, *Love Motive*, 13.

[691]Ury, *Trinitarian Personhood*, 11,280.

[692]Kinlaw, *Let's Start With Jesus*, 71-106.

ness of his glory. By love man is not only made like God, but in some sense one with him."[693]

The image has also been explained as functional, describing how humanity exercises stewardship or dominion over creation. Each concept makes a positive contribution, but all three views — substantive, relational, functional — need to be held in tension.

Wesley, in solidarity with the Reformers, understood the image of God to consist of three components: the moral image, the natural image, and the political image.

• The Moral Image

The moral image is spirituality — righteousness and holiness. This primitive holiness produces an innocence toward sin, a relative perfection, as well as an enlightened understanding of God and a will wholly inclined toward him.

Nor is the image of God an innate aspect of Adam's character apart from the influence of the Holy Spirit. Whedon insisted that Adam had moral excellence but not ethical holiness.[694]

According to Hebrews 12:9, God is the Father of our spirits. Essentially, the moral image includes the communicable attributes of God. This moral image of God within man was lost in the fall. Man is a spiritual being, but through sin he has lost his relationship with God (1 Cor 2:14-15).

Spiritual death is the separation of the human spirit and the Holy Spirit. However, the soul of man is immortal even if the sinner exists in a state of spiritual death. Thus, Paul explained to the Ephesians that they were dead in their transgressions and sin (Eph 2:1). However, we must remember that Paul's use of *death* to describe our natural state is an analogy. In v 2 he continues by saying that those who were dead *walked* in sin. Elsewhere, in

---

[693]Wesley, "The One Thing Needful," Sermon 146, 2.2.

[694]Whedon, *Freedom of the Will*, 300-316.

Romans 6:20, 7:14, and 2 Timothy 2:26 Paul uses the analogy of slavery to describe the life of sin. Scripture also uses the analogy of sickness in Isaiah 1:5-6.

First Corinthians 2:11 explains that we know a person's thoughts because we also have a spiritual relationship with that person. Because all men are spiritual, they are capable of having a relationship with each other and with God. Ladd wrote, "This seems to be a psychological statement that is universal in its application." He continued to explain that before salvation our relationship with God was dead, but we still possessed spiritual capabilities.[695] Wesley described this state as "absolutely void of all spiritual life."[696] Spiritual death indicates a deprivation of all spiritual life. This is a living death. Samuel Wakefield described this death as

> a separation of the soul from communion with God, and is manifested by the dominion of earthly and corrupt dispositions and habits, and an entire indifference or aversion to spiritual and heavenly things. All who have not been made alive by the power of divine grace are regarded as being in this state of spiritual death.[697]

The regenerate are spiritually alive because they have the Holy Spirit. According to 1 Corinthians 15:45-49, the first man was a living soul and the last Adam is a life-giving spirit. The first man was first created from the dust, then he received the breath of life. The contrast is not between soul and spirit but between the first man, who received life, and the last man, who gave life.

In 1 Corinthians 2:14-3:3 and 15:44-46 Paul uses the adjective or adverb forms of *soul* and *spirit*. Here he teaches that

---

[695]Ladd, *Theology of the New Testament*, 463.

[696]Wesley, *Notes*, 491.

[697]Wakefield, *Christian Theology*, 1:291.

Christians who still live primarily on the basis of their old life are *soulish* or natural. Paul admonishes them to become more *spiritualish*.

According to Gordon Fee, Paul is not suggesting classes of Christians or grades of spirituality in 1 Cor 3:1-3. He is trying to get the Corinthians to stop acting like people of the present age.[698] Thus, there are two categories — natural and spiritual.

Regarding the doctrine of the immortality of the soul, two errors must be refuted. First, this doctrine does not imply the pagan notion of preexisting souls, as Plato taught.[699] The soul of man is immortal but not eternal.

Second, the teaching of conditional immortality must also be rejected. The soul of man will continue to exist forever in a state of life or death.

• **The Natural Image**

The natural image encompasses all that distinguishes human life from animal life, since the image of God is what sets man apart from the rest of creation. Since mankind retains this image, we either sanctify or profane God's name by our lives.

The natural image is largely relational. It is also grace-infused capabilities.[700] It is reflected in the intellectual power of reason, self-consciousness, conscience, and self-expression, such as language, literature, the arts, and culture.

Conscience involves a perception of moral distinctions, a sense of obligation to do right, and a feeling of self-justification or condemnation which results from choosing right or wrong.

---

[698]Fee, *NICNT* 122.

[699]Tertullian affirmed Plato's teaching that "Every soul is immortal" [*On the Resurrection of the Flesh*, *ANF*, 3:547], but in *A Treatise on the Soul* refutes Plato's teaching concerning its preexistence [*ANF* 3:184].

[700]Collins, *Theology of John Wesley*, 53.

After the fall of mankind, the work of the Holy Spirit through conscience is part of preliminary grace.[701] Romans 9:1 is the only reference which directly connects the Holy Spirit and conscience. Conscience is also influenced by social taboos and cultural expectations which may not be biblical.

The natural image is summed up in the word *personality*. Personality incorporates intellect, emotions, and will. With regard to our will, the image of God in man is reflected in self-determinism. Freedom is the power of contrary choice. Freedom of choice means that man is held responsible for sin. He was created in a state of probation.

Thus, divine law existed from the time man was created. The law of God is holy, just, and good (Rom 7:12). Theologians often refer to a covenant of works, implied in Hosea 6:7, but Scripture never describes a covenant of works with Adam.[702]

While the term *covenant* (*berith*) does not appear until the covenant with Noah in Genesis 6-9, yet the elements of a covenant are present with Adam. Two parties are named, a condition is laid down, a promise of reward for obedience is clearly implied, and a penalty for transgression is threatened.[703] Adam was the *federal head* or legal representative for mankind. While we cannot be saved by keeping the covenant of works, the notion that grace has replaced law is wrong.

But how can mankind be free if God is sovereign? The tension between divine sovereignty and human responsibility has been expressed in Calvinism as *compatiblistic* liberty. This means that man's freedom is compatible with God's determinism. Thus, man was not coerced to sin, even if his original sin was predestined. He is free to comply with God's decisions, but he is not free not to comply.

---

[701]Wesley, "Scripture Way of Salvation," Sermon #43, 1.2.

[702]Noble, *Christian Theology* 1 3:660.

[703]Berkhof, *Systematic Theology*, 213.

Thus, man sins because he is a sinner. But Adam was not created as a sinner. Sin is not part of man's basic essence. Jesus was fully human, but he did not sin. We were not created to be sinners. Sin was the result of a historical event.

In contrast to the theology of Luther and Calvin, Edwards presented a rationalistic argument that the will is free, but free only to choose evil. Edwards defined *freedom* as the ability to act in accordance with one's own choices. Edwards asserted that a person never "wills anything contrary to his desires, or desires anything contrary to his will."[704] However, since mankind is totally depraved he will never choose anything but evil and sin.

Thus, his concept of freedom is compatible with determinism. But a free will that is compatible with determinism is not free since it is the only choice possible. Edwards' book, along with Luther and Calvin, also advocates the bondage of the will even though he has redefined bondage as freedom. Edwards reflects the New England model of Calvinism. He rejected libertarian freedom but upheld moral responsibility. However, only those who were elect and because of their election were sovereignly regenerate would repent as the fruit of their regeneration.

Wesley responded, "There is no blame if they are under a *necessity* of willing. There can be no moral good or evil, unless they have *liberty* as well as *will*."[705]

Wesley took special delight in citing the language of the Calvinistic Westminster Confession which stated, "God hath endued the will of man with that natural liberty that is neither forced, nor by an absolute necessity of nature, determined to do good or evil."[706]

The Arminian answer is *libertarian* freedom. We are not autonomous, but God confers to us our freedom. Our actions are foreknown but not predetermined by God. Thus, true freedom

---

[704]Edwards, *Freedom of the Will*, 139.

[705]Wesley, *Thoughts Upon Necessity*, 3.7; *BE Works*, 13:539.

[706]Oden, *John Wesley's Teachings*, 2:180.

contains the option of contrary choice. It is significant that John Frame concedes this was the position of the early church until the time Augustine debated Pelagius.[707]

Man was also created immortal. While Job asked, "If a man dies, will he live again?" (14:14), this was a rhetorical question, not the question of an agnostic. Life after death was part of Israel's faith. Assuming that Job was not part of Israel, I am not sure how much revelation Job had. But in Job 19:26-27 he declared emphatically that he would see God after his death.

Watson argued for the immortality of man's body *and* soul.[708] If physical death is the result of sin (Rom 5:12), then it can be logically inferred that man was originally created to live forever. Some theologians argue that the human body was created mortal and that the tree of life symbolizes the providential means through which God would have sustained human immortality. The only debate, then, is whether immortality was unconditional or conditional. However, the Pelagian argument that Adam would have died anyway must be rejected.[709] The Council of Carthage in AD 418 declared,

> If any man says that Adam, the first man, was created mortal, so that, whether he sinned or not, he would have died from natural causes, and not as the wages of sin, let him be anathema.[710]

- **The Political Image**

Genesis 1:26 connects the image of God and man's dominion over creation. The political image is the responsibility of

---

[707]Frame, *Doctrine of God*, 138.

[708]Watson, *Theological Institutes*, 2:386.

[709]Wakefield, *Christian Theology*, 1:291.

[710]McCall, *Against God and Nature*, 322.

mankind as steward and caretaker of creation. The political image means that man has dominion over the earth. He is to rule it under God. "The highest heavens belong to the Lord, but the earth he has given to man" (Ps 115:16).

This is the basis of the cultural mandate and it references our relationship with creation and nature. "You made [man] a little lower than the heavenly beings and crowned him with glory and honor. You made him ruler over the works of your hands; you put everything under his feet" (Ps 8:5-6).[711]

The implications of this dominion include our stewardship of the earth itself. While we do not worship nature, we do not have the right to destroy it. While "green theology" tends toward pantheism, and while radical feminism has developed an extreme worldview in which the earth is sacred and needs to be liberated from male domination, Christians should lead the way in commonsense ecology — although our ethic comes from a different rationale. Thus, a comprehensive theology of stewardship is not a fad or trend to adapt. The basis for such thinking can be found in OT case law which prohibited the use of fruit trees in siege warfare (Deut 20:19-20).

Life must go on. War is not to be waged against the earth. The vineyard represents an inheritance from the past and the fruit tree represents a heritage for the future. Thus, wanton destruction is not permitted.

Furthermore, the nation of Israel was required to clean up after themselves as they passed through the wilderness on the way to land that was promised to them (Deut 23:9-14).

Thus, man has the capacity and responsibility for dominion because he is the image of God. Yet, the image of God cannot be defined as our body, our experience, or our function.

The natural image and the political image of God was marred — not completely lost — but greatly damaged. The moral

---

[711]Yet Heb 2:8-9 shifts to a specific reference to Jesus Christ, the representative man. He alone is the perfect fulfillment of Ps 8:4-6.

image was totally destroyed. Salvation is the restoration of the fallen image (Eph 4:24; Col 3:10).

If our identity is defined by the image of God in which we were created, sin is the rejection of our identity. Mankind is a magnificent ruin due to the results of sin. Blaise Pascal said that man is "the glory and refuse of the universe."[712] Yet that image of God in man still exists in some sense.

Both man and woman are created in God's image and are given dominion (Gen 1:26-28). Women are presented in the Bible as no less intelligent than men nor any less capable of redemption. The Hebrew word *adam* comprises both male and female. While 1 Corinthians 11:7 specifies males as the image and glory of God, as a present reality after the fall, Paul is here emphasizing that women honor both God and man. He is delineating role distinctions. This does not imply that women are not the image of God, however, since men too are also in relationships of subordination — yet that does not imply that they are not in the image of God. Jesus himself was subordinate to his Father and even became subordinate to human structures in order to redeem us. Yet he was still the exact image of God (Col 3:15).

At issue is not male superiority or female inferiority. Nothing about the term *helper* (*ezer*) in Genesis 2:18 implies inferiority. The same word is used of God in Psalm 118:6. Again, in 1 Peter 3:7 *weaker* does not mean inferior. Because women are *weaker* we treat them with respect, not contempt.

The issue concerns roles. Evangelical feminists want to abolish all gender roles in society, church, and home. Scripture, however, teaches equal worth but different roles just as each member of the Trinity has distinct roles or functions.

---

[712]Pascal, *Pensées*, frag. 131.34.

The Unity of the Race

Cultural anthropology deals with the similarities and differences within the human race. They have identified approximately 24,000 ethnic units or people groups. Jesus used the term *ethnos* in Matthew 28:19. From a Jewish perspective, these non-Jews are the *goyim* or gentiles, but Jew and gentile are both part of the same race.

Race is a social construct developed from human interrelationships, not from God's design. Race has been defined as, "any of the major biological divisions of mankind, distinguished by color and texture of hair, color of skin and eyes, stature, bodily proportions."[713] Both the Old and New Testament show that God does not assign any significance to race. In Genesis 1:27 God said, "Let us make *humanity* in our image."

Theories of racial supremacy are myths. Basic genetic differences within an *ethnos* are often greater than genetic difference between ethnicities. In 2000 the human genome project found that we all came from the same DNA.[714]

Before Darwin, the term *race* was largely a political and geographical term. In Romans 9:3, 16:7,11,21, Paul uses the Greek word *suggenes* to refer to his kin. Some translations employ the word *race*, but Paul is actually referring to his kinsmen according to the flesh. Jesus is called the *monogenes*, the only begotten. Paul has simply changed the prefix from *mono* to *syn*, which means *with*.

In 1859 Charles Darwin published his famous book, *On the Origin of Species by Means of Natural Selection, or the Preservation of Favored Races in the Struggle for Life*. However, Scripture teaches that every human being is our relative. We all have a common ancestry in a historic Adam and Eve. According

---

[713]*Webster's New Twentieth Century Dictionary*, 1484.

[714]International Human Genome Sequencing Consortium Announces "Working Draft" of Human Genome (June 2000).

to Genesis 3:20, Eve is the mother of all the living. Acts 17:26 teaches that every nation (*ethnos*) of men come from one. And Romans 5:12 teaches that humanity was corporately implicated in Adam's original sin. Therefore, we should not distinguish between races but between ethnicity.

Just as Nazi Germany employed Darwin's racism to advocate a pure Aryan race, American southern churches employed the same argument in favor of segregation. A survey of the literature will reveal that the argument for segregation was based on genetics, not on Scripture.

However, the "Christian" defense of slavery was based largely on a distortion of the curse of Ham, the relationship of Philemon and Onesimus, and such passages as 1 Peter 2:18-20 and Ephesians 6:5-9. The first mention of slavery in the Bible is Genesis 9:25-26. Noah placed a curse on Canaan, not Ham, and this curse was not the color of his skin.

Racism is based on a false assumption that there is more than one race of human beings. God does not show partiality to any ethnicity (Acts 10:34-35). If we compile the guilt for the sins of every generation back to Adam and transfer that cumulative guilt to the next generation, future generations could never make adequate reparation. This attempt becomes an attempt to save ourselves, or justify ourselves, through our good works. It is also a form of racism — that certain ethnic groups are automatically culprits and other ethnic groups are automatically victims.

If the guilt of Adam's original sin was not imputed to the human race, as an unconditional benefit of the atonement, this concept may help us answer the question of reparations. While we deplore slavery, and its justification through the abuse of Scripture, the guilt of a previous generation cannot transfer to future generations. According to Ezekiel 18:20, "The soul who sins is the one who will die. The son will not share the guilt of the father, nor will the father share the guilt of the son." While children are harmed by the sins of their parents, they are not liable. Every pot sits on its own bottom. According to Ezekiel 18:20,

The son who sins is the one who will die. The son will not share the guilt of the father, nor will the father share the guilt of the son. The righteousness of the righteous man will be credited to him, and the wickedness of the wicked will be charged against him.

According to Deuteronomy 24:16, "Fathers shall not be put to death for their children, nor children put to death for their fathers; each is to die for his own sin." We cannot resolve the injustices of previous generations by punishing the present generation. However, we should make restitution, to the degree that it is possible, when we have personally hurt other people. This concept of personal restitution is founded in Exodus 21-22, Luke 19:8, and perhaps 2 Corinthians 7:11. According to Exodus 22:3, a thief who cannot make restitution could be sold into slavery until the debt was paid. However, restitution is not the basis of salvation, but rather the fruit of genuine repentance.

Justice is defined within the ten commandments. However, modernists tends to define "social justice" in terms of identity politics. Everyone is grouped as either the oppressed or the oppressor. But Jesus identified with the entire human race through his incarnation, since both groups are sinners.

When individuals are categorized in terms of race, sex, or economic identity, then it is claimed that wherever inequality exists one collective group must repay another collective group. However, this Marxist class warfare often results in justified injustice when freedom of speech exists only for the oppressed and when equity of outcomes, not just equity of opportunity, must be enforced by big government. Marxism claims that there must be a redistribution of wealth, enforced by the same government which they say must be overthrown.

Who decides who owes what to whom? We have all sinned against each other. We cannot atone for our own sins, much less those of our ancestors. Modernism assumes that certain groups are innocent because they have suffered injustice and that other groups are guilty, and thus are disenfranchised, simply because of their ancestry. We cannot save ourselves through masochism. "The political cultivation of guilt is a central means to power, for guilty men are slaves; their conscience is in bondage, and hence they are easily made objects of control."[715]

We have a common ancestry, and the result is that we are all sinners. Our salvation is not through human government enforcing a particular view of social justice. Our salvation is through the atonement of Christ, which alone can restore what Adam forfeited. We all need to start fresh through the grace provided in Christ's atonement.

When Does Life Begin?

In Psalm 139:13-16 David described the development of an unborn child. David wrote in Psalm 51:5, "Surely I was sinful at birth, sinful from the time my mother conceived me." At the moment of conception, this new life has a self-identity and a sinful nature.

Human life, whether born or unborn, was protected in the OT (Exod 21:22-25). The Bible treats the unborn as fully human. The penalty for death to a fetus is the same as murder to any other human being. The *Didache*, written about 100, stated the ethics of the Christian church. "Thou shalt not murder a child by abortion nor kill that which is begotten."[716]

All the genetic information to make an individual is present at conception, so right from the start a fertilized human egg cell is totally human. There is no biological basis for drawing any other line for when we "become" human. Every human is fully human, from conception to the end of life.

Therefore, the issue of family planning and birth control falls under human responsibility. Marital sex was created by God for more than the propagation of the race.

---

[715]Rushdoony, *Politics of Guilt and Pity*, 19.

[716]*Didache, ANF* 7:377.

The Constitution of Man

• *The human body*

The body (*soma*) was formed from the dust of the earth and will return to dust (Gen 3:19). We are fearfully and wonderfully made (Ps 139:14).

In contrast to a Christian worldview which respects the body, gnosticism teaches that the body is the prison house of the soul and that the body is sinful. The Greek view is that we are an eternal soul which dwells temporarily inside a body.

The word *flesh* (*sarx*) occurs 150 times in the New Testament. It can refer to humanity, the human body, the incarnation of Christ, the unregenerate nature in man, or the remaining sinful nature in the regenerate. The majority of the occurrences refer to the physical body, but Paul also uses it to refer to the carnal or sinful nature, especially in Romans 7-8.

In 2 Corinthians 10:2-3 Paul distinguishes between walking according to the flesh and walking in the flesh. Although we live in a human body, we do not live according to the sinful nature. We must not conclude that the human body is sinful, because Jesus became flesh (John 1:14) but did not become sinful. The incarnation of Jesus Christ implies the dignity of man. Thus, the flesh itself is not sinful, but it provides channels through which sinful desires assert themselves.

The human body is usually over-indulged or over-restrained. Some teach that we attain holiness by disciplining or abusing the body; others believe we can never be holy as long as we are in the body. In contrast Scripture teaches the body is to be the temple of the Holy Spirit (1 Cor 3:16-17). First Corinthians 6:12-20 teaches that our bodies are for his service and our bodies are his temple to indwell. Our bodies are members of Christ, therefore our spiritual relationship with him also includes our physical relationship with others. We are to glorify God in our bodies. There is some profit in physical exercise (1 Tim 4:8). This emphasis on the dignity of the body also impacts the doctrine of physical healing.

A proper understanding of the mind-body dualism is important. Secular psychology has moved toward behaviorism, which believes that a person's behavior has been preconditioned by his heredity and controlled through his environment. Thus, B. F. Skinner in 1971 wrote *Beyond Freedom and Dignity* in order to dismiss the idea that man amounted to anything more than a machine which needs to be programmed.

Marxism, which teaches dialectical materialism, holds that since matter is the only reality, man is only physical. Thus, man's identity is found in his labor. Marx taught, "From each according to his ability, to each according to his needs." While this motto sounds noble, it does not take into account the basic selfish nature of mankind or the basic flaws of communism.

In contrast to Marxism, which reduces mankind to the survival of the fittest, we view our vocation as the ministry God does through us. Our vocation is how we bring glory to God, but it should not define us. We have intrinsic worth because we are created in the image of God.

According to 1 Corinthians 10:31: "So whether you eat or drink or whatever you do, do it all for the glory of God." In Ephesians 6:6 we are told that we should not simply work when someone is looking, but we should work as if we were serving God. Colossians 3:22 contains a similar admonition. And the next verse declares, "Whatever you do, work at it with all your heart as working for the Lord, not for men." 1 Corinthians 15:58, "Always give yourselves fully to the work of the Lord, because you know your labor in the Lord is not in vain."

The *Protestant work ethic* is based on human responsibility, faithfulness, and excellence. Apparently this phrase was coined by Max Weber in 1905.

Christianity undercut slavery by giving dignity to work, no matter how seemingly menial that might be. Traditionally, labor which might be performed by slaves was despised as degrading to the freeman. Christian teachers said that all should work and that labor should be done as to Christ as master and as to God and in the sight of God. Work became a Christian duty.[717]

Yes, we are saved by faith and not by works. God does not need our good works, but Luther reminded us that our neighbor does! Before sin ever entered the world, Adam and Eve were given a task. We will continue to work and serve in heaven, for John wrote, "His servants will serve him" (Rev 22:3). Adam and Eve worked before the curse. We will work even after the curse has been lifted. There will be no unemployment in heaven. We will serve him "day and night" (Rev 7:15-16).

Unless we know who we are in light of the Creator's revelation, we are likely to be manipulated by Satan. Karl Marx taught that history is the class struggle within society which results in the survival of the fittest. For Marxism, man lives for bread alone, and we work merely in order to satisfy our physical needs.

Jesus did not say that we can become so spiritual that we no longer have physical needs, however. Eastern mysticism says that we can become so spiritual, so absorbed into the divine, that we do not need bread. But true spirituality is not the result of withdrawing from life, taking a vow of poverty, chastity, and obedience. Jesus is not teaching that we deny ourselves by refusing to take a bath or depriving ourselves of sleep.

The Bible teaches that we are embodied souls. We have physical needs and spiritual needs. God cares about the whole person. Thus, John Wesley taught that a proper love of self "is not a sin, but an indisputable duty."[718] And so Jesus did not teach in Luke 9:23 that we are to deny our existence or our needs, but he taught in Matthew 6:33 that we are to put his agenda above our own. In this way we entrust ourselves into the care of our heavenly Father. We cannot satisfy our spiritual needs through materialism. We cannot be reduced to money, sex, and power.

---

[717]Latourette, *History of Christianity*, 1:246.

[718]Wesley, *Notes*, 500.

For Augustine, all sexual activity, even marital sex, is tainted with sin. He wrote that carnal concupiscence, while tolerated in marriage, is not good but rather an evil which is the accident of original sin.[719] He taught that sexual relations within marriage which were not for the purpose of procreation were venial sins.[720] Yet sexual relations within marriage are commanded and not restricted to the purpose of procreation.[721]

However, the Song of Solomon teaches otherwise. Until the nineteenth century this book was usually treated as some type of allegory.[722] While it is true that there is symbolism within the book, the allegorical approach is too subjective. Nothing in the text indicates the author's intention was to allegorize.

> To read a single allegorical interpretation is to be impressed, and to wonder if the author is on to something profound; to read a hundred allegorical interpretations is to be depressed, and to want to discard the whole.[723]

Yet the church has often been embarrassed by a straightforward reading of this book, preferring to spiritualize it as referring to Christ and the church. The church adopted a negative view toward marriage. Celibacy and chastity were considered superior, due to the Greek philosophy of dualism and gnosticism. While

---

[719]Augustine, "On Marriage and Concupiscence," ch. 19; *NPNF*1 5:271.

[720]Augustine, "On the Good of Marriage," ch. 6; *NPNF*1 3:402.

[721]This is implied in such passages as Prov 5:15-20, Song of Solomon, 1 Cor 7:5, Heb 13:4.

[722]See Martin, "The Song of Songs," 775-786 for an analysis of the views of James Strong and Milton S. Terry which interpret this book generally the same way I am suggesting. Similar counsel in Prov 5:15-20 negates the allegorical approach.

[723]Garrett, *WBC*, 23B:74. Adam Clarke made similar comments [*Commentary*, 3:843-849].

marriage does illustrate the spiritual union between Christ and his church, Song of Solomon is dealing with marital love. Hebrews 13:4 teaches that sexual relations within marriage are not sinful. The translation *bed* is a euphemism for *koite* and the *bed* is to be kept pure by not having sexual relations outside marriage. Charles Carter wrote that Paul traces the corruption of man's moral nature to the fall rather than to a basic sex drive.[724]

Scripture commands modesty in passages such as 1 Timothy 2:9 and 1 Peter 3:3. While these passages forbid extravagance, modesty also includes a proper covering of the body. Proper dress should be economical, plain, appropriate, and sufficient.

Sexual Confusion: Sins Against the Body

Romans 1:24-27 describes and condemns homosexual practice. This passage begins with the assertion that God has sufficiently revealed himself so that no one has an excuse for denying his existence. However, men suppress the truth and the result is that their mind is darkened. Three times we are told that God gives them over to their sinful desires.

Just as idolatry is the exchange of the truth about God for the darkness of worshiping creation, so homosexuality is the exchange of the truth about male/female sexuality for the darkness of same-sex practices. In both cases, it is foolishness, deception, and shameful.

In v 25 Paul compares idolatry with homosexuality. Because they refuse to acknowledge God, they dishonor themselves. While idolatry is a sin of the mind, homosexuality is a sin of the body. But in both cases there is an exchange. Idolatry is an exchange of God for idols; homosexuality is the exchange of the natural for the unnatural. In both cases God gives them over to

---

[724]Carter, *Contemporary Wesleyan Theology*, 2:980; see also Lawson, *Introduction to Christian Doctrine*, 74; Noble, *Holy Trinity: Holy People,* 120.

absurdity, deception, and shame. Sexual perversion is rejected both on the authority of special revelation and natural revelation.

Thomas Oden noted that in Scripture "the prevailing analogy for sexual debauchery is idolatry." Oden also observed that Wesley made this point in his *Notes*; that just as idolatry brings dishonor to God, so also homosexuality brings dishonor to the person made in God's image.[725] Homosexuality dishonors the body like idolatry dishonors God. Wesley's actual comments on v 27 read, "Their idolatry; being punished with that unnatural lust, which was as horrible a dishonor to the body, as their idolatry was to God."[726] Sproul wrote, "When men refuse to honor God, they begin to dishonor themselves. Wherever the glory of God is attacked, sooner or later the dignity of man suffers."

Romans 1:27 describes males, having left behind the natural use of the female regarding sexual intercourse, are inflamed, set on fire, consumed with intense desire[727] for one another. Homosexual practice, whether among males or females, is the prime example of ungodliness and unrighteousness (Rom 1:18).

In the largest and most in-depth biblical study of homosexuality from a conservative position, Robert Gagnon pointed out that both idolatry and homosexuality are denials of natural revelation. In their vertical relationship with God, Gentiles ignore the truth about God and pursue idolatry, which is an absurd course of action. In their horizontal relationship with each other, Gentiles ignore the truth about the complementary nature of male and

---

[725]Oden, *Requiem*, 155-156.

[726]Wesley, *Notes*, 364.

[727]*Orexis* means a reaching or stretching after, a grasping or yearning. It is not restricted in meaning to sexual desire, nor does Scripture always use it in a negative connotation. As a verb it is used twice in a positive sense (Heb 11:16; 1 Tim 3:1) and once as a negative desire for money (1 Tim 6:10). Rom 1:27 is the only occurrence as a noun. See the comparison of it with *pathema* and *epithumia* in Trench, *Synonyms*, 323-327.

female and pursue the absurd course of action of attempting to have sexual intercourse with members of the same gender.[728]

Just as the glory of the incorruptible God has been changed (Rom 1:23) and the truth of God has been changed (v 25), so normal sexual relations have also been changed (v 26). Homosexuality is practiced only where the fear of God has been lost.

Watson said God gave them up by withdrawing the influences of the Holy Spirit. They provoked the Spirit to depart by their determined wickedness.[729] Wesley said much the same thing in the phrase "withdrawing his restraining grace."[730]

In Genesis 1:27 God created both male and female in his image, then told them to be fruitful and increase in number. According to Genesis 2:21-25, God gave woman to man, and only a husband and wife are to become one flesh. Neither man nor woman is complete without the other, nor can they engage in a one-flesh act without the opposite sex. Matt Chandler described this one-flesh marital love as two bodies as well as "two souls mingling together."[731]

In Genesis 19:1-11 we find the first reference to perverted sexuality. God destroyed Sodom and Gomorrah because of this wickedness. According to Leviticus 18:22 and 20:13 homosexuality was a capital offense, an abomination to God. Nothing in the New Testament indicates God has changed. When a people reach a certain level of depravity, punishment ceases to be particular and becomes general.

First Corinthians 6:9 refers to *malakoi* [effeminate; male prostitutes] and *arsenokoitai* [abusers of themselves with mankind; homosexual offenders]. The first word carries the meaning

---

[728]Gagnon, *Bible and Homosexual Practice*, 267-268.

[729]Watson, *Exposition*, 472.

[730]Wesley, *Notes*, 364.

[731]Chandler, *The Mingling of Souls*, 17.

of *soft* and it was used of young boys who were sexually abused by older men. This was the most common form of homosexuality among the Greeks and Romans; today it is called pedophilia. Fourteen of the first fifteen Roman emperors practiced homosexuality.

The second word is a compound word made up of the Greek word *male* (*arsen*) + "sexual intercourse" (*koite*; our word is coitus). How could God's Word be any plainer? But notice v 11, "And that is what some of you were." There is no more important past tense anywhere in God's Word. The new birth not only brings justification, the forgiveness of past sins, but it washes us from sinful practices and sanctifies us. Contrary to the propaganda that homosexuality is predestined, that it is a genetic determination, these people have been delivered from it through salvation.

According to 1 Corinthians 11:8-9, woman was created for man to be his helper, but at vv 11-12 man is not independent of woman. In other words, both sexes are dependent upon each other in order to be fruitful. We cannot redefine "marriage" or "family" because they were defined by God in creation.

First Timothy 1:10 also uses the word *arsenokoitai* which is translated *defile themselves with mankind* or perversion.

Properly understood, homosexuality is not an identity, but a behavior. Thus, we can love the sinner while hating the sin. Romans 1 lists twenty-two types of sin. This is only one manifestation of rebellion against God. It is not a predestined genetic determinism.

The homosexual is not a special type of person, but an ordinary sinner who engages in a specific sin.

The church cannot conform to the social pressure to accept or condone it. We must warn those who do such things that they will not enter heaven. "Have nothing to do with the fruitless deeds of darkness, but rather expose them" (Eph 5:11).

Deuteronomy 22:5 describes transvestites. Pagan worship incorporated perverted sexual activity. This is a reference to cross-dressing. We will later notice the comparison in Romans between idolatry and sexual sin. And we will notice the confusion that exists today. God does not want male/female roles or identity confused. God created man and woman. Computer technology and cyberspace have provided an alternate reality and for the first time in history people are attempted to decree their own sexual identity.[732]

The concept of transgender sexual identity is based on the assumption that the human body is not an essential part of our being. Essentially this is a modern application of the old gnostic heresy. This assumption allows for a fluid or subjective concept of gender identity. Thus, gender is a choice and even a human right.

While it does not change the objective reality of male or female identity as God created us, our rejection of God results in our foolish hearts becoming so darkened that we do not even know whether we are male or female (Rom 1:21). Even if a man becomes a transgendered "female," he will not menstruate. There are only X and Y chromosomes.

In 2011, *The American Psychological Association Handbook of Sexuality and Psychology* described sexual orientation as fluid and changeable.[733] If this is true, then no person is created homosexual or born with a "gay gene." Thus, in secular anthropology, *process* is replacing *predestination*.

As it is used today, the term "gender identity" refers to a person's self-perception. Today, it is claimed that gender is unattached to sex. We are the first generation that can medically make gender the result of sexual preference. However, as early as Deuteronomy 22:5, the practice of cross-dressing was prohib-

---

[732]Carl R. Trueman, *The Rise and Triumph of the Modern Self* (2020).

[733]Haynes, "The American Psychological Association Says Born-That-Way-And-Can't-Change is Not True of Sexual Orientation and Gender Identity" (2016).

ited. God has always required a clear distinction between the sexes.

Transgender is an umbrella term for all types of situations in which a person's perceived gender does not match his or her genetic sexual identity. *Gender dysphoria* is the term used to describe people who have a disconnect between their genetic sexual identity and what they think about themselves. This confusion is not inherently sinful. We are all born in sin and broken in different ways. But it is sinful to surgically alter our body to conform with our confusion. Statistically, those who undergo sex reassignment surgery do not experience higher levels of happiness.

This is part of a neo-Marxist agenda promoted under the innocuous label of "social justice," which can be defined as:

> The tearing down of traditional structures and systems deemed to be oppressive, and the redistribution of power and resources from oppressors to victims in pursuit of equality of outcome.[734]

Marx failed with his economic paradigm to account for the social constructs which kept those with power in power and those without power from rising up. To remedy this, the rejection of traditional historical narrative, morality, and absolute truth coupled with Critical Race Theory is used to develop a cultural shift or uprising. The result is a cultural revolution that will bring about the economic revolution resulting in communism. This is at the heart of Critical Race Theory and is the root of Social Justice.

Critical Race Theory establishes a four-stage approach to Social Justice.

• Identify the disadvantaged group or groups.

---

[734]Allen, *Why Social Justice is not Biblical Justice*, 43.

- Assess the inequality of outcomes for the disadvantaged groups.
- Assign blame for disparate outcomes by identifying the perceived power group.
- Redistribute power and resources from the "power group" to the disadvantaged groups.

The goal of Social Justice isn't justice or redemption, it is chaos and vengeance. Ibram X. Kendi, a black author and anti-racist activist, states, "The only remedy to past discrimination is present discrimination. The only remedy to present discrimination is future discrimination."[735] In contrast, biblical justice is:

Conformity to God's moral standard, particularly as revealed in the Ten Commandments and the royal law: "love your neighbor as yourself" (James 2:8). There are two kinds of justice. (1) Community justice is living in right relationship with God and with others. Giving people their due as image-bearers of God. (2) Distributive justice is impartiality rendering judgment, righting wrongs, and meting out punishment for lawbreaking. Distributive justice is reserved for God and God-ordained authorities, including parents in the home, pastors in the church, and civil authorities in the state.[736]

The Marxist social justice gospel appeals to Wesley, but misrepresents his theology.[737] However, true freedom comes when we submit to truth. It does not come by allowing a person to claim he is ten inches taller than he actually is. The Creator

---

[735] Allen, *Why Social Justice is not Biblical Justice*, 5.

[736] Allen, *Why Social Justice is not Biblical Justice*, 24.

[737] Jennings, *Good News to the Poor* (1990); "What Wesleyans Can Learn from Lenin" (2007); Marquardt, *John Wesley's Social Ethics* (1992), first published in German in 1976.

created male and female (Gen 1:27), and he has more knowledge about his creation than creation itself has. Jesus also affirmed in Matthew 19:4-6 that there are only two genders. Men and women are different but of equal worth.

But we also have natural revelation. Our anatomy tells us what gender we are. Our bodies do not lie to us. It really is not possible to transition from one sex to another.

- ### *The human spirit*

The soul (*psyche*) or spirit (*pneuma*) refers to the immaterial aspect of man. God formed him from the ground, breathed into him, and he became a living soul (Gen 2:7). Thus, creation was a two-step act. Theistic evolution is not implied. God did not breathe on a previously created animal form or on living dust. Furthermore, Eve is a separate and direct act of God.

Grudem asks, "What can the spirit do that the soul cannot do? What can the soul do that the spirit cannot do?"[738] The words *soul* and *spirit* are often used interchangeably:

- "Now is my soul troubled" (John 12:27); Jesus was troubled in spirit (John 13:21).
- "My soul magnifies the Lord and my spirit rejoices" (Luke 1:46-47). This is parallelism.
- Jesus gave up his *psyche* (Matt 20:28); he gave up his spirit (Matt 27:50).
- The good shepherd lays down his *psyche* (John 10:11); in John 19:30 he gave up his spirit.

All trichotomists are also dichotomists, but they have attempted to divide soul and spirit. We must be careful about overanalyzing or attempting to impose our philosophy on Scripture. Although the trichotomy model is trinitarian, it is contrived

---

[738]Grudem, *Systematic Theology*, 477.

and actually originated with Plato's trichotomy of *nous* (mind, intellect), *psyche* (soul), and *soma* (body).[739] It is impossible exegetically to distinguish between spirit, soul, mind, and heart. These words are used almost interchangeably, and the attempt to distinguish between them is arbitrary. Thomas Summers called trichotomy a "baseless theory."[740]

According to Luke 10:27, we are to love God with our whole spirit, mind, soul, and body. Are we then comprised of four parts? Romans 12:1; 1 Thessalonians 5:23; Hebrews 4:12 are the three passages where our spiritual nature is divided in its description. With regard to Romans 12, Pope agreed that the body presented by the spirit is representative of a whole life dedicated to God.[741] With regard to 1 Thessalonians, in his *Notes*, Wesley argued

> That man cannot possibly consist of three parts, appears hence: The soul is either matter or not matter: there is no medium. But if it is matter, it is part of the body: if not matter, it coincides with the spirit.[742]

Wesley also implied a dichotomy in his statement, "The soul and the body make a man."[743]

Howard Marshall argued that Paul in 1 Thessalonians 5:23-24 is distinguishing between three aspects of Christian personality. Paul lists them together to emphasize that it is "indeed the whole person who is the object of sanctification."[744]

---

[739]Plato, *Timaeus*, 122-128; Wiley, *Christian Theology*, 2:17.

[740]Summers, *Systematic Theology*, 1:202.

[741]Pope, *Prayers of St Paul*, 134.

[742]Wesley, *Notes*, 532. See also Wesley, *BE Works*, 14:596.

[743]Wesley, "Causes of the Inefficiency of Christianity," Sermon #122, ¶ 7.

[744]Marshall, *NCC*, 163.

Hebrews 4:12 declares that the Word of God can divide the indivisible,[745] but theologians cannot inductively distinguish between the soul and the spirit. While doctrine should not be based on biblical assumptions which cannot be substantiated, the trichotomy assumption is the basis of the "carnal" Christian teaching. By making a distinction between the soul and the spirit, it is claimed that the Christian is converted but still "carnal" until he is Spirit-filled.

In 1918 Lewis Sperry Chafer wrote his influential antinomian book, *He That Is Spiritual*, which began by asserting three classes of men: natural, carnal, and spiritual.[746] Thus, Keswick teaching holds that the new Christian is "soulish" and may become "spiritual" if he is Spirit-filled. Such teaching is also found in *The Scofield Reference Bible*.

However, Romans 8:6-9 teaches that the person under the control of the carnal mind is spiritually dead and that Christians are under the control of the Holy Spirit. Thus, those who reject the "carnal" Christian teaching also tend to be dichotomists. James R. Graham objected to

> three classes of men, the natural man, the carnal man and the spiritual man. The natural man is, of course, the unsaved child of the world. The carnal man is a saved man who, however, still walks in the flesh. The spiritual man is the higher quality of saved man, who walks in the Spirit and in the course of obedience.[747]

The nature of mankind, as well as reality, is dual — material and nonmaterial. While materialism holds that matter alone

---

[745]Cockerill, *NICNT*, 216.

[746]Chafer, *He That Is Spiritual*, 3-14. Ryrie managed to affirm a dichotomy and maintain the notion of a "carnal" Christian [*Basic Theology*, 195-196, 338-339].

[747]Graham, "Are There Carnal Christians?" 156-164.

exists, not the mind, this is self-defeating since the theory of materialism itself is not matter.[748] C. S. Lewis explained:

> Supposing there was no intelligence behind the universe, no creative mind. In that case nobody designed my brain for the purpose of thinking. It is merely that when the atoms inside my skull happen for physical or chemical reasons to arrange themselves in a certain way, this gives me, as a by-product, the sensation I call thought. But if so, how can I trust my own thinking to be true? It's like upsetting a milk-jug and hoping that the way the splash arranges itself will give you a map of London. But if I trust my own thinking, of course, I can't trust the arguments leading to atheism, and therefore have no reason to be an atheist, or anything else. Unless I believe in God, I can't believe in thought; so I can never use thought to disbelieve in God.[749]

In another context, Lewis pushed the implications of materialism against evolution.

> If the solar system was brought about by an accidental collision, then the appearance of organic life on this planet was also an accident, and the whole evolution of Man was an accident too. If so, then all our thought processes are mere accidents — the accidental by-product of the movement of atoms. And this holds for the materialists' and astronomers' as well as for anyone else's [thought processes]. But if their thoughts — i.e., of Materialism and Astronomy—are merely accidental by-products, why should we believe them to be true? I see no reason for believing that one accident

---

[748]Lewis, *Miracles*, 15.

[749]Lewis, *The Case for Christianity*, 32.

would be able to give correct account of all the other accidents.[750]

The opposite extreme, idealism, holds that only minds and ideas exist. But it begs the question by assuming the very conclusion it intends to demonstrate. The power of the mind is exaggerated by rationalism and overlooked in agnosticism.

The Role of Psychology

The humanistic view holds that human reason is the source of truth. While Elihu considered himself wise and well-informed, he also conceded his limitations in Job 37:19.

Humanism believes human nature is basically good, that people have the answers to their problems within themselves, and that the basic problem is guilt.

The opposite position accepts nothing but the Bible as the basis for psychology. This position denies natural revelation and common or preliminary grace. They see man as so sinful that he is incapable of observing any truth apart from the revelation of Scripture. The tendency of this position says that all emotional problems are sin.

The compartmentalized view teaches two realms of truth. Religion and psychology operate in separate categories.

Integrated truth holds that all truth is from God. We have the disclosed truth of Scripture and the discovered truth of general revelation. I am arguing for this integrated view. We can accept the validity of any psychological insight so long as it does not contradict Scripture.

Jesus is our *wonderful counselor* (Isa 9:6). However, the Great Physician often works through human physicians and the Great Counselor can also work through human counselors. The goal of biblical counseling is holy living. We need not reject

---

[750]Lewis, *God in the Dock*, 52-53.

psychology categorically, but we must develop a more biblical psychology. It is a mystery why the good and godly W. B. Pope spent the last seventeen years of his life in seclusion and emotional darkness as the result of a mental breakdown.[751]

Scripture speaks of the heart as the vital center of life. The heart is the seat of feeling, thought, and action. Thoughts, imaginations, purposes, memory, reflection, judgment, belief, and emotions originate in the heart. The Bible often connects the terms *heart* and *soul*. Sometimes the biblical writers refer to the kidneys, the intestines, and even the liver (Lam 2:11) as the seat of our emotions. Although the brain is the chief organ of the mind, they are speaking phenomenally instead of scientifically. Thus, a study of the biblical terms for mind, heart, soul, and spirit does not resolve philosophical questions about man's nature.

How is the soul propagated?

There is no biblical support for the concept of reincarnation. The transmigration of souls only transfers the question from the present to the past. Origen was the only church father who ever adopted this theory.

Wiley stated that the origin of souls is not a tremendously important question in Arminian theology.[752] John Frame, a modern Calvinist, is also ambivalent between creationism and traducianism.[753] However, Charles Carter argued for traducianism.[754]

Creationism, in this context, is the theory that each soul is a direct creation from God. This requires God to continue cre-

---

[751]Moss, *W. B. Pope*, 119-121.

[752]Wiley, *Christian Theology*, 2:28.

[753]Frame, *Salvation Belongs to the Lord*, 93.

[754]Carter, *Contemporary Wesleyan Theology*, 1:270.

ation when God rested from creation (Gen 2:2), but separates man from the fall of Adam. Theoretically, the soul could be created at a different time than conception.

Traducianism holds that the soul originates in connection with the origin of the body. The soul was originally created in Adam, and instrumentally through parents. Thus, humanity is involved in procreation. Wiley explained "it is the whole man who begets and is begotten."[755]

The first man was the direct creation of God, yet God propagates human life through a human father and a mother. The first woman, Eve, came from a man, but every man since Adam came from a mother's womb. *Procreation* means that God shares the act of creation with us. We are not gods, but God allows us to reflect his creative nature in reproduction. According to Genesis 5:3, Adam propagated a son like himself. This statement does not imply that Seth was identical to Adam, but that he inherited the Adamic nature.

---

[755]Wiley, *Christian Theology*, 2:29.

CHAPTER EIGHT
The Doctrine of Sin

Sin is rebellion against God. However, the Bible distinguishes between types and degrees of sin. Sin is a condition and an act. There are sins of commission and sins of omission. There are unintentional as well as deliberate sins. There are also personal sins as well as corporate or systemic sins. However, liberation theology tends to exploit the concept of systemic sin under the heading of "social justice." But sin cannot be reduced to specific "social" sins which certain segments of society must rectify through self-atonement.

The original sin occurred in heaven when Satan rejected the truth and became the father of lies. However, the first human sin was committed by Eve in the garden of Eden. Because Adam was the head of the human family, however, he is charged with the original sin. God did not predestine Adam and Eve to sin, but he foreknew their free choices. The first human sin occurred when they chose to fulfill legitimate desires illegitimately. However, sin cannot be defined as simply being human. If that were the case, God would have created sin.

This choice to break God's law resulted in alienation from God, as well as the judgment of God. Humanity has lived under the curse of sin from that moment forward. The permanent results include a deprivation of original righteousness. We are totally depraved — meaning our whole personality — intellect, will, and emotions are corrupt.

Whether we were charged with the liability of Adam's original sin and that charge was dropped in view of a future unconditional benefit of the atonement or whether we were never charged with Adam's guilt and only inherited his sinful nature — the result is the same. No one is consigned to eternal punishment merely for Adam's sin.

However, everyone has personally sinned; and when they are conscious of that choice, they are held liable for their sins. The wages of sin is death. We are completely unable to save ourselves. Our only hope is through the substitutionary atonement of Jesus Christ. No sin is beyond his ability to forgive, but those who have been justified are warned that apostasy is a real possibility. Thus, we cannot presume that we are unconditionally secure while persisting in defiance and disobedience. Our entire life is a probationary state. It is always possible for the Christian to forfeit saving grace, but it is never necessary.

The Biblical Doctrine of Sin

Sin is rebellion against God's sovereignty. It is the violation of God's law. Man has been tempted ever since the fall to express his freedom through disobedience. Sin is the breach of fellowship which God intended to maintain with man. Sin is autonomy, in which we set ourselves up as gods. It results in man, and not God, being at the center.

Sin is also contrary to nature and religion.[756] Biblically, the essence of sin is unbelief, pride (self-centeredness), disobedience (self-assertion), and sensuality (self-gratification). Wesley identified five elements which constitute the root of sin: atheism, idolatry, pride, self-will, and love of the world.[757] Mark Mueller

---

[756]McCall, *Against God and Nature*, 218-240.

[757]Wesley, "Original Sin," Sermon #44, 2.4-9; 3.1; see also Chiles, *Theological Transitions*, 119; Lindström, *Wesley and Sanctification*,

wrote that the universal antecedent of all sin was the historic fall of Adam.

- Atheism is the universal cause of all sin
- Self-idolatry is the universal nature of all sin
- Self-pride is the universal attitude of all sin
- Self-will is the universal assertion of all sin
- Love of the world is the universal desire of all sin.[758]

Only a biblical worldview takes the fall into account and thus understands that we are now abnormal. Other worldviews assume that the way things are now are the way they have always been.

According to dualism, sin is an evil power which has coexisted eternally along with God. For Plato the basis of sin is privation. According to Aristotle it is inappropriate desire. It is ignorance according to Socrates, Buddhism, Hinduism, and Confucianism.[759] According to Christian Science, sin is an illusion. It has also been explained as an evolutionary lag, which was Bowne's explanation.[760]

The basic meaning of *sin* in the Old Testament is to miss or transgress an implied absolute standard of God. The Hebrew language has at least eleven words for sin that correspond roughly to the Greek vocabulary of the New Testament. This is more terms than the Hebrew language has for *goodness*.

There are three Hebrew words which carry a unique meaning: *amal* describes the burden and travail of sin, *maal* is a breach or betrayal of trust, and *aven* means vanity or nothingness.

27; Collins, *Theology of John Wesley*, 69-70.

[758]Mueller, "A Biblical Examination," 21.

[759]Bloesch, *Jesus Christ*, 28-32.

[760]Lawson, *Introduction to Christian Doctrine*, 78-79; Bowne, *The Atonement*, 69.

The basic New Testament meaning is to miss the mark (*hamartia*). This word was used in the Septuagint translation of Judges 20:16, "each of whom could sling a stone at a hair and not *miss*." Used over two hundred times in the New Testament, *hamartia* can refer to sin in the abstract or to sinful acts.[761]

The New Testament contains twenty-eight synonyms for sin, derived from eight different roots. They carry these variations in meaning and emphasis: wrongdoing, unrighteousness, injustice, overstepping, transgression, disobedience, failure to hear, carelessness, trespass, a false step, oversight, error, mistake (unintentional), lawlessness, iniquity, godlessness, falling short, an error, ignorance, a defect, loss, a fault, a crime, evil, wicked, unbelief.

Several of these words, *asebeia*, *anomia*, and *adikia* refer to an inward orientation toward sin. Kinlaw observed that in Romans 1:18-32 Paul uses *asebeia* first and then speaks of *adikia*. The point is that *asebeia* describes a relationship with God that is not proper and *adikia* describes all other relationships which are not right. Thus, *asebeia* is cause and *adikia* is the result.[762]

Other phrases in the New Testament, such as *filthiness* (2 Cor 7:1), *the body of sin* (Rom 6:6), *the sin which does so easily beset us* (Heb 12:1), and *moral filth and the evil that is so prevalent* (Jas 1:21) also denote inward depravity.

There may be sin without guilt imputed when the person is not conscious that an action is sinful. According to Romans 5:13, sin is not charged where there is no knowledge of God's law. The biblical concept of sin is blurred, however, when it is assumed that all of man's deeds are sinful merely because he is human.

---

[761]Trench, *Synonyms*, 241.

[762]Kinlaw, *Let's Start with Jesus*, 122.

All sin is not equal.[763] All sin is not treated the same. There are degrees of sin. Wesley expressed concern that Calvinism tended to confound all types of sin together.[764]

Numbers 35 distinguishes between an accidental killing and an intentional murder. The charge of *murder* is not attributed to the man who kills accidently. Passages such as Matthew 10:15, 12:31; Luke 12:47-48, John 9:41, 19:11 also imply a graduated view of sin. Arminius rejected the Stoics' teaching which makes all sin equal.[765] Calvin also acknowledged a gradation of sin.[766] Commenting on 1 John 3:4, John Calvin acknowledged that John did *not* make all sin equal, but Calvin's editor offered a "correction," that all sin is the same.[767]

A careful study of the terms used to describe sin will bear out these distinctions:

- sin as a condition and as an act
- sins of commission and sins of omission
- unintentional and deliberate sin

Leviticus 4 also refers to inadvertent errors, which are still called *sin*. Restitution to man and a sacrifice offering to God were required for these unintentional sins. Leviticus 4-5 uses the verb *shagah* which means to go astray. As a noun it describes the sin of error, inadvertence. This word is set over against sins of

---

[763]McCall, *Against God and Nature*, 248.

[764]Wesley, *Letter* to Elizabeth Bennis, 16 June 1772.

[765]Arminius, *Works*, 2:160.

[766]Calvin, *Institutes*, 4.12.4.

[767]Calvin, *Commentary* 22:208-209. The editor, John Owen (not to be confused with the Puritan who lived in the 17th century), corrected Calvin in 1849.

intention.[768] However, Leviticus 5:17 declares that the person who sins ignorantly is still guilty and thus is responsible to offer a guilt (*asham*) offering. Even in our civil law, ignorance is no excuse.

Numbers 15:22-31 makes a distinction between unintentional and defiant sin. No sacrifice was prescribed for defiant sin, but Morris argued that sacrifice is implied for such serious offenses.[769] Hamilton notes that the types of sin mentioned in Leviticus 6:1-7 have to involve deliberate sin. But according to Numbers 5:6-8 confession and restitution must precede atonement. It is not the deliberate sinner who is excluded from sacrifice, but the unrepentant sinner.[770]

However, some sin was so serious that it resulted in that member being removed from the covenant community. George Allen Turner wrote that the Old Testament treats sin in three broad categories: deliberate acts of rebellion, sins of ignorance, and a chronic disposition to sinfulness.[771] Psalm 19:12-13 makes a distinction between errors and hidden faults and willful or presumptuous sins. If I am kept from willful sins, I am blameless and declared innocent of great transgression. Clarke defined "great transgression" as habitual sinning, apostasy, and besetting sin.[772] Benson said that innocence from great transgression meant to be kept pure from the guilt of presumptuous sins, which are, indeed, very great transgressions.[773]

In the New Testament the result of sin is *fault* (*aitia*). A second word, *enochos*, describes the bond of obligation when

---

[768]BDB, *Lexicon*, 993. A form of this word is used seven times in Lev 4-5.

[769]Morris, *The Atonement*, 51-52.

[770]Hamilton, *Handbook on the Pentateuch*, 245-246.

[771]Turner, *The Vision Which Transforms*, 26.

[772]Clarke, *Commentary*, 3:283.

[773]Benson, *Notes*, 2:714-715.

someone is liable for their sin. Romans 3:19 uses a third word, *hupodikos*, to declare that the whole world is guilty and liable for punishment.

Romans 10:3 implies that the Jews, in their ignorance of salvation, are still guilty. Hebrews 10:26 speaks of sinning deliberately, which implies that Christians may also sin inadvertently. There is no atonement for those who draw back (v 38) into total apostasy.[774] Paul said he was once the foremost sinner, yet two verses earlier, in 1 Timothy 1:13, said he had acted in ignorance.

W.T. Purkiser argued that the category "sins of ignorance," which is found sparingly in Leviticus and Numbers, refers to unconscious transgressions of the ceremonial law with its many requirements. However, even in the Old Testament, the prevailing use is that which regards sin as rebellion against God.[775] Yet Wesley said of New Testament believers,

> The best of men still need Christ, in his priestly office, to atone for their omissions, their shortcomings (as some not improperly speak), their mistakes in judgment and practice, and their defects of various kinds. For these are all deviations from the perfect law, and consequently need an atonement. Yet that they are not properly sins, we apprehend, may appear from the words of St. Paul: "He that loveth hath fulfilled the law; for love is the fulfilling of the law." Now mistakes, and whatever infirmities necessarily flow from the corruptible state of the body, are no way contrary to love, nor therefore, in the Scripture sense, *sin*.[776]

---

[774]Dale Moody connected Heb 10:26 with Num 15:30 [*Apostasy*, 53].

[775]Purkiser, *Exploring Our Christian Faith*, 292.

[776]Wesley, *BE Works*, 13:169.

Kenneth Kinghorn asserted there is no precise biblical definition of sin. The Bible is more concerned with the remedy for sin than with a definition of sin. Sin is both willful transgression and falling short. It is both objective and subjective, both ethical and legal. Kinghorn concluded that sin is essentially a wrong relationship with God.[777] Because there are degrees and types of sin, there are various definitions of sin found in Scripture.

- *Sin* is not believing in Christ (John 16:9).
- *Sin* is suppression of the truth (Rom 1:18).
- *Sin* is defiance against God's law (Rom 8:7).
- *Sin* is whatever does not come from faith (Rom 14:23).
- *Sin* is lawlessness (1 John 3:4).
- *Sin* is refusal to do good (Jas 4:17).

According to Gary Anderson, the predominate Old Testament metaphor for sin is the picture of sin as a weight or burden. But Jesus never talked about sin as an enormous weight. Instead, he depicted sin predominately as debt. Thus, he taught us to pray "forgive our debts." This carries the idea of God deciding not to collect.[778]

The classic New Testament passage on sin is Romans 1:18-3:20. In Romans 1:29-31 Paul begins with four vices with which we are *filled to the brim* — unrighteousness, evil, greed, and depravity. Then Paul lists five vices: envy, murder, strife, deceit, and a tendency to put the worst construction upon everything. Finally Paul lists twelve additional vices: whisperers, back-talkers, God-haters, those who insult, arrogant, boastful, inventors of evil, disobedient to parents, senseless, faithless, loveless, and merciless.

---

[777]Kinghorn, "Biblical Concepts of Sin," 21; 23-26.

[778]Wilson, "The Evolution of Sin," 30-33. The interview of Gary Anderson was based on his book *Sin: A History*.

In Romans 2 Paul shifts from the rebellious sinner to the religious sinner and argues that those with greater privilege are liable to greater punishment. In Romans 3:9-20, Paul closes his argument by indicting the whole human race as sinners. In a corporate sense, we all sinned with Adam and continue to fall short.

While we walk in obedience, our fellowship with God remains unbroken and the blood of Christ continually cleanses us from unconscious sin (1 John 1:7). In contrast, Finney taught that sanctified Christians were dependent upon the atonement only for their past sins.[779] However, Wesley wrote,

> There cannot be a more proper phrase than that you used, and I will understand your meaning; yet it is sure you are a transgressor still — namely, of the perfect, Adamic law. But though it be true all sin is a transgression of this law, yet it is by no means true on the other hand (though we have so often taken it for granted) that all transgressions of this law are sin: no, not at all — only all voluntary transgressions of it; none else are sins against the gospel law.[780]

Wesley declared, "*All* deviation from perfect holiness *is sin*."[781] But he also spoke of sin, properly so called, and sin, improperly so called.[782] Here he distinguishes between willful sins and unintentional sins. He defined sin, properly so called, as a "voluntary transgression of a known law of God." But he also

---

[779]Finney, *Lectures to Professing Christians*, 393.

[780]Wesley, *Letter* to Jane March, 31 May 1771.

[781]Wesley, *Notes*, 641.

[782]Wesley, *BE Works*, 13:169.

referred to "sins of infirmity," as involuntary transgression of the perfect law.[783]

Wesley also defended his definition of sin as "a voluntary transgression of a known law," as the definition of "all such sin as is imputed to *our* condemnation." Regarding whether we should call mistakes "sin," Wesley replied, "*Call* them just what you please."[784]

J. T. Crane defended Wesley's distinction between sins of ignorance and presumption. "There are cases where ignorance is itself a grievous sin." Yet they do not result in peace with God being forfeited. "So far as the ultimate salvation of the soul is concerned, the difference between Wesley and Calvinism is that what Wesley concludes in regard to the believer's involuntary infractions of the perfect law Calvinism affirms in regard to all manner of deliberate sin."[785]

Diane Leclerc acknowledged that these omissions are sin.[786] In the sense that we could always care for more of the poor, visit more of the sick and imprisoned, and do more acts of mercy — everyone sins through omission. But these sins of omission are not imputed to us if we are walking as 1 John 1:7 describes.

Therefore, Wesleyans have not necessarily redefined sin, but instead teach that it is not imputed unless willful. This concept is implied in John 9:41, "If you were blind, you would not be guilty of sin; but now that you claim you can see, your guilt remains."

W. B. Pope explained that the Methodist doctrine did not lower the law, but instead taught that Christian perfection is an obedience which is counted as perfection.[787] Referring to 1 John

---

[783]Wesley, *BE Works*, 13:469.

[784]Wesley, *Letter* to John Hosmer, 7 June 1761.

[785]Crane, "Christian Perfection and the Higher Life," 710-711.

[786]Leclerc, *Discovering Christian Holiness*, 162.

[787]Pope, *Higher Catechism*, 273.

3:9, Wesley explained that whoever is born of God does not sin habitually or wilfully. He does not sin through unholy desires nor through his infirmities — since they exist without the agreement of his will and thus are not properly sin.[788] He explained in a letter,

> Nothing is sin, strictly speaking, but a voluntary transgression of a known law of God. Therefore, every voluntary breach of the law of love is sin; and nothing else, if we speak properly. To strain the matter farther is only to make way for Calvinism. There may be ten thousand wandering thoughts and forgetful intervals without any breach of love, though not without transgressing the Adamic law. But Calvinism would fain confound these together. Let love fill your heart, and it is enough.[789]

Other systems tend to make little distinction between these issues, assuring us that we all sin daily because we are human or finite. This popular attitude toward sin discounts the possibility of deliverance from willful sin. Yet Sam Powell argued that Wesley did not intend for this definition to be a complete or adequate definition. Sin is multidimensional and therefore no brief definition of sin can be adequate. "There is much to sin besides voluntarily transgressing the command of God. It is therefore a mistake to think that the Wesleyan view of sin is principally about voluntary transgressions of God's law."[790]

However, Calvinists such as Charles Hodge believed that Wesley had a deficient view of sin.[791] Calvinists basically hold a legal definition of sin as any transgression of the law of God.

---

[788]Wesley, "Salvation by Faith," Sermon #1, 2.6.

[789]Wesley, *Letter* to Elizabeth Bennis, 16 June 1772.

[790]Powell, *Discovering our Christian Faith*, 116.

[791]Hodge, *Systematic Theology*, 3:254-255, 258.

While Wesley recognized the reality of involuntary transgressions, he felt they were covered under the unconditional benefits of the atonement. So long as the human will was not in rebellion, man did not incur any guilt or punishment. The Old Testament law did make a distinction between voluntary and involuntary transgressions. According to W.E. Vine, *para-ptoma* is a stronger term than *hamartema* because it describes the breach of a known law.[792] Thus, both the Old and New Testaments appear to make the distinction Wesley also made.

Wesley wrote that those cleansed from all sin are the most deeply conscious of their need of Christ both as prophet, priest, and king.

> "But are they not sinners?" Explain the term one way, and I say, "Yes," another, and I say, "No." "Are they cleansed from *all sin*?" I believe they are; meaning all sinful tempers. "But have they then need of Christ?" I believe they have.

Wesley then argued that this position was no contradiction, that it was consistent with right reason, and the whole oracles of God.[793]

While Wesley's view has received much criticism, the Scriptures do distinguish between being blameless and faultless. The difference is that faults are not imputed as sin when the motive was pure before God. Even R. J. Rushdoony, a proponent of Calvinism, conceded, "In this life, we can be perfect in the sense of being blameless in our faithfulness to God's purpose, but to be blameless does not mean being faultless."[794] Wesley explained,

---

[792]Vine, *Expository Dictionary*, 4:155.

[793]Wesley, *Letter* to Samuel Furly, 15 Sept 1762.

[794]Rushdoony, *Institutes of Biblical Law*, 629.

1) Every one may mistake as long as he lives. 2) A mistake in *opinion* may occasion a mistake in *practice*. 3) Every such mistake is a transgression of the perfect law. Therefore, 4) Every such mistake, were it not for the blood of atonement, would expose to eternal damnation. 5) It follows, that the most perfect have continual need of the merits of Christ, even for their actual transgressions, and may say for themselves, as well as for their brethren, "Forgive us our trespasses."

This easily accounts for what might otherwise seem to be utterly unaccountable; namely, that those who are not offended when we speak of the highest degree of love, yet will not hear of living *without sin*. The reason is, they know all men are liable to mistake, and that in practice as well as in judgment. But they do not know, or do not observe, that this is not sin, if love is the sole principle of action.[795]

Using relational language, Wynkoop described sin as "self-separation from God" in moral unlikeness and spiritual alienation.[796] She said sin must be interpreted in keeping with the existential terminology of Scripture and the terms are all very personal. "God seeks our love and gives His love without measure. Sin is simply the absence of this relationship because man has repudiated it." "Sin is love, but love gone astray. . . . Sin is love locked into a false center, the self." It is perverted love.[797] We have turned every one to his own way (Isa 53:6). Luther described this condition as *in se curvatos* (the heart turned in upon itself).[798]

---

[795]Wesley, *BE Works*, 13:168.

[796]Wynkoop, *Theology of Love*, 51.

[797]Wynkoop, *Theology of Love*, 150, 154, 157-158, 155, 252.

[798]*Luther's Works*, 10:241; 25:245, 291, 313, 345, 351, 513; 33:175.

Sam Powell wrote that sin is the revival of chaos. "In creation God overcomes the power of chaos and thus fashions a world for our existence. But chaos is not utterly destroyed; it is only kept at bay. . . . Sin is the power of chaos manifesting itself in human being, resisting and distorting the creative power of God's coming into the world." Yet sin is more than relational; it is an independent reality which is a distortion of God's creation. He observed that John wrote of the *world* both as God's creation and as the system of sin. Paul's favorite term for the corporate nature of sin is *flesh*.[799]

Liberalism does not view the fall as ontological, as happening in time and space and resulting in a state of sinfulness. The relationship was never severed as far as God was concerned. Instead, they explain sin as relational.[800] The truth is that sin is a state or condition which results in a broken relationship with God and broken relationships within mankind.

Roman Catholics distinguish between *venial* and *mortal* sin. A sin may be willful, but considered *venial* if it is a small matter. "A sin can be venial in two ways: (1) when the evil done is not seriously wrong; (2) when the evil done is seriously wrong, but the sinner sincerely believes it is only slightly wrong or does not give full consent to it."[801] Augustine held that while a man might avoid all mortal sin, venial sins were absolutely unavoidable and the holiest men often fell into them.[802]

The problem with this rationale is that *little* sins often open the door to *big* sins. Wesley, in contrast, distinguished between willful sins and unintentional sins.[803]

---

[799]Powell, *Discovering our Christian Faith,* 111,128-131.

[800]Dunlap, "Methodist Theology in Great Britain," 42,111.

[801]Noll, *Father Smith Instructs Jackson,* 76.

[802]Peck, *Christian Perfection,* 98.

[803]Wesley, *BE Works,* 13:469.

Roman Catholic theology also teaches there are seven deadly sins. They are called *capital sins*, not because they are the worst sins but because they are the chief reasons why men commit sin. They amount to our besetting sin; the sin that so easily entangles (Heb 12:1). By their definition, the "seven deadly sins" are: pride, covetousness, lust, anger, gluttony, envy, and sloth.

A distinction is also made between personal sin and corporate or systemic sins. The concept of corporate guilt is implied in Psalm 9:17, where nations are punished. However, this does not imply the liberation theology reduction of sin to class oppression and exploitation. It is misleading for Oord to identify Christian social justice with liberation theology.[804]

Slavery will always exist. However, God did not predestine that some skin colors were intended to be on the bottom of a caste system. Bondage occurs whenever men and women decide they have to have what they want now and agree to restrictions in order to realize their desires. According to 2 Peter 2:19, we are slaves to whatever has mastered us. However, salvation is liberation from sin.

According to Luke Keefer, Wesley decried miscarriage of justice in the court systems, corrupt election practices, and government policies that adversely affected the nation, especially the poor. He wrote vigorously in behalf of better prison conditions. He boldly called for the elimination of slavery and the slave trade.

> One can hardly be thoroughly acquainted with the Wesleyan sources and be unimpressed with Methodist social achievements. If one compares the Methodist record from 1725-1850 (which some see as the pre-liberal days) to that of any other organized group of the period — sacred or secular, one cannot help but conclude that

---

[804]Oord, "Social Justice," 506.

no other group can match it at the point of social service.[805]

Yet Wesley and early Methodism did not embrace liberation theology. Davies explained,

> If a liberation theologian accepted any form of Marxist determinism, that would indeed disqualify that person from any claim to thinking with Wesley. Economic determinism is, after all, the modern equivalent of predestination.[806]

Liberation theology is a political movement which interprets the teaching of the Bible in terms of deliverance from unjust economics, political and social conditions. It began as a movement within the Roman Catholic Church in Latin America in the 1950s-1960s. The term was coined in 1971 by Gustavo Gutiérrez, a Peruvian priest. In his book *A Theology of Liberation* Gutiérrez wrote, "The God of Exodus is the God of history and of political liberation more than he is the God of nature." Thus, the exodus of Israel is reinterpreted as a political event. "The Exodus is the long march toward the promised land in which Israel can establish a society free from misery and alienation. Through the whole process, the religious event is not set apart."[807]

One of the keys to Liberation Theology is its emphasis and the meaning it places on the word *praxis*. Where orthodoxy works from the biblical text, historical theology, the creeds, and then the application, liberation theology works from the point of praxis, that is to say, the act of some injustice, and then brings that event to the biblical record to find some sympathy. In other

---

[805]Keefer, "John Wesley, Methodists, and Social Reform," 10.

[806]Davies, "Justification, Sanctification and Liberation," 71.

[807]Gutiérrez, *A Theology of Liberation*, 157-158.

words, it works backward from the praxis into the text where the text applies to a particular situation, not from the text to bring order to the action to be taken. Thus, liberation theology is a theology of praxis first and foremost as it relates to a certain injustice.

This injustice toward the disadvantaged is identified with the human suffering of Jesus found in the Gospels. In so doing, one is absolved from his or her personal sin or transgression. Since this is a political ideology more than a biblical theology, it seeks to move upon the atonement in a horizontal-political manner. It speaks overwhelmingly to the injustices that are performed by corporations, institutions, and governments against those who have suffered, the disenfranchised poor and politically exploited. Vanhoozer writes,

> It sees the atonement to be made, not toward the person but the systematic problem of those governing or in authority. Any suffering Jesus has done to save is strictly on a humanitarian level. That is, the death of Jesus as the historical outcome of the kind of life he lived. His suffering for the cause of justice becomes the central challenge for discipleship today. Such an approach is to be questioned if, by overemphasizing the political significance of Jesus' death, it overall does not pay enough attention to the biblical material about the soteriological significance of that death.[808]

Liberation theology insists that there is a new understanding of the gospel and that the Bible must be re-read from that new perspective. This new perspective emphasizes the creation of a new, just society and denigrates Western culture and capitalism. They equate this with the kingdom of God. They identify with

---

[808]Vanhoozer, *Dictionary for Theological Interpretation*, 454-55.

socialism and communism, justifying oppressive conditions in such countries while belittling those who oppose communism.

Liberation theology portrays Jesus Christ as a political revolutionary, justifies revolutionary violence, and demands that Christians participate in the liberation struggle. Thus, Yoder wrote, "Jesus was, like themselves, a social critic and an agitator, a drop-out from the social climb, and the spokesman of a counter-culture."[809]

Liberation theology twists the biblical concept of love to justify a violent revolution as a prelude to the establishment of a just society. Out of the chaos a new world order will arise. It dismisses biblical passages which teach obedience to government and appeals to the Exodus account to justify overthrowing government.

Feminist theologies also tend to describe sin in terms of cultural systems or institutional sins. Thus, sin results in injustice. However, the sins of the oppressed are not adequately acknowledged. It is assumed that certain groups are innocent because they have suffered injustice and that other groups are guilty, and thus are disenfranchised, simply because of their ancestry. This is itself a form of racism and discrimination.

Christian theology should not accept the Marxist view of social justice since Marxism itself was the most oppressive political philosophy of the twentieth century. Feminism may be a type of liberation for women, the prosperity gospel may be a type of liberation from poverty, and healing a type of liberation for the charismatic; but liberation theology tends to prescribe a Christianized Marxism as the standard solution. Oden gave this analysis,

> Consciousness raising was for Marx the raising of the consciousness of the underclass to become outraged at the injustices of class oppression, calling upon people

---

[809]Yoder, *The Politics of Jesus*, 1.

to unite and break their chains of economic bondage through revolution. Now we find that their revolution over time became a poverty machine, which itself has required the release of new freedoms to overcome. Such is the history of sin.[810]

In such systems it is always capitalism which must be overthrown. However, W. B. Pope declared that Scripture does not sanction communism. The community of goods referenced in Acts 4:32 was extraordinary and voluntary.[811] In Acts 4:32-37 the early church pooled their resources and the apostles managed the collective resources. This was communism, but not Marxism.

- It was not mandatary, but voluntary (Acts 5:4).
- It was not commanded. Acts is a book of history, not of doctrine.
- It did not work. In Acts 11:30 relief was raised for the brethren living in Judea. There was a great famine in the whole world in the days of Claudius Caesar. This voluntary plan, which seemed so successful at first, had utterly failed within fifteen years.

In Romans 15:26 Paul again collected an offering from the gentile churches for the poor saints in Jerusalem around AD 52-57. Why were they poor? They did not have any assets and were relying on the benevolence of others. Such benevolence cannot be sustained long-term. The general principle is personal responsibility. "If a man will not work, he shall not eat" (2 Thess 3:10).

While the spread of the gospel should result in an end to discrimination, racial prejudice, and inequality, it cannot be reduced to social justice. Our basic problem is still sin, and sin cannot be reduced to racism or capitalism.

---

[810]Oden, *John Wesley's Teachings*, 1:202.

[811]Pope, *Compendium*, 3:249-250.

Oden observed, "Few liberal Protestants have ever heard a sermon on original sin, except in the guise of a political appeal against economic injustice or war or racism or social oppression."[812] Oden also wrote that liberals reduced justification to deliverance of the oppressed from social and political bondage.[813]

Gutiérrez insisted that when instituting public policy one must always keep the "preferential option for the poor" at the forefront of one's mind. Accordingly, this doctrine implies that the moral test of any society is how it treats its most vulnerable members. They claim God sides with the poor against the rich. And here *poor* is expanded to mean all who are disenfranchised or oppressed. But we are not saved through our good works *or* through our poverty. We are saved by grace through faith. "There is neither Jew nor Greek, slave nor free, male nor female, for you are all one in Christ Jesus" (Gal 3:28).

Justice must be blind. "Acquitting the guilty and condemning the innocent — the Lord detests them both" (Prov 17:15). According to Exodus 23:3 the poor man is not to be shown favoritism. However, in v 6, justice is not to be denied to the poor. Thus, the Bible does not advocate a "preferential option for the poor." Rather, it demands justice regardless of economic status.

Liberation theology claims that God is always on the side of the poor. Thus, the poor may take from the rich. The poor are then told that God allows them as a class to vandalize, loot, or steal from the rich class. This is called the politics of envy. If I can't have it, you will not enjoy it either! After the community organizers have successfully implemented this policy, no one has anything left—except for them. The communist leaders always did well for themselves!

Biblical justice teaches that God is on the side of those who keep covenant with him by obeying his commandments. Deuter-

---

[812]Oden, *John Wesley's Teachings*, 1:201.

[813]Oden, *The Justification Reader*, 22.

onomy 19 instructs that the judges must make a thorough investigation and if the witness proves to be false, which is perjury, the false witness is to receive the same punishment which would have been inflicted upon the accused. This passage explains that such justice will prove to be a deterrent. "The rest of the people will hear of this and be afraid, and never again will such an evil thing be done among you. Show no pity: life for life [capital punishment], eye for eye; tooth for tooth, hand for hand, foot for foot." This is biblical social justice. To the degree that this justice is violated, we need prison reform.

Mercy is always the prerogative of the individual who has been victimized, but it can never be presumed. The opposite of justice is injustice. Mercy goes beyond justice. However, when government requires productive taxpayers to support those who are unwilling to carry their own weight, the government at that point takes on the role of a predator. The confiscation and redistribution of what has been earned by one who works and given to one who will not work is injustice. Nor is such redistribution of wealth the legitimate function of government. Charity must be voluntary. Christians should have the prerogative to give in the name of Jesus (Mark 9:41), not have their earnings confiscated by an ungodly state.

On the other hand, prosperity theology insists that God wants us all to be rich. In both cases *salvation* has been reduced to an economic status. How we manage what we have been made stewards of may be a good indicator of what we really believe.

Philanthropy was not exclusively a Christian innovation. However, Christianity taught that giving was the obligation of *every* Christian, whether rich or poor. The motive was love, in response to the love of Christ, who, though he was rich, became poor for our sake. The object of benevolence became the Christian widows, orphans, sick, and disabled, as well as those who had lost their job because of their Christian faith, or were imprisoned for their faith. While Christian charity was not restricted to members of the church, Galatians 6:10 specified that charity *begins* within the household of faith. Christian charity was not impersonal, but focused on individuals, each as having distinct worth in the sight of God.[814]

The Historic Fall of Mankind

Humanity was created holy, with an inclination or tendency toward God and good. That holiness was more than innocence, it was an enlightened understanding of God and a will wholly inclined toward spiritual things.[815]

We were originally created in the image and likeness of God. The problem in the Garden of Eden was not that the fruit was poisonous; the problem was that Adam and Eve made a choice to disobey God. Satan had nothing of his own to offer, so he offered a perversion of God's gifts.

Eating the forbidden fruit was an act of disobedience. Adam and Eve were promised they would experience good and evil. Wiley explained the distinction between a knowledge about evil and an experiential knowledge of evil.[816] They experienced the loss of good and the consequences of evil. They knew evil by participating in it, and the knowledge they gained was knowledge about their own resultant sinfulness.

When God said, "Let there be" — whatever he commanded happened, whether it was light or sky or dry land or vegetation or sun and moon or life. There was not a chance that it would not happen. But God also made us in his image and gave us the freedom to choose. When he gave the first negative command, not to eat of this tree, he suspended his sovereignty and allowed the possibility that we might not obey his command. However, the loyalty of the first pair had to be tested. This loyalty is always the test of covenant faithfulness.

---

[814]Latourette, *History of Christianity*, 1:247-248.

[815]Wiley, *Christian Theology*, 2:44-45.

[816]Wiley, *Christian Theology*, 2:56.

Adam and Eve were created without sin (Gen 2:25) and in God's image (Gen 1:26). Adam was commanded not to eat from the tree of the knowledge of good and evil (2:17). This was before Eve was created (2:21). Therefore, the tempter went to Eve, who was the first to sin (1 Tim 2:13-14). She rebelled against her husband and against God. Adam, however, was held responsible as the head (1 Cor 15:22). Satan used an animal to appeal to the woman to reject her husband's authority, then Adam blamed God (Gen 3:12). Thus, Satan perverted the chain of authority.

The Steps of Temptation

Satan suggested doubt to Eve regarding God's goodness (Gen 3:1). Eve mistakenly attempted to reason with him. She added to God's law by reporting that she must not even touch the tree. Satan then boldly denied God's command, thus questioning the authority of God's Word. Satan appealed to the illusion of freedom from God. His big lie was that we would be like God. Yet, Adam and Eve were already created in the likeness of God. Satan's appeal was to become autonomous from God. However, any autonomous "freedom" results in bondage. The result of sin was that man did come to know good *and* evil (v 22), but this acquired knowledge of evil did not lift him to a higher level. Instead, man fell and the image of God was marred.

The desire for elevated knowledge, independent from God, led to deception. This rebellion is inherent within false religion. Hinduism teaches that the goal of every Hindu is to realize that he is God. Thus, illumination is the realization that the individual self is really the universal self. Pope explained that when this goal is reached, all distinction between God and his creation is destroyed.[817]

---

[817]Pope, *Compendium*, 3:77.

Mormonism teaches, "As man is, God once was; as God is now, man may become."[818] Mormon theologian Sterling W. Sill taught, "Adam fell, but he fell in the right direction. He fell toward the goal. . . . Adam fell but he fell upward."[819] According to Brigham Young, "The devil told the truth . . . I do not blame Mother Eve. I would not have had her miss eating the forbidden fruit for anything in the world."[820]

Humanism teaches, "No deity will save us, we must save ourselves."[821] Satanism is a religion of indulgence and controlled selfishness.

This lust for forbidden knowledge is deceptive. We are like goldfish who demand to live outside the bowl as an expression of our freedom. This knowledge of good and evil provides knowledge we never had previously. It is like being told not to put your hand in the fire. We never knew how good it felt not to be burnt, and we never knew how badly it felt to be burned before we put our hand in the fire!

Adam and Eve did gain knowledge. They learned that they would have been better off had they obeyed God and not eaten what he had forbidden. But by the time they learned that lesson, it was too late. They chose the wrong tree. This acquired knowledge of evil did not lift them to a higher level. Instead, they opened the door to sin and Satan — not only for themselves, but for us all.

Eve saw the forbidden fruit was good for food, pleasing to the eye, and desirable for gaining wisdom. This appeal corresponds to the lust of the flesh, the lust of the eye, and the pride of life in 1 John 2:16. Thus, she was attracted to sin as personal fulfillment.

---

[818]Snow, *Biography of Lorenzo Snow*, 46-47.

[819]Sill, "Church Section," *Deseret News* (31 July 1865) 7.

[820]Young, *Deseret News* (18 June 1873) 308.

[821]The Humanist Manifesto 2 (1973).

But how can an innocent person, who was created good, choose evil? Can he choose contrary to his nature? God cannot be tempted, for he is self-sufficient. He needs nothing. However, we are finite and have needs. Temptation appeals to our desires (Jas 1:13-15). The word *epithumia* need not have a bad connotation. The KJV translation *lust* is misleading and the NIV *evil desire* even more misleading. The word *evil* is not in the Greek text.

Epithumia is a neutral word. It is used in a positive sense in Matthew 13:17; Luke 22:15; Philippians 1:23; 1 Thessalonians 2:17. Human desires *become* sin when we choose to fulfill them contrary to God's law. Wrong desires lead to sin, and sin leads to death (Jas 1:15). Thus, the choice to sin was an abuse of the gift of freedom.

Since God foresaw this apostasy, could he not have prevented it? And if so, how do we reconcile the fall of man with divine goodness? Wakefield answered that God did foreknow the fall of man and could have prevented it. It was not necessary for God to create man. Thus, he could have prevented the fall by refraining from creating mankind. He could have also prevented it by withholding moral agency from us.

A moral agent is capable of making moral choices. Thus, he is responsible. This concept assumes that God has given his law so that we know right from wrong. It also assumes mankind has been given libertarian freedom, the freedom of contrary choice. But God would receive greater glory if humanity freely chose to serve him than if we had no alternative. Part of being created in his image was this freedom to determine our destiny.

It was not improper for God to create us as moral agents because he did not create evil. Nor was it necessary for us to commit sin. However, it was appropriate for us to be placed under probation. It was appropriate for us to be tempted. God created us as moral agents, foreknowing what we would do, because ultimately more good than evil would result from our creation and freedom. Thus, Wakefield employed the *greater good* theodicy.[822] However, the concept of moral agency or free agency should not be defined to mean natural ability.

Liberalism and the Fall

While Genesis 3 is the classic Old Testament passage on sin, most modern scholars reject the idea of a historic fall. For the first seventeen hundred years of church history the opening chapters of Genesis were regarded as historical. Watson, Wakefield, Ralston, Raymond, as well as Pope, defended a literal interpretation of Genesis 3, arguing that the historic account is the basis for the symbolic references in the book of Revelation.[823]

Pope contended that the "Mosaic account of the Probation and Fall of the First Pair is an inspired narrative of the origin of sin in the human race."[824] Dunlap explained that for Pope, "It is neither myth, allegory, legend, nor any combination thereof with history." However, Pope felt that there was nothing inconsistent with maintaining that the narrative is historical and at the same time symbolic.[825]

The serpent, as well as the tree of life, would have no estab-lished meaning if they were not based on a historical precedent. Biblical symbolism relies heavily upon the preceding history. However, Genesis 1-3 has no past history upon which to build. It has no store of persons and events to produce images. Its

---

[822]Wakefield, *Christian Theology*, 1:286-287. Ralston employs the same argument [*Elements of Divinity*, 105-106. This appears to be an expansion of the same *greater good* theodicy by Philip Doddridge cited by Watson [*Theological Institutes*, 1:434-435]. See also 1:278-279.

[823]Watson, *Theological Institutes*, 2:20-30; Wakefield, *Christian Theology*, 1:281-283; Ralston, *Elements of Divinity*, 104-105; Raymond, *Systematic Theology*, 2:50-54; Pope, *Compendium*, 2:6-11.

[824]Pope, *Compendium*, 2:6.

[825]Dunlap, "Methodist Theology in Great Britain," 310.

presence in Scripture is the beginning of the store from which future biblical writers will draw.[826]

With the advent of Enlightenment philosophy, Baruch Spinoza was one of the first to reject the biblical account. Jean-Jacques Rousseau is considered to be the first to formulate a secular version of the fall, teaching the inherent goodness of mankind.

Georg Hegel introduced an evolutionary model, teaching it was both necessary and good for Adam to eat the forbidden fruit. By the twentieth century, liberal theologians had abandoned Genesis for Darwin.

In 1973, psychiatrist Karl Menninger published *Whatever Became of Sin?* His point was that sociology and psychology tend to avoid terms like *evil*, *immorality*, and *wrongdoing*. He detailed how the theological notion of sin became the legal idea of crime and then the psychological category of sickness.

Kierkegaard held that Genesis 3 was not literal but was an existential cross section of the primal act of sinning. Tillich held that Genesis 3 was a symbol for the human predicament and should not be taken literally. Barth declared that Genesis 3 was not history but a saga. Emil Brunner, Reinhold Niebuhr, and Donald Bloesch held Genesis 3 was myth. Even Clark Pinnock, Millard Erickson, and Bernard Ramm, who are all regarded as evangelical theologians, do not think Genesis 3 is necessarily literal history.

But the origin of sin in the human race must be a space and time historical event, argued David L. Smith. A meta-historical fall would be unjust.[827] Liberals want us to believe that Adam is theologically significant even though he did not exist historically. But theological significance must be grounded in historical reality. The man through which sin entered the world must be the father of our race, not just an abstract concept. Romans 5:12-21

---

[826]Weeks, *The Sufficiency of Scripture*, 116,104.

[827]Smith, *With Willful Intent*, 107-119,146, 339-343.

teaches that what one man got us into the other man got us out of. If Christ is historical, Adam cannot be mythical. Furthermore, Jesus regarded the creation narrative as literal history (Matt 19:4-6; Mark 13:19). Paul does as well in Romans 5, 1 Corinthians 15:45, and 1 Timothy 2:13-14.

It is legitimate to describe the effects of sin in relational language provided the historic fall is not denied or explained exclusively in terms of existential philosophy. Donald Metz warned that a relational idea of original sin is more in harmony with evolutionary naturalism than it is with traditional Wesleyan theology. Metz then argued that Wesley regarded both original righteousness and original sin as more than relational. He argued that such righteousness and sin were substantive states. Yet some of his citations from Wesley seem to also convey a relational dimension.[828]

Colin Williams reinterpreted the whole Adam story as a myth which did not happen historically but is still true existentially. While Williams reinterpreted Wesleyan thought in liberal terms which rejected the historic fall, it does not necessarily follow that all relational explanations of sin amount to liberalism.[829]

However, a mythical view of the fall tends toward a psychological view of sin. For Friedrich Schleiermacher sin is misspent energy which interferes with God-consciousness. For Tillich sin is existential estrangement from the "Ground of his being." For process theologians, sin is perverted or misdirected love.

Søren Kierkegaard, as well as Reinhold Neibuhr, also explained original sin psychologically. When faced with the freedom of choice, Adam and Eve felt anxiety. They chose to leap from freedom into sin and this resulted in more anxiety. While the presence of God had originally kept anxiety at bay, after his relationship with mankind was estranged, despair and dread

---

[828]Metz, *Some Crucial Issues*, 145-149.

[829]Williams, *John Wesley's Theology Today*, 55-56.

amount to the original sin which resulted. But what was it that broke the relationship? Perhaps anxiety and dread are conditions that make us vulnerable to temptation.

But is sin defiance or weakness? The emphasis in liberal theology is not on rebellion or guilt, but on the fractured self. According to Kierkegaard, we become sinners when we also leap into sin. This is our original sin. And salvation, for Adam or any one of us, is a wholeness which results from a leap of faith back toward God.[830]

But this leap of faith is not based on propositional truth. The subjectivity of existentialism must be balanced by the objectivity of propositional truth. Kierkegaard declared that man is not born as a sinner in the sense that he is presupposed as being a sinner before he is born.[831] Thus, there is no sinful nature passed on from Adam.

Calvinism and the Fall

According to John Frame, "Sin did not take God by surprise. God planned it, and if he planned it, he certainly planned it for a holy and good purpose."[832] This conflates providence with determinism and sovereign control. The result is that there is no true human freedom. Somehow Calvinism must uphold the goodness of God and yet explain how he has ordained our evil acts. In contrast, Arminius held that God's knowledge of evil does not imply that he is its cause. God did not decree sin, but neither did he restrain it.[833]

Calvinism also speculates on the chronological order of God's decrees regarding election. *Supralapsarianism* holds that

---

[830]Leclerc, "Holiness: Sin's Anticipated Cure," 114-126; *Discovering Christian Holiness*, 167-169.

[831]Bretall, *Kierkegaard Anthology*, 218.

[832]Frame, *Salvation Belongs to the Lord*, 102.

[833]Pope, *Compendium*, 1:453.

before creation God foreordained certain individuals to everlasting life and others to eternal destruction. Unless eternal perdition is somehow defined as good, the supralapsarian position holds that God decreed something for evil. Thus, reprobation precedes sin.

> Franciscus Gomarus was a superlapsarius
> (He actually gave Adam an excuse)
> Saying God had decreed,
> Foreordained Adam's deed,
> God had pre-cooked Adam's goose.

Infralapsarianism teaches that *after* creation, God decreed the salvation of the elect. Therefore, the main difference is whether the decree to save the elect comes before or after the fall. Arminius concluded that infralapsarianism also failed to avoid the conclusion that God is the author of sin.[834] He asked, "Does the Justice of God permit Him to destine to death eternal a rational creature, who has never sinned? We reply in the negative."[835]

The Bible does not address the issue of an order of God's decrees. This is nothing more than speculative theology. John Frame urged an *agnostic* position regarding lapsarian views.[836] Peterson and Williams declared that both infralapsarianism and supralapsarianism "are unsatisfying."[837] Yet their presentation of Calvinism was essentially a pre-Dort position. The Council of Dort solidified a rigid, five-point Calvinism which became the new standard of orthodoxy and affirmed infralapsarianism.

---

[834]Arminius, *Works*, 1:648.

[835]Arminius, *Works*, 2:352.

[836]Frame, *Doctrine of God*, 335-337.

[837]Peterson and Williams, *Why I Am Not An Arminian*, 98.

Rushdoony declared that all lapsarian theories "involve a blasphemous presumption on the part of the mind of man and a projection of human thought processes into the mind of God." However, Rushdoony accepted Calvin's view of predestination.[838]

In his *Declaration of Sentiments* (1608) James Arminius taught that God's first decree was to appoint Christ to redeem sinful people. Second, he decreed to receive those who repent, believe, and persevere. Third, he decreed preliminary grace, enabling everyone to repent and believe. Fourth, God decreed to save or damn individuals based upon his foreknowledge of who will repent, believe, and persevere.[839] This fourth degree assumes the concept of middle knowledge.

Since the Scripture does not address this topic of decrees, theologians such as Wiley and Wynkoop felt that Arminianism does not need a doctrine of decrees. However, Carl Bangs explained that Arminius attempted to be as conciliatory as possible with the Calvinists of his day.[840]

The Results of the Fall

The results of sin: corruption, catastrophe, confusion are all found in Genesis. Adam and Eve were alienated from God (Gen 3:8). According to Sam Powell, the twofold consequence of living in the world of sin is *alienation*, which manifests itself as spiritual death, and *judgment*, which implies separation and the wrath of God.

The Eastern Orthodox Church believes humans are born under the curse of sin, which is mortality, but they do not believe

---

[838]Rushdoony, *Systematic Theology*, 1:69.

[839]Gunter, *Arminius and His Declaration of Sentiments*, 135.

[840]Grider, *Wesleyan-Holiness Theology*, 249.

that humans are born in sin.[841] They believe that there was a fall and death resulted from that ancestral sin. We are born into a web of sin which has accumulated across history, but we are not born with a sinful nature. Their misunderstanding is similar to that of Pelagius.

While the Western church views sin as a legal problem, the Eastern church sees sin as a disease. While the analogy of sin as disease is legitimate, Scripture also teaches that the disease of sin is hereditary.

Another result of sin is *corruption*, manifested as wrong desire, loss of true freedom, distortion of thought and ethical conduct, and in wickedness.[842] Cornelius Plantinga observed, "Sin is more than the sum of what sinners do. Sin acquires the powerful and elusive form of a spirit."[843]

The whole earth was cursed (Gen 3:16-19; Rom 8:20-22). Death entered the world (Rom 5:12-18). If Adam opened the door to sin and death, then there would be no death of "prehistoric" animals prior to Adam's sin. Nor could the fossils of dead animals be properly dated millions of years before Adam. Theologically, an evolutionary theory puts death before the creation of mankind. Thus, death becomes eternal.

However, McCall argued that animals died before sin entered the world. Evolutionists see death as entirely natural and inevitable.[844] Yet Romans 8:20-22 teaches that the entire created order came under the curse of sin through no fault of its own. In

---

[841]Harakas, *Toward Transfigured Life*, 81-84.

[842]Powell, *Discovering our Christian Faith*, 139-143.

[843]Plantinga, *Not the Way it's Supposed to Be*, 75.

[844]McCall, *Against God and Nature*, 312-323,383-403. McCall also misrepresented W. B. Pope as supporting evolution on p. 389. If the quote is read in context [*Compendium*, 1:404-405], it will become clear that Pope was merely summarizing a position which he rejected. Pope's rejection of evolution can be found in his *Compendium*, 1:150, 366, 398, 404-405,419.

his sermon, "The General Deliverance," John Wesley taught that the brute creation was also created immortal,[845] a fact which did not escape the attention of C. S. Lewis.[846]

While Wesley is not infallible and at this point he is relying on the theology of John Hildrop, if creation was implicated by Adam's fall and death was the result, then the reversal of the fall would mean that animals would also regain, or even surpass, what was lost in cosmic redemption. Wesley also asserts this in his sermon, "The New Creation."[847]

Ultimately, Christian theology does not advance by accommodating evolutionary theory which is based on a completely different worldview. The natural world became "red in tooth and claw" *after* the fall. Placing this animal predation before the fall contradicts Genesis 1:29-31. Putting millions of years before the fall implies millions of years of animal death, disease, and extinction and other natural evils such as asteroid impacts, hurricanes, and earthquakes before Adam sinned resulting in God's curse on creation. Millions of years of natural evil is actually an assault on the character of the Creator. Bertrand Russell noted,

> Religion, in our day, has accommodated itself to the doctrine of evolution. . . . We are told that . . . evolution is the unfolding of an idea which has been in the mind of God throughout. It appears that during those ages . . . when animals were torturing each other with ferocious horns and agonizing stings, Omnipotence was quietly waiting for the ultimate emergence of man, with his still more widely diffused cruelty. Why the Creator should have preferred to reach His goal by a process, instead of

---

[845]Wesley, "The General Deliverance," Sermon #60, 1.5.

[846]Lewis, *The Problem of Pain*, 136.

[847]Wesley, "The New Creation," Sermon #64, § 17.

going straight to it, these modern theologians do not tell us?[848]

Jacques Monod wrote,

[Natural] selection is the blindest, and most cruel way of evolving new species, and more and more complex and refined organisms. . . . The struggle for life and elimination of the weakest is a horrible process, against which our modern ethics revolts. An ideal society is a non-selective society, one where the weak is protected; which is exactly the reverse of the so-called natural law. I am surprised that a Christian would defend the idea that this is the process which God more or less set up in order to have evolution.[849]

David Hull added:

The evolutionary process is rife with happenstance, contingency, incredible waste, death, pain, and horror. Whatever God implied by evolutionary theory and the data of natural history may be like, He is not the Protestant God of waste not, want not. He is also not a loving God who cares about His productions. He is not even the awful God portrayed in the book of Job. The God of the Galápagos is careless, indifferent, almost diabolical. He is certainly not the sort of God to whom anyone would be inclined to pray.[850]

Genesis 9:6 and James 3:9 teach that part of the divine image still remains. If the image of God is what distinguishes

---

[848]Russell, *Religion and Science*, 73.

[849]Gadsby, "Jacques Monod and Theistic Evolution," 18-19.

[850]Hull, "The God of the Galápagos," 486. Darwin did research in the Galápagos Islands in 1835.

humanity from the rest of creation, and that image is completely lost, we would be robbed of our humanity. Therefore, the moral image of God was lost, the natural image marred, and the political image imperiled. Sin broke our relationship with God, humanity, self, and nature.

At first man doubted God, then disobeyed God, then hid from God. God sought Adam, not because Adam was lost from his knowledge, but from his communion. Then they blamed someone else (Gen 3:12-13,16). As a result of sin, the desire of the wife will be against her husband and he will attempt to dominate her. This word for desire, *teshuqah*, is used in the Old Testament only two other places: Genesis 4:7; Song of Solomon 7:10. Based on the use of the word in the nearer context, it would refer to a sinful desire to possess or control her husband. The phrase can be translated "your desire shall be *against* your husband."

Dennis Kinlaw explained that Adam and Eve together chose a relationship of personal distrust, distance, suspicion, and disobedience. Because they turned their faces away from God, the result was a chasm, and God's face could no longer be seen. This amounted to a deliberate reorientation away from God and toward our own way. The result was a self-centered inversion; a kingdom within the self where the *I* could reign unchallenged.[851]

The effects of the fall on gender are evident in every area of life. In Genesis 1-3 man and woman are presented as equal under God, co-laborers together in performing the tasks of their Creator. They come together to have children. They rule over the earth as overseers of God's creation. Yet their failures are distinct because their created purpose is distinct. The woman abdicates her helping role by disregarding the Word of the Creator and disregarding the leadership of her husband. The man abdicates his role by disregarding the Word of the Creator and shifting blame to his helper.

---

[851]Kinlaw, *Let's Start with Jesus*, 111-125, 137.

Their punishment, therefore, was different. Gordon Wenham explained, "The sentences on the man and woman take the form of a disruption of their appointed roles."[852] The resulting issue for the woman becomes one of safety. It is difficult for the man to lead because the woman and the ground now "fight back." Therefore he copes by abdicating his leadership and focusing on whatever he perceives to be his competency.[853]

Romans 7 describes the divided self. The imagination pulls toward temptation, while the conscience reminds us of God's law. There is a struggle between what I want and what I ought. Our affections are alienated, our intellect is darkened, and our will is perverted.

When man rebelled under God, nature rebelled under man (Gen 3:17-19). According to Romans 8:18-25, the entire creation was subjected to suffering through Adam's choice. The verb *was subjected* is in the passive voice, indicating that creation was acted upon. However, the text does not indicate who did the acting. According to Genesis 3:17, God cursed the ground, which indicates that it was God who brought the creation under this frustration. But the One who brought the frustration also promised hope. The hope of final salvation also includes the liberation of the entire creation.

Wesley preached that creation and all the elements are off course and fighting against man. Human sin also cut the rest of creation off from the blessings of God. Just as man lost his perfection, so the beasts lost their perfection, which included a "loving obedience to man." The beasts became savage and cruel, destroying the weaker and being destroyed by man. But nothing can be clearer than the fact that they will not always remain in this condition.[854]

---

[852]Wenham, *Genesis 1-15*, 81.

[853]Talley, "Gender and Sanctification," 6-16.

[854]Wesley, "The General Deliverance," Sermon #60.

Original Sin

"Original sin refers to a state of sin in us due to that original act of sin on Adam's part."[855] Sam Powell wrote that original sin is more than simply the first sin. "*Original* means *universal*."[856] Thus, humanity is radically lawless, broken, and out of joint with its original purpose.[857] Technically, the original sin was the fall of Satan, but the term is used theologically to refer to a corrupt nature that mankind inherited due to that original act of sin on Adam's part. That original act of sin has been imputed to us since we are connected to Adam as head of the race. Wesley explained

> that as Adam was a public person, who acted in the stead of all mankind, so was Christ. As Adam was the first general representative of men, Christ was the second and the last. And what they severally did, terminated not in themselves, but affected all whom they represented.[858]

Watson explained that Adam was "a *public man*, the *head* and *representative* of the human race."[859] John Fletcher noted that the passages which Paul quotes in his conclusion (Rom 3:10-18) affirm both the universality of human corruption, as encom-

---

[855]Grider, *Wesleyan-Holiness Theology*, 277.

[856]Powell, *Discovering our Christian Faith*, 134.

[857]Curtis, *The Christian Faith*, 202.

[858]Wesley, *Notes*, 444.

[859]Watson, *Theological Institutes*, 2:52. This language apparently originated in the Westminster Larger Catechism and was used by Wesley [*BE Works*, 12:240].

passed in the word *all*, and the extent of human corruption, affecting the whole person.[860]

We have inherited Adam's sinful tendency. According to Genesis 5:3 Adam "had a son in his own likeness, in his own image." Wesley explained,

> Adam was made in the image of God; but when he was fallen and corrupted, he begat a son in his own image, sinful and defiled, frail and mortal, and miserable like himself; not only a man like himself, consisting of body and soul; but a sinner like himself, guilty and obnoxious [liable], degenerate and corrupt.[861]

Watson wrote that the three consequences imputed to mankind through the sin of Adam were physical death, spiritual death, and eternal death.[862] Arminius explained that the first sin of the first man resulted in mankind falling under the displeasure and the wrath of God. We became subject to a double death, and were deprived of primeval righteousness and holiness, "in which a great part of the image of God consisted."[863] Arminius explained the "double death" was physical and spiritual (Gen 2:17; Rom 6:23).[864]

> The whole of this sin, however, is not peculiar to our first parents, but is common to the entire race and to all their posterity, who, at the time when this sin was committed, were in their loins, and who have since descended from them by the natural mode of propaga-

---

[860]Fletcher, *Works*, 3:254.

[861]Wesley, *Notes*, 1:26.

[862]Watson, *Theological Institutes*, 2:55.

[863]Arminius, *Works*, 2:151.

[864]Arminius, *Works*, 2:156.

tion, according to the primitive benediction: For in Adam "all have sinned" (Rom 5:12). Wherefore, whatever punishment was brought down upon our first parents, has likewise pervaded and yet pursues all their posterity: So that all men "are by nature the children of wrath" (Eph 2:3), obnoxious [liable] to condemnation, and to temporal as well as to eternal death; they are also devoid of that original righteousness and holiness (Rom 5:12,18-19).[865]

Pelagianism, however, denies original sin. This historic controversy began late in the fourth century between Pelagius, a British monk, and Augustine. Pelagius argued that Adam had set a bad example, but that his descendants did not inherit his corruption. Every person has the same choice that Adam and Eve had in the garden. Pelagius taught that it is possible to live without sinning. He held that if an act is necessary, it is not sin. If it is voluntary, it can be avoided.[866]

Augustine was quite libertarian in his earlier writings. Then he rejected this position for a compatibilist position in his debate with Pelagius. Late in his life, he reverted back to libertarian free will.[867]

The early Methodist position was that the will was corrupted by the fall and that man could will to do right only under the influence of preliminary grace. Wesley declared, "Since the fall,

---

[865] Arminius, *Works*, 2:156-157.

[866] Augustine, *Treatise Concerning Man's Perfection*, 2.1; *NPNF*1 5:160. None of the writings of Pelagius are extant. This summary comes from his opponent, who is actually describing the teachings of Celestius, a disciple of Pelagius. Wesley expressed some ambiguity about the man. However, he condemned the theological position we have labeled as *Pelagian* [Campbell, *John Wesley and Christian Antiquity*, 6].

[867] McCall, *Against God and Nature*, 287.

no child of man has a natural power to choose anything that is truly good."[868] Wesley claimed this doctrine as "the first grand distinguishing point between heathenism and Christianity."

> Is man by nature filled with all manner of evil? Is he void of all good? Is he wholly fallen? Is his soul totally corrupted? Or, to come back to the text, is "every imagination of the thoughts of his heart evil continually?" Allow this, and you are so far a Christian. Deny it, and you are but an heathen still.[869]

Yet Milton S. Terry wrote, "The real cause of the first sin as of every other subsequent act of sin, is to be sought in the sinner himself."[870] Terry reflected a Pelagian view which rejects original sin. Across the twentieth century Methodist theologians such as Borden Parker Bowne, Albert C. Knudson, Edgar Brightman, Harris Franklin Rall, Vincent Taylor, L. Harold DeWolf, and Georgia Harkness *did* deny original sin. Harkness is famous for her 1929 statement, "The doctrine of 'original sin' is fast disappearing — and the sooner it disappears, the better for theology and human sympathy."[871]

Karl Barth eventually made the doctrine of sin popular again with his 1919 commentary on the book of Romans. However, with his usual dialectic doublespeak, he taught that sin was an ontological impossibility since God created him and everything

---

[868]Wesley, *BE Works*, 13:398.

[869]Wesley, "Original Sin," Sermon #44, 3.1-2.

[870]Terry, *Biblical Dogmatics*, 97; 84.

[871]Harkness, *Conflicts in Christian Thought*, 221. See also Knudson, *Basic Issues in Christian Thought*, 99; 119.

God created was good.[872] Yet Barth also claimed that man was "radically and totally evil."[873]

But the doctrine of original sin was fundamental to Methodism. John Wesley only wrote one full-length systematic treatise, *The Doctrine of Original Sin: According to Scripture, Reason, and Experience* (1757). In it he declared without this doctrine "the Christian system falls at once."[874]

Kenneth Collins explained: "a weak doctrine of original sin could only result in an equally weak doctrine of the new birth. For if the extensiveness of the problem was relinquished or soft-pedaled, the radical nature of the solution would be lost as well."[875] Since we were born in sin, we must be born again. Oden explained, "A high doctrine of original sin is the premise and companion of a high doctrine of grace."[876]

Lindström explained what original sin meant for Wesley,

The Fall, he believed, had deprived man of his original perfection and occasioned total corruption of human nature. Consequently, Adam's descendants are spiritually dead at birth and utterly devoid of the righteousness and holiness in which he himself was created. Sometimes original sin is described as an inclination to evil, or a condition in which all the faculties of man, understanding and will and affections, have been perverted. But he can use stronger language, defining it as total corruption of the whole of human nature.[877]

---

[872]Barth, *Church Dogmatics*, IV/2, 441.

[873]Barth, *Church Dogmatics*, IV/1, 500.

[874]Wesley, *BE Works*, 12:158.

[875]Collins, *Wesley on Salvation*, 22.

[876]Oden, *John Wesley's Teachings*, 1:215.

[877]Lindström, *Wesley and Sanctification*, 27.

Wesley's evangelical sermons were based on three main assumptions:

- natural man is totally corrupt
- this corruption is the result of original sin
- man can be justified only through God's grace in Christ[878]

In America, however, Daniel Whedon and John Miley undermined the doctrine of original sin by their stress on responsible guilt and freedom.[879] Writing in 1897, Daniel Steele complained that the doctrine of original sin, "a poison stung into humanity by the sin of Adam," had "quite generally dropped out of our pulpits."[880]

In 1864 Daniel Whedon wrote *The Freedom of the Will as a Basis of Human Responsibility and a Divine Government.* Whedon wrote a rebuttal to Jonathan Edwards' view of compatabilistic free will. "Is the Will at liberty to choose otherwise than it does, or is it not?"[881] Whedon's answer was based more on philosophy than on Scripture.

He placed more emphasis on human ability and less emphasis on preliminary grace. This power of contrary choice, for Whedon, was the result of the atonement, not preliminary grace. This transition from free grace to free will resulted in semi-Pelagianism.

Formulated by John Cassian in the fifth century, after Pelagianism had been condemned, the semi-Pelagian view accepts original sin but believes that man can still choose salvation on his own. We are fallen, but retain free will and the ability to seek God apart from any special grace. Essentially, when we take

---

[878]Lindström, *Wesley and Sanctification*, 21.

[879]Chiles, *Theological Transitions in American Methodism*, 199.

[880]Steele, *Gospel of the Comforter*, 288.

[881]Whedon, *Freedom of the Will*, 23. Fletcher had originally asked Augustus Toplady this same question [*Works*, 2:452].

the first step toward God, he will meet us the rest of the way.[882] This concept is sometimes expressed by mystics as a pearl in the heart of every person which is untouched by sin. Wesley was neither Pelagian nor semi-Pelagian. Oden declared,

> When Wesley is mistakenly portrayed today as a Pelagian or semi-Pelagian, the portrayer owes it to fairness to read *The Doctrine of Original Sin*. When Wesley is portrayed as a cheery humanistic type of Arminian who supposedly stressed the natural abilities of man, the critic reveals ignorance of the defining Doctrinal Minutes of August 1745 instructing all preachers in Wesley's connection.[883]

Wesley himself described the inability of the awakened sinner to choose salvation:

> Now he truly desires to break loose from sin, and begins to struggle with it. But though he strive with all his might he cannot conquer; sin is mightier than he. He would fain escape; but he is so fast in prison that he cannot get forth. He resolves against sin, but yet sins on . . . . Such is the freedom of his will — free only to evil. . . . Thus he toils without end, repenting and sinning, and repenting and sinning again, till at length the poor sinful, helpless wretch is even at his wit's end, and can barely groan, "O wretched man that I am, who shall deliver me from the body of this death?"[884]

It might appear in this statement of Wesley, which states that humanity in their fallen state are free only to choose evil,

---

[882]Schaff, *History of the Christian Church*, 3:858.

[883]Oden, *John Wesley's Teachings*, 2:158.

[884]Wesley, "Spirit of Bondage and Adoption," Sermon #9, 2.7-8.

amounts to compatibalistic freedom. It is true that we are so bound by sin that left to ourselves, our choices are always evil. Our freedom from evil can never be effected merely by an act of our will alone. But God has not left us to ourselves. Thus, preliminary grace breaks the determinism of Calvinism. Arminius emphasized a freed will. Wesley emphasized free grace, not free will.

Gunter concluded that neither Arminius nor Wesley taught a human-centered voluntarism that initiates even the slightest move apart from grace in the direction of salvation. That human will is free to respond to God's overtures and offer of salvation is the result of being *set free* by the Holy Spirit.[885]

James Arminius taught that while we did not lose our will, we lost the power to will any good thing.[886] He explained,

> But in his *lapsed and sinful state*, man is not capable, of and by himself, either to think, to will, or to do that which is really good. . . . The Free Will of man towards the True Good is not only wounded, maimed, infirm, bent, and weakened; but it is also imprisoned, destroyed, and lost: And its powers are not only debilitated and useless unless they be assisted by grace, but it has no powers whatever except such as are excited by Divine grace.[887]

Thus, Wesley declared, "No man that ever lived, not John Calvin himself, ever asserted either original sin or justification by faith in more strong, more clear and express terms, than Arminius has done."[888] The early Methodists declared they were

---

[885]Gunter, "John Wesley, Representative of Arminius," 78-82.

[886]Arminius, *Works*, 3:178.

[887]Arminius, *Works*, 2:192.

[888]Wesley, *BE Works*, 13:407.

within a hair's breadth of Calvinism because they ascribed all good to the free grace of God, denied all natural free will and all power antecedent to grace, and excluded all merit from man, even for what he has or does by the grace of God.[889]

While Methodism was shifting toward semi-Pelagianism, the American holiness movement was influenced by the Pelagianism of Charles Finney. Pope objected to Finney's Pelagianism and his denial of original sin.[890]

Recent Nazarene theologians have articulated an orthodox understanding of original sin, including Wiley, and Grider who said that Finney

> sometimes tended to be Pelagian and humanistic, as for example when he wrote, "The human will is free, there-fore men have the power or the ability to do all their duty."[891]

Writing from a feminist perspective, Diane Leclerc argues that the primary definition of original sin is relational idolatry.[892] Brad Mercer explained original sin as inadequate self worth and identity. Holiness, then, is finding our worth and identity through our relationship with Christ. Such descriptions are more psychological than theological.[893]

---

[889]Wesley, *BE Works*, 10:153.

[890]Pope, *Compendium*, 3:73-74.

[891]Grider, *Entire Sanctification*, 20. However, Timothy L. Smith declared that Finney was "never a Pelagian" ["Doctrine of the Sanctifying Spirit," 104].

[892]Leclerc, *Singleness of Heart*.

[893]Online: Mercer, "Sin and Holiness."

Original Guilt

It is one thing to teach that we share in the effects of the fall, another to teach that we incur the guilt of this fall. Arminius affirmed original sin, but denied original guilt. This position was adopted by John Miley.[894] However, Wesley ascribed to Adam's posterity an element of imputed guilt. He explained that we were "so *constituted sinners* by Adam's sinning as to become liable to punishment threatened to his transgression."[895] Wesley taught that original guilt was cancelled as an unconditional benefit of the atonement.[896]

Romans 5:12-19 teaches that in Adam all sinned. Death reigned, even over those who did not sin by breaking a command, as did Adam (v 14). Wesley noted "even over infants who had never sinned, as Adam did, in their own persons."[897]

Hebrews 7:10 illustrates the doctrine of imputation. Since death is the penalty of sin, therefore all men are born guilty of original sin because all men die. In his *Notes* Wesley explained, "infants themselves not excepted."[898] Fletcher also included infants.[899] But Wesley also believed the "free gift" of Romans 5:16 was that original guilt had been absolved as a universal benefit of the atonement. Wesley held,

> That all men are liable to these [to all punishments in this world and that which is to come] for Adam's sin alone, I do not assert; but they are so, for their own

---

[894]Stanglin and McCall, *Jacob Arminius*, 149-150, 194-195.

[895]Wesley, *BE Works*, 12:234.

[896]Wesley, *Letter* to John Mason, 21 Nov. 1776; "God's Love to Fallen Man," Sermon #59, 2.14.

[897]Wesley, *Notes*, 375.

[898]Wesley, *Notes*, 375.

[899]Fletcher, *Works*, 1:161.

outward and inward sins, which, through their own fault, spring from the infection of their nature.[900]

Wesley also said, "I believe none ever did, or ever will, die eternally, merely for the sin of our first father."[901] Unlike later Methodists who argued against original guilt on the basis of logic, Wesley was trying to formulate doctrine on the basis of Scripture. Paul states in Romans 5:12 that death came *because* all sinned.

The realist position, as advocated by Augustine, is that we all sinned with Adam. The Pelagian interpretation is that we sin independent of Adam's sin. A third interpretation explains that the result of Adam's sin is that we all sin.

We were involved in some way with Adam's sin. The question is whether we sinned in Adam. This view implies that Adam was our federal head. Or were we involved in Adam's sin? This interpretation implies realism. Or do we sin consequently to Adam's sin? Do all sin *like* Adam or *with* Adam?

Stott framed the question as one of imitation or participation. He argued that since all died from Adam to Moses, and death is the penalty for sin, but the law was not given until Moses, that all sinned in and through Adam. Stott also noted that in Romans 5:15-19, five times Paul states that the trespass or disobedience of one man brought death. Thus, universal death is attributed to a single sin. Stott also argued that we are justified on account of what Christ did, just as we are condemned on account of what Adam did. There is a correspondence between Adam and Christ which must be preserved. "If death comes to all because they sin like Adam, then by analogy we would have to

---

[900]Wesley, *BE Works*, 12:271.

[901]Wesley, *BE Works*, 12:307.

say that life comes to all because they are righteous like Christ."[902] Therefore, Stott argued that we sinned *with* Adam.

Pelagianism categorically denies the doctrine of imputation and therefore concludes that there is no necessary connection between Adam's sin and our sin. However, Romans 5:19 declares that through the disobedience of Adam many *were* constituted sinners. Yet if the Pelagian emphasis on free will is taken consistently, Adam's sin would not necessitate our sin.

Pope pointed out that Ephesians 2:3 does not separate condemnation from depravity, but instead taught that we are by our sinful nature the children of wrath. Yet he went on to explain that the wrath of God was upon those who live after this sinful nature, rather than the nature itself.[903]

American Methodist theology in the nineteenth century moved away from this earlier view. The newer view placed a much greater emphasis on individualism and free will. They denied that we could be punished for Adam's sin or that Christ was punished for our sin. Yet the theme of this section in Romans is the representative work of Adam and Christ. If we reject the concept of headship and representation, denying that Adam's disobedience was imputed to us, then we are at a loss to explain how we can be saved by faith in the obedience of Christ and how his righteousness can be imputed to us.

Paul views Adam as the head of the race and sees us in solidarity with Adam. Chrysostom preached, "Thus once Adam fell, even those who had not eaten of the tree became mortal because of him."[904] Fletcher wrote that in Adam all mankind was "seminally and federally collected in one individual."[905] The punishment of Adam's sin was not forgiven, but suspended so

---

[902]Stott, *Romans*, 150-152; see also Erickson, *Christian Theology*, 636-639.

[903]Pope, *Compendium*, 2:54-55.

[904]Bray, *ACC*, 136.

[905]Fletcher, *Works*, 3:251.

that the human race might continue. Yet, in deferring the punishment, the disease was also passed on.

Wesley held that there were two kinds of guilt: personal and corporate.[906] Wesley declared, "God does not look upon infants as innocent, but as involved in the *guilt* of Adam's sin." Yet two paragraphs earlier he declared, "But with regard to parents and their posterity, God assures us, children 'shall not die for the iniquity of their fathers.' No, not eternally. I believe none ever did or ever will die eternally, merely for the sin of our first father."[907]

Wesley held that we were guilty *corporately* through Adam but that this guilt was not imputed through preliminary grace and cancelled through the unconditional benefits of the atonement.

> Therefore no infant ever was, or ever will be "sent to hell for the guilt of Adam's sin;" seeing it is cancelled by the righteousness of Christ, as soon as they are sent into the world.[908]

The natural depravity of infants is not eliminated, but conditionally covered through the atonement until the infant reaches a level of moral accountability. Paul described this concept in Romans 7:9.[909]

Isaiah 7:15-16 describes a child who was not old enough to choose right and reject wrong, but then he arrives at that knowledge. The interpretative question is whether the subject is the Messiah, promised in v 14, or whether Isaiah is referring to the son of Ahaz. I understand that the subject is the Messiah who

---

[906]Cox, *Perfection*, 31; 49; Lindström, *Wesley and Sanctification*, 34-37.

[907]Wesley, *BE Works*, 12:307.

[908]Wesley, *Letter* to John Mason, 21 Nov 1776; "God's Love to Fallen Man," Sermon #59, 2.14.

[909]Bruce, *TNTC*, 147.

would be born into poverty and who would also develop a moral consciousness normally. This seems to be what was described in Luke 2:49. Since Jesus was twelve years old, this gave support to the notion that the age of accountability was reached at twelve years of age. The Jewish custom was that boys became men when they were brought to the temple for their bar mitzvah, although scholars are not certain whether bar mitzvah can be dated to this early period.

Millard Erickson, while not a Wesleyan-Arminian theologian, came to the same conclusion. He holds that we were all involved in Adam's sin and thus receive both the corrupted nature that was Adam's after the fall, along with the guilt and condemnation attached to his sin.

> With this matter of guilt, however, just as with the imputation of Christ's righteousness, there must be some conscious and voluntary decision on our part. Until this is the case, there is only a conditional imputation of guilt. Thus, there is no condemnation until one reaches the age of responsibility. If a child dies before he or she is capable of making genuine moral decisions, there is only innocence, and the child will experience the same type of future existence with the Lord as will those who have reached the age of moral responsibility and had their sins forgiven as a result of accepting the offer of salvation based upon Christ's atoning death.[910]

The basis for the doctrine of infant justification is a logical deduction from the fact that God warned Adam that in the day he ate of the forbidden fruit he would die. While Adam did die immediately, meaning that he was separated from God, the preservation of the race was an unconditional benefit of a future

---

[910]Erickson, *Christian Theology*, 639.

predestined atonement. Pope wrote, "There was in heaven an Atonement before the Atonement."[911]

As the second man, Jesus Christ also acted on behalf of the entire race. He chose life for us collectively. Thus, we are covered by the benefits of Christ's atonement until we are awakened to our personal responsibility. Because infants are not capable of a voluntary rejection of this preliminary grace, they are saved.[912]

However, it is important to distinguish between salvation and regeneration. Every child who is dedicated to God, regardless of whether they are baptized or not, is a Christian. Their Christian identity was decided on their behalf by their parents. But when they come to the age of accountability or personal responsibility, if they have the ability to choose sin, they also then have the responsibility to choose Christ and salvation personally.

Jesus declared that minor or under age children are in his kingdom (Matt 19:14; Mark 10:14; Luke 18:16). Therefore, such children are invited to come to Christ in baptism and the baptism of infants is not to be forbidden.[913]

However, Jesus also taught that unless a person has been born again he cannot enter or even see the kingdom of God (John 3:3-5). The proper function of systematic theology is to reconcile such apparent discrepancies.

While Matthew used the term *kingdom of heaven*, the other gospels use the term *kingdom of God* interchangeably. Therefore, no valid distinction can be maintained. Baptismal regeneration is not taught in Scripture and baptism is not a stipulated require-

---

[911]Pope, *Compendium*, 2:284.

[912]Watson, *Theological Institutes*, 2:59; Wakefield, *Christian Theology*, 1:295; Fletcher, *Works*, 1:283-285; Clarke, *Commentary*, 6:74-75; Raymond, *Systematic Theology*, 2:311-312; Summers, *Systematic Theology*, 2:39. See also Reasoner and O'Neal, "The Salvation of Infants," 5-8.

[913]Jeremias, *Infant Baptism*, 50, 53.

ment for these under age children to be in Christ's kingdom. Sacramentalists argue from John 3:5 that the Holy Spirit accompanies infant baptism, regenerating the infant. But Jesus declared that all children are in his kingdom, regardless of whether or not they were baptized. Some Calvinists would answer that elect children are in the kingdom, but Jesus did not make that stipulation either. Nor can we say that those children who are in the kingdom are those whom God foreknows will believe.

Nicodemus would see the kingdom of heaven once it came at Pentecost if he was born again after the Holy Spirit came. The new birth is an absolute requirement for entrance or membership in the church or kingdom of Christ only for those who have been awakened to their unregenerate condition and have heard the gospel call. However, those who die before birth, infants, under-age children, those with mental handicaps, and those who never heard the gospel may be saved through unconditional benefits of Christ's atonement and thus belong to the kingdom in spite of the fact that they have not exercised saving faith and received the Holy Spirit. The entire human race reaps the benefits of this kingdom influence even if they have not been born again.

John Fletcher was aware of this interpretive question when he wrote that the disciples before Pentecost were already partially regenerated.[914] His extended answer employed his doctrine of dispensations. Essentially, he said that under-age children were under the dispensation of the Son but not the Spirit. Certainly, Fletcher was on solid ground by affirming the justification of all infants based on the unconditional benefit of Christ's atonement and the nonimputation of Adam's sin to them.

According to Romans 5:18, this free gift of preliminary grace was extended to all mankind. The only other interpretation of this verse would lead to universalism. Either all *were* saved, all *are* saved, or, according to Calvinism, *all* cannot mean *all*.[915]

---

[914]Fletcher, *Works*, 3:151.

[915]Reasoner, *Romans*, 1:316-317.

Fletcher taught that all infants are saved until they sin away their justification. Therefore, universalism was a past reality, not a future possibility.[916] Matlock explained that this general work of Christ in justifying infants is an integral part of Methodist doctrine. "If all men are not justified at birth, then some are condemned; they must be eternally reprobated in Adam."[917]

In his *Treatise on Baptism* Wesley taught that Romans 5:12 included infants. Since they die, they too have sinned, but the guilt of original sin is washed away in infant baptism.[918] Perhaps it would be more consistent to say that infant baptism is an outward sign of inward preliminary grace, which is an unconditional benefit of the atonement.

Whether original guilt is rejected on the basis of logical assumptions or its consequences are suspended by virtue of the unconditional benefits of Christ's atonement, both positions end up with the same conclusion. However, this conclusion is arrived at through different processes. Wesley's view is an attempt to deal with the scriptural implications, while the view of Arminius is based more upon logical assumptions. Of course, there is a logical process involved in scriptural interpretation, but we should always start with an exegesis of Scripture, not *a priori* assumptions.

Total Depravity

This inherited sin, which results in the total inability to save ourselves, is taught throughout the Bible. Apart from enabling grace, the plight of mankind is hopeless. When his disciples asked Jesus who can be saved, he replied, "With man this is

---

[916]Fletcher, *Works*, 1:283-285; see also Clarke, *Commentary*, 6:74-75.

[917]Matlock, *The Four Justifications*, 19.

[918]Wesley, *Works*, 10:190-193.

impossible, but with God all things are possible" (Matt 19:25-26).

Apart from grace, every inclination of the thoughts of man's heart is only evil all the time (Gen 6:5). The Hebrew word *yetser*, translated *imagination*, means propensity, tendency, or direction. It describes the formation of thoughts. Thus, the rabbis used the term *yetser hara, the evil tendency*, as their expression for original sin.[919]

We have all turned aside and become corrupt. There is no one who does good, not even one (Ps 14:2-3, 53:3). We are sinful from the moment of conception (Ps 51:5). The wicked are estranged from the womb; they go astray from birth (Ps 58:3). The heart is deceitful above all things (Jer 17:9). Jesus said we are evil (Matt 7:11; Luke 11:13). We are all under sin (Rom 3:9). There is not even one who is righteous (Rom 3:10-18; Ps 143:2). We are dead in transgressions and sins, gratifying the cravings of our sinful nature (Eph 2:1-3). Our old self is corrupt through deceitful desires (Eph 4:22). We are helpless (Rom 5:6). We are sold as a slave to sin (Rom 7:14). We are subject to "the law of sin and death" (Rom 8:2). The flesh is at war with God (Rom 8:7). We have a sinful nature (Rom 8:8).

We quarrel and fight, covet and murder because we have passions warring within (Jas 4:1-2). Sinful desire is the corruption that is in the world (2 Pet 1:4). All have sinned (Rom 3:23) because all are sinners. Sinful actions proceed from a sinful heart (Mark 7:21-22). Anyone who claims to be without a sinful nature is thus deceived and the truth is not in him (1 John 1:8). The sinner is:

- energized by Satan (Eph 2:1-2)
- blinded by Satan (2 Cor 4:3-4)
- controlled by Satan (1 John 5:19)

---

[919]Purkiser, *God, Man, and Salvation*, 85-86.

Every sinner is not demon-possessed, but every sinner is bound by sin. Even without the work of the devil, the sinful nature controls him. His sin condemns him. He not only has inherited depravity, but he acquires more depravity by wrong choices. He stands guilty before God because of his sins. The wages of sin is death (Rom 6:23). The sinner is dead in sin (Eph 2:1). The sinner faces the second death, eternal separation from God (Rev 2:11, 20:14, 21:8).

This depravity is *total* since it affects the entire being of man:

- the affections are alienated
- the intellect is darkened. Semi-Pelagianism, however, holds that man's reason is only relatively impaired. For them, faith is a reasonable decision based upon rational reflection.
- the will is perverted

John Fletcher wrote that "the whole head is sick" (Isa 1:5), including our understanding, imagination, memory, reason, will, conscience, and affections.[920]

Francis Schaeffer wrote, "Since the Fall, there is no truly healthy person in his body, and there is no completely balanced person psychologically. The results of the Fall spoils us as a unit and in all our parts."[921] While normalcy is established as the 80% within the Bell curve, every person on the human spectrum is abnormal in comparison with God's original intention.

We are deprived of all that is good (Rom 7:18). There was a total loss of original righteousness.[922] But Scripture teaches more than a deprivation of original good. Watson taught that

---

[920]Fletcher, *Works*, 3:280-283.

[921]Schaeffer, *Works*, 3:321.

[922]Wakefield, *Christian Theology*, 1:299.

original sin is "a depravation arising from deprivation."[923] This means that the sinfulness of man is the result of his separation from God, as well as his inherited nature from Adam. Thus, we are inclined to evil continually (Gen 6:5). Leclerc affirmed total deprivity *and* total depravity.[924] McCall concluded that sin is best understood as a parasite on goodness.[925]

G. K. Chesterton called the doctrine of original sin the only empirically verifiable Christian doctrine.[926] While Arminius never used the term *total depravity*, he did affirm the concept.[927] Samuel Wakefield declared,

> True Arminianism, therefore, as fully as Calvinism, admits the total depravity of human nature in conse-quence of the fall of our first parents; and to represent this doctrine as being exclusively Calvinistic, which has often been done, is an entire delusion.[928]

Modernism is essentially Pelagian in its denial of original sin. Both liberalism and Pelagianism teach that man is born morally neutral and is condemned only for his own sinful choices. Both positions exalt human nature and human potential, believing people will do right because of an inner imperative. A

---

[923]Watson, *Theological Institutes*, 2:79.

[924]Leclerc, *Discovering Christian Holiness*, 158-159.

[925]McCall, *Against God and Nature*, 233.

[926]Chesterton, *Orthodoxy*, 28. This quip has also been attributed to Reinhold Niebuhr. The same argument is eloquently made by Fletcher [*Works*, 3:251-342].

[927]Stanglin and McCall, *Jacob Arminius*, 150.

[928]Wakefield, *Christian Theology*, 1:291; see also Watson, *Theological Institutes*, 2:48; Harrison, *Arminianism*, 234.

liberal theologian who denied total depravity admitted, however, that "the disorder runs pretty deep."[929]

On the other hand, neo-orthodox theologians such as Reinhold Neibuhr and Barth have made the sinfulness of man so inherent in his nature as to be irremediable. We are helpless, but not hopeless. Without God's grace we cannot be saved, but without our grace-enabled participation, God's grace will not irresistibly save us.[930]

Five misconceptions concerning total depravity
- **Total depravity is not transmitted physically.**

Because we are charged with Adam's sin we are deprived of the Spirit of God who makes us holy. Thus, we experience a lost relationship. And because of our identification with Adam, we inherit a propensity or inclination to sin. Wiley said original sin is a depravity that results from deprivation. He also explained, "This depravity must not, however, be regarded as a physical entity or any other form of essential existence added to man's nature."[931]

Sin is not in the blood or in the DNA. It is not a physical substance that can be eradicated. Scripture does not teach that sin is genetically transferred by our parents to us. Wesley explained that sin was transferred to us legally because Adam was our legal representative or federal head.

Sin is entailed upon me, not by my *immediate* but by my first parent. "In Adam all died;" "by the disobedience of one, all men were made sinners" — all men

---

[929]MacQuarrie, *Principles of Christian Theology*, 61.

[930]Maddox, *Responsible Grace*, 19.

[931]Wiley, *Christian Theology*, 2:119.

without exception who were in his loins when he ate the forbidden fruit.[932]

Richard Treffry explained that parents propagate their species but not their endowments.[933]

Concerning the transmission of original sin, Wesley replied to a correspondent who had asserted that "there are but three opinions" that "I care not if there were none. The fact I know, both by Scripture and by experience. I know it is transmitted; but *how* it is transmitted I neither know nor desire to know."[934]

> And if you ask me how, in what determinate manner, sin is *propagated*, how it is transmitted from father to son, I answer plainly, I cannot tell. No more than I can tell how man is propagated, how a body is transmitted from father to son. I know both the one and the other fact. But I can account for neither.[935]

However, Pope attempted to explain what Wesley avoided by distinguishing between our being susceptible to punishment, which was passed on to all men through Adam, and our being held responsible and therefore guilty for Adam's sin.[936]

Pope said that depravity is twofold, "the absence of original righteousness and the bias to all evil."[937] Because we are charged with Adam's sin we are deprived of the Spirit of God who makes us holy and thus our relationship with God is lost. Because of

---

[932]Wesley, *BE Works*, 13:173; "God's Love to Fallen Man," Sermon #59, ¶ 1; *Notes*, 376.

[933]Treffry, *Treatise on Christian Perfection*, 61-62.

[934]Wesley, *Letter* to Dr. John Robertson, 24 Sept 1753.

[935]Wesley, *BE Works*, 12:329.

[936]Moss, *Pope*, 81; see also Pope, *Compendium*, 2:48-51.

[937]Pope, *Compendium*, 2:59.

our identification with Adam, we inherit a propensity or inclination to sin; and thus the condition of sinfulness is transferred.

If we reject the doctrine that sin is transmitted genetically, we cannot claim that homosexuality is predetermined genetically. Homosexual practice is a choice based on depravity.

- **Total depravity does not mean that every person is as thoroughly depraved as he can possibly become.**

Maddox explained that even Reformed theologians did not believe that every person is as evil as he could possibly be. Rather *total* means that the corruption of sin affects every faculty of our personality.[938] Thus, it is pervasive. Whedon distinguished between *extensive* and *intensive* depravity.[939]

Through continued rejection of God's law and continued choices to sin we become even more depraved. While Pelagians affirm only this acquired depravity, the reality is that depravity is both inherited *and* acquired.

- **Total depravity does not mean that the sinner has no innate knowledge of the will of God or conscience.**

Paul wrote in Romans 2:15 that even the pagans have the law written upon their hearts, and their consciences both accuse and defend them. Although we are fallen, we still have a consciousness of right and wrong. Although we have a bias toward sin and our tendency is to choose wrong, through preliminary grace we are given the possibility of choosing right; and we are held responsible for our choices. Wesley wrote,

---

[938]Maddox, *Responsible Grace*, 82.

[939]Whedon, *Statements*, 331. See Carter's discussion [*Contemporary Wesleyan Theology*, 1:268-270].

Natural free will, in the present state of mankind, I do not understand: I only assert, that there is a measure of free will *supernaturally* restored to every man, together with that *supernatural* light, which "enlightens every man that cometh into the world."[940]

- **Total depravity does not mean that sinful man is incapable of good acts toward man.**

Watson rejected the view that there is nothing virtuous among men before they are regenerated.[941] We can do relatively good, but not love God and our neighbor as we should.

Wesley explained: "All works done before justification are not good, in the Christian sense, forasmuch as they spring not of faith in Jesus Christ."[942] Oden explained, "Total depravity does not mean that there is nothing good in human creation, but that sin taints every corner and aspect of human choosing."[943]

- **Total depravity does not mean that every sinner will indulge in every form of sin.**

Nor can original sin be reduced to one expression of sin. Anselm and Thomas Aquinas held that it was the lack of original righteousness.[944] For Augustine and Peter Lombard, however, original sin was concupiscence. The Greek word *epit-humia* was translated *concupiscence* by the KJV in Romans 7:8; Colossians 3:5; 1 Thessalonians 4:5. In all three references it has a negative connotation, but its meaning is broader than sexual lust. Most

---

[940]Wesley, *BE Works*, 13:287.

[941]Watson, *Theological Institutes*, 2:83. See also Wakefield, *Christian Theology*, 1:307.

[942]Wesley, "Justification by Faith," Sermon #5, 3.6.

[943]Oden, *John Wesley's Teachings*, 1:205.

[944]Stanglin and McCall, *Jacob Arminius*, 146-147.

translations of Romans 7:8 render it *covetousness* because of the subject established in the previous verse.

The Danger of Apostasy

The Greek word *apostasia* occurs only twice: to describe Jews forsaking Moses (Acts 21:21) and to describe a rebellion or falling away at the end of the millennium (2 Thess 2:3).

A related word, *apostasion*, is used three times for *divorce*. And so we have the concept of departure, but always in a negative connotation.

Our study of apostasy must also consider synonymous words such as *aphistemi*, which literally means *to stand apart from*. It is sometimes used in narrative passages to describe departure from a location, to leave a person, or to take something away. Doctrinally, it is used in Luke 8:13 to describe those who believe for a while but fall away. In 1 Timothy 4:1 it describes those who will abandon the faith. It is used in a positive sense in 2 Timothy 2:19, "Everyone who confesses the name of the Lord must *turn away* from wickedness." But Hebrews 3:12 warns against turning away from or forsaking the living God.

Pipto is a third word used for apostasy. Normally it is used to describe a literal fall, but 1 Corinthians 10:12 describes falling from grace. In 2 Peter 3:17-18 there is a warning against falling from our secure position. Here the compound verb is *ekpipto*. Joseph Benson preached that growth in grace is the only security against falling from it.[945] According to 2 Peter 1:10, those who keep on confirming their salvation shall never *ptaio* stumble, trip, sin, fail, or fall. This verb was used in the LXX translation of Deuteronomy 7:25 to describe apostasy. The previous verse, 2 Peter 1:9, warns that the only protection against apostasy is to keep going forward.

---

[945]Benson, *Sermons*, 7:230-232. Sermon #251.

A fourth word, *aphiemi*, can be used in a positive sense to describe the release of forgiveness. It can also refer to the release of permission. But in Revelation 2:4 it describes the Ephesians who have left or abandoned their first love. The result was that their light was removed.

First Timothy 5:12 describes widows who have broken their pledge, but the Greek text is stronger than the NIV translation. They *atheteo* or set aside, cast off, or rejected their previous faith. In 2 Timothy 4:10, Demas abandoned or forsook Paul (*egkataleipo*). Clarke explained that Demas preferred Judaism to Christianity.[946] While this is a case of apostasy, the text does not reveal any formal renunciation of Christ, only a love for this present world. That same love for the world causes many to forsake (same Greek word) the assembly of believers. Perhaps apostasy is more prevalent than we recognize.

Romans 14:15 warns that a brother's faith can be destroyed. This destruction comes in stages. He is first distressed or grieved. Ultimately he is destroyed. This word, *apollumi*, means damnation.

Three times in Romans 1:24-28 God gave up the reprobate. In all three instances the verb *paradidomi* is used. It describes a giving up or giving over through the withdrawal of the influence and restraint of the Holy Spirit. The word used to describe the reprobate is *adokimos* which denotes the negation of approval. The depraved mind has been rejected by God because it has first rejected God. Paul used the same word, *adokimos*, in 1 Corinthians 9:27 to say that he himself could become disqualified or a castaway if he did not mortify the deeds of the flesh. Thus, the elect could become the reprobate.

In 2 Peter 2:22 the graphic depiction of apostasy uses the Greek verb *hupostrepho* to describe the dog returning to his vomit and a sow back to the mud.

The NT also contains metaphors for apostasy.

---

[946]Clarke, *Commentary*, 6:638.

- In 1 Timothy 1:18-19 we are warned that some did not maintain their hold on faith and their faith was *shipwrecked*.
- Romans 11:17 describes Israel as a branch which was broken off because of unbelief (v 20).
- Jude 12 describes apostates who are twice dead. They were originally dead in trespasses and sins, but they had been made alive. Now they are once more dead. Jude describes them as trees without fruit. Revelation 3:2 also describes those who are ready to die. Apostasy is the sin which leads to spiritual *death* (1 John 5:16).

John is not making a distinction between venial and mortal sins. The expression *sin unto death* comes from Numbers 18:22 where sacrilege was denoted as a capital offence. Daniel Steele explained,

> This sin is not limited to a single act, such as a crime worthy of punishment by death, or a manifestly Divine visitation, or a sin punished by the church with excommunication. It is rather a course of wilful sin in defiance of the known law of God persisted in so obstinately against the influences of the Holy Spirit, that repentance becomes a moral impossibility, just as a man may starve himself so long as to lose the power to appropriate, digest and assimilate food.[947]

- Apostasy is a removal of the candlestick (Rev 2:5).
- Apostasy results in a name taken from the book of life (Rev 3:5). Robert Thomas conceded, "The promise to the overcomer is an empty one unless the possibility exists that such blotting out could occur. What incentive is furnished

---

[947]Steele, *Half-Hours with St. John's Epistles*, 144.

by being promised deliverance from something that could not happen?"[948]

In order to maintain his presupposition of unconditional security, Thomas explained that everyone's name is in the book, and those who never trust in Christ are erased. However, Revelation 17:8 teaches that not every name is written in the book of life.

There are also five warning passages in Hebrews. In Hebrews 2:1-4 the warning is against drifting away, slipping away, or losing sight (*pararheo*). They neglected their salvation. *Pararheo* occurs only here in the NT. It is debated whether this word depicts a drifting ship or a leaking vessel. Regardless of whether the metaphor is a ship drifting off course or a vessel which runs dry, the result is still the same — a gradual backsliding which ultimately results in the loss of salvation.

The second warning is Hebrews 3:7-4:13. The verb *aphistemi* has already been noted, but in the context this turning away is the result of hardening the heart. This hardening comes as a result of disobedience, and the result is falling short. Dale Moody says that *apistia* is a synonym for apostasy. It is used in Hebrews 3:12,19 and means unbelief. A second synonym is *apeitheia* (disobedience; 4:6,11).Thus, hardness of heart is the result of falling away, unbelief, and disobedience. He also says that *hustereo*, falling short (4:1), is a synonym of *aphistemi*, falling away (3:12).[949]

The third warning is Hebrews 5:11-6:12.The danger is that those who have not reached maturity may fall away. Here the verb is a compound form of *pipto* — *parapipto* and the meaning is not simply to fall away, but to deliberately turn away. According to Grant Osborne, to repudiate the Son, as described in Hebrews 6:4-6 is to commit the unpardonable sin.

---

[948]Thomas, *Revelation 1-7*, 261.

[949]Moody, *Apostasy*, 29-30.

Wesley also interpreted Hebrews 6 as "absolute, total apostasy." He felt that Hebrews 6:4-6 and 10:26-27 describes such a case."[950] Yet he continues in the same sermon to declare, "A believer may fall, and not fall away. He may fall and rise again. And if he should fall, even into sin, yet this case, dreadful as it is, is not desperate." But Wesley went on to warn that a believer may "sink lower and lower till he wholly fall away."[951] Elsewhere he described the warning in Hebrews 6 as a formal renunciation of Jesus of Nazareth as an impostor, a deceiver, and deserving of the cross.[952]

Not all Arminians agree that Hebrews 6 is necessarily warning of final apostasy. Robert Shank defined apostasy as "any departure from God and saving grace, whether deliberate or casual."[953] Shank devoted an entire chapter to the question, "Is apostasy without remedy?" Shank argued that even the warning in Hebrews 6 is regarding not merely a past defection, but a present deliberate hostility toward Christ.[954]

This is also the position of Boyce Blackwelder who explained that the temporal force of the two present participles in Hebrews 6:6, *while crucifying* and *while putting to open shame*, "implies that if a person guilty of such sin will cease it, and repent, they can be reclaimed."[955]

The fourth warning, in Hebrews 10:19-39, is to those who deliberately keep on sinning or persist in wilful sin. Osborne

---

[950]Wesley, "Sermon on the Mount, IV," Sermon #24, 1.9; "Call to Backsliders," Sermon #86, 2.3.i. See also his *Notes* on Heb 6:6. Ironically, he seems to conflate his interpretation of Hebrews 6 with the blasphemy of the Holy Ghost in "Call to Backsliders," 2.5.i.

[951]Wesley, "Sermon on the Mount, IV," 1.9.

[952]Wesley, "Call to Backsliders," 2.4.

[953]Shank, *Life in the Son*, 312.

[954]Shank, *Life in the Son*, 318;

[955]Blackwelder, *Light from the Greek New Testament*, 103-104.

declared that Heb 10:26 was the closest thing to a definition of apostasy in Hebrews.[956] They cast away or throw off (*apoballo*) their confidence (v 35) and draw back (*hupostole* - noun form of *hupostello* used in v 38) unto destruction (v 39).

The final warning, Hebrews 12:14-29, is against falling behind or lacking (*hustereo*) the grace of God which results in a bitter root which grows up to cause trouble and defile.

Thus, the NT uses at least twelve synonyms and five metaphors to define apostasy. While many of the passages do not describe *how* apostasy occurs, at least four of the five warnings in Hebrews seem to be describing a gradual process.

Having surveyed the warnings in the NT against apostasy, we must now draw some theological conclusions. Calvinism denies the possibility of apostasy for the elect.[957] Theologically, Calvinism may interpret these warnings as hypothetical, but that violates the graphic language of Hebrews 6:4-5. To conclude that those who depart from the faith actually never were elect violates the very concept of apostasy. One cannot abandon what he never possessed. John Frame wrote, "This is a troubling passage. It is hard to see how the description could fit someone who is unregenerate."[958] Yet his theological presuppositions force him to that conclusion.

Thus, Calvinism teaches that those who commit the unforgiveable sin are those who are predestined by God to hear and receive the gospel. They are also predestined to *initially* respond in faith to the gospel. But they are also predestined to reject Jesus Christ because his atoning work was never intended for them. Thus, they are predestined to commit the unforgiveable sin.[959]

---

[956]Osborne, "Classical Arminian View," 120.

[957]Feinburg, "God Ordains All Things," 35.

[958]Frame, *Doctrine of God*, 436.

[959]McCall, *Against God and Nature*, 256.

Some who embrace unconditional eternal security want to reject the predestination of Calvinism but embrace the perseverance of the believer. They, too, must dismiss the possibility of apostasy.

Ultimately Arminius held that it is impossible for believers, as long as they remain believers, to decline from salvation, but that a believer who ceases to trust God is no longer a believer.[960] According to McCall and Stanglin, Arminius taught that true believers can fall away and that in most cases they can be brought back. A true believer can apostatize either by rejecting the faith or by committing sins out of a malicious heart that is inconsistent with saving faith.[961]

There can be degrees of apostasy. Apostasy is the final step in backsliding. Not all apostasy is final. Adam Clarke wrote, "It is utterly absurd to say that the day of grace may end before the day of life. . . . while there is life there is hope." [962] Steve Harper declared, "Even when we fall *from* grace, we do not fall *beyond* grace."[963] Even in Romans 11 the national apostasy of Israel was *not* final. Verse 26 promises that all Israel will be saved. The Remonstrants taught that one can be renewed should he fall away.

> Yet though true believers sometimes fall into grievous sins, and such as destroy the conscience, we do not believe that they immediately fall away from all hope of repentance; but we acknowledge this to be an event not impossible to occur, that God, according to the multi-

---

[960]Arminius, *Works*, 3:470.

[961]Stanglin and McCall, *Jacob Arminius*, 172-175, 207.

[962]Clarke, *Letter* to Samuel Dunn in Hare, *Life of Adam Clarke*, 218.

[963]Harper, "Wesleyan Arminian View," 241.

tude of His mercies may again call them by His grace to repentance.[964]

Wesley reported that some who were backslidden were restored to their first love. And his general conclusion is that we should not give up on those who have no hope of restoration.[965] He even claimed that he knew of several thousand real apostates who were restored.[966] Thus, apostasy was not always final (see Hos 14:4).

Grant Osborne, writing as a Classical Arminian, concludes that we can backslide by allowing sin to crowd Christ out of our life. This kind of apostate can be brought back to Christ. But we can actually repudiate Christ, and this type of apostate will never want to come back, nor will God ever convict that person again.[967]

Apostasy is the culmination of backsliding, and that backsliding is the result of sin. Apostasy is not merely a hypothetical possibility, nor can it be committed by the nominal Christian who never was regenerate. It cannot be relegated to another dispensation, or exclusively to Israel or the church corporately. The warning in Hebrews 3:12 and 4:1 is to individuals — "none of you."

Apostasy is not necessarily a decisive renunciation of Christ or attributing his works to the power of Satan. Most cases of apostasy are not that dramatic or decisive. The more dramatic and decisive mode is more properly associated with committing the unpardonable sin. However, Wilson Hogue, a Free Methodist bishop, taught the blasphemy against the Holy Spirit was not

---

[964]Article 5, Proposition 5 in Watson, *Dictionary*, 898.

[965]Wesley, "Call to Backsliders," § 5; 2.1.v; 2.4-6.

[966]Wesley, "Call to Backsliders," 2.2.

[967]Osborne, "Classical Arminian View," 87. Harper also articulates two ways in which apostasy may occur ["Wesleyan Arminian View," 244].

some isolated and independent act. He described it as a culminating transgression, "the final link in a long chain of malignant and rebellious acts. . . .This state is usually reached through a protracted series of resistances against the drawing and impulses of the Spirit."[968]

It seems, then, that both *final* apostasy and the blasphemy of the Spirit occur gradually; and the only real difference is that only true believers may become apostate, while nonbelievers may blaspheme the Spirit. Thus, apostasy may occur incrementally or decisively.

According to the warning passages in Hebrews, apostasy results when believers drift away, disobey, harden their hearts, and fall short. They deliberately persist in wilful sin. The root of bitterness springs up because they fail to appropriate the grace of God.

We are either moving forward or sliding backward. Anyone who is sliding backward is in danger of apostasy. The only question is how far back do they have to slide? And is apostasy always irreversible?

Our entire life is a probationary period. It is possible to forfeit saving grace, but never necessary.

---

[968]Hogue, *Holy Spirit*, 385-391.

CHAPTER NINE
The Doctrine of Atonement

Mankind is under the wrath of God because of our rebellion against him. We are hopelessly doomed to eternal judgment because of our sins against God. While God was under no obligation to rescue us, if we were ever to be saved *he* would have to provide our salvation. Moved by love, he chose to provide a way of salvation. However, his plan had to be consistent with his own nature. God could not simply decree that guilty sinners were released from the debt of sin.

The atonement of Jesus Christ does not automatically save anyone, but it provides a plan which includes everyone. Thus, it is universal in provision, but it is effectual only for those who believe.

Because God had predestined this atonement before we were ever created, the human race did not experience the full punishment of God when we sinned. Every believer before the cross was provisionally saved by that future fact. And every human is saved through the unconditional benefits of this atonement until he willfully chooses to sin.

The justice of God was satisfied through a voluntary, innocent substitute taking the penalty of guilty sinners on their behalf. This substitute would have to be sinless himself or else he would be in need of a substitute. He would also have to be part of the human race. In that case there could be a transfer of punishment from one guilty sinner to one innocent man. Because Jesus Christ was also fully God, however, his substitution was of infinite worth. He overpaid for all the cumulative sins the human race will ever commit. That is why the only adequate plan of salvation for the human race required the God/man.

Jesus Christ gave his life for our sins. Because blood is equated with life, the atonement is made more graphic when the Scriptures teach that we are redeemed through his *blood*.

Thus, this satisfaction of divine justice turns away the wrath of God against guilty sinners. This atonement reconciles us with God, provides full restoration from the fall, and gives us victory over sin and Satan. It is the ultimate expression of divine love for fallen man.

The cross is the heart of the gospel. Reconciliation, redemption, justification, regeneration, sanctification, and glorification are all present or future benefits of the atonement. The potential exists for us to gain more through Christ than we ever lost through Adam. Ultimately we will receive a new body, no longer under the curse of sin, and our immortality will be restored. The entire creation will be saved from the curse of sin.

A Survey of Atonement in Scripture

The basis of our salvation is the grace of God through the atonement of Jesus Christ. The atonement is the heart of the gospel. Paul declared, "May I never boast except in the cross of our Lord Jesus Christ" (Gal 6:14). "Christ died for us" (Rom 5:8) is the most basic statement of the atonement. Yet the preaching of the cross is a stumbling block to the Jews and foolishness to the Greeks (1 Cor 1:22).

The atonement is the satisfaction of God's justice. When we believe on the Lord Jesus, who has borne the penalty for our sins, God accepts Christ as our substitute and us as his children. We are redeemed from the bondage of sin and are reconciled with God. The atonement of Christ reveals the love of God, the wisdom of God, and turns away the wrath of God.

God began teaching the necessity of atonement as early as Genesis 3. While Adam and Eve were conscious of their guilt, they did not repent. Instead they attempted to cover themselves with fig leaves (v 7). God covered them with animal skins. Something living had to die to adequately cover the guilty pair. This was the first time Adam and Eve had ever encountered death. The sacrificial system delineated in the OT was not invented by the Jews nor copied from the pagans. It was based on a direct revelation of God.

The Hebrew word *kaphar* means *to cover*. It is first used in Genesis 6:14 to cover over the ark with pitch. It was the pitch that shielded Noah's family from the water of God's judgment, coming between death outside the ark and the salvation of Noah's family on the ark.

Yom Kippur (a variation of *kaphar*) is the Day of Atonement. In Leviticus 16 the verb *kaphar* occurs sixteen times. The purpose for the Day of Atonement was to provide a covering which protected Israel from the wrath of God. Sinful humanity does not need a covering of leaves or pitch. We need a blood covering.

The priestly ritual included sprinkling blood on the *mercy seat*. More literally, *kapporeth*, the noun form, should be translated *the place of propitiation*. This noun occurs seven times in the same chapter. The mercy seat is referenced in Hebrews 9:5 where the Greek adjective *hilasterion* is used to refer to the lid on the ark of the covenant. This word also refers to propitiation. According to Leviticus 16:2, God appeared in a cloud of glory situated over this mercy seat. We cannot experience his shekinah presence without the covering of his atonement.

Exodus 12 described the deliverance of Passover. A lamb without blemish is slain and its blood brushed on the door frames in the outline of the cross. According to 1 Corinthians 5:7 Jesus is our Passover lamb.

The priesthood was instituted in Exodus. Jesus Christ is both our great high priest and the sacrificial lamb. On the Day of Atonement (Lev 16), the high priest slew one goat and sprinkled its blood in the Holy of Holies. He laid his hands on the head of the other animal, the scapegoat, and confessed the sins of the people. This goat was led into the wilderness. This ritual symbolized imputation and substitution; the removal of guilt and the offering for sin.

Atonement was the basic principle underlying all blood sacrifices. Archer explained,

> In token of this substitution the offerer laid his hand upon the victim's head, thus identifying himself with it as his representative. To signify his acceptance of the just penalty of death, he himself slew his victim, and then turned it over to the priest for the completion of the ceremony.[969]

Leviticus 17:11 explains that the life of a creature is in the blood. God said, "I have given it to you to make atonement for yourselves." Treffry wrote, "Nothing, surely, can more clearly convey the notion of transfer and substitution."[970]

The blood explains why Abel's sacrifice was accepted (Heb 11:4).[971] The Greek word for *sacrifice* (*thusia*), is based on the verb which means to slay or kill. It implies a violent act. *Blood* is a metaphor for death.[972] Yet the blood of bulls and goats can never adequately substitute for human sin (Heb 10:4).

In Numbers 21 the people of Israel were dying from snake bites. The Lord told Moses to make a snake and put it up on a pole. Anyone who was bitten could look at it and live. This deliverance symbolized Jesus hanging on the cross. Jesus taught, "Just as Moses lifted up the snake in the desert, so the Son of

---

[969]Archer, *Survey of Old Testament Introduction*, 231.

[970]Treffry, *Letters on the Atonement*, 96.

[971]Watson, *Theological Institutes*, 2:173-188.

[972]Stibbs, *Meaning of the Word "Blood" in Scripture*, (1948).

Man must be lifted up" (John 3:14). "But I, when I am lifted up from the earth, will draw all men to myself. He said this to show the kind of death he was going to die" (John 12:32-33).

But why did Moses put a snake on the cross? Word of Faith teachers say that Jesus actually took on the nature of the devil.[973] This is blasphemy. The devil did not go to the cross for us. Jesus is not a snake; nor did Christ actually become a sinner. Through symbols God taught us that sin is like a fatal snakebite. The snake on the cross represents the antidote. Christ took our punishment into his own body in order to produce a cure for sin. Jesus is the only physician who can cure his patients by taking their disease. "Christ redeemed us from the curse of the law by becoming a curse for us, for it is written: Cursed is everyone who is hung on a tree" (Gal 3:13). We must look to the cross to be saved. God sent his own Son in the likeness of sinful man to be a sin offering (Rom 8:3).

To use the figurative language of Genesis 3:15, the snake bit the heel of Jesus Christ. He took our punishment into his own body in order to produce a cure for sin. Medical laboratories search for someone who has contracted a specific disease, and from the blood of that person who has overcome they produce a serum for the victim. The blood of Jesus is the only antitoxin in the world that will cure the snakebite of sin.

The book of Ruth tells the story of a kinsman-redeemer. The Hebrew term *gaal* describes a near relative who was responsible to buy back property which the family once owned. Thus, Boaz illustrates the fact that before Jesus Christ could become our redeemer he had to become our kinsman.

In the NT the word *atonement* is found only once in the King James Version, at Romans 5:11. However, four Greek words are used in the NT, borrowed from the home, the temple,

---

[973]Hanegraaff, *Christianity in Crisis*, 175. For example, Hinn, "The Person of Christ," 2 Dec 1990; Hagin, *The Name of Jesus*, 31; Copeland, "What Happened from the Cross to the Throne?" side 2.

the court, and the marketplace, to illustrate the basic meaning of atonement. However, these metaphors routinely overlap:

- **Relational**. *Katallasso* means to reconcile or make peace. It conveys the theme of restored relationship. This concept is conveyed in at-one-ment. God reconciled the world to himself through Christ (2 Cor 5:19). Christ is the mediator (1 Tim 2:5). The result is fellowship.
- **Sacrificial**. *Hilaskomai* means to propitiate; to turn away the anger of God. Various forms of this word occur six times in the NT. Christ was our merciful and faithful high priest who offered himself as the once and for all sacrifice for our sins, turning away the wrath of God. The result is forgiveness.
- **Legal**. *Parakaleo* means to make an appeal or act as an advocate. In the OT the high priest not only offered the sacrifice, but he made intercession. According to 1 John 2:1, Jesus Christ speaks to the Father, our judge, in our defense. Christ Jesus who died is at the right hand of God (Rom 8:34; Heb 7:25, 9:24, 10:12). The result is satisfaction of divine law and our forensic justification.
- **Commercial**. *Lutroo* means to redeem or ransom. It conveys the commercial theme. We are bought with a price (1 Cor 6:20). Christ gave himself for us to redeem us from all wickedness (Titus 2:14). Thus, he taught us to pray, "Forgive us our debts" (Matt 6:12). The verb *aphiemi* is used in the NT both of the release from sin and the dismissal of a debt. The result is deliverance and freedom.

The apostolic fathers tended to repeat the Scriptures related to the atonement without formulating a theological statement. However, all of the essential elements of a theology of the atonement were expressed or implied in their writings. Polycarp,

Ignatius, Barnabas, and Clement of Rome clearly stated a vicarious satisfaction understanding.[974]

A proper view of the atonement takes into account the love of God and the wrath of God, the satisfaction of his law and moral government, substitution, the active/passive work of Christ, victory over Satan, and reconciliation with God. In some cases particular theories exaggerate one aspect and omit other key elements.

Thomas Noble suggested that instead of using the word *theory*, we should discuss *models* of the atonement since the atonement is not a matter of theoretical speculation.[975] Jesus Christ actually completed the work of atonement. We are simply discussing the most adequate way to express its significance, given the metaphors utilized in Scripture.

It is also crucial to understand that the atonement was objective, or directed toward God, in contrast to subjective concepts of the atonement which are directed toward mankind. Thus, an objective view sees the atonement as necessary for our salvation, while a subjective view sees the atonement as arbitrary.

The Necessity of the Atonement

The atonement was not a divine necessity since God was not obligated to redeem fallen humanity. But if we were ever to be saved, it *was* necessary.

Jesus explained in Matthew 16:21 that he *must* go to Jerusalem and suffer and be killed and be raised. In Luke 24:44 he taught that everything written in the OT must be fulfilled. The verb *dei* was used in both passages to emphasize his death as an absolute necessity. While only the Textus Receptus includes *dei* again in v 46, and thus only the KJV and NKJV include the phrase *it behooves* or *it was necessary*, the necessity for Christ

---

[974]Pope, *Compendium*, 2:299.

[975]Noble, "The 'Necessity' of Anselm," 55.

to suffer on the cross is implied from v 44 and connected to the three infinitives in v 46. It was necessary to suffer, to rise, to be preached.

As sinners, we are under the wrath of God. "The sinful mind is hostile to God. It does not submit to God's law, nor can it do so" (Rom 8:7). There are over 580 references to the wrath of God in the Old Testament.[976] Over twenty Hebrew words are used to express this wrath. "God is angry with the wicked every day" (Ps 7:11). We must flee the wrath to come (Matt 3:7). We need propitiation. Yet Islam rejects the cross. They see no need for a Savior. In five passages the Quran rejects the possibility of substitution, since "each man shall reap the fruits of his own deeds."[977]

The doctrine of total depravity teaches that man can do nothing to save himself. If we are saved, God must provide atonement. We can assume that he would not have paid the supreme price of his Son if a lesser price would have paid for our sins.

If God is sovereign, why could he not forgive our sin without any atonement? Since all have sinned, surely God will "grade on the curve." Voltaire said that God is bound to forgive because that's the business he's in.[978] Apparently, this is the basis for the popular view that it is man's nature to sin and God's nature to forgive. Thus, we both keep each other in business. Of course, this reflects a trite view of sin and holiness.

God is bound by his truthfulness and justice. Justice and holiness demand punishment. The demands of the law must be satisfied. Sin deserves punishment. God said the penalty for sin was death (Gen 2:17; Rom 6:23). He must keep his word, for he cannot lie (John 17:17; Rom 3:4; Titus 1:2; Heb 6:18). Thus, clemency would imply that God's word could not be trusted.

---

[976]Morris, *The Atonement*, 153.

[977]Stott, *The Cross of Christ*, 40-41.

[978]Wells, *Cross Words*, 14.

God was under no obligation to rescue us, but because of his love he chose to do so. However, his plan to save us must not violate his nature. "But the Lord Almighty will be exalted by his justice, and the holy God will show himself holy by his righteousness" (Isa 5:16).

How can he be both just and the one who justifies guilty sinners (Rom 3:26)? He cannot gratify his love without satisfying his justice. Too often mercy and grace are pitted against justice. The result is a defective view of God. Richard Treffry explained that the atonement of Christ was the grandest judicial proceeding that ever took place in the universe and the most convincing demonstration of the righteousness of God.

> Now, the great object of the atonement of Christ was to demonstrate the righteousness of God, and thus enable him, without any dishonor to his attributes and government, to show mercy to the sinner. I have before remarked, that the pardon of sin, as an act of prerogative, would practically annul the divine government. In order, therefore, that God might prove himself just as well as good, Christ was appointed to undergo, in his own person, the punishment due to our sin.[979]

In the atonement Christ offered, "Love and faithfulness meet together; righteousness and peace kiss each other" (Ps 85:10). Wesley explained that the great work of Christ clearly manifested God's mercy in redeeming Israel and in the conversion of the gentiles; his truth in fulfilling the great promise of sending his Son, his righteousness in punishing sin on his Son, and in conferring righteousness upon guilty and lost creatures; and his peace or reconciliation to sinners.[980]

---

[979]Treffry, *Letters on the Atonement*, 117, 58.

[980]Wesley, *Notes*, 3:1750-1751.

Wesley wrote, "Nothing in the Christian system is of greater consequence than the doctrine of Atonement. It is properly the distinguishing point between Deism and Christianity."[981]

Richard Watson explained that while the law condemns us, the atonement meets the demands of justice, because it presents, as a satisfaction to it, the death of a Being of infinite dignity in the place and stead of guilty man. The wisdom of God, as well as his love for us, is demonstrated through his exaction of the penalty of his violated law from his own Son and in leaving still under the curse all who refuse to repent, forsake their sins, and believe in Christ.[982] This definition summarizes five major truths regarding the nature of the atonement.

The Atonement is Universal

First of all, the atonement is *universal*. Jesus is the Lamb of God who takes away the sin of the world (John 1:29). "For God so loved the world that he gave his only begotten Son" (John 3:16). Pope declared, "We should take it for granted that so glorious a Person would not be sent on a partial and limited errand; that, supposing Him to visit this earth, He would embrace its whole compass in His mission."[983]

The burden of proof is for Calvinists to demonstrate why they can legitimately say that *world* means only the world of the elect. While they typically point out that Christ laid down his life for his sheep (John 10:11) and that he died for his church (Eph 5:25), they fail to demonstrate that atonement was made *only* for those who constitute his church. Their logic raises the suspicion that they believe the elect are actually saved by divine predestination.

---

[981]Wesley, *Letter* to Mary Bishop, 7 Feb 1778.

[982]Watson, *Conversations,* 341-342.

[983]Pope, *Compendium*, 2:295.

According to 1 John 2:2, Christ is the propitiation for the sins of the *whole* world. John uses this word *world* (*kosmos*) twenty-three times in his first letter. The uniform meaning of the word is the entire unbelieving world, in contrast to the church or Christians. In the nearest context, the *whole world* is referenced in 1 John 5:19 and it does not describe the elect. The adjective *holos* means all, the total, the entire, or the complete. "There is not one place in the entire NT where 'world' means 'church' or 'the elect.'"[984] Grant Osborne concluded, "In John's writings *kosmos* occurs 115 times, always of the world of unbelievers who are hostile to God and yet are the object of God's love and mission."[985] Yet Berkhof attempted to redefine *world* to mean that "the blessings of the gospel were extended to all nations."[986]

In Romans 5:17-21 *the many* describes the actual effect of Adam's disobedience and *the many* also describes the potential effect of Christ's obedience. Mickelsen argued that Paul has not changed the extent of *the many* on either side of this comparison.[987]

According to 2 Corinthians 5:14-19, Christ died for all in order to reconcile the world to God. Christ gave himself a ransom for all (1 Tim 2:6). There is no grammatical or contextual indication that *pas* does not mean *everyone*. He tasted death for everyone (Heb 2:9). Yet Berkhof claimed *all* "really means all classes of men."[988]

Titus 2:11 teaches that preliminary grace has appeared to all men for the purpose of bringing salvation. According to 2 Peter 3:9, God wants everyone to come to repentance. No valid dis-

---

[984]Elwell, "Extent of Atonement," 100.

[985]Osborne, *Perspectives on the Extent of the Atonement*, 108.

[986]Berkhof, *Systematic Theology*, 395-396.

[987]Mickelsen, *Wycliffe Bible Commentary*, 1199.

[988]Berkhof, *Systematic Theology*, 396.

tinction can be made between God's desires and his decrees. He does not have two wills.

However, Thomas Schreiner attempted to make this argument.[989] John Piper also does in his chapter, "Are There Two Wills in God."[990] Carl Trueman, while defending Calvinism, conceded that "there are no real practical gains to be made from the two-will idea."[991] Thomas Coke wrote, "He has no secret will contrary to, and inconsistent with his revealed will."[992] Jack Cottrell asked,

> How shall we evaluate this attempt to explain the inconsistency between God's so-called decretive will and his revealed will? We certainly can accept the idea of "mystery" and "multi-formity" in God's will. What we are asked to accept here, though, goes far beyond mystery and manifoldness. In this Calvinist explanation we are dealing, plainly and simply, with contradiction. A basic law of logic (and logic is grounded upon and derived from God's own nature) is the law of non-contradiction. This law says that no statement can be both true and not true, in the same sense, at the same time. But the Calvinist says that it IS God's will that all the lost be saved, and it is NOT God's will that all the lost be saved. Assigning the first desire to one level of God's will and the second to another level of his will does not remove the contradiction: it is the same God in both cases, and the desire is sincere in both cases. The same God decrees things to happen that he does not

---

[989]Schreiner, *1,2 Peter, Jude*, 381-382.

[990]Schreiner and Ware, *Still Sovereign*, 122-124.

[991]Naselli and Snoeberger, *Perspectives on the Extent of the Atonement*, 30,209-210.

[992]Coke, *Commentary*, 6:844.

desire to happen, things that are the opposite of what he desires.[993]

Calvinists and Arminians debate whether the mission of Christ was to atone for the sins of the whole world or only for the elect. Arminians contend that the provision is for all, but it is effectual only for those who believe. Calvinism holds to a limited atonement, but often they prefer the terms *definite atonement* or *particular redemption*. At this point they conflate atonement with salvation.

Calvinism can certainly produce a list of proof texts which they claim infer a limited atonement. Arminians can also produce their list of proof texts which they claim infer a universal atonement. However,

> The task of harmonizing those various Scriptures poses a far greater problem for those who hold to a limited atonement than it does to those who hold to an unlimited position. Those who hold to an unlimited atonement recognize that some Scriptures emphasize the fact that Christ died for the elect, for the church, and for individual believers. However, they point out that when those verses single out a specific group they do not do so to the exclusion of any who are outside that group since dozens of other passages include them. The "limited" passages are just emphasizing one aspect of a larger truth. In contrast, those who hold to a limited atonement have a far more difficult time explaining away the "unlimited" passages.[994]

Calvinism, however, argues that Christ did not intend to die for everyone, but those he died for are actually and certainly

---

[993]Cottrell, *How Do Calvinists Explain 2 Peter 3:9?*

[994]Lightner, "For Whom Did Christ Die?" 166.

saved. They make the benefit of salvation unconditional and definite for the elect, based on their interpretation of Romans 8:29-32 as a *golden chain* which cannot be broken.

Robert Lightner responded that if the atonement of Christ included the sin of unbelief, why does God ask men to believe — since they would not be lost for not believing? What does it matter whether or not men believe if they are already saved by virtue of election?

Faith, in actuality, becomes unnecessary and salvation has no condition whatsoever. The necessity of faith for salvation in Scripture serves to demonstrate the provisional aspect of atonement. The sin of unbelief is a problem for the limited redemptionists, for if their view is carried through consistently, it would mean the elect would not even be born in sin and thus would not be subject to the wrath and condemnation of God before they believe, nor would they ever need to be forgiven and declared righteous before God since that has already been done on the cross.[995]

We must distinguish between atonement *accomplished* and atonement *applied*. The atoning sacrifice was made for all and sufficient for all, but effective only for the faithful. It is accomplished for all, but applied and efficacious only for believers, that is, the elect.

Even the elect were at one time enemies of God (Rom 5:10; Col 1:21) and children of wrath (Eph 2:3), and thus did not have the atoning benefits applied. This proves that the atonement, as accomplished and as applied, are two distinct categories — even if one holds to unconditional election and/or irresistible grace. Lightner observed,

> The Bible does not teach that Christ's death saves apart from faith. The accomplishments of the cross must be appropriated by those who would be saved and until

---

[995]Lightner, *The Death Christ Died*, 100-101.

such a time as faith is exercised the elect are just as lost as the nonelect.[996]

John 3:18 declares that whoever believes in him is not condemned, but whoever does not believe stands condemned. Thus, faith is mandatary. Lightner continued,

> The cross does not apply its own benefits . . . No elect person was saved at the time of Christ's dying. All men, including the elect, live some part of their lives in open rebellion to God, thus demonstrating that the finished accomplishments of Calvary must be applied by faith to reach an individual before any saving value comes to that individual.[997]

In fact, if the cross alone saves, without or prior to faith, as some limited atonement individuals seem to think, then the regenerating, convicting, enlightening work of the Spirit is completely superfluous and the centrality of faith is removed, which is a biblically untenable conclusion.[998]

Calvinism, however, has the problem of explaining how they can preach a bona fide offer of salvation to the whole world if only the elect can be saved. Here Berkhof resorted to the "secret council of God."[999] This echos Calvin's comment,

> But it could be asked here, if God does not want any to perish, why is it that so many do perish? To this my answer is, that no mention is here made of the hidden purpose of God, according to which the reprobate are

---

[996]Lightner, *The Death Christ Died*, 94.

[997]Lightner, *The Death Christ Died*, 97.

[998]Lightner, *The Death Christ Died*, 131.

[999]Berkhof, *Systematic Theology*, 393-399.

doomed to their own ruin, but only of his will as made known to us in the gospel. For God there stretches forth his hand without a difference to all, but lays hold only of those, to lead them to himself, whom he has chosen before the foundation of the world.[1000]

If God has another side, so secret that it is not revealed in Scripture, how did Calvin know about it? When the logical inconsistencies of Calvinism threaten to destroy their whole system, they adopt a position of agnosticism. We are told God's election and human believing cannot be put into a logical relationship to one another.[1001] When their golden chain of logic snaps, they dismiss logic and scold us for trying to grasp what is incomprehensible.

John MacArthur wrote that God loves everyone — even the non-elect. He argued that his love for the non-elect is genuine, demonstrated through common grace, compassion, admonitions to the lost, and through the gospel offer to them. According to MacArthur, God's universal love is revealed in his constant warnings to the reprobate of their impending fate. But while God pleads with them to repent, they cannot because God has not chosen them for salvation. Yet MacArthur insisted that God loves the reprobate because he has offered them the gospel. MacArthur declared that this offer is sincere even though God has not chosen them[1002]

MacArthur stated that God is absolutely and utterly sovereign over all that happens. God takes no pleasure in the death of the wicked, but desires that they turn from their ways and live (Ezek 33:11). If God is utterly sovereign, why do any of his actual desires remain unfulfilled? MacArthur's answer is that "His *decrees* do not always reflect His *desires*; His *preferences*

[1000]Calvin, *Commentary*, 22:419-420.

[1001]Carson, *Divine Sovereignty and Human Responsibility*, 201-222.

[1002]MacArthur, "Love of God for Humanity," 232-252, 168.

do not necessarily dictate His *purposes*." But it is little comfort to the reprobate to learn that although God decreed their damnation from all eternity, God still loves them and desires to see them saved even though they were not included in the atoning work of Christ.

This contradicts the clear statement of God's love in Romans 5:6-8. According to Calvinism, the love of God unconditionally chooses the elect and unconditionally rejects the reprobate. Speaking as a Calvinist, at least Arthur Pink was more candid when he wrote that God really does not love everyone.[1003]

The majority position in the Christian church has been on the side of universal atonement.[1004] Augustine was the only advocate of limited atonement in the early church, and he makes no explicit or extended defense of the position. Chris Bounds concluded that belief in unlimited atonement was the consensual exegesis and understanding of the first five hundred years of Christianity.[1005]

Wesley argued for the universal atonement because the prophets, Christ himself, and his apostles affirm it. There is not one Scripture that says he did not die for all or affirms that he died only for some. Any interpretation that *all men* means *all men of the elect* or that *the world* means only the world of believers is a "senseless evasion." God has commanded that the gospel should be preached to every creature. God calls all men everywhere to repent (Acts 17:30). Those who perish are damned for not believing in Christ; therefore he died for them or else they are damned for not believing a lie. Those who perish might have been saved (2 Thess 2:10). While 2 Peter 2:1 speaks of

---

[1003]Pink, *The Sovereignty of God*, 314.

[1004]Elwell, "Extent of Atonement," 100.

[1005]Bounds, "Scope of the Atonement in the Early Church Fathers," 26.

those who deny the Lord that bought them, they could not have done this if Christ had not bought them by his death.[1006]

Adam Clarke argued that if humanity is of one race and if Christ took on himself the nature of man and in human nature made expiation for the sins of nature, then redemption is general and the benefits of his death must necessarily apply to every human being who has descended from Adam. All who share the human nature have a right to apply to God, by virtue of that redemption, for remission of sins.[1007]

Fred Sanders concludes that objectively salvation is accomplished for all through the Son, but subjectively salvation is accomplished particularly when each person hears and responds to the gospel. This is what Pope meant by distinguishing between universal redemption in general and special redemption of the individual. It is also what Oden meant that the atonement is universal in it sufficiency and conditional in it efficacy. It is limited to those who accept God's offer of salvation through Christ.[1008]

The Atonement Is Substitution

Second, the atonement is *substitutionary*. The Latin word is *vicarious*. Pope wrote that the very heart of the doctrine of atonement is its substitutionary nature. If this is taken away, the whole vocabulary of the NT would have to be fundamentally changed.[1009]

There are only two ways the debt of sin could be paid. If punishment is inflicted upon the transgressor, the debt is satisfied and the sinner is destroyed. The only other way is through a

---

[1006]McGonigle, *Sufficient Saving Grace*, 141-142.

[1007]Clarke, "Fragment in Favor of General Redemption, *Works*, 8:439-440.

[1008]Sanders, "Wesleyan View," 169, 175.

[1009]Pope, *Person of Christ*, 50.

substitute. If we are under the sentence of death and Christ gave his life so that we would not have to die, his substitutionary death makes it possible for us to live and be reconciled.

But not any substitute would be acceptable to God. Our substitute must be identified with the human race in order for there to be a transfer of sin's punishment. Hebrews 2:17 states that he had to be like us in every way in order to make atonement for us. He had to be our representative before he could become our substitute.

Our substitute could not himself be a sinner or he, too, would stand in need of a substitute. One sinless human being would substitute for one sinful human being. However, there are no sinless humans. Any concept of salvation by human works is an insult to the value of Christ's sacrifice and his finished work. Therefore, according to Psalm 49:7, "No man can redeem the life of another or give to God a ransom for him." The following verse gives the reason, "The ransom for a life is costly, no payment is ever enough."

Only Christ qualifies as our substitute because he alone is fully human, yet sinless. The incarnation was necessary for this reason. "God made him who had no sin to be a sin offering for us, so that in him we might become the righteousness of God" (2 Cor 5:21). However, the incarnation limited Christ to becoming a substitute for the human race. No salvation was provided for fallen angels. In fact, even the holy angels long to stoop down and investigate the redemption provided for humanity (1 Pet 1:12).

Is it right for the innocent to suffer for the guilty? Jesus declared, "No one takes [my life] from me, but I lay it down of my own accord" (John 10:18). In this case the innocent volunteered and the judge accepted him as our substitute. They were both moved by love.

The concept of substitution is unique to the Bible. Oden pointed out that in the NT it is not humans who come to God with a compensatory gift, but rather God who comes to humanity in self-giving.[1010]

Substitution is prefigured as early as Genesis 22:8. Substitution is clear foreseen by Isaiah 53:5. Alec Motyer wrote that "this verse cannot be understood without the idea of substitution."[1011] According to Oden, there are eleven different metaphors for substitution in Isaiah 53.[1012]

Matthew 20:28 and Mark 10:45 both teach that Christ came "to give his life as ransom *for* (*anti* - in place of) many." Romans 5:6-8 declares, "When we were still powerless, Christ died for (*huper* - in behalf of; for the sake of) the ungodly. . . . But God demonstrates his own love for [to] us in this: While we were still sinners, Christ died for (*huper*) us." In 1 Timothy 2:6 the text is clear that Christ paid the ransom himself in the place and on the behalf of (*huper*) all men. According to 1 Peter 2:24, he bore our sins in his body. In 1 Peter 3:18, Peter teaches that Christ suffered and died for sins once for all, the righteous for (*huper*) the unrighteous, not a repeated sacrifice every time the Mass is offered.

According to 2 Corinthians 5:21 Christ became a sin offering for (*huper*) us. This verse connects with Isaiah 53:10 where the Messiah is made a guilt or trespass offering. Leviticus 5:1-6:7 discusses the guilt offering. Motyer said it could be called the satisfaction offering.[1013]   However, Jesus did *not* become a sinner. Oden explained that while substitution did not make Christ a sinner, he was viewed and dealt with as such. He was not a sinner in our stead in the sense that he himself sinned.[1014]

[1010]Oden, *The Word of Life*, 352.

[1011]Motyer, *TOTC*, 335.

[1012]Oden, *The Word of Life*, 379.

[1013]Motyer, *TOTC*, 18:338.

[1014]Oden, *The Word of Life*, 384.

Penal substitution means that he was punished for our sins. Some theologians prefer to say that he *suffered* for us, but that seems ambiguous since he suffered tremendously *before* he ever arrived at Calvary. Other theologians worry that if we say he was *punished* for our sins, it implies that he became a sinner. If we say that the *penalty* for our sin was imputed to him, them some theologians argue that either the whole world or the elect are automatically saved. Since Christ is God, his life was of infinite value. The payment of Christ was sufficient, but not an exact equivalent.

Oden explained that Christ's penal satisfaction is function-ally equivalent to all human sin, but not identical nor equal.[1015] The emphasis should not be upon the quantity of suffering, but the quality of the one suffering. The proper emphasis is not the extent of his suffering but the value of the sacrifice. Faith is not the exact equivalent of righteousness, but God accepts it as sufficient for him to impute righteousness to us.

The sacrifice of Christ was once for all (Heb 10:10). As both the High Priest and the sacrificial offering, he obtained eternal redemption (Heb 9:11-12). However, if animal sacrifices were merely a ritual expression of thanks, there would be no reason to discontinue them. Since they were ordained by God to function as a temporary substitute for punishment, since blood had to be shed, they became obsolete after the finished work of Christ.

Prior to the atonement of Christ, sin, which was confessed to the priest and dealt with according to Levitical ritual, was not punished due to the forbearance of God. But their redemption was contingent upon the atonement of Christ (Heb 9:15) since it was impossible for the blood of bulls and goats to take away sins (Heb 10:4). According to Acts 17:30, God overlooked ignorance in times past, but now he commands all people everywhere to repent.

[1015]Oden, *The Word of Life*, 387.

Romans 2:4 and 3:26 both use *anoche* which means "a holding back." John Murray wrote, "This by-passing is not to be equated with remission. Suspension is not equivalent to forgiveness.... 'Passing over' is not justification."[1016] Yet David's experience of forgiveness is cited in Romans 4:6-8. While OT forgiveness was real, it was contingent upon the future work of Christ.

Jews who lived by God's law and who relied on the sacrificial system to turn away God's wrath when they fell short, were accepted by God on the basis of the future atoning work of Christ. God did not impute sin to the pagans who were ignorant of God's law (Rom 5:13; Acts 17:30), but followed the law as revealed to their conscience. They were also accepted by God on the basis of the atoning work of Christ. Yet God had something better (Heb 11:39-40). Through substitution, which is God's just action, the just character of God is satisfied and the sinner is justified.

It was necessary for Christ to die because death was the penalty for sin. There was no redemptive significance in the obedience of Christ during his life before the cross. Nor is his righteousness imputed as a covering for our unrighteousness.

Wesley rejected the idea that Christ's death was substitutionary in the sense of fulfilling all righteousness in our place. He affirmed that Christ fulfilled the law of God, but denied that he did this to purchase redemption for us. This was done through his death in our stead.

We are saved by his substitutionary death, not by the example of his life or the imputation of his obedience. Death without Christ does not produce an atonement; Christ without death does not either. If we are unable to lift ourselves because of our sinful condition, the moral influence of Christ is insufficient. Salvation comes from the atonement, not the incarnation.

[1016]Murray, *NIC*, 1:119.

Liberal Pelagian theology, which denies the sinful nature of man, emphasizes only the moral example of Christ as a teacher. No atonement is necessary. Since Christ perfectly obeyed the Father, he has set the perfect example and he has great influence with the Father if we ever need forgiveness. In 1937 Richard Niebuhr described liberalism as teaching, "A God without wrath brought man without sin into a kingdom without judgment through the ministrations of a Christ without a cross."[1017]

Liberation theology teaches that Christ was a revolutionary who died as the victim of a corrupt political system. He was a martyr for the cause. We must continue his fight. However, our battle is not against flesh and blood (Eph 6:12) and our weapons are not of the flesh (2 Cor 10:4).

The feminist attack on penal substitution argues that it portrays God as vengeful and unable to have a loving relationship with his son Jesus. It is even called "cosmic child abuse."[1018]

The Blood of Christ

Harry Emerson Fosdick, a liberal Protestant pastor who was famous for his 1922 sermon, "Shall the Fundamentalists Win?" spoke with disgust of those who believe "that the blood of our Lord, shed in a substitutionary death, placates an alienated Deity and makes possible welcome for the returning sinner."[1019] Fosdick often criticized the fundamental Christian doctrine of the atonement as a "slaughterhouse religion."

On the other hand, many gospel songs emphasize *the blood* while never defining its significance. "The life of a creature is in the blood, and I have given it to you to make atonement for

---

[1017]Niebuhr, *Kingdom of God in America*, 193.

[1018]Noble, *Christian Theology* 1 3:904-905, 927.

[1019]Fosdick, "Shall the Fundamentalists Win?" 713-717. This sermon provided impetus for J. Gresham Machen to write *Christianity and Liberalism* (1923).

yourselves on the altar; it is the blood that makes atonement for one's life" (Lev 17:11). "Without the shedding of blood there is no forgiveness" (Heb 9:22). However, "It is impossible for the blood of bulls and goats to take away sins" (Heb 10:4). Therefore, a body was prepared for Christ (v 5). It was not his teaching, his moral example, his obedient life, or his sufferings that saved us. We are saved through his blood. *Blood* is a metonymy or synecdoche for *atonement*. In other words, to speak of *the blood* is to utilize a figure of speech in reference to the atonement, in order to emphasize substitution by using a more forceful word.

First Peter 1:19 calls the blood of Christ *precious*. Blood represents life, and for Christ to shed his blood means that he had to die. To pay the price in blood was to pay with your life. Jesus had to die a violent death to redeem us with his blood.[1020] His blood is our ransom price (Acts 20:28; 1 Cor 6:20; 1 Pet 1:18-20; Col 1:14, some mss v 20). Through the blood we are redeemed from the guilt and power of sin.

- The blood makes propitiation (Rom 3:25); it satisfied the justice of God (Isa 53:11). It is the blood applied that turns away the judgment of God. God promised, "When I see the blood I will pass over you" (Exod 12:13).
- We are justified by his blood (Rom 5:9).
- We have redemption through the blood (Eph 1:7). This states the cost of the atonement.
- We are brought near through the blood of Christ (Eph 2:13). It is the blood applied that marks us as owned by God; we have been purchased by God and Satan has no claim on us. Acts 20:28 refers to the church which Christ purchased with his own blood.
- The blood provides reconciliation (Col 1:20).

[1020]Morris, *The Atonement*, 52-65.

- The blood ratified and inaugurated the new covenant between God and his people (Heb 9:16-18).
- The blood gives us access to the presence of God (Heb 10:19).
- The blood makes us holy (Heb 13:12).
- The blood purifies us from all sin (1 John 1:7). Zechariah prophesied, "On that day a fountain will be opened to the house of David and the inhabitants of Jerusalem, to cleanse them from sin and impurity" (13:1). Revelation 7:14 describes a multitude who have washed their robes and made them white in the blood of the Lamb.
- We are washed in the blood (Rev 1:5, some texts have *freed us*).
- The blood makes us overcomers (Rev 12:11).

First Peter 1:2 says that we are "sprinkled" by his blood. At Mt Sinai the people entered into covenant with God (Exod 24:3-8). Moses took the blood of bulls and sprinkled half of it on the altar. He read the covenant to the people and when they agreed to it, he sprinkled them with the other half of the blood. The book of Hebrews picks this up and teaches that the blood of Christ sprinkles the altar in heaven, the very throne of God. This satisfies God's justice and makes atonement for our sins. This is what happened at the Passover when blood was sprinkled on the door post to outline a cross and the death angel passed over.

But we are sprinkled with the other half to mark God's claim upon us. Through the sprinkling of this blood we enter into covenant with God. The blood of Jesus does more than pay the penalty for our sin; it actually makes us part of God's family. We are connected with Christ and are to abide in him as the vine and branches are connected.

In the Lord's Supper, just as the bread represents our participation in the body of Christ, so the cup represents our fellowship in the blood of Christ (1 Cor 10:16). Moses said, "This is the blood of the covenant that the Lord has made with you" (Exod 24:8). Jesus said, "This cup is the new covenant in my blood" (1

Cor 11:25). Unless you drink his blood, you have no life in you (John 6:53).

God owns those who have been sprinkled by his blood. Those who engage in spiritual warfare talk about "pleading the blood." We are told that Satan cannot touch us if we "plead the blood." These are not magic words. Instead, they convey the concept that if God has redeemed us by his blood, Satan has no claim on us. If God has sprinkled us by his blood, he owns us and we are "a people belonging to God" (1 Pet 2:9).

Christ triumphed over the claims of Satan (1 Cor 15:24-25; Col 2:15). To plead the blood means we claim the victory of the cross (John 12:31-33) and the redemption from sin. Satan has no claim on us. His claims are dismissed. Jesus declared in John 14:30 that Satan had nothing in him. Westcott explained,

> There was in Christ nothing which the devil could claim as belonging to his sovereignty. In others he finds that which is his own, and enforces death as his due; but Christ offered Himself voluntarily.[1021]

Because Christ was dying as our substitute and not for his own sin, there was no sin in Christ through which the devil could control him. Likewise, Satan has nothing on those who are in Christ. He has nothing on those who are forgiven, and he has nothing in those who are cleansed.

When Jesus declared, "It is finished," he said *tetelestai*. This Greek word often appeared on receipts and could be interpreted as "paid in full."[1022] Thus, the atonement can be understood as a satisfaction of the penalty for our sin debt, so long as this metaphor is not distorted.

[1021]Westcott, *Gospel According to St. John*, 2:187.

[1022]Moulton and Milligan, *Vocabulary of the Greek Testament*, 630.

The Atonement Is Propitiation

Third, the atonement is *propitiation*. The purpose of substitution is propitiation. "And he himself is the propitiation for our sins, and not for ours only but also for the sins of the whole world" (1 John 2:2). The purpose of propitiation is satisfaction, and satisfaction was provided through substitution. If we reject the concept of satisfaction, we must replace the word *propitiate*.

The usual choice is *expiate* — an impersonal word meaning to make amends for a wrong.[1023] According to Romans 3:25 God *passed over* sin and suspended punishment before the atonement of Christ, but justification required propitiation made by the blood of Jesus. Pope wrote that expiation refers to the sacrifice, while propitiation means that God's holy wrath is turned away. The first term is borrowed from the temple, while the second comes from the court.[1024]

Properly understood, *propitiation* does not describe an act of appeasement to a pagan deity in an attempt to "get on his good side;" it refers to the satisfaction of divine justice. Stott pointed out that in a pagan context it is always humans who seek to avert divine anger either through rituals, magic, or sacrifices. However, the biblical doctrine of propitiation is based on the premise that we can do nothing to compensate for our sins or turn away God's anger. Therefore, God takes the initiative and himself provides the propitiation in the person of his Son.[1025]

Ben Witherington conceded, "It is hardly possible to remove the notion of anger or wrath and the notion of appeasement or satisfaction from these discussions, and have anything significant

---

[1023]Morris, *The Atonement*, 151-176.

[1024]Pope, *Compendium*, 2:274-275.

[1025]Stott, *The Cross of Christ*, 173-175.

left to say about the atonement . . . Sins do not need atoning for, if God does not need to be propitiated."[1026]

The Atonement Is Satisfaction

Fourth, the purpose of propitiation was the *satisfaction* of the justice of God. Numbers 35:30-33 taught that no ransom or satisfaction was acceptable for a murderer. Three times in this passage the Hebrew word for atonement, *kopher*, was used.

The purpose of Christ's substitution was to provide satisfaction. "He shall see the travail of His soul and be satisfied. By his knowledge my righteous Servant shall justify many"(Isa 53:11). The death of Christ is both a demonstration of God's love and the satisfaction of God's law.

John Stott observed that "no two words in the theological vocabulary of the cross arouse more criticism than 'satisfaction' and 'substitution.'"

Summers wrote that the propitiatory sacrifice of Christ embraced the "twofold idea of satisfaction and substitution." Summers went on to say that 1 Peter 2:22-24,3:18 taught satisfaction; Christ suffered for (*peri*) sins; it taught substitution, the just for (*huper*); and it taught reconciliation, in order that (*hina*) he might bring us to God.[1027] Wiley also conceded that the two words substitution and satisfaction necessarily belong to the word atonement.[1028]

The concept of satisfaction has been understood in various ways. One view is that the devil was overthrown by satisfying his demands. Others speak of satisfying God's law, his honor, or his justice. Still others see the atonement as satisfying the moral

---

[1026]Witherington, "Death of Sin in the Death of Jesus," 8, 18.

[1027]Summers, *Systematic Theology*, 1:225-228.

[1028]Wiley, *Christian Theology*, 2:282.

order of the world. "The biblical doctrine of atonement is of God satisfying himself by substituting himself for us."[1029]

William Burt Pope wrote that the vicarious sacrifice of Christ avails because

> it is no less than the satisfaction, provided by Divine love, of the claims of Divine justice upon transgression: which may be viewed, on the one hand, as an expiation of the punishment due to the guilt of human sin; and, on the other, as a propitiation of the Divine displeasure, which is thus shown to be consistent with infinite good-will to the sinners of mankind. But the expiation of guilt and the propitiation of wrath are one and the same effect of the Atonement. Both suppose the existence of sin and the wrath of God against it. But, in the mystery of the Atonement, the provision of eternal mercy, as it were, anticipates the transgression, and love always in every representation of it has the pre-eminence.[1030]

Pope also wrote that the perfect submission of Christ to the will of the Father required the surrender of his life as the penalty of guilt.[1031] Binney explained that God was seen as just in punishing sin and as justifying the sinner because "Christ thus became the sinner's substitute, and his death a satisfaction to justice."[1032]

[1029]Stott, *The Cross of Christ*, 111-123; 160.

[1030]Pope, *Compendium*, 2:264.

[1031]Pope, *Compendium*, 2:265.

[1032]Binney, *TPC*, 403.

The Ultimate Exhibition of Love

Fifth, the atonement demonstrates the *love* of God. Although God foreknew who would believe, he provided a universal atonement which demonstrates the extravagance of his love. And he receives the maximum glory from the millions who freely chose to serve him, even though they had the power of contrary choice.

Calvinism, on the other hand, emphasizes limited atonement by saying that God gets exactly what he paid for. If he paid for the salvation of ten souls, then ten souls are saved. That view suggests the miserliness of his love.

While his anger is righteous, his justice is tempered by love. He should not be characterized as a bloodthirsty tyrant who would have destroyed the human race had Jesus not come between and bore the brunt of his rage. God is love, but he cannot be reduced to simply one attribute. His wrath is his resistance to everything unholy. Both his love and his wrath are holy. The problem is not with God; the problem is with humanity.

The atonement is the revelation of God's glory, his justice, his mercy, his wisdom, his power, and his love. Nor can God the Father be depicted as different from God the Son, since the Son is the perfect representation of the Father.

James Denney argued, "If the propitiatory death of Jesus is eliminated from the love of God, it might be unfair to say that the love of God is robbed of all meaning, but it is certainly robbed of all its apostolic meaning."[1033]

Thus, atonement is a holy love which provides a substitute. However, some have emphasized the subjective influence of this love at the expense of the objective, legal efficacy of the substitutionary atonement.

We must emphasize that Christ died because of our sin against God *and* because of God's love toward us. These contrasting emphases were represented by two medieval theologians

---

[1033]Denney, *Atonement and the Modern Mind*, 58.

of the twelfth century. While Anselm taught satisfaction, Abelard taught the efficacy of the atonement was largely the moral influence it exerts. Stott concluded, "In general terms, Anselm was right to understand the cross as a satisfaction for sin, but he should have laid more emphasis on God's love. Abelard was right to see the cross as a manifestation of love, but wrong to deny what Anselm affirmed. . . . For it was precisely in making a just satisfaction for sin that the manifestation of love took place."[1034]

The Theology of the Ransom Model

"You were bought at a price" (1 Cor 7:23). Wrapped up in the word *redemption* is the idea of the payment of a price or a ransom. The ransom model teaches that we were captured by the devil and held in bondage. Satan held us hostage knowing that if God kept his Word he would either have to punish us or, if God was just, he would have to release us and him. But God kept his own word and released us by providing a substitute. Jesus paid our ransom price. We were delivered from a situation we could have never delivered ourselves from.

While ransom is still connected with satisfaction, this metaphor can be distorted. *Redemption* should not be interpreted to mean that we were ransomed from Satan. The Bible never speaks of a ransom paid to the devil. "Satisfaction is to be made, not to the jailer, but to him whose law has been violated."[1035] God never owed the devil anything and doesn't do business with him. We were trapped by our sinful nature and Christ paid the price of our freedom. Thus, the satisfaction view corrects this distortion by clarifying that God paid the ransom to himself in order to satisfy his own justice. Stott explained,

---

[1034]Stott, *The Cross of Christ*, 221.

[1035]Watson, *Theological Institutes*, 2:126.

The cross was not a commercial bargain with the devil, let alone one which tricked and trapped him; nor an exact equivalent, a *quid pro quo* to satisfy a code of honor or technical point of law.[1036]

The notion that God had outwitted Satan was put forward by Irenaeus.[1037] According to Gregory of Nyssa, Satan was caught like a fish by the bait.[1038] In *The Lion, the Witch, and the Wardrobe*, C. S. Lewis utilized this theory. Jesus was the ransom paid to the devil in order to free the sinner. But once the devil gained control of Jesus, he could not hold him. Thus, the deceiver himself was tricked. While Acts 2:24 explains that death could not hold him, Scripture never legitimizes the claims of Satan. Satan was not involved in the atonement. God satisfied his own law, paid our ransom to himself, and declared us righteous in his sight through faith. Satan is only a tempter, an accuser, and a jailer.

The Theology of the Penal Satisfaction Model

Penal substitution means that Christ took upon himself our penalty for sin. Penal satisfaction means that as our substitute he satisfied the just demands of the law. However, the two terms, satisfaction and substitution, are often confused. Properly understood, they illustrate the role of Christ as the mediator between God and man.

In 1098 Anselm, the Archbishop of Canterbury, wrote *Why the God-Man?*, building on the groundwork laid by Athanasius seven hundred years earlier. James Denney called Anselm's book

---

[1036]Stott, *The Cross of Christ*, 159.

[1037]Irenaeus, *Against Heresies*, 5.1.1; *ANF*, 1:527.

[1038]Gregory, *The Great Catechism*, ch 24; *NPNF2* 5:494.

"the truest and greatest book on the atonement that has ever been written."[1039]

Athanasius accepted the concept of substitutionary atonement and related the suffering of Christ to the satisfaction of divine law, not a ransom to Satan. He taught repentance was not sufficient for salvation because it does not satisfy divine justice.

This title, *Why the God-Man?* indicates that Anselm's thesis is that the purpose of the incarnation was atonement. Thus, both the incarnation and the atonement were logical necessities. While *necessity* can be based simply on deductive logic, Thomas Noble explained that Anselm's necessity was based on revealed truth. Anselm was not providing a logical syllogism, but rather an internal coherence of the Christian faith in the cross of Christ.[1040]

Anselm taught the satisfaction theory based on the affront of sin to the honor of God. Yet God's honor is inseparable from his goodness. Love, justice, and holiness are all necessary for real atonement. His righteousness cannot contradict itself. His justice is the basis of his universal government.

Noble also explained that *debt* does not force a commercial model of atonement. Nor does *honor* imply a feudal model based on medieval society.[1041] Anselm viewed sin as a debt, based on the word in the Lord's prayer. God cannot just arbitrarily forgive. The debt remains unpaid. Punishment could be inflicted upon the transgressor, but then no one could be saved. The only other way the debt can be paid is through a substitute. According to Psalm 49:7 the payment offered must be greater than the total of all finite creation. Only deity can satisfy this claim, but only humanity can render the satisfaction for his own sin. Thus, the satisfaction must be rendered by the God-man whose satisfaction is greater than our sin and is accepted by God.

[1039]Denney, *The Death of Christ*, 188.

[1040]Noble, "The 'Necessity' of Anselm," 66.

[1041]Noble, "The 'Necessity' of Anselm," 62.

Anselm's concept of satisfaction was expanded by Bonaventure, who taught that it was fitting for humanity to be restored by God. If God does not restore us, it cannot be done. There is no more fitting method for restoring humanity than by a satisfaction of justice. This maintains the balance between God's attributes of justice, wisdom, omnipotence, and majesty. He is both merciful and just. However, it was necessary that God be just, not that he show mercy. Forgiveness without sacrifice is not a greater manifestation of love. "Greater love has no one than this, that he lay down his life for his friends" (John 15:13). However, a sinless creature could not render satisfaction for the whole human race. A single creature is finite and on a level with all other finite creatures. Infinity alone can save us. Sinful man cannot make satisfaction for his own sin, because he would then incur eternal death and could not be redeemed. God was obligated to accept the satisfaction made by Christ, however, since he was behind the offer. Thus, the satisfaction of Jesus Christ is the most fitting and only way atonement could be made.

The Reformation theologians modified Anselm's doctrine to include the subjective element of faith. Anselm had never specified how the atonement is appropriated. Faith does not justify, but it accepts that which does justify. They also developed a concept of Christ's active and passive righteousness. They emphasized penal satisfaction based upon the broken law of God.

We must avoid any concept of the atonement that results in automatic salvation. The atonement makes salvation possible for all but completed for none. The atonement makes us *savable*. According to scholastic logic, if the death of Christ was the formal cause, the only options would be either a limited atonement or universalism.

Although some isolated Scripture verses can be cited which appear to teach universalism, the doctrine that in the end all human beings will be saved is heresy. Origen misinterpreted Hebrews 2:9 to include redemption of the whole universe of evil, including Satan. His universalism was condemned by the Synod of Constantinople in AD 544. No one enters the kingdom of God after this life. There is a place of everlasting punishment. The Bible offers no hope after this life (Heb 2:3, 10:26-31).

Calvinists object that there are no conditions to be met — salvation is wholly the work of God. They teach God's grace is irresistible. Eternal security is based upon the particular atonement for the elect. Jesus suffered the exact amount necessary to pay the sins of the elect. Since two people cannot be punished for the same offence, those for whom Christ died will be saved. However, the work of Christ is universal in its extent; and the work of Christ is conditional, becoming effectual if it is accepted by faith.

Richard Treffry, in his *Letters on the Atonement* (1839), explained the terms of the covenant:

- That there shall be no obligation on the sufferer.
- That he shall himself be the subject of reward.
- That the ends of justice shall be more fully answered by the suffering of the substitute than by that of the actual offender.
- That the offended party shall be satisfied with the substitute and shall afford sufficient evidence of his admission of it.
- That the offender shall accept the suffering of the substitute upon such terms as he shall be pleased to propose.[1042]

Essentially, God has offered to accept the suffering of Christ in lieu of the eternal punishment of the human race. Christ offered himself as our substitute. In return, he becomes Lord over a redeemed race (Ps 110:1). However, each person must also accept the terms individually in order for God to declare him justified. There must be a voluntary agreement among all parties in this covenant of salvation. While a covenant is unconditional in the sense that it cannot be negotiated, it is conditional in the sense that it must either be ratified or rejected.

[1042]Treffry, *Letters on the Atonement*, 118.

The payment of Christ is not reckoned to our account until we believe. This condition of faith is stated in Romans 3:25 and Galatians 3:14. According to 1 Timothy 4:10, Christ has provided universal salvation, but it is realized only by those who believe.

Penal satisfaction is *objective*. Its object is to satisfy the justice of God. According to 2 Corinthians 5:19, God reconciled the world to himself in Christ. Thus, God is both the reconciler and the reconciled.

Subjective Views of the Atonement

The atonement is necessary for our salvation. It originates outside ourselves and is directed toward God as its object apart from any human response. The thrust of R. W. Dale in *The Atonement* (1875) was to demonstrate that the atonement had to first be objective before it could have a subjective influence. Subjective views include, not only the governmental view, but the formation of a new race of men and victory over Satan.

The Theology of the Moral Government Model

Hugo Grotius, an Arminian lawyer and statesman, formulated the governmental theory in 1636. Grotius emphasized the necessity of satisfaction to uphold God as governor, not his satisfaction as judge.[1043] The work of Christ is seen as an exhibition of the evil of sin rather than turning away the judgment of God. In other words, if punishment is not administered when a command is broken, we would lose respect for God, and his government of the world would break down. God demonstrates how serious sin is through the greatness of the sacrifice he re-

---

[1043]McCall and Stanglin, *After Arminius*, 59. Arminius wrote *A Defense of the Catholic Faith concerning the Satisfaction of Christ, against Faustus Socinius* (1617).

quired. However, Grotius did not abandon the aspect of penal substitution.

In 1879 John Miley dropped substitutionary atonement for what he called the governmental theory of Grotius in *The Atonement of Christ*. In his *Systematic Theology*, Miley devotes 188 pages to the doctrine of the atonement. He began with a definition of the atonement that is misleading.

> The vicarious sufferings of Christ are an atonement for sin as a conditional substitute for penalty, fulfilling, on the forgiveness of sin, the obligation of justice and the office of penalty in moral government.[1044]

Initially, he also affirmed propitiation and substitution, but eventually he began to qualify what these terms mean in "a consistent Arminian theology." After surveying numerous theories of the atonement, he declared that there are really only two theories: absolute or conditional substitution. I would counter that there are really only two theories: objective or subjective.

Thus, the atonement was arbitrary for Miley. It is directed toward mankind in order to evoke a loving response. Although the alleged purpose of the atonement is to insure moral government, the premise that God does not have to uphold his own law or can relax it if he chooses tends to antinomianism. They imply that since God is the moral governor of the universe, he can change his own laws. God's law is a reflection of his nature, not simply an expediency in deterring mankind.

The governmental theory, like the more liberal moral influence theory developed by Abelard, tends to denies that the law is an expression of the nature of God. God could have set aside his law, but penalized sin to deter men from future offenses. The punishment of Christ might make a profound impression on the

---

[1044]Miley, *Systematic Theology*, 2:68.

sinner, but how could it act as a deterrent if man was sinful by nature?

Abelard rejected the doctrine of original sin. He argued that the atonement was motivated by love and that satisfaction for sin was not necessary. In reaction to the moral influence theory of Abelard, Anselm said, "You have not yet considered the seriousness of sin."[1045]

If mankind is totally depraved, we can neither be drawn by God's love nor deterred from our sin by the example of Christ's suffering and death. If Christ came merely to influence us to live better, he failed. We need more than an example to follow; we need a Savior to deliver. Commenting on Hebrews 9:22, "without the shedding of blood there is no forgiveness of sins," Witherington wrote, "So much for the modern notion that Jesus' death was not absolutely necessary in order for God to forgive our sins."[1046] We need more than an example; we need a Savior.

Toward the end of his life, Richard S. Taylor abandoned the governmental theory for a penal satisfaction view that is provisional and conditional. He wrote,

The twin notions that in any kind of penal satisfaction theory true forgiveness is impossible, and that, because the principle of double jeopardy all for whom Christ died must be saved unconditionally, are hobgoblins of constricted definitions. A biblical doctrine of penal satisfaction does not carry these implications. The rectoral or governmental principle in the Atonement is sound as a subordinate principle, but not as the primary principle. In attempting to avoid the unsavory implications of Calvinism as popularly taught and understood,

---

[1045]Stott, *The Cross of Christ*, 220.

[1046]Witherington, "Death of Sin in the Death of Jesus," 15.

Arminians are in danger of losing the true depths of the Atonement.[1047]

Therefore, he concluded,

If Christ's blood was not primarily penal in nature and directly a means of satisfying the moral and legal claims against the sinner, but rather merely a means of proclaiming God's wrath against sin for the sake of upholding moral government, then the connection between Christ's death and the Old Testament breaks down.[1048]

The Theology of the Racial Model

Olin Curtis, a Methodist theologian writing in 1905, said that the ultimate object of the atonement was a new humanity. God's purpose in redemption was to obtain a race of holy persons. Thus, his purpose in redemption was the same as it had been in creation. Jesus is the last Adam and the second man (1 Cor 15:45-47). Those who have been born again are a new race.

Ephesians 2:13 says those who were far off were brought near; the rejected now belong; the outsider is now an insider. Man-made distinctions are destroyed by the creation of a new race. When 1 Peter 2:9 says we are a chosen race, the word literally is *genos.* The destruction of a race is called *genocide.* In Ephesians, Paul speaks about the creation of a third race, and in 1 Corinthians 10:32 he speaks of Jew, Greek, and the church of God as three categories.

Yet Curtis wrote that Jesus Christ, as the representative of the race, endured the precise racial penalty for human sin, which expressed God's hatred of sin. It would seem, then, that the ultimate object of the atonement was to satisfy God's penalty for

---

[1047]Taylor, *God's Integrity and the Cross*, 19.

[1048]Taylor, *God's Integrity and the Cross*, 96.

sin, and the consequence of that satisfaction was this new re-deemed race of holy persons. Curtis saw the eschatological consequences of the atonement by stating that this new race will "be the victorious realization of God's original design in creation."[1049]

Curtis held that it is the satisfaction of divine holiness, by the full expression of it, not divine justice, which made the atonement an absolute necessity. But there is no need to separate the divine attributes. Even if God's justice made the atonement necessary, certainly the provisions of the atonement result in the ethical expression of holiness in the lives of the redeemed.

The Theology of the Christus Victor Model

"And having disarmed the powers and authorities, he made a public spectacle of them, triumphing over them by the cross" (Col 2:15). Gustaf Aulén built on the writings of Irenaeus and his recapitulation concept using the parallelism of the first Adam/second Adam. Wesley explained that God's plan to gather together all things into one meant that God "might recapitulate, reunite, and place in order again, under Christ, their common Head, all angels and men, whether living or dead in the Lord."[1050]

Wesley stated, "He triumphed over all his enemies, Satan, sin, and death, which had before enslaved all the world." Christ first conquered Satan, then sin in his death, and finally death in his resurrection.[1051] Yet Deschner reminded his readers that Wesley emphasized penal satisfaction, not victory.[1052]

Martin Luther also emphasized the atonement as divine conflict with the evil powers of the world and victory over Satan.

[1049]Curtis, *The Christian Faith*, 316-334.

[1050]Wesley, *Notes*, 490.

[1051]Wesley, *Notes*, 496, 442.

[1052]Deschner, *Wesley's Christology*, 121.

Christ is victor. Christ in his death and resurrection overcame the hostile powers that held humanity in subjection, those powers variously understood as the devil, sin, the law, and death. Although it is God who suffers most in the conflict, yet he emerges victorious. In the crucible of the cross, Christ assumed the full consequences of man's sin in himself. God's love met all the demands of his holiness, all the requirements of his justice, and all the claims of his law. Thus, Aulén restates the objective necessity of the atonement while developing another consequence of that atonement.

While this theory affirms our guilt for getting ourselves into this predicament, beginning with the original sin of Adam and Eve, it emphasizes our victimhood, not our guilt. The main human problem is that we are trapped and we need to be rescued.

Richard Mouw wrote, "*Christus Victor* also runs the risk of down-playing our sinfulness. It is easy to depict *enslavement* to rebellious spiritual powers in terms of victimhood, rather than to acknowledge our own guilt."[1053] Mark Galli wrote,

> Substitutionary atonement focuses on our guilt. In Christus Victor, we are liberated from hostile powers out there. In substitution, we are forgiven, and liberation is from ourselves and our addiction to *our* sin. Naturally, both models speak to truths of the human condition! And both have nuances worth exploring. But I'm concerned at the rising popularity of Christus Victor *when it comes at the expense of subs-titution.*[1054]

[1053]Mouw, "Why *Christus Victor* Is Not Enough," 31.

[1054]Galli, "Problem with Christus Victor."

Benefits of the Atonement
Unconditional Benefits

Universal grace restores human personality to native dignity, human responsibility to everlasting reality, and human perfection to gracious possibility.

"Every blessing known to man is the result of the purchase price of our Lord Jesus Christ, and comes down from the Father of lights."[1055] Unconditional benefits of Christ's atonement include a suspension of the death penalty. The race was allowed to continue since the penalty for sin, physical death, would be satisfied in the death of Christ. The continued existence of the human race is a benefit of the atonement. However, Adam and Eve died spiritually when they sinned.

Unconditional benefits of Christ's atonement include the salvation of all who die in infancy. Original guilt is not imputed. Calvinism has traditionally held that only elect infants go to heaven when they die. Fletcher observed that in his day Calvinists were beginning to teach that all infants were elect, but when they grew up they were not necessarily so.[1056] Historically, Calvinism has held that children of believers are elect. Other Calvinists hold that all babies are elect.[1057] However, since everyone came into this world as an infant, and since this decree of election and reprobation supposedly occurred either before creation or after the fall, how can the same individual be elect as an infant and potentially reprobate as an adult?

The restoration of all men to a state of salvability is an unconditional benefit. Although we are totally depraved, we are

---

[1055]Wiley, *Christian Theology*, 2:297.

[1056]Fletcher, *Works*, 1:284-285.

[1057]Spurgeon, "Infant Salvation," Sermon #411; Warfield, *Development of the Doctrine of Infant Salvation* (1897); Hodge, *Systematic Theology*, 1:27; MacArthur, *Safe in the Arms of Jesus* (2003); Mohler, "Salvation of the 'Little Ones.'"

also under preliminary grace. Thus, preliminary grace is an unconditional benefit of the atonement.

> For allowing that all the souls of men are dead in sin by *nature*, this excuses none, seeing there is no man that is in a state of mere nature; there is no man, unless he has quenched the Spirit, that is wholly void of the grace of God. No man living is entirely destitute of what is vulgarly called "natural conscience." But this is not natural; it is more properly termed "preventing grace."[1058]

Calvinism teaches that *common grace* is an unconditional benefit of the atonement. Herman Bavinck taught that common grace was restricted to God's elect.[1059] Gary North explained, "God gives rebels enough rope to hang themselves for all eternity. This is the fundamental implication of the doctrine of common grace."[1060] This is essentially a restraint upon the wicked.

Thus, for Calvinists the atonement provides collective benefits for all mankind, but the atonement is salvific only for the elect. Thus, common grace does not lead to salvation in Calvinistic theology. However, according to Romans 2:4 the purpose of God's kindness is to lead us toward repentance. We need not reject the doctrine of common grace, which includes the positive blessings stated in Matthew 5:45. But unlike the exclusive nature of Calvinistic theology, the purpose of all grace is to lead toward salvation. Thus, for Wesleyan theology preliminary grace is a more extensive term. Allan Coppedge explained,

> The difference between Wesley's prevenient grace and the Calvinists' common grace was that while both provided a restraining influence on the evil in human be-

---

[1058]Wesley, "Working Out Our Own Salvation," Sermon #85, 3.4.

[1059]Bavinck, *Reformed Dogmatics*, 2:214.

[1060]North, "Common Grace, Eschatology, and Biblical Law," 17.

ings so that society could exist, prevenient grace also restored the capacity of every man to accept salvation, whereas common grace did not.[1061]

According to Oden, common grace "enables society to live together in a proximately just and orderly manner, and enables it to cultivate scientific, rational, and economic pursuits of civilization."[1062]

Conditional Benefits

The entire plan of salvation: reconciliation, redemption, justification, regeneration, sanctification, glorification — everything going forward in systematic theology now hinges on the atonement. The church has been purchased by his blood. The Son redeemed the world and inherited it upon his inauguration, which followed his atonement (Ps 2:7-8).

Pope explained that faith in the atonement of Christ provides release from condemnation and the restoration of the Holy Spirit. We are released from bondage as well as having our inheritance restored. This dual blessing is stated in Galatians 3:13-14, where faith is also stated as the condition.[1063]

Is physical healing provided in the atonement?

This question cannot be addressed until we define *atonement*. Must the wrath of God be turned away because we are sick? Do we need reconciliation because we are ill? Is redemption necessary in order to be healed? Is sickness the breach of divine law which must be satisfied through a substitute? Sin alone requires atonement.

[1061]Coppedge, *John Wesley in Theological Debate*, 136.

[1062]Oden, *Transforming Power of Grace*, 63.

[1063]Pope, *Compendium*, 2:292.

However, we know that sickness, disease, and even death came into this world as the result of sin. Christ came to destroy the hold of sin on our life. Ultimately we will be delivered from the effects of sin when we get an immortal body. The curse of sin is being broken. In this life we can be delivered from the power of sin, but not necessarily from all infirmities. Yet Gordon Fee declared, "God *must* do *nothing*! God is free to be God. He is sovereign in all things and is simply not under our control. . . . Healing, therefore, is not a divine obligation; it is a divine gift."[1064]

However, God does heal often because of his love and grace. The basis for praying for divine healing is God's nature, as well as the gifts of the Spirit, not Christ's atonement or the intensity of our faith. According to Exodus 15:26 it is God's nature to heal. The healing referred to in Isaiah 53:4-5 is spiritual healing. In Matthew 8:16-17 when Jesus cast out demons and healed the sick, Matthew said this was in fulfillment of Isaiah 53:4. Adam Clarke explained that while Isaiah was describing the taking away of sin through the atonement, these acts of healing and deliverance were symbolic of salvation.[1065]

Millard Erickson concluded that Isaiah is referring to physical and mental illnesses. The Hebrew word for grief (*chali*) is predominately used for physical sickness and the word for sorrows (*makov*) conveys the idea of mental pain, sorrow, or distress. However, Isaiah does not say that Jesus has vicariously borne them in our place. Rather, he entered into the same conditions we experience through his incarnation and thus he is able to sympathize with us.[1066]

Everyone who calls upon the name of the Lord will be saved (Acts 2:21) but not necessarily healed. Perfect health is not a present, but a future benefit of the atonement. Physical healing

---

[1064]Fee, *Disease of the Health and Wealth Gospel*, 31.

[1065]Clarke, *Commentary*, 5:104.

[1066]Erickson, *Christian Theology*, 839-841.

is a foretaste of the resurrection of the body. If God has the power to raise from the dead, he has power to heal the sick. God cares about the whole person and the Greek word *soteria*, usually translated *salvation*, is also used of physical healing. Yet the redemption of the body is described in Rom 8:23 as future. Any physical healing prior to the resurrection is temporary.

In 1650 Richard Baxter wrote *The Saints' Everlasting Rest*. While he urged his readers to become more heavenly minded, he also advised them "neglect not the due care of thy bodily health."[1067]

Wesley did not advocate an attitude of resignation—that sickness was sent by God and should be borne in submission. Over time, Wesley grew more convinced that God's ultimate healing work extended to both soul and body. He encouraged his followers to expect both dimensions of healing in the present life. In a letter he wrote,

> Give yourself up to the Great Physician, that He may heal soul and body together. And unquestionably this is His design. He wants to give you and my dear Mrs. Knox both inward and outward health. . . . Look up, and wait for happy days![1068]

Wesley believed that healing could come through medicine and through prayer. He believed that God has more than one method of healing either the soul or the body.[1069] Accounts of miraculous healings are sprinkled throughout his *Journal*.

But Wesley put more emphasis on the ordinary means of maintaining and restoring health than he did on supernatural healing. Here again we see the moderation between the two polar opposites. While Calvinism tends to assert that the age of mira-

---

[1067]Baxter, *The Saints' Everlasting Rest*, 335.

[1068]Wesley, *Letter* to Alexander Knox, 26 Oct 1778.

[1069]Wesley, *Journal*, 18 May 1772.

cles is over, and the charismatic movement purports to cast out the demon of gluttony, Wesley advised his people to take responsibility for their health and trust God for healing. He advocated hygiene, diet, exercise, emotional health, and prayer. "I earnestly advise everyone, together with all his other medicines, to use that medicine of medicines, *prayer*." He called prayer the universal medicine.[1070]

Thus, if a Christian is ill, he should take an aspirin and pray. If he does not get relief, he should see his doctor and pray. We should not demand that God do supernaturally what can be done through the natural means which he has instituted. All healing comes from God, whether naturally or supernaturally.

However, when the ministry of the medical community has reached an impasse, the Christian should call for prayer at his local assembly. The procedure outlined in James 5:14-16 does not assume that anointing the sick is the specialized ministry of a professional faith healer. Rather, it is assumed to be part of the worship in a local body of believers.

Charles Farah concluded that much of what passes for faith today is in fact presumption. "Failure to distinguish the difference between these two has caused untold anguish to thousands of sincere and dedicated Spirit-filled Christians for whom the ordinary formulas have not worked."[1071] The modern teaching of faith as a leap in the dark is based on presumption. This is faith in faith.[1072]

Prosperity teachers claim that words create reality. Words are the containers of faith. They are magical. Even God cannot do anything except by faith. They teach that the substance God used in Hebrews 11:1 was faith. But God created and sustains everything through the word of his power (Heb 1:3). Yet Ken-

---

[1070]Wesley, *BE Works*, 32:404-405.

[1071]Farah, *From the Pinnacle of the Temple*, 205.

[1072]For example, Charles Capps, *How to Have Faith in Your Faith* (1986).

neth Copeland declared, "Faith is a power force. It is a tangible force. It is a conductive force."[1073] He teaches that faith is God's source of power.[1074]

For the child of God, the future breaks into the present in the kingdom of God. And while divine healing is possible now, then there will be a general resurrection. We are *already* in the kingdom and have tasted the power of the world to come (Heb 6:5), but we are still under the curse of sin, and our bodies will die regardless of what we confess. However, Isaiah 65:20 implies that health will improve as the kingdom advances.

The influence of the gospel will bring healing to the nations of the world. Thus, the healing through Christ extends beyond mere physical healing which would be temporary and personal. Second Chronicles 7:14 promises the healing of the land of God's covenant people. God will flood this world with his Spirit and bring healing to the nations (Ezek 47:1-12; Rev 22:2).

Knight concluded that we need a theology of healing that maintains the tension between God's faithfulness and freedom, between the *already* and the *not yet*. For Wesley,

> Healing was important, because it was important to a loving God who will ultimately put an end to sickness and death. But it was not as important as salvation itself. . . . Consequently to elevate healing to the level of salvation is as great an error as to ignore it.[1075]

Van Baalen referred to the "unpaid bills of the church." He argued that elements of truth which become neglected by the church tend to become distorted by cults. He concluded that the rise of many mind-healing and faith-healing cults is the result of

---

[1073]Copeland, *The Force of Faith*, 10.

[1074]Copeland, *Freedom from Fear*, 12.

[1075]Knight, *Anticipating Heaven Below*, 181-182.

the church not preaching a balanced message that God is the healer of the body as well as the soul.[1076]

Future Benefits of the Atonement

According to Romans 8:18-25, all creation, except those members of the human race who are finally impenitent, will be influenced by the glory reflected from the children of God. While it was Adam who subjected the creation to this bondage, it will be through the redeemed of Adam's race that the creation will be released.

Wesley preached that creation and all the elements were off course and fighting against man. Man's sin cut the rest of creation off from the blessings of God. Just as man lost his perfection, so the beasts lost their perfection, which included a "loving obedience to man." The beasts became savage and cruel, destroying the weaker and being destroyed by man. But nothing can be clearer than the fact that they will not always remain in this condition.[1077]

Mickelsen wrote that "tornadoes, hurricanes, earthquakes, drought, floods are just a few evidences of the imbalance of nature." While part of the world suffers drought, another part is flooded. But God has promised that "the very creation which has been enslaved to deterioration and corruption will be set free from this condition."[1078]

Thus, Paul personifies creation in order to illustrate the cosmic significance of man's fall and the believer's restoration. Romans 8:19 contains a compound word *apekdechomai*, made up of *apo* (from) + *kara* (the head) + *dokeo* (to watch). Trans-

---

[1076]Van Baalen, *The Chaos of Cults*, 390, 393.

[1077]This paragraph is a summary of Wesley, "The General Deliverance," Sermon #60. Yet it must also be understood that nature is still subservient to God.

[1078]Mickelsen, *Wycliffe Bible Commentary*, 1207.

lated *earnest expectation* in the KJV, this word depicts watching with outstretched head; to strain forward for an eagerly awaited event. The prefix *apo* adds the idea of watching with concentration for that which is anticipated, emphasizing the difference between the present and future. The word, in its noun form, is found only here and in Philippians 1:20. J. B. Phillips translated it, "the whole creation is on tiptoe."[1079] The creation waits in eager expectation and preparedness—all of which is implied in the verb again in Romans 8:23, 25.

The entire creation was subjected to this suffering through Adam's choice. The verb *was subjected* is in the passive voice, indicating that creation was acted upon. However, the text does not indicate who did the acting. According to Genesis 3:17, God cursed the ground, which indicates that it was God who brought the creation under this frustration. But the One who brought the frustration also promised hope. The hope of final salvation also includes the liberation of the entire creation.

Christians have the firstfruits of the Spirit. But they also groan along with the rest of creation, suffering under the curse of sin. While we have already been adopted, we are not yet recipients of our full inheritance. We who are now adopted internally await the final, external phase, the redemption of our bodies. While we are *now* the sons of God, the world does not yet recognize us (1 John 3:1-2). Someday the true identity of the sons of God will be revealed (Rom 8:19) and their inheritance fully realized.

Revealed is *apocalupsis*, the same word which begins the book of Revelation. The true identity of the sons of God will be revealed when we regain the dominion over the earth which Adam lost. "The liberation of all creation awaits the apocalypse of man, man's assumption of his dominion mandate," wrote Rushdoony.[1080] Along with creation, we are also on tiptoes, in

---

[1079]Phillips, *New Testament in Modern English*, 324.

[1080]Rushdoony, *Romans & Galatians*, 137.

eager anticipation (Rom 8:19, 23) of our revelation, which is our public adoption by God. Verse 23 ties this to the redemption of our bodies, which refers to the general resurrection following Christ's return. While deliverance, in an absolute sense, will not occur until the second advent, there can be a progressive deliverance, leading up to that climatic event, as the world realizes the victory of the cross.

Creation was implicated by Adam's fall. The new redeemed race will be used by God to release all creation. Science and technology are not the savior of the world. The salvation offered which Christ alone brings, however, it is not limited to the spiritual nature of man. Victory over sin, in the regenerate, is just the start. Through his Spirit he enables his people to bring his grace and truth into every sphere of creation. Someday the meek will inherit the earth. Believers will realize their full authority. The emphasis in this passage, Romans 8:18-25, is not upon the destruction, but upon the transformation of the world.

The gospel not only provides a present deliverance from sin but a future hope of glory (Col 1:27). Christianity alone offers hope for all of God's creation. We alone understand that creation's groan as the pain of childbirth. A new world is coming (2 Pet 3:13).

CHAPTER TEN
The Doctrine of Salvation

The salvation process is always initiated by God. In his preliminary grace, administered through the work of the Holy Spirit, a sinner who is dead to God and asleep to spiritual concerns comes under this divine influence. This gospel call is always a genuine call to salvation. No one can or will choose to be saved without being drawn. But neither is the call valid only for the unconditionally elect.

During this window of opportunity, the sinner becomes awakened to his true spiritual condition and alarmed over his final destiny. It is common for an awakened sinner to feel more miserable than he did while he was asleep to his true condition. However, he cannot save himself through an attempt at moral reform. The harder he tries to keep God's commandments, the more aware he becomes that he is completely unable to do so on his own.

While he cannot initially resist this preliminary grace, which at some time and in some manner works in every heart, he can resist this temporary awakening and return to the sleep of death.

While the Holy Spirit will not repent for him, the Spirit is faithful to convict him of his sin. And the Spirit will enable him to confess and repent with godly sorrow. The law of God serves as a diagnostic tool to reveal our sin. The law cannot save us, but we are oblivious to our need of salvation until divine law arrests us.

While the Holy Spirit will not believe on his behalf, the Spirit will enable the repentant sinner to believe. Faith begins with the persuasion that God is right and we are wrong. Thus, our mind assents to the truth of God's Word — at least to the degree that we comprehend it. But true faith moves past intellectual persuasion to a point where we consent and submit to God. We deliberately decide to accept Christ as our substitute and trust in him alone for our salvation.

This saving faith brings divine assurance that we are forgiven and accepted. No true believer should ever accept anything less than confidence and assurance. As a result of this inward work, we should submit to water baptism, in any mode, as an outward testimony of our conversion.

This salvation includes justification. We are legally forgiven by the God whom we have offended. He declares that on the basis of Christ's atoning death all the claims of his law against us are satisfied and our sin is no longer imputed against us.

The Holy Spirit also gives us a new spiritual life. We are born again or born from above. We receive a new beginning. We have put off the old life and put on the new life. The baptism with the Holy Spirit initiates us into the Christian church, the spiritual body of Christ. The same Holy Spirit remains in us, empowering us to live righteously. This imparted holiness is initial sanctification. We are also adopted into the family of God. We also share the authority of Christ. We have victory over sin and Satan.

The direct assurance we have as God's Spirit continues to bear witness with our Spirit is confirmed by the indirect reality of a changed life. The fruit of the Spirit in our lives is ethical holiness. We love God. We obey his commandments. And we love the people of God.

While we are secure in Christ, this security is conditioned upon an obedient faith. It is always possible to cease believing; but so long as we are believing, with all that such faith implies, we are secure. And we have a continuous assurance regarding our present relationship with God.

When there is a lapse in our faith, leading to a lapse in our obedience, we should immediately confess our sin, and the blood of Christ continues to cleanse us from all sin. All of life is probationary. While it is possible to leave the Christian faith, becoming apostate, it is never necessary. We are empowered to be overcomers.

The Synergism of Salvation

The doctrine of sin reveals our need of salvation. The doctrine of atonement reveals God's provision for salvation. Now we are looking at the plan and order of salvation. Pope described salvation as "the administration of redemption."[1081] The Calvinist theologian Louis Berkhof acknowledged the differences between his understanding of theology and that of Pope, but wrote this phrase, *the administration of redemption*, is "indeed a very good term."[1082]

The Divine Initiative

Grace is God in the soul of man through the Holy Spirit. Thus, grace describes divine influence on the soul and derives its name from the effect of this great favor of God to mankind. Grace is the unmerited work of God for us, in us, and through us. Grace is pardon and empowerment.

The extensive grace of God makes salvation possible for everyone. The intensive grace delivers from all sin. The free grace of God includes creation, preliminary grace, regeneration, and entire sanctification; they are gifts and do not involve human merit.

[1081]Pope, *Compendium*, 2:319.

[1082]Berkhof, *Systematic Theology*, 415.

Preliminary Grace

Through preliminary grace our faculties are restored in the wake of total depravity, making us savable. God restores conscience, the freedom to receive, a knowledge of the moral law, and a knowledge of God. In a cumulative sense, the result is that power of sin over us is broken. We are awakened, convinced, and convicted.

Colin Williams concluded that Wesley's emphasis on preliminary grace enabled him to break "the chain of logical necessity" which seemed to be the inevitable consequence of original sin.[1083] Wesley taught "the grace or love of God, whence cometh our salvation, is free in all, and free for all."[1084] Grace, which is free *for all,* answers the artificial distinction made by Calvinism between common grace and irresistible grace. Grace which is free *in all* describes preliminary grace. Picirilli concluded that Calvin's doctrine of irresistible regeneration is unnecessary in light of the doctrine of preliminary grace.[1085] This initial overture by God is described or implied throughout Scripture.

Genesis 6:3, "My Spirit will not contend with man forever." While this conviction does not necessarily result in salvation, yet it is necessary if anyone is saved.

Preliminary grace is described in Psalm 80:3 as God shining upon us that we may be saved. In Psalm 85:4 the prayer for restoration is itself instigated through the preliminary work of the Spirit.

Isaiah explains that God reveals himself to those who did not ask for him. God was found by those who were not seeking him. God depicts himself with outstretched hands to an obstinate people (Isa 65:1-2).

[1083]Williams, *John Wesley's Theology Today*, 44.

[1084]Wesley, "Free Grace," Sermon #110, ¶ 2.

[1085]Picirilli, *Free Will Revisited*, 96.

God drew Israel with loving-kindness (Jer 31:3). Jeremiah describes her repentance after God has disciplined her (Jer 31:18-19).

In Hosea 11:4 God drew Israel with cords of human kindness, with ties of love.

Zechariah 4:6 declares that salvation is not by human might or power, but by the Spirit.

While these OT references tend to be more corporate, salvation has always been by grace through faith. In the NT the ministry of the Holy Spirit becomes more personal.

Luke 24:13-33 describes the burning heart, the awakening, the revelation, and the restoration of faith to the two disciples who had lost faith.

John 1:9-13 teaches that Christ brought sufficient light into the world to graciously illuminate every person. That illumination does not guarantee the salvation of anyone, but it makes the choice of salvation possible. While everyone may not have the same amount of light, those who miss heaven will be denied on the basis that they rejected whatever amount of light they did receive.

John 6:44, 65 does not imply irresistible grace, but it does promise an enabling grace which is necessary for a person to respond in faith to the offer of eternal life.

According to John 12:32 all men are drawn to Christ. This gracious drawing is resistible, but it provides everyone with the opportunity to believe.

Jesus taught in John 15:5 that apart from him we can do nothing. Therefore, God must initiate the process of salvation and enable us to respond.

In John 16:8-11 the ministry of the Spirit is to convict the entire fallen world of mankind of their sin of unbelief.

After Peter's sermon at Pentecost, his hearers were cut to the heart and asked, "What shall we do?" (Acts 2:37; see also Acts 16:30). According to Acts 5:31, God enables repentance. In Acts 8:14-17, the Samaritans had accepted the Word of God and had been baptized, but they had not received the Holy Spirit. Yet the Holy Spirit was already at work in their lives.

In Acts 8:26-40 we see the Ethiopian eunuch was moved by the Spirit to read Isaiah and Philip was led to join him in the Bible study.

Paul was also under preliminary grace for three days until he received the Holy Spirit (Acts 9:4-18, 22:16). Cornelius feared and obeyed God before he was born again, but he was given repentance unto life (Acts 10:35,11:18). After Paul and Barnabas left the Jewish synagogue, they urged the congregation to continue in the grace of God (Acts 13:43). Yet they were not yet born again. Ultimately, all who were ordained for eternal life believed (v 48). The text does not say they were foreordained, but it describes an operation of divine grace working in their hearts while they were hearing the gospel.

Lydia's heart was opened to the gospel and she became a believer (Acts 16:14-16). She was faithful to the grace she had received, so God gave her more grace. Regarding both the travelers on the Emmasus Road and Lydia, Oden explained, "Their eyes became open not because they sought God, but because God sought them (John 9; Acts 9:18)."[1086]

God promised protection to Paul and disclosed that he was at work in Corinth (Acts 18:10). Many there had not resisted the Spirit and were under his influence, ready to embrace the gospel when Paul arrived to preach it.

Apollos was awakened and came to saving faith through the ministry of Aquila and Priscilla (Acts 18:24-26). The disciples at Ephesus were also led into saving faith through the preaching of the gospel (Acts 19:3-4).

Romans 2:4 teaches that God continues to lead sinners to repentance. Verse 14 describes the work of conscience within pagans who do not have the Scriptures. Romans 5:16-18 teaches

---

[1086]Oden, *Transforming Power of Grace*, 38.

that the gracious gift came to all who sinned. However, all men are not saved. The gracious gift, then, is preliminary grace.

Preliminary grace is the God-given desire to please God and obey his law (Rom 7:16, 22). The preaching of the gospel enables anyone to believe (Rom 10:8-21). Paul explained that his preaching was accompanied by the power of the Holy Spirit (1 Cor 2:4; 1 Thess 1:5). The power of the gospel comes from God (2 Cor 3:5). Yet that preliminary grace may be thwarted (2 Cor 6:1-2; Gal 2:21; Heb 10:29).

However, that grace is able to bring to life those who are spiritually dead (Eph 2:1-8). Scholars often debate whether it is faith, grace, or salvation which is the gift of God. But salvation is *all* of grace, beginning with the moment the sleeper is awakened (Eph 5:14).

It is God who is at work enabling us to do his will (Phil 2:13). God chose some in Thessalonica to be the first converts there. He called them and they believed. This was all through the sanctifying work of the Spirit which began as preliminary grace (2 Thess 2:13). Peter wrote that God called Jews who were dispersed throughout the Roman provinces and enabled them to obey Jesus Christ (1 Pet 1:2).

Titus 2:11 teaches that God's grace has appeared to bring salvation to all men. Syntactically, the word *all* corresponds to *salvation*. The text does not say that the grace of God has appeared to *offer* salvation to all (NIV), but to say that "the grace of God hath appeared, bringing salvation to all men" (RSV) sounds like universalism. We cannot conclude that all men will be saved. While this grace may be resisted, its purpose is to bring salvation. Yet the sinner cannot initiate it. It is preliminary grace. First John 4:19 explains that God loved us first and thus initiated the process of salvation. Collins argued that this preliminary grace is irresistible grace.

> Irresistibility in this context pertains not to the call or
> overtures made to these faculties (that can be resisted)

but to the reestablishment of these faculties that constitute responsible personhood and accountability.[1087]

The process of salvation begins irresistibly in every heart, but every person while under that grace must choose to respond and cooperate with God in order to be finally saved. Thomas Oden wrote that this grace which prepares the way illumines the intellect, strengthens the will, and guides the senses. It is necessary for the very inception of faith.[1088]

In his survey, Brian Shelton also found passages that dealt with enlightenment, with drawing, and with gracious assistance. "All of these verses come together to evidence a biblical principle that God enables sinners to believe by a means that is gracious, and not deterministically based."[1089]

McCall pointed out that Arminius affirmed and employed the concept of preliminary grace, but it did not originate with him. Augustine also made repeated use of the concept.[1090]

The Second Council of Orange, which convened in AD 529, declared, "Prevenient grace is necessary for the very inception of faith."[1091] Reformation scholars Martin Bucer and Philipp Melanchthon also endorsed the doctrine of preliminary grace. Oden described this preparatory grace as the lowest gear in the drive train of grace that enables one to move from inertia until we are gradually brought up to speed.[1092]

[1087]Collins, *Theology of John Wesley*, 80-81; see also Fletcher, *Works*, 1:407-408.

[1088]Oden, *Transforming Power of Grace*, 38-46, 120.

[1089]Shelton, *Prevenient Grace*, 24-57.

[1090]McCall, *Against God and Nature*, 357.

[1091]Oden, *Transforming Power of Grace*, 120. *Prevenient* is the older term.

[1092]Oden, *John Wesley's Teachings*, 2:138.

Wesley understood that the grace of God enables a sinner to repent and believe.

Salvation begins with what is usually termed (and very properly) "preventing grace;" including the first wish to please God, the first dawn of light concerning his will, and the first slight, transient conviction of having sinned against him. All these imply some tendency toward life, some degree of salvation, the beginning of deliverance from a blind, unfeeling heart, quite insensible of God and the things of God.[1093]

Wesley said that preliminary grace included

all the "drawings" of "the Father," the desires after God, which, if we yield to them, increase more and more; all that "light" wherewith the Son of God "enlighteneth everyone that cometh into the world," *showing* every man "to do justly, to love mercy, and to walk humbly with his God;" all the *convictions* which his Spirit from time to time works in every child of man. Although it is true the generality of men stifle them as soon as possible, and after a while forget, or at least deny, that ever they had them at all.[1094]

Wesley taught there is no man that is in a state of mere nature; there is no man, unless he has quenched the Spirit, that is wholly void of the grace of God. No man living is entirely destitute of what is vulgarly called "natural conscience." But this is not natural; it is more properly termed "preventing grace."[1095]

[1093]Wesley, "Working Out Our Own Salvation," Sermon #85, 2.1.

[1094]Wesley, "Scripture Way of Salvation," Sermon #43, 1.2.

[1095]Wesley, "Working Out Our Own Salvation," Sermon #85, 3.4.

He stated that what was usually meant by "natural conscience" was more properly a supernatural gift of God.[1096]

The Gospel Call

The gospel call is the drawing of the Spirit. Jesus said, "No one can come to me unless the Father who sent me draws him" (John 6:44). Yet all men *are* drawn (John 12:32). When Christ is preached as the object of our faith, the Holy Spirit draws all men to Christ. While this is a supernatural tug, the Greek verb *helkuo* does not mean that God irresistibly draws the elect. There is no implication that the drawing is either selective or irresistible.

The call is stated in passages such as Isaiah 55 and Matthew 11:28-30. This call involves a proclamation of the gospel, the genuine offer of salvation based on the condition of faith, and the command to submit to the authority of Christ. The Holy Spirit is the agent and the call comes through the Word of God. While this call is stated in Scripture, the church is also commissioned to go into all the world and declare the terms of salvation. The Holy Spirit usually draws sinners to Christ through the preaching of the gospel (Rom 10:14).

God's purpose in saving the world is made known to everyone by a proclamation of the free offer of grace. The call must be as universal as the atonement. Thus, the Spirit's calling is efficacious since he makes all who hear it conscious of their responsibility and capable of obedience.

Calvinism, however, teaches that a general or external call is to be preached universally, but that the call is effectual or inward only in the elect. This creates a moral dilemma for the conscientious Calvinistic evangelist which borders on false advertizing. Louis Berkhof, a Calvinistic theologian, wrote that missionaries cannot

---

[1096]Wesley, "On Conscience," Sermon #105, 1.5.

go out and give their hearers the assurance that Christ died for each one of them and that God intends to save each one; but it does mean that they can bring the joyful tidings that Christ died for sinners, that He invites them to come unto Him, and that He offers salvation to all those who truly repent of their sins and accept him with a living faith.[1097]

In other words the evangelist can issue a general call, but it will be irresistible only for those who are elect. This destroys the *good news* of the gospel for the reprobate or non-elect.

Actually this call is resistible. Jesus taught that "many are called, but few are chosen" (Matt 22:14). He warned that the Jews "refuse to come to me to have life" (John 5:40). Like their fathers, they "always resist the Holy Spirit" (Acts 7:51). Judas was one of the elect, yet he forfeited his election (John 6:70). Therefore, we must make our calling and election sure (2 Pet 1:10) by enduring to the end (Matt 24:13). If God is no respecter of persons, Wesley asked how, then, can we believe that he places one person, as it were, suspended between heaven and hell, while he fixes another one, before he is born, under the absolute impossibility of missing heaven?[1098] Oden explained, "The freedom to hear implies also the freedom not to hear, or to hear and to decline the invitation."[1099]

In Luke 14:23 the church is commissioned to persuade sinners to come to God's house. However, the verb *anagkazo* cannot imply forcing them against their will.

Acts 13:48 does not say those gentiles were irresistibly saved. The passage does say that there were Jews who did not believe. If the Jews had a choice in whether or not to accept Christ, apparently the gentiles did as well. Both Jew and gentile

---

[1097]Berkhof, *Systematic Theology*, 463.

[1098]Wesley, *Letter* to Elizabeth Bennis, 20 July 1771.

[1099]Oden, *Transforming Grace of God*, 49.

had the power of contrary choice. What was foreordained by God was not the individuals who were "elect," but his plan to include the gentiles.

Acts 22:14 refers to an individual, Paul, and not to corporate election. However, what God appointed was the opportunity for Paul to encounter him. God did not necessarily appoint Paul's choice — although his Damascus Road experience was powerful. In Paul's case, it is helpful to understand, along with Wesley, that Paul was awakened on the Damascus Road and born again three days later. Wesley said that Paul was in the pangs of the new birth for three days.[1100]

Romans 2:4-5 teaches that the purpose of God's kindness, tolerance, and patience is to lead the sinner toward repentance. While the context here refers specifically to the Jew, it is obvious that they are not unconditionally elect. It should also be noted that *ago*, which is translated *lead* does not necessarily imply the idea of force or that grace is irresistible.

The word *also* in Romans 2:14-15 indicates the Gentiles are called as well. The preliminary grace of God informs their conscience to the extent that they are also without excuse if they resist.

Scripture does not distinguish between a general call and an effectual call. While Calvinism teaches that the call of God is irresistible and the election of God is unconditional, Peter taught a synergism. "Therefore, my brothers, be all the more eager to make your calling and election sure (2 Pet 1:10). Then he states a condition. "For doing these things, you will by no means ever fall."The implication is that if we do not follow through on our commitment, we will fall. But what does it mean to fall? 2 Peter 1:11 explains that those who do not fall away will be welcomed into heaven. The implication is that those who do fall away will not be welcomed into heaven. Those who accept the divine call

---

[1100]Wesley, *Notes*, 299.

are the elect. "Election always presupposes the call; but the call does not always issue in election."[1101]

Calvinists object that God is sovereign and his call cannot be resisted. We affirm the sovereignty of God, but believe that God can choose to limit his power. His call is an invitation, not a conscription.

Conviction and Awakening

Wesley's "invariable method to present his hearers with the demands of the moral law, before he spoke of the Savior who had paid the price of their release." Wesley urged the evangelical preacher to "preach the law in the strongest, the closest, the most searching manner possible, only intermixing the gospel here and there." Only after sinners were awakened did Wesley advise the preacher to "mix more and more of the gospel."[1102]

John 16:8-11 describes the convicting work of the Holy Spirit. The Greek word *elegcho* means to convince. We are convicted over sin, and the ultimate sin is to deny Christ. We are convicted over our unrighteousness. Christ returned to heaven, but we are not fit for heaven. We are convicted over the coming judgment.

In some theological systems, that consciousness of sin and that concern over that sin is considered sufficient evidence that a person is born again. Martin Luther's famous statement, *simul justus et peccator*, means that a person is both justified and yet a sinner. Luther's advice to "sin boldly" is also well-known. Martyn Lloyd-Jones said, "If your presentation of the gospel does not expose it to the charge of antinomianism you are probably not putting it correctly."[1103] More recently Kevin DeYoung de-

---

[1101]Pope, *Compendium*, 2:345.

[1102]Wood, *The Burning Heart*, 242.

[1103]Lloyd-Jones, *Righteous Judgment of God*, 186-187; *The New Man*, 8-9.

clared, "If people hear us talking about justification and don't almost think that we are giving them a license to sin, we aren't preaching grace strong enough."[1104] But preliminary grace teaches us to say *no* to ungodliness and worldly passions (Titus 2:11-12). The devil does not need any help in providing us with an excuse for sin.

Neo-orthodoxy rejects the notion of a transformed life. Karl Barth taught that sin was inevitable. In this life we will always be prisoners of the devil and evil.[1105] Barth described himself as a man who has sinned, is sinning, and will sin, and who can recognize himself as nothing else than lost. Yet he is acknowledged by God in Jesus Christ.[1106] Emil Brunner wrote, "The believer is always the unbeliever, the sinner."[1107]

Evangelicalism today is plagued with an easy believing that bypasses conviction and repentance. Too often this approach only inoculates against real salvation. Many think they are going to heaven merely because they have repeated a prayer for salvation. The "sinner's prayer" was first developed for counselors to pray individually with seekers *after* it was determined they had demonstrated repentance and submission. Then it was prayed with all seekers as a group at the close of their counseling. Then it was prayed with all who came forward *before* their counseling. Finally, it was prayed in mass without any counseling.

Ralph Winter wrote,

It is not necessary to assume that our instant-conversion salvation formulas are entirely faithful to the Bible. We need to look for those who are hungering and thirsting after righteousness, not those who are basically seeking

---

[1104]Wax and Olsen, "The Justification Debate," 36.

[1105]Barth, *The Christian Life*, 17-25.

[1106]Barth, *The Christian Life*, 12-13.

[1107]Brunner, *The Divine Imperative*, 30, 199.

adventure in Western ways. We need to reread the New Testament emphasis on salvation as growth in grace over time.[1108]

Francis Schaeffer said if he had an hour to present the gospel to modern man, he would use forty-five minutes to show the man his dilemma.

> Then I'd take ten or fifteen minutes to preach the gospel. . . . I believe that much of our evangelism and personal work today is not clear simply because we are too anxious to get the answer without having a man realize the real cause of his sickness.[1109]

The Function of the Law

The law is an expression of God himself since God and his will cannot be separated.

- The law defines sin (Rom 7:7).
- The law convicts of sin (Gal 3:19). This is the ordinary means through which sinners are convicted.
- The law even provokes sin (Rom 7:7-8).
- The law drives us to Christ who alone can save us (Gal 3:24).

The one thing the law cannot do, however, is save the sinner. According to Galatians 3:21, the law cannot impart life. Yet it is indispensable as a diagnostic tool. It is like a mirror which reveals our flaws but cannot remove them.

[1108]Winter, "Editorial Comment," 11.

[1109]Schaeffer, *Works*, 4:251.

- The law instructs us as believers (Gal 5:14). Keeping the law does not earn salvation, but it is an expression of salvation. It serves as the standard of obedience for Christians (Rom 6:14-23).
- The law is a restraint to evil (Rom13:3). It provides the order for all aspects of society; it is the law by which society is governed. Thus, the law is holy, righteous, and good (Rom 7:12).

Wesley said the most common way for the law to be nullified is not to preach it at all. He also said the law is made void when it is taught that faith supersedes holiness. However, the popular teaching is that we are not under law but grace. Three times the Bible makes such a statement (Rom 6:14-15; Gal 5:18). In what sense are we no longer under the law?

- The justified are no longer under condemnation for past transgressions.
- The regenerate are no longer under the dominion of sin, but are enabled to keep the law.
- We are not under the ceremonial law.

Although every believer is free from the Jewish ceremonial law, the entire Mosaic dispensation, and even the moral law as a means of procuring justification, we are not through with the law.[1110] The moral law cannot pass away since it is a reflection of God's nature. In 1 Corinthians 9:20-21 Paul says he is not under the law, yet in the next verse he clarifies that statement to mean that he is not free from God's law. He is still under the law of Christ. According to Romans 8:2 we are under a new law — the law of the Spirit of life. Wesley argued that Christ did not

---

[1110]Wesley, "Sermon on the Mount, V," Sermon #25, 1.1.

free us from his own law.[1111] According to James 1:25, those who continue to live by the perfect law, motivated by love, are free. Those who do not live by the law of God are slaves to sin and criminals before God.

In contrast, *legalism* is the attempt to earn salvation through our good works. Under legalism the basis of assurance is self-righteousness, and religion becomes primarily a set of rules and regulations. While Wesley taught salvation by grace, along with James 2:18, he taught that saving faith will produce good works. Salvation is not *of* works, but *for* good works (Eph 2:10). "This little word *for* reconciles St. Paul and St. James better than all the commentators."[1112] Works do not believe, but faith works.

Kenneth Kinghorn wrote that most leading Protestant thinkers allow that there is a legitimate place for works in the Christian life, but there is no precise agreement as to the place of works.[1113] However, we reject the Roman Catholic concept of *supererogation*, which teaches that the total merits of Christ exceeded what was necessary for our salvation.[1114] According to this dogma, the saints also did more than was required for their salvation. Therefore, a treasury of merit exists at the disposal of the Roman Catholic Church. At the discretion of the pope, this surplus may be transferred to those who fall short and imputed to their account. However, there is always an administrative "fee" charged!

Scripture teaches that the fruit of Christianity is not an imputed transfer of merit from someone else, but personal transformation. Thomas Oden demonstrates inductively in *The Good Works Reader* that classic Christian teaching of good works is grounded in salvation by grace through faith. We can neither

---

[1111]Wesley, "Dialogue between Antinomian and Friend," *BE Works*, 14:52-55.

[1112]Adolphe Monod quoted by Findlay, *Ephesians*, 116.

[1113]Kinghorn, "Faith and Works," 11.

[1114]Oden, *Life in the Spirit*, 147.

seek righteousness through our works nor pretend righteousness without good works.[1115]

Along with John, Wesley believed that those who love God will keep his commandments (John 14:15, 23, 15:10; 1 John 5:3; 2 John 6). Thus, Wesley disagreed with Martin Luther who pitted law against grace and provided the basis for the teaching, "No works, no law, no commandments."[1116] In contrast, Wesley held that the opposite of law was lawlessness.

The regenerating grace of the Holy Spirit restores the love of holiness and the power to practice it. "I run in the path of your commands, for you have set my heart free" (Ps 119:32, 45).

The Awakened State

The awakened state is an important concept. This awareness that we are a sinner and have fallen far from God's original intention for us is often referred to as being *awakened*. According to Psalm 36:1-2, the wicked do not know their true state. Paul cried out, "Wake up, O sleeper, rise from the dead, and Christ will shine on you" (Eph 5:14).

Oden gave this word picture:

> Think of a child playing near a cliff. Unawareness of the danger does not make the situation less dangerous, but more. This is the condition of the natural self. While one is playing perilously on the edge of a measureless moral abyss (final judgment), one remains totally unaware of it. . . . How does it happen that the moral drifter moves toward becoming morally serious? Each person's story is unique.[1117]

[1115]Oden, *The Good Works Reader*, 2, 7. See also McCall and Stanglin, *After Arminius*, 91-92.

[1116]Wesley, *Journal*, 15 June 1741.

[1117]Oden, *John Wesley's Teachings*, 2:195-197.

According to John Fletcher, the ordinary methods of awakening are affliction, Christian conversation (witnessing), and the preaching of the Word.[1118]

In our natural condition, we are said to be both spiritually asleep and spiritually dead. The natural man neither fears nor loves God. He is not troubled by his sin. But perhaps in a moment, perhaps by degrees, the eyes of his understanding are opened and he sees the danger he is in. He is now awakened to his need and is under the conviction of the law. He has a desire to please God. He fears God but does not yet have a relationship with God. He is a servant but not yet a son. This dawning of preliminary grace is stifled as soon as possible by most people; but God visits every soul, though most forget or deny the experience.[1119] Awakening is analogous to conception. Conception will lead to the new birth unless the gestation process is aborted. Second Peter 1:19 describes awakening as the day star dawning in our hearts.

Romans 7 is a watershed chapter, and how it is interpreted will largely determine our theology of salvation. Alexander Whyte, often called "the last of the Puritans," once told his Edinburgh congregation, "You'll never get out of the seventh of Romans while I'm your minister."[1120]

"Most of the reformers believe that when referring her to his struggles with sin, Paul is speaking of himself as a regenerate person."[1121] However, in his *A Dissertation on the True and Genuine Sense of the Seventh Chapter of the Epistle to the Romans* (1612), Arminius demonstrated that for the first four

---

[1118]Fletcher, *Works*, 4:127.

[1119]Wesley, "Scripture Way of Salvation," Sermon #43, 1.1-2. See also "Working Out Our Own Salvation," 3.4 where Wesley drew on John 1:9 as his principal text.

[1120]Packer, *A Quest for Godliness*, 197-198; *Keep in Step with the Spirit*, 129.

[1121]Adams, *RCS* 7:386.

hundred years of the church, Romans 7 was generally regarded as pre-Christian experience.[1122]

In Romans 7 the awakened sinner finds the pleasure of sin is gone. Although he purposes to improve his life, he discovers he is bound by sin. Sin is the problem. It causes a breakdown between us and God. It causes a breakdown in human relationships.

Romans 6 asserts that justification and initial sanctification are bound together and we cannot have the one without having the other. Sin is not to reign. We have been set free from sin. It is inconsistent with Scripture to teach that one can become born again without any change and to teach that a believer can switch back and forth between the old life and the new life.

In Romans 7, Paul flashes back to his pre-Christian experience. Although Paul shifts to the present tense in vv 14-25 this should be understood as the historical present, in which a past event is viewed with the vividness of a present occurrence.[1123]

Romans 7 then is the classic psychological description of an awakened sinner struggling to please God without the enablement of the Holy Spirit. The struggle in Romans 7 is between conscience and will. It is the struggle between what we ought to do and what we want to do. Unless our desires are transformed by grace, desires will win out over conscience. We may approve of right, but eventually we find ourselves doing wrong.

[1122]"Most of the Fathers believed that here Paul was adopting the persona of an unregenerate man, not describing his own struggles as a Christian" [Bray, *ACCS* 6:189].

[1123]Dana and Mantey, *Grammar*, 185; Blackwelder, *Light from the Greek New Testament*, 67. In *Toward Understanding Romans* Blackwelder claimed the use of the historical present was common in Koine Greek and that the use of *gar* (translated *for* in the KJV and not translated in the NIV) "connotes an explanation and continuation of the thought of the previous section" [54-55].

Is there any deliverance from sin? "Who will rescue me from this body of death?" (v 24). In some theological systems this consciousness of sin and this concern over it is considered sufficient evidence that a person is born again. But the harder the awakened sinner tries to live holy, the more impossible it will become. "I have the desire to do what is good, but I cannot carry it out" (v 18).

According to Romans 8:9, if anyone does not have the Spirit of Christ, he does not belong to Christ. We receive the Holy Spirit when we get saved; and if we are saved, we walk in the Spirit. The description in chapter 7 then is of someone who is *not* saved.

John expressed wonder at the present status of believers that *now* we are the children of God (1 John 3:1-2). Paul follows this same pattern in Romans. "We did not receive again the spirit of slavery, but the Spirit of sonship. And if we are now sons we are also heirs who will share in his glory" (Rom 8:14-17). The difference in the relationship of the Spirit to believers in the OT and the NT is illustrated by Paul with the image of a master to a servant and a father to a son.

In Wesley's *Notes* on 1 John 4:18, he wrote, "A natural man neither fears nor loves God. One that is awakened, fears without love. A babe in Christ loves and fears. A father in Christ loves without fear."

Galatians 4:21-31 illustrates the difference between servant and son. Abraham's two wives, Hagar and Sarah, represent two covenants. John Fletcher felt that Galatians 3 clearly distinguishes between Jewish and Christian faith, although many nominal Christians live below their privileges.[1124] Here Paul uses Isaac and Ishmael as an allegory. There are four major points made:

[1124]Fletcher, *Works*, 1:573-574.

- **The new birth is supernatural.**

Ishmael had an ordinary birth; Isaac had a supernatural birth. Abraham fathered Ishmael in an attempt to help God. Fourteen years later Abraham and Sarah were too old to reproduce and Isaac's birth was a miracle. The new birth is always a miracle. It is not based upon our works. The true seed of Abraham are those who by faith in Jesus Christ have been born again (Gal 3:26-29).

- **The new birth produces freedom.**

Ishmael's identity is associated with servanthood. Five times in this section he is described as the son of a slave woman. Isaac is associated with freedom. Four times he is spoken of as the son of the free woman. In order to understand the significance, we have to go back to the previous section in Galatians 3:26-4:20. Here Paul teaches that when we are baptized into Christ, we are no longer servants but sons.

- **The new birth is adoption.**

The major difference between a servant and a son is that one is in the family while the other is not. How do we know we are in the family? According to Galatians 4:6 we have the Spirit's witness. Those who do not have this witness are still servants.

Kenneth Collins has observed that while all servants lack assurance and are under the spirit of bondage, not all who lack assurance are necessarily servants nor under the spirit of bondage. There are exceptional cases which are usually the result of bodily infirmaries or ignorance of the gospel promises.[1125] But assurance is the birthright of every believer.

[1125]Collins, *Scripture Way of Salvation*,136-144]. One exceptional case was Wesley's own brief bout with depression, recorded in his *Journal*, 4 Jan 1739.

Notice that both the servant and the son experience training and discipline, but the difference is that only the son has the promise of a future. Isaac alone is the heir to the promises made to Abraham. While sons and daughters still obey the Father, the servant has no relationship with the Father.

- **The doctrine of the new birth is opposed.**

Ishmael persecuted Isaac. The religious who have never been born again will always fight this message. That is why Paul persecuted the church before his conversion. The new birth is not a popular teaching, but it will bring revival. The new birth has always been a predominate theme in true revival.

The Human Response

God must initiate the process of salvation, enabling man to respond. In conversion, divine sovereignty and human responsibility work synergistically. *Synergism* comes from the Greek word *sunergeo*. It is the basis for our word *energy* with a prefix *sun* which means *with*. As a noun it occurs thirteen times and as a verb five times in the NT. However, each of these references is not necessarily an instance of preliminary grace. Passages such as Philippians 2:12-13 do describe the ongoing divine/ human cooperation in the Christian life. Regarding synergistic grace, Wesley taught,

> God worketh in you; therefore you can work — otherwise it would be impossible. If he did not work, it would be impossible for you to work out your own salvation. . . . First, God works; therefore you *can* work: Secondly, God works, therefore you *must* work.[1126]

[1126]Wesley, "Working Out Our Own Salvation," Sermon #85, 3.2-3.

Augustine said, "He that made us without ourselves, will not save us without ourselves." Wesley called this one of the most noble sayings Augustine ever uttered.[1127] The later Augustine, in his overreaction against Pelagius, moved toward predestination and monergism.

God initiates the process, but does he do it all? Certainly, God created alone, without any human participation. Preliminary grace is also monergistic in the sense that God initiates the process of salvation. But his preliminary grace enables synergism. The act of forgiveness is also a sovereign act of God. Nor do we do nothing to regenerate or adopt ourselves. But at strategic points, we are commanded and enabled to cooperate.

Conversion (*epistrepho*) describes a turning or return from darkness to light. It is the process by which the sinful soul, enabled through preliminary grace, turns away from sin in repentance and turns to God through faith in Christ. In Acts 3:19 conversion is the result of repentance. In Acts 11:21 conversion is the result of faith. In Acts 11:35 faith is implied.

James Dunn wrote that Luke used three principal words to describe faith. Each word describes it from a different angle. The Greek verb *metanoein*, the word for *repent*, means to turn away (*apo*) from sin. The verb *epistrephein*, the word for *convert*, means to turn to (*epi*) God. And *pisteuein*, the word for *believe*, means commitment to (*eis*) Christ.[1128]

Repentance

What is the awakened sinner to do? He is called upon by Scripture to repent. Repentance is the first step in human response. Yet even our response is enabled by grace. Repentance is the gift of God. It is an element of preliminary grace. According to Acts 5:31,11:18, God granted even the Gentiles repentance

---

[1127] Wesley, Sermon #63, ¶ 12; Sermon #85, 3.7.

[1128] Dunn, *Baptism in the Holy Spirit*, 91.

unto life. 2 Timothy 2:25 teaches that God will grant them repentance leading them to a knowledge of the truth. This was Paul's experience on the Damascus Road.

However, we will have no inclination to repent until we are convicted. *Confession* means to agree with the charges brought by the Holy Spirit. It means that we plead guilty. Repentance is a change of mind about sin that results in a turning from sin. In the Greek language, *metanoeo* describes a change of mind, while *metamelomai* can mean regret. Oden wrote, "True repentance elicits a fundamental *behavioral reversal*."[1129]

Sinners are commanded to repent in Mark 6:12; Luke 13:3; Acts 8:22, 17:30. True repentance means that we begin to feel a deep sorrow of heart for our sin. We deplore ourselves for having lived so foolishly. We thought we were wise, but begin to realize that in truth we have been a fool. We are grieved to recognize that we have trampled both the laws of God and the blood of his Son under foot.

Repentance is not false humility. Nor is repentance a matter of making excuses. It is not the fear of getting caught nor grief over the consequences of bad choices.

Repentance is a radical change of heart. It is a deep remorse and regret over hurting others, condemnation for violating our own integrity, and most of all sorrow over offending God.

Repentance is a radical change of mind. Sin is not caused by our heredity or environment, our physiological temperament or the sign of the stars under which we were born. To repent means we accept personal responsibility for our sin and have changed our way of thinking. It is an ax wielded at the root of a tree (Matt 3:10). Thus, the sinner is not trimming leaves or merely cutting back. Nor is he cutting off an entire branch. This is a radical change in which the whole life of sin must go.

Repentance is a commitment to the truth which produces a change in our conduct, as God enables us. It is a change of val-

---

[1129]Oden, *John Wesley's Teachings*, 2:124.

ues in which we turn from the value system of the world and adopt the values taught by God's Word.[1130]

Psychologically, a convicted sinner must avoid despair, fatalism, and even suicide. The psychological term *compensation* means to become overly strict in one area to compensate for a deficiency in another area. The sinful mind is also capable of rationalization and self-justification. Repentance is a radical change of will in which we surrender control over our life and submit to the Lordship of Jesus Christ.

> Repent! Turn away from all your offenses; then sin will not be your downfall. Rid yourselves of all the offenses you have committed, and get a new heart and a new spirit (Ezek 18:30-31).

Under this conviction we see ourselves as desperately wicked (Jer 17:9). We will never repent unless we are first convicted, but God will not repent for us. "God commands all people everywhere to repent" (Acts 17:30).

The desire for forgiveness and acceptance by God grows stronger as our sorrow over sin deepens. We attempt to reform our life by leaving off the sins of the past and striving to obey God's commands. We try to turn away from idols and serve the living God. We pray for forgiveness and request mercy as we begin to honestly acknowledge all of the known sin that has been in our life.

Antinomianism, however, denies that one must repent in order to be saved. Saving faith involves only accepting Christ as Savior. Submission to Christ is an optional later step that is not required for salvation. This false teaching was stated by Lewis Sperry Chafer who wrote, "The New Testament does not impose

---

[1130]Oden, *Life in the Spirit*, 85-108.

repentance upon the unsaved as a condition of salvation."[1131] Dave Hunt also left repentance out of his book, *The Nonnegotiable Gospel* (2007).

Antinomians assert that repentance does not involve a turning from sin and that faith does not include obedience. They insist that a sinner can trust in Christ but may never obey him as Lord. They say that since God changes people by grace — we can do nothing. We do not even stop sinning to get saved. Thus, Charles Stanley wrote,

> It is not lying, cheating, stealing, raping, murdering, or being unfaithful that sends people to hell. . . . Neither do we become unsaved by acting unsaved. . . . Even if a believer for all practical purposes becomes an unbeliever, his salvation is not in jeopardy.[1132]

The truth is that God's grace convicts us of sin and it also enables us to repent and believe. Paul distinguished between the sorrow of the world and godly sorrow which produces repentance. "See what this godly sorrow has produced in you: what earnestness, what eagerness to clear yourselves, what indignation, what alarm, what longing, what concern, what readiness to see justice done" (2 Cor 7:10-11). The result is behavioral change.

Jesus preached repentance as a condition to salvation in at least nineteen passages. He declared, "Unless you repent, you too will all perish" (Luke 13:3). Yet we are not saved by repentance alone. We must trust in the atoning work of Christ. Jabez Bunting explained,

> Our *Repentance* is neither the meritorious cause, not the immediate instrument of our Justification. For although

---

[1131]Chafer, *Systematic Theology*, 3:376. This view is also defended by Zane Hodges, *The Gospel Under Siege* (1981).

[1132]Stanley, *Eternal Security*, 70-71, 94.

no man is justified *without repenting*, yet it is equally true that none is justified merely *for or by his repentance*. Repentance makes no atonement for sin; and therefore cannot be allowed to supersede the blood of Jesus.[1133]

Verses like Mark 1:15 command us to repent and believe. Why, then, did Paul tell the jailer simply to "believe on the Lord Jesus Christ" (Acts 16:31)? Why did Peter preach "repent and be baptized" (Acts 2:38) and not mention faith at all?

The NT prescribes faith, without any mention of repentance, 115 times. However, in other passages repentance is used to cover the whole process while faith is not mentioned (Luke 24:47; Acts 2:38, 3:19, 5:31). Jesus preached repentance as a condition to salvation at least 19 times. Sometimes faith includes repentance even if repentance is not specifically mentioned. Actually, both repentance and faith constitute a single act; repentance is turning away from sin and faith is turning toward grace. Strictly speaking faith is the only condition of conversion, but repentance is a part of faith.[1134] Repentance results when we believe what the Holy Spirit reveals about our sin.

"There is not true saving faith without repentance, just as there is not true repentance without saving faith."[1135] "Repentance is not, strictly speaking, a condition of justification, but rather a turning from evil that is presupposed in faith's reception of God's justifying action."[1136]

Another weakness of modern evangelicalism is that salvation has been reduced to a standardized formula. We fail to realize that each person may be at a different point in their spiritual

---

[1133]Bunting, *Justification by Faith*, 28.

[1134]Oden, *Life in the Spirit*, 79-108.

[1135]Dobson and Hindson, "Is Repentance Part of the Gospel?" 10-11.

[1136]Oden, *Life in the Spirit*, 132.

journey. Jesus and his apostles did not counsel all seekers alike. Some seekers were told to make restitution; some were told to have faith; some were told to repent. Each case was diagnosed individually and given instructions which varied, but were all part of the same general order of salvation.

The nature of faith

Christ is the meritorious cause of justification. Faith is the instrumental cause or act by which we apprehend Christ. Thomas Summers wrote,

> Faith is a receiving and appropriating grace. It receives and appropriates the merit of Christ for justification, and also the power of the spirit for sanctification and every good work.[1137]

Wesley preached that faith is the only necessary condition of justification. The very moment God gives faith to the ungodly, that faith is counted to him for righteousness.[1138]

Pope explained that the faith that lays hold of Christ is the highest moral act of a state of penitence: nothing more, but nothing less. Thus, the faith which precedes repentance is a belief in God, his Word, and his righteous judgment against sin. But a saving trust can spring up only in a contrite heart, so that repentance precedes saving faith.[1139]

Although Luther's *Preface* defines several key terms and then summarizes each chapter in Romans, the section being read at Wesley's conversion was where "Luther teaches what faith is,

---

[1137]Summers, *Systematic Theology*, 2:142.

[1138]Wesley, "Justification by Faith," Sermon #5, 4.5.

[1139]Pope, *Compendium*, 2:382-385, 371.

and also that faith alone justifies."[1140] In that section Luther wrote:

> Faith is not the human notion and dream that some people call faith. When they see that no improvement of life and no good works follow — they fall into the error of saying, "Faith is not enough; one must do works in order to be righteous and be saved." This is due to the fact that when they hear the gospel, they get busy and by their own powers create an idea in their heart which says, "I believe"; they take this then to be a true faith. But, as it is a human figment and idea that never reaches the depths of the heart, nothing comes of it either, and no improvement follows.
>
> Faith, however, is a divine work in us which changes us and makes us to be born anew of God, John 1:12-13. It kills the old Adam and makes us altogether different men, in heart and spirit and mind and powers; and it brings with it the Holy Spirit. It is a living, busy, active, mighty thing, this faith. It is impossible for it not to be doing good works incessantly. It does not ask whether good works are to be done, but before the question is asked, it has already done them, and is constantly doing them. Whoever does not do such works, however, is an unbeliever. He gropes and looks around for faith and good works, but knows neither what faith is nor what good works are. Yet he talks and talks, with many works, about faith and good works.
>
> Faith is a living, daring confidence in God's grace, so sure and certain that the believer would stake his life on it a thousand times. This knowledge of and confidence in God's grace makes men glad and bold and happy in dealing with God and with all creatures. And

---

[1140]Tyerman, *Life and Times of John Wesley*, 1:180.

this is the work which the Holy Spirit performs in faith. Because of it, without compulsion, a person is ready and glad to do good to everyone, to serve everyone, to suffer everything, out of love and praise to God who has shown him this grace. Thus it is impossible to separate works from faith, quite as impossible as to separate heat and light from fire. Beware, therefore, of your own false notions and of idle talkers who imagine themselves wise enough to make decisions about faith and good works, and yet are the greatest fools. Pray God that he may work faith in you. Otherwise, you will surely remain forever without faith, regardless of what you may think or do.[1141]

Just as there is a period of gestation prior to the instant of birth in the natural world, so in the spiritual realm the awakening process may be gradual, but the new birth is itself instantaneous. Scripture does not describe the new birth as a process which has not yet been completed. The relevant passages describe the new birth in the past tense, utilizing either the aorist or perfect tense.

However, the term *salvation* is a broader concept and Scripture describes it as a process. Scripture describes salvation as a past event, an ongoing present reality, and a future hope.[1142] While the atonement is finished, the complete recovery of all that was lost in the fall has not yet been realized. Thus, the new birth, though it is a supernatural beginning, is not the end.

After his conversion, John preached

Christian faith is then not only an assent to the whole gospel of Christ, but also a full reliance on the blood of Christ, a trust in the merits of his life, death, and resurrection; a recumbency upon him as our atonement and

---

[1141]Luther, *Luther's Works*, 35:370-371.

[1142]Oden, *Life in the Spirit*, 84-85.

life, as *given for us*, and *living in us*. It is a sure confidence which a man hath in God, that through the merits of Christ *his* sins are forgiven, and *he* reconciled to the favor of God.[1143]

Wesley distinguished between the faith of a heathen who believes in God but does not know Jesus Christ and the faith of a demon, referred to in James 2:19, which is simply an intellectual knowledge. He distinguished the faith of a servant who tries hard to live according to God's will with saving faith, or the faith of a son, who relies on God for everything. "It is born out of utter despair of ourselves and a deep need of God." While a servant works for a future reward, the faith of a son enjoys the great privilege of the present relationship.[1144] He also distinguished between the faith of the disciples before Pentecost and Christian faith.[1145]

The Word of God is the basis of faith (Rom 10:17). The atoning work of Christ is the object of faith. "The sole cause of our acceptance with God . . . is the righteousness and the death of Christ, who fulfilled God's law, and died in our stead."[1146]

The Holy Spirit gives the gift of faith. Acts 3:16 speaks of "the faith which is by him." Wesley observed that God is the source, as well as the object, of our faith.[1147] No one can say, "Jesus is Lord," except by the Holy Spirit (1 Cor 12:3). According to Hebrews 12:2, God is the author of faith.

Faith is not an irrational leap, nor is the gospel uncertain. The Christian faith is not proven true by a pragmatic leap in which the hearer is challenged to give it a try. To believe without

---

[1143]Wesley, "Salvation by Faith," Sermon #1, 1.5.

[1144]Mitton, *Clue to Wesley's Sermons*, 28-31.

[1145]Wesley, "Salvation by Faith," 1.3; *BE Works*, 10:192.

[1146]Wesley, *BE Works*, 13:37.

[1147]Wesley, *Notes*, 282.

evidence is gullibility. *Faith* is more than a way of describing the opinion we hold. The Greek word for *faith* (*pistis*) comes from the verb *peitho* which means to persuade. The result is that faith is a conviction based on evidence (Heb 11:1).

Faith is depicted as looking to Jesus (John 3:14-15; Num 21:9). It is described as eating and drinking (John 4:14, 6:50-58, 7:37). It is symbolized as coming to Christ (John 5:40) or receiving him (John 1:12).

In Romans 4, Paul speaks of belief in the aorist tense (vv 3,17-18), which resulted in righteousness being imputed. But Paul also speaks of belief as present tense (vv 5, 11, 24) which results in a present imputation (v 5) and a future imputation (v 11). In v 11 righteousness is imputed as we believe, but v 24 probably refers to the day of judgment when God will justify.[1148] Romans 3:30 also refers to a future justification. Therefore, we must keep on believing if we hope to receive final justification.[1149] Faith must continue or else we will be "cut off," as Romans 11:22 warns.

Thus, faith is both the condition and the result of salvation. Adam Clarke preached, "The way to obtain salvation, and the way to retain it are the same."[1150]

Faith is stated as the condition of salvation in Romans 1:17. According to Romans 3:22, "This righteousness from God comes through faith in Jesus Christ to all who believe." In Romans 5:16-17 the free gift of grace which brings justification comes to those who *receive* it. Here the condition of faith is described as *receiving*, which is a present active participle.

[1148]Dunn, *WBC* 38A:223.

[1149]On the doctrine of final justification, see Fletcher, *Works*, 1:275; Matlock, *The Four Justifications*, 81-89.

[1150]Clarke, *Works*, 5:129.

While faith is required as the condition of salvation, R. C. Sproul, reflecting his Calvinism, claimed regeneration *precedes* faith. "Faith is regeneration's fruit, not its cause."[1151]

Mark 11:22; Romans 3:3,22,26; Galatians 2:16,20, 3:22,26; Ephesians 3:12; Philippians 3:9; Colossians 2:12; Revelation 14:12 all say that faith is *of* God or *of* Jesus. The question is whether *through faith in Jesus Christ* should be translated the *faith of* or *faith in* Jesus Christ. Grammatically, is this phrase an objective genitive, in which the noun in the genitive case *receives* the action, or a subjective genitive, in which the noun in the genitive case *produces* the action? Those who argue for a subjective genitive are also divided as to whether it means *the faith given by Jesus Christ* or *the faithfulness of Jesus Christ.*

In either case, this righteousness of God comes through faith in Jesus Christ, through the faithfulness of Jesus Christ, or through the faith given by Jesus Christ, *to all who believe.* Scholars agree that the previous matter cannot be resolved syntactically. While there is no doubt that Jesus Christ is the proper object of faith, does the fact that *faith* is a noun instead of a verb move away from the idea of human response? The faith of Jesus Christ as a divine gift and faith in Jesus Christ as a human response.

While both Calvinists and Wesleyan-Arminians hold that faith is in some sense a gift, they differ on whether it is given only to the passive elect as a result of their regeneration or to those who repent and is the basis of their justification. Wesleyan theology is a mediating position between the extremes of a presumptuous faith which leads to antinomianism and a passive faith which is based on fatalism.

Faith is the gift of God (Eph 2:8; Phil 1:29), yet we are commanded to believe. Adam Clarke explained,

---

[1151]Sproul, *Willing to Believe*, 23.

Is not *faith* the *gift of God*? Yes, as to the *grace* by which it is produced, but the *grace* or *power* to believe, and the *act* of *believing* are two different things. Without the *grace* or *power* to believe no man ever did or can believe; but with that *power* the *act of faith* is a man's own. God never believes *for* any man, no more than he *repents* for him. . . . This, therefore, is the true state of the case: God gives the power, man uses the power thus given, and brings glory to God; without the power no man can believe; with it, any man may.[1152]

Leroy Forlines argued,

There can be no faith on the part of a human being without the active involvement of his personality. It is a contradiction of the facts of human personality to think that a person can believe and it be totally the work of God with no human involvement.[1153]

Ralph Winter wrote that faith as a noun is the gift of God. "Those to whom faith has been given are often, in a human sense almost 'victims' of that faith. They do not ask for it any more than Abraham asked for his summons from Ur of the Chaldees." Believing, however, is a verb and refers to what we do, not what God gives. "Belief is our response to faith."[1154]

Faith always contains an unknown element. It always contains action. And it always contains strong assurance. But faith cannot be totally monergistic, whether it comes before or after regeneration. And yet Alister McGrath claimed that God provides everything necessary for justification so that all the sinner

---

[1152]Clarke, *Commentary*, 6:439, 1069.

[1153]Forlines, "Election in Romans 9," 7-8.

[1154]Winter, "Theology of Redemption, Part 4," 15.

needs to do is receive it. "In justification, God is active, and humans are passive."[1155]

Saving faith is a gift in the sense that the Holy Spirit enables faith, but there must be human consent. Otherwise, justification is by divine decree and not by faith. Wesley argued that if salvation is by absolute decree, it is not by works, but neither is it by faith. "For *unconditional* decree excludes faith as well as works."[1156]

George Bryson wrote, "While Calvinists give *theological lip service* to the place and importance of faith, Calvinists do not see faith as a *condition of salvation*, but instead they reduce it to a mere *consequence of election*."[1157] Picirilli concluded, "I think it is obvious that Calvinism's salvation is not *by* faith but *to* faith. In that system of theology regeneration logically (if not chronologically) precedes faith."[1158]

According to Romans 5:1, "We have been justified through faith." Here justification is described as the result of faith. The preposition *ek*, which is translated *through*, denotes the basis or condition of justification. Again, Romans 10:9-10 clearly makes faith the condition of salvation.

It is absurd to argue that saving faith is a meritorious work, because saving faith is total reliance on the work of another. Our faith is a required condition, but not a meritorious work which obligates God. Frederick Godet wrote that faith cannot be meritorious, since faith consists precisely in renouncing all merit and in the humble acceptance of the free gift.[1159] Furthermore, faith

---

[1155]McGrath, *Reformation Thought*, 100.

[1156]Wesley, *BE Works*, 13:554.

[1157]Bryson, "Is Faith Really a Condition of Salvation?" 38.

[1158]Picirilli, *Free Will Revisited*, 133.

[1159]Godet, *Commentary*, 348-349.

cannot be a meritorious work since it is the gift of God.[1160] Faith is not a righteous act of merit, but an active reception of merit.[1161] Richard Hooker wrote in 1593, "God doth justify the believing man, yet not for the worthiness of his belief, but for his worthiness who is believed."[1162] Arminius gave this example:

> A rich man bestows, on a poor and famishing beggar, alms by which he may be able to maintain himself and his family. Does it cease to be a pure gift, because the beggar extends his hand to receive it? Can it be said with propriety, that "the alms depended partly on the *liberality* of the Donor, and partly on the *liberty* of the Receiver?[1163]

The emphasis on saving faith in the NT is on a present-tense faith. The Greek verb *pisteuo* occurs 248 times in the NT. While many references in the Gospels and Acts are a matter of historical record, of particular interest are some ninety references which state general commands to believe or offer promises to those who believe. While there are a few instances of commands which emphasize the initial act of faith, every stated promise of eternal life or final salvation to those who believe is based on a present-tense, continuous faith.[1164]

Saving faith produces good works. Twice in Romans Paul uses the phrase "obedience of faith" (1:5,16:26). In Romans 10:16 Paul equates obedience with faith. Douglas Moo wrote,

---

[1160]Outler made this point in his annotation to Wesley's sermon "Justification by Faith," Sermon #5, 4.5. *BE Works*, 1:196.

[1161]Hicks, "Theology of Grace," 92-93.

[1162]Stott, *The Cross of Christ*, 190.

[1163]Arminius, *Works*, 2:52.

[1164]Reasoner, "The Faith Factor," 1-3. See also Greenlee, *Words from the Word*, 49-52.

"Obedience always involves faith, and faith always involves obedience. They should not be equated, compartmentalized, or made into separate stages of Christian experience."[1165]

As we live by faith, Romans 1:17 also teaches that we grow in faith. Romans 6 asserts that justification and initial sanctification are bound together. We cannot have the one without having the other. The term *old man* occurs three times in Paul's writings. In Romans 6:6 Paul states that our old man was crucified with Christ. Colossians 3:9 declares that believers have put off their old way of life. Ephesians 4:22 is an imperative for Christians to put it off.

It is inconsistent with Scripture to teach that one can become born again without any change. The goal of predestination, according to Romans 8:29, is conformity to the image of Christ both now and more fully in the age to come. Two natures may exist in the life of the justified, but only one can be in control. Wesley taught that while the old nature remained, the new nature reigned.[1166] Those who are born again do not walk after the flesh, but after the Spirit (Rom 8:4).

Therefore, Romans teaches that saving faith is the condition of justification, enabled by preliminary grace, and is a present, continuous faith. It results in obedience, producing good works, and bringing assurance. Faith cannot be reduced to the righteousness of Christ which the elect passively have imputed to their account as evidence of their regeneration.

But while the Scriptures teach imputation, they do not affirm everything that is taught about imputation. Faith is initially imputed for righteousness, but the righteousness of Christ is not imputed in lieu of any subsequent obedience.

Paul affirmed "that a man is justified by faith without the deeds of the law" (Rom 3:28). We do not pay our sin debt through good works. Arminius stated that his desire was to

---

[1165]Moo, *Romans 1-8*, 44-45.

[1166]Wesley, "On Sin in Believers," Sermon #13, 4.3.

appear before the tribunal of God with this confidence or trust in Christ, as a propitiation through faith in his blood. To be judged otherwise is to be condemned. God is the primary cause of our justification. Faith is the requirement of God and the act of the believer. Christ is the object of our faith. "Faith is imputed for righteousness on account of Christ, the object which it apprehends."[1167]

Stages of Faith

Faith is the assent of the mind to the truth of the Word. It is also the consent of the will to obey the Word. And it is the trust of the heart in the living Word.[1168]

Faith begins as an intellectual acceptance of the truth. Our faith must have content. Our faith is not in the power of faith. Francis Schaeffer wrote about "pre-evangelism." We cannot presume the sinner has a Christian framework of truth. A person cannot put faith in a Christ he knows nothing about.[1169] Yet faith must go beyond mental assent. The demons *believe* in the sense that they know certain truths to be true, yet they remain demons (Jas 2:19).

Faith also involves the consent of the will. There must be a deliberate decision to accept Christ as my substitute and trust solely in his atoning work.

But are we saved because we have determined that we have sufficiently believed? How do we know when we have sufficiently believed? This can easily degenerate into rationalization and logical deductions. If "the heart is deceitful above all things" (Jer 17:9), it is not safe to make these assumptions.

Faith also includes assurance or confirmation that we are forgiven and accepted. According to Hebrews 11:1 true faith

---

[1167]Arminius, *Works*, 2:46-51.

[1168]Oden, *The Justification Reader*, 155.

[1169]Schaffer, *Works*, 1:151-160.

produces assurance or confidence. The word *hupostasis* was found in papyri sources to denote a title deed.[1170] William Lane translated this opening phrase, "Now faith celebrates the objective reality of the blessings for which we hope."[1171] In Acts 17:31 and 2 Timothy 3:14 the Greek word for *faith* is translated *assurance*.

Pope declared that, although there is a difference between faith and assurance, the same Spirit who brings faith to life gives the internal assurance that it is fulfilled in such swift succession that it is impossible to distinguish between faith and assurance.[1172] Yet Wesley wrote "a conviction that we are justified cannot be implied in justifying faith."[1173] The assurance of *provision* is an aspect of saving faith. The assurance of *possession* is the witness of the Spirit.

Thus, saving faith involves the whole personality — intellect, will, and emotions. This needs to be understood and incorporated into evangelism. Some churches bypass the intellect and will and appeal directly to the emotions. Sinners experience an emotional high during corporate worship, but there is no change in their life. Other churches assume that if an applicant for membership affirms certain doctrinal propositions that they are Christians.

Often there must be pre-evangelism, even apologetics. A sinner cannot believe over the top of genuine doubt. In contrast to teaching and lectures, evangelistic preaching must push awakened sinners to the point of decision when they make a volitional choice to trust in Christ alone.

[1170]Moulton and Milligan, *Vocabulary of the Greek Testament*, 660.

[1171]Lane, *WBC* 47A:325.

[1172]Pope, *Prayers of St. Paul*, 214-215.

[1173]Wesley, *Letter* to Richard Thompson, 5 Feb 1756.

Conversion

Just as the atonement is described in commercial, legal, relational, and sacrificial terms, so the new birth is described in legal, relational, and biological terms. The offender is forgiven, the accused is pardoned, the offense is remitted, and the lost child is welcomed home.

Justification is a legal change, while regeneration is a restorative change. Oden observed that the Protestant reformers emphasized justification, but "the new birth has sometimes been insufficiently emphasized."[1174] Baptist theologian A. H. Strong noted,

> It was John Wesley who did the most to establish the doctrine of regeneration. He asserted that the Holy Spirit acts through the truth, in distinction from the doctrine that the Holy Spirit works solely through the ministers and sacraments of the church.[1175]

Adoption is a positive relational change, and sanctification is a negative relational change — separation from the world. We are forgiven from the guilt of past sin, we are delivered from the power of present sin, and we are released from the fear of future punishment.

Wesley also described sin as disease and salvation as restoration to health. Oden explained,

> God is able and willing to destroy all sin in all that believe. Sin is not intrinsic to humanity as created by

---

[1174]Oden, *John Wesley's Teachings*, 2:219-220.

[1175]Strong, *Systematic Theology*, 816.

God, but a malformation, a disease of humanity that God is in the process of correcting.[1176]

Wesley preached that the religion of Jesus Christ is God's method of healing a diseased soul. "Hereby the great Physician of souls applies medicine to heal *this sickness*; to restore human nature, totally corrupted in all its faculties."

If mankind was not thus fallen, there would be no need of anything more than outward reformation. But the Word of God teaches otherwise.

> Know your disease! Know your cure! Ye were born in sin; therefore "ye must be born again," "born of God." By nature ye are wholly corrupted; by grace ye shall be wholly renewed. . . . Now "go on" "from faith to faith," until your whole sickness be healed.[1177]

There are eight gracious blessings associated with conversion. While systematic theology may separate justification, regeneration, and initial sanctification for purposes of analysis, they are experienced concurrently.

1. Justification

According to Romans 8:33-34, *justification* is the antonym of condemnation. Richard Watson agreed with John Calvin that the imputation of righteousness was simply the non-imputation of sin, or the remission of sins.[1178] In a letter to John Newton, John Wesley declared that he was in agreement with Calvin on

---

[1176]Oden, *John Wesley's Teachings*, 2:93.

[1177]Wesley, "Original Sin" Sermon #44, 3.3-5.

[1178]Watson, *Theological Institutes*, 2:215, 233, 241.

justification. "In this respect I do not differ from him a hair's breadth."[1179]

Justification is both positive and negative. Negatively, God does not count our sins against us. David described the blessing of justification in Psalm 32:1-2 by saying that the Lord does not count our sins against us. Paul cites these verses in Romans 4:7-8. The result is that "There is now no condemnation"(Rom 8:1).

Positively, God counts our faith as righteousness and we have peace with God (Rom 5:1). This is not legal fiction, as Roman Catholics charge. He declares us to be without guilt and imparts his righteousness. To justify means to make just. The same word *dikaios* is translated in Romans *just* four times and *righteous* three times.

Paul makes two statements in Romans which give the positive and negative side of this judicial act of God. "Since we have been justified through faith, we have peace with God" (Rom 5:1). I am reconciled. I am brought near through the blood of Christ. "There is now no condemnation for those who are in Christ Jesus" (Rom 8:1). My sins are not imputed to my account. I am forgiven. The demands of the law have been satisfied.

In justification God both forgives and forgets (Jer 31:34; Isa 43:25, 44:22; Ps 51:1, 5). Although omniscient, God chooses to blot out of his memory and remember our sins no more.

Jabez Bunting provided this classic definition of justification:

> To justify a sinner, is to *account* and consider him *relatively righteous*, and to *deal* with him *as such*, notwithstanding his past unrighteousness; by clearing, absolving, discharging, and releasing him from various penal evils, and especially from the wrath of God, and the liability to eternal death, which by that past unrighteousness he had deserved; and by accepting him as if

---

[1179]Wesley, *Letter* to John Newton, 14 May 1765.

just, and admitting him to the state, the privileges, and the rewards of righteousness.[1180]

We were under condemnation, facing the wrath and judgment of God. Through faith we trust in Christ as our propitiation and God justifies us. Justification is a judicial act of God in which he declares on the basis of Christ's death that all the claims of the law are satisfied with respect to the sinner. The vocabulary of justification includes *pardon, remission, blotting out, acceptance, reconciliation, non-imputation of sin*, and the *imputation of righteousness.*

Justification has always been by faith. Because of his faith, Abel was commended as a righteous man (Heb 11:4). Enoch was commended as one who pleased God (Heb 11:5). Noah became heir of the righteousness that comes by faith (Heb 11:7). Paul refers to Abraham and David as examples of justification by faith (Rom 4:3-6). However, regeneration is a NT blessing since the Holy Spirit was not given until after Christ completed the atonement (John 7:39).

According to Romans 3:24, we are justified freely by his grace. We have nothing of which to boast (v 27). Here Christian faith differs from all the religions of the world. They all teach that we are in some way justified before God by human effort. Scripture teaches we are justified by what Christ has done.

Justification by Faith

Because we are cleared from our guilt through faith in the substitutionary atonement of Christ, we are no longer held liable for our past sins. Faith is the condition of salvation, not its consequence. God imputes righteousness to us when we trust in the atoning work of Christ, but the non-imputation of sin is limited to past sin. Thus, the doctrine of non-imputation does not pro-

---

[1180]Bunting, *Justification by Faith*, 10.

vide a Protestant indulgence for present and future acts of sin. While we insist upon personal righteousness as the mark of a true Christian, we are emphatic that this holiness does not originate with us. It is the ongoing work of the indwelling Spirit.

While these concepts are intertwined, I want to develop them in a logical sequence, distinguishing first between Roman Catholic and Protestant theology, then distinguishing between Calvinism and Arminianism. This analysis is part of the larger discussion on the eight blessings which accompany conversion. It also demonstrates the *via media* or middle road between two extremes.

- **The difference between Roman Catholic and Protestant theology**

The historic debate between Roman Catholic and Protestant theology is focused on the question, Is justification a declaration of righteousness and acceptability to God or is it a process whereby we are made righteous? The Roman Catholic statement "On Justification," Canon 14, from the Council of Trent:

> If anyone saith, that man is truly absolved from his sins and justified, because that he assuredly believed himself absolved and justified; or, that no one is truly justified but he who believes himself justified; and that, by this faith alone, absolution and justification are effected: let him be anathema [cursed].[1181]

In *The Justification Reader*, Thomas Oden demonstrated inductively that for the first five hundred years of the church, justification by grace alone through faith alone was taught. He also rejected the common Protestant assumption that Luther finally got right what Augustine got wrong. While acknowledg-

---

[1181]Schaff, *Creeds of Christendom*, 2:113.

ing some abuse or inconsistency in the interpretation of Paul's writings, Oden claimed this was an exaggeration. Oden contended that what the Protestant Reformation did was to rescue the doctrine of justification from distortions of patristic thought that developed in the late Middle Ages.[1182]

Commenting on Romans 3:3-8, Greathouse wrote, "Here is the basis for the Protestant doctrine of *sola fide*, 'by faith alone.'"[1183] Paul is explicitly declaring both *how* we are saved and *how* the people of God maintain their covenant relationship with God. Therefore, justification is a declaration of righteousness and acceptability to God, and sanctification is the process whereby we are made righteous.

- **The difference between Wesleyan-Arminian and Calvinistic theology**

However, while Methodism is Protestant and Reformed, we broke with the major Protestant Reformers on the *results* of justification. While Wesley upheld the Protestant view that the *basis* of justification is faith alone, he did not accept the majority Protestant view that the Christian is at once just and yet a sinner.

John Wesley's theology is Reformed. His theology stands with Protestantism regarding the *nature* of justification, as a forensic declaration by God in which he graciously forgives and accepts sinners.

Faith is the only condition necessary for salvation. Properly understood, repentance is an act of faith. Faith cannot be separated from obedience. The Greek verb *pitho*, which is often translated trust, having confidence, assurance, or being persuaded, is translated six times as *obey* in the KJV. Hebrews 3:18 said the Israelites did not enter into God's blessing because of disobedience. The very next verse says they did not enter in

---

[1182]Oden, *The Justification Reader*, 20, 24-25, 29, 143.

[1183]Greathouse, *Beacon Bible Commentary*, 8:95.

because of unbelief. Faith and obedience are two sides of the same coin.

Roger Olson labeled as a myth the accusation that Arminian theology denies justification by grace alone through faith alone.[1184]

Wesley agreed with Luther that the church stands or falls with this doctrine of justification by faith.[1185] However, Fletcher warned that the term *solifidianism* means more. According to Fletcher, Solafidians assert or insinuate

> that true faith is inamissible [cannot be lost], that it can live in a heart totally depraved, that a man's faith can be good when his actions are bad, detestable, diabolical; in a word, that true Christians may go any length in sin, may plunge into adultery, murder, or incest, and even proceed to the open worship of devils, like Solomon, without losing their title to a throne of glory, and their justifying, sanctifying, saving faith![1186]

Solafidians not only hold that sinners are justified solely by faith in the day of conversion, but that because faith is the sum total of salvation, they deny the final justification by works of faith at the day of judgment. Thus, Fletcher labeled *solafidianism* "a softer word for *Antinomianism*."[1187] Fletcher warned against two extremes, of legalism and of solafidianism.

[1184]Olson, *Arminian Theology,* 200-220.

[1185]Wesley, *Journal*, 1 Dec 1767; "The Lord our Righteousness," Sermon #20, ¶ 4.

[1186]Fletcher, *Works*, 1:554; see also Oden, *Life in the Spirit*, 125; Bloesch, *The Holy Spirit*, 324.

[1187]Fletcher, *Works*, 1:370.

Philip Melanchthon, early Lutheran theologian, said that it is faith alone which saves, but the faith that saves is not alone.[1188] Repentance and faith are two sides of the same coin. Repentance means to turn away from the old life while faith makes possible the new life in the Spirit. A person cannot turn toward Christ without turning away from sin. The seeker who turns to Christ for salvation must also turn away from sin.

2. Imputed Righteousness

In Romans 4 Paul uses *logizomai* eleven times. This key word means to reckon, credit, rank with, calculate, consider, deliberate, grasp, draw a logical conclusion, decide, or impute. Romans 4:3-8 teaches that faith in the atoning work of Christ is imputed to the believer for righteousness.

However, imputed righteousness must be balanced with imparted righteousness. *Imputed righteousness* is a negative grace. It is absolution from our sin. *Imparted righteousness* is positive grace. It is the infusion of a new nature. In his explanation of 2 Corinthians 5:21, Wesley wrote that the believer is invested with that righteousness, "first imputed to us, then implanted in us, which is in every sense the righteousness of God."[1189]

The concept of *imputation* is important at four points in systematic theology:

- The imputation of Adam's sin to his descendants.
- The imputation of the sinner's punishment, not his sins, to Christ
- The imputation of righteousness for faith
- The imputation of perfection for love.

[1188]Oden, *Life in the Spirit*, 148; see also Watson, *Theological Institutes*, 2:249.

[1189]Wesley, *Notes*, 458.

The scriptural teaching is not that the *obedience* of Christ is credited to us, but that our *faith* is credited to us as righteous. The result is that we are both declared justified and made righteousness.

While J. I. Packer admitted that the phrase "the imputation of Christ's righteousness" is not found in Paul's writings, he argued that the concept was biblical.[1190] However, some late seventeenth-century Puritans, such as Richard Baxter, Christopher Cartwright, John Goodwin, and Benjamin Woodbridge, disputed the notion that justification was the imputation of Christ's righteousness. Instead they held to the *imputation of faith* as the formal cause of justification.[1191]

Michael Bird concluded that there is no text in the NT which categorically states that Christ's righteousness is imputed to believers.[1192] Robert Gundry also concluded that the biblical texts used to support the popular misconception of imputed righteousness do not espouse it.[1193]

Paul used *dikaiosune* thirty-six times in Romans. While it is translated *righteousness*, the older English spelling was *rightwiseness*. It refers to the character or quality of being right or just in the sight of God. In Romans 5, five related words are used which all come from the root word *dike*, which means *justice*. The KJV translates them as *justified, justification, righteousness, righteous,* and *righteousness*. The righteous act of Jesus Christ provides justification. Through faith in him we were justified and made righteous. According to A. T. Robert-

---

[1190]Packer, "Justification," 648.

[1191]McGrath, *Iustitia Dei*, 2:103, 1167. Wesley abridged Goodwin's *A Treatise of Justification* (1642) and it is found in Wesley's *Works*, 10:316-346.

[1192]Bird, *Saving Righteousness of God*, 2.

[1193]Gundry, "Nonimputation of Christ's Righteousness,"17-45. See also Gathercole, "What Did Paul Really Mean?" 22-28.

son, when Paul used the word *righteousness*, he meant both justification and sanctification. The gospel reveals both "the righteousness that God has and that he bestows."[1194]

Wesley objected to a distortion of the doctrine of imputation which results in God being deceived in those whom he justifies, "that he thinks them to be what in fact they are not, that he accounts them to be otherwise than they are. . . . He can no more in this manner confound me with Christ than with David or Abraham."[1195] Wesley affirmed imputed righteousness, but then explained how it can be distorted.

> But when is it imputed? When they believe. In that very hour the righteousness of Christ is theirs. It is imputed to every one that believes, as soon as he believes: faith and the righteousness of Christ are inseparable. . . . I believe God *implants* righteousness in every one to whom he has *imputed* it. . . . In the meantime what we are afraid of is this: lest any should use the phrase, "the righteousness of Christ," or, "the righteousness of Christ is imputed to me," as a cover for his unrighteousness. We have known this done a thousand times. A man has been reproved, suppose, for drunkenness. "Oh," said he, "I pretend to no righteousness of *my own*: Christ is *my righteousness*." Another has been told, that "the extortioner, the unjust, shall not inherit the kingdom of God." He replies with all assurance, "I am unjust in myself, but I have a spotless righteousness in Christ." And thus though a man be as far from the practice as from the tempers of a Christian, though he neither has the mind which was in Christ nor in any respect walks as he walked, yet he has armor of proof

---

[1194]Robertson, *Word Pictures*, 4:327.

[1195]Wesley, "Justification by Faith," Sermon #5, 2.4.

against all conviction, in what he calls the "righteous-ness of Christ."[1196]

The teaching that we are forgiven of all past, present, and future sins leads to antinomianism. Wesley declared, "I cannot find anything in the Bible of the remission of sins past, present and to come."[1197] Yet William G. T. Shedd declared,

All the sins of the believer, past, present, and future, are pardoned when he is justified. The sum-total of his sin, all of which is before the Divine eye at the instant when God pronounces him a justified person, is blotted out or covered over by one act of God.[1198]

The issue is whether Christ's *active* obedience to the precepts of the law is imputed to the believer in lieu of righteousness. The meritorious cause of man's justification is based on Christ's *passive* obedience unto death. We are saved by his atoning death, not through his sinless life. In his substitutionary death Christ did not become a sinner. Our sins were not transferred to him, but the penalty of our sins was laid upon him. He became a sin offering, not a sinner.

The active obedience of Christ's sinless life meant that he was not disqualified to become our substitute in the passive obedience of his passion and death. If our sin was so imputed to him that he became a sinner, he would have been disqualified to have become our atoning sacrifice. The Scripture is abundantly clear that Christ did not sin. Here again, the issue of imputation must be defined. Those who teach that he *really* became sin have moved beyond simply a legal concept of the transfer of penalty.

[1196]Wesley, "The Lord our Righteousness," Sermon #20, 2.1,12,19.

[1197]Wesley, *BE Works*, 9:176.

[1198]Shedd, *Dogmatic Theology*, 2:545; see also Berkhof, *Systematic Theology*, 514.

3. Regeneration

God not only forgives our sins, he gives us a new nature — the righteousness of Christ. Justification is what God does *for* us; regeneration is what God does *in* us. *Regeneration* is related to the word *genesis* which means beginning. This word *palingenesia* occurs in Matthew 19:28 and Titus 3:5. Regeneration or restoration is a new beginning. It means to be born again or born from above. It is the impartation of spiritual life. It is not a change of degree, but an instantaneous gift of grace. Richard Watson gave this definition,

> It is that mighty change in man, wrought by the Holy Spirit, by which the dominion which sin has over him in his natural state, and which he deplores and struggles against in his penitent state, is broken and abolished, so that, with full choice of will and the energy of right affections, he serves God freely.[1199]

Scripture describes regeneration as a birth. Twice the Bible uses the term *born again* (*anagennao* - 1 Pet 1:3, 23). We are born of God (1 John 5:1). We are born from above (John 3:3, 7). We are born of water and the Spirit (John 3:5). This is a hendiadys in which *water* is used figuratively for the Holy Spirit. Nicodemus was familiar with the Jewish rituals of sprinklings and ablutions. Jesus was describing something with which he was *not* familiar, an inward cleansing. Regeneration is a washing (Titus 3:5), but not simply the removal of dirt from the body (1 Pet 3:21). Cullman warned against separating water and Spirit baptism. Forgiveness of sins must always be connected with the gift of the Holy Spirit.[1200]

[1199]Watson, *Theological Institutes*, 2:267.

[1200]Cullman, *Baptism in the New Testament*, 12-13.

We are made alive (Eph 2:5). Regeneration is a spiritual resurrection (John 5:25; Eph 2:1). It is new creation (2 Cor 5:17). We are created in Christ Jesus (Eph 2:10). We are given a new heart (Ezek 36:26). Some Methodist theologians have also included the metaphor of circumcision as a picture of the new birth. I see it as a metaphor for entire sanctification and will deal with it under that topic.

We put off the old man and put on the new man (Rom 6:6; Eph 4:22; Col 3:10). Regeneration is the renewal of the divine image (Col 3:10-11; 2 Cor 3:18). It is participation in the divine nature (2 Pet 1:4). It is being united with Christ and abiding in him (John 15:4). It is entrance into the kingdom of God (John 3:5).

Union with Christ is described both as Christ in the believer, as well as the believer in Christ (Eph 1:3-10). This union should not be conceived pantheistically or mystically, in which the believer is absorbed into the divine so that he loses his personal identity. Yet it is more than a friendship. Nor should it be explained sacramentally, that we actually take Christ into ourselves through our participation in the sacraments.

Our union with Christ must be understood as the basis of our spiritual life which results in our participation in the corporate life within his spiritual body, the church. This union with Christ is the result of the Holy Spirit who regenerates us, baptizing us into the body of Christ (1 Cor 12:13).

Regeneration was promised in Ezekiel 36:25-27,

I will give you a new heart and put a new spirit in you; I will remove from you your heart of stone and give you a heart of flesh. And I will put my Spirit in you and move you to follow my decrees and be careful to keep my laws.

However, no one in the Old Testament is ever said to be regenerated. Regeneration was "their hope, not their experience."[1201]

4. The Baptism with the Holy Spirit

The apostolic order of salvation is stated in Acts 2:38. There are two imperatives. Everyone is commanded to repent. Forgiveness *and* the Holy Spirit are promised to all who repent.

The second command is singular. Baptism is not commanded for everyone. It is only commanded for the one who has repented. The Greek preposition *eis* (*for*) has a causal meaning. The question is whether this is an objective or subjective genitive. If it is objective, the noun (*repentance*) receives the action. This would mean that baptism led to repentance. If it is subjective, the noun (*repentance*) causes the action. This would mean that repentance led to baptism.

The Greek syntax could go either way. However, if we look for the same construction elsewhere in the NT, such as Matthew 3:11; Mark 1:4; Luke 3:3, there are no other cases where *eis* is used in the objective sense. There are no other instances where baptism brings or causes repentance. If this was what Peter was trying to say in Acts 2:38 he could have employed a *hina clause*, which would mean that we must be baptized *in order that* we might be forgiven.[1202] However, Peter himself clears up any ambiguity in Acts 3:19, "Repent, then, and turn to God, so that your sins may be wiped out."

Water baptism is the outward testimony that I have received Spirit baptism. That baptism is a public confession that we believe *upon* (*epi*) the name of Jesus (v 36) and because (*eis*) we have been forgiven.[1203] We are to believe what that name repre-

---

[1201]Büchsel, "ἀναγεννάω," *TDNT* 1:674-675; Wesley, *Notes*, 3:2209.

[1202]Mantey, "The Causal Use of *eis* in the New Testament," 45-48.

[1203]Wallace, *Grammar*, 369-371.

sents — that he is both Lord and Christ. Peter said this promise of forgiveness and the Holy Spirit is valid for all whom the Lord shall call (v 39). All who receive the gospel message are called (v 41) and they are baptized and added to the church (v 47).

This order of salvation does not teach baptismal regeneration or baptism in Jesus' name only. Acts 2:38 is a trinitarian verse which references all three members of the godhead. It does not separate the gift of the Holy Spirit as a blessing to be received after the new birth, nor does it teach that the initial evidence of the Spirit is speaking in unknown tongues. It does not teach that only those who are unconditionally elect may be saved, nor does it teach that one may believe in Jesus as Savior but not as Lord.

Regeneration is accomplished through the baptism with the Holy Spirit. Oden explained,

> It is not as though one first believes and later the Spirit comes to dwell. Rather, saving faith embraces the indwelling Spirit. Precisely in believing, the Spirit indwells. . . . Though indwelling is not precisely the same as the baptism, sealing, and filling of the Spirit, none of these is detachable from new birth through the Spirit and baptism in the Spirit. . . . The New Testament understands baptism of and by the Spirit as the privilege of all who have faith, all Christians, all who belong to the body of Christ. . . . Baptism by the Spirit is not subsequent to conversion or faith, but intrinsic to it.[1204]

Zechariah 13:1 promised that a fountain would be opened for sin and uncleanness. According to Titus 3:5 this washing of regeneration is accomplished through the baptism with the Holy Spirit.[1205]

[1204]Oden, *Life in the Spirit*, 178, 182.

[1205]Pope, *Compendium*, 3:13.

The baptism with the Spirit is never mentioned in the OT. The promise of John the Baptist that Christ will baptize you with the Holy Spirit is recorded in Matthew 3:11; Mark 1:8; Luke 3:16; John 1:33. The second cluster of references is the promise of Jesus that the disciples would be baptized with the Holy Spirit (Acts 1:5,11:16).

In the book of Acts the terms *baptized* (1:5), *come upon* (1:8), *filled* (2:4), and *receiving the gift of the Holy Spirit* (2:38), all refer to the same event and that event is regeneration. Biblical writers refer to the giving of the Holy Spirit as being filled, being baptized, being endued with power. The Spirit was sent, given, poured out, and fell. These terms are synonymous and cannot be used to make artificial distinctions. Luke used seven different phrases a total of 23 times, in Luke and Acts, to describe the coming of the Spirit, and they are merely different aspects of the same operation.

The term *filled with the Spirit* is used only by Luke and in Ephesians 5:18. Pentecostal scholar Howard Ervin agreed that the terms *baptism in the Holy Spirit* and *filled with the Holy Spirit* are used interchangeably "as related aspects of the same experience." Ervin is also correct that *came upon, filled with, received, fell upon,* and *poured out* all amount to the same experience.[1206] However, Ervin understood this experience as subsequent to regeneration. "It is a consensus of the classical Pentecostal view that the baptism of the Holy Spirit (Acts 2:4) is *subsequent* to conversion and the new birth."[1207] However, Robert Lyon demonstrated that "baptizing, coming upon, filling, pouring out, receiving — are equivalent expressions" and all believers receive the Holy Spirit in his fullness at conversion.[1208]

All believers have the Holy Spirit (Rom 8:9), and there is no command in the NT for Christians to receive the baptism with

---

[1206]Ervin, *Spirit-Baptism,* 25-26, 44.

[1207]Ervin, *Conversion-Initiation*, vii.

[1208]Lyon, "Baptism and Spirit-Baptism,"18, 24.

the Holy Spirit. Any person who does not have the Spirit of Christ dwelling in him and governing him is "not a Christian; not in a state of salvation," according to Wesley.[1209]

Baptism is initiation through which we enter the church. Baptism is a once-for-all experience. Therefore, the phrase *baptism of the Holy Spirit* is stressing the initial work of the Holy Spirit. The phrase *gift of the Holy Spirit* emphasizes that this is something that God gives to us, not something that we earn through observing some spiritual formula.

The *filling of the Holy Spirit* stresses the result of our encounter with the Holy Spirit, but does not describe a single experience in a Christian's life. If you are baptized, even by immersion, in a short time you will be dry, and you will only have a memory of your experience. However, if you fill something, it is likely to remain in that condition much longer. The results of the filling will continue for a long time. Thus, the filling of the Holy Spirit is primarily stressing the result of the encounter with the Holy Spirit that we have when we are baptized by the Holy Spirit.

Murphree reminds us that the phrase *filled with the Spirit* is a metaphor which uses a spatial analogy. But we are talking about something that is not spatial. The Holy Spirit is not a physical substance and we are not receptacles. Thus, we actually mean that we are united with and controlled by the Spirit. Every Christian is filled with the Spirit *to the extent* that he or she is emptied of self and surrendered to Christ. No Christian is filled with the Spirit, in the sense of being full, until that person is fully surrendered. A person cannot be occupied with the presence of Christ so long as he or she is preoccupied with self.[1210]

It is like the difference between a wedding and marriage. Though we use the two words somewhat interchangeably, the wedding is like the baptism. It is a once-for-all event and only

---

[1209]Wesley, *Notes*, 381.

[1210]Murphree, *Love Motive*, 62; 65.

lasts a short time. However, marriage is like the filling. When one gets married, that marriage lasts for the rest of our life. The command in Ephesians 5:18 is a present tense command to keep filled with the Spirit.

No one is filled permanently. It is a mistake to conceive of a container which is filled at a point in time and neither gains nor loses any of the contents. According to Wesley, Hebrews 2:1 describes water leaking out of a barrel.[1211] The verb is used only here in the NT and it seems to convey the image of a drifting ship, not a leaking barrel. The leaking barrel metaphor has been connected to Ephesians 5:18, but the Hebrews passage does not reference the infilling of the Holy Spirit. The Christian life is like a conduit which has a continual infilling and a continual outflowing. This flow of the Spirit may be restricted or blocked by anything which is inconsistent with divine love.

Paul states in Romans 6:3 that when we are baptized into Christ Jesus, we are uniting with him in his death and resurrection. Through this baptism we die to the old life of sin and are raised from the dead that we may live a new life. Although many people see the word *baptize* and immediately associate it with water, it is questionable whether Paul is speaking of the ritual of water baptism here.

James Dunn says *baptism into Christ Jesus* is a metaphor.

> It is drawn from baptism, but does not itself describe baptism, or contain within itself the thought of the water-rite, any more than did the synonymous metaphors of putting on Christ (Gal. 3:27) and being drenched with the Spirit (1 Cor. 12:13).[1212]

It is through this baptism with the Spirit that we are added to the body of Christ (1 Cor 12:13; Gal 3:27). Water baptism is

---

[1211]Wesley, *Notes*, 566.

[1212]Dunn, *Baptism in the Holy Spirit*, 140.

an outward sign of the inward work of Spirit baptism. When Paul states in Ephesians 4:5 that there is one baptism, it is best to understand that water baptism and Spirit baptism are two parts of that one baptism.

Robert Tuttle explained:

> The new birth is the side of conversion that denotes a turning to righteousness — what God does in us by the Holy Spirit. It is the beginning of an imparted righteousness or that which is realized in us through the power of the Holy Spirit — a real change. In most instances Wesley would have associated the outset of this transformation into the likeness of Jesus Christ with the "baptism of the Holy Spirit."[1213]

The Fallacy of Teaching Two Baptisms

It has been claimed that there are two baptisms; that the Holy Spirit baptizes believers into the body of Christ, and that subsequent to the new birth Christ baptizes believers with the Holy Spirit. However, according to Ephesians 4:5 there is only one baptism.

Theologically, it is absurd to divide up the Trinity and teach that the Holy Spirit baptizes every believer into Christ at the new birth but that Christ has not baptized every believer with the Spirit at that time. If there is a baptism by the Son and a baptism by the Spirit, why not also a baptism by the Father?

Christ is always the baptizer. He baptizes *with* the Spirit *into* the body of Christ or *into* the realm of the Spirit and the church (the body of Christ). By making the baptism with the Holy Spirit an experience subsequent to entrance into the kingdom of God, the modern holiness movement has obscured the significance of water baptism. Water baptism and Spirit baptism are two halves

---

[1213]Tuttle, *Sanctity without Starch*, 104.

of one act or the one baptism. That one act or baptism is entrance into the kingdom of God. Baptism consists of an inward effusion of the Holy Spirit, outwardly typified by the application of water as its emblem. Water baptism, properly understood, is an outward sign of this inward grace. This is one event, not two; it is an act of initiation which occurs at the time of regeneration.[1214]

5. Initial Sanctification

Initial sanctification begins at the new birth. Wesley declared that "none can be holy except he be born again."[1215] But his statement also implies that those who are born again are holy.

Wesley believed the new birth to be an entire change of our inmost nature from the image of the devil (in which we were born) to the image of God, a change from the love of the creature to the love of the Creator.[1216] "At the same time that we are justified, yea, in that very moment, sanctification begins."[1217] James Bartlet wrote,

Thus sanctification begins subjectively as faith (see Acts 26:18), or trustful self abandonment to God's revealed will, and ends as love. Attitudes pass into character, the soul becoming assimilated to its object, the God to whom it is consecrated. This means that Justification, which involves regeneration, is implicit Sanctification; and actual Sanctification means the

---

[1214]Reasoner, *Holy Living*, 1:277-286; Oden, *Life in the Spirit*, 181-182.

[1215]Wesley, "The New Birth," Sermon #45, 3.2.

[1216]Wesley, *Journal*, 13 Sept 1739.

[1217]Wesley, "Scripture Way of Salvation," Sermon #43, 1.4.

subjective attitude of the justified becomes explicit in moral life.[1218]

According to 1 Corinthians 6:9-11, those in the Corinthian congregation who were justified were also washed and sanctified to the extent that they were set apart from the outward expression of sin. This same deliverance from sin is taught in 1 Thessalonians 4:3.

In the NT every Christian is a *saint* or holy one. The process of being made holy begins upon receiving the Holy Spirit in regeneration. At the new birth we are cleansed from acquired depravity (Titus 3:5; 1 Cor 6:11). This is initial sanctification. While inherited depravity or original sin remains, it no longer controls. It remains, but does not reign. Wesley explained, "Certainly before the root of sin is taken away, believers may live above the power of it."[1219]

Saint or *holy one* is the primary NT term for a Christian and is used as such over sixty times. The NT, however, uses the term *saints* or *holy ones* (*hagioi*) to refer to believers not yet entirely sanctified (for example, see 1 Cor 1:2 and Eph 4:12). Five of Paul's letters are addressed to the saints or *holy ones* (*hagioi*) at a particular church.[1220] They have already been separated to God as his possession (1 Cor 6:18-19), separated from the common or ordinary, and separated from all that is sinful (1 Pet 1:14-16; 2 Pet 1:4; 1 John 3:9).

Yet while they are initially sanctified, Paul urges them on to entire sanctification. But he acknowledges that they are already holy. "Clearly, the term 'saint' is used in Scripture to refer to the believer and 'sinner' is used in reference to the unbeliever." The NT uses terms such as believer, saint, disciple, and brother to identify the Christian, but it never uses *sinner*. "Though believers can still sin, the New Testament uses the term 'sinners' only of

---

[1218]Bartlet, "Sanctification" 4:394.

[1219]Wesley, *Letter* to Hester Ann Roe-Rogers, 3 May 1776.

[1220]1 Cor 1:2, 2 Cor 1:1, Eph 1:1, Phil 1:1, Col 1:2.

unbelievers."[1221] In thirty-eight NT passages where the Christian is described, they are never referred to as *sinners*. The only possible exception might be 1 Timothy 1:15-16 where Paul describes himself twice as a sinner. But the question is whether that is his present state or his previous identity. Verse 13 seems to settle the question, that Paul was recalling his previous state.

While all true Christians are holy, according to 2 Corinthians 7:1 that holiness may be perfected. The tension between the indicative mood and the imperative mood is seen in comparing Ephesians 4:27 and Colossians 3:9. The Colossians passage indicates that the readers at Colossae had put off the old life, while the imperative in the Ephesian passage commands the readers at Ephesus to put off their old life. Thus, Paul is teaching that while believers have already put off the old life, they must continue to do so.[1222]

Wesley preached, "When we are born again, then our sanctification, our inward and outward holiness, begins. And thenceforward we are gradually to 'grow up in him who is our head.'"[1223] This phrase *inward and outward holiness* implies not only an inward cleansing but an outward righteousness.

Where the Bible speaks of *sanctification*, it is initial sanctification unless qualified by an adjective such as *entire* or *wholly*.[1224] Those who are born again are holy because they have

---

[1221]Anderson and Saucy, *The Common Made Holy*, 42.

[1222]Wesley, "Deceitfulness of the Human Heart," Sermon #128, 2:5.

[1223]Wesley, "The New Birth," Sermon #45, 4.3. According to Sangster, Wesley taught that justification was the first stage of sanctification [*Pure in Heart*, 186]. See also Cox, *Perfection*, 97.

[1224]Wesley, *BE Works*, 10:195; 13:160; Steele, *Love Enthroned*, 9; Wilcox, *Profiles in Wesleyan Theology*, 2:236. Incredibly, Laurence Wood has it exactly backwards, "It was normal for Wesley and his preachers to mean full sanctification when they simply used the term sanctification. If they were denoting initial sanctification, they usually

received the Holy Spirit. The Holy Spirit delivers them from sinful habits. They walk in the Spirit and have assurance that they have been adopted into the family of God. They manifest the fruit of the Spirit in their lives and are used by God to lead sinners to Christ.

We are free from sin and the wrath of God. We are free from the Mosaic law. We are free from the bondage of extrabiblical legalism, and we must not allow ourselves to be burdened by the yoke of human rules (Gal 5:1). We live in the freedom of the Spirit.

Participation in the divine nature produces victory over sin. God's seed remains in us enabling us not to sin (1 John 3:9; 1 Pet 1:23). This is Peter's primary emphasis because of the clause which follows. The result of partaking of the divine nature is that we escape the corruption in the world caused by corrupt desires (2 Pet 1:4).

The change of prepositions in 1 Peter 1:23 from *ek* to *dia* indicates that the Word itself is not the seed, but rather the means by which the new life is mediated. We are saved *through means of* the Word. According to Romans 10:17 faith comes by hearing the Word. Yet the Word alone does not save us. Rather it tells us how to be saved. We have been born again by incorruptible seed. This *spora* is synonymous with the *sperma* in 1 John 3:9 and is a reference to the nature of God implanted by the Holy Spirit.

When do we escape this corruption? Some theologies say only at death, but the aorist participle in 2 Peter 1:4 puts that deliverance in the past. According to 2 Peter 2:20 we escaped the corruption of this world by knowing our Lord and Savior Jesus Christ. Therefore, the new birth enables us to live a victorious life, in contrast to the defeated life described in Romans 7. Second Corinthians 5:17 teaches deliverance from sin. We die to the old life. We are transferred from one kingdom to another (Col 1:13).

---

spoke of justifying faith" [Wood, *Meaning of Pentecost*, 288].

"No one who is born of God will continue to sin, because God's seed remains in him; he cannot go on sinning, because he has been born of God" (1 John 3:9). According to Nathan Bangs, the believer might turn away from the holy commandment as easily as Eve and Adam did, but he cannot sin so long as the seed remains in him as a living, active principle and so long as his heavenly Father purges him that he might bring forth more fruit.[1225] Thus, grace is not only exhibited in the forgiveness of sin, but grace is power over sin.[1226]

The Scriptures do not speak of the regenerate as *carnal*. While popular teaching defines a carnal Christian as a Christian who has not grown up yet, the terms *carnal* and *Christian* are mutually exclusive. One is either *carnal* or a *Christian*.

True Christians are not in the flesh (*sarx*), but in the Spirit (Rom 8:9). Those who are carnal (*sarx*) cannot please God (Rom 8:8), but the regenerate please God because they have their mind set on what the Spirit desires (Rom 8:5). Therefore, the regenerate are not carnal.

To be *in the flesh* is to be unregenerate. Wesley distinguished between being *controlled* by the carnal mind and having the carnal mind *remaining*.

According to 1 Corinthians 2:14-15 there are two spiritual classes: the natural man and the spiritual man. The men Paul addressed in 1 Corinthians 3:1 were not spiritual. Anthony Hoekema wrote that there is no biblical basis for the distinction between *carnal* and *spiritual* Christians. The Bible never speaks of a third class of people called "carnal Christians."[1227] This is clearly articulated by James R. Graham.

> Some say that there are three classes of men: the natural man, the carnal man, and the spiritual man. The natural

---

[1225]Bangs, *Necessity, Nature, and Fruits*, 109-110.

[1226]Bunting, *Justification by Faith*, 20.

[1227]Hoekema, *Five Views on Sanctification*, 189.

man is, of course, the unsaved child of the world. The carnal man is a saved man who, however, still walks in the flesh. The spiritual man is the higher quality of saved man, who walks in the Spirit and in the course of obedience. Much of this is directly contrary to the teaching of the eighth chapter of Romans ... the teaching, then of the three classes: natural man, carnal man, and spiritual man is deeply pernicious and is deluding many who are continuing in sin into thinking they are saved. . . . It is the worst kind of antinomianism and is part of the base alloy of fundamentalist instruction that is abroad today. . . . The Scripture knows of two places—heaven and hell; two beings—God and Satan; two ways—the narrow way that leadeth to life and the broad that leadeth to destruction; two principles of walk—the Spirit principle and the flesh principle.[1228]

When the new birth is reduced to a decision, to the result of a human action, or to a religious ceremony — nothing supernatural occurs. While there must be a human response to the gospel call, enabled by preliminary grace, salvation is the plan of God, provided by Jesus Christ, and administered through the Holy Spirit. Too often, the work and ministry of the Holy Spirit is relegated to a second blessing *after* salvation, which is optional according to some theological systems.

6. Adoption

In Romans 8:15 the Holy Spirit is termed the "Spirit of adoption." J. I. Packer wrote that adoption was the highest privilege that the gospel offers, even higher than justification, because of the richer relationship with God that it involves. Thus, Packer said that the NT could be summed up as teaching "adoption

---

[1228]Graham, "Are There Carnal Christians?" 158-164.

through propitiation."[1229] While Wesleyan-Arminians would say that Christian perfection is the highest privilege the gospel offers, we still affirm the blessing of adoption. According to Watson,

> Adoption, then, is that act by which we who were alienated, and enemies, and disinherited, are made the sons of God, and heirs of his eternal glory.[1230]

Adoption is that work of the Spirit by which we are received into the family of God. Adoption is a legal means by which a child not of the family can be taken into the family with full rights and privileges of that relationship. We who were created by God were disinherited by sin and had become aliens and outcasts. Yet through faith in Christ we are received into the family of God and given the privileges of sonship (Rom 8:15,17,23; Gal 4:5-7). We are no longer aliens, outcasts, or disenfranchised.

By faith we enter into a covenant relationship with God and he adopts us. Romans 4:16-18, 9:7-8 teaches that by faith we have become the seed of Abraham. Romans 2:28-29 says that we have become Jews by spiritual circumcision. Romans 10:12-13 teaches that there is no difference between Jew and gentile — salvation is for all. Romans 11:17 teaches that we have been grafted into the salvation tree.

The Father-son relationship is not described in the OT. John writes, "Now we are the sons of God" (1 John 3:2). Rarely did anyone address God as father. Jesus scandalized his hearers by using this as his regular address. *Abba* is a term of intimacy — dear father.[1231]

Jewish slaves were never allowed to address their master as *father*. Muslims object to calling God our father, considering it

---

[1229]Packer, *Knowing God*, 186-194.

[1230]Watson, *Theological Institutes*, 2:269.

[1231]Pope, *Compendium*, 3:16-20.

blasphemy to say *my father*. They also object to Jesus being called the "Son of God." They insist that God has no children and call themselves "servants of God."[1232]

According to Romans 5:5, however, the Holy Spirit pours the love of God into our hearts. This Spirit of adoption causes us to cry, Abba, Father. *Abba* is the Aramaic word for *father*. It is followed by the Greek word *pater*. No matter what language we speak, we have the same Father if we have faith in his Son.

Paul alone uses the analogy of adoption. However, John 1:12 explains that those who receive Christ through saving faith are given the authority or right to become children of God. Those who are adopted into God's family have been given freedom from bondage. "So if the Son sets you free, you will be free indeed" (John 8:36).

We are also given the advantages of election. Israel was chosen, thus they were adopted (Rom 9:4). "In Christianity the election is still synonymous with adoption, but it is personal and not national." Pope then clarified that the elect are foreknown corporately, "even as they are one by one gathered out of the world into the Divine household through their obedience to the evangelical call."[1233]

We are also given the constant guidance of the Holy Spirit. "Those who are led by the Spirit of God are sons of God" (Rom 8:14). And we are given the earnest of inheritance. If we are children, then we are heirs (Rom 8:17). Our inheritance is the privilege of the covenant. We are predestined to be conformed to the image of his Son (Rom 8:29). "Now we are the children of God, and what we will be has not yet been made known" (1 John 3:2). "The inheritance of Christians is in its deepest meaning *reserved in heaven*" (1 Pet 1:4). Thus, we who are adopted await the redemption of our bodies (Rom 8:23).

[1232]Hansen, "Son and the Crescent," 19-23.

[1233]Pope, *Compendium*, 3:17-18.

7. The Authority of the Believer

The centurion in Matthew 8:8-9 understood the principle of authority because he was a man *under* authority (v 9). Then he proceeds to describe his authority. Those under him do what he says. He has authority *over* a hundred men. He realizes that he has authority *over* a realm only so long as he is *under* authority.

God gives us authority now to prepare us to reign with him later. Sitting with Christ is our spiritual position to be realized by faith. John MacMillan explained:

> Christ's seat is at the right hand of God. His people, therefore, occupy "with him" the same August position. This honor is not to a chosen few, but is the portion of all those who share the resurrection of the Son of God. It is the birthright of every true believer, of every born-again child of God.[1234]

This authority includes

• The Authority to Cast Out Demons
• Freedom from sin
• The Authority to Resist Satan
• The Church has Authority to Discipline its Own
• The Authority to Bind and Loose
• The Authority to Expose Deception
• The Authority to Declare the Gospel

8. The Witness of the Spirit

Justifying faith implies not only a divine evidence or conviction that "God was in Christ, reconciling the world unto himself," but a sure trust and confidence

---

[1234]MacMillan, *Authority of the Believer*, 13-14.

that Christ died for *my* sins, that he loved *me* and gave himself for *me*.[1235]

This knowledge comes from an external source, the Holy Spirit, who brings an inner confidence. Confidence should be the default position of a true Christian. Four times in 1 John the Greek word *parrhesia* occurs.[1236] This word describes boldness, confidence, and the absence of fear.

A doctor working in a mental hospital in Tennessee said, "Half of my patients could go home in a week if they knew they were forgiven."[1237] If we confess our sins, he is faithful and just and will forgive us our sins (1 John 1:9). We can only confess *known* sin. It is a contradiction to confess unknown sin — except theoretically. Therefore, I understand 1 John 1:9 to imply that if we will acknowledge and confess known sin, the intercession of Christ covers all of those unknown sins as an unconditional benefit of the atonement.

Some passages of Scripture attribute the enlightenment of the believer to an act of God the Father (Matt 16:16). As a result of God's illumination, the Christian possesses the Word of God in himself (1 John 1:10, 2:14). Another group of passages attributes enlightenment to the Son (Matt 11:27). Some passages refer to a great inward saving operation of the Holy Spirit (John 3:1-16). A number of passages attribute the certainty of Christian consciousness to the inward action of the Holy Spirit (Col 2:2; 1 Thess 1:5; 2 Thess 2:13). Our consciousness of salvation is the result of the action of the Holy Spirit. In Galatians 4:6 it is the Spirit who cries *Father*, and in Romans 8:15-16 it is the believer who cries *Father*. In both instances the participle or verb *cry* is in the present tense implying that this action is continuous.

[1235]Wesley, "Justification by Faith," Sermon #5, 4.2.

[1236]1 John 2:28, 3:21, 4:17, 5:14.

[1237]Seamands, *Healing Grace*, 7.

Romans 8:16 uses the compound verb *summartureo*. The normal verb for *testify* has the prefix *sun*, which means *with*. Ramm explained, "There are not two cries but one cry. They are like two forks of the same pitch which vibrate sympathetically and harmoniously together. We *both* cry; we *both* cry *Father* — it is the same cry, the same content, to the same God."

Some passages show the strong connection between the Holy Spirit and the Word of truth (John 6:63,14:17). Some passages show an interesting reversal of the relationship between the Word and the Spirit by speaking of a test for spirits by the Word (1 Cor 12:3; 1 John 4:1-6).[1238]

There is no uniform procedure by which the Spirit bears his witness, but the result is *plerophoria* or spiritual certainty. Noah and Abraham had such assurance, as well as pagans who heard and believed without the Scriptures.[1239]

The verb *plerophoreo* is made up of two words: *full* and *to carry*. It means to be fully assured. As a noun this word occurs in Colossians 2:2, 4:12; 1 Thessalonians 1:5; Hebrews 6:11,10:22. A second word for assurance is used more frequently, *parrhesia*. It describes confidence or boldness. "The full assurance of faith relates to present pardon; the full measure of hope, to future glory."[1240]

Wesley taught, "The plerophory (or full assurance) of faith is such a divine testimony, that we are reconciled to God, as excludes all doubt and fear concerning it."[1241] Pope explained that at every level of Christian privilege the Holy Spirit imparts to the believer the full assurance of his participation. At every level the same Spirit bestows the privileges on everyone who complies with his conditions. "In other words, we preach the

---

[1238]Ramm, *Witness of the Spirit*, 42-61.

[1239]Ramm, *Witness of the Spirit*, 65, 76, 85.

[1240]Yates, *Doctrine of Assurance*, 128-132.

[1241]Wesley, *Letter* to Elizabeth Ritchie, 6 Oct 1778; see also *Letter* to Hester Ann Roe, 10 April 1781.

testimony of the Holy Ghost in the heart of the believer as the common prerogative; and further, the attainableness in this life of a state of entire sanctification and acceptableness in the sight of God."

This witness of the Spirit is not based on sacramentalism, priestly absolution, or mysticism which is independent of the means of grace.[1242] Calvinism, as well as fundamentalism, has tended to emphasize this assurance as attestation of scriptural reliability more than personal assurance of adoption. Without discounting the *testimonium spiritus sancti* regarding the Scriptures, the same Spirit also testifies regarding our personal forgiveness and adoption. Pope explained that the blessing of this assurance is the gift of the Holy Spirit. It is his office to bear his witness *to* our conscience concerning justification. It is also his office to bear his witness *with* our spirit concerning adoption. He also bears his witness *in* our soul concerning sanctification. This assurance produces faith for the present, hope for the future, and understanding as the basis for confidence.[1243] According to Wesley,

> The testimony of the Spirit is an inward impression on the soul, whereby the Spirit of God directly "witnesses to my spirit that I am a child of God"; that Jesus Christ hath loved me, and given himself for me; that all my sins are blotted, out, and I, even I, am reconciled to God.[1244]

Wesley taught,

> The *manner* how the divine testimony is manifested to the heart, I do not take upon me to explain. "Such

---

[1242]Pope, *Peculiarities of Methodism*, 11-13.

[1243]Pope, *Compendium*, 3:115-116.

[1244]Wesley, "Witness of the Spirit, I," Sermon #10, 1.7.

knowledge is too wonderful and excellent for me; I cannot attain unto it." "The wind bloweth, and I hear the sound thereof;" but I cannot "tell how it cometh, or whither it goeth." As no one knoweth the things of a man, save the spirit of a man that is in him; so the *manner* of the things of God knoweth no one, save the Spirit of God. But the fact we know; namely, that the Spirit of God does give a believer such a testimony of his adoption that while it is present to the soul he can no more doubt the reality of his sonship than he can doubt of the shining of the sun while he stands in the full blaze of his beams.[1245]

Thus, Methodism rejected the *naked faith* which Phoebe Palmer later advocated. For Palmer, no confirmatory feeling was necessary. A person was saved or sanctified by a deliberate act of the will. Any assurance was based on a logical inference. Essentially, this is faith in faith.

While Palmer urged a leap of faith, that for Wesley would amount to claiming something one did not really know.[1246] Wesley required evidence, but Palmer taught that only *bare faith* was necessary. David Bebbington explained, "For Wesley the empiricist, evidence was needed in experience; for Phoebe Palmer, in keeping with Romantic currents of thought, bare faith was all that was required. A new era had dawned in holiness teaching."[1247]

In contrast, Samuel Wesley admonished his son, John, "The inward witness, son, the inward witness, that is the proof; the strongest proof of Christianity."[1248]

[1245]Wesley, "Witness of the Spirit, I," Sermon #10, 1.12.

[1246]Raser, *Phoebe Palmer*, 263-276.

[1247]Bebbington, *Dominance of Evangelicalism*, 203.

[1248]Wesley, *Letter* to John Smith, 22 March 1748, ¶ 6.

Many who cling to the teaching of unconditional security have no confidence that they were ever accepted by God. Watson said, "Some persons confound this assurance of present acceptance with an assurance of final salvation. The one is very distinct from the other. I find no authority for the last in the book of God."[1249]

The emphasis should be placed upon assurance of our present relationship, not presumption about unconditional security for the future. Romans 8:31-39 promises security to the believer, but Romans 8:15-16 also promises assurance to the believer. Unless we have assurance that we are now born again, we should not presume on the eternal security of the believer.

The Conditional Security of the Believer

Romans 8:13 warns the believer that if he persists in living according to the sinful nature, he will die. Since this warning comes in the same chapter which declares that the believer is secure, the proper debate is whether security is conditional or unconditional.

"Once saved, always saved" or unconditional eternal security was not a doctrine that was taught by the ancient church, nor for that matter by any well-known theologian before John Calvin. While the first extensive discussion of the doctrine of the perseverance of the saints is found in Augustine's *Treatise on the Gift of Perseverance*, written around AD 429, Augustine believed it was possible to experience the justifying grace of God and yet not persevere to the end. Augustine did believe God's elect would certainly persevere to the end, but he denied that a person could know they were in the elect; and he also warned it was possible to be justified but not among the elect. Not until Calvin

---

[1249]Watson, *Sermons*, 2:349.

were unconditional election, permanent regeneration, and certitude of final perseverance all connected.[1250]

Wesleyan theology strongly upholds Christian assurance. Romans 8:16 describes a direct and present-tense witness of the Spirit which is the birthright of every believer. Yet this is assurance regarding a present condition, not of a past election nor a future perseverance. Perseverance is a command (Rom 11:22), not an unconditional promise. We must persevere in faith or be "cut off."

All of life is a probationary period. While it is possible to lose salvation, it is never necessary. The grace of God is adequate to keep us.

Above the doorway of the Pastor's College in London, Charles Spurgeon affixed the words, "Holding, I am held."[1251] These words reflect the tension between Jude 21, "keep yourself" and Jude 24, "who is able to keep you from falling."

All Scripture is inspired by God and is profitable for doctrine (2 Tim 3:16). Some Scriptures apparently teach unconditional eternal security; other Scriptures seem to deny that our security is unconditional. God has not contradicted himself. Our doctrine of assurance must take seriously both columns of texts listed below. Each passage should be studied within its context. We must believe everything stated in both columns. But we must construct a systematic theology that reconciles the conditions in the second column with the promises in the first column.

Both positions have a doctrine of assurance. The unconditional position teaches that once we are saved we can never lose salvation, but relies on a logical deduction from Scripture to assure us that we received that salvation.

The conditional position teaches that we have divine assurance through the Holy Spirit that we have been saved, but that we can be sure of salvation only as we continue to believe and be

---

[1250]Davis, "Perseverance of the Saints," 213-228.

[1251]Shank, *Life in the Son*, 282.

assured by the Spirit. Deliberate sin which remains unconfessed grieves the Holy Spirit, resulting in a loss of assurance and jeopardizing the salvation covenant.

Passages apparently teaching unconditional security

John 5:24 Whoever believes him who sent me has eternal life and will not be condemned; he has crossed over from death to life.

John 6:35-40 He who comes to me will never go hungry, and he who believes in me will never be thirsty. . . . All that the Father gives me will come to me, and whoever comes to me I will never drive away. . . . And this is the will of him who sent me, that I shall lose none of all that he has given me. . . . For my Father's will is that everyone who looks to the Son and believes in him shall have eternal life, and I will raise him up at the last day.

John 10:28-29 I give them eternal life and they shall never perish; no one can snatch them out of my hand. My Father, who has given them to me, is greater than all; no one can snatch them out of my Father's hand.

John 17:11-15 Protect them by the power of your name . . . While I was with them, I protected them and kept them

Passages apparently teaching conditional security

Ezek 18:24 If a righteous man turns from his righteousness and commits sin and does the same detestable things the wicked man does, will he live? None of the righteous things he has done will be remembered . . . he will die (see also v 26, 33:12-18).

John 8:31 If you hold to my teaching, you are really my disciples.

John 15:6 If anyone does not remain in me, he is like a branch that is . . . thrown into the fire and burned.

1 Cor 15:2 By this gospel you are saved, if you hold firmly to the word I preached to you. Otherwise, you have believed in vain.

2 Cor 13:5 Examine yourselves to see whether you are in the faith; test yourselves. Do you not realize that Christ Jesus is in you - unless, of course, you fail the test?

Gal 5:4 You have fallen away from grace.

safe by that name you gave me. None has been lost except the one doomed to destruction so that Scripture would be fulfilled. . . . Protect them from the evil one.

Rom 5:8-9 Since we have now been justified by his blood, how much more shall we be saved from God's wrath through him.

Rom 8:38-39 Neither death nor life, neither angels nor demons, neither the present nor the future, nor any powers, neither height nor depth, nor anything else in all creation, will be able to separate us from the love of God that is in Christ Jesus our Lord.

Rom 11:29 God's gifts and his call are irrevocable.

1 Cor 1:8-9 He will keep you strong to the end, so that you will be blameless on the day of our Lord Jesus Christ. God, who has called you into fellowship with his Son Jesus Christ our Lord, is faithful.

Eph 1:13 Having believed, you were marked in him with a seal, the promised Holy Spirit, who is a deposit guaranteeing our inheritance until the redemption of those who are God's possession.

Col 1:23 If you continue in your faith, established and firm, not moved from the hope held out in the gospel; **2:19** He has lost connection with the Head.

1 Tim 4:1 Some will abandon the faith, **vv 15-16** Be diligent . . . watch your life and doctrine closely. Persevere in them, because if you do, you will save both yourself and your hearers.

2 Tim 2:12 If we endure we will also reign with him; **v 18** They destroy the faith of some.

Heb 6:4-6 It is impossible for those who have once been enlightened, who have tasted the heavenly gift, who have shared in the Holy Spirit, who have tasted the goodness of the word of God and the powers of the coming age, if they fall away, to be brought back to repentance while to their loss they are cruci-fying the Son of God all over again.

Heb 10:26-29 If we deliberately keep on sinning after we have received the knowledge of the truth, no sacrifice for sins is left, but only a fearful expectation of judgment and of raging fire that

Eph 4:30 The Holy Spirit of God, with whom you were sealed for the day of redemption.

Phil 1:6 Being confident of this, that he who began a good work in you will carry it on to completion until the day of Christ Jesus.

2 Thess 3:3-4 The Lord is faithful and he will strengthen and protect you from the evil one.

1 Pet 1:3-5 He has given us . . . an inheritance that can never perish, spoil or fade - kept in heaven for you who through faith are shielded by God's power until the coming of the salvation that is ready to be revealed in the last time.

Jude 1 To those who have been called, who are loved by God the Father and kept by Jesus Christ. **v 24** To him who is able to keep you from falling and to present you before his glorious presence without fault and with great joy.

will consume the enemies of God.

Heb 12:15 See to it that no one misses the grace of God.

Jas 5:19-20 If one of you should wander from the truth and someone should bring him back, remember this: Whoever turns a sinner from the error of his way will save him from death and cover over a multitude of sins.

2 Pet 1:10-11 Be all the more eager to make your calling and election sure. For if you do these things, you will never fall.

2 Pet 2:20-22 If they have escaped the corruption of the world by knowing our Lord and Savior Jesus Christ and are again entangled in it and overcome, they are worse off at the end than they were at the beginning. It would have been better for them not to have known the way of righteousness, than to have known it and then to turn their backs on the sacred command that was passed on to them.

Rev 2:5, 7 You have forsaken your first love. . . . If you do not repent, I will come to you and remove your lampstand. **v 11** He who overcomes will not be hurt at all by the second death. **3:5** He who overcomes . . . I will never blot out his name from the book of life.

Four Views of the Plan of Salvation

There are four views on salvation. These theological positions are based on two issues: original sin and the resulting human depravity. The first question is how extensively humanity has been damaged by the fall. The second question relates to the relationship between divine sovereignty and human responsibility.

Modernism denies the doctrine of original sin and sees salvation as monergistic, entirely the work of humanity. Thus, preliminary grace is the innate and undestroyed capacity of the soul for good — even a bias toward good. Early in the twentieth century, the emphasis in Methodism was shifting from radical conversion to a gradual nurturing process.[1252]

Historically, the terms for this position have been *Pelagianism* and *Socinianism*. The Third Ecumenical Council at Ephesus in AD 431 condemned Pelagianism as heresy. The optimism of psychologists such as Abraham Maslow and Carl Rogers reflect a Pelagian worldview.[1253] Robert Schuller also denied human depravity.[1254]

This humanism teaches that mankind is morally neutral, but has a *spark of goodness*. We can either choose salvation or we can reject it. Great emphasis is put upon the freedom of the will.

[1252]Sheldon, "Changes in Theology Among American Methodists," 50.

[1253]Oden, *Transforming Power of Grace,* 109.

[1254]Schuller, *Self-Esteem,* 67.

The moral example of Christ should inspire us to make the right choices, and we respond to the love exhibited by Christ on the cross.

Semi-Pelagianism, the second answer, accepts the doctrine of original sin, but believes that mankind inherently has the power to repent and believe independent of divine grace. Thus, there is a synergism in which God responds by forgiving and redeeming man. God has done his part. Now we have to do our part. We must exercise faith. We can choose salvation at any time. Tozer objected:

> The trouble is that the whole "Accept Christ" attitude is likely to be wrong. It shows Christ applying to us rather than us to Him. It makes Him stand hat-in-hand awaiting our verdict on Him, instead of our kneeling with troubled hearts awaiting His verdict on us.

Tozer concluded that it was not a matter of whether we have accepted Christ, but whether Christ has accepted us.[1255]

Wesley held that no cooperation with God is possible without grace.[1256] Grider reflects this understanding when he declares that salvation is not an act of human will. He cautioned the Arminian-Wesleyan evangelist not to tell a congregation, "You do your part and God will do His part." He also argues against the promise that "God will meet you halfway." Grider explains, "We cannot initiate our own salvation. . . . God must come all the way to where we are and initiate in us our 'first faint desire' to turn to Christ."[1257]

It is possible to affirm total depravity in theory and reject it in practice. Preliminary grace must not be understood as universal and continual. God's Spirit will not always strive with us

---

[1255]Tozer, *That Incredible Christian*, 18.

[1256]Oden, *John Wesley's Teachings*, 2:180.

[1257]Grider, *Wesleyan-Holiness Theology*, 246-247.

(Gen 6:3). Wesley said any man may be saved if he will, though not when he will.[1258]

Some modern descriptions of preliminary grace seem to be describing a *spark of goodness* within every person or human personality. Oden explained that preparatory grace is sometimes misunderstood in a Pelagian sense of natural ability.[1259]

Both Arminius and Wesley held that mankind is totally unable to do anything to save himself. Wesley explained that if original sin is denied, then either death is not the wages of sin or there is punishment without guilt. If we are not totally depraved, then mankind commits sin without that choice stemming from a sinful nature. Thus, the fruit grows without a root. If we are not ruined by the first Adam, neither are we saved by the second. If the sin of Adam was not imputed to us, neither is the righteousness of Christ. Infants would have no need of Christ to save them.

> Finally, a denial of original sin contradicts the main design of the gospel, which is to humble vain man, and to ascribe to God's *free grace*, not man's *free will*, the whole of his salvation. Nor indeed can we let this doctrine go without giving up at the same time the greatest part, if not all, of the essential articles of the Christian faith.[1260]

The third position is the **semi-Augustinian** position. This position is the orthodox Wesleyan-Arminian position. God must initiate the process through preliminary grace. Chris Bounds explained,

---

[1258]Wesley, *Letter* to Isaac Andrews, 4 Jan 1784.

[1259]Oden, *John Wesley's Theology*, 2:152; see also Pope, *Compendium*, 2:386.

[1260]Wesley, *BE Works*, 12:441-442.

As such, only in moments when the Holy Spirit is awakening people from their spiritual slumber, can they be awakened; only in moments in which the Spirit brings repentance, can people repent; and only when the Spirit creates and *enables saving faith* in people can they be converted.

Therefore, people cannot choose the "day or the hour" in which they are saved. The experience of new birth, conversion, can only happen in the moments in which God gives grace capable of creating saving faith.[1261]

The Plan of Salvation According to Calvinism

This is the fourth option and the polar opposite from Pelagianism. In this monergistic view, mankind is unable to do anything to save himself. Therefore, God must do it all. Yet Berkhof acknowledged that man cooperates in conversion. He observed that the NT represents conversion as a deed of man twenty-six times and speaks of it only two or three times as an act of God. After reminding us that "this activity of man always results from a previous work of God in man" (which is what Arminians mean by preliminary grace), he explained that man is active in conversion.[1262]

As a Calvinist, Berhkof is able to maintain his monergistic position by separating regeneration from conversion. Thus, he understood regeneration as a sovereign act of God in which the elect are first brought to spiritual life through an "effectual calling," and then they manifest evidence of that regeneration through repentance and faith. The result is justification. Biblically, however, regeneration is not separate from conversion. It is one aspect of conversion.

[1261]Bounds, "How Are People Saved?" 9.

[1262]Berkhof, *Systematic Theology*, 490-491.

This convoluted order of salvation is the result of the Calvinistic misunderstanding of the nature of freedom of choice. Their "freedom" is compatible with their determinism. Since they believe mankind does not have the ability, naturally or supernaturally, to choose anything other than sin, God must first save us while we are totally passive. Then *after* we are saved, we then participate in the process of salvation. But preliminary grace enables us to respond and cooperate. We need not substitute regeneration for preliminary grace.

Calvinism begins with total depravity and then constructs a logical sequence which they call an unbroken chain. Since they teach a limited or particular atonement, only those predestined to salvation will be called.

There is no significant theological distinction between *predestination* and *election*, except that *predestination* implies a time element by its prefix. Prior to Augustine the consensus within the Christian church was that election and predestination were conditional. Modern Calvinism cannot trace its doctrine back any further than the later Augustinian teachings in the fifth century.

From Romans 9:11 Calvinists conclude that God chooses some to salvation and that his election is unconditional. Thus, for them salvation is monergistic. Bloesch wrote, "I cannot subscribe to the radical monergism of R. C. Sproul, who sees regeneration clearly before the advent of faith or even the beginnings of seeking for faith."[1263]

The most crucial passage Calvinism relies upon in support of these conclusions is Romans 9. Their assumption is that Paul is answering the question, "Has the word of God failed if most of the Jews are excluded?" But the real question is, "Has the word of God failed if those Jews who seek salvation *by keeping the law, not by faith*, are rejected?"[1264] And Paul's answer is that

---

[1263]Bloesch, *The Holy Spirit*, 388-389.

[1264]Arminius, *Works*, 3:488.

both Jew and Gentile are justified by faith (Rom 9:30-32). Thus, Paul is teaching that election is conditional, and that condition is faith. If Israel's election was unconditional, Paul would not write in Romans 11:17-20 that they were cut off. Nor would Zechariah warn in 11:10-14 that God would revoke his covenant with Israel.

Calvinism sees the most complete order of salvation stated in Romans 8:29-30. If this is true, then man is completely passive. However, there is another order of salvation stated in Romans 10:9-15. If we adopt this order, salvation is completely a human endeavor. We must merge both orders with the result that God initiates and man is enabled to respond.

God in his foreknowledge knows that mankind will sin. God predestines the plan of salvation. Christ makes full atonement on the cross. The preacher is called, trained, and sent to proclaim the gospel. The message of the gospel is preached. Sinners hear the gospel. Sinners hear the gospel call, the drawing of the Holy Spirit. Through the work of the Spirit sinners are awakened, convicted; they are under preliminary grace. Sinners are enabled to repent and call on the name of the Lord. Sinners are enabled to believe on Christ. Sinners are justified. They are also regenerated. They receive the baptism of the Holy Spirit. They are initially sanctified. They are adopted into God's family. They receive assurance of their forgiveness and acceptance through the direct witness of the Holy Spirit. They confess with their mouth and through water baptism. As they trust and obey the Holy Spirit continues the progressive work of sanctification. They experience entire sanctification. They experience final sanctification or glorification.

The question is not "*who* are the objects of this predestination, but *what* they are predestined to?"[1265] In Ephesians 1:4 Paul

---

[1265]Cremer, *Lexicon*, 462.

also teaches a corporate election. God, motivated by love, has chosen that those who are in Christ should be holy.[1266]

The Plight of Those Who Never Heard

What about those who never heard the gospel? It is our responsibility to make sure that they *do* hear the gospel. The consciousness that there must be a higher power is not the equivalent for the good news that God loves us and has provided a substitute for our sin.

We cannot say how God will handle exceptional cases. However, Herbert Kane summarized the popular argument, "There is only one way to be saved and that is through faith in Christ; the heathen, having never heard of Christ, cannot exercise faith; consequently he is doomed to everlasting punishment for something quite beyond his capability."

Kane argued that this concept is based on a false assumption, that all men will be judged on the same basis — failing to believe the gospel. Kane argued that Romans 2 makes it plain that all men will not be judged on the same basis. Rather they will be judged according to the light they had. "No man will be judged by light he did not possess."[1267]

Thomas Oden wrote that "the New Testament was written primarily for those who have had a reasonable chance to hear the gospel. It does not often focus speculatively on what might be the possible destiny of those who never have had such an opportunity."[1268] In *The Transforming Power of Grace*, Oden declared the sufficiency of grace for those who have had no reasonable opportunity to hear the gospel and respond.[1269]

[1266]Oden, *Transforming Power of Grace,* 141-142.

[1267]Kane, *Understanding Christian Missions*, 134-137.

[1268]Oden, *Life in the Spirit*, 448-450.

[1269]Oden, *Transforming Power of Grace*, 78-79.

Those who reject Jesus Christ are damned, but those who have never heard the gospel may be accepted by God through the unconditional merits of Christ's atonement. A. Berkeley Mickelsen wrote that Romans 2:12-16 may shed some light upon the eternal destiny of those who have never heard the gospel. If God judges everyone according to the light they have, does this nullify the principle of salvation by faith? Mickelsen argued that faith is essential for those who obey conscience, law, or the gospel. "But how much richer and fuller is our knowledge of God as revealed through his Son!"[1270]

C. S. Lewis began *Mere Christianity* with the observation that the moral teachings of diverse cultures are remarkably similar. "Human beings, all over the earth, have this curious idea that they ought to behave a certain way, and cannot really get rid of it."[1271] He argued that God was behind this law of nature. God has preprogrammed us with a consciousness of himself.

Yet, Watson warned against reading too much into Romans 2:14-15.

> From this passage of St. Paul respecting the Gentiles, many erroneous conclusions have been drawn. Here it has been pretended we see the foundation of natural religion, and the sufficiency of unassisted reason to discover the existence of God, and to arrive at the knowledge of his will; "therefore there is a law of nature which is a true guide."[1272]

Romans 2:14-15 is sometimes also misused to teach multiple plans of salvation. Yet all who are saved are saved by grace. And grace is not limited only to those who have the revealed law or have heard the gospel.

[1270]Mickelsen, *Wycliffe Bible Commentary*, 1189.

[1271]Lewis, *Mere Christianity*, 17-39.

[1272]Watson, *Exposition*, 482.

Nor is this passage teaching salvation apart from Jesus Christ any more than it teaches the sufficiency of natural law. In Romans 2:16 Jesus Christ will be the judge on that final day. His standard of judgment will differ, but his verdict will be the same—all have sinned. But to ask, Will anyone be saved who has not consciously trusted in the name of Jesus Christ? is to ask a different question. We must reject the pluralist view which teaches salvation is possible through all religions. But does that force us to conclude that no one can be saved apart from explicit faith in Jesus Christ? Some who answer *yes* have reduced saving faith to nothing more than a one-time decision for Christ, which amounts to little more than "saying the magic word," without requiring any subsequent obedience of faith which requires walking in light.

The Athanasian Creed closes with the declaration that what has been stated is the catholic faith, and unless a man believe it faithfully, he cannot be saved. Watson wrote, however, that the creed addressed only those to whom the evidence of the gospel had been fully set forth. "The state and lot of the Heathen world are quite out of the question." It does not apply to those who "sit in darkness and the shadow of death."[1273]

What, then, is the plight of those who never heard the gospel? Romans 2 reveals that all mankind is both under law and under grace. But while all mankind is under grace, that grace has not necessarily led all men to salvation. All salvation comes through Christ. There are not multiple avenues of salvation. Yet we are saved by grace, not through knowledge. Therefore, even where Christ is not known, it is he who has made grace possible. God will justify anyone who will appropriate the available grace and, through faith, obey God's law, to the extent it has been revealed to him. Thus, all salvation is through Christ, and all who are damned have no one to blame but themselves.

[1273]Watson, *Dictionary*, 259-260.

CHAPTER ELEVEN
The Doctrine of Sanctification

Holy living begins with the baptism with the Holy Spirit when we are regenerated. Initial sanctification results from imparted righteousness. After we are born again, sin remains within us but it no longer controls us. The bondage to sinful practice has been broken, and possibility exists within divine grace for us to be purified from the sinful nature.

Obedient believers will become increasingly convicted of the nature of sin which still remains. As they walk in the Spirit, they will be led to a full cleansing from the inner nature of sin and filled with a holy love toward God and their neighbor.

There is no stopping point required in Scripture. The babe in Christ is urged to realize his full stature. This optimism of grace means that we are always capable of becoming more like Christ. It is possible to love God with our whole heart and to love our neighbor as we love ourselves. This entire sanctification implies neither the end of growth or progress, nor absolute perfection. It is a relative perfection in which God imparts holiness and imputes perfection to those who are governed by and who continue to develop in his holy love. Whether in a single crisis moment, or through more gentle steps over a longer period of time, all believers are exhorted to press forward and not to stop short of the fullness of this blessing.

So long as we are full of that love, it displaces everything which is contrary to its nature, and God imputes perfection to us. In an absolute sense, perfection is an attribute which God does not share. But in a relative sense, there is a Christian perfection in which the believer becomes all that God intended for him to become.

The Christian walk is a walk of faith. Our faith is based upon the Word of God. The promises of Scripture, the commands of Scripture, the examples of Scripture, and the prayers recorded in Scripture for the church all assure us that there is much more for us to realize now that our new life in Christ has begun. God is sovereign over sin and he is able to do much more than we can even imagine is possible.

As the new believer continues to walk in the light, he should expect every moment that God can make him all that God intended him to be. However, this state of grace does not come simply because we have said the magic words. Our progress is aborted whenever we resist the sanctifying operation of the Holy Spirit. This reality may necessitate frequent surrender and consecration to the perfect will of God.

We are not purified by an act of our will. We are cleansed from all sin through the sanctifying work of the Holy Spirit. One danger is that we are instructed that this sanctification will always be in process but never realized in this life. The opposite danger is that we imagine that our sinful nature is uprooted once-for-all and we are never troubled with it again after that second crisis. We are not delivered from our humanity in this life. Nor are we delivered from all of the shortcomings which accompany humanity. However, sin is not a basic component of human nature as God created us. Today it is a basic component of humanity without enabling grace. Grace can expel sin. Our complete sanctification is a moment-by-moment reality based upon a moment-by-moment faith.

This wonderful privilege has often been diminished by extra-biblical standards which assume that we make ourselves holy through self-denial, through conformity to a subculture within the church, resulting in an attitude of superiority to *average* Christians. The opposite danger is that we become lawless and disregard the plain commands of Scripture. We must distinguish between a separation from sinful practices and withdrawing from the world —even other believers. God wants us to be conduits of his holy love to a lost world with nothing blocking that flow.

Scriptural Sanctification

The doctrine of sanctification is based on the doctrine of sin. Those who deny man's total depravity cannot be right about sanctification. In the new birth the bondage of sin is broken. Sin remains, but does not reign. Isaiah 53:5 promised that Christ would become the substitute for our transgressions and our iniquities. The Hebrew word for *transgressions* is *pesha*, describing outward, deliberate sin and rebellion. The word for *iniquities* is *avon*, describing inborn crookedness and perversion. David prayed for cleansing from secret faults and from presumptuous sins (Ps 19:12-13). Both the words of our mouth and the meditations of our heart need to be accepted by God (Ps 19:14). We need clean hands and a pure heart (Ps 24:4).

Romans 6:6 teaches that the old life is crucified and also that the body of sin may be destroyed or abolished. This remaining nature of sin is described in Galatians 5:16-18. The Greek verb in Romans 6:6, *katargeo*, means to put away, to render inoperative, inactive, or powerless. It is also used in 1 Corinthians 13:11 where we are to put childish ways behind us.

All theological systems teach a doctrine of sanctification, but they disagree as to how much progress can be made. It has been reduced to a philosophy. For others it is a mystical or charismatic experience. In other cases it is a doctrinal proposition to be affirmed. It has also been presented as an ascetic state we arrive at through extra-biblical rules. It has also been taught as a condition that occurs when we belong to a corporate organization. In still other emphases, it amounts to a private pietism.

Wesleyanism is pessimistic about man's nature, but optimistic about God's grace. "He who calls us is faithful and will do it" (1 Thess 5:24). God can save completely or to the uttermost (Heb 7:25). This phrase, *eis to panteles* means salvation is to the farthest extent, to the greatest degree, to the most distant point. Full salvation is not only freedom from the guilt, the bondage, and the power of sin, but cleansing from the pollution and nature of sin and ultimately deliverance from the very presence of sin.

How much of this complete salvation may be experienced in this life? "Now to him who is able to do immeasurably more than all we ask or imagine, according to his power that is at work with us" (Eph 3:20). "No limit is set on Christian privilege."[1274] Sangster argued that "no man has a right to put a limit on what the grace of God can do."[1275] There is more grace available in this life than most theological systems allow. If God is sovereign, there is no limit to the grace he can extend. Outler explained, "For Wesley, the doctrine of perfection was yet another way of celebrating the *sovereignty* of grace!"[1276]

This sanctifying work of the Spirit occurs in all true believers, whether or not they embrace Wesleyan theology. While it is not necessary to adhere to a particular theological system to experience perfecting grace, it is the duty of the church to counsel, teach, and provide spiritual guidance for believers. The Wesleyan synthesis is the most adequate framework in which to diagnose spiritual needs, discern spiritual unbalance, and direct spiritual formation. Yet, we must concede some people are more spiritual than their theology, and the Holy Spirit works in all true Christians regardless of their theological bias. It should not be assumed that affirming the Wesleyan doctrine automatically produces spiritual maturity.

[1274]Platt, "Perfection," 9:728.

[1275]Sangster, "The Church's One Privation," 493-507.

[1276]Outler, *John Wesley*, 253.

Inadequate teachings on the holy life

In *Holy Living* (2012), I devoted almost five-hundred pages to an analysis of the doctrine of sanctification, attempting to trace the historical development by evaluating seventeen approaches.[1277] This section is a summary.

The humanistic view is that we perfect ourselves by choosing what is right. This ignores our depravity. The positive confession teaching counsels people to *just say it*. However, we are not made holy merely because we profess it, claim it, or confess it to be so. Early Methodism was quick to seek and slow to profess Christian perfection.

The biblical doctrine of a holy life has also been obscured by the teaching that a holy life is possible only after death or that holiness is possible at the hour of death. Death is our enemy (1 Cor 15:26), not our friend. We can serve God in holiness and righteousness "all our days" (Luke 1:75).

We can be preserved blameless until the coming of our Lord Jesus Christ (1 Thess 5:23). The preposition *en* can mean *at* or *until*. Warfield taught that entire sanctification is obtained *at* the second advent.[1278] But the return of Christ will not remove sin since he already put away sin at his first appearing.[1279] He will bring final sanctification or glorification at his second advent.

The promises and commands of Scripture imply that entire sanctification is possible before death and that the believer may be preserved in this condition culminating, not beginning with Christ's return.

It has been asserted that regeneration and entire sanctification occur simultaneously. Wesley refuted this view.

[1277]Reasoner, *Holy Living*, 305-792.

[1278]Warfield, *Studies in Perfectionism*, Abridged, 462-464.

[1279]Pope, *Compendium*, 3:51.

1) There is such a thing as *perfection*; for it is again and again mentioned in Scripture.
2) It is not so early as justification; for justified persons are to "go on to perfection."
3) It is not so late as death; for St. Paul spake of living men that were perfect.[1280]

It is widely taught that there is no deliverance from sin in this life. This is based on a dualistic view that anything physical is sinful, therefore the body is sinful and we will be sinful until we leave the body. Thus, any holiness, then, is positional or imputed. The obedience of Christ is imputed or reckoned to our account so that a person who is morally impure is accounted as holy. Our standing in Christ may be very different from our actual state.

Mysticism has emphasized perfection is attained through the loss of self-consciousness. The finite is absorbed by the infinite. How would you know if you had arrived at this state of perfection since you would have lost all self-consciousness?

Monasticism has been called the greatest organized pursuit of perfection in history.[1281] Monasticism emphasized holiness through withdrawal from the world and vows of poverty, chastity, and discipline. "Such regulations indeed have an appearance of wisdom, with their self-imposed worship, their false humility and their harsh treatment of the body, but they lack any value in restraining sensual indulgence" (Col 2:23; Gal 3:3). In contrast, Wesley taught a social holiness. "The Gospel of Christ knows of no religion, but social; no holiness but social holiness."[1282] He advised, "It is a blessed thing to have fellow travelers to the New

---

[1280]Wesley, *BE Works*, 13:187.

[1281]Harnack, *History of Dogma*, 5:10; Flew, *Idea of Perfection*, 158.

[1282]Wesley, *BE Works*, 13:39.

Jerusalem. If you cannot find any, you must make them; for none can travel that road alone."[1283]

Supernatural manifestations such as tongues and miracles do not necessarily lead to a holy life (Matt 7:21-23). A leading Pentecostal scholar conceded that the baptism in the Holy Spirit "is not of itself a sanctifying experience."[1284] For Jimmy Swaggart "the message of the cross" is that the sinful nature can be controlled by the cross itself. Swaggart interprets this to mean that Christ did it all. This is an adaptation of "the finished work of Calvary" doctrine articulated by William Durham in 1910.[1285]

While the sacraments are a means of grace, the symbols do not necessarily produce a holy life. Sacramentalism is a corporate view of perfection that believes the body is holy even if all its parts are unholy.

A deeper life convention held annually in Keswick, England teaches the Holy Spirit counteracts the sin nature and helps us suppress it. We agree that this is our condition in regeneration (Gal 5:17-24), but we believe God's grace can take us beyond this condition.

Eradicate means to pull up by the roots. The danger in using this term is that it conveys the concept that sin is a physical substance that can be removed once and for all, like a tooth is extracted or the roots of a tree dug out. This amounts to reification, the practice of making something concrete out of an idea or abstraction.[1286]

Is all pride, anger, jealousy, and desire removed or redirected? A holy person is fully human and no human emotion is destroyed. If holiness is full conformity to the image of Christ

---

[1283]Wesley, *Letter* to Francis Godfrey, 4 Aug 1789.

[1284]Horton, "The Pentecostal Perspective," 132.

[1285]Reasoner, *Holy Living*, 2:723.

[1286]Truesdale, "Reification of Sanctification," 102.

and Christ was angry, we should not pray for anger to be removed but redirected.

Meekness (*prautes*) is defined as the balance between excessive anger and passivity. A man who is meek is the man who is always angry at the right time and never angry at the wrong time.[1287]

If the American holiness movement put too much emphasis on a crisis experience, their scholars today have put too much emphasis on process. It is not necessary to embrace process philosophy in order to understand that sanctification is both crisis and process. Although salvation is an ongoing process, however, there must be a first moment of actualization. If everything is process, there is no victory. Nothing is decisive. But justification and regeneration are instantaneous because they are sovereign works of God. Entire sanctification is also a sovereign free gift of grace. It is not accomplished by submission or consecration. And because it can only be realized through faith in the atonement of Christ, the cleansing can happen in a moment of time.

Four Stages of Sanctification
- ### Initial Sanctification

Initial sanctification is closely related to regeneration. All true Christians are holy, but according to 2 Corinthians 7:1 that holiness may be perfected.

- ### Progressive Sanctification

The gradual or *progressive* work of *sanctification* is the work of the Spirit beginning with preliminary grace and continuing until final glorification. Christ continually purges everyone who is abiding in him (John 15:2). Discipleship is essentially progressive sanctification. "In its broadest sense discipleship is

---

[1287]Barclay, *New Testament Words*, 241.

the metaphor most descriptive of the doctrine of 'progressive sanctification.'"[1288]

The word for *discipleship* (*mathetes*) occurs 269 times in the four Gospels and Acts. The verb form is used three times in Matthew and once in Acts. This word occurs in no form after Acts. Yet the concept of discipleship continues throughout the NT. Why didn't Paul use this word *disciple*? In Greek culture disciples followed many philosophers. The term *Christian* specifies a disciple of Christ (Acts 11:26). While the Gospels and Acts demonstrate private discipleship, the epistles of Paul show how the local church exists to disciple corporately.

The Means of Grace

A spiritual discipline which people use to express their faith and receive God's grace is called a *means of grace*. We must remember that these spiritual disciplines are means, and not the end in themselves.

By "means of grace" I understand outward signs, words, or actions, ordained of God, and appointed for this end — to be the ordinary channels whereby he might convey to men, preventing, justifying, or sanctifying grace.[1289]

The Roman Catholic Church even considers relics and images as means of grace. On the other hand mysticism tends to reject any external means as unnecessary. It is possible to make too much of the means, by trusting in them instead of what they represent. And it is also possible to make too little of them.

However, the means of grace are divinely appointed channels through which the Holy Spirit influences the soul. Wesley

---

[1288]Wilkins, *Following the Master*, 343.

[1289]"The Means of Grace," Sermon #16, 2.1.

distinguished between the instituted means of grace which are works of piety ordained by God and the prudential means of grace which are spontaneous, practical works of mercy.

Prayer and fasting, daily Bible reading and the reading of devotional literature, spiritual conversation, public worship and the sacraments, accountability to a small group, and financial giving are all instituted means of grace. While baptism is a sacrament, since it is not repeated, it is not usually listed. The sacraments will be addressed under the doctrine of the church. Nor did Wesley cite financial giving.

Works of mercy include feeding the hungry, clothing the naked, entertaining the stranger, visiting those who are sick or imprisoned, instructing the ignorant, awakening the sinner, quickening the lukewarm, comforting those who are struggling, encouraging those who are tempted, and in any way contributing to the saving of souls from death. While we should be zealous for works of piety, Wesley taught that we should be *much more* zealous for works of mercy (Hos 6:6; Matt 9:13, 12:7).[1290]

Dallas Willard taught that the spiritual disciplines were a means of constant interaction with the kingdom of God. *The Spirit of the Disciplines*, the title of his 1988 book, describes the love of Jesus which produces a resolve to be like him. This is a contemporary statement of Thomas à Kempis, *The Imitation of Christ*, first printed in 1471. While Wesley felt that Kempis was too rigid,[1291] he appreciated the emphasis on simplicity and purity. Much later Søren Kierkegaard would write, "Purity of heart is to will one thing."[1292]

Willard quoted Wesley's statement, "The soul and the body make a man; the spirit and discipline make a Christian." Wesley

---

[1290]Wesley, "On Zeal," Sermon # 92, 2.9. See also "The Scripture Way of Salvation," Sermon # 43, 3.9-10.

[1291]Wesley, *Journal*, 24 May 1738; ¶ 4; *Letter* to Susanna Wesley, 28 May 1725.

[1292]That is the title of his book, translated into English in 1938.

said this implied that no one could be a real Christian without the help of Christian discipline. "But if this be so, is it any wonder that we find so few Christians, for where is Christian discipline!"[1293]

• Entire Sanctification

Entire sanctification is the condition of loving God with all our heart. This love expels all sin, cleansing the heart from all unrighteousness. This term corresponds with the term *Christian perfection*, but neither term implies the end of growth or progress.

No one can understand entire sanctification until they understand the new birth. No one can understand the NT until they understand Pentecost.

Wesley believed that the new birth was an entire change of our inmost nature from the image of the devil to the image of God.[1294] But we did not get all that God has provided through the atonement when we were born again. The distinction between birth and maturity must be maintained. Since baptism implies initiation, Spirit baptism should not be equated with Christian maturity.

There is not a complete deliverance from the remains of sin in the new birth. *Entire* sanctification is *entire* in the sense that total depravity is *complete* inability. Thus, the cure goes as deep as the disease. Entire sanctification is a "second work of grace" in the sense that sin has a two-fold nature. Therefore, salvation also has a two-fold deliverance. The cure goes as deep as the disease.

Wesley counseled that it was not necessary to testify to having attained a specific blessing.

[1293]Wesley, "Causes of the Inefficiency of Christianity," Sermon #122, ¶ 7. Quoted by Willard, *Spirit of the Disciplines*, 16-17.

[1294]Wesley, *Journal*, 13 Sept 1739.

Avoid all magnificent, pompous words. Indeed you need give it no *general* name. Neither "perfection, sanctification, the second blessing, nor the having attained." Rather speak of the *particulars* which God has wrought for you.[1295]

Wesley argued for entire sanctification on the basis of God's promises, his commands, scriptural examples, and scriptural prayers.[1296]

- **Entire sanctification is promised.**

"And he will redeem Israel from all his iniquities" (Ps 130:8). Wesley said this promise was expanded upon in Ezekiel 36:25, "I will sprinkle clean water on you, and you shall be clean from all your uncleanness, and from all your idols I will cleanse you." Wesley declared, "No promise can be more clear." Paul clearly is referring to this promise, "Since we have these promises, beloved, let us cleanse ourselves from every defilement of body and spirit, bringing holiness to completion in the fear of God" (2 Cor 7:1). In Deuteronomy 30:6 Moses promised, "And the Lord your God will circumcise your heart and the heart of your offspring, so that you will love the Lord your God with all your heart and with all your soul, that you may live."

Circumcision was required because human nature was unclean. All that we procreate is a reproduction of our sinfulness. Under the new covenant God requires circumcision of the heart (Rom 2:29, 4:9-12; Col 2:11-13). Yet even under the old covenant it was described as circumcision of the heart, which delivered them from being stiff necked (Deut 10:16).

God used the graphic analogy of circumcision to teach us that our hearts are impure and that he wants to do spiritual sur-

---

[1295]Wesley, *BE Works*, 13:122.

[1296]Wesley, *BE Works*, 13:65-68.

gery on us. The context of Colossians 2:11 implies that when we were living in sin we were uncircumcised, but at the moment of regeneration Christ circumcised us. We are the circumcision (Phil 3:2-3). This work of the Spirit is part of the new covenant (Jer 31:31-34).

"The reason the Son of God appeared was to destroy the works of the devil" (1 John 3:8). "Christ loved the church and gave himself up for her, that he might sanctify her, having cleansed her by the washing of water with the word, so that he might present the church to himself in splendor, without spot or wrinkle or any such thing, that she might be holy and without blemish" (Eph. 5:25-27). "By sending his own Son in the likeness of sinful flesh and for sin, he condemned sin in the flesh, in order that the righteous requirement of the law might be fulfilled in us, who walk not according to the flesh but according to the Spirit" (Rom 8:3-4). "He has given us his very great and precious promises, so that through them you may participate in the divine nature and escape the corruption in the world caused by evil desires" (2 Pet 1:4).

First John 1:9 encompasses entire sanctification as well as justification. Both *forgive* and *cleanse* are aorist active subjunctives. The timing of these actions is relative to the main verb *confess*. When we confess our sins, God is faithful to forgive us. When we receive a deeper revelation of our sinful nature and confess that, God is faithful to cleanse us from all iniquity.

The present tense cleansing, described in v 7, is the continuation of that initial sanctification and includes cleansing from the actual practice of sin, and as we seek for a deeper cleansing, cleansing from the sinful nature. Wesley understood the cleansing of v 7 to include cleansing from both original and actual sin, which resulted in taking away all the guilt and all the power.[1297]

•

[1297]Wesley, *Notes*, 631.

- ### Entire sanctification is commanded.

"Walk before me and be perfect" (Gen 17:1). "Serve him with a perfect heart and a willing mind" (1 Chr 28:9). "You therefore must be perfect, as your heavenly Father is perfect" (Matt 5:48). The perfection or completeness commanded is explained in v 43 where Jesus said we are to love even our enemies. Thus the context prior to v 48 is dealing with perfect love and v 48 is a concluding statement which begins with the connecting word *therefore*. According to E. Stanley Jones, there are twenty-seven marks of the perfect life in Matthew 5.[1298]

"You shall love the Lord your God with all your heart and with all your soul and with all your mind" (Matt 22:37; Mark 12:30). Paul commanded the Corinthian believers to "be perfect" (2 Cor 13:11). "You shall be holy, for I am holy" (1 Pet 1:16). These verbs are all future indicatives and express a command — "you will be" or "you will." Thus, they are classified as imperative future. This compares to *el* (not) with the imperfect form of the Hebrew verb used in the Ten Commandments. "You will not ever. . . ." Some OT scholars hold that the Ten Commandments do not merely contain negative commands, but actually give promise of future conformity to them.[1299]

In addition to the imperatives just cited, a second class of texts could be categorized as exhortations: "I urge you to present your bodies a living sacrifice, holy, acceptable to God" (Rom 12:1). Under the old covenant worship involved offering sacrifices to God. There were burnt offerings, grain or meat offerings, peace offerings, guilt or sin offerings. Normally animals were put to death. This symbolized substitution as human guilt was transferred to the animal sacrifice. By the time of the temple in Jerusalem, so much blood was spilled into the drainage system that the brook Kidron, into which it dumped, ran red.

[1298]Jones, *Christ of the Mount*, 36, 194.

[1299]Ferguson, *The Holy Spirit*, 141.

Then Christ came and became our sacrifice, doing away with animal sacrifices. The worship of the church in Rome, with its breaking of the bread and sharing of the communion cup, must have appeared strange to the Jews, because there were no animal sacrifices, and to the Romans because there were no sacrifices offered to Caesar. Although God took the blood out of sacrifice, he did not take the sacrifice out of worship. Now he calls on us to present ourselves as *living* sacrifices. This is a paradox since the very word *sacrifice* implies to kill or slay. *Thusia* is from the root *thuo* which means *to kill in sacrifice* or *slay*. It occurs for the first and only time in Romans at 12:1. But God wants us to live for him as a freed servant (see Exod 21:2-11), not necessarily to die for him.

- **The NT gives examples of entire sanctification.**

Paul included himself with all those of whom he exhorted in Philippians 3:15, "Let those of *us* who are perfect think this way." Three verses earlier Paul declared that he was not already perfected in the sense that he had not already been resurrected from the dead. Here he does testify to Christian perfection, even if not to final perfection. This is obscured by some translations, but in v 12 the verb is *teleioo* and in v 15 the adjective is *teleios*, both from the root word *telos*.

Paul wrote to the Thessalonians, "You are witnesses, and so is God, of how holy, righteous and blameless we were among you who believed" (1 Thess 2:10). All three of these adverbs describe Christian perfection.

John included himself with all those of whom he said, "By this is love perfected with us, so that we may have confidence for the day of judgment, because as he is so also are we in this world" (1 John 4:17). Thus we reflect the likeness of Christ now, as a student reflects the character of his teacher (Luke 6:40).

In 1 Corinthians 13 Paul describes mature Christianity. Paul used *agape*, the word for commitment or covenantal love. The Greek language used four different words for *love*: *eros*, *philos*, *storgos*, and *agape*. All of these types of love are legitimate. However, *agape* is a completely different dimension of love. This Christian *agape* love is not a substitute for the other loves, but it is a quality of the entire person as it is centered in Christ. Thus, it becomes our goal to bring Christian character into *eros, storgos*, and *philos*.

The word *agape* occurs nine times in 1 Corinthians 13. When we are born again, this *agape* love is poured out into our hearts (Rom 5:5). Yet according to 1 John 4:17-18 this love can grow to a state of completeness or perfect love. Therefore when perfection comes, it brings to an end (*katargeo*) that which is imperfect, immature, and childish. Thus, Wesley concluded,

> There is nothing higher in religion; there is, in effect, nothing else; if you look for anything but *more love* you are looking wide of the mark, you are getting out of the royal way. And when you are asking others, Have *you* received this or that blessing? if you mean anything but *more love*, you mean wrong; you are leading them out of the way, and putting them upon a false scent. Settle it then in your heart, that from the moment God has saved you from all sin, you are to aim at nothing more, but more of that love described in the thirteenth of the Corinthians. You can go no higher than this, till you are carried into Abraham's bosom.[1300]

- **NT prayers for entire sanctification.**

Many of these NT prayers utilize the optative mood, which expresses a wish or prayer. Pope observed that all of Paul's prayers are more or less devoted to the grand concept of the perfect Christian life. "The word Perfection is the seal with

---

[1300]Wesley, *BE Works*, 13:114.

which they are all alike stamped, and that ideal which is found in them is to be personally realized."[1301]

Wesley declared that if there were no such thing as entire sanctification, such prayers "would be mere mockery of God." Wesley also explained that if we pray, as Jesus taught us to pray, "Deliver us from evil" (Matt 6:13), "when we are delivered from all evil, there can be no sin remaining." Thus, Wesley understood 1 John 1:8 to refer to any person *before* the blood of Christ has cleansed him.[1302] First John 1:8 cannot be interpreted so as to contradict 1 John 1:7 and 9 or 1 John 3:9.

Most of Paul's letters contain prayers for Christian perfection. They are typically addressed to the saints (*hagioi*) or literally to the holy ones. They are initially sanctified, but not entirely. However, there are no such prayers in the pastoral letters. The significance may be that Timothy and Titus were already mature believers.

In Romans 15 the example of Christ is held up in vv 3-4,7-8. We are told not to please ourselves, but rather that each of us should please his neighbor (vv 1-2). The mature Christian should thus exemplify a spirit of consideration and a spirit of cooperation. The prayer of Paul in Romans 15:5-6 is for the grace of unity between Jewish and Gentile believers within the Roman church. Paul prayed that they might receive patience and encouragement. The example of Christ teaches his people to endure the contempt of the world and to bear with each other. The basis of this patient endurance is hope. Christian maturity should produce hope (see vv 4-5,12-13).

Paul also prays that we might be filled with *all* joy and peace. This implies the displacement of anything inconsistent with the fruit of the Spirit.

In 2 Corinthians 13:9 Paul declared,"Our prayer is for your perfection." This is a prayer for restoration and wholeness. This

---

[1301]Pope, *Prayers of St. Paul*, 29-30.

[1302]Wesley, *Notes*, 631.

includes a restoration of order in the Corinthian church, as well as the recovery of moral purity. But the prayers of Paul always rise above their immediate occasion. Although this prayer scarcely mentions the individual believer, every application of scriptural truth must find its way to the individual, and only through the individual will it reach the community.

Originally this word *perfection* was used for setting dislocated bones. Even after we are born again, there are areas of our personality that are out of alignment and need to be relocated. These idiosyncrasies should not be excused. Verse 11 tells us to aim for perfection. In v 9 the noun *katartisis* comes from the same root word as *katartizo*, the verb in v 11. The meaning is to mend, restore, or perfect. This concept of perfection is implied in Ephesians 4:12-13 which also uses *perfecting, perfect,* and *full stature* (v 13).

In Ephesians 1:15-23 Paul prays that God would give the saints in Ephesus the Spirit of wisdom and revelation so that they may know him better. The Spirit inspired the revelation of the mind of God through Scripture, but he is also in every believer revealing Christ as a personal Savior. Pope asserted that the same Spirit who presided over the inspiration of Scripture presides over this personal revelation. Nothing less than this will satisfy the language of the prayer nor should satisfy the aspiration of the Christian.

The believer has already received the seal of the Spirit (v 13), an internal assurance of acceptance which no mere rational assent could bring. Yet there is more to behold: the hope of his calling, the riches of our glorious inheritance, and the might of the divine power made available to us.

We are called to experience the treasury of blessings for the people of God in time and in eternity. This resurrection power has already raised the dead sinner to life and will raise our bodies from physical death in the future. In the present, we sit in heavenly places with the resurrected Christ and he exercises his authority through us.

Paul resumes this prayer in Ephesians 3:14-21, praying that we might become mighty through the Spirit (v 16). Not only does Paul pray for a supernatural empowerment, in v 17 Paul prays that Christ may dwell in our hearts through faith. While the Spirit of Christ indwells all believers, here Paul uses a compound word *kata + oikeo*, meaning to settle down or to make a home in your hearts. The Spirit makes himself at home in the sense that we become rooted and grounded in love. When we are justified by faith, the love of God is poured out into our hearts (Rom 5:5). Now Paul prays that we might become established in love. In this deeper relationship, we are enabled to realize the magnitude of God's love — how wide, how long, how high, and how deep. As our spiritual capacity increases, we can receive a fuller measure of the Holy Spirit.

While all true Christians have the Spirit, Daniel Steele explained, "The vessel is too weak and too small to contain all that God desires to pour into it. It must be enlarged and strengthened."[1303] To be filled with God is to be emptied of self. John Wesley commented that this describes "a perfection far beyond a bare freedom from sin."[1304] While we can never contain the fullness of God, we can be filled unto the full measure of blessing and maturity God has for us. This does not indicate a static state of fullness, but rather a progressive filling.

In Philippians 1:4-6, Paul prays that the Spirit will carry his ongoing work in us unto completion or perfection. According to verses 9-11 this would produce

- a love growing in knowledge of the truth and discernment which is able to react properly in every crisis
- an ability to discern the more excellent way. Love functions as an internal monitor "instructing us always what to believe and what to reject, what to do and what to shun, what to

---

[1303]Steele, *Half-Hours with St. Paul*,18; *Love Enthroned*, 86-97.

[1304]Wesley, *Notes*, 495.

leave behind us as unworthy and what to make the mark of our supreme pursuit."[1305]
- a purity of character that reflects sincerity (simplicity of motive) and is not offensive
- a fullness of the fruit of righteousness, which Wesley defined as "all inward and outward holiness."[1306] All Christians have an imputed righteousness that comes through faith in Christ (Phil 3:9), but here Paul describes a condition of being full of this righteousness."Here also the apostle is far from speaking of justification only."[1307]

In Philippians 3:10-11 Paul himself longs to know Christ better. While Christ suffered and died, then was resurrected, the order for the Christian is reversed. First he is raised from spiritual death. Thus, we first know God in the power of Christ's resurrection. Then we come to know Christ through the fellowship of his sufferings. The only suffering which becomes a means of grace is suffering which causes us to look away from ourselves and focus upon his passion.

The third level of intimacy with God is through death. This seems like a paradox, but it is a deeper death to self-centeredness. It is the death of what remains of the old life. This sinful propensity remains after the new birth. Many who profess to be Christians are not truly Christian, yet it seems that most who are Christians are still interested in very little beyond themselves. Paul complained that everyone looks out for his own interests (Phil 2:21). But perfect love is not self-seeking (1 Cor 13:5). Jesus taught us to seek first his kingdom (Matt 6:33), but few Christians do. The perfecting grace of God turns the heart outward.

[1305]Pope, *Prayers of St. Paul*, 264.

[1306]Wesley, *Notes*, 506.

[1307]Wesley, *Notes*, 512.

Thus, entire sanctification is a spiritual death. It is a more perfect conformity to the nature of Christ. The word translated *conformable* or *becoming like him* is *summorphizo*. Paul took the word *morphe*, which means *form*, and added the prefix *with*. Just as Paul distinguished between Christian perfection and bodily perfection in Philippians 3: 12,15, so he distinguished between a conformity to the image of Christ in v 10 and the future change of our physical bodies in v 21.

In Colossians 1:9-14, Paul continued to pray that they would have a growing knowledge of God's will which would result in a practical conformity with that will in three areas:

- more fruit — the holiness of the regenerate life is the fruit of a tree of life within as well as his own habits and acts. But the fruitfulness of the Christian life knows no limits. As our knowledge of God's will grows the fruits of obedience will also grow.
- a greater power in our lives producing more strength, endurance, patience, and joy
- thankfulness — gratitude for the benefits of redemption

Yet we are not to be passive in this process. Paul said he labored, struggling with all the energy he could muster, counseling and teaching so that every person might be presented perfect (*teleios*) in Christ (1:28-29).

In Colossians 4:12 a colleague of Paul also prays earnestly for two things — that we may stand perfect or complete (*teleios*) and fully assured, having a greater sense of God's presence and acceptance.

In the first letter written to the church at Thessalonica we read that they are in God the Father and in the Lord Jesus Christ (1:1). If any man be in Christ, he is a new creation (2 Cor 5:17). According to v 4 they are brethren, elect by God. In 4:8 we also discover that they have the Holy Spirit. God is giving them (present tense) the Spirit. And he came in much assurance (1:5). He also gave them joy (1:6).

According to 1 Thessalonians 1:3, their faith produced good works; their love prompted labor, and their hope inspired endurance. According to 1:7 they were a model or pattern. Verse 8 records their witness was like a trumpet blast that covered all of Macedonia. They had turned from idols to serve the living and true God and the news of their conversion had covered their whole region.

Timothy had returned to Paul bringing a good report (1 Thess 3:6) about their faith and love but they needed an increase in love (1 Thess 3:12). According to 1 Thessalonians 1:3 their labor was prompted by their love. They had love, but they needed more love. God's love can flow from us only when he continually flows into us. God wants to increase our intake and our outflow. Sometimes, however, it seems the demand is greater than the supply. But God can enlarge our capacity to love each other and to love everyone. Paul seems to indicate in the last part of v 12 that he has that kind of love for them. And he is praying that they will also have that kind of love.

They also needed more stability (1 Thess 3:13). It is God's plan to so cleanse the church that they are holy and blameless (Eph 5:27). Paul testified in 1 Thessalonians 2:10 that he had lived holy, righteous, and blameless among them. Now he is praying that they may be established blameless in holiness (3:13); and again in 5:23 he prays that their spirit, soul, and body be kept blameless. In Philippians 2:15 and 1 Thessalonians 3:13 *amemptos* (*blameless*) is used as an adjective. In Ephesians 1:4, 5:27; Colossians 1:22; Jude 24; Revelation 14:5 a related adjective *amomos* is used. In 1 Thessalonians 2:10, 5:23 it is used as an adverb (*amemptos*).

To be holy is to be morally blameless. In this life we will never know freedom from ignorance, mistake, temptation, or a thousand infirmities, but we can be blameless. Our motives can be pure.

There is a state possible to Christians, corresponding to the ideal of their calling, in which they can be described as "unblamable in holiness," and into which they may be brought by the grace of God in this life.[1308]

Part of what it means to be blameless is stated in Philippians 2:14, "Do everything without complaining or arguing so that you may become blameless and pure." According to Colossians 3:13-14, if any man have a complaint we are to bear with each other, forgive each other [not cast blame], and above all put on love, which binds them all together in perfect unity.

God can deliver from a complaining spirit. In Ephesians 5:27 Paul says he can cleanse us — that is the negative side. First Thessalonians 3:12-13 is the positive answer — he strengthens, establishes, reinforces, and braces in holiness. This results in an increase and overflow of love.

The Thessalonians already had some holiness, but it needed reinforcement. God can provide extra bracing that will stabilize us. Notice this stabilization is not provided by death nor by the return of Christ. Paul's prayer was that they would be found blameless and holy *when* the Lord Jesus appeared. This appearing of Christ will then confirm us in a permanent state of holiness which implies the end of probation.

They needed a completion of sanctification. They were already initially sanctified. In 1 Thessalonians 4:3 Paul teaches that their sanctification was God's will. Paul says it is God's will that they should keep on abstaining (present imperative) from these sexual sins. Thus, they were already partially sanctified and separate from sexual impurity. So were the Corinthians. Paul wrote that some of them were involved in sexual sins, "but you were washed, you were sanctified, you were justified" (1 Cor 6:11). This is initial sanctification which comes along with justification. God calls all believers to live such a holy life (1 Thess 4:7).

[1308]Bartlet, "Sanctification," 4:393.

But in 1 Thessalonians 5:23 this is more than a wish, although in the optative mood. It is the desire of the Spirit that our sanctification or holiness be entire. This is the only place in the NT where *holoteles* occurs. It is comprised of *holos*, meaning all, whole, or entirely and *telos* which means to perfect. It speaks strongly of a completeness to sanctification. The second word *holokleros* means entire, complete, sound in every part. These words are synonyms.[1309]

The prayer for the noun cannot be understood apart from the action of the verb. Although *wholly* is an adjective, which technically modifies the noun, the subject and verb cannot be separated. If *wholly* does not modify the verb *sanctify*, the prayer for the subject cannot be understood. Therefore, Paul prays that something will happen to us which will make us complete. Since the verb is *sanctify*, the focus of the prayer is that we are sanctified completely. The process of sanctification may occur in stages or degrees, but Paul's concept is that it can reach a point of completeness. Hermann Cremer wrote that *telos* never refers merely to an end with regard to time or space in and for itself. It always includes the idea of an inner completion or qualitative end.[1310]

Paul prays that they would completely attain the goal. This prayer was expressed for those who had experienced the grace of God. Paul said in 1 Thessalonians 3:10 that he prayed earnestly night and day that God would supply what was lacking in their faith. He prays for sanctifying grace that reaches the whole life and the whole person. All believers are cleansed as they walk in light, so that their mistakes and shortcomings are not imputed against them; but this is a deeper cleansing which leaves nothing out, penetrating body, soul, spirit, and cleansing through and through, entirely and completely. While the Savior prayed for the unity of his spiritual body in John 17, here Paul prays for the

---

[1309]Trench, *Synonyms*, 74-77.

[1310]Cremer, *Biblico-Theological Lexicon*, 541.

individuals comprising that body that this entire sanctification will pervade their whole being. What will this entire sanctification do? First Thessalonians 5:12-22 imply at least nine graces:

- It will give us a respect for spiritual authority and for preaching (v 20)
- It will help us live in peace with one another (v 13b)
- It will give us a sensitivity to spiritual needs. The lazy need to be admonished, the fearful need to be encouraged, the weak need to be propped up — it will take patience to deal with them all (v 14).
- It will deliver us from a vindictive, get-even spirit (v 15) and make us kind.
- It will make us joyful and deliver us from blaming and grumbling (v 16)
- It will make our prayer life more consistent (v 17)
- It will make us more thankful; thankful in all circumstances (v 18). Actually vv 16-18 describes unbroken praise to God, unbroken communion with God, and unbroken awareness of God. Wesley said this is Christian perfection.[1311]
- It will make us more obedient to the Spirit and more discerning of the Spirit (vv 19, 21)
- It will help us live more consistently and avoid every evil and questionable practice (v 22)

Then Paul prayed that this condition be maintained in them until the return of Christ. According to 1 Thessalonians 5:24, the one who calls you is faithful and he will do it, not simply impute it. John Wesley said no man can live higher than this, but no man need to live short of this. "Farther than this we cannot go; and we need not stop short of it."[1312] "Now to him who is able to do immeasurably more than all we ask or imagine, according to his

---

[1311]Wesley, *Notes*, 531.

[1312]Wesley, *Notes*, 531.

power that is at work within us" (Eph 3:20). The process has already begun. The Holy Spirit is already at work. And so with Charles Wesley we sing,

Finish then thy new creation,
Pure and spotless let us be;
Let us see thy great salvation
Perfectly restored in thee;
Changed from glory into glory,
Till in heaven we take our place,
Till we cast our crowns before thee,
Lost in wonder, love, and praise.[1313]

In 2 Thessalonians 1:11-12 Paul prayed that the church, who were called out of sin and called unto holiness, be deemed worthy of this calling and thus be glorified by the grace that counts them and makes them worthy.

In 2 Thessalonians 2 Paul again prays. He prays in vv 16-17 that the Thessalonian Christians be consoled and established. Through the love and grace of God they have already experienced everlasting comfort and good hope. According to Pope "everlasting consolation" implies nothing less than the healing of the great wound of sin and the removal of its consequences. *Good hope* describes that part of the everlasting gift which has reference to the future. Paul prayed that the Lord himself, in unity with the Father, console their inner man by the word that invigorates and keeps their outer life steadfast in every good work and in every good doctrine.

While they had already received eternal encouragement, Paul is concerned that they not become quickly unsettled or alarmed (2 Thess 2:2). Therefore he prays that their hearts will be kept strong in this same consolation and their life established in obedience.

[1313]Wesley, *BE Works*, 7:547.

In 2 Thessalonians 3, Paul has been requesting prayer for himself when he breaks out in prayer for them at v 5. Paul prays for their direction into the love of God and into the patience of Christ. Then Paul literally prays for the steadfastness of patience that is Christ's. This will result in the steadfast obedience described in v 4. The specific meaning of this prayer is that it may please the Lord to remove every hindrance to our perfect union and harmony with our Lord in his example of endurance unto death. Carl Henry wrote,

> Many fillings, many deepenings, many enablings follow the initial yielding of one's life to God. Yet the New Testament says even more. It assures us that even here and now in this life God's people may live victoriously over sin. "Sin shall not have dominion over you . . . under grace," Paul writes the Romans (6:14). Amid the conflict of rival powers to subdue him, the believer whose life is open to the fullness of the Spirit will love in victory and in expectation of growing conformity to the indwelling Christ.[1314]

At 2 Thessalonians 3:16 Paul returns to conclude his prayer. He prays that the Savior himself administer the blessings of his peace. That peace abides on the entire assembly through the abiding presence of the Lord. He can give us peace at all times and in all circumstances. The result is that we may expect a permanent, uninterrupted assurance of his acceptance. This peace of Christ incorporates all that is included in perfect spiritual prosperity. Yet this bold petition also demands that the rage of Satan and the wrath of men should not only praise God, but be turned to the deeper joy of his servant. The previous verses teach the Thessalonians to expect that the unrest and disorder of evil men should result in a far more exceeding peace for the devout.

[1314]Henry, *GRA* 6:338.

The voice of the Lord may not always hush the storm around or within the soul, but always and by all means he will give his peace in that inner man which ought never to be penetrated by anxiety.

In Hebrews 13:20-21, the writer prays, "May God equip you with everything good for doing his will." Here the verb *equip* is *katartizo* one of the NT words for perfection. Then the God of holiness is petitioned to do his own good pleasure within us so that we are able to manifest his good pleasure externally. He works internally, conforming us to his own image; and thus we are enabled to do every good work.

Finally, Peter prays, "And the God of all peace, who called you to his eternal glory in Christ, after you have suffered a little while, will himself restore you and make you strong, firm and steadfast. To him be the power for ever and ever. Amen" (1 Pet 5:10-11).

Here the emphasis is not upon suffering, but upon grace. Suffering demonstrates our need for growth in grace. Although Peter's emphasis in this first letter is that Christians will suffer (see 1:6) and that trials should not take us by surprise (4:12), persecution and stress, trials and afflictions do not sanctify — they reveal to what degree we are sanctified.

Wesley believed that most who are justified gradually die to sin and grow in grace, until at or near the point of death God perfects them in love.

> God usually gives a considerable *time* for men to receive *light*, to grow in *grace*, to *do* and *suffer* his will, before they are either justified or sanctified; but he does not invariably adhere to this. Sometimes he "cuts short his work." He does the work of many years in a few weeks — perhaps in a week, a day, an hour. He justifies or sanctifies both those who have *done* or *suffered* noth-

ing, and who have not had *time* for a gradual growth either in *light* or *grace*.[1315]

While this statement is open to misunderstanding, the bottom line is that often we need to go through some things before we become aware of a deeper need.

There are four synonyms, all future tense verbs, in 1 Peter 5:10 which are a promise of what God's grace can do in us between now and the end. He can *restore* (*katartizo*). He can supply what is lacking in our faith (1 Thess 3:10 - same word *katartizo*).

He can *establish* (*sterizo*). Peter says the grace of God will confirm and support us. The word is used in v 9 where it tells us to stand firm in the faith. We have an invisible means of support. God has the grace to help us stand firm; make you hard, firm, solid. In Acts 14:22 Paul and Barnabas strengthened the disciples and encouraged them to remain true. They preached that we must go through many hardships to enter the kingdom of God. The kingdom is both now and later. We enter the kingdom now through the new birth; we enter heaven later by remaining true. We need this establishing grace so that we will persevere. Paul ends Romans with this same word: "Now to him who is able to establish you by my gospel" (Rom 16:25). In the LXX, *sterizo* is used to describe the support of Moses by Aaron and Hur. They put a stone under the hands of Moses and then supported his hands, one on the one side and one on the other (Exod 17:12).

He can *strengthen* (*sthenoo*). Although this is the only place this verb is found in the NT, it is found in noun form in the LXX, where Eliphaz speaks of the strength of a lion (Job 4:10). Satan roars *like* a lion (1 Pet 5:8), but he is not a real lion. Jesus is the lion of the tribe of Judah and he gives us his strength. Grace will keep us from collapsing.

[1315]Wesley, *BE Works*, 13:106.

He will *settle* (*themelioo*). He will establish us on a firm foundation. Grace will prevent you from being swept away. S*terizo* denotes solid support *around* us; *themelioo* describes a secure foundation *under* us.

Every true Christian hungers for these dynamics. Some theologies offer little encouragement, but Pope declared that "no desire of holiness can be vain."[1316] Even though Calvinism teaches there is no deliverance from sin in this life, there is still among godly Calvinists a God-given desire to rise above it. "I often pray, Lord, make me as holy as a pardoned sinner can be made," confessed Robert Murray M'Cheyne.[1317]

Randy Maddox said that Wesley's view of entire sanctification convinced him that the Christian life did not have to remain a life of perpetual struggle.[1318] According to Romans 5:20 grace is more powerful than sin.

• Final Sanctification

Final sanctification is attained in the resurrection when we are delivered from the very presence of sin. Paul makes this distinction in Philippians 3:12,15. This category comes under eschatology.

Christian Perfection

Holiness and *perfection* are related terms. Frederic Platt observed that "many Christians who urge the possibility of holiness plead the impossibility of perfection."[1319] Oscar Cullman

---

[1316]Pope, *Compendium*, 3:56.

[1317]Bonar, *Memoirs of McCheyne*, 209.

[1318]Maddox, "Reconnecting the Means to the End," 44; *Responsible Grace*, 188.

[1319]Platt, "Perfection," 9:728.

said that *teleioo* (to make perfect) is "almost a synonym for *hagiadzo* (to sanctify)."[1320]

Perfection, in its absolute sense, is an attribute of God alone. Yet Christ commands us to *be perfect* (Matt 5:48). Plato concluded that only God was perfect, but Aristotle defined perfection as that which accomplishes the purpose for which it was created. Both philosophers were right, in a sense, although both were pagan. Aristotle was aligned with stoicism and Plato with asceticism. God alone is *absolutely* perfect. However, there is a *relative* perfection in which we love God with our total being and our neighbor as ourselves. That perfect love displaces everything contrary to it. When that love is the ruling motive of our life, God imputes perfection to us.

Pope explained, "As faith is reckoned for righteousness, so faith working by love is reckoned for perfection."[1321] Noble wrote,

> The Christian who is no longer divided in heart and mind is an integrated person, a whole person. There is no longer the divided mind which makes him unsteady or which makes her unreliable.[1322]

This *perfection* does not imply sinlessness. Wesley stated "'sinless perfection' is a phrase I never use, lest I should *seem* to contradict myself."[1323] He replied, "'Absolute or infallible perfection?' I never contended for it. Sinless perfection? I do not contend for this, seeing it is not scriptural."[1324] Wesley wrote,

---

[1320]Cullmann, *Christology of the New Testament*, 100.

[1321]Pope, *Compendium*, 3:96-98.

[1322]Noble, *Holy Trinity: Holy People*, 23.

[1323]Wesley, *BE Works*, 13:170.

[1324]Wesley, *Letter* to Penelope Maitland, 12 May 1763.

If you say that "'Coming short' is sin," be it so; I contend not. But still I say: "There are they whom I believe to be scripturally 'perfect.' And yet, these never felt their want of Christ so deeply and strongly as they do now."[1325]

Wesley explained his use of the term *perfection*,

As to the *word*, it is scriptural. Therefore neither you nor I can in conscience object to the word, unless we would send the Holy Ghost to school and teach him to speak who made the tongue. By that word I *mean* (as I have said again and again) "so loving God and our neighbor as to rejoice evermore, pray without ceasing, and in everything give thanks." He that experiences this is scripturally perfect. . . . What, then, does their arguing prove who object against "perfection?" Absolute and infallible perfection? I never contended for it. Sinless perfection? Neither do I contend *for this*, seeing the term is not scriptural. A perfection that fulfils the whole law, and so needs not the merits of Christ? I acknowledge none such — I do now, and always did, protest against it.[1326]

Wesley taught that the best of men still need the intercession of Christ to atone for their omissions, their shortcomings, their mistakes in judgment and practice, and their defects of various kinds.[1327] Yet he is routinely accused of teaching sinless perfection. Calvinists, who reject this straw man, then proceed to teach what we are trying to say. Often their exegesis is better than their theology.

[1325]Wesley, *Letter* to Samuel Furley, 15 Sept 1762.

[1326]Wesley, *Letter* to Penelope Maitland, 12 May 1763.

[1327]Wesley, *BE Works*, 13:169.

After rejecting what he thought was Wesley's "heresy," Rushdoony defended almost the same concept:

> The law does not command us to do what man cannot do. . . . The Old Testament words translated as "perfect" mean upright, having integrity, blameless, and the New Testament words have the meaning of mature, complete. . . . Perfection means uprightness and maturity in terms of a goal or purpose, and end established by God. . . . In this life, we can be perfect in the sense of being blameless in our faithfulness to God's purpose, but to be blameless does not mean being faultless.[1328]

John Frame also distinguished between sinless perfection and a relative perfection or uprightness.[1329] He explained that although we are not sinlessly perfect in this life, the Lord is working to perfect in us the image of Christ (Jer. 32:39-40; Eph. 5:25-27). "So we pray that God will enable us to please him, for we know that this is his will, and that only he can make that happen (Col. 1:10-12)."[1330]

Much of the difficulty is centered on the fact that *perfect* has more than one meaning. Yet Jesus commanded us to be perfect (Matt 5:48) and it is crucial to determine what he meant and did not mean.

The Latin word *perfectus* means unimprovable. This is a static state. But Wesley defined perfection based on the Greek word *teleios*, which means maturity or completeness. It does not connote a static state, but rather an ongoing life of wholeness. It is perfecting grace.

[1328]Rushdoony, *Institutes of Biblical Law*, 628-629; *Law and Society*, 620.

[1329]Frame, *Doctrine of God*, 453; 403-404.

[1330]Frame, *Doctrine of God*, 76.

Entire sanctification should not be understood as a state or higher level which we attain. We are cleaned from sin as we walk in the light. "We teach, therefore not a *state of purity*, but a *maintained condition of purity*, a moment-by-moment salvation consequent upon a moment-by-moment obedience and trust."[1331] Christian holiness is sustained on a moment-by-moment basis. As we trust and obey, our love for God expels sin. If we love God with all our heart, sin is expelled because there is no room for it.

A perfect Christian would not be as absolutely holy as God. He would not have the knowledge of angels. He would not have the innocence as Adam and Eve before the fall.[1332] The highest perfection man can attain in this life does not exclude ignorance, error, and a thousand other infirmities.

However, 1 John 2:12-14 does imply a maturity in the faith. While every believer is a child of God, they are divided into three categories. *Little children* have the forgiveness of sins. They have been initially sanctified.

Young men have a strong faith through which they have won some battles and overcome the evil one. They are being progressively sanctified.

Fathers have known God from the beginning point of the new birth and still know him. They are entirely sanctified. While the new Christian both fears and loves God, the mature Christian has a perfect love which drives out fear (1 John 4:17-18).

Full sanctification was provided by the atoning work of Christ as a present possibility (Eph 5:25-26). Other theological systems teach it is possible only after this life. This deeper relationship is entered and maintained by faith. "Did you receive the Spirit by observing the law, or by believing what you heard? Are you so foolish? After beginning with the Spirit, are you now

---

[1331]Cook, *New Testament Holiness*, 43.

[1332]Wesley, "On Perfection," Sermon #76, 1.1-2.

trying to attain your goal by human effort?" (Gal 3:2-3). Our faith must be in the atoning work of Christ, not in our works.

Crisis points

John Wesley emphasized both crisis and process. And the process may not be exactly the same for each believer. Kenneth Kinghorn also explained:

Growth in the Lord, for most Christians, involves both moments of crises and periods of process. By crises I mean those special times when we consciously make deeper commitments to Christ, as the Holy Spirit reveals personal needs and deeper possibilities. By process I mean the daily growth in grace that we undergo as we walk in faithful obedience to Christ.[1333]

Thomas Ralston wrote,

It matters but little whether this eminent state of holiness be gained by a bold, energetic, and determined exercise of faith and prayer, or by a more gradual process, whether it be *instantaneous* or *gradual*, or both the one and the other.[1334]

Can sanctification be entire? We cannot put limits upon the grace of God, but we are usually cleansed to our level of consciousness. There will be many crisis points when we realize an attitude, a word, or a deed was not Christlike. We should repent, surrender anew to his lordship, and trust him for cleansing.

However, there can be a decisive moment of deliverance. Wesley reasoned,

---

[1333]Kinghorn, "Question and Answer," 9.

[1334]Ralston, *Elements of Divinity*, 470.

A man may be *dying* for some time; yet he does not, properly speaking, *die* till the instant the soul is separated from the body. And in that instant he lives the life of eternity. In like manner he may be *dying to sin* for some time; yet he is not "dead to sin" till sin is separated from his soul. And in that instant he lives the full life of love. . . . Yet he still grows in grace, in the knowledge of Christ, in the love and image of God; and will do so, not only till death, but to all eternity.[1335]

We surrender to the lordship of Christ when we are regenerated. As sinners we were afraid of God's wrath. However, we did not really know at that time what God's will would involve. There may be many points in time in which we accept the will of God as it unfolds. The Spirit of God will convict us of inner attitudes which are inconsistent. As a child of God our consecration is based on love, not fear. Wesley counseled,

Conviction is not condemnation. You may be convinced, yet not condemned; convinced of useless thoughts or words, and yet not condemned for them. You are condemned for nothing if you love God and continue to give him your whole heart. . . . You are a child of God, a member of Christ, an heir of the kingdom. What you have hold fast (whatever name is given to it), and you *shall have* all that God has prepared for them that love him.[1336]

The same Greek word *paristemi* is used in Romans 6:13 to describe the surrender of a sinner and in Romans 12:1 to describe the consecration of a believer. However, we cannot purify our hearts through consecration. That would amount to sanctification

[1335]Wesley, *BE Works*, 13:175.

[1336]Wesley, *Letter* to Jane March, 11 Nov 1760.

by works, not by faith. The holiness movement tends to teach sanctification through consecration. A more biblical understanding sees consecration as a prerequisite for sanctification in which we release control so that the Holy Spirit can purify our hearts.

"To obey is better than sacrifice" (1 Sam 15:22). Obedience is submission to God. Sacrifice can refer to sacrificial offerings which God prescribed. However, sacrifice can also be our attempt to compensate for our sin through our own legalism. It is possible to practice a self-imposed lifestyle of self-denial and yet be in rebellion against God. Wesley explained, "Therefore thy gross disobedience to God's express command, is not to be compensated with sacrifice."[1337]

Progressive growth

Holiness theology often implies there can be no growth prior to a radical sanctification experience after the new birth. New Christians are urged to profess the second blessing as soon as possible so they will not lose what they have. Holiness advocates often teach entire sanctification as purity and what follows as maturity.

In contrast, Wesley taught that Christian perfection was usually attained much later in the Christian life. "Generally speaking, it is a *long time*, even many years, before sin is destroyed."[1338] It may take some time for a true Christian to see his need for a deeper work. Methodism taught regeneration as a purifying work (Titus 3:5) and Christian perfection as maturity. Wesley counseled, "Unless we grieve the Holy Spirit, He will never take away what He has given. On the contrary, He will add

---

[1337]Wesley, *Notes*, 2:941.

[1338]Wesley, *BE Works*, 13:106.

to it continually, till we come to the measure of the full stature of Christ."[1339]

The older view in the holiness movement was that the second blessing was crisis with a view to a process. But now all crisis has been eradicated and the process is endless. Somehow the balance has been lost as the scale is tipped too far to the other side in order to compensate for excesses of the past.

Process philosophy holds an attraction to some contemporary holiness theologians because it offers a way to reconcile and explain process and crisis. But the explanation raises more questions than it answers. The problem is that this model is built upon evolutionary presuppositions in which God himself is portrayed as being in process.

Process theology overreacts to a rigid view of God found within some Calvinistic theologians in which God is immutable and incapable of relationships. It is claimed that the traditional view of God originated in Greek philosophy, not Scripture.

Yet in their attempt to correct our understanding of God, process theology proposes a God who is relational but finite. This God can only exist by being in the process of change. The result is a God who needs the world as much as the world needs him. Thus his sovereignty is diminished and our freedom is magnified. We resemble God and he needs us. Process thought seems to lean toward Pelagianism in its denial of original sin and emphasis on human ability. Yet without a proper view of sin there cannot be a proper understanding of sanctification. Process sanctification seems to infer that we can evolve beyond sin and the result is that we are moving toward universal salvation.

About all that remains of the doctrine of Christian perfection is the assertion that while the church remains susceptible to sin, there are moments when we fully walk in the Spirit. But to accept the concept of progressive sanctification does not mean it is based upon process philosophy. The concept of progressive

---

[1339]Wesley, *Letter* to Molly Marston, 26 Aug 1770.

sanctification is not in error because of its emphasis on the process of sanctification. The error is to project this process on the nature of the God who is sanctifying us. Our perfection may be in process, but the perfection of God is absolute. According to a process theology application to the doctrine of Christian perfection, Matthew 5:48 would need to be amended to read, "Become perfect, therefore, as your heaven Father is becoming perfect."

Is such a God in any position to make us what he himself has not yet become? And would such a God even know whether or not we will ever be made perfect in love? If God is the source of our holiness and he is in process, how can we know what holiness is? Thus, the goal of Christian perfection becomes a moving target.

Thus Wesley wrote, "I believe this perfection is always wrought in the soul by a simple act of faith; consequently, in an instant. But I believe in a gradual work, both preceding and following that instant."[1340] He preached

Exactly as we are justified by faith, so are we sanctified by faith. Faith is the condition, and the only condition of sanctification, exactly as it is of justification. It is the condition: none is sanctified but he that believes; without faith no man is sanctified. And it is the only condition: this alone is sufficient for sanctification.[1341]

Because this sanctifying grace is by faith and not by works it can happen in a moment and ought to be expected every moment. He wrote, "Strongly exhort all believers to expect full sanctification now by simple faith."[1342]

[1340]Wesley, *BE Works*, 13:199.

[1341]Wesley, "Scripture Way of Salvation," Sermon # 43, 3.3; see also Wesley, *Letter* to Ann Foard, 12 Oct 1764.

[1342]Wesley, *Letter* to John Ogilvie, 7 Aug 1785.

Believe . . . that he is not only able, but willing to do it *now*! Not when you come to die; not at any distant time; not tomorrow, but *today*. He will then enable you to believe, *it is done*, according to his word.[1343]

However, expecting this gracious gift any moment does not mean that we must first claim it in order to receive it. Phoebe Palmer advocated a naked trust in the naked Word of God. What Palmer called *faith*, Wesley would have called *presumption*.[1344] The early Methodists were quick to seek sanctifying grace, but slow to profess it.[1345] They did not claim it without the fruit. They did not wait passively, but continued to attend to all the means of grace.

The Bane of Legalism

Wesley wrote, "I cannot find in my Bible any such sin as legality. I am not half legal enough, not enough under the law of love."[1346] However, the context of his letter indicates he is not advocating the doctrine of salvation by good works, but rather is speaking of the law of love which Christians should live under. Christians should keep God's law, and that is not properly *legalism*. Keeping the law does not earn salvation, but it is an expression of salvation. It is the standard of obedience for Christians.

In reaction to legalism, there has always been a tendency to antinomianism. Ironically, it is possible to substitute man's rules for God's commands and be both legalistic and antinomian. Wesley himself was accused of legalism because he taught the necessity of keeping God's law.

[1343]Wesley, "On Patience," Sermon #83, § 13.

[1344]See Reasoner, *Holy Living*, 544-562 for a more extensive evaluation of Palmer's theology.

[1345]Tracy, "Entire Sanctification and Uncertain Trumpets," 6-7.

[1346]Wesley, *Letter* to Mary Bishop, 27 Nov 1770.

Virtually any person who believes that there are conditions to be met, commandments to obey, and New Testament standards and principles to which Christians must adhere, will not escape being called a legalist, even while he daily trusts in the merits of Christ and His shed blood for redemption and purchased salvation.[1347]

However, Wesley also wrote the same person a few months later,

Legality, with most who use that term, really means tenderness of conscience. There is no propriety in the word, if one would take it for seeking justification by works. Considering, therefore, how hard it is to fix the meaning of that odd term, and how dreadfully it has been abused, I think it highly advisable for all the Methodists to lay it quite aside.[1348]

Words change their meaning over time, and words which were plainly understood in the 18th century are used differently in the 21st century — such as *enthusiasm* and *prevenient*. However, *legalism* carried more than one connotation in the 18th century. In the 21st century, it means the attempt to earn salvation through works or make oneself holy through extra-biblical rules and standards. Thus, the basis of assurance is self-righteousness. Religion becomes primarily a set of rules and regulations. Over time the Pharisees added their traditions to God's commandments and developed a slavish bondage to regulations and rituals. Jesus kept God's law, but he offended the Pharisees because he did not conform to their expectations.

[1347]McPherson, "What Meaneth the Outcry Against Legalism?" 1.

[1348]Wesley, *Letter* to Mary Bishop, 16 Feb 1771.

In the literature of the early church there are tendencies toward legalism in the *Didache*,[1349] *The Shepherd of Hermas*,[1350] and parts of *The Instructor* by Clement of Alexandria. Wesley was initially inspired by Clement's description of a perfect Christian.[1351] Yet, later in life, Wesley wrote that he saw a Stoic and a Christian were different characters. He said he did not admire the description of Clement as he previously had.[1352]

The Shepherd of Hermas even taught that it is possible to do more than God commands and thus gain more abundant glory.[1353] Legalism was emphasized even more within the monastic movement. Pope cautioned against the undue emphasis on human effort and asceticism.[1354]

The bottom line is the authority of Scripture. We cannot demand or require anything which is not required by Scripture. Wesley taught salvation by grace, not works. In *The Character of a Methodist* he wrote, "Our religion does not lie in doing what God has not enjoined or abstaining from what he hath not forbidden."[1355]

In the book of Galatians, Paul refutes the notion that faith in Jesus Christ is not sufficient for salvation and that some observance of the law is necessary. "Having begun by the Spirit, are you now being perfected by the flesh?" (Gal 3:3).

[1349]The *Didache* was a church manual from the last half of the second century. See the evaluation of Bounds, "Doctrine of Christian Perfection in the Apostolic Fathers," 14-16.

[1350]*The Shepherd of Hermas* was written before AD 150.

[1351]Clement's *Stromateis*, also called *Miscellanies*, Book Seven [Outler, "Introduction," Wesley *BE Works*, 1:75].

[1352]Wesley, *Letter* to Jane C. March, 30 Nov 1774.

[1353]On these works of supererogation, see Flew, *The Idea of Perfection*, 133-134.

[1354]Pope, *Compendium*, 3:65-66.

[1355]Wesley, *BE Works*, 9:34.

The weakness of the law was its powerlessness to produce the love which motivates a person to please God. According to Romans 8:3 the sinful nature overrides any desire to please God in the life of the unregenerate. The law reveals God's holy nature and man's sinful nature. The law demonstrates man's need for salvation. Wesley thought the ceremonial law was added as punishment for sin (Gal 3:19).[1356] Yet the law cannot save. The law drives man to Jesus Christ who alone can save (Gal 3:24). But the law defines how a believer is to walk *after* he is saved (Gal 5:14).

However, we must distinguish between the law and legalism. Legalism is the attempt to earn salvation through works. The Hebrew word for law is *torah* which means instruction or guidance. It refers to a way of life. John Barton explained that "'Torah is a system by which to live the whole of life in the presence of God. . . . ethics is not so much a system of obligations as a way of communion with God, which is the cause of joy."[1357] Thus, the Torah defines holiness not as rigid adherence to regulations but as life lived in obedient love. This definition of godly character, through the giving of the law, implies that God wants us to take on his holy character.

The entire book of Galatians is a warning against legalism. Legalism is the attempt to earn salvation and assurance through works. But salvation is a relationship. Whenever religion loses the supernatural emphasis, it will always revert into legalism and works. The legalist will attempt to justify himself or herself through strict rules. Whenever they fall into difficulty they will try harder, but they do not have the Spirit, they do not have victory over sin, nor do they have any assurance. This is also the situation found in Romans 7. With legalism religion becomes primarily a set of rules and regulations. The basis of assurance is then self-righteousness.

[1356]Wesley, *Notes*, 479.

[1357]Barton, "Approaches to Ethics in the Old Testament," 120.

Legalism is inherent within Pelagianism and liberal Arminianism because they deny original sin. Thus, mankind is born morally neutral and is condemned only for his own sin. For Pelagius, human perfectability is the result of man's freedom and moral nature. Pelagius maintained that the will is naturally free to do good and is not at all impaired by the fall, that there are not special influences of the Spirit in regeneration, but all the help that is necessary in that work is instruction. Through such education a man can perfectly keep the law.[1358] Arminius labeled such a view as "heretical."[1359]

Yet legalism cannot be restricted to any denomination or doctrine. Both legalism and/or antinomianism may crop up within any movement or theological position. Sanctification is distorted when it is reduced to separation or consecration. While it incorporates a proper separation and consecration, if these elements alone define sanctification, the danger is that we then attempt to sanctify ourselves through our works. This is another distortion.

A third distortion is that many have been instructed to sanctify themselves by presumption. But to simply claim sanctification through a misguided understanding of faith does not necessarily produce a holy character.

While the believer should be separate from sin, all too often believers have separated from each other over nonessentials. An emphasis on separation from the world can be Manichaean, based on the belief that the physical world is evil and that we should retreat from it. This can lead to monasticism or legalism. While we are not to love the world system (1 John 2:15), we must realize that the earth is the Lord's and everything in it (Ps 24:1).

Jesus Christ paid the full price of our salvation at the cross. We can add nothing to his finished work. Salvation is a salvation

---

[1358]Peck, *Christian Perfection*, 90; Pope, *Compendium*, 3:70.

[1359]Arminius, *Works*, 1:684-688

from the bondage and power of sin, but that salvation is the gracious gift of God. We cannot make ourselves holy. Paul warned in Colossians 2:21-23,

"Do not handle! Do not taste! Do not touch!" These rules, which have to do with things that are all destined to perish with use, are based on merely human commands and teachings. Such regulations indeed have an appearance of wisdom, with their self-imposed worship, their false humility and their harsh treatment of the body, but they lack any value in restraining sensual indulgence.

With the slogan "Do not handle! Do not taste! Do not touch!" Paul is ridiculing such a reduction of spirituality to a graceless set of regulations. In the 4th century, Chrysostom wrote, "Mark how he makes sport of them, 'touch not, handle not, taste not,' as though they were cowards and keeping themselves clear of some great matters, 'all which things are to perish with the using.'"[1360]

Holy living does involve orthodoxy and orthopraxy. While such holy living cannot be legislated, the believer and the body of Christ collectively must be led by the Spirit. That which the Scriptures do not address cannot be elevated to the level of scriptural authority. We must, however, allow both for personal conviction and tolerance. Basic principles include love, responsibility, liberty, stewardship, modesty, discernment, and deference.

Ethical purity

The Wesleyan emphasis is not upon the OT ceremonial holiness which is so important in high church liturgy. Nor is it the emotional emphasis of pentecostalism. Instead our emphasis

---

[1360]Chrysostom, *Homilies on Colossians. NPNF*1 13:289.

is upon an ethical holiness which is exhibited by conformity to the law of God. Anyone who claims holiness or perfection while living a lawless lifestyle is a fanatic.

R. Newton Flew argued, "The ultimate consideration is not whether human beings have ever attained, but whether it is God's will that they should."[1361] Edward Sugden taught that Christian perfection is an ideal "to which the believer approximates ever more closely, though it may be impossible to say that he has absolutely attained it."[1362] However, the preaching of our age tends to justify Christians in their lukewarmness instead of urging them on to a higher standard. Flew concluded,

> Since holiness is given in response to faith, and since faith is no mere single response but a continuous succession of responses to the divine Giver, it follows that the ideal life is a 'moment-by-moment' holiness.[1363]

As we trust Christ each moment we are cleansed by his blood and filled with his Spirit. The Holy Spirit develops Christian character and maturity within those who are consistently led by the Spirit. Those who walk closest are the most conscious of their imperfections. Yet they can be cleansed at least from all conscious sin. The fruit of the Spirit can be increased in quality and quantity.

"Thus, as a possibility and an obligation, Christian perfection signifies the full cluster and maturity of the specifically Christian graces which give the Christian character its completeness for life and service within the conditions of its earthly environment."[1364] As we endure trials and persevere in faith, the full

---

[1361]Flew, *The Idea of Perfection*, 402.

[1362]Sugden, *Works of John Wesley*, 2:150.

[1363]Flew, *The Idea of Perfection*, 405.

[1364]Platt, "Perfection," 9:728.

effect is that we are perfect and complete, adorned with every Christian grace (Jas 1:4). Wesley said that joy was the highest degree of patience or perseverance and contains all the rest.[1365]

The mature Christian can have a greater delight in God's law and a greater consistency in keeping it. He may enjoy a greater sense of God's favor and a full assurance of faith. He can have a greater sensitivity and compassion for his neighbor. This is Christian perfection.

Psychology and Sanctification

Too much or too little can be made of psychology. The healing of the soul cannot be the result of secular psychotherapy. When theology is reduced to propositional statements, the role of psychology is often discounted. But we do have a soul. The Greek word for *soul* is *psuche*, which is the basis for the word *psychology*. The issue is whether the psychological model we embrace is compatible with biblical teaching or not. Any approach to psychology which affirms the basic goodness of mankind is incompatible with the biblical doctrine of total depravity. Modernism looks to human reason as the ultimate source of truth. This leads to the belief that people have the answers to their own problems within themselves. Some psychological models believe the basic human problem is guilt. And they often blame Christianity for reinforcing guilt. Yet it is the work of the Holy Spirit to convict of sin. The opposite extreme holds that all emotional problems are the result of personal sin.

Jesus Christ is our *wonderful counselor* (Isa 9:6). Yet he often works through human physicians and counselors. A *counselor* has been defined as a temporary assistant to the Holy Spirit. The work of the Holy Spirit in sanctification is to restore the balance of our personality which was lost in the fall. Forgiveness, faith, prayer, meditation, and submission all have powerful

---

[1365]Wesley, *Notes*, 597.

psychological consequences. Bitterness, legalism, perfectionism, fear, and confusion also have negative psychological consequences.

Since Wesleyan theology emphasizes a right relationship with God, with mankind, and peace within, the role of psychology is more important to us than to a system which is merely propositional. We affirm a salvation that we know and a peace that we can feel. If Christian perfection is to be filled with perfect love, this goes beyond mere propositional affirmations. The nature of this secondness is psychological. After the new birth we are not immediately aware of the remaining problem of sin. This remaining sinful nature must be realized before we seek cleansing.

The Hebrew word *shalom* describes a condition of wholeness or completeness. "Sanctification is God's method of healing a soul."[1366]

The purpose of sanctification is wholeness. The grace of God can reverse the effects of the fall. When Paul prayed for the perfection of those in Corinth (2 Cor 13:9-11), he used the Greek word *katartisis*. The verb form is used in v 11. This word was originally used to describe the setting of dislocated bones. God's grace can realign us and restore us.

However, we should not expect Christian maturity to produce uniformity. Charles Rishell explained

Since perfect love is consistent with many mistakes and imperfections, and since these are not identical in any two individuals, there is no absolute standard. The ideal of one may be far higher than that of another.[1367]

Thus, Wesley taught that Christian perfection was a dynamic that can be constantly improved and can always be forfeited. He

[1366]Wynkoop, *Foundations of Wesleyan-Arminian Theology*, 117.

[1367]Rishell, "Doctrine of Sanctification," 528.

was impressed with a phrase from Fénelon, *moi progressus ad infinitum*, "my progress is without end."[1368] Wesley preached, "There is no perfection which does not admit of a continual increase."[1369]

[1368]Tuttle, *Mysticism in the Wesleyan Tradition*, 156.

[1369]Wesley, "Christian Perfection," Sermon # 40, 1.9.

CHAPTER TWELVE
The Doctrine of the Covenant

A covenant is a contract that also creates a relationship. Because God is a covenant-making and covenant-keeping God, he desires to enter into such a relationship with mankind. Yet such a compact cannot be negotiated. God himself controls the terms of the covenant. In order for us to enter into a covenant with God, we must accept his terms. While the intention of the covenant is to form an eternal relationship, the covenant is conditional since we are required to keep the terms. It is outside the nature of God to break his word, but it is possible for us to break covenant with him. God promises blessing to those who keep covenant with him and a curse upon those who break covenant.

God first made a covenant with Adam, who was the legal representative for the entire human race. When Adam broke covenant with God, the entire human race was implicated. Therefore, God offered a new covenant through Jesus Christ. He made provision to restore that broken relationship and provided the enabling grace of his Spirit which makes it possible for us to keep covenant. Until the fullness of time when Christ came, God continued to make covenants.

The covenants with Abraham, Moses, and David should not be contrasted with each other. Rather they were all the same covenant of grace which anticipated the coming of Christ. Dispensationalism tends to dissect these covenants from God's overarching covenant program instead of understanding their continuity. The result is multiple plans of salvation, each unique to a specific period of time. Thus, there are actually only two covenants in Scripture—the covenant of works with Adam and the covenant of grace.

Because we are created in the image of a covenant God, we also make covenants. God, who has all authority, has delegated some of that authority to three covenant institutions which he has ordained. Thus, the kingdom of God includes the family, the church, and the state. None of these institutions can be properly understood, nor can they properly function, without an adequate covenant theology.

Roman Catholic theology tends to consolidate the authority of all three institutions under the pope. Thus, during the medieval period Rome dictated polity to the state. However, the state does not have authority over the church, either. There has always been a present danger — that the state will subsume the family and the church. And there has been tension within marriage ever since the fall. The authority of all three covenant institutions, however, is limited, as is authority within the institution. All three realms must answer ultimately to Almighty God. No human being can exercise authority without first submitting to authority.

The divine Trinity is the ultimate demonstration of how the Father, the Son, and the Spirit can all have specific functions while always working in harmony.

The Covenant God

God is a covenant-keeping God. The word *hesed* means that God is faithful to his covenant. It is translated *loving kindness* or *mercy*. God is motivated by a steadfast love. *Hesed* occurs 246 times in the OT and it has no cognate in any other Semitic language.[1370] There was no covenant relationship between god and

---

[1370]Baer and Gordon, "חסד" *NIDOTTE* 2:211-218.

man in pagan religions. God's covenant reveals his character, the character he wants within us, as well as the problem of sin which keeps us from keeping covenant.

That the transcendent God would condescend to enter into partnership with his own creation is indeed cause for worship. He is not dependent upon us for anything, nor do we have anything to offer him which he has not first given us. Yet he desires to cut a covenant with mankind and enter into a personal relationship with his creation.

The concept of covenant permeates the Jewish understanding of their relationship with God. Yahweh, the self-existent God, initiates and keeps covenant with man.

> The ruling idea of the Old Testament is the idea of Covenant. The term is found in the documents of all periods, but even where the term is absent the idea is present. Apart from one or two such small books as the Song of Songs, it is the presupposition of every book in the Old Testament. Without this idea, no Hebrew story would have a *motif*, no Hebrew prophet a message, no Hebrew psalmist a plea.[1371]

Because God's nature is covenantal, we who are created in his image also make covenants. The Hebrew word *berith* is used over 280 times in the OT to describe treaties, alliances, or leagues between men. It is used to describe a constitution between a ruler and his subjects. And it is used of a relationship between God and his people.

The basic pattern for a covenant, whether secular or sacred, contained a preamble, in which the initiator is identified; a historical prologue describing previous relations between the parties; stipulations and demands which were to be read publicly at

---

[1371]Smith, *Bible Doctrine of Salvation*, 16.

regular intervals; swearing of an oath with blessings and curses; the designation of witnesses and successors.[1372]

These components are observable in the Code of Hammurabi and other ancient treaties and alliances. Such a pattern is also observable in the book of Deuteronomy. This reaffirmation of the covenant, first given at Mt. Sinai, begins with the transcendence of God's sovereignty (Deut 1:1-5). The next section establishes a hierarchy. Moses described the history of Israel in terms of God's leading and blessing (Deut 1:6-4:49).

The heart of the covenant deals with ethics (Deut 5-26). This section defines how God's people are to live so that they can be his holy nation.

The fourth section (Deut 27-30) deals with oaths or vows. Inherent within any covenant is blessing for faithfulness and judgment for those who break covenant. In Nehemiah 9:29 it is stated that a man will live if he obeys the covenant. In Nehemiah 10:29 the people acknowledge that they are under a curse if they break their vows. This is described as a self-maledictory oath. Therefore, Scripture warns that it is better not to vow than to make a vow and not fulfill it (Eccl 5:5).

The final section (Deut 31-34) deals with succession. This section addresses the heirs of the covenantal blessing. God intends for the covenant to continue from generation to generation.

Every covenant was ratified by a sign or seal (Neh 9:38). Under the Mosaic covenant circumcision was the sign of the covenant (Gen 17:11). According to Colossians 2:11-12, baptism has replaced circumcision. Through Scripture, covenants were ratified by a rainbow (Gen 9:15-17), blood (Gen 15:9-21), exchanging names (Gen 17:5,15), exchanging salt (Num 18:19; Lev 2:13; 2 Chr 13:5), exchanging sandals (Ruth 4:1-8), or rings (Gen 38:18; Jer 22:24; Hag 2:23).

The Greek word *diatheke* occurs thirty-three times in the NT. In the King James Version it is translated *covenant* twenty

---

[1372]Sutton, *That You May Prosper*, 14-17.

times and *testament* thirteen times. A *diatheke* was a will that distributed the property after the owner's death. According to Hebrews 9:16 a will became legally valid only through the death of the testator.

It is important to grasp that God's covenants are unilateral in their formulation, that there is a historical continuity in his covenant plans, and that his people must keep the conditions within the covenant in order to enjoy the blessings of the covenant.

God's covenants are unilateral in their formulation

A *diatheke* is completely one-sided; the terms are controlled by the initiator. The ordinary Greek word for covenant was *syntheke*; but since the prefix *syn* means *together with*, it was not used in the NT lest it suggest an equality of partners.

We cannot negotiate a covenant with God. It is always God who makes covenant with someone; never that God and someone make a covenant. Covenants are unilateral, not bilateral. He is the initiator and we either accept or reject his terms. To accept the terms of the covenant involves an unconditional surrender on our part. But we must not only pledge our faith, we must keep faith, since the very nature of a covenant is relational. The church is comprised of those who express their faith through obedience to the covenant. While it is contrary to God's nature to break covenant with us, the history of man's relationship with God is one of broken covenants.

While the term *covenant* does not appear until the covenant with Noah in Genesis 6-9, the elements of a covenant are present with Adam. Two parties are named, a condition is laid down, a promise of reward for obedience is clearly implied, and a penalty for transgression is threatened. Adam was the *federal head* or the legal representative for mankind. The covenant with Adam promised life to those who obeyed God's law, but made no provision for transgressors.

The Historical Continuity of God's Covenants

The term *dispensation* (*oikonomia*) literally means house law or management. The Greek word occurs in Luke 16:2-4 (three times), 1 Corinthians 9:17, Ephesians 1:10, 3:2, 9; Colossians 1:25, and 1 Timothy 1:4. It is best translated *stewardship* or *management*. It can refer to either a method or plan of management or administration or to the one who is given authority to carry out the plan, but never a period of time.[1373]

Dispensational theology, which originated with John Darby (1800-1882), arbitrarily divided human history into *dispensations*, marked by some change in God's method of dealing with mankind. C. I. Scofield defined a dispensation as "a period of time during which man is tested in respect to his obedience to some specific revelation of the will of God."[1374] Scofield taught seven dispensations, each of which ends in judgment marking man's utter failure.[1375] Thus, God's plan is accomplished through his sovereignty, without human participation. A more Wesleyan covenant understanding of synergism acknowledges the role of human responsibility.

According to dispensational theology, God's relationship to man changes with each dispensation. But Bass wrote, "Of such divisions and differentiated relations the historic Christian faith knows nothing."[1376] A belief in progressive revelation or two covenants does not necessarily lead to dispensational theology. In contrast to modern dispensationalism,

Although God made covenants with mankind, this fact is misinterpreted by dispensationalists. For example, Dwight Pente-

---

[1373]Vine, *Expository Dictionary*, 1:321.

[1374]Scofield, *Scofield Reference* Bible (1909), 5; *New Scofield Reference Bible* (1967), 3; Scofield, *Rightly Dividing the Word of Truth*, 19.

[1375]Scofield, *Rightly Dividing the Word*, 19.

[1376]Bass, *Backgrounds to Dispensationalism*, 21.

cost referred to five major covenants, implying that there were at least five different dispensations.[1377]Progressive dispensationalism blurs the distinction even more, saying that dispensations are ways of relating to covenants.[1378]

I am not quibbling over the terms *covenant* or *dispensation*. If a dispensation is a method of administration, the term *dispensation* could be a near synonymous term with covenant. The real distinction is that covenant theology sees continuity, while dispensationalism teaches a split covenant between Israel and the church.

Dispensationalism imposes a discontinuity upon the plan of God. Bill Arnold explained:

So-called covenant theologians assume that the biblical covenants have an organically unified character, while advocates of classical dispensationalism assume that there are a number of distinct dispensations (often seven), each governed by its own covenant. The idea of dispensations with distinct covenants assumes a particular eschatological perspective that is foreign to Wesleyan thought. Wesleyans tend to focus on the unity between the Bible's two Testaments; it is thus more natural to think of the continuity of the OT's four covenants, illustrating that covenants may be developed and adapted, but not superseded. The Mosaic covenant does not make null and void the Abrahamic covenant, no more than Zion (Davidic) supersedes Sinai (Mosaic). The distinctions between the OT covenants are differences of degree rather than kind. Ultimately then, the

---

[1377]Pentecost, *Things to Come*, 67.

[1378]Blaising and Bock, *Progressive Dispensationalism*, 123-126.

NT builds upon and assumes the OT, without nullifying or replacing it.[1379]

In his article, Arnold listed the four covenants as the Edenic or creation covenant, the Abrahamic or land covenant, the Mosaic or national covenant, and the Davidic or family covenant. Arnold explained that the biblical concept of covenant established a relationship between two parties that did not previously exist. Thus, covenant theology see a progressive continuity, while dispensationalism sees a basic discontinuity.

In contrast with the discontinuity of dispensationalism, a covenant understanding provides a more adequate framework. Christ was the *federal head* of the covenant of grace. God's covenant with Noah extended grace. The covenant with Abraham anticipated the coming of Christ. The Mosaic covenant, while called the old covenant, also anticipated the coming of Christ (Gal 3:19) in types and shadows. Jeremiah 31:31 promised a new covenant. Ezekiel 36:22-27 promised the enabling grace of the indwelling Spirit in order to keep the new covenant.

Three times in the book of Hebrews Jesus is identified as the mediator of the new covenant (Heb 8:6, 9:15, 12:24). While Hebrews 8 declares that the new covenant is *better*, there is still a continuity in God's covenants. They all contained law and grace. The difference between the old covenant, with its prescribed forms, and the new covenant, is a new life not a new prescription.

Wesley explained that what was better about the new covenant was that after Pentecost believers "were made more than conquerors over sin by the Holy Ghost given unto them." For Wesley, the fullness of time came at Pentecost and "the kingdom of heaven is now set up on earth."[1380] While Jesus explained that his kingdom was not of this world (John 18:36), he did not say

---

[1379]Arnold, "Covenant," 95-96.

[1380]Wesley, "Christian Perfection," Sermon #40, 2.11,13.

that his kingdom was not *in* this world. According to Matthew 11:1,16:28, Luke 16:16, the kingdom began with the preaching of the gospel.

However, Scofield insisted that Scripture never mixes these two principles. "Law always has a place and work distinct and wholly diverse from that of grace. Law is God prohibiting and requiring; grace is God beseeching and bestowing."[1381]

The new covenant has a better high priest. It is based on better promises (Heb 8:6). These promises are based on Jeremiah 31 and Ezekiel 36. Essentially, Jeremiah 31:31-34 teaches that the new covenant would bring a new inclination of the heart to obey the commands already stated in the old covenant. This passage, cited in Romans 11:27 and Hebrews 8:8-12, 10:16, anticipates the gospel not the millennial kingdom. This contradicts the dispensational position that the new covenant was made only with Israel.[1382] Chafer even suggested a separate new covenant for the church.[1383]

Romans 9 answers the question, "Has the word of God failed if those Jews who seek salvation *by keeping the law, not by faith*, are rejected?" Paul's answer is that both Jew and Gentile are justified by faith (Rom 9:30-32). Thus, Paul is teaching that election is conditional and that condition is faith. If Israel's election was unconditional, Paul would not write in Romans 11:17-20 that they were cut off. Nor would Zechariah warn in 11:10-14 that God would revoke his covenant with Israel.

In a general sense, the old and new covenants are the holy Scriptures. They cannot lie either since they are God's revelation and he is a God of truth. God is faithful to his Word, but his

---

[1381]Scofield, *Rightly Dividing*, 42-43; *Scofield Reference Bible*, 1115.

[1382]Henzel, *Darby, Dualism, and the Decline of Dispensat-ionalism*, 127-150.

[1383]Chafer, *Systematic Theology*, 7:98-99. See also Henzel, *Darby, Dualism, and the Decline of Dispensationalism*, 151-190.

Word contains both promises and warnings. The unfaithfulness of the Jews broke the covenant (see Rom 9:6-14), but did not nullify the faithfulness of God to his Word and his promises to Abraham. According to Galatians 3:19 the law of Moses was added because of transgressions. It was a temporary arrangement until the promised Messiah came. It did not come directly from God to man. It was complex. Peter described it as an unbearable yoke (Acts 15:10).

According to 2 Corinthians 3 the new covenant is better because it is life-giving, not killing, emancipating, not enslaving, inward, not outward, and transfiguring, not condemning.[1384]

A belief in progressive revelation or two covenants does not necessarily lead to dispensational theology. Therefore, it was misleading for Walvoord to argue, "All theologians have some sort of a dispensational division if no more than to divide the Old and New Testament." Walvoord then quoted Chafer who said, "Anyone is a dispensationalist who no longer offers lambs on brazen altars or who does not observe Saturday as the day of rest."[1385] However, Fuller pointed out that it was not proper for Ryrie to call *dispensational* every system which divides redemptive history into periods. He explained that Ryrie was defining the same term generically and then by Darby's specialized usage.[1386]

Peter Gentry and Stephen Wellum wrote in *Kingdom Through Covenant* that dispensationalists reject the idea that covenants, and especially the progression of the covenants, serve as *the* backbone of the Bible's story. The Israel-church distinction is what is distinct to dispensational theology. They believe that the church began at Pentecost.[1387]

[1384]Mantle, *Better Things from Above*, 89-95.

[1385]Walvoord, "Dispensational Premillennialism," 11–13.

[1386]Fuller, *Gospel and Law*, 10.

[1387]Gentry and Wellum, *Kingdom Through Covenant*, 54-56.

Dispensationalism is a theology of discontinuity, in which God has multiple plans of salvation. Chafer explained that the dispensational hermeneutic necessitated two ways of salvation.[1388] While the 1967 Scofield edition added that salvation has always been by grace through faith, this understanding seems to be both asserted and contradicted. For example, John Walvood wrote that during a future tribulation period believers would not be indwelt by the Holy Spirit, but that conditions would revert back to OT norms. He also wrote that during a future millennial age the baptism of the Spirit will become the baptism of fire.[1389] John Hagee holds that Jewish people do not need to be saved since they are under a different covenant.[1390] This two-covenant theology holds that Gentiles are saved by faith in Christ while Jews are saved by keeping the law. However, Paul prayed for Israel "that they may be saved" (Rom 10:1-2), instead of insisting that they already were. Salvation has always been by grace through faith. Justin Martyr condemned Judaism because Christianity had inherited all that was valuable, religiously, doctrinally, and messianically, in Judaism. Therefore, Jews need to be converted.[1391]

An inductive study of the Scripture reveals that there are eighteen descriptions of Israel given in the OT which are transferred to the Christian church in the NT. There are also sixteen passages in the OT referring to Israel which are quoted in the NT as referring to Christians.[1392]

[1388]Chafer, "Dispensationalism," 390-449.

[1389]Walvoord, The Holy Spirit, 230; 21.

[1390]House, "Summary Critique," 50-52. Franz Rosenzweig (1886-1929) taught two separate but equal ways to God [Gudel, "To the Jew First," 36-42].

[1391]Justin Martyr, Dialogue with Trypho, ch. 137; ANF 1:268.

[1392]Provan, The Church is Israel Now (1987).

However, dispensationalism rejects this conclusion as "re-placement theology." They claim that God's covenant with Israel is unconditional and therefore he cannot break his word. But we must recognize both a continuity and discontinuity. The butterfly does not exactly replace the caterpillar. It is a new phase of existence which actually surpasses the caterpillar. The church is a continuation and expansion of Israel, not necessarily a replace-ment. Oden explained, "The new Israel does not destroy but fulfills the promise of the old."[1393]

Both Old and New Testament saints make up the church, the bride of Christ, in Revelation 21:9-14. The New Jerusalem has twelve gates with the names of the twelve tribes of Israel. It has twelve foundations which contain the names of the twelve apos-tles. Therefore, the conditional privilege of old Israel has been transferred to the church. Jesus warned in the parable of the tenants that the vineyard would be taken away from those who neglected it and given to others (Luke 20:9-18). Yet Romans 11:26 foretells that they will be grafted back into the new cove-nant. But how could they be restored if they were never cut off?

Charles Ryrie insisted that it is mandatory for dispensationalists to separate Israel and the church. He said this distinction between Israel and the church is probably the most basic theological test of whether or not a person is dispensational.[1394] This insistence on discontinuity has led dispensationalism to interject a secret rapture of the church into God's plan, so that God could revert back to Israel. Walvoord explained, "It is therefore not too much to say that the rapture question is determined more by ecclesiology than eschatol-ogy."[1395] F. F. Bruce observed,

---

[1393]Oden, *Life in the Spirit*, 269.

[1394]Ryrie, *Dispensationalism Today*, 44-45; see also 47, 96, 159.

[1395]Walvoord, *The Rapture Question*, 15-16. This concession is found in the 1957 original edition, but was expunged from subsequent editions from 1970-1979.

One cannot logically retain Darby's eschatology and reject his ecclesiology, as some schools of thought in our own day attempt to do. (I have never known anyone who accepted his ecclesiology without at the same time accepting his eschatology.)[1396]

In this case, a whole system of eschatology is built on the false premise that covenants are unconditional. They hold that the church did not exist until Pentecost and that it is a digression from God's original plan. Showers wrote, "In contrast with the Covenant Theology view, Dispensational Theology declares that the Church did not begin until the Day of Pentecost of Acts 2."[1397]

But God does not have two people nor two plans. Both Jew and Gentile are to be incorporated into "one new man." The dividing wall has been destroyed (Eph 2:14-15). According to Peter, God put no difference between Jew and Gentile (Acts 15:9). Ray Dunning wrote, "The most pervasive metaphor used in the New Testament for the Church is 'the new Israel.'" He then rejected dispensationalism. "The distinction between Israel and the Church, so widely embraced among conservative Christians, simply will not stand the test of biblical exegesis."[1398]

In Scripture, the term *Israel* is not identical with the Jewish race. Qualifications for inclusion in *Israel* were the same for Jew and Gentile: obedience to God and covenantal loyalty. Thus, Jews could be cut off from Israel according to Exodus 30:33, 38,

---

[1396]Bruce, foreword to Rowdon, *The Origins of the Brethren*, xii.

[1397]Showers, *There Really Is a Difference*, 169.

[1398]Dunning, *Grace, Faith, and Holiness*, 511-512. On p. 587 Dunning rejected the distinction between Israel and the church as based upon a Calvinistic view of unconditional covenants. Dunning is correct in his analysis that this invalid conclusion is based on the false premise of unconditional covenants, but Calvinism rejects dispensationalism as adamantly as true Wesleyan-Arminians.

31:14; Leviticus 17:14, 18:29, 20:18, 23:29; Numbers 9:13, 19:13. Therefore, Paul could write in Romans 9:6 that not all who are descended from Israel are Israel. And any Gentile proselyte who adopted covenant stipulations could be welcomed into Israel (Exod 12:48-49).[1399]

God has always had a people. We see the beginnings of the church within the first family. Adam was the first priest and he led his family in worship through sacrifices. As the world became apostate, God called Noah and his family out. The basic meaning of *ekklesia* is called out. Abraham was also called out.

In the LXX *ekklesia* refers to Israel in references such as Joshua 8:35; Ezra 2:64; and Joel 2:16. Acts 7:38 refers to Israel as the "church in the wilderness." Clarke observed that the Israelite church consisted of twelve tribes but they were one family.[1400] Beale explained,

> The word *church*, however, must also be understood against the background of the Greek Old Testament, where the word repeatedly refers to the gathered congregation of Israel. In this light, the Thessalonian church was part of the true Israelite congregation of God's people who had been established by Messiah Jesus' later-day redemptive work.[1401]

By the NT, the church was no longer national, but international. Paul revealed God's mystery in Ephesians that God intended both Jew and Gentile to be one body. Thus, Wiley said that the church took its visible form in the covenant with Abraham and that the Christian church is the continuation of the Abrahamic covenant. Pentecost was the birthday of the *Christian*

[1399]Gregg, *There is Another King*, 53.

[1400]Clarke, *Works*, 5:219.

[1401]Beale, *1-2 Thessalonians*, 42.

church, but not the birth of the church.[1402] However, Scofield claimed that the church is distinct from Israel and not mentioned once in the OT.[1403] While it has been assumed that the words of Jesus in Matthew 16:18, "I will build my church" implies that the church was only a future reality at that time, the church was a present reality in Matthew 18:17.

Dispensationalism also emphasizes the failure of each dispensation.[1404] Darby believed "the church age" would end in apostasy, just like every other dispensation. He taught that we should expect the progress of evil. The hope that Christendom could be restored was an impossibility. The church was apostate and in ruins. Any attempt to restore the church will result in utter failure and is sinful.[1405] In fact, Darby taught that anything which looked like church prosperity is a delusion. "The year-books of Christianity are the year-books of hell." Thus, Daniel Steele characterized dispensational premillennialism as *pessimistic*.[1406]

God's Covenant Blessings are Conditional

The Jews seemed to think that for God to condemn a Jew would be a violation of his promises to them and that God would then be unfaithful. This thinking was based on the false assumption that God's covenants are unconditional. Paul declared that God is faithful, even if every man is unfaithful (Rom 3:3-4). But will God maintain his covenant with covenant breakers?

The very nature of a covenant implies mutual obligations. We are not discussing a blank check or an outright grant with no

---

[1402]Wiley, *Christian Theology*, 2:329; 3:107,185-186.

[1403]Scofield, *Rightly Dividing*, 11-12.

[1404]Scofield, *New Scofield Reference Bible*, 3; *Rightly Dividing the Word of Truth*, 19.

[1405]Bass, *Backgrounds to Dispensationalism*, 46-47,100-108.

[1406]Steele, *Substitute for Holiness*, 77-78,9.

strings attached. Stipulations are inherent within covenants. Richard Watson defined the essence of a covenant as mutual stipulations between two parties. "It could not be a covenant unless there were terms, something required, as well as something promised or given, duties to be performed, as well as blessings to be received."[1407] Not only are there blessings promised for those who keep covenant, whoever breaks covenant has brought a curse upon himself. Therefore, Scripture warns that it is better not to vow than to make a vow and not fulfill it (Eccl 5:5).

Wesley raised the question "whether this covenant between God and man be unconditional or conditional?" Wesley went back to the covenant made with Abraham. While the covenant was everlasting, Wesley demonstrated it was also conditional.[1408] The terms of a covenant are everlasting (Jer 50:5). A covenant cannot be made on a trial basis. But a covenant is also conditional in the sense that both parties must maintain their eternal agreement. Adam was forbidden to eat from the tree, Noah was required to build an ark, Abraham had to leave home and later be willing to offer his son. For Moses the requirement was the law given at Mt. Sinai.

In Psalm 89, the covenant made with David was conditioned upon the obedience of David and his family. God promised David that his seed would reign forever (2 Sam 7:11-16). While Psalm 89:29 sounds like an unconditional covenant, Wesley pointed out that it was "accomplished only in Christ."[1409] The conditional nature is stated in Psalm 132:12.

After twenty-two sons of David ruled over Judah, there was no son of David on the throne from 587 BC to the coming of Christ. If this covenant was unconditional, then God broke it. Yet it was David's heirs who broke covenant with God. In Zechariah

---

[1407]Watson, *Dictionary*, 153.

[1408]Wesley, *BE Works*, 13:297-298.

[1409]Wesley, *Notes*, 3:1756.

11:10-11, God broke his covenant with Israel. The verb used in vv 10 and 14, *parar*, was also used in Isaiah 10:33 to signify cutting down a tree and in 1 Samuel 2:31 for bringing a family line to an end. In the context of Zechariah the breaking of the covenant is connected with the betrayal of Jesus (v 12). Symbolically, Zechariah says Jesus was *paid* because he was being *let go*. Thus, Israel broke covenant with God.

While we cannot be saved by keeping the covenant of works, the notion that grace has replaced law is wrong. The giving of the law was an essential part of the establishment of the covenant. The terms *covenant* and *commandments* were interchangeable. To keep the commandments was to maintain the covenant relationship.

This distinction between the ceremonial law and the moral law is implied in such passages as Psalm 40:6-8, 51:16-17; Isaiah 1:11-17; Hosea 6:6; and Micah 6:6-8. Jesus taught in Matthew 12:11-12 that some ritual laws could be preempted by acts of mercy. In Matthew 23:23 Jesus taught that justice, mercy, and faithfulness carried more weight than the ritual duty of tithing herbs, which were not specifically covered in Leviticus 27:30 and Deuteronomy 14:22. Paul also distinguished between the importance of dietary law and sexual morality (1 Cor 6:13).

Moral law reflects God's character, while ritual law symbolized, through memorial or anticipation, acts of God which were more important than the ritual itself. Such distinctions are common to covenant theology.

However, the category of moral law is rejected by dispensationalists because they relegate it to the Mosaic dispensation. Showers argued that, in contrast with covenant theology, dispensationalism holds the position that "Christians today are not under any aspect of the Mosaic Law, even the moral aspect."[1410] Thus, it may be easier to get the Ten Commandments

---

[1410]Showers, *There Really Is a Difference*, 187.

posted in the courthouse than preached in some evangelical churches.

When law is separated from grace, as in dispensationalism, the result is antinomianism. John Gerstner bluntly declared, "Dispensationalism is inseparably connected with antinomianism."[1411] Their hermeneutic requires any OT command must be renewed under the new covenant in order to be valid.[1412]

The practical consequence of such a belief is that the OT becomes little more than a book of history. However, John MacArthur declared:

> The age of law/age of grace distinction in particular has wreaked havoc on dispensationalist theology and contributed to confusion about the doctrine of salvation. Of course, there is an important distinction to be made between law and grace. But it is wrong to conclude, as Chafer apparently did, that law and grace are mutually exclusive in the program of God for any age. Actually, elements of both law and grace are part of the program of God in every dispensation.[1413]

God always intended for his covenant with mankind to be an everlasting covenant, but he always included conditions which he enabled his covenant people to keep. Wesley demonstrated that the Davidic Covenant was conditional and concluded that, even when not explicitly stated, conditions are implied in all covenants.[1414] Ray Dunning declared, "The Wesleyan commitment to

---

[1411]Gerstner, *Primer on Dispensationalism*, 29.

[1412]Moo, "A Modified Lutheran View," 376.

[1413]MacArthur, *Gospel According to Jesus*, 25-26.

[1414]Wesley, *BE Works*, 13:244.

synergism rejects the idea that God enters into unconditional covenants with humankind."[1415]

However, the Calvinist Gary DeMar, who would affirm monergism, also rejected dispensationalism on the basis that covenents are conditional. Thus, DeMar argued that the promises of land to Israel were conditional, according to Leviticus 18:24-30. He concluded,

> If the promises to Israel are unconditional, then no matter what Israel does, she still inherits all the promises. . . . There can be no "spewing out," no kingdom "taken away," and no coming to remove your lamp-stand.[1416]

Apparently, DeMar makes a distinction between unconditional personal election and conditional corporate covenants. Louis Berkhof observed that even the law of Moses is not devoid of promises and that the gospel also contains demands. Christ did not fulfill the law for us as a rule of life. "It is pure Antinomianism to maintain that Christ kept the law as a rule of life for His people, so that they need not worry about this any more."[1417]

Dispensationalism, however, teaches the unconditional nature of covenants. While a covenant is unconditional in the sense that it cannot be negotiated, it is conditional in the sense that it must either be ratified or rejected. Every biblical covenant has stated or implied conditions. Yet dispensationalism is characterized by the assumption that covenants are unconditional. At a personal level, this leads to antinomianism — the belief that once we possess faith in Christ we are unconditionally secure regardless of whether we obey the commands of Christ.

[1415]Dunning, "Presuppositions of a Wesleyan Eschatology," 198.

[1416]DeMar, "Effects of the Dispensational Parade," 2.

[1417]Berkhof, *Systematic Theology*, 612-614.

At the corporate level, this leads to the belief that God's covenant with Abraham was unconditional. Therefore, God was obligated to keep covenant with Israel even through Israel rejected his Messiah. John MacArthur declared that because of God's holy nature he could not renege on his promise to Israel.[1418] Showers argued that the unconditional nature of the Abrahamic covenant guarantees Israel permanent existence as a nation and it guarantees Israel permanent ownership of the promised land.[1419]

John Hagee insists that Israel must gain control over a land mass that is thirty times its present size.

> The Royal Land Grand that God, the original owner, gave to Abraham, Isaac, and Jacob and their seed forever, includes the following territory which is presently occupied by Israel, the West Bank, all of Lebanon, one half of Syria, two-thirds of Jordan, all of Iraq, and the northern portion of Saudi Arabia.[1420]

This belief has led some dispensationalists to advocate a position of unconditional support for the nation of Israel.[1421] Dwight Wilson concluded,

> Although it is difficult to prove from direct statements, when one analyzes the premillenarians' response to Israel, the inescapable conclusion is that their philosophy of history in many cases is equivalent to the antinomian heresy. . . . If every action is preordained, then there is no need to measure one's actions by moral

---

[1418]MacArthur, *Romans 1-8,* 171.

[1419]Showers, *There Really Is a Difference,* 69-72.

[1420]Hagee, *Should Christians Support Israel?* 99.

[1421]Weber, *On the Road to Armageddon,* 213-248.

law, since the decision to obey or disobey the standard has already been made. If Israel is the elect, and Jewish history is predetermined by God and foretold by prophecy, then ordinary rules of international law (morality) do not apply to God's chosen people; and there is no absolute standard by which they can be judged.[1422]

This worldview is a variation of the Calvinist view that might makes right. It also creates an unnecessary barrier in Arab evangelism. Mark Hanna argued that when the Bible refers to Israel as a nation it means *a people*, not a territory of state. Hanna wrote, "Israel today is not the people of God." He argued that the people of God today are not Israelis or Jews or Gentiles, but regenerated believers in the gospel of Christ.[1423]

Although dispensationalists consider it futile for Christians to be involved in the political process, according to them the highest eschatological purpose for the church is to lobby for the nation of Israel. This position is known as *Christian Zionism*. Stephen Sizer explained that dispensationalism and covenantalism disagree over whether unconditional support for the nation of Israel is biblical.[1424]

Fuller explained that it was necessary for dispensationalism to insist the Abrahamic covenant was unconditional and the blessings physical so that Israel and the church could be kept distinct.[1425] Thus, some dispensationalists have been forced by

---

[1422]Wilson, *Armageddon Now!* 143, 217.

[1423]Hanna, "Israel Today," 14-17. This article in *Christianity Today* was followed by an attempted rebuttal by Jerry Falwell entitled "Jerry Falwell Objects," 14-17. In his agenda for the Moral Majority, Falwell declared, "To stand against Israel is to stand against God" [*Fundamentalist Phenomenon*, 215]. However, Falwell was advocating a political agenda.

[1424]Sizer, *Christian Zionism*, 19.

[1425]Fuller, *Gospel and Law*, 136.

their own presuppositions to hold to two new covenants, one for Jews and one for Gentiles.[1426]

Yet Zechariah 11:10-14 warned that God would revoke his covenant with Israel. Jesus warned that the kingdom of God would be taken away from them and given to a nation producing fruit (Matt 21:45). Wesley explained that the Jews who did not receive the Lord became reprobated, "For they no longer continued to be the people of God."[1427]

The Three Covenant Institutions

The term *theocracy* refers to the sovereignty of God. Neither the family, the church, nor the state is a theocracy. There is a division of authority under God. However, the Roman Catholic Church sees itself as the church *and* the state. The pope regards himself as the *pontifex maximus*, a title appropriated from the Roman emperors. Pope Innocent III declared that Christ left to Peter the governance not of the church alone, but of the whole world.[1428]

Nor is there any separation of church and state in the eastern church. The control of the church by the emperor is known as *caesaropapism*. Thus, the church was subordinate to the state and this dynamic probably accounts for its tendency to stagnation.

• The Institution of Marriage

God instituted marriage in Genesis 2:24-25. Marriage was designed to be a permanent union, as well as an intimate relationship. Marriage is based upon mutual respect and commitment. In the marriage covenant there is a transfer of authority.

[1426]Walvoord, *The Millennial Kingdom*, 209-214; Ryrie, *Basis of the Premillennial Faith*, 107.

[1427]Wesley, *Notes*, 385.

[1428]Latourette, *History of Christianity*, 1:483.

Eve sinned first, then Adam. In desiring to be as God, Adam became less than man by submitting to his wife. However, the Scripture always holds Adam responsible (for example, see 1 Cor 15:22).

What Adam was to the entire human family, each husband is for his own immediate family. The Bible is consistent at this point. The wife is under her husband's authority (Num 5:29) and the husband has *veto power* over any vow made by his wife (Num 30:8).

While marriage is not a sacrament, because it is not commanded, it serves at least six purposes. We were not created for marriage, but marriage was created for humanity. Thus, marriage is not the end of our existence, but the means to these ends:

- Marriage illustrates the relationship between Christ and his church (Eph 5:32; Rev 19:7).
- Marriage propagates the race (Gen 1:27-28). According to Psalm 127:3-4, children are God's gifts. Parents also enter into a covenant to train up their children in the nurture and admonition of the Lord. While infant baptism is a legitimate sign and seal of that covenant, a dedication, without such a sign and seal, also constitutes a covenant.
- Marriage provides companionship and encouragement. God set the lonely in families (Ps 68:6).
- Marriage provides sexual satisfaction and prevents immorality (Prov 5:18-19; 1 Cor 7:1-5). However, no sexual practice should be insisted upon when it includes a violation of conscience or requires medical risk.
- The marriage relationship forces both partners to deal with their inherent self-centeredness and to put their partner ahead of themselves. Thus, God designed it to be part of the sanctifying process.
- Marriage advances God's kingdom (Gen 1:28). A Christian home demonstrates God's order and harmony. According to Proverbs 13:22 we are to leave a heritage. As generations of

Christians multiply, Christianity can expand on earth through the multiplication of Christian children.

According to 1 Corinthians 7:14 an unbelieving spouse is sanctified through their covenant relationship with a believing spouse. This does not mean that an unbeliever is saved by proxy, but that he or she benefits from a relationship in which grace is at work. And their offspring are spiritually circumcised even though father or mother is spiritually unclean.

In the beginning, God created marriage and it was beautiful. God designed this relationship to be based on mutual respect. But marriage has been under attack ever since the fall. One of the consequences, stated in Genesis 3:16, is that women want to control their husband and the husband will have a tendency to be domineering. Both of these tendencies are sinful and must be addressed by the purifying grace of God if the marriage is suc-cessful. When the opportunity affords itself, males tend to exploit females. And if they have the leverage, females tend to exploit males. When men and women are born again, they receive a new nature, but they still retain this old nature. Although it remains, it has been rendered powerless. It has not been eradicated and it can regain control even in Christian marriages.

The word *desire* (*teshuqah*) in Genesis 3:16 is only used in two other places: Genesis 4:7 and Song of Solomon 7:10. Based on the use of this word in the nearer context, it would refer to a sinful desire to possess or control. The phrase could be translated "your desire shall be *against* your husband."

Likewise, the statement "he shall rule over you" indicates a tendency to be overbearing. The Hebrew verb *mashal*, which is translated *rule*, occurs in Genesis 3:16 and 4:7. Because of man's sinful nature, women have been abused and oppressed. The feminist movement is a reaction against overbearing men and fathers who have abandoned their responsibility. It can also be an expression of the woman's sinful nature.

In Genesis 4:7 sin is personified as lurking and poised ready to exploit any situation which arises. Much the same picture is expressed in 1 Peter 5:18 where Satan is compared to a lion on the prowl.

Cain was told that he must master this desire, and so must we— whether husband or wife. The husband is not ordained to be the master of his wife. Nor is she ordained to control him. Rather, both husband and wife must master this sinful urge to control and exploit each other. Essentially, the besetting sin of men is to become harsh and overbearing or to abdicate their role as head of the family. While the besetting sin of women is to control their husband, he must maintain his role as leader using the minimum degree of assertion necessary to fulfill his responsibilities.

The perfecting grace of God will address this tendency, and great progress can be made in a marriage where both partners are being filled with perfect love. Yet this perfection is not static. Every marriage encounters times of crisis. We are constantly changing, for better or worse, by the choices we make.

Equal worth, different roles

At issue is not male superiority or female inferiority. Both male and female are created in God's image and are given dominion (Gen 1:26-28). *Man* is the generic Hebrew term, *adam*, for *mankind*. Nothing about the term *helper* in Genesis 2:18 implies inferiority. The same word is used of God in Psalm 118:6. *Weaker*, in 1 Peter 3:7, does not mean inferior. Because women are physically *weaker*, we treat them with respect, not contempt.

According to 1 Peter 3:1, part of her role is to submit to her husband, and if she does not submit to her husband *her* prayers may be hindered. The pronoun *your* in v 7 is plural. Since they are joint-heirs, either party may hinder their vertical relationship with God by being out of line in their horizontal relationship with their spouse.

The controversy in marriage concerns roles. Evangelical feminists want to abolish all gender roles in society, church, and home. Their key verse is Galatians 3:28, "There is neither Jew nor Greek, slave nor free, male nor female, for you are all one in Christ Jesus."

The feminist argument is that submission is a result of the curse. Since the cross delivers from the curse, in Christ submission is no longer required. Therefore, marriage should be an egalitarian relationship with no male headship nor submission by the wife.

This interpretation goes far beyond what Paul wrote. Galatians 3:28 affirms the basic equality of male and female, but it does not abolish their roles. The verse does not negate racial, economic, or sexual differences. The phrase *neither male nor female* does not mandate homosexuality. The verse never mentions the husband/wife relationship. It does not change the relationship of husband and wife any more than it changes the relationship of parents and children. Furthermore, submission was God's plan before the fall and was not part of the punishment. Paul's basis for male headship is based on creation order, not the fall (1 Tim 2:13).

Christ and the church

The Bible never commands a husband to submit to his wife. Colossians 3:18, Titus 2:5, Ephesians 5:22, and 1 Peter 3:1 specify that it is the wife who is to submit. Ephesians 5:21 is often quoted in support of *mutual submission*. Even good authors often use this term carelessly. Both partners are to be considerate and thoughtful, but no institution can function without a system of authority. Someone has to take responsibility. Both cannot come under each other. A committee of two with no chairperson will not work! Ephesians 5:21 is an introduction to the concept that everyone must live under authority. Then three examples are given: wife/husband, slave/master, and child/parent.

If one of the primary purposes of marriage is to symbolize the union of Christ and the church, then an egalitarian marriage destroys the symbolism. C. S. Lewis is often quoted as saying,

"Only a man in masculine uniform can represent God to the church, since the church is essentially feminine to God."[1429]

Paul taught that Christ is head of the church and that the husband is head of the home. Paul taught that the head of woman is man in the same sense that God the Father is head over God the Son (1 Cor 11:3).

Orthodox Christianity understands that Christ is of the same essence as God the Father. However, Christ did not consider his equality with the Father something to cling to (Phil 2:6). In the salvation order the Father sent the Son and the Son sent the Spirit.

Two lessons should be drawn from the harmony within the Trinity. First, husband and wife are of equal value to God in the same way that Father and Son are both God. Second, just as the Son willingly submitted to the Father's will, so the wife is to voluntarily submit to her husband.

A woman should not marry a man she is unwilling to follow. God designed marriage and the terms of the covenant cannot be altered. Those who attempt to set up a different structure only increase the tension.

This truth must be balanced, however, by the statement that no husband has unlimited authority. He is not God. Sapphira was judged by God because she did not disobey her husband. Acts 5:29 teaches that no person can take the authority of God. Since there is only one Sovereign, we believe in limited human government and limited human authority.

Jesus explained that while Moses permitted divorce, that was never God's intent (Matt 19:8). Within the terms of the covenant, "until death do us part," is stipulated. Scripture allows for the marriage covenant to be broken only because of death, desertion (1 Cor 7:15) or adultery. Jesus allowed divorce in the case of fornication (*porneia*). This word refers to sexual sin. One type of *porneia* is *adultery*, a sexual sin which can be committed only by someone who is married or with someone who is mar-

---

[1429]Lewis, *God in the Dock*, 234-239.

ried. Adultery is even more serious because it violates the marriage covenant. Thus, the marriage bed is defiled (Heb 13:4).

Proverbs 2:17 and Malachi 2:14 both describe marriage as a covenant. However, because covenants are conditional, God allows divorce when there has been marital unfaithfulness. The verb used in Matthew 5:32 and 19:9, *apoluo*, implies that the marriage is dissolved. Just as a man and a woman cut the covenant of marriage, so their divorce cuts off that relationship. While the marriage union must involve mutual consent, the dissolution of marriage does not. If one party of the covenant breaks faith, the union is potentially broken. The innocent party cannot maintain the vows of marriage alone.

Historically, the Roman Catholic Church has contended that marriage is a sacrament, that the state does not have jurisdiction over marriage, and that the state cannot pronounce a divorce. However, Vatican II made major changes. Today the Roman church teaches that marriage is a sacrament and the ceremony of marriage is a liturgical act to be celebrated in the public liturgy of the church. According to Canon 1124, marriage between a Romanist and a baptized non-Romanist is prohibited. However, a bishop may allow the marriage if the non-Romanist promises not to try to "pervert" the Romanist spouse. They both must agree in writing that their children would be baptized as Roman Catholics and raised in the Romanist faith.

Roman Catholic dogma teaches four types of marriage. Marriage between two baptized Roman Catholics and performed by the Roman Catholic Church is regarded as sacramental. *Sacerdotalism*, whether Roman Catholic or high-Anglican, believes that marriage is a sacrament. Therefore, if vows are exchanged between two baptized Roman Catholics, no power on earth can dissolve a sacramental marriage because it is a supernatural union. Protestants who claim that the vows of marriage are indissoluble reflect either a more Roman Catholic theology or at least a misunderstanding of the nature of covenants.

A "mixed marriage" is a marriage between a Roman Catholic and a baptized non-Roman Catholic. Such a marriage needs the express permission of the Roman Catholic Church. Any permission presupposes that both parties accept the baptism and education of their children into the Roman church.

A marriage between a Roman Catholic and a non-baptized person requires even greater concern. Such a marriage is not considered on the same level as a marriage between a Roman Catholic and a baptized non-Catholic.

A fourth category, "common law" marriage, is based on an implied consent, without any covenant vows. It may be recognized as legal by some civil governments. However, a marriage tribunal of the Roman church has the power to judge whether a sacramental marriage actually did occur. On the basis of "Pauline privilege," supposedly based on 1 Corinthians 7:15, the Roman church teaches that a marriage between Protestants, or between unbelievers, can be dissolved when one member converts to their church and the spouse is unwilling to also "convert." A marriage can also be annulled either by a dispensation from the pope if one or both parties claim that it was not consummated or if one party takes the vow of chastity to become a monk, a priest, or a nun.[1430]

While the Roman church teaches that a sacramental marriage cannot be dissolved, it permits the physical separation of the couple. The Roman church does not recognize divorce pronounced by civil law. According to Roman Catholic theology, marriage is under the jurisdiction of the church, which they define as themselves exclusively. A marriage between those who have been validly married by a priest is consummated after they have engaged in sexual intercourse.

These artificial distinctions disregard the covenantal nature of marriage, as well as the separation of powers between church and state. Pope Innocent III taught that civil authority is inferior to papal authority as the moon is to the sun. Thus, they tend to disregard the authority of the state regarding marriage. He also

---

[1430]Boettner, *Divorce*, 33-38.

taught that the clergy was independent from the law of the state and subject only to the church.[1431]

If the Roman church determines that a sacrament did not occur, they can authorize an annulment which frees the parties to remarry within the Roman church since the first marriage was deemed to be defective and not sacramental.

Those who remarry without a church nullification are barred from communion because they are living in a state of adultery. However, if they have repented from their illicit union, but remain together for the sake of children, they may live together as "brother and sister," avoiding sexual relations, and they may receive communion provided scandal can be avoided—that most people are unaware of their remarriage. If a scandal cannot be avoided, they must either separate or refrain from communion.

While conservative Protestants may, at times, find more common ground with conservative Roman Catholics than with liberal Protestants, we have a fundamental difference in the division of covenant institutions. We reject papal authority as the final authority over the family, the church, *and* the state.

In Mormonism, the only way a man can attain godhood is through eternal marriage. Their doctrine of celestial marriage allows for polygamy. According to Orson Pratt,

> Each God, through his wife or wives, raises up a numerous family of sons and daughters. . . . Each father and mother will be in a condition to multiply forever. As soon as each God has begotten many millions of male and female spirits . . . he, in connection with his sons, organizes a new world . . . where he sends both the male and female spirits to inhabit tabernacles of flesh and bones. . . . The inhabitants of each world are required to reverence, adore, and worship their own

---

[1431]Latourette, *History of Civilization*, 1:483.

personal father who dwells in the Heaven which they formerly inhabited.[1432]

In contrast, a covenant theology of marriage does allow for divorce under biblical circumstances. It also acknowledges the role of the state, as separate from the church, in permitting marriage. The state has a compelling interest in the health and education of the children which will be the fruit of the new marriage. The state can also prohibit near relatives from marriage, since the risk of such marriages can provide handicapped children who will likely become wards of the state. Wiley observed that the state and the church both have a role in creating the family.[1433]

Where the state permits that which Scripture prevents, Christians must adhere to the higher standard; and the Christian church must not redefine marriage in accordance with pagan definitions.

In cultures where Roman Catholic theology prevails, there are often two marriage ceremonies, a civil wedding and a church wedding. But the couple is not considered *fully* married until they have their church wedding. From a covenantal standpoint, the couple is as married as they ever will be when they have concluded exchanging their covenant vows — regardless of whether that ceremony was conducted by civil or church authorities.

Initially, Christians were not required to seek the blessing of the church in order to validate their marriage. However, by the time of Tertullian writing around AD 202, he observed that Christians were requesting marriage from their priests. Thus, it became customary to have a Christian ceremony.[1434]

[1432]Pratt, "Pre-Existence of Man," 37. See also *Doctrines and Covenants*, 132:18-22.

[1433]Wiley, *Christian Theology*, 3:81-82; Watson, *Theological Institutes*, 2:546.

[1434]Latourette, *History of Christianity*, 1:204-205. See Tertullian's two letters to his wife, *ANF*, 4:48.

While the divorce rate may be higher in cultures with a Protestant and covenant understanding of marriage, that is only because the Roman theology does not allow for the "sacrament" of marriage to be broken. It does not insure a higher state of morality. The Roman priesthood may be under the vow of celibacy which prohibits their marriage, but they have never been under a vow of chastity which prohibits their sexual promiscuity. Celibacy is not a higher spirituality than marriage. Marriage is the gift of God and celibacy is a gift only in extenuating circumstances, such as the "present crisis" of first-century persecution (1 Cor 7:26). Marriage is not to be forbidden (1 Tim 4:3). It is a misunderstanding to claim that one is married to Christ or the church in lieu of marriage to a husband or wife. The church is the community of all those who have saving faith in Jesus Christ. All within the church are spiritually the bride of Christ, but that spiritual relationship does not replace the institution of marriage.

Marriage is more than a civil contract which can be negotiated. Since it is a divinely instituted covenant relationship, God alone has the authority to establish the terms. Thus, same-sex relationships do not constitute marriage. Jesus explained that God created two genders, male (*arsen*) and female (*thelus*). In the marriage covenant a man is united to a woman (Matt 19:4). In Matthew 19:5 and the parallel passage in Mark 10:7, the Greek word *anthropos* is used. This word can mean a male or it can be used generically of mankind. However, in this context it is used as a synonym with *arsen* in the previous verse. Jesus cited Genesis 2:24 where the Hebrew word *ish* is the gender-specific word for a male and *ishshah* is a gender-specific word for a female. Further, two humans of the same gender cannot become "one flesh." While *one flesh* may imply more than sexual intercourse, according to 1 Corinthians 6:16 it does include it.

The state does not have the authority to usurp the normal functions of the family, including its right to private property. The belief that a man's house is his castle assumes the proposition that liberty and property are inseparable. Thus, the right to bears arms in order to defend our family and property is implied in such passages as Luke 22:36-38 where Jesus approved of his disciples being armed.

In Exodus 22:2, case law allowed householders to defend their property. In the KJV, Luke 3:14 was translated, "Do violence to no man." More specifically this describes robbery through shaking someone violently. However, it is not an act of violence to defend ourselves, our family, or our nation.

• The Institution of the Church

Second, God instituted the church. I will deal with the doctrine of the church in chapter 13. However, 1 Timothy 3:5 suggests that the church is an extended family.

• The Institution of the State

Third, God instituted the state. It is not a priesthood nor a kingdom. It exists by divine right, but it cannot usurp the ultimate authority of the God who delegated limited authority to it (Rom 13:1). Hegel's statement, "The state is god walking upon earth,"[1435] destroys the biblical concept that the state is instituted by God and is under his authority. Hegel viewed the state as the incarnation of God. For many who came after Hegel, as well as many before him, the state is the only god they recognize. However, a biblical understanding of a big God should result in small government. God delegated, but did not divest himself of absolute authority on earth. The *higher powers* are always subject to the highest power—the Almighty.

The word *nation* is from the Latin word *natus* which means birth. *Nation* is the place where one is born. Patriotism comes from the Latin root *pater*. Thus, one's nation is the land of one's

---

[1435]Lindsay, "German Philosophy," 58.

mother and father. Our nation, therefore, is sometimes called our *fatherland*.

It is proper for Christians to have a loyalty to their nation. In fact, we are commanded to pray for our national leaders (1 Tim 2:2; 1 Pet 2:13-17) and submit to their authority when it is legitimate (Rom 13:1-7). However, Christians should not be blindly allegiant to their nation. Our primary loyalty is to the kingdom of Christ. While that kingdom is international, we do not embrace globalism, internationalism, or a one-world civil government. God appointed the boundaries of nations (Deut 32:8; Acts 17:26) and by implication the nations themselves. The word *politeia* in Acts 22:28 and Ephesians 2:12 describes the relationship a citizen has to the state. In this sense Wesley said it was the duty of every minister to preach on politics.[1436]

Psalm 33:12 declares, "Blessed is the nation whose God is the Lord." This implies that God has a plan for all nations. However, Psalm 9:17 warns, "The wicked shall be turned into hell, and all the nations that forget God." Deuteronomy 28 promises blessing for national obedience and judgment for national disobedience. Solomon's prayer in 1 Kings 8, a reaffirmation of the Davidic covenant, is a reversal of Deuteronomy 28.

Psalm 11:3 asks, "When the foundations are being destroyed, what can the righteous do?" The language of 2 Chronicles 7:14 is covenantal. Since God ordained three covenant institutions, big government usurps the institution of the family and the church. Religious liberty is not bestowed by the state, nor is church tax-exempt status a privilege bestowed by the state. God has ordained the institution of government as one of three delegated authorities. The state only has the authority which God has granted it. Rutherford argued that Romans 13 indicates all power is from God, but government which contradicts God's law

---

[1436]Wesley, "Duty of a Christian Minister to Preach Politics," *Works*, 11:154-155.

is illegitimate. According to Scripture, government has six basic functions:

- to defend against international aggression
- to promote justice
- to ensure honest weights and measures
- to protect private property
- to quarantine general health risks
- to protect religious freedom[1437]

In order to defend against international aggression, nations may have to go to war. While war and fighting is a prime indication of mankind's sinful nature (Jas 4:1), the precedent for just war is established in Genesis 14. Abraham's 318 armed servants amounted to a small army.

In Matthew 17:24-27 Jesus taught that the payment of taxes is an implicit acknowledgment of submission. In that instance he voluntarily chose to comply. He made it clear that he was exempt because he was the king, not a subject, and the king is not required to pay taxes to himself. The Son of God could not be required to pay an ecclesiastical tax for use of the house of God. Jesus argued that the son cannot be required to pay a tax to his own father. Certainly a minor age son is required to obey his father, but in the nature of the essential Trinity the Son is equal to the Father. Every institution God ordained, the state and the church, as well as the family, all answer to God and do not have authority over each other.

However, the church cannot arbitrarily overrule civil law. Today "sanctuary cities" have been declared, making a zone in which anarchy exists. The basis for this concept is found in Numbers 35:11-28; Deuteronomy 4:41-43, 19:2-3; Joshua 20:2. However, the original purpose was to insure due process, not protect anarchy. The concept of *sanctuary* is a religious concept

---

[1437]DeMar, *Ruler of the Nations*, 76-84.

based on the idea of sacred space — where the divine and human realms intersected. In the OT, this was the tabernacle or temple. In the NT it is the people of God themselves. Therefore, a church building is not intrinsically holy. Essentially, a sanctuary is wherever God's people meet to worship. Therefore, it is a distortion of this sanctuary concept to allow criminals a safe haven all in the name of a holy God.

The Biblical Model for Civil Government

In the book of Exodus, God asked the people of Israel three times if they would accept and live by the terms of the covenant before it went into effect. If God himself required the consent of the people, then all government must be based on the consent of the governed.

For a period of 300-400 hundred years Israel had no king. After their freedom from Egyptian bondage and after Joshua led them into the promised land, we come to the period of the judges. Between the extremes of the tyranny of foreign oppression and the chaos of internal anarchy, the book of Judges describes a society which had private ownership of land, no police, no standing army, no prisons, welfare without bureaucracy, and honest commerce. They elected their own leaders (Deut 1:3-13). Some early New England pastors saw this as a prototype for American government.

While the theme of Judges, that there was no king in Israel and everyone did what was right in his own eyes (Judg 17:6, 18:1, 19:1, 21:25), is generally interpreted as a description of moral chaos, during most of this period what was right in God's sight was also deemed right by the people. The contrast was not between personal license to do as one pleased or doing right in the sight of God. The contrast was between having an earthly king or a heavenly King. The result of living under God's law resulted in freedom instead of tyranny under human kings.[1438]

The government at this time was a confederacy of local government in which the twelve tribes provided assistance to one another in case of foreign aggression, which provided safe conduct and decent treatment to travelers from other tribes, which respected the property rights of other tribes and their members, which required extradition to their members who were accused of serious crimes against other Israelites.

Israel was also the first nation which could read.[1439] Tyrants did not want their slaves to be able to read. While the first alphabet is thought to have been developed by the Sumerians in ancient Mesopotamia, the Hebrew language is a slight variation. It is possible that the Sumerians borrowed their alphabet from the Jews.

Across this four hundred-year period there was an ebb and flow. Sometimes they drifted away from God and he used foreign powers to threaten their freedom. But every time the people cried out to God, God raised up a deliverer and their freedom was restored. By the end of this period, however, everyone did what was right in his own eyes. They valued freedom, but had abandoned personal responsibility.

Modernism sees bigger government as the solution to civil issues because liberalism is humanistic. By 1 Samuel 8, Israel demands a king like all the other nations. Yet all human kingdoms were oppressive. The Pharaohs of Egypt, the Assyrian kings, the Babylonian kings, the Medes and the Persians, the Greek monarch, and the Roman emperor all required worship. Daniel 2 describes four world empires as one man, symbolizing their continuity. Daniel 7 also covers the same span of history, but instead of shining metal, they are carnivorous beasts consuming anything that stands in their way.

[1438]Gregg, *There is Another King*, 55-59.

[1439]Cahill, *Gifts of the Jews*, 11, 150, 208.

Across thousands of years, mankind individually and collectively lived in bondage. First Egypt, then Assyria, Babylon, the Medes and Persians, the Greeks, and finally Romans all held the world under oppressive regimes. But at just the right time, Christ came. He came to set us free in every sense (Luke 4:18; Gal 5:1). At first his spiritual kingdom was itself brutally persecuted by the Roman Empire, but gradually salvation penetrated the darkness. Where the Spirit of the Lord is, there is freedom (2 Cor 3:17).

After Christ established his kingdom, the only king by divine right was Jesus Christ. Before the kingdom of Christ was established, the war between God's covenant people and their enemies was fought against tyrannical world empires. Under the new covenant our primary battle is against principalities and powers who bind the hearts and minds of men through deception and fear.

Gradually, the followers of Christ grew to the point they were able to influence society. The status of women was elevated. Slavery was abolished. Christians cared for the handicapped, built hospitals and orphanages, taught people to read, gave them an education, and raised the standard of living.

Too often, however, government was still corrupt. While Scripture does not necessarily prescribe a particular form of government, the implication is that there should be liberty and justice for all. Corrupt leaders tended to appeal to a concept they abused — the divine right of kings. They claimed that God had appointed their family to rule and it was the duty of their subjects to obey them unconditionally. Especially, if those subjects were Christians, they obeyed God by obeying the king. But in most cases, the monarch, once established, had no further use for God. They continued to abuse their subjects with the justification that God willed it. However, the kings of Israel were not only chosen by God but also ratified by the people (1 Sam 10:17-24; 2 Sam 5:1-3; 16:18; 1 Chr 28:1-8; 2 Chr 10:1; 22:1; 26:1; 36:1).

Centralized human power in the hands of one person results in tyranny. "Power corrupts," as Lord Acton articulated, "and absolute power corrupts absolutely."[1440] Such tyranny is empirical proof that mankind is totally depraved.

Across European history the king was propped up by an appeal to the "divine right of kings." Thus, the king told his subjects that God told him to tell them to do whatever he commanded. However, he regarded himself as above God's law.

In the OT, however, the covenant was presented to the king of Judah by the priest (2 Kgs 11:12,17). At the inauguration of a king there were two covenants: the first between God, the king, and the people; the second between the king and the people. The people pledged to obey the king only after the king pledged to obey God.

Eventually, Christians began to realize that if God gave them freedom, they could surrender that freedom only on a voluntary basis. This voluntary surrender is based on the ethics of the greater good. I could choose to forfeit some personal freedom in order to love my neighbor as myself. But we should guard our freedom and be reluctant to barter it away. Once it has gone, it is hard to retrieve. More importantly, however, is that our freedom cannot be taken from us; we must give it up voluntarily.

As the Reformation spread and the Bible was translated into the common languages, people began to realize that the kingdom of Christ provided freedom, not bondage.

In 1644 Samuel Rutherford wrote *Lex Rex*, which declared that human leaders were also subject to God's authority. Rutherford was pushing against the popular concept that the king is the law unto himself or that might makes right. While the title literally says that the law is king, the concept is that the king must come under the authority of God's law, since God himself is bound to keep his own law. When Saul disobeyed God, he was replaced as king (1 Sam 15:22-23). David was then chosen by God based on his submission to God, as was Solomon (2 Chron 7:17-18).

[1440]Acton, *Letter* to Mandell Creighton, 5 April 1887.

The first act of a newly installed king was to write out the law of God as a reminder that he was under that law (Deut 17:18). The implications are that God alone is sovereign, but he delegates authority to the family, the church, and the state. Here we see the development of a biblical theology of civil government.

Civil government is no longer based on divine right but upon covenant. Here are the implications of Rutherford's theology:

- The duty of civil leaders is to uphold God's law in society.
- No leader has the authority to violate God's law. This means that no president, governor, or mayor has the authority to tell the church or the home to do something contrary to God's Word.

Centralized power in the hands of one person results in tyranny. Tyranny is satanic because it takes our God-given freedom. Any leader who mandates or decrees actions contrary to God's Word has nullified their delegated authority and must be resisted. If the king broke God's law, it was the duty of Christians to resist his tyranny since tyranny is satanic and we are commanded to resist the devil.

- This resistance may involve civil disobedience in order to force the issue to go to court.
- Tyranny is satanic at its root, and we are told to resist the devil (Jas 4:7). This does not imply that an elected official is actually the devil, but it does imply that he or she may be acting like the devil in the abridgement of freedom. It was on this basis that the American Colonies declared their independence from King George III.

The Bible does not prescribe a particular form of government. Whatever form government takes, the greatest virtue of good government is freedom. The nature of God is the basis of freedom. To be created in his image means that he has shared his freedom with us. True freedom always implies more than one option. Love is not real unless it involves choice. When God created mankind, he put a forbidden tree in the garden. He wanted to see if we would choose to love him. At some point Satan tempted the first pair to eat of the forbidden fruit. He promised that our rebellion would result in true freedom. Instead, it resulted in bondage and the loss of privilege. Before we sinned, somehow Satan himself also chose to rebel.

The basis of liberty is the atonement. It was on the Day of Atonement that the jubilee year was proclaimed (Lev 25:9-10). In the Christian era, there is no *day* of atonement since Christ provided a once-for-all atonement. Through saving faith we enjoy freedom from sin. We are commanded to stand firm in the freedom that Christ has provided and refuse to be burdened again by the yoke of slavery (Gal 5:1). According to 1 Peter 2:16 Christians are to live in freedom. This freedom is comprehensive, encompassing both freedom from sin and freedom from political tyranny. While we are free from legalism, we are not free to live lawlessly. We are still servants of God.

Leviticus 25:10-54 ties freedom to the ownership of private property. We must not steal a person's freedom through slavery, his life through murder, his property through stealing, or his right to worship through government interference.

God created us to be free and intends for us to have the liberty to do everything consistent with his will. However, slander and libel are not protected forms of speech. We have the right to speak the truth without intimidation even if we are politically incorrect. However, we must speak the truth in love (Eph 4:15). We must be sensitive. It is not always necessary to say everything we think.

Today the state has usurped the functions of the church and the family in its attempt to foster a secular millennium. The family has been weakened as a result of multi-genenerational state welfare; and the church has often found it necessary to step

in and do what the family should have done, all the while dependant upon voluntary contributions.

CHAPTER THIRTEEN
The Doctrine of the Church

The church is comprised of all who are in covenant with Christ. Before Pentecost, old covenant believers were in covenant with God in anticipation of the coming Messiah. Since Pentecost, those who are believing on the Lord Jesus Christ for salvation are baptized by the Holy Spirit into the body of Christ. Thus, water baptism, by whatever mode, is the outward declaration of identification with Christ and assimilation into his universal church. Thus, water baptism is valid for those who personally enter into covenant with Christ and those who make covenant on behalf of their children.

There has always been only one church, comprised of everyone in heaven and on earth who is saved through the merits of Christ's atonement — whether they lived before his finished work on the cross or after salvation was completed. Thus, the church is the new Israel of God.

The church is catholic or universal. It is holy because those who comprise it are at least initially sanctified. Through the means of grace and accountability, believers urge and inspire each other on to more consistent holy living. The church is also apostolic, which means that it affirms and proclaims the faith which was once-for-all given through the prophets and apostles.

The church is also the local assembly of believers. Christians gather, usually on the first day of the week, to commemorate the resurrection of their Head, to hear the Word of God preached, to participate in the sacraments, and to submit to discipleship. Participation in the sacraments of the church does not save the participant, but it is an outward sign and seal of the covenant for those who are trusting or who are acting on behalf of those who are unable to reject the covenant. No one who is trusting in Christ should refrain from the sacraments.

Every member has been given at least one spiritual gift for the good of the whole congregation, but God also calls leaders to the office of pastor and deacon. Within different structures, the names of the offices may differ, and there is not necessarily only one divinely sanctioned structure.

The church locally and collectively is committed to the worship of God, fellowship with each other, and world evangelism. The church is God's only plan to save civilization and the only means through which his kingdom is advanced. Ultimately, the church will be successful in her mission.

The Body of Believers

The church is the community of the redeemed. It is composed of those who have responded to God's call and are saved through Christ. They are under the leadership of the Spirit and they are the instruments of God through which he carries out his purposes in the world.

Irenaeus declared, "Where the Church is, there is the Spirit of God; and where the Spirit of God is, there is the Church, and every kind of grace."[1441]

Believers are in solidarity with each other across time and across location. Death does not even separate the fellowship of the saints in heaven and on earth. While we commonly distinguish between the church militant, as the church on earth, and the church triumphant, as the church in heaven, the church on

---

[1441]Irenaeus, *Against Heresies*, ANF 1:458.

earth is also triumphant even on earth, although we have not yet won the final battle. "But thanks be to God, who always leads us in triumphal procession in Christ" (2 Cor 2:14).

According to Ephesians 3:10 the church is the prototype of God's master plan. God used Paul to explain his strategy for the church. The church is God's instrument in effecting world reconciliation. It is God's pilot project for universal reconciliation. The church reveals God's secret in action and proclaims to demons their defeat.

The church is also an army. God is the Lord of armies, and the church is his army. In Ephesians 6 we are armed as Christian soldiers. In 2 Corinthians 10:3-5 we battle deception — even breaking down the gates of hell (Matt 16:18). Thus, the Word of God is our defensive armor and our offensive weapon. John Wesley called the church the "theater of divine wisdom."[1442] Certainly the church is no parenthesis in God's original plan. If God's eternal purpose will be carried out through the church, how can dispensationalism teach the church was not part of God's original plan? However, they hold a low view of the church, believing that only a remnant of the church will not become apostate in the end times. Yet Martyn Lloyd-Jones declared,

> The Church, far from being an afterthought, is the brightest shining of the wisdom of God. It is equally wrong to say that the Church is only temporary, and that a time will come when she will be removed and the gospel of the kingdom will again be preached to the Jews! The Church is the final expression of the wisdom of God, the thing above all others that enables even the angels to comprehend the wisdom of God.[1443]

[1442]Wesley, *Notes*, 495.

[1443]Lloyd-Jones, *Unsearchable Riches of Christ*, 86.

Archibald Hunter wrote,

> When men say . . . that Jesus never intended to create a church, they show that they do not understand what the Kingdom of God means. The idea of the *Ecclesia* has deep roots in the purpose of Jesus. His message of the Kingdom implies it. His doctrine of Messiahship involves it. His ministry shows him creating it.[1444]

At his first advent Christ became the head of the NT church and he also established his kingdom. There is no significant distinction between Christ as *head* and Christ as *king*. Both terms suggest the concepts of sovereignty and subjection.[1445]

We know that his kingdom is here because we have authority over the demonic world (Matt 12:28-29), we are born again (John 3:3-5), and we have received the Holy Spirit (Rom 14:17). Thus, the church is sent into the world to preach that the kingdom of Christ has come. The church has the *keys of the kingdom* (Matt 16:18-19).

The church, then, is that corporate dimension of believers, whether on earth or in heaven. The church is the means through which the kingdom of Christ will expand and cover the earth. The kingdom is the universal realm in which Christ reigns, and this is the goal of the church.

The Origin of the Church

When did the church begin? Wiley said the church first took its visible form in the covenant with Abraham and that the Christian church is the continuation of the Abrahamic covenant. Pen-

---

[1444]Hunter, *Introducing New Testament Theology,* 34.

[1445]Gregg, *There is Another King,* 43.

tecost was the birthday of the *Christian* church, but not the birthday of the church.[1446]

God has always had a people. We see the beginnings of the church within the first family. Adam was the first priest, and he led his family in worship through sacrifices. As the world became apostate, God called Noah out. The basic meaning of the Greek word for church, *ekklesia*, is called out. The ark is an illustration of the church. We are called out of this world to be saved from coming judgment.

Abraham was called out and entered into a covenant agreement with God. By the time of Moses the family had grown into a nation. The nation of Israel was God's church in the OT.

In the LXX *ekklesia* is used to refer to Israel in places such as Joshua 8:35; Ezra 2:64; Joel 2:16; Acts 7:38 refers to the Israelites as *the church in the wilderness*. By the NT the church was no longer national, but international. The mystery referred to by Paul was that God intended both Jew and Gentile to be one body (Eph 3:4-6).

Dispensationalism teaches, however, that the church did not exist until Pentecost and that it is a digression from God's original plan. However, God does not have two peoples. Both Jew and Gentile are to be incorporated into *one new man* (Eph 2:15). Some have inferred from the words of Jesus in Matthew 16:18, "I will build my church," that the church was not a present reality when Jesus spoke. But in Matthew 18:17 the church is functioning as a present reality.

Christ reformed the old church (Heb 9:10), and the new church was built upon the foundation of the old (Eph 2:20). The new church began at Pentecost with the sending of the Spirit. After Pentecost, believers believed not only in the Father, but in the Son; and when we believe in the Son we are baptized by the

---

[1446]Wiley, *Christian Theology*, 2:329; 3:107, 185-186; see also Wakefield, *Christian Theology*, 2:566.

Spirit into the body of Christ. All who are saved are added to this church (Acts 2:47).

Abraham is the father of all who believe (Rom 4:12,16). We are chosen by grace, not race (Rom 2:28-29). Those who belong to Christ are Abraham's seed and heirs according to the promise (Gal 3:29). The church is described as the children of God, heirs according to the promise and sharing in the inheritance promises to Abraham (Rom 4:13). We are the new Israel (Gal 6:16; Eph 2:12,19). According to John Lawson, "The most comprehensive and fundamental definition of the Christian Church in the New Testament is that it is 'the new Israel' (Gal 3:7-9, 29; 6:16; Phil 3:3; Jas 1:1; 1 Pet 2:9)."[1447]

Attributes of the church
- ## The church is universal yet local

The word *catholic* means universal. As Protestants, we affirm that the church is catholic. The term *Roman Catholic*, however, refers to the denomination centered in Rome. The Roman church cannot be catholic because it has anathematized Eastern Orthodox, as well as Protestant, Christians.[1448] The headquarters for the true catholic church is in heaven, not Rome. Kenneth Collins objected to the Roman use of the word *catholic*.

First, it maintains that the word "catholic" refers to the universal, comprehensive church; second, it then identifies that universal, catholic church specifically with itself in a move of generalization in which a part, that is, a particular theological tradition, is mistaken for the whole.[1449]

[1447]Lawson, *Introduction to Christian Doctrine*, 137.

[1448]Latourette, *History of Christianity*, 2:841.

[1449]Collins and Walls, *Roman but Not Catholic*, 98.

The OT church was limited to a small part of Palestine. Many of the laws and ceremonies were only adaptable locally. However, God intended Israel to bless the world. The prophets foretold worldwide influence.

When Jesus came, however, he found God's people proud and uninterested in outreach. Christ made it clear the new church was to be universal. The gospel is for all the people (Luke 2:10). Jesus told the Samaritan woman that the time was coming when true worship would not be limited to Jerusalem (John 4:21). The church is commissioned to make disciples of all nations (Matt 28:19). The church is universal because:

- we are all under the same Lord
- we are all adopted into the same family
- our mission is a world vision
- our sacraments are universally adaptable

God has determined that the church will be made up of all nations (Rev 7:9). Often when *church* is used in the singular and is not qualified by a location, it is referring to the universal church. For example, Matthew 16:18 does not promise that a local assembly cannot close, but that the universal church will never fail.

The most common usage in the NT for the word *church*, however, is in references to local congregations. *Ekklesia* is used 115 times in the NT; most references are to local congregations.

NT congregations cooperated in these areas:

- they shared a common faith
- they shared a common Scripture
- they sent letters of commendation to each other
- they cooperated in discipline
- they helped each other financially
- they cooperated in missions by financially supporting Paul

- ## The church is united yet diverse

"There is one body" (Eph 4:6). Jesus prayed that "they all may be one" (John 17:21). Wesley taught that the church is *ever one* because "in all ages and nations it is the one body of Christ."[1450] However, does this oneness refer to the invisible fellowship of the saints on earth and in heaven, or must we work for a visible unity within the institutional church?

God does not want division (Rom 16:17; 1 Cor 1:10). There are now around 33,820 denominations and para-denominations worldwide.[1451] The result is overlapping ministries, a competitive spirit, and confusion.

The Roman church has unity, but no liberty. Protestants have liberty, but no visible unity. The ecumenical movement is willing to sacrifice truth in order to have visible unity. Oden complained,

> Too many pretentious pseudoecumenical efforts have been themselves divisive, intolerant, ultrapolitical, misconceived, utopian, abusive, nationalistic, and culturally imperialistic. All this has occurred under the banner of modern bulldozer ecumenism. Hence modern ecumenical movements are themselves called to repentance on behalf of the unity of the Church.[1452]

Throughout church history would-be reformers have denounced all denominations as sectarian, and to solve the problem of disunity they began a new denomination. The best approach is to recognize the unity of God's people and demonstrate a spirit

---

[1450]Wesley, *Journal*, 19 Feb 1761.

[1451]Barrett, *World Christian Encyclopedia*, 1:10.

[1452]Oden, *Life in the Spirit*, 309.

of cooperation. Unity cannot be legislated or organized. Rather, it is a spiritual reality to be recognized.[1453]

There need not be uniformity. Cultural difference will exist in a worldwide church. Local congregations may have different personalities, gifts, and ministries, yet they can complement not compete with each other.

However, *sectarianism* is a sin. Romans 16:17-18 mentions *divisions* or standing apart. The Greek word *hairesis* is translated *factions*, *divisive*, *differences*, or *sect* by the NIV and *heresies* in the KJV (Acts 24:14; 1 Cor 11:19; Gal 5:20; Titus 3:10).

A synonym, *schisma*, meant to tear, split, or divide. Heresy and schism are not exactly the same, but they are different manifestations of the same disease. "Heresy is theoretical schism; schism is practical heresy."[1454] Thomas Oden confessed that as a career liberal, he was in love with heresy. His technique was to learn to sound Christian while undermining traditional Christianity.

"Heresy is any self-willing choice that departs from apostolic teaching."[1455] Oden explained that *heresy* is the pretense of transcending apostolic truth. It is the proud imagination that we can improve on the gospel. *Schism*, however, refers to tearing the fabric of unity. Today we are faced with similar questions of inward schism and outward separation, especially regarding human sexuality. Ordained ministers are officiating at weddings that neglect the classic Christian teaching of covenant fidelity in marriage between one man and one woman.

> Though the separation is usually portrayed as the splitting off of evangelicals from liberally dominated churches, the more accurate way of portraying it is the splitting off of liberal clergy from their roots. The

---

[1453]Lloyd-Jones, *Basis of Christian Unity*, 8-47.

[1454]Nevin, *Antichrist*, 20. See also Pope, *Higher Catechism*, 328.

[1455]Oden, *Life in the Spirit*, 364.

threatening schism is not fueled by laity who are faithful to the classic Christian tradition but clergy who are unfaithful to it.[1456]

The term *cult* is not necessarily a negative term, but in this context it describes a religious group that is exclusive, secretive, and authoritative. Based on new revelation, they have a new and better way. In contrast with orthodox Christianity, such cults rely on extra-biblical authority to uphold heresy. They have a charismatic leader who often provides the rationale for members to engage in aberrant morality. Such cults use controlling methods, even intimidation, to keep members from leaving. Furthermore, to leave this only "true" religion is to forfeit eternal salvation.

The Holy Spirit has faithfully preserved orthodoxy across the centuries and God does not rely on leaders of questionable integrity to "restore" truth.

• **The church is holy yet imperfect**

The Roman church teaches there is no salvation outside the church. Since the separation in AD 1054, the Roman Catholic Church has no greater claim to catholicity than does the Eastern Orthodox Church.

Other mainline denominations tend to teach that salvation comes sacramentally and therefore salvation comes through the church. There are other denominations which do not believe there is salvation outside their name or rituals. Often faith is reduced to the affirmation of a creed. The invisible church is defined as the mystical body of Christ across the span of time, regardless of denomination.

Against the accusation that they were separated from the one true church, the Protestant Reformers taught that the true church

---

[1456]Oden, *John Wesley's Teachings*, 3:227-230. This seemed to be Wesley's point [*Notes*, 431].

existed where the Word of God was faithfully taught, the sacraments faithfully administered, and discipline enforced.

These are the marks of the church. The antinomianism within modern evangelicalism destroys the concept that there are necessarily *any* distinguishing marks of the saved. Not only must the Word of God be preached, it must also be lived.

The faithful exercise of discipline is the third mark. However, it must be understood that discipline includes discipleship and accountability and should not be misunderstood as simply excommunication. The purpose of discipline is the restoration of the believer who is going astray, if possible (Gal 6:1). It is also to keep the sin from spreading to others and to protect the purity of the church. Matthew 18:15-20 gives the process of discipline. Excommunication is the final step (1 Cor 5:5, 11; 2 Thess 3:14; 1 Tim 1:20).[1457]

Technically, *excommunication* means to be barred from the Lord's Supper. In its broader application it means to be disfellowshipped.

The commandment to love one another, which Jesus gave in John 13:34-35, is also intended to be a distinguishing mark of the church. Francis Schaeffer called Christian love the "final apologetic."[1458]

According to Philip Schaff, the Reformation was the greatest act of the catholic church.[1459] Thus, the Protestants recaptured the ecumenical doctrine of the apostolic church by returning to *sola scriptura*, *sola gratia*, and *sola fide*, while Rome basically affirmed *sola Rome*.

Martin Luther said the surest mark of the true church is that in it one hears the pure gospel proclaimed. Furthermore, no secular organization has the authority to administer the sacra-

---

[1457]Grudem, *Systematic Theology*, 894-900. See also Adams, *Handbook of Church Discipline* (1986).

[1458]Schaeffer, *Works*, 4:188-204, 151-152.

[1459]Schaff, *The Principle of Protestantism*, 49.

ments. John Calvin concluded that where there is a good faith effort to maintain purity of preaching, lawful sacramental life, and discipline in earnest, one may conscientiously embrace a church even if blemished.[1460] Oden agreed with Calvin on this point. He quoted Melanchthon who remarked, "Let us not praise those tramps who wander around and unite with no church, because they nowhere find their ideals realized [because] something is always lacking."[1461]

When people join a self-conscious non-church (no sacraments, no creeds, no system of institutional discipline) in the name of joining the "true church," you can write off that group historically. It has moved into the fringe. It will not survive the death of its Pope, or at least the struggle that follows his death.

While the church is a spiritual organization, Scripture reported that local congregations had problems. This was especially true at Corinth and five of the seven churches in Revelation 2-3. Some people may be visible members of a local congregation who do not belong to God's church. Pastors sometimes must allow weeds and wheat to grow side by side until the harvest (Matt 13:24-30, 36-43). And they also have to deal with goats who have mixed in with the sheep (Matt 25:31-46).

• **The church is apostolic yet contemporary**

According to 1 Corinthians 3:10-11 Jesus Christ is the church's one foundation. However, in Ephesians 2:20 the apostles were given the authority to lay the foundation, which was based on their instruction from Jesus Christ. In 1 Timothy 3:16 Paul lists six pillars of truth. The church is built upon this foundation of truth.

[1460]Calvin, *Institutes,* 4.1.12.

[1461]Oden, *Life in the Spirit*, 302, 324.

The church is to teach the apostles' doctrine. There are three positions regarding how the church today is connected to the apostles:

- ***Apostolic* churches claim they are led by living apostles.**

Are there apostles today? According to Scripture, *apostles* were defined as those who had seen Christ (1 Cor 9:1, 15:8) and did miracles (2 Cor 12:12). They had authority to appoint leadership (Acts 14:23; Titus 1:5) and rule on doctrine (1 Cor 7:12). Thus, these contemporary "apostolic" churches are forced to redefine apostleship. Those who make this claim usually believe also that revelation is open. In contrast to classic Pentecostal teaching, which holds that the gift of apostleship enables apostles to perform miraculous signs to confirm the gospel, the New Apostolic Reformation holds that present-day apostles have governing authority equal to the original apostles.

- ***Apostolic succession* claims that Peter is the foundation rock and that he passed down his authority by ordination.**

However, apostolic authority cannot be passed on since it was foundational. Peter was not the "rock" which Jesus referenced in Matthew 16:18. Jesus said to *Petros* (a masculine noun) that upon *taute te petra* (dative feminine singular) he would build his church. The imagery of a rock is used in Scripture to describe divine character and attributes. It would be highly unusual for our Lord to apply this image to Peter instead of to himself. The change in syntax is too abrupt to have no meaning. If the two rocks are synonymous, why does Jesus switch from masculine to feminine? Even if Jesus originally spoke these words in Aramaic, we are dealing with the Greek text which Matthew wrote under the inspiration of the Holy Spirit. Even Augustine held that Peter was not the foundational rock.[1462]

History disproves the notion of an unbroken line of succession. The assumption of an unbroken line of bishops all the way back to Peter cannot be substantiated historically. However, history does record the existence of heretical popes, immoral popes, and the spectacle of two popes simultaneously, only to be outdone by the spectacle of three popes. In what was termed "the Great Schism," from 1378 to 1417, the Roman Catholic Church had at least two rival popes. The Council of Pisa deposed them both in 1409 and appointed a third. Since the two existing popes did not accept the decision of the council, the result was there were three popes.

Furthermore, the Roman Catholic Church did not evolve until AD 590, when Gregory, the bishop of Rome, declared himself to be the first among equals.

• **The priority of apostolic *doctrine*.**

A church is apostolic when it preaches the apostles' doctrine (Acts 2:42). Christ empowered the apostles and they left no successors. Their authority remains in their letters which comprise the NT. These letters give the qualifications for the selection of leadership (1 Tim 3; Titus 1).

Timothy George suggested, "Perhaps evangelical catholicity today is best seen in its worldwide missionary vision."

Evangelicals, no less than Roman Catholics, claim to be apostolic in this sense. But the two traditions differ sharply in understanding the transmission of the apostolic witness from the first century until now. Catholics believe that the church continues to be "taught, sanctified, and guided by the apostles ... through their succes-

---

[1462]Augustine, *Sermons on New-Testament Lessons*, *NPNF*1 6:340.

sors in pastoral office: the college of bishops, assisted by priests, in union with the successor of Peter, the church's supreme pastor." As heirs of the Reformation, evangelicals do not define apostolicity in terms of a literal, linear succession of duly ordained bishops. They point instead to the primordial character of the gospel, the inscripturated witness of the apostles, and the succession of apostolic proclamation.[1463]

Thus, apostleship is no longer an office within the church. The whole church is apostolic to the degree that it is faithful to the apostolic witness. There has been an uninterrupted apostolic witness to the gospel through a faithful community and faithful ministers down through history.

The term *apostolic*, however, has been subjected to reductionism. There have been many movements to restore apostolic or primitive Christianity which consisted in little more than advocating a particular mode of baptism or church government, Saturday worship, or speaking in tongues. Dunning wrote, "All restorationist movements are misguided when they identify the essence of the Church with its forms of worship or organizational structure(s) or practices."[1464]

The church is God's appointed means of upholding truth (1 Tim 3:15). Yet while doctrine, experience, and the mission of the church do not change, methodology and forms do change. Outler concluded that the catholicity of the church is defined by the universal outreach of redemption, the unity of the church is based upon Christian fellowship (*koinonia*) in the Holy Spirit, the holiness of the church is grounded in the discipline of grace which guides and matures the Christian life, and the apostolicity

---

[1463]George, "What I'd Like to Tell the Pope," 43.

[1464]Dunning, *Grace, Faith, and Holiness*, 536.

of the church is gauged by the succession of apostolic doctrine.[1465]

Illustrations of the Church
• Sheep/Shepherd

The flock belongs to the shepherd (John 10). Christ purchased us with his own blood (Acts 20:28) and appoints undershepherds. He is the *great shepherd* (Heb 13:20) and the *chief shepherd* (1 Pet 5:4).

• Branches/Vine

Israel was a vine planted by God. It brought forth sour grapes (Isa 5:1-7; Jer 2:21; Ezek 15:1-5,19:10-14) In John 15 we are the branches and are connected to Christ.

• Building/Cornerstone
The church has divine and human architects (1 Cor 3:10). It has a divine and human foundation—the twelve apostles. In the OT it was the tabernacle; later the temple. Today believers are the temple of God (1 Cor 3:16). Collectively, the church is the temple of the Holy Spirit. This building is still under construction (Eph 2:20-22; 1 Pet 2:5).

• Body/Head

This is Paul's favorite metaphor which he used over forty times (1 Cor 12; Eph 1:22-23; Col 1:24). The Bible never calls a local church the body. We must realize that we are part of something bigger. The body is to be visible. It has an invisible connection to the Head.

[1465]Outler, "Do Methodists Have a Doctrine of the Church?" 19.

- **Bride/Groom**

Israel was the bride of God. She broke her covenant by committing spiritual adultery. God made a new covenant (Jer 31:31-34) which also included Gentiles in the bride. Thus, the church is always referenced with feminine pronouns. Ephesians 5:25-29 describes Christ's love for the church using the illustration of marriage.

Offices in the Church

The common distinction between clergy and laity is not biblical. Yet Latourette claimed by the end of the second century, the clergy had clearly become a separate order.[1466] First Peter 2:9 describes the entire church as a priesthood and as a people belonging to God. The word *people* is *laos* from which we get *laity*. In 1 Peter 5:3 the entire church is called God's *heritage*. The Greek word *kleros* is the basis for our word *clergy*. Furthermore, all Christians are to be ministers or servants. The usual word here is *diakonos*. Yet the word also has a specialized usage. God does call and the church does set apart those for special ministry through ordination. No longer is the ministry a Levitical dynasty. Instead, God calls, the Holy Spirit equips through his gifts, the church trains through the seminary, and then acknowledges God's call through a process which eventuates in ordination.

The Christian ministry is a vocation, not a profession. It is the highest calling which God bestows upon men because of the extent of its responsibilities. The subject of this call must have a clear conviction of his duty. Just as Jesus called the twelve, so men are called into the ministry today. From the case of Samuel we see at first the call was unclear. The call continued to grow stronger, and the call was confirmed by the church. A valid call

---

[1466]Latourette, *History of Christianity*, 1:133.

also consists in the recognition and approval of the church that the subject is gifted and called. Purity in character must be maintained, and the church has the right to administer discipline.

John Calvin explained that *clergy* was an ancient way of describing the whole order of ministers. He expressed regret that the early fathers used this terminology,

> for what Scripture ascribes in common to the whole Church, it was by no means right to confine to a few men. And this way of speaking was spurious, at least it was a departure from apostolic usage. Peter, indeed, expressly gives the churches this title.[1467]

Writing in *Matthew Henry's Commentary*, Zechariah Merrill wrote that the word *clergy* is never restricted in the NT to the ministers of religion.[1468] Today the term *clergy* is the general name given to those who are set apart by ordination. Without necessarily contending for the term, it is clear from Ephesians 4:11 that there were men who were separated to the work of the Christian ministry. Martin Luther taught, "It is true that all Christians are priests, but not all Christians are pastors."[1469]

Whatever the NT says about sacrifices either refers to the priestly ministry of all believers or applies figuratively to the functions of the ministry. There is no separated order of priests who perform sacerdotal ministries. No church official is ever given the title of *priest* in the NT.

While Ephesians 4:11 refers to apostles, prophets, evangelists, pastors and teachers, this does not necessarily denote a "five-fold ministry." Pope regarded the offices of apostle, prophet, and evangelist to be extraordinary and transitional. The

---

[1467]Calvin, *Commentary*, 22:146.

[1468]*Matthew Henry's Commentary*, 6:1033.

[1469]Krey, *RCS* 8:122.

offices of pastor and deacon constitute the regular ministry.[1470] Wiley explained,

> With the passing away of the apostles, the passing of the evangelist as an assistant of the apostle, also passed away; but as an irregular and proclaiming ministry of the church it continued, and must continue, if the church is to extend her borders.[1471]

Pastor/teacher is one office with three distinct descriptions:

- *Elder* (*presbuteros*) normally refers to an old man. However, in the church it is used to emphasize spiritual maturity, not chronological age. The emphasis is on character and integrity; being not doing.
- *Pastor* (*poimen*) is usually translated *shepherd*. *Pastor* is the Latin equivalent to the Greek word for *shepherd*. According to 1 Peter 5:1-2 *elders* are to do the work of a pastor-shepherd and to serve as *overseers*. The command to watch over the church is *episkopeo*, the verb form for *episkopos* which is usually translated in the KJV as *bishop*.

In Acts 20:17 Paul sent for the *elders*. He charged them in v 28 to guard the flock as an overseer or *bishop* and to be shepherds or *pastors*. The term *elder* refers to spiritual maturity, the term *bishop* refers to the task of leading, and the term *pastor* refers to the task of feeding. Ephesians 4:11 connects pastoring with teaching.

The pastor is called by God and by the local congregation. By voting for the pastor the congregation is agreeing to his leadership.

[1470]Pope, *Compendium*, 3:337-342.

[1471]Wiley, *Christian Theology*, 3:131.

- *Bishop* (*episkopos*) describes the function of *looking* or *watching over*. This oversight involves the function of administration and leadership.

A prophet used to be called a *seer* (1 Sam 9:9). There were three Hebrew words utilized in the OT. *Nabi* meant to announce. *Raah* meant to see. *Chozeh* meant to give a vision. All three terms are found in 1 Chronicles 29:29. The old prophet had nothing to announce until he had seen something. He warned of future events functioning as a watchman. Now that the office of a prophet has ceased, in a sense the *seer* has transitioned into an *overseer*. Leadership within the church today involves seeing the present, understanding what is seen, and knowing what ought to be done (1 Chr 12:32).

In Titus 1:5-9 the *elder* is also called a *bishop*. Thus, the same individual is given two titles. Later we will deal with church government. In an episcopal form of government, these two titles indicate two separate offices. However, regardless of denominational structure, the minister of the local church must be both a person of maturity *and* a leader — even if there is a hierarchy above him.

In Acts 20:17 Paul sent for the elders of the church. In v 28 he told them to be both overseers and pastors. If the basic meaning of *bishop* is to lead, the basic meaning of *pastor* is to feed.

In 1 Peter 5:1-2 the elders are told to *shepherd* the flock and take the *oversight*.[1472] Christ holds both offices (1 Pet 2:25).

The best model for ministry is the life of Jesus Christ — our prophet, priest, and king. In our prophetic role we preach, proclaiming God's Word to the people. In our priestly role, we administer the sacraments and counsel. Oden said that our word *priest* is derived from *presbuteros*.[1473] Yet the word *presbuteros* means *elder*. The Greek word for *priest* is *hiereus*, and no church

---

[1472]*episkopeo* is found in most mss.

[1473]Oden, *Pastoral Theology*, 68.

official is ever given this title. No designated church office functioned as a mediator. Strictly speaking, however, the pastor is not a priest in the OT sense that ministry is restricted to him alone. Their entire body of Christ is a priesthood of believers. In the kingly role the pastor is to administer wisely and effectively the resources God has given the church.

- Deacon (*diakonos*) denotes a servant. This office originated in Acts 6, although the word is not used in that context. However, see vv 1-2 where a form of the word is used. In 1 Corinthians 12:5; 2 Corinthians 9:12 *diakonia* is translated *administration* in some versions. The qualifications are essentially the same as for pastors.

The word *diakonos* often is used in the general sense of ministry, but sometimes it refers to a special office. The office of deacon originated in Acts 6 so that the apostles could give themselves to prayer and the ministry of the Word. While the word *deacon* is not used in this account, v 3 speaks of their *business* or *responsibility*. The Greek word here means *office*. Their first assignment was to serve tables (v 2) and this Greek verb is *diakonein*. Philippians is addressed to bishops and deacons (1:1). 1 Timothy 3 is devoted to the qualifications for a bishop first and then for a deacon.

The apostles would not have instituted a permanent office to support the temporary office of apostle. Therefore, deacons were ordained to assist the pastor, and the pastor is to continue the priority of giving himself to prayer and ministry of the Word.

The Bible gives no specific job description for deacons, but delineates the office of pastor fairly well. Therefore deacons fill in the gaps which may include:

- overseeing the finances
- overseeing the maintenance
- ministry to the poor
- care for temporal needs with the congregation

- assisting the pastor with the sacraments

While the Bible does not say anything directly about the pastor's wife, it does address the deacon's wife in 1 Timothy 3:11. Phoebe was a deaconess (Rom 16:1). Wesley said that during the apostolic age some grave and pious women were appointed deaconesses in every church. "It was their office not to teach publicly, but to visit the sick, the women in particular, and to minister to them both in their temporal and spiritual necessities."[1474]

Apparently the office of deaconess existed for the first thousand years of the church.[1475] While the authority for church leadership rests with her husband, yet deaconesses have had significant responsibility.
- they assisted in the baptism of women
- they visited and nursed the sick
- they cared for guests, showing hospitality to traveling evangelists
- they ministered to believing women in unbelieving homes
- they administered help to the poor and orphans
- they taught younger women

Some churches have *stewards*. This word comes from *oikonomos*, from which we get *economics*, refers to one who manages the household (Matt 13:52). Eliezer had such a function in Genesis 15:2. In Titus 1:7 part of the job description of a bishop is to manage God's house.

Models of Church Government

Usually when there is no formal organization there are unwritten rules. However, sound doctrine must be upheld and the

---

[1474]Wesley, *Notes*, 404.

[1475]Weinrich, "Women in the History of the Church," 263-266.

proper conduct of the ministry must be enforced. Everything is to be done decently and in order (1 Cor 14:40). The purpose of the church must be insured.

A church is to be *set in order* (1 Cor 11:34). The Greek word *diatasso* means to appoint, arrange, charge, give orders. In Titus 1:5 *epidiorthoo* means to set straight.

It is popular to reject "organized religion," but there is no advantage to disorganized corporate spirituality. Any attempt at corporate worship, be it two or more gathered, *must* incorporate some elements of organization.

• Episcopal Government

In an episcopal structure the office of bishop is superior to the officers of local churches, based on the premise that the apostolic office has continued. In an episcopal form of government, local leaders are appointed. The Roman Catholic Church has the greatest hierarchy. Some Protestant churches have an archbishop who is over many or all other bishops.

According to J. B. Lightfoot the explanation that those who were first apostles were later designated as bishops is baseless. Instead, he explained that the episcopate was created out of the presbytery.

> It is clear that at the close of the apostolic age, the two lower orders of the threefold ministry were firmly and widely established; but traces of the third and higher order, the episcopal, properly so-called, are few and indistinct.[1476]

[1476]Lightfoot, *Philippians*, 195-196.

- **Presbyterian Government**

After the extraordinary ministry vested in apostles, prophets, and evangelists ceased, Watson explained that the highest offices of teaching and government in the church are vested in the presbyters. Terms such as *pastor*, *presbyter*, and *bishop* were used interchangeably.[1477]

In the fourth century, Jerome wrote that bishops are greater than presbyters rather by custom than by appointment of the Lord, and that still the church ought to be governed by both.[1478]

The term *presbyter* is from the Greek word *presbuterion*. The word *presbys* simply means *old*. Thus, in the church the *elders* are those with spiritual maturity.

This word *presbuterion* was used in Luke 22:66 and Acts 22:5 to describe the Jewish Sanhedrin. Apparently the early Christian church followed this same structural model. In 1 Timothy 4:14 it was the *presbuterion* who ordained Timothy.

In time the presbyterian or elder-team structure became distinct from the episcopal hierarchy. Thus, the presbyterian structure is a representative form of government. In a presbyterian government the congregation elects elders who rule the local church, much like Americans elect representatives to civil government. It is not a direct democracy.

The local church is governed by a group of elders called a *session*. The session is composed of ruling elders and teaching elders. Members of the session from several local churches in an area comprise the presbytery. Some members of the presbytery also serve as members of a general assembly.

[1477]Watson, *Theological Institutes*, 2:576.

[1478]Jerome, *Letters*, *NPNF*2 6:288-289.

- **Congregational Government**

This model holds that Christ has invested authority in the entire body. Congregationalism is distinguished by the autonomy or independency of the local church.

According to Beyer, Hebrew 12:14 teaches the whole church has an essential episcopal ministry and office.[1479] Thus, the final authority rests with the body. Yet every pastor needs a pastor. And Acts 15 implies authority above the local level. Therefore, the question is whether this early independency was prescribed by the head of the church or whether these citations are simply descriptive of a fledgling church.

The autonomy of the local congregation must be balanced by the concept of inter-dependency and connection. The apostles did hold a council which set policy for all congregations (Acts 15). The early church held seven worldwide or ecumenical councils which clarified church doctrine.

Probably the most widely used model is single-elder congregationalism in which the local church is overseen by one elder or pastor chosen by the congregation. He is assisted by or in some cases supervised by a group of deacons. A plurality of elders model is similar to presbyterianism, except the elders have no authority outside their local church.

Which model is scriptural? Watson said the NT contains no formal plan of church government.[1480] Any system can work under spiritual leadership. No system will work with unregenerate leadership. Different personality temperaments may work better under different systems. I have observed a continuous realignment from one end of the spectrum to the other because there can be abuse under any structure.

Charles Kraft feels that the NT prescribes no form and allows the freedom to adapt to culture. He sees these models as

---

[1479]Beyer, "ἐπισκέπτομαι," *TDNT* 2:604.

[1480]Watson, *Theological Institutes*, 2:582.

cultural and suggests the church should adopt the prevailing model of the culture. They should contextualize the indigenous church model to fit their particular society.[1481]

The Priority of Preaching

Martyn Lloyd-Jones declared, "Preaching is the primary task of the Church."[1482] According to Douglas Crossman, "Only a service where the Word of God is read and expounded, is a truly Christian service." Duane Litfin wrote, "Anything less than expository preaching is technically not really preaching at all." It is merely the subjective opinion or experience of the speaker.[1483] Ray Dunning also upheld the superiority of expositional preaching.[1484]

Expositional preaching finds its sole source in Scripture. The message is extracted from Scripture through careful exegesis. The message preparation correctly interprets Scriptures in its normal sense and its context. The message clearly explains the original God-intended meaning of Scripture. The message applies the scriptural meaning for today. We see examples of true preaching in Nehemiah 8:8, when Ezra read from the Book of the Law of God, making it clear and giving the meaning so that the people could understand what was being said. During their Babylonian exile the Jews had lost their command of the Hebrew language, and so the text had to be explained. The great revival described in Ezekiel 37 happened as the Holy Spirit brought life when the prophet preached the Word of God.

Philip asked the Ethiopian, "Do you understand what you are reading?" The Ethiopian official answered, "How can I unless

---

[1481]Kraft, *Anthropology for Christian Witness*, 130.

[1482]Lloyd-Jones, *Preachers and Preaching*, 26.

[1483]Litfin, "Theological Presuppositions and Preaching," 169-170.

[1484]Dunning, *Grace, Faith, and Holiness*, 535.

someone explains it to me?" (Acts 8:30-31). The word for *explain* or *guide* is *hodogeo*, which means to lead in the way.

In Acts 20:27 Paul declared that he had preached the whole will or all of the counsel of God. Bloesch wrote that this includes law as well as gospel, sin as well as salvation, hell as well as heaven, and obedience as well as faith.[1485]

Such preaching requires divine anointing and a human preparation. *Homiletics* (*homilos*, to assemble together) in theology is the application of the general principles of rhetoric to the specific department of public preaching.

Exegesis is like a diver bringing up pearls from the ocean bed; an expositor is like the jeweler who arrays them in orderly fashion and in proper relation to each other. According to John Stott in *Between Two Worlds* (1982), we must bridge the gap between our minds and the minds of the biblical writers.

In the OT the high priest was anointed, set apart, and consecrated for God's service. Then God's Spirit was poured out. The NT uses three words for rubbing or spreading ointment:

- *chrio* – used figuratively for appointment or commissioning; Luke 4:18
- *aleipho* used literally of applying ointment or perfume to the body; Luke 7:38
- *chrisma* focuses on that with which one has been anointed. In 1 John 2:20,27 *unction* means *anointing*. This refers to the enabling power of the Holy Spirit to declare the Word of God.

Can women preach? In the OT only men were priests and in the NT only men are to be pastors and deacons. Both are to be "the husband of one wife" (1 Tim 3:2,12). God's standard for church leaders is that first they be in control at home (1 Tim 3:4-5,12). It would be a confusing situation if the husband was over

---

[1485]Bloesch, *Essentials of Evangelical Theology*, 2:83.

the wife at home, but she was his leader at church. That is why Paul stated, "I do not permit a woman to teach or to have authority over a man" (1 Tim 2:12). It is inconsistent to contend for an egalitarian marriage and a church hierarchy.

However, under the new covenant women can be personally baptized. The sign and seal of the old covenant was circumcision, and therefore women could only be included by proxy—either through the circumcision of their father or their husband.

Furthermore, Joel prophesied that in these last days the Holy Spirit would be poured out on everyone. Both sons and daughters would prophesy (Joel 2:28). Therefore, the question is whether prophecy is the same as preaching. I have already defined prophecy as anointed preaching. In Bible times a teacher exercised great authority. Students were required to submit to the teacher who was an elder or community leader. But the gift of teaching may be exercised by women without the implications that she has rabbinical authority.

Therefore the question is not whether or not women can minister. Every Christian is a minister. Neither is there any scriptural inference that certain spiritual gifts are not available to women. However, certain church *offices* are not available to women. Isaiah 3:12 expresses contempt that men are not ruling, not contempt for women who find it necessary to rule because men will not. The Bible does not condemn Deborah for her leadership, but it does condemn Barak for shirking his responsibilities (Judg 4:8-9).

Recognizing that churches are structured differently and that the same terms mean different things in different settings, Susan Foh concluded that a woman may do anything except exercise the authority of an elder. In her Presbyterian setting, elders rule and deacons serve. She allows for a woman to be a deacon or an administrator. Women may have delegated authority, but not leadership authority.[1486]

The Sacraments

Rob Staples explained that sacraments are visual parables. However, there are rituals of worship which are sacramental in tone and effect. Roman Catholics tend to employ the term *sacramental* to refer to any kind of action that may be used to further the notion that God is at work in his world conveying grace to those who seek it.[1487] Yet we must distinguish between the means of grace and the sacraments. Wesley defined a sacrament as "an outward sign of inward grace, and a means whereby we receive the same." His definition abridged the Anglican Catechism, which stated, "An outward and visible sign of an inward and spiritual grace given unto us; ordained by Christ himself, as a means whereby we receive the same, and a pledge to assure us thereof."[1488] This definition aligned Wesley with Luther and Reformation theology.

Beet explained the parallel between word and sacrament.

Therefore, just as in the preached word there is, in some sense to all who hear it and in the fullest sense to those who receive it by faith, the real, living, active, objective presence of the crucified and living Savior, so we need not hesitate to say that in the same sense, but in a more conspicuous because unexpected manner, He is present in the sacramental feast. . . . To the eye of faith the

---

[1486]Foh, "Male Leadership View," 94-102.

[1487]Staples, *Outward Sign and Inward Grace*, 89-96.

[1488]Staples, *Outward Sign and Inward Grace*, 89-90.

symbols disappear, and the infinite and amazing reality alone remains.[1489]

While preaching the Word is a priority, the Lord's Supper also constitutes preaching. According to 1 Corinthians 11:26, the Lord's Supper is the proclamation of the Lord's death. The verb used, *kataggello*, means to herald, proclaim, or preach. Thus, the church emphasizes *both* preaching and the sacraments.

A *sacrament* is a pledge of fidelity. The Roman army soldiers were required to pledge obedience to the commander, and this act was called a *sacrament*. Baptism and the Lord's Supper are a pledge of our faith.

In 1 Peter 3:21 baptism is described as a pledge (*eperotema*). Wesley translated this word as *stipulation, contract, or covenant.*[1490]

The Latin Vulgate translated the Greek word *musterion* in Ephesians 5:32 and Revelation 1:20 as *sacramentum*. This emphasizes their symbolic nature and does not imply any gnostic tendencies.

In 1439 the Roman church established their dogma of seven sacraments. However, a sacrament must be instituted by divine authority. Christ, the head of the church, observed and instituted both baptism and communion. A biblical sacrament must also be commanded by our Lord. And it must have a symbolic meaning. Only two ordinances fit the criteria of being a sacrament. Water baptism is commanded (Matt 28:19) and the Lord's Supper is commanded (1 Cor 11:24,26). Therefore, as Protestants we reject confirmation, penance, extreme unction, ordination, and matrimony as sacraments. Ironically, no one within the Roman church can receive more than six, since priests cannot marry and married persons cannot be priests.

[1489]Beet, *The Lord's Supper,* 174-175, 177.

[1490]Wesley, "Treatise on Baptism," *BE Works,* 14:283.

Nor is foot washing a sacrament. In John 13:15 Jesus explained that foot washing was an *example* (*hupodeigma*) and that his disciples should do *as* or *similar* (*kathos*) to what he had done. Jesus gave them a sample and then makes a simple indicative statement. Had Jesus intended for his church to wash feet he could have used *hupogrammos*, which was used in 1 Peter 1:21 to describe the process of copying by exactly tracing the letters. However, when Jesus instituted the Lord's Supper he said *do this* (Luke 22:19; 1 Cor 11:24-25). He gave a direct command in the imperative mood.

First Corinthians 11:2 calls the Lord's Supper an *ordinance* which has been passed down from Christ. While the Lord's Supper is commanded, if it is nothing more than an ordinance to observe — it is merely an act of obedience, not a means of grace. Sacraments are signs and seals, they are ordinances *and* means of grace. They are a pledge of fidelity. Possessing symbolic character, a sacrament is an outward and visible sign of an inward grace. It is also a seal of the covenant. The sacraments are covenantal, converting, confirming, and sustaining.

The sacraments are physical signs, which Augustine described as visible words.[1491] We are embodied spirits and the sacraments engage our physical senses. The sacraments serve as a seal to the covenant. Lutheranism teaches that the sacrament holds virtue, while Calvinism puts more emphasis on the concurrence of the Holy Spirit. In this realm of theology the Methodist position is more in line with Calvinism.

The Sacrament of Baptism

Under the OT there were several baptisms. The Bible speaks of Jewish baptism or ablution, baptism of utensils (Mark 7:4,8), baptism into Moses (1 Cor 10:2), John's baptism (Mark 1:4-8), baptism for the dead (1 Cor 15:29), the baptism of suffering

---

[1491]Augustine, *Homilies on the Gospel of John*, *NPNF*1 7:344.

(Matt 20:22-23; Luke 12:50), and the baptism of fire (Mark 3:11-12). Hebrews 9:10 says there were various baptisms until the time of the new order. We are also admonished to leave the elementary teachings about baptism (Heb 6:2).

Under the NT there is *one* baptism (Eph 4:5). Therefore, we must understand water baptism and Spirit baptism to be two aspects of that *one* baptism. Clarke wrote, "To say that water baptism is nothing, because a baptism of the Spirit is promised, is not correct."[1492] But neither should the outward sign suffice for the inward grace.

Water baptism is the outward sign and Spirit baptism is the inward grace. Both parts may be described as initiation. Water baptism is also a public identification with Christ in which we become members of his visible church. Thus, a private baptism is abnormal. Infant baptism also recognizes children as members of the visible church.

As a sign, baptism signifies our entrance into the church. Through it we identify with the death and resurrection of Christ. It is a testimony to the outpouring of the Holy Spirit into our heart.

As a seal we pledge ourselves to God, we bind ourselves to God, and the covenant of salvation is sealed.

The Proper Subjects for Baptism

Believers should be baptized as a testimony of their faith in the Lord Jesus Christ. The church was commanded by Christ to make disciples of all nations, baptizing them (Matt 28:19). Jesus set the example by submitting to John's baptism (Matt 3:13-15). According to Acts 2:38 those who have been forgiven and who have received the gift of the Holy Spirit are commanded to be baptized in the name of the Father and of the Son and of the

---

[1492]Clarke, *Commentary*, 5:531.

Holy Spirit. F. F. Bruce declared that "the idea of an unbaptized Christian is simply not entertained in the New Testament."[1493]

However, the command in Acts 2:28 to be baptized in the name of Jesus is not exclusive. We are not commanded to be baptized *only* in the name of Jesus. As early as AD 65-80, the *Didache*, the oldest extant non-canonical literature, prescribed baptism in the triune name.[1494]

Nor does the Bible teach that we are regenerated through water baptism. John 3:5 and Titus 3:5 have often been used to teach baptismal regeneration. Wesley explained that the washing of regeneration was the outward sign, signified by baptism. However, initial sanctification, which purifies the soul, is the work of the Holy Spirit.[1495]

We are saved by grace through faith alone. The Roman Catholic Church teaches that the rite of baptism effects salvation *ex opere operato*. This Latin phrase literally means *by the work worked* and it implies the belief that by virtue of the ritual the candidate is saved, independent of any merit by the minister or the candidate. In *Popery Calmly Considered*, Wesley wrote:

> The grace does not spring merely *ex opere operato*. It does not proceed from the mere elements, or the words spoken; but from the blessing of God, in consequence of his promise, to such as are qualified for it.[1496]

Wesley also taught that there is no intrinsic power in any means.[1497] The Reformed position is *nullum sacramentum sine fide* (no sacrament apart from faith). Lutheranism, however,

---

[1493]Bruce, *Acts*, 70, 363.

[1494]*Teaching of the Twelve Apostles*, ANF 7:379.

[1495]Wesley, *Notes*, 559.

[1496]Wesley, *BE Works*, 14:227.

[1497]Wesley, "The Means of Grace," 2.3.

understands baptism as regenerative. There are many positions within the Campbell-Stone Restoration Movement, but Alexander Campbell declared that regeneration is consummated by immersion and that the Holy Spirit did not call anything regeneration except the act of immersion.[1498]

According to Mark 16:15 those who believe will be baptized, but those who do not believe are condemned, regardless of whether or not they were baptized. 1 Peter 3:21 does not teach that we are saved by water. Those who were saved in Noah's day were saved *in* the ark and *through* the water. The word *water* does not appear in the Greek text. Some translations have supplied the wrong antecedent. The flood water did not save; the ark did!

Infant baptism is also valid. Historically termed *paedobaptism*, this practice anticipates the response of the individual to the call of Christ once they reach the age of accountability. Children of believers belong to God until they choose to break that covenant through willful sin. Romans 4:11 teaches that circumcision was a sign and a seal of the covenant. Just as circumcision was the sign of the old covenant, so baptism is the sign of the new covenant (Col 2:11-12).

This interpretation is as old as Justin Martyr.[1499] Infant baptism does not mean that the baby has been born again, but that the child is under the preliminary influence of the Holy Spirit and has been inducted into the covenant community. However, Arminius was clear that children are under preliminary grace whether or not they are baptized.[1500]

In the case of an adult baptism, a person believes first and then is baptized. In the case of an infant, the child is first baptized, then believes. Thus, baptism is the starting point of faith; and in the case of infants, the faith of believing parents covers

---

[1498]Campbell, *The Christian System*, 60, 202.

[1499]*Dialogue with Trypho, ANF* 1:216.

[1500]Arminius, *Works*, 2:12; Summers, *Systematic Theology*, 2:33.

the child until he or she reaches the age of accountability. This reflects the corporate faith of a believing community. Scot McKnight asserted, "Infant baptism is the first public step in nurturing our children into the faith."[1501]

However, unbaptized infants do not go to limbo. All children are saved, whether or not they have been baptized, until they reject that unconditional benefit of the atonement.[1502] Jesus declared in Mark 10:14 that children were part of the kingdom of God. Thus, the Apostolic Constitutions, compiled around AD 390, taught:

> Baptize your infants also and bring them up in the nurture and admonition of God. For He says, "Allow the little children to come unto me and do not forbid them."[1503]

Yet I would distinguish between justification, as the non-imputation of sin, and regeneration, as the impartation of righteousness. I would prefer to explain that infants are saved but not born again. According to 1 Corinthians 7:14, children are made holy through the covenant and through their relationship to the believing parent.

Those who appeal to historical precedent tend to find what they are looking for. Therefore, we must study Scripture *and* history inductively, but we will be greatly influenced by either covenant or dispensational assumptions.

Acts 16 teaches household salvation. Paul not only preached personal salvation to the jailer, but taught that both he and his house should believe and be saved. In v 31 the command to the jailer is second person singular. He believed, but his entire house was catechized (v 32) and saved (v 34). Parents have the author-

---

[1501]McKnight, *It Takes a Church to Baptize*, 1.

[1502]Raymond, *Systematic Theology*, 2:311-312.

[1503]*Apostolic Constitutions*, ANF 7:457.

ity to make covenants for their entire family by proxy. Thus, Joshua declares that he and his house would serve the Lord (24:15). According to Peter, the Pentecostal promise was for his hearers and their children (Acts 2:39).

Those who claim that we cannot be sure there were any infants in these examples miss the point. The point is that a head of family or parent, whether the jailer, Lydia, or Stephanas made a commitment on behalf of those under their authority. Parents who present their infant for baptism today are doing the same thing.

When the jailer put his faith in Jesus Christ, his entire house was baptized. This truth is also emphasized in Acts 16:15 where Lydia and her entire household were baptized and in the case of Stephanas in 1 Corinthians 1:16. Those who advocate infant baptism cannot prove that there were any infants present in any of these three cases, and those who oppose infant baptism cannot prove that there were not. However, the case of the jailer does explicitly demonstrate that heads of household can make covenants on behalf of their children. Furthermore, Jeremias argued that when Gentiles became proselytes to the Jewish faith it was completely taken for granted that at the same time the children also, including even very young children, should be received into the Jewish faith. This would include circumcision to every male who was at least eight days old. The description of baptism as "Christian circumcision" makes it very probable that children of every age were baptized along with their parents when the parents were converted to the Christian faith.[1504]

The purpose of systematic theology is not to provide ammunition for argumentation, but to promote consistency. Many Baptists who are horrified at the thought of *infant* baptism have no qualms about baptizing *adolescents* at a very early age. Furthermore, many *adults* who are baptized upon their profession of faith know next to nothing about the Christian faith. They are

---

[1504]Jeremias, *Infant Baptism in the First Four Centuries*, 37, 40.

baptized on the basis that they have gone forward and made a decision. Statistically, most who do go forward and make a decision never become faithful church members.[1505] The usual figure is 3%-6%. Therefore, adult or believer's baptism sometimes is as shallow in terms of faith and commitment as an infant's faith.

The Proper Mode of Baptism

Baptism is initiation into the visible church. It is a sign and seal of the covenant. It is identification with Christ. Sprinkling, pouring, and immersion are all valid modes of baptism. Yet baptism is not immersion, sprinkling, or pouring. Therefore, we cannot claim that a person has not been baptized merely because they have not submitted to our preference regarding the external ritual.

The Greek word *baptisma* means identification, incorporation, and initiation. Its use in passages such as Mark 7:4; Luke 11:38; and 1 Corinthians 10:2 indicate a broader meaning than simply *immerse*. Watson declared that it is a comparative trifle to attach undue importance to the mode of baptism. The word *baptizo* proves nothing.[1506]

Wesley allowed for immersion, but did not restrict the meaning of baptism to immersion.[1507] Wesley wrote,

Baptism is performed by *washing*, *dipping*, or *sprinkling* the person in the name of the Father, Son, and Holy Ghost. . . . I say "by washing, dipping, sprinkling" because it is not determined in the Scripture in which of these ways it shall be done — neither by any express

---

[1505]McIntyre, *The Graham Formula*, 12.

[1506]Watson, *Theological Institutes*, 2:747, 650; Clarke, *Commentary*, 5:51.

[1507]Wesley, *Notes*, 376, 15, 299.

precept, not by any such *example* as clearly proves it, not by the *force* or *meaning* of the word "baptize."[1508]

The Calvinistic perspective is no different:

No prescription of a particular mode of baptism can be found in the New Testament. The command to baptize may be fulfilled by immersion, dipping, or sprinkling; all three modes satisfy the meaning of the Greek verb *baptizo* and the symbolic requirement of passing under, and emerging from, cleansing water.[1509]

Ezekiel 36:25-27 provides the biblical basis for sprinkling. "I will sprinkle clean water upon you and you will be clean." According to Isaiah 52:15, "So will he sprinkle many nations." Moses baptized the congregation of Israel by sprinkling (Heb 9:19). "Let us draw near to God with a sincere heart in full assurance of faith, having our hearts sprinkled to cleanse us from a guilty conscience and having our bodies washed with pure water" (Heb 10:22).

The biblical basis for pouring is found in Joel 2:28, "I will pour out my Spirit upon all flesh." According to Romans 5:1-5, having been justified through faith, God has poured out his love into our hearts by the Holy Spirit, whom he has given us.

The biblical basis for immersion is found in Romans 6:3-4, which teaches that we were buried with him through baptism and that just as Jesus was raised from death through the glory of the Father, so we are raised to a new life. However, it must be demonstrated that Romans 6 is speaking of *water* baptism.

Colossians 2:12 also speaks of being buried with Christ in baptism. The amount of water is not significant any more than

---

[1508]Wesley, *BE Works*, 14:279.

[1509]Sproul, *Reformation Study Bible*, 1776.

the amount of bread and wine in communion. Rob Staples explained,

> The preference for immersion basically rests on the idea that the more water there is, and the more of the body that is covered by it, the more valid the baptism is. . . . But, by the same logic, if more water meant better baptism, then in the Lord's Supper a scrumptious feast at a table loaded with food would seem to be a more fitting symbol of the coming Heavenly Banquet, of which the Eucharist is a foretaste, than the small amounts of bread and wine usually consumed by the communicant.[1510]

The Sacrament of Communion

Just as baptism replaced circumcision, so the Lord's Supper replaced Passover. Scripture uses seven terms for this sacrament. When Jesus took the bread and the cup, he gave thanks (Matt 26:26-27). This verb *eukaristeo* is the basis for the term *eucharist*. First Corinthians 10:16 also speaks of the cup of blessing. This word *eulogia* is the basis for our word *eulogy*. Literally it is a *good word* or a proclamation.

In Luke 22:19, as well as 1 Corinthians 11:24,26, Jesus called it a *memorial*. In Acts 2:42 it is called *the breaking of the bread*. This phrase occurs sixteen times in the NT. Four times it describes the miracle of the loaves and fishes. Twice it refers to eating in general. Ten times it describes the Lord's Supper.

In Acts 2:42 one of the four marks of the apostolic church was their fellowship. This Greek word (*koinonia*) is used twice in 1 Corinthians 10:16 to describe *communion*. Apparently, Luke uses it in Acts 2:42 in the more general sense of fellowship, then employs "the breaking of the bread" to describe the Lord's Supper so that there not be any confusion.

[1510]Staples, *Outward Sign and Inward Grace*, 275.

In 1 Corinthians 11:2 it is called an *ordinance* (*paradosis*) in the KJV, but this word really describes a tradition which has been handed down. In v 20 it is called the Lord's Supper.

The Lord's Supper is also an eschatological banquet. Jesus promised to share the cup with us in his Father's kingdom. In the meantime, we observe this sacrament in anticipation of that climactic event (1 Cor 11:26).

Before Christ's return we are to compel as many as we can to accept the invitation and prepare to attend (Luke 14:15-24). Every time we partake of the Lord's Supper we anticipate the marriage supper, and every time we evangelize we are inviting sinners to supper.

There is still room at the table! Someday the entire church of all races, languages, nations, and periods of history will gather at one table. On that day we will come from the north and the south, the east and west. We will sit down with Abraham, Isaac, and Jacob, and all the prophets to eat and drink (Luke 13:29). Christ himself will be the host. His body will be our bread, and his blood will be our wine (John 6:53-56). We will be sustained eternally through the merits of the atonement. John 6:58 teaches that we will live eternally as we feed on Christ.

The first time the Lord's Supper was observed there were only eleven; the last time there will be a number too great to count. The first time it was called the last supper because it was the last time Christ was physically present; but he is always spiritually present. It was also the last time Passover was observed. Passover looked back to deliverance. The Lord's Supper not only looks back, but it looks forward. We are to continue to do this until he comes. At Passover, they ate the lamb, but at the marriage supper the Lamb will eat with us.

Henry Alford observed that in 1 Corinthians 10:16 the pronouns were first person *plural*. Thus, this was an act of the whole congregation, not simply the minister.[1511]

[1511]Alford, *Greek Testament*, 2:558.

On the basis of the priesthood of all believers, Martin Luther believed that any Christian may bestow baptism and preside at communion. Luther also asserted the special office of the clergy in order to maintain church order and discipline. He believed that while all Christians are priests, only a few are ministers through their ordination.[1512]

In AD 109 Pliny described Christian worship in which Christians assembled at sunrise on Sunday and pledged themselves by an oath. The Latin word used is *sacramentum*.[1513]

By the fourth to sixth centuries the Roman church began to teach the Lord's Supper was a sacrifice because the elements were literally changed into the body and blood of Christ. The word *mass* was from the Latin phrase *to dismiss* the people. However, the Roman mass carries this idea of sacrifice which we reject (Heb 10:1,11-14,18). The once-for-all sacrifice was offered by Christ on the cross. If the Lord's Supper is a sacrifice, then ministers are priests. However, the element of sacrifice at the Lord's Table is explained in Romans 12:1. We present *ourselves* as *living* sacrifices.

The Roman church teaches *transubstantiation*. They teach that in the miracle of the mass, the substance of bread and wine changes or is transformed into the substance of the body and blood of Christ. However, the accidents of bread and wine remain the same. In philosophical language the *accident* is incidental to the essential substance of body and blood. There is a supposed change in reality but not in perception.

John Wycliffe declared that the bread and wine remain after consecration and that Christ's body is present only figuratively or tropically in the eucharist.[1514] At that time *transubstantiation* was a relatively new doctrine dating back to the thirteenth century. In *On the Eucharist* (1379), Wycliffe affirmed the real

---

[1512]Bloesch, *Essentials of Evangelical Theology*, 2:112.

[1513]Schaff, *History of the Christian Church*, 2:222.

[1514]Schaff, *History of the Christian Church*, 6:320-321.

presence of Christ, but taught that he is present spiritually not corporeally. The Lollards argued that Christ sitting at the last supper could not give his disciples his living body to eat.

Luther protested that this doctrine involves two miracles, one to have the substance of a thing present without its accident before the mass, and another to have the accident present without the substance after the miracle of transubstantiation. Luther charged that this was a frivolous and unnecessary appeal to philosophical logic.[1515]

Martyrs such as Hugh Latimer, Thomas Cranmer, and Nicholas Ridley were burned at the stake in 1555 for rejecting transubstantiation. Latimer declared, "There is no other presence of Christ required than a spiritual presence. And the same presence may be called a real presence." However, Latimer did not want to be identified with the Anabaptists, who made the sacrament nothing else but a bare and naked sign.[1516]

These English Reformers understood clearly that the claim of papal authority was built upon the foundation of transubstantiation. The power of the priesthood, the infallibility of the pope, and the supremacy of tradition and the church over the Scripture were all based on the manner of Christ's presence at the communion altar. Since Scripture does not teach transubstantiation, tradition must supercede Scripture in order to bolster this doctrine. Thus, tradition was called the Word of God unwritten. Without this authority of tradition, the priest has no supernatural powers nor is the word of the pope infallible.

Rattenbury developed a Methodist understanding of Holy Communion based on the Wesleys themselves. He analyzed their Eucharistic hymns under six headings:

- As a memorial of the sufferings and death of Christ
- As a sign and means of grace

[1515]Sproul, *Not a Chance*, 111-112.

[1516]Stuart, *Latimer*, 308.

- The sacrament as a pledge of heaven
- The holy Eucharist as it implies a sacrifice
- Concerning the sacrifice of our persons
- After the sacrament[1517]

Real Presence

There is a divine-human encounter at the Lord's table in which we are given an intimation of Christ's suffering and a foretaste of his coming glory. Pope explained,

> There is a real presence by the Spirit, who specially reveals Christ as the Bread of Life to the faith of the recipient, at once assuring him of his communion with the life of his Head and strengthening that life.[1518]

The Reformers did not agree on the doctrine of the Lord's Supper. Zwingli held that the Lord's Supper was a memorial. This view has been facetiously termed "a real absence." Luther affirmed *consubstantiation*, holding to a real physical presence. This means that the bread and wine *contain* the physical body and blood of Christ, but they are *not* the physical body and blood of Christ.

Calvin taught a real spiritual presence — that the bread and wine *spiritually contain* the body and blood of Christ. Steve Harper explained that the Methodist position is in line with Calvin.

> By his own choice the risen Christ is truly present whenever the Lord's Supper is observed. Christ does

---

[1517]Rattenbury, *Eucharistic Hymns of John and Charles Wesley*, 14-15.

[1518]Pope, *Higher Catechism*, 347.

not come through the bread and cup; he comes through the Spirit. But Christ is *really* there.[1519]

The Scriptures teach that Christ is present in the sacrament of communion through his Spirit. His presence makes the feast (Luke 24:13-35). The Gospel accounts teach that both the bread *and* the body of the Lord are present in communion; both the wine *and* the blood of Christ are also present. Paul clearly states in 1 Corinthians 10:16 that when we receive the Lord's Supper we are *eating bread* and *drinking the cup*, but he goes on to say that those who eat this bread and drink this cup are also partaking of the true body and blood of Christ.

The observance of the Lord's Supper has been the means of revival.[1520] It was during the time of preparation for the communion cycle that revival broke out on the Kentucky frontier at Cane Ridge in 1801.

Open Communion

Reflecting the catholic nature of the church, communion should be open to believers of other denominations. However, it need not be open to everyone who happens to feel a desire to participate without any commitment to accountability.

The real issue is that we must avoid partaking of the Lord's Supper in an unworthy manner (1 Cor 11:27). The problem within the Corinth congregation was the division described in vv 18-19. The poor were discriminated against and the rich received preferential treatment. This practice did not square with the purpose of the Lord's Supper. Instead, it was divisive. Earnest seekers and sincere believers need a good reason *not* to obey the Lord's command to meet him at his table. No one should stay

---

[1519]Harper, *Devotional Life*, 38; George, "The Real Presence," 183.

[1520]Schmidt, *Holy Fairs: Scottish Communions and American Revivals* (1989).

away simply because they do not feel worthy of the atoning sacrifice which Christ made on our behalf. While there is a particular condemnation upon those who partake unworthily, there is also a particular blessing for those who partake worthily. Thus, Wesley argued that it is the duty of every Christian to receive the Lord's Supper as often as possible. "I ask, then, why do you not accept of his mercy as often as ever you can? God now offers you his blessing: why do you refuse it?"

Wesley said the most common excuse for not obeying the Lord's command to do this in remembrance of him is that we are unworthy. But he pointed out that the text does not forbid those who are unworthy to eat and drink. Rather, the text warns against eating and drinking *unworthily*.[1521] Clarke wrote,

> "But I am not worthy." And who is? There is not a *saint* upon earth, nor an *archangel* in heaven, who is worthy to sit down at the table of the Lord. "But does not the apostle intimate that none but the *worthy* should partake of it?" No: He has said nothing of the kind; he solemnly reprehends those who eat and drink *unworthily*, and consequently approves of those who partake *worthily* . . . but there is an essential difference between eating and drinking *unworthily*, and being *worthy* thus to eat and drink. . . . Thus, none are excluded but the *impenitent*, the *transgressor*, and the *profane*. Believers, however *weak*, have a right to come; and the strongest in faith need the grace of this ordinance.[1522]

The necessity of accountability

Ecclesiastes 4:1-10 illustrates the dangers of isolation and the benefits of connection. We must rediscover the power of

---

[1521]Wesley, "Duty of Constant Communion," Sermon #101, 2.5; 8.

[1522]Clarke, *Discourse on the Holy Eucharist*, 87.

being connected. We are vulnerable when we minister in isolation.

Too often fundamentalism has become merely the affirmation of certain propositions. But the demons believe (Jas 2:19). On the other hand propositional truth is denied by modernism and replaced by a relational psychology/theology. But discipleship does have a relational aspect. Jesus spent half of his time, during the years of public ministry, living with twelve men. The marks of the new birth in 1 John are propositional, relational, *and* behavioral. We must believe rightly, we must obey, and we must love.

The small group as a tool for discipleship is not unique to Methodism. Wesley adapted the Methodist practice from the Moravians who carried on this tradition from the early church. While discipleship would seem more necessary to those who believe salvation could be forfeited, often it is more intentional among those who believe in unconditional security. Bloesch wrote,

> Orthodoxy, right belief, is intimately related to *orthopraxis*, right actions. There can be no apprehension of the gospel apart from obedience to the imperatives of the gospel. Yet we cannot do the truth unless we are in the truth. Being grasped by the truth of the gospel is prior to obeying the gospel, though a fuller or deeper understanding of the gospel comes through obedience.[1523]

The mission of the church

The church has a threefold mission of worship, discipleship, and evangelism. This mission is irreducible, and any organization

---

[1523]Bloesch, *Theology of Word and Spirit*, 141.

which does not attempt to practice all three priorities does not properly constitute a Christian church.

- ## Worship is our responsibility toward God

The Father seeks true worship (John 4:23). Worship is a holy waste of time! The Westminster Catechism of the 17th century asked, "What is the chief end of man?" The answer given was, "To glorify God and to enjoy him forever."

> Missions is not the ultimate goal of the church. Worship is. Missions exist because worship doesn't. Worship is ultimate, not missions, because God is ultimate, not man. When this age is over, and the countless millions of redeemed fall on their faces before the throne of God missions will be no more. It is a temporary necessity. But worship abides forever.[1524]

Wesley said that God instituted the Sabbath for the preservation of the church and marriage for the preservation of mankind.[1525] God instituted the Sabbath to commemorate creation, as a memorial of deliverance from bondage, and as a reminder of the rest that remains at the right hand of God.[1526] The Sabbath was an eschatological act for the Jew. He lived in eternity one day a week. It was a consecration of a part of time for the whole of life. We acknowledge that God is the lord over all our income by tithing, and we acknowledge that God is lord over all our time by setting apart one day per week.

"There remains, then, a Sabbath-rest for the people of God" (Heb 4:9). *The Lord's Day*, as used in Revelation 1:10, means that the kingdom is here. As the kingdom of Christ expands,

---

[1524]Piper, *Let the Nations Be Glad*, 17.

[1525]Wesley, *Notes*, 1:13.

[1526]Clarke, *Commentary*, 1:752.

peace will come to earth. Pope said the Sabbath was a permanent divine ordinance of worship.[1527] Wesley regarded it as a means of sanctification.[1528]

The word *Sabbath* means *rest* and does not specify a particular day of the week. While the ceremonial aspects have been abolished in Christianity (Col 2:16), Jesus Christ is the Lord of the Sabbath (Mark 2:28). Jesus did not destroy the moral law, but he relaxed its severity. It is a sacrament of holy time, which sanctifies the rest of the week. It is the day in which the Christian church assembles to worship, and that assembly must not be forsaken (Heb 10:25).

Liturgy is the formal worship of the church. Liturgy implicitly reveals theology. The issue in worship is not traditional or contemporary forms, but worship which glorifies God and sanctifies man. Proper worship of God is sanctifying. Misguided worship becomes entertainment. Psychological or cultural worship cannot sanctify because it does not glorify. Worship should include our reason, emotions, and will. Where Christians gather, there is the church. Where the church is, there is Christ. A. W. Tozer described worship:

> Worship is to feel in your heart and express in some appropriate manner a humbling but delightful sense of admiring awe and astonished wonder and overpowering love in the presence of that most ancient Mystery.[1529]

- **Discipleship is our responsibility to each other**

In the Great Commission the main verb is to *make disciples* of all nations. This involves going, baptizing, and teaching (Matt 28:19-20). Discipleship involves teaching, edification, fellow-

---

[1527]Pope, *Compendium*, 3:290.

[1528]Wesley, "On the Sabbath," Sermon #139, 1.3.

[1529]Tozer, *Keys to the Deeper Life*, 80.

ship, and counsel. We are dependant upon the body of Christ to receive these ministries. Steven Harper wrote,

> No one can develop a mature spirituality alone. To be a Christian is to be called into community. It is to become a functioning part of the body of Christ.[1530]

Dunning addressed the same issue, declaring that in the NT "there were no 'free-lance' believers. When a person became a believer in Christ, he was therewith incorporated into the community through the rite of baptism."[1531]

The *one another* (*allelon*) passages in the NT exhort us to "make every effort to do what leads to peace and to mutual edification" (Rom 14:19). "Build yourselves up in your most holy faith" (Jude 20). "The whole body grows and builds itself up in love as each part does its work" (Eph 4:16). "You are able to admonish one another" (Rom 15:14). "Let us consider how we may spur one another on toward love and good deeds. Let us not give up meeting together . . . but let us encourage one another" (Heb 10:24-25).

We are to comfort one another (1 Thess 4:18, 5:11), encourage one another (Heb 3:13), confess to one another (Jas 5:16), pray for one another, and carry each other's burdens (Gal 6:2).

We are commanded to live in harmony with one another; be sympathetic, love as brothers, be compassionate and humble (1 Pet 3:8). This love for each other is a prerequisite for evangelism. "By this all men will know that you are my disciples, if you love one another" (John 13:35).

[1530]Harper, *Devotional Life*, 54.

[1531]Dunning, *Grace, Faith, and Holiness*, 506-507.

- **Evangelism is our responsibility to the world**

Evangelism means to preach or proclaim the gospel. Oden declared that a church which is uncommitted to taking the whole message everywhere cannot be *catholic*.[1532] We are to give an answer to everyone who asks the reason for the hope we have (1 Pet 3:15).

Jesus taught us to pray, "Thy will be done on earth as it is in heaven." Part of the gospel is the call to repentance. The church must stand against sin and call the world to turn from sin. We are our brother's keeper (Gen 4:9). Thus, the church should be involved in social action.

The word *missionary* means *sent out*. It describes someone who crosses cultural or geographic barriers to carry out the Great Commission. The urgency of evangelism is threatened by four false views of salvation. Two threats come from modernism, while the other two can be found among those who are conservative in their theology.

- **The denial of depravity undermines evangelism**

Pelagius maintained that the will is naturally free to do good and is not impaired by the fall. He taught that there are no special influences of the Spirit in regeneration, but instruction is all the help that is necessary. He also taught that man can perfectly keep the law through instruction.

Pelagianism and liberal Arminianism both deny original sin. They hold that man is born morally neutral and is condemned only for his own sin. They exalt human nature and human potential believing people will do right because of an inner imperative. But this teaching does not square with the description of mankind given in Romans 7:19.

[1532]Oden, *Life in the Spirit*, 339.

If man is basically good, he only needs the right environment, heredity, and circumstances. If man is not connected with Adam, but is neutral or born with a blank slate, he only needs to be encouraged toward the light. But if man is basically sinful, he cannot save himself and needs God's help.

- **The problem of predestination undermines evangelism**

Universal redemption leads to the recognition that every person needs salvation which is available only in Christ. The urgency of this salvation leads to an appeal to every individual for repentance and faith.

However, rigid Calvinism teaches that God unconditionally chooses those whom he wills to save, and that Christ made atonement only for the elect and that those for whom Christ has died *will* be saved through irresistible grace.

I am especially concerned with the Calvinist understanding of evangelism. The first issue is whether persons actually are born again or whether they become convinced that they were included in God's election. In other words, are we saved by faith in Christ alone or by affirming a Calvinistic view of election?

The second issue relates to the order of salvation. According to Calvinism, the elect are first regenerated, then they repent and believe.

The third issue deals with the necessity of evangelism. How can an evangelist make a bona fide offer of salvation indiscriminately when he does not know whom God has chosen or for whom Christ died?

- **The heresy of universalism undermines evangelism**

A third teaching which blunts evangelism is *universalism*. This teaching combines the Calvinist view that the atonement is effectual, actually providing salvation for whom Christ died, with the Arminian emphasis that Christ died for the whole human race. Therefore, universalism teaches that all are saved but do not know it, or that all will be saved.

Universalism is a heretical position within liberal Calvinism. Arminianism affirms libertarian free will and therefore affirms that salvation is resistible. While God desires that all be saved, some sinners will remain unrepentant. Orthodox Arminian theology teaches that while
the atonement was made for the whole race of humanity, it is effectual only for those who believe.

Universalism may also be viewed as the progressive evolution of everyone toward salvation. Thus, Bloesch explained,

> If many roads lead to God, we should then respect other religions and philosophies and feel free to draw on them in constructing our own worldview. Christians no longer need to have compassion for the lost, since there are no spiritually lost.[1533]

A Methodist bishop said, "Our trouble is that we don't believe anymore that people are lost."[1534] Or as Thomas Starr King concluded, "Universalists believe God is too good to damn us for ever; and you Unitarians believe you are too good to be damned."[1535]

- **The distortion of dispensationalism under-mines evangelism**

Modern dispensationalists have sometimes carried their doctrine of the carnal Christian to such absurdities that a "carnal believer" cannot be distinguished from a lost man or woman

---

[1533]Bloesch, *The Church*, 238.

[1534]Coleman, *Nothing to Do But to Save Souls*, 48.

[1535]Frothingham, *Tribute to Starr King*, 121.

because they both act the same way. This debate is sometimes referred to as "lordship salvation." Dispensationalism holds that Jesus can be a personal Savior without necessarily becoming Lord. Tozer rightly called this teaching *heresy*,

> The Bible never in any way gives us such a concept of salvation. Nowhere are we ever led to believe that we can use Jesus as a Savior and not own Him as our Lord. He is the Lord and as the Lord He saves us, because He has all of the offices of Savior and Christ and High Priest and Wisdom and Righteousness and Sanctification and Redemption! He is all of these things and all of these are embodied in Him as Christ the Lord. . . . It is either all of Christ or none of Christ![1536]

John MacArthur pushed back against the teaching that believers out of fellowship may be "unbelieving believers," even agnostics or atheists, yet even those who deny God are still eternally secure.[1537]

Those who are not delivered from the practice of sin are not truly saved. There is not much emphasis on imparted holiness, however.

It should also be understood that while dispensationalism is committed to world evangelism, they reject the hope of world conversion, believing that only a remnant will be saved.

Purpose Driven

The irreducible minimum for the church is the threefold priorities of worship, evangelism, and discipleship. The task of an overseer, regardless of the type of church government he functions in, is to make sure the church is fulfilling its mission.

[1536]Tozer, *The Tozer Pulpit*, 2:26.

[1537]MacArthur, *Gospel According to Jesus*, 98.

What we do flows from our purpose. Thus, the church should be *purpose-driven*. Our doctrines are absolute and never change. Our threefold purpose has been established by Christ, but we need to formulate long-range objectives. We need to think ahead four generations. According to 2 Timothy 2:2, Paul mentored Timothy. Timothy discipled reliable men. Those reliable men trained those who would teach others.

We also need short-term goals. Thus, absolutes determine the purpose, the purpose determines the objectives, the objectives determine the goals, and the goals determine the methods.[1538] "To fail to plan is to plan to fail." George Hunter says over 80% of all churches in North America "plan to fail."[1539]

[1538]McIntosh, *Church That Works*, 187-192.

[1539]Hunter, *Leading and Managing a Growing Church*, 39.

CHAPTER FOURTEEN
The Doctrine of Last Things

The church will complete its mission to take the gospel to the whole world. The world will be evangelized, meaning that the gospel will take root in every political nation, every language, and every culture before Jesus returns. Thus, the world will be converted and the enemies of Christ will be subdued.

The *millennium* is a figurative expression describing the kingdom of Christ, which extends from his first coming to his second advent. Christ will physically and literally return, not to become king and establish a Jewish kingdom on earth, but he will return as king to a world which is under his lordship.

The decisive victory of Jesus Christ occurred at the cross when he finished his mission. The kingdom he established at that time is progressively advancing across time. The final victory of Christ will occur at his return. This optimism is based on the sovereignty of God, the victory of Christ, the power of the Holy Spirit, the trustworthiness of Scripture which foretells it, and the success of the church in preaching the gospel to the whole world. The whole gospel preached to the whole world under the anointing of the Holy Spirit has the potential to effect world revival.

It is also the most consistent view for Wesleyan-Arminians to adopt because it is a corporate extension of the doctrine of Christian perfection which is promised to the individual believer. However, because of the systematic nature of systematic theology, as theologians continue to draw conclusions from unestablished premises — it is to be expected that by the time they arrive at their position on eschatology that there will be as many conflicting views as there are unestablished premises. The most simple explanation is often the correct one. Detailed charts and diagrams are not usually helpful.

When Christ returns there will be a general resurrection and a general judgment. Sinners will be consigned to eternal punishment in hell. Believers will be given eternal life in heaven.

The fact that God reveals what will happen indicates that he is in control of human destiny. Thus, he has corporately predestined that the church will fulfill its mission, his kingdom will cover the earth, and that all who believe will live forever where he is. Yet he does not override the free choice every sinner has been given to decide which side he or she will be on.

The final apostasy should not be interpreted as the ultimate failure of Christ's kingdom, but the ultimate decision of mankind whether to submit or rebel. In the end, sinners will reject all the blessings of Christ's kingdom, but their futile attempt will do nothing to dethrone Christ as king or to derail God's plan to restore everything that was lost in our fall to those who keep covenant with him.

The Last Days

The Greek word for last things is *eschatos*. *Eschatology* refers to the biblical teachings concerning events which will occur at the end of world history. History is linear and not a meaningless repetition. We are moving toward the consummation of God's master plan. The theme of eschatology is paradise restored.

The *last days* is the period between Christ's first advent and second advent (Acts 2:16-17, 3:24; Rom 16:20; 1 Cor 10:11; Heb 1:1-2, 9:26; 2 Tim 3:1; 1 Pet 1:20, 4:7; 1 John 2:18). The first eschatological event was the resurrection of Jesus Christ. Therefore, Oden explained, "If the resurrection takes place in our midst, then we are already at the end."[1540] Miner Raymond also said that the last days began at Pentecost.[1541] There will also be a *last day* when Christ returns.

Approximately 20-25% of the Bible was prophetic when written. Prophecy serves to

- authenticate the Scripture. However, when prophecy "experts" make outlandish claims which do not come to pass, the Bible is discredited.
- give hope to the Christian that God is in control. History is linear, not circular. Human existence has meaning as we move toward God's ultimate purpose.
- warn the sinner of coming judgment.

We must be cautious about making dogmatic assertions concerning the future. The professional scholars in Jesus' day expected two Messiahs, one to suffer and one to reign. They expected the establishment of a political kingdom which would overthrow Rome. Christ fulfilled 332 distinct prophecies, yet he was rejected because he did not meet their expectations. If the experts missed it concerning his first advent, we should guard against prophetic speculation regarding his second advent.

The second advent will be the final victory. In between the first advent and the second advent there is a progressive victory. Christ will not return to introduce victory, but to consummate victory. Hebrews 2:8 explains that everything is under the authority of Christ. "Yet at present we do not see everything subject to him." The decisive victory was won at the cross and that victory cannot be reversed. Daniel explained that once the kingdom of Christ has been established, it would crush all humanistic

---

[1540]Oden, *The Word of Life*, 457.

[1541]Raymond, *Systematic Theology*, 3:385.

kingdoms, that it would endure forever, and fill the whole earth (Dan 2:35, 44).

And yet the progress of this kingdom has been uneven. Church historian Kenneth Scott Latourette divided church history into seven segments.

- During the first five centuries, Christianity won the professed allegiance of the large majority of the population of the Roman Empire.
- Between AD 500-950 Christianity suffered the greatest losses which it has ever encountered. Its very existence was threatened. Yet even during this decline, the gospel advanced geographically to new regions.
- This reversal was followed by four centuries of advance.
- Between AD 1500-1750 a series of awakenings revitalized the Christianity of Western Europe and missionaries carried Christianity to a larger portion of the earth than had ever been evangelized previously.
- Latourette called the period from AD 1750-1815 a *pause*. However, while menaced by a series of events and movements, there were few actual losses, and new movements would later advance Christianity to a new high level of vigor.
- From AD 1815-1914 the faith was threatened by forces which were openly or tacitly hostile to Christianity. But new life in Christianity swelled to a flood.
- The last period which Latourette surveyed began with AD 1914 and continued into the mid-twentieth century.

He concluded that Christianity has become the most potent single force in the life of mankind. In a supplemental chapter, Ralph Winter concluded that "by 1975 Christianity had clearly outpaced and was continuing to outgrow all other religious movements in global size and influence."[1542]

With another fifty years with which to evaluate this seventh period, Maxie Dunnam wrote in 1996 that 70% of all the people who have ever come to know Christ have been saved since 1900. 70% of that group have come to Christ since World War II. 70% of that group have come to Christ in the last three years.[1543] Since 1970 the growth of evangelical Christianity has been more rapid than the increase in population on every continent.[1544]

We have no way of knowing how much more time will elapse until the end. We should expect uneven progress. However, those who live through a particular period of decline tend to have a warped sense of pessimism, unless they have grasped the reality that since this fifth kingdom of Daniel was established, it will never be replaced by anything else.

We now live in between the first and second advent, assured of victory but still engaged in fierce conflict. The kingdom (or millennium) is already present, but not yet in its zenith. Thus, the best is yet to come.

Yet across history the influence of this kingdom has already elevated the status of women and abolished slavery. It has cared for the handicapped, built hospitals and orphanages, taught people to read and given them an education, and raised the standard of living.[1545]

[1542]Latourette, *History of Christianity*, 1:xxii-xxiv, 270, 275; 2:xii, 995, 1506.

[1543]Dunnam, "Renewal and Revival," 3-5.

[1544]Anonymous, "A Century of Growth," 50-51.

[1545]Schmidt, *Under the Influence: How Christianity Transformed Civilization* (2001); Garlow, *How God Saved Civilization* (2000); Tennent, *How God Saves the World* (2017); Hudson, *How Jesus Changed the World* (2016); Hill, *What Has Christianity Ever Done for Us?* (2005); D'Souza, *What's So Great About Christianity?* (2007).

Five Prophetic Fundamentals

Unfortunately, those who have the most incomplete understanding of Scripture are often the most dogmatic in their insistence that we make secondary eschatological issues a test of fellowship. There are five basic doctrines about the future that must be insisted upon in order to be true to Scripture. The early Arminians held no animosity toward those who disagreed with them on secondary issues. They only requested that their views be permitted to exist. In *The Character of a Methodist*, Wesley wrote, "But as to all opinions which do not strike at the root of Christianity; we 'think and let think.'"[1546] We can agree to disagree on the secondary issues, but we must defend these five fundamentals. Often, however, they get lost in all the speculation.

- **The literal return of Jesus Christ**

It is claimed that the second coming of Christ is mentioned over three hundred times in the NT. Not every *coming* of Christ, however, is the second advent. The second advent is Christ's return to complete all things pertaining to his work of redemption. "It is very important to note that this great event is always connected with a complete end and consummation of that work which the Lord began in His first appearance" (Heb 9:28).[1547]

Other references to his *coming* imply that

- Christ came to the disciples after his resurrection.
- Christ came on the day of Pentecost.
- Christ came in judgment on Jerusalem in AD 70.[1548]
- Christ comes for the Christian at death.

[1546]Wesley, *BE Works*, 9:33-34.

[1547]Pope, *Compendium*, 3:389.

[1548]Steele, *Half-Hours with St. John's Epistles*, xii.

- Christ comes often in judgment (Rev 2:5,16).
- Christ comes often in revival.
- Christ comes to the believer in salvation.

We know if a passage is describing the second advent by its immediate context. At the second advent he is coming in great glory to judge the world.

> The distinguishing mark of the Last Day is that the dead will be raised. The Resurrection of all men is, in the nature of the case, unrepeatable. It is not a continuing motif, but rather a part of the final eschatological event. Therefore, wherever the Bible mentions the Resurrection, it is speaking of the Last Day — the final Judgment, the ultimate Day of the Lord.[1549]

Three Greek words, *parousia, apokalupsis,* and *epiphaneia* are utilized to describe one great future event. Those who make a distinction between the *rapture* and the *revelation* or *return* of Jesus Christ also base their teaching on the use of three Greek words. *Parousia* is said to refer to the rapture and *apokalupsis* and *ephiphaneia* are said to refer to the revelation. However, in 2 Thessalonians 2:8 both *parousia* and *ephip-haneia* are used in the same verse to describe the same event. If this artificial distinction is followed, the *blessed hope* promised in Titus 2:13-14 would not be the rapture since the word *ephiphaneia* is used. This is also true of 2 Timothy 4:8.

Some also say Christ must first come *for* his saints in the rapture and then after a disputed length of time come *with* his saints in revelation. They use 1 Thessalonians 3:13 as a proof text since it uses the word *with*. However, the Greek word used is *parousia*, and by their definition this word refers to the rapture. John Walvoord conceded this point. Most dispen-

---

[1549]Chilton, *Paradise Restored*, 140.

sationalists changed their presentation, but not their conclusions, in the 1940s.[1550]

First Thessalonians 4:15-17 is the most commonly used passage to support the idea of a secret rapture. I affirm what it teaches, but I deny that it teaches a secret return of Christ for his church which may be as long as seven years before his second advent. The text does compare his coming to a thief who comes unexpectedly, but nothing about this coming is secret. On the contrary, it will be loud enough to raise the dead! Proof-texts for the rapture are usually describing the general resurrection, not a secret rapture. The blessed hope, described in Titus 2:13, is not a secret rapture, but the visible appearing of Jesus Christ at the end of time.

Dispensationalists hold that the rapture is *imminent*, meaning that it could happen at any moment. "In no respect is the inconsistency of Dispensationalists more glaringly apparent than in their persistent efforts to discover *signs* of an event which they emphatically declare to be *signless*."[1551]

Not only do premillennialists disagree as to whether this rapture is to be pre-trib, mid-trib, post-trib, or pre-wrath, but some teach a partial rapture in which only those members of their select group will miss the tribulation period.

After surveying the major passages used to prove two phases to Christ's return, George Eldon Ladd summarized his findings:

> The vocabulary used of our Lord's return lends no support for the idea of two comings of Christ or of two aspects of his coming. On the contrary it substantiates

---

[1550]Walvoord, "New Testament Words for the Lord's Coming," 284-289; Reiter, "Development of the Rapture Positions," 30.

[1551]Boettner, *The Millennium*, 332.

the view that the return of Christ will be a single, indivisible, glorious event.[1552]

Christ declared that "the wheat and the tares are to remain together in the field until the harvest" or end of the age. The secret rapture theory, however, teaches that all the wheat is removed and the tares left standing before the end. We are assured that Christ will come "the second time without sin unto salvation" (Heb 9:28), but there is no clear teaching scripturally that he will come a third or fourth time. In contrast to premillennial speculation Pope declared, "There is but one visible appearance of Christ set before the expectation of His people."[1553]

Premillennialism frequently appeals to Zechariah 14:4 as proof of a physical return. Of course, the literal and physical return of Christ is accepted across all orthodox millennial views. However, this passage says nothing about a physical and literal Jewish kingdom established *after* the return of Christ. Grider pointed out that even in this description of his literal return, symbolic language is still utilized.

> Those who want to take all these statements literally, surely must have trouble avoiding the figurative altogether. For example, if Jehovah's feet are on a mountain, the expression must be figurative, especially when this mountain is *cleft in the midst* so that *a very great valley* is formed between its two sides.[1554]

The second coming of Christ did *not* occur in the first century. This heretical position claims that the events of the book of

---

[1552]Ladd, *The Last Things*, 57; *The Blessed Hope*, 70. See also Wiley, *Christian Theology*, 3:250.

[1553]Pope, *Compendium*, 3:399.

[1554]Grider, *Wesleyan Bible Commentary*, 3:786.

Revelation *and* the second advent of Christ are both in the past. Proponents of this view claim to be consistent preterists. They teach there are no future prophetic events. This position was advocated by J. Stuart Russell in *The Parousia* (1878). Liberal preterists recognize the AD 70 foci of many passages, but deny the predictive nature of inspired prophecy. Hyper-preterists focus all eschatological statements on AD 70, including the general resurrection, the great judgment, and the second advent of Christ. Jonathin Seraiah advocated that this position be termed *pantelism*, in distinction from the orthodox preterist position.[1555] *Pantelism* is from the Greek words meaning "all is completed." Moderate preterists teach a *parousia* of Christ to judge Jerusalem in AD 70, but still advocate a future second advent.

- **The resurrection of all mankind from the dead**

Death is the last enemy (1 Cor 15:26). The resurrection of the dead will be the first act of the consummation of Christ's redeeming work. The soul is immortal, but the body will be resurrected. Jesus taught that through faith our spirit can cross over from death to life and it can be born again. But a time is coming when dead bodies will also hear his voice and will come to life (John 5:24-25). This resurrection of the body is described in 1 Corinthians 15. This resurrection will be universal. E. M. Bounds wrote,

> The resurrection of the body will be universal and personal, general and particular, of every one good and bad, or, in the language of the Bible, "a resurrection of the just and unjust." It will take place generally and at the last day.[1556]

[1555]Seraiah, *The End of All Things*, 13.

[1556]Bounds, *The Resurrection*, 34.

According to Philippians 3:21, Christ will transform our lowly bodies at his second advent so that they will be like his glorious body — incorruptible and immortal. Thus, the resurrected body is substantively the same body that died.

Oden said, "The glorified body is not a different body, but a different form of the same body."[1557] It is buried in corruption, dishonor, weakness, and in a natural state, but raised in incorruption, glory, power, and a spiritual state (1 Cor 15:42-44).

The Bible does not teach *conditional immortality* — that hell is the grave. Advocates teach that eternal life is conditional and only the righteous are raised from the grave while the rest sleep in a state of annihilation. First Thessalonians 4:14 employs the term *sleep* in a figurative sense. The dead in Christ are resting in him. Thus, death is not to be feared. Revelation 14:13 describes the saints resting from their labor, but this does not imply soul sleep or a state of unconsciousness.

The concept of rest in scriptural usage carries the idea of satisfaction in labor or joy in accomplishment, not the cessation of activity.[1558] The rich man was also tormented while in hades (Luke 16:23).

Connected with conditional immorality is the teaching of *annihilation*. Annihilation teaches that the only hell is the grave. *Annihilation* also describes hell in terms of fire that consumes rather than fire which torments. But how can extinction be considered punishment? It's like digging up a dead man and hanging him to teach him a lesson. The Bible teaches a resurrection of the body to eternal life for the just *and* the unjust.

John said that at the coming of Christ death gave up the dead (Rev 20:13). This describes a general resurrection when the sea and death and hades (the grave) surrender every person back to life. This description alone destroys the teaching of conditional

---

[1557]Oden, *Life in the Spirit*, 402.

[1558]Boettner, *Immortality,* 92.

immortality and annihilation. Oden wrote concerning Wesley's teaching on hell,

> Wesley spoke with Scripture of an all-too-real hell as eternal separation from the source of all good. Whatever path modern Wesleyans have taken, Wesley himself held fast to the clear preaching of Jesus concerning a real hell more horrible than our worst imaginings. When we come up before the final divine judgment, we will see that the real judgment is far more devastating than our most terrible visualizations.[1559]

Most biblical descriptions of the resurrection depict both good and bad who are raised. The pertinent passages to be evaluated are: Job 21:25-27, Daniel 12:2,[1560] John 5:28-29, 1 Corinthians 15:42-44, and Revelation 20:12-13. At the second advent, all who are dead will be resurrected and receive their eternal bodies.

In contrast to the belief in a general resurrection, the premillennial view, that there are two physical resurrections a thousand years apart, is based upon only one passage, Revelation 20, which is found in a figurative context. Amos Binney wrote,

> If the doctrine of two literal resurrections, one thousand years apart, be a revealed truth, it is strange that it should be directly and explicitly taught in one passage only. The uniform testimony of all other Scripture is to the effect that there is but one literal resurrection, and universal, and simultaneous with the second coming of

---

[1559]Oden, *John Wesley's Teachings*, 2:301.

[1560]Daniel is describing the spiritual revival of Israel which is also foretold in Ezekiel 37 [Clarke, *Commentary*, 4:617; Jordan, *The Handwriting on the Wall*, 616-618].

Christ, to judge the righteous and wicked together, at the end of the world.[1561]

The intermediate state

Death is the last probationary event for mankind. It ushers us into an intermediate state to await the final consummation of Christ's coming. The intermediate state is a state of conscious blessing or torment. Those who die in the faith are present with the Lord the moment they are separated from the body (2 Cor 5:6). Jesus promised the thief on the cross that today he would be with him in paradise (Luke 23:43). But the dead are not in purgatory. It is appointed for us to die and after death no second chance is promised — only judgment (Heb 9:27). Probation ends at death. But the resurrection does not occur at the moment of death.

The most graphic passage depicting the intermediate state is the account of the rich man and Lazarus in Luke 16:19-31. Jesus is describing *hades* and not *gehenna*. Both men are in *hades*. But the passage is generally considered a parable, although Luke does not introduce it as such.[1562] Hermeneutically, a parable cannot be analyzed for doctrinal specifics since it was given to illustrate one main concept. Thus, I am not sure how much can be inferred about the afterlife from this account. However, Erickson wrote, "While it was not Jesus' primary intent here to teach us about the nature of the intermediate state, it is unlikely that he would mislead us on this subject."[1563]

[1561]Binney, *TPC*, 701.

[1562]Trench, *Notes on the Parables of Our Lord*, 161-171. Commentators also disagree over whether 2 Cor 5:1-9 describes the intermediate state or the resurrected body. Ladd argued that it was the resurrection body [*The Last Things*, 35-37].

[1563]Erickson, *Christian Theology*, 1177.

- ## The final judgment

The final judgment is the consummation of God's judicial administration which has always been at work in the world. It involves a separation of those who are condemned from those who are justified. Benjamin Field wrote, "The day of judgment is not to make God Himself better acquainted with the character of men, but to make both men and angels better acquainted with the character of God."[1564]

"If the righteous receive their due on earth, how much more the ungodly and the sinner!" (Prov 11:31) Peter's logic is irrefutable in 1 Peter 4:17-18. If even good people suffer and if hypocrites are judged, there is no escape for the ungodly and the sinner. Peter asserts, *How much more* will God judge the wicked. If the best people do not escape judgment, the worst people are not going to get by either. When the Lord Jesus is revealed from heaven in blazing fire with his powerful angels, he will punish those who do not know God and do not obey the gospel of our Lord Jesus. They will be punished with everlasting destruction [not annihilation] and shut out from the presence of the Lord and from the majesty of his power (2 Thess 1:5-9).

According to Acts 17:31; 1 Corinthians 4:5; and Revelation 22:12, the judgment will follow Christ's return. All will be judged, according to Romans 14:10-12; 2 Corinthians 5:10; and Revelation 20:12-13.

The basis of judgment will be our works. We are saved by faith, but faith is an inward persuasion. We demonstrate true faith by good works (Jas 2:17-18). If our works are imputed and not actual, and if the basis of judgment is our works, then the nominal Christian would be condemned along with the sinner. To handle this dilemma dispensationalists have adopted a division of judgments with one for sinners on the basis of works and

---

[1564]Field, *Student's Handbook of Christian Theology*, 397.

one for believers to determine the degree of reward. Some have taught numerous judgments:

- The believer's sin is judged at the cross. Thus, all past, present, and future sins are forgiven. Scofield wrote that the believer "can never again be put in jeopardy."[1565] This means any future judgment for believers would only concern the degree of reward.
- The believer's reward at the *bema* judgment. However, the description of the *bema* seat or step in 2 Corinthians 5:10 does not describe a separate judgment of believers after the rapture merely to determine reward.
- The judgment of the Jews. Again, dispensationalism keeps Israel separated from the church.
- The judgment of nations based on their treatment of Israel.
- The Great White Throne Judgment

In 1927 H. A. Baldwin wrote *The Coming Judgment* in which he argued for a general judgment and attempted to resist the influence of Scofield and Blackstone within the holiness movement. He felt the teaching of a divided judgment opened the door for endless speculation "which approach is dangerously near to higher criticism." Baldwin demonstrated that the leading dispensational writers of that period did not agree among themselves as to how many judgments there would be. After demonstrating that the early church fathers taught a general judgment, Baldwin examined the scriptural basis for multiple judgments as presented by dispensationalists. He concluded that there was no scriptural basis for inserting a period of a thousand years into such texts as Acts 10:42; 2 Timothy 4:1; and 1 Peter 4:4-5 which all speak of judging the quick or living and the dead.

[1565]*New Scofield Reference Bible*, 1144.

The reader can look in vain for any intimation or for the least suspicion that the judgment of the two classes will not synchronize. To separate them, the theory must first be framed and then the texts "split" to accommodate the theory.[1566]

This general judgment will be based upon works. There are forty-two instances in Scripture where we are told we will be judged on the basis of our works.[1567] When we are first saved, our works are filthy before God (Isa 64:6). Therefore, our faith is imputed to us for righteousness (Rom 4:6). We are not only justified; we are given the new life of the Holy Spirit and were created in Christ Jesus to do good works (Eph 2:10). We demonstrate true faith by good works (Jas 2:17-18).

While we are initially saved by faith alone, genuine faith will produce good works. The Greek word used is *ergon*. A frequent theme in Revelation is this final judgement of works or deeds (see 2:2,5-6,19,22-23,26, 3:1-2,8,15, 9:20, 14:13, 16:11, 18:3-6, 20:12-13, 22:12).

Good works do not merit salvation and eternal life, but they are signs or manifestations of inward grace. In both cases it is the value of deeds as manifesting something which stands in the foreground, rather than being a matter of performance. Works are not understood primarily as proof of performance but as a means of knowing and assessing.

In Romans 2:6-11 the emphasis is not on rewarding achievement, but upon the relevance of good and evil deeds in the judgment as the means of recognizing the inner character of the person. In Galatians 5:19-26 the fruit of the Spirit is not meritorious human achievements, but the produce of the new Spirit-worked inner reality.

[1566]Baldwin, *The Coming Judgment*, 14, 184.

[1567]Smith, *Revelation*, 279.

This corresponds with the OT emphasis that deeds are not merits which gain entry into a particular status with God. Instead, they reveal the status which one has already gained through election and covenant.[1568]

Travis wrote that such passages as Romans 2:1-11; 1 Corinthians 6:9; Galatians 5:21, and Ephesians 5:5 teach that works bear testimony to the depths of a man's character and show whether his relationship to God is fundamentally one of faith or unbelief.

> For Paul this is the crux of the matter. Works are not the criterion of possession of the inheritance. Rather they are the revelation of a person's character, the evidence of whether he is "in Christ" or not.[1569]

Thus, the apparent contradiction between Paul and James — justification by faith and judgment according to works — are two sides of the same coin. Justification involves more than simply a legal acquittal. Simultaneous with justification is regeneration, which results in imparted righteousness.

• An eternal heaven

The Hebrew language did not have a specific word for the universe, so in the OT there are frequent references to "heaven and earth." The Hebrew word *shamayim* literally means *the heights*. The Greek word *ouranos* means *that which is raised up*.

In 2 Corinthians 12:2 Paul refers to the third heaven where God is. Clarke explained that the first heaven is the atmosphere. The second heaven is the sun, moon, planets, and stars. The third

---

[1568]Yinger, *Paul, Judaism, and Judgment*, 160-161.

[1569]Travis, *Christ and the Judgment of God*, 61, 57.

heaven is the throne of divine glory.[1570] The Bible uses *heaven* in six senses:

- the sky (Gen 1:8).
- the celestial heaven (Gen 1:14-18).
- the abode of God and angels (Ps 103:19).
- the kingdom of heaven — which is the reign of God. The term *kingdom of heaven* occurs 34 times in Matthew and nowhere else in Scripture.
- intermediate paradise or punishment between death and resurrection (2 Cor 5:6).
- the final consummated eschatological heaven — the eternal abode of the redeemed (John 14:2-3).

Heaven is a real place (John 14:2-3). It is a place of rest (Rev 14:13, but not inactivity (Rev 7:15, 22:3). Heaven will be deliverance from temptation, Satan, infirmities, pain, and death (Rev 21-22). We are told 51 times that heaven is forever. We will dwell in the house of the Lord *forever* (Ps 23:6).

Heaven will also be full of praise and music (Rev 14:2). It will be a place of reunion with loved ones who have died in the faith. Most importantly we will see God (1 John 3:2).

Revelation 21-22 tells us more about heaven than any other passage in the Bible. And yet heaven is not the primary subject. The bride of Christ is the subject. The place called *heaven* is only referred to directly three times in these two chapters, as the eternal abode of the church.

Jesus told his church before he left, "And if I go to prepare a place for you, I will come back and take you to be with me that you also may be where I am" (John 14:2-3). The glory of the church is that God dwells with his people, and the hope of the church is that they will dwell with him. Heaven is our reward (Rev 22:12) and our inheritance (1 Pet 1:3-4).

[1570]Clarke, *Commentary*, 6:367.

There will be no more sorrow, pain, or death because the curse of sin has been reversed. In heaven everything will be *new* (Rev 21:5). The word *kainos* means newness in kind or fresh. The old heaven and earth will be renovated by fire — not annihilated but purified. While we do not affirm that matter is eternal, however we can affirm the conservation of matter (Ps 148:6).

The most radical change will be that death has died. According to 1 Corinthians 15:26 the last enemy to be defeated is death. Death will never enter heaven.

Heaven is the location of God's throne (Rev 22:3). Heaven is a place of holiness. Its citizens have experienced final sanctification. The walls are a symbolic barrier to sin. Fletcher explained,

> But suppose it were possible for thee, O sinner, to enter into heaven without having experienced the new birth. What wouldst thou do there? Drunkard! there is no strong drink in heaven. Sensualist! thou must leave flesh and blood behind, and how great would be the disappointment to be deprived of all the means of thy present happiness. Heaven itself would be no heaven for thee; and thy discontent would even prove a kind of hell.[1571]

The Bible, however, teaches that where he is there we will be also (John 14:3). All of God's people will be with him. The only separation is between saved and unsaved. We can gather very little, however, about the location of heaven and earth. The *coming down* is a description of the bride coming down the aisle (Rev 21:2). In v 10 the city is coming down. Both the city and the bride are metaphors or symbols for the people of God.

Death means separation, not annihilation. I am actually more alive after I die, but I am simply no longer present on earth. We

---

[1571]Fletcher, *Works*, 4:144.

need not become so heavenly minded that we think of heaven in terms of escape from that which is earthly. Heaven is more like a redeemed earth. In heaven the sky will be blue and the grass will be green, but there will be no sin. The greatest distinction between heaven and earth will be that absence of sin in heaven.

While the Bible has more to say about hell than about heaven, perhaps God wants his covenant people just to trust him. We can infer more about heaven based on the character of God than we can inductively conclude from Scripture. If God is the highest good, and if in his providence he is working the greatest good for us, then heaven will be a reflection of his goodness. I suspect that the humor in heaven will be based upon inadequate earthly concepts of heaven.

In the consummation of all things, there will be a new heaven and a new earth (2 Pet 3:13). The earth will be purified, but nothing God made will be destroyed. Peter tied the concept of a future renovation by fire with the historic judgment by water in the days of Noah. Peter does not describe the annihilation of creation, but its renovation. While this renovation does not imply the eternity of matter, it does imply the conservation of matter (Ps 148:6).

The divine ideal will be realized and the redeemed will be perfected, but individual identity will not be merged with the corporate body of Christ any more than the corporate body will be merged in God. The glorified saints will see God. This hope is termed the *beatific vision*. Now we see through a glass darkly, but then we will see him face to face. That continuous vision of him will transform us into his likeness.

First John 3:2 describes the beatific vision, the vision of God in heaven permitted to the blessed. "Blessed are the pure in heart, for they will see God (Matt 5:8). We shall see him as he is (1 John 3:2). Now we see through a glass darkly, but then face to face (1 Cor 13:12; Ps 17:15). We will see the face of God (Rev 22:4).

• An eternal hell

The Bible has more to say about hell than about heaven. The Hebrew *sheol* and the Greek *hades* usually refer to the grave, but sometimes they specifically mean a place of torment. In the KJV *sheol* is translated *grave* 31 times, *hell* 30 times, and *pit* 3 times.

Does that mean *hell* is simply the grave? The Greek words *gehenna* and *tartaroo* (to cast into hell) are also translated *hell*, and these words describe a place of torment. The verb *tartaroo* occurs in 2 Peter 2:4. *Gehenna* is used twelve times in the NT and always refers to a place of torment.

The dead are conscious. All go to the grave, but not all to the same state. In Luke 16:22-30 one man is in torment and one man is in Abraham's bosom. There is a great chasm between them — yet both are in *hades*.

It is often asked how a loving God can send people to hell. But God is not only a God of love, but of holiness (Hab 1:13), justice (Rev 15:3), and mercy (Mic 7:18). Those who go to hell have rejected God's mercy and his offer of salvation. He did not unconditionally predestine anyone to go there.

While hell was prepared for the devil and its angels (Matt 25:41), Jesus taught that people will also go to this place. Revelation 20:15 describes their being cast into the lake of fire. A. T. Robertson wrote, "There is no room here for soul sleeping, for an intermediate state, for a second chance, or for annihilation of the wicked."[1572] Carson wrote that 20:15 and 21:8 affirm explicitly that all unbelieving people will suffer the punishment of *the lake of fire*, the very same *lake of fire* into which the devil, the false prophet, and the beast will be thrown.[1573]

Peter Head wrote that John knows of no difficulty in the continuing existence of the wicked under the judgment of God (Rev 21:27, 22:14). The final triumph of God is not deemed

---

[1572]Robertson, *Word Pictures in the New Testament*, 6:465.

[1573]Carson, *The Gagging of God*, 527-528.

incompatible with a continued exclusion and punishment of the godless. In fact, the final triumph of God's justice is seen in the salvation of the saints and the punishment of the wicked. There is no escaping the fact that Revelation clearly teaches and assumes the continued existence of the wicked in a destructive punishment primarily intended for Satan and his operatives. The eternal fire was designed for the devil and his angels, but human beings experience this judgment by virtue of their association with the Devil as children of wrath and their opposition to Jesus Christ. "The fiercest New Testament language is reserved for outspoken and blatant opponents of the gospel and persecutors of Christians."[1574]

C. S. Lewis explained that heaven is the habitation of those who say to God, "Thy will be done," and hell is the abode of those to whom God says, "Thy will be done."[1575] Thus, hell is the conclusion of man's insistence upon autonomy. "In hell, all is chaos, waste, and ruin; all things are unrelated and beyond communication. There is no community in hell."[1576]

In 1861 Methodist theologian William F. Warren explained that just as libertarian freedom explains the existence of sin, so it also vindicates the benevolence of God although he permits the full, eternal fruition of sin's consequences. God's final treatment of the sinner does not imply a vindictive spirit. The conditions for the exercise of pardoning mercy would no longer subjectively exist as sinners persist in their lack of desire for salvation. Is hell hopeless? Warren explained that it is hopeless because its inmates have been so loved, and yet have rejected that love, that no new or higher manifestation is possible in which to hope.[1577]

[1574]Head, "Duration of Divine Judgment," 226-227.

[1575]Lewis, *The Great Divorce*, 75.

[1576]Rushdoony, *Politics of Guilt and Pity*, 34.

[1577]Scott, "Methodist Theology in America," 272-273.

Universalism teaches that everyone will ultimately be redeemed and restored — some even include Satan. Advocates like to utilize the vague phrase *the wideness of God's mercy*. But Scripture teaches that *today* is the day of salvation (2 Cor 6:2). Also called *restorationism*, universalism teaches that sinners will have a second chance after death. Since Christ died for everyone, the promise of salvation was without limitation, whether it happened in this life or the next. This final restitution would come when every tongue confessed that Jesus Christ is Lord (Phil 2:10-11).

The Duration of Hell

There will be no change in our eternal condition (Rev 22:11). Everyone will not ultimately land in heaven. Hell is eternal. Revelation 20:10 says those in the lake of fire will be tormented day and night for ever and ever. This phrase *for ever and ever* is the strongest term in Greek. Arndt and Gingrich defined it as "without beginning or end."[1578] It is also used to refer to the duration of God's own existence in Revelation 1:18, 4:9-10, 10:6, 15:7.

Revelation 14:11 describes the smoke of torment rising forever and ever. The consequences of rejecting the eternal gospel are eternal consequences. Mounce wrote, "The punishment of the damned is not a temporary measure."[1579] The Greek word for *torment, basanismos,* is never used in the Bible to describe annihilation.[1580]

According to Matthew 25:46 the duration of heaven is the same length as the duration of hell because the same adjective, *aionios*, is used to describe both places. Raymond explained that the doctrines of heaven and hell interpenetrate each other. Each

---

[1578]Arndt and Gingrich, *Lexicon*, 28.

[1579]Mounce, *Revelation*, 274.

[1580]Osborne, *Revelation*, 547-548.

implies the other. If there is a heaven, there is also a hell. If one is a condition of happiness, the other is a condition of misery. If heaven is a place, so is hell. And if heaven is eternal, so also is hell.

In Romans 2:12 Paul warns that the wicked will perish. This word *apollumi* means to destroy. Oepke wrote that it describes "definite destruction, not merely in the sense of the extinction of physical existence, but rather of an eternal plunge into Hades and a hopeless destiny of death."[1581]

According to 2 Thessalonians 1:9 the wicked will be punished with everlasting destruction. The Greek word for *destruction, olethros*, means ruin, doom, or death, but not annihilation.

The word *hell* does not appear in the NIV translation of Revelation. The four places it does appear in the KJV it should be translated *hades*. However, the doctrine of hell is stated clearly in the rest of Scripture and hell is described symbolically in Revelation as:

- the lake of fire and brimstone or sulfur. This combines the imagery of the destruction of Sodom and Gomorrah with the opening of the ground to swallow Korah in Numbers 16. The lake of fire is John's symbolic description of the utter defeat and complete destruction of these enemies in their attempt to seize the kingdom.[1582] If fire produces light, and hell is a place of outer darkness, it follows that the fire is not literal but a metaphor describing divine judgment and human suffering which never burns out.

- The second death symbolizes eternal separation from God. Just as there is a new and higher life in the Spirit, so there is also a second and deeper death. "The essence

---

[1581]Oepke, ἀπόλλυμι, *TDNT* 1:396.

[1582]Chilton, *The Days of Vengeance*, 491.

of hell is final exclusion from communion with God because of one's own fault."[1583]

To say these expressions are symbolic in no way tones down the awfulness of eternal punishment. Martin Luther said that no picture of hell could be as bad as the reality.[1584] Sometimes preaching has centered on the physical suffering and pain, but John uses words such as fire and death to describe something which is even worse.

Secondary Issues

There is a great deal of speculation and carnal curiosity about such secondary issues as: the timing of the great tribulation, the identity of the antichrist, the nature of the mark of the Beast, the nature of the battle of Armageddon, as well as Gog and Magog, the timing of the rapture, and the nature of the millennium. Often these subjects overshadow the primary doctrine of Christ's second coming. I am not advocating latitudinarianism, the position that doctrinal concepts do not matter. I am not advocating an agnostic position, that we cannot know anything about the future. We can know with certainty what God has clearly revealed. However, I reject any appeal to extra-biblical revelation. I am advocating an attitude of humility expressed in the words of Oliver Cromwell, "I beseech you, in the bowels of Christ, think it possible that you may be mistaken."[1585]

All prophetic teaching should be evaluated on the basis of ten basic truths:

• Jesus Christ is the central theme of Bible prophecy.

[1583]Kasper, *Church's Confession of Faith*, 347.

[1584]Oden, *Life in the Spirit*, 452.

[1585]Carlyle, *Cromwell's Letters and Speeches*, 1:448.

- Christ conquered Satan at the cross and established his kingdom.
- Christ's kingdom will overcome the kingdom of Satan and exercise world-wide dominion.
- Christ will remain at the right hand of the Father until all enemies are put under his feet.
- Christ will come to raise the dead and to judge the whole world.
- No one can get saved after the return of Christ.
- No one can enter Christ's kingdom except through saving faith in his atoning work.
- God has not unconditionally selected any race or group of people.
- Christ is coming after a holy, not a defeated church.
- Christians are to live by faith in the victory of the cross and in hope of world revival.

Daniel's vision of seventy sevens (Dan 9:20-27) foresaw a period of 490 years which included judgment, redemption, and completed revelation. Jesus expanded upon this same period of time in his Olivet Discourse (Matt 24; Mark 13; Luke 21). John's record is expanded in his Revelation.

The time frame of the book of Revelation — preterist, historicist, or futurist is an interpretative issue. Dispensationalism pushes much into the future, because of the gap they impose on Daniel's seventy weeks, pushing week 70 into the future.

During this 490-year period of time which Daniel foresaw (Dan 9:24-27), the old covenant came to an end and the temple was left in desolation as the apostate Jewish nation was punished for its rejection of its Messiah. Those who did not enter into the new covenant at Pentecost faced a holocaust. Thus, the great tribulation was that period of struggle between two kingdoms as Satan attempted to stop the establishment of Christ's kingdom.

However, dispensationalism arbitrarily interjects a gap between week 69 and week 70 of Daniel's vision. The irony is that the gap inserted between Genesis 1:1-1:2 distorts our perspective of creation and this gap in Daniel 9 distorts our perspective of future events.

Daniel 9:24-27 foresees the end of the old covenant and the establishment of the new covenant. In a period of 490 years Jerusalem would be rebuilt, the Messiah would come to make an end of sins, make reconciliation for iniquity, bring in everlasting righteousness, cause sacrifice to cease, and establish the new covenant. After that the old temple will be destroyed because it has become obsolete. While the new covenant began at Pentecost, apparently there was an overlap of the two covenants between AD 30 and AD 70.

Once we settle *when* the kingdom is established, then we can pinpoint the time of great tribulation. Since the kingdom was established at the crucifixion, resurrection, and session of Christ, I understand the great tribulation to be the siege of Jerusalem from AD 67-70. Therefore, the seals, trumpets, and bowls of Revelation should be interpreted as symbolic of events which occurred in the first century. The people of God will always be tested, however. "Everyone who wants to live a godly life in Christ Jesus will be persecuted" (2 Tim 3:12).

Clearly, the kingdom was established at Pentecost. Yet God in his infinite mercy gave the Jews one generation to repent. In a real sense Jesus came in AD 70, but that was not his second advent. He came in judgment on those who rejected him as Messiah. Daniel 7:9-22 described the verdict pronounced by the Judge. The time of this event was the ascension and session of Christ. Yet, according to v 25, the saints will have to resist the devil for 3½ years—even though he is already under the sentence of death! There is often a time interval between the rendering of a verdict, the declaration of the sentence, and the execution of judgment.

Jesus taught that war, famine, pestilence, earthquake—the events of the seals, trumpets, and bowls—were not the end, but the beginning (Matt 24:6-8; Luke 21:9-10). He also taught clearly that the great tribulation would not occur at the end of time. He said, "For then there will be great distress (or tribulation), un-equaled from the beginning of the world until now and never to be equaled again" (Matt 24:21).

The popular teaching of a future tribulation period is based upon the shaky theory of a postponed kingdom. Not until the mid 1800s did the church ever hear about a postponed kingdom. While Harry Ironside himself advocated this view, he conceded that until Darby this idea "is scarcely to be found in a single book or sermon through a period of sixteen hundred years."[1586]

In his doctoral dissertation, William E. Bell set out to examine what was taught in the church prior to 1830. He said that any of the following items would be of crucial importance:

- Any mention that Christ's second coming was to consist of more than one phase, separated by an interval of years.
- Any mention that Christ was to remove the church from the earth before the tribulation period.
- Any reference to the resurrection of the just being in two stages.
- Any indication that Israel and the church were to be clearly distinguished, thus providing some rationale for a removal of Christians before God again deals with Israel.

Bell concluded, "No trace of the doctrine is to be found in church history after the Ante-Nicene fathers until the nineteenth century."[1587]

The most basic eschatological issue that separates Bible-believing theologians is whether God's plan should be understood covenantally or dispensationally. The result of this disagreement is the plethora of prophetic charts which exist in order to maintain the dispensational hermeneutic of separation. The

---

[1586]Ironside, *The Mysteries of God*, 50-51.

[1587]Bell, "Critical Evaluation of the Pretribulation Rapture Doctrine," 26-27.

greatest eschatological concept is the kingdom of Christ. Covenantally, we understand that his kingdom was established at his first advent. In the language of Daniel 9:24 the kingdom of everlasting righteousness was brought in.

However, dispensationalism has a very different understanding of the kingdom. For them, it is a Jewish kingdom which is established at the return of Christ and after the rapture of the church. Thus, Ryrie wrote, "The church is not part of this kingdom at all."[1588]

According to dispensationalism, during the millennial period Jesus will sit on a literal throne within a rebuilt temple in Jerusalem. By their count this would be the fourth temple. First, there was Solomon's temple, then the rebuilt temple under Ezra. They teach there will be a rebuilt temple during a future, seven-year tribulation, and finally a millennial temple described by Ezekiel.

From a covenantal understanding, this future millennium would be a regression in God's plan. The church is the temple of God. Christ's kingdom is universal, and he has been seated at the right hand of God since his ascension and session. His kingdom is primarily spiritual.

Revelation 20:1-6 is the only biblical passage which speaks of a millennium or thousand year period. Milton S. Terry wrote, "No doctrine which rests upon a single passage of Scripture can belong to fundamental doctrines recognized in the analogy of faith."[1589]

The Greek term *chilia ete* occurs six times in Revelation 20:1-6. There is disagreement over whether this is a literal or symbolic number. John Walvood declared that a literal interpretation of prophecy is the basis of premillennialism.[1590] The hermeneutic of dispensationalism is literal whenever possible. But in a genre which employs symbolism, literalism will eventually

---

[1588]Ryrie, *Basic Theology*, 398-399.

[1589]Terry, *Biblical Hermeneutics*, 581.

[1590]Walvoord, *The Millennial Kingdom*, v-vi.

break down. Why take the wrong road until it dead ends then abandon it? A consistent hermeneutic is preferable — one that acknowledges the inherent symbolism within apocalyptic literature. Crenshaw and Gunn analyzed 97 OT prophecies cited in the book of Matthew. Only 34, or 35%, were literally fulfilled.[1591]

No one interprets the book of Revelation in a consistently literal way. Commenting on Revelation 20, Beale explained,

> Because the objects he sees and what he hears are seen and heard in a vision, they are not *first* to be understood literally but viewed as symbolically portrayed and communicated, which is the *symbolic* level of the vision. That this vision is shot through with symbols is apparent merely from the obviously symbolic nature of such words as "chain," "abyss," "dragon," "serpent," "locked," "sealed," and "beast."[1592]

In reaction to those who fail to grasp the poetic style of the book of Revelation, Chesterton said, "Though St. John the Evangelist saw many strange monsters in his vision, he saw no creature so wild as one of his own commentators."[1593]

Since the book of Revelation declares itself to be symbolic some nine times,[1594] the burden of proof is for dispensationalism to demonstrate why *chilia ete* should be taken literally. In the Greek language *chilia* was the highest numerical concept. To go

---

[1591]Crenshaw and Gunn, *Dispensationalism Today, Yesterday, and Tomorrow*, 22.

[1592]Beale, *Revelation*, 974. See also Tenney, *Interpreting Revelation*, 186-193.

[1593]Chesterton, *Orthodoxy*, 29.

[1594]Rev 1:1, 12:1, 3, 15:1 uses the Greek word *semaino*, which means to express by signs or symbols. In 11:1 the word *spiritually* is used to indicate the same thing. In 1:20, 10:7, 17:5, 7 the term *mystery* is used to make the same statement.

beyond a thousand you had to say "thousands and thousands," as John did in Revelation 5:11.

There is also disagreement over whether we are now in this period or whether it constitutes a future age. The word *chiliast*, as well as *millennialism* and *adventism*, denotes *premillennialism*. The premillennial position, in general, sees the millennium as a future period of time inaugurated by a cataclysmic event — the return of Christ to earth. Actually, the great cataclysmic defeat of Satan occurred in the middle of history, not at the end.

In fairness, a distinction must be made between historic or covenantal premillennialism and the more recent variety of premillennialism, dispensationalism. Dispensationalists claim antiquity for their view by equating premillennialism with dispensationalism. However, dispensationalism was not developed until the nineteenth century. Some of the early church fathers held a historic premillennial view, but it was never the predominate view. None of the major creeds of the early church affirmed premillennialism.[1595]

The premillennial emphasis was imported into the Christian church from Jewish converts who carried over the Pharisees' doctrine of the Messianic kingdom. Rall notes that premillennialism originated in the Jewish apocalyptic literature of the inter-testamental period.[1596] They anticipated that after their return from exile, God would reestablish the Jewish kingdom. This misconception is implied in the question of Acts 1:6, "Lord, are you at this time going to restore the kingdom to Israel?"

Dispensationalism insists on a distinction between Israel and the church which historic premillennialism does not advocate. Historic premillennialism exalted the church and its role in the

---

[1595]Lightner, *The Last Days Handbook*, 158.

[1596]Rall, *Modern Premillennialism and the Christian Hope*, 54.

kingdom. However, it claimed that the kingdom would be brought to earth only with the return of the King.

Dispensationalism is also based on a pessimism concerning the success of the church. They teach that the dispensation of the church will end in failure. Incredibly, Dave Hunt wrote, "The millennial reign of Christ far from being the kingdom, is actually the final proof of the incorrigible nature of the human heart, because Christ Himself can't do it."[1597]

Dispensationalists believe the kingdom of heaven refers to the earthly, nationalistic rule which Jesus offered to the Jews but which they rejected. Thus God's program for Israel had to be postponed until later, and "the church age" became God's interim program. The church will secretly be raptured out of this world so that God can resume his original plan of establishing a Jewish earthly kingdom. Dispensationalists disagree, however, concerning whether this rapture of the church will be pre-tribulational, mid-tribulational, pre-wrath, post-tribula-tional, or partial.

However, there are no biblical passages which teach the rapture of the church as a distinct event from the second advent (see 1 Thess 3:13). Historic premillennialists, amillennialists, and postmillennialists all agree at this point.

Premillennialism must impose the second advent somewhere in Revelation 19. Walvoord declared that vv 11-13 were "one of the most graphic pictures of the second coming of Christ to be found anywhere in Scripture."[1598] But this is an *a priori* assumption imposed upon the text. The passage says nothing about his return to earth. None of the three Greek words, *parousia*, *apokalupsis*, and *epiphaneia*, used to describe the second advent, occur in this chapter. Additionally, there are two more general Greek verbs which can refer to the second advent: *erkomai* and *horao*. Revelation 19:7 says the marriage supper of the Lamb has come (*erkomai*). Revelation 19:10 commands John to see that he

---

[1597]Hunt, *Beyond Seduction*, 250.

[1598]Walvoord, *Revelation of Jesus Christ*, 274.

not worship the angel. Here the verb *horao* is used. But neither reference describes the second advent. Ray Summers wrote,

> Christ is pictured as coming down from heaven, but this does not picture the second coming of Christ which we find discussed elsewhere in the New Testament. This scene graphically represents his coming to the aid of persecuted Christians with heavenly assistance in their spiritual struggles.[1599]

Revelation 19:6 describes his present reign and kingdom expansion. This chapter portrays Christ riding from victory to victory across history. According to Whedon, Revelation 19 describes Christ going forth as the Word of God, "marching as a conqueror and subduing the nations to his triumphal sway, fulfilling the mission of the second Psalm."

> As the gospel progresses throughout the world it will win, and win, and win, until all kingdoms become the kingdoms of our Lord, and of His Christ; and He will reign forever and ever. We must not concede to the enemy even one square inch of ground in heaven or on earth. Christ and His army are riding forth, conquering and to conquer, and we through Him will inherit all things.[1600]

His second advent occurs *after* the millennium of Revelation 20:1-6. He comes in vv 7-14 to raise the dead and judge the world.

The premillennial millennium, no matter whether the historic view or the dispensational view, is a very confused state of affairs. King Jesus reigns from Jerusalem, but many of his sub-

---

[1599]Summers, *Worthy is the Lamb*, 199.

[1600]Chilton, *Paradise Restored*, 192.

jects are unconverted. It is only through force that his will can be imposed, and at their first opportunity, his subjects rebel. Thus, this "dispensation" ends in failure like all the rest! But while it lasts, the subjects of the millennial kingdom consist of Christians who have died, been resurrected, and brought back to earth, along with living Christians who have been "raptured" and given glorified bodies. They apparently will live side by side with human beings who still have their mortal bodies.

In contrast, covenant theology sees more continuity. For us, the great cataclysmic event which divided human history was the coming of Christ to establish his kingdom. His kingdom, described symbolically in Revelation 20 as the *millennium*, will continue to expand until it fills the whole earth. Then Christ will return at the end of time. Those who reject the premillennial view are called *amillennialists*. This term does not mean that we reject the teaching of Revelation 20, only that we reject the premillennial *interpretation* of Revelation 20. John Walvood reflects a very distorted view of the amillennial position:

> It is also clear that Christ is not reigning on earth in any literal sense. Jerusalem is not His capital nor are the people of Israel responsive to His rule at the present time. To attempt to find fulfillment in the present age requires radical spiritualization and denial of the plain, factual statements related to the kingdom.[1601]

Historically, the debate within the church has been between premillenialism and postmillennialism. All postmillennialists are amillennial regarding the *nature* of the millennium, and all amillennialists are postmillennial regarding the *timing* of Christ's return. The term *amillennial* was not coined until the 1930s.

In addition to interpretative disagreements over when the kingdom of Christ began and its length, there is also a third

---

[1601]Walvoord, *Major Bible Prophecies*, 108.

difference — regarding the *nature* of the kingdom. The millennium is not to be anticipated as a Jewish kingdom. Nor is amillennialism adequate. Amillennialism understands the present reality of the kingdom but does not see any future expansion. They expect a continuous development of good and evil in the world until the second coming of Christ. The only problem with this position is that it does not do justice to the many wonderful promises cited which describe the kingdom of God extending into the world through the preaching of the gospel and the work of the Holy Spirit. They do not believe that the world will eventually be Christianized or that there will be a long period of righteousness and peace before the return of Christ. For them the kingdom of God is entirely a spiritual kingdom.

If Daniel's first four kingdoms were political in nature, should not the fifth kingdom have a political influence as well? However, the primary power of the church to change society is not through political strategy but by moral example and spiritual influence.

The basic distinction between a literal earthly reign of Christ from a throne in Jerusalem and the spiritual growth of Christ's kingdom has been debated within the church for the better part of two thousand years. In the final analysis, I am not attempting to defend a term either. I am contending for an eschatology of hope. Wesley declared,

> Give me one hundred preachers who fear nothing but sin and desire nothing but God, and I care not a straw whether they be clergy or laymen, such alone will shake the gates of hell and set up the kingdom of heaven upon earth.[1602]

[1602]Wesley, *Letter* to Alexander Mather, 6 Aug 1777.

Such a statement is implicitly postmillennial, since premillennialism does not believe this kingdom can be set up until Christ returns.

Athanasius was the bishop of Alexandria, Egypt in the fourth century. At that time it was part of the Roman empire and a pagan city of learning. He wrote:

> Since the Savior has come among us, idolatry not only has no longer increased, but what there was is diminishing and gradually coming to an end: and not only does the wisdom of the Greeks no longer advance, but what there is is now fading away: And demons, so far from cheating any more by illusions and prophecies and magical arts, if they so much as dare to make the attempt, are put to shame by the sign of the Cross. And to sum the matter up: behold how the Savior's doctrine is everywhere increasing, while all idolatry and everything opposed to the faith of Christ is daily dwindling, and losing power, and falling. And thus beholding, worship the Savior "Who is above all" and mighty, even God the Word; and condemn those who are being worsted and done away by Him. For as, when the sun is come, darkness no longer prevails, but if any be still left anywhere it is driven away; so, now that the divine Appearing of the Word of God is come, the darkness of the idols prevails no more, and all parts of the world in every direction are illuminated by His teaching.[1603]

John of Damascus recorded a similar statement in the eighth century.[1604] While it could be argued that the kingdom has subsequently lost ground in these regions, there has been a net increase internationally. "More people from different countries, who

---

[1603]Athanasius, *Incarnation of the Word*, *NPNF*2 4:66.

[1604]John of Damascus, *On the Orthodox Faith*, *NPNF*2 9:75.

speak different languages, and who are part of different cultures, worship Jesus Christ than at any time in the history of the world."[1605] And the reversals were not predestined. They were the result of the church leaving its first love.

The Final Apostasy

Revelation 20:7-10 describes the end of the millennial period. After many have professed faith in Christ and the world has known its greatest prosperity, then Satan is released, deceives the nations, and gathers together a rebellion numbering as the sand of the sea.

Luke 17:26-30; 1 Thessalonians 5:3; 2 Timothy 3:1-5 all describe complacency, worldliness, materialism, and hedonism as prevailing conditions immediately prior to the Lord's return. John Jefferson Davis places the time frame of these texts as after the millennium and before the second advent.[1606]

If Christ were physically present on this earth and imposing his will by force, how could such a rebellion ever get off the ground? To teach, as some do, that Christ personally and bodily rules on earth, only to have a revolt at the end, involves a second humiliation of Christ. His own people, as a nation, rejected him when he came the first time. He humbled himself and died on a cross, as the famous passage in Philippians 2:6-8 detailed. Yet the following verses (9-11) inform us that Christ has been exalted by the Father. He will never suffer humiliation again.

This section in Revelation 20:7-10 corresponds to 2 Thessalonians 2:1-12 which teaches that Christ will come *after* the apostasy.[1607]

If sin could enter a perfect environment with Adam and Eve (Gen 3), sin will be present during the millennium. The millen-

---

[1605]Tennent, "Global Community Formation," 3.

[1606]Davis, *Christ's Victorious Kingdom*, 111-112.

[1607]Davis, *Christ's Victorious Kingdom*, 98.

nium will not be a utopian society since Satan, sin, and death will not then be completely destroyed. The kingdom will be perfectly consummated only at the second advent. After the human race universally experiences the blessings of Christ's kingdom, many will choose to rebel. This reality does not mean Christ's kingdom failed or that the millennial "dispensation" ends in failure. It means that God still gives libertarian freedom.

One thing is certain, a world which does not know Christ as Savior cannot fall away from what they never knew. There must first be world conversion, then there will be a short-lived apostasy. When Satan finally leads this rebellion, it will be a rebellion against a Christian civilization.

The Sequence of Last Events

The church must take the gospel into all the world. There will be opposition and persecution, but gradual success. There will be many *times of refreshing* (Acts 3:19). John Fletcher wrote, "We can patiently and confidently expect those times of refreshing which shall assuredly come from the presence of the Lord looking forward to that promised restitution of all things."[1608]

And there will be a latter-day rain of the Spirit which was predicted by Hosea. "As surely as the sun rises, he will appear; he will come to us like the winter [later] rains, like the spring [former] rains that water the earth (6:3)." Joel's reference to these rains comes in the context of his great pentecostal prophecy (2:23). Zechariah encourages us to *ask for rain* (10:1).

The early rain was needed so that the planted seed would germinate. The latter rain was necessary for the plant to fill out and produce fruit. The purpose of the latter rain is to guarantee an abundant harvest. Just as Pentecost was the early rain which established the kingdom, the latter rain, which we are to pray for,

---

[1608]Fletcher, *Works*, 2:165.

will produce a great end time harvest of souls.   As a result of the atoning death of Christ and the drawing of the Holy Spirit there will be people in heaven from every *nation, language,* and *ethnic group*, according to Revelation 5:9, 7:9, 10:11, 11:9, 13:7, 14:6, 17:15. If everyone seen in heaven was saved on earth, the church must first evangelize the whole world by penetrating every political division, every linguistic barrier, and every cultural identity. This phrase is so significant that it occurs in some form seven times in Daniel and seven times in Revelation. I understand a fourth term, *ethnos*, to be the most general term which includes nation, language, and ethnic or cultural group.

"All Israel shall be saved" (Rom 11:26). Peace will come to the mid-East. "In that day there will be a highway from Egypt to Assyria. . . . In that day Israel will be the third, along with Egypt and Assyria, a blessing on the earth. The Lord Almighty will bless them, saying, 'Blessed be Egypt my people, Assyria my handiwork, and Israel my inheritance'" (Isa 19:23-25).

The earth will know a time of peace as the rule of Christ extends from sea to sea (Zech 9:10). Nations will be governed by the law of God, and the knowledge of the glory of the Lord will fill the earth (Hab 2:14). After the world has known peace and prosperity for an indefinite period of time, Satan will be loosed for a short time — in contrast to a "thousand" years — to test the nations.

If sin could enter a perfect environment tempting Adam and Eve, so it is only fair that those who have seen the golden age also are tested. The millennium will not be a perfect world, but it will be a relative perfection.

And so Paul explained to the church in Thessalonika that Christ had not already returned. He will not return until after a falling away (2 Thess 2:1-12). The final apostasy cannot happen until the world has first turned to Christ. Then there will be a short-lived rebellion, in contrast to a thousand-year age of blessing. Satan will try one final time to overthrow the kingdom of God, but Christ will return like fire coming down from heaven.

Satan will be cast into the lake of fire, the dead will be raised, and all the world judged by Christ.

Paul tells us that Satan will be overthrown with the breath of his mouth and the splendor of his presence. John, in Revelation 20:9, describes the coming of Christ like fire which falls from heaven and consumes them. All who have rejected Christ will be cast into hell, and all who have overcome will enter heaven.

After death, the final enemy, has been destroyed and every enemy has been vanquished, Jesus Christ will deliver the kingdom back to the Father (1 Cor 15:24-28). Wesley explained that the Father would not reign eternally without the Son. The Son will not cease to reign because passages such as Luke 1:33; John 17:5; Hebrews 1:8; and Revelation 22:15 imply that Jesus Christ will reign eternally. But while the Father and the Son will reign jointly, something will change. The mediatorial kingdom of Christ will be terminated since Christ will no longer need to intercede on behalf of his own church, nor would it avail to intercede for those who are consigned to a place of everlasting punishment.[1609]

It is quite possible that I am wrong at some point in my understanding of eschatology and the biblical sequence. But I will not do any harm so long as I emphasize nine fundamental themes in biblical prophecy.

- **The Centrality of Jesus Christ**

Jesus Christ is the theme of all Scripture, including prophecy. The book of Revelation is the revelation of Jesus Christ. We must avoid conspiracy theories, preoccupation with identifying antichrist, and trying to locate when and where the battle of Armageddon will be fought. "For the testimony of Jesus is the spirit of prophecy" (Rev 19:10).

[1609]Wesley, *Notes*, 442.

Richard Bauckham argued in *The Theology of the Book of Revelation* (1993), the central symbol of Revelation is the throne, and the central question the book of Revelation answers is, "Who is really Lord of this world?" The God who came to us in Jesus Christ is Lord of all, and all other aspirants to kingship are pretenders. Jesus is, in fact, King of kings and Lord of lords (Rev 17:14, 19:16).

• The Dominion of God's People

Christ came to redeem mankind and reinstate his redeemed to rule this world as his vice-regents. A proper view of authority leads to the conclusion that the reign of Christ is not determined by his physical location. Christ rules this world through his church. Fear is not from God, and the believer need not live in fear of "doomsday."

Christ rules from his heavenly throne until every enemy on earth is subdued. Psalm 110:1 is quoted in the NT more frequently than any other OT verse. It is quoted or alluded to 23 times in the New Testament. It is quoted in eleven of the 27 NT books and by seven of the nine NT authors.

• The Conditional Nature of Covenants

The assumption that Israel is the focus of biblical prophecy, in spite of their rejection of Christ, has created a two-track understanding of God's plan for the future. While his plan includes the salvation of Israel (Rom 11:26), his plan is universal in scope and does not revolve around Israel.

• The Victory of the Cross

The cross was the turning point in redemptive history. A universal atonement is the basis of universal hope. Ultimately, all things will be reconciled to Christ and he will have dominion over everything (Col 1:18-20). The universal atonement of the last Adam not only counteracts the sentence of death incurred by the first Adam, but the victory of Christ is superabundant, restoring much more than was ever lost (Rom 5:20). While everyone will not be saved, the race as a whole will be redeemed. Mankind as a race will be saved. However, this concept of redemption accomplished does not imply universalism, the annihilation of those who are not redeemed, nor the salvation of a mere remnant who alone are elect.

• **The Establishment of the Kingdom**

The kingdom of Christ was established at his first advent. In his Pentecostal sermon, Peter links the resurrection, the ascension, and the outpouring of the Holy Spirit, all as evidence that the kingdom of Christ had begun (Acts 2:32-36). The gift of the Spirit was confirmation that Christ was indeed seated at the Father's right hand. The meaning of Pentecost is that Christ has been seated and has poured out the Holy Spirit. We know the kingdom has come because we have received the Spirit (Rom 14:17).

This much is clear from biblical prophecy, once this kingdom has been established there can be no reversal. The decisive victory of Christ was won at the cross. The progressive victory of Christ is accomplished through his church across human history. However, Latourette explained that Christianity has spread by pulsations of advance, retreat, and advance. Each major advance carried it further than the one before it, and each major recession has been less severe than the previous one.[1610] The final victory will be his second advent.

Christ will return a second time. There will be a general resurrection and judgment. Yet the popular view is that God's plan is on hold until Christ returns. This misunderstanding stems from a failure to recognize his present kingdom on earth. It leads

---

[1610]Latourette, *History of Christianity*, 2:1468.

to disastrous results to believe that the church plays no significant role in society until he returns. Although this kingdom had a small beginning, Jesus taught it was like yeast which would silently and slowly permeate the whole world (Matt 13:31-35).

- ## The Urgency of Evangelism

The gospel must be preached to the whole world which exists at the time of Christ's return, before his return (Matt 24:14). As a premillennialist, Walt Russell believes that Christ will return to complete his kingdom on earth when the church has finished her task of evangelism.[1611] This was the theology of A. B. Simpson.[1612] But it may be a "thousand years" after the gospel is preached to the world that Christ returns.

On the other hand preterists often assert that the gospel *was* preached to the known world (*oikoumenes*, not *kosmos*) and that the end of the age did come, along with the coming of the new age of the Spirit. Those who take this view tend also to teach that the coming (*parousia*) of Christ also occurred when he came in judgment at AD 70. Thus, for them the three questions asked by the disciples all have the same answer. Certainly all three were connected in the minds of the disciples, but they were wrong.

Is Matthew 24:14 then past or future? Since the second advent did not occur in the first century, Matthew 24:14 is future. It is a summary of what must occur before Christ returns at the end of the world. Jesus disassociates the last two questions of the disciples from their first question and gives them hope that, although the early church will go through the great tribulation, ultimately the gospel will succeed. Since the prevailing condition at the time of his coming is that the world will be evangelized, each new generation of the church has a responsibility to evangelize their world. The timetable for Christ's return is in the Fa-

---

[1611]Russell, "Do We Need to Evangelize?"14-16.

[1612]Wood and Takenaga, "Bring Back the King!" 11-13.

ther's hands, but any time period in which the church has failed to finish the great commission is a time period in which conditions are not right for the Lord to return.

This is *the sign*, the only sign, he gave us. The nations must be discipled (Matt 28:18). If there will be people in heaven from every political nation, language, and subculture — they must come to Christ on earth in this life. We have no basis for a second chance. Thus the urgency of evangelism is thwarted when we deny the existence of hell.

The boundaries of the kingdom expand as we disciple the nations.

> Eventually, through evangelism, the reign of Christians will become so extensive that "the earth will be full of the knowledge of God as the waters cover the sea" (Isa 11:9). Edenic blessings will abound across the world as God's law is increasingly obeyed (Lev 26:3-13; Deut 28:1-14). What a tremendous motive for worldwide evangelism![1613]

But nominal conversion which does not produce transformation is not true conversion. Discipleship will produce an ethical transformation, and this world will change as the gospel changes lives one at a time.

• **The Social Responsibility of the Church**

Conservatism tends to emphasize withdrawal from the world and liberalism tends to substitute government programs for cultural salvation. Liberals try to reform the world without the converting work of the Holy Spirit. Conservatives emphasize personal evangelization while often denying that society can be changed.

[1613]Chilton, *Paradise Restored*, 200.

The dispensational tradition is famous for asking, "Do you polish brass on a sinking ship?" Yet the *ship* is sinking because those with the answer have withdrawn. Rall explained, "Wesley's plan was to save the ship and not simply to take off a few souls from a doomed vessel, as premillennialism suggests."[1614]

While we are instructed to separate from sinful practices, we are not instructed to separate from society. The captives from Israel were instructed to immerse themselves in the Babylonian culture (Jer 29:4-28). Scripture describes the influence of the church as salt and light (Matt 5:13-16).

- ## The Necessity of Holy Living

This kingdom is a spiritual kingdom. We enter it through the new birth (John 3:5), which is the first resurrection (Rev 20:6). It is righteousness, both imputed and imparted, as well as peace and joy in the Holy Spirit (Rom 14:17).

Christ is presently at work conforming his church into his image. We can be made morally perfect now and absolutely perfect through our glorification at his coming. We will be presented to him without the stains of sin (Eph 5:27). We can be kept blameless until he comes (1 Thess 5:23). Since the day of the Lord will come unannounced, we must live holy lives on a daily basis so that when he comes we will be found without spot and unblemished (2 Pet 3:10-14). He is able to keep us and present us in this condition (Jude 24). If sin keeps sinners out of heaven, what hope do "carnal" Christians have of eternal life?

The return of Christ is therefore a major incentive to holy living. No passage in Scripture which deals with future events completely answers all our questions. But these passages typically move to an emphasis upon the necessity of holy living. Our complete holiness is the present provision of Christ, and by

---

[1614]Rall, *Modern Pre-Millennialism and the Christian Hope*, 237. However, Rall, himself, imbibed too much modernism.

appropriating faith we must be found in this condition when he returns. The reality of a final apostasy, described in 2 Thessalonians 2:1-12 and Revelation 20:7-10, warns us of the reality of sin and the necessity to persevere in faith.

- ## The Hope of Revival

The gift of the Holy Spirit is the gift of new life. Yet kingdom growth usually comes slowly. First the blade, then the ear, then the full ear of corn (Mark 4:28). This maturing process requires time and patience. While the gift of evangelism is a legitimate spiritual gift, modern evangelists often tend to force God's hand because of their theology of revivalism. However, Eugene Peterson described the pastor who works for long-term subversion.[1615]

True revival, however, is the acceleration of kingdom work. The normal process of conviction, awakening, repentance, faith, and assurance is accelerated. But true revival involves both divine sovereignty and human responsibility. Jonathan Edwards observed, "When God has something very great to accomplish for his church, it is his will that there should precede it the extraordinary prayers of his people."[1616]

Wesley noted that Martin Luther believed that a revival of religion usually lasted about fifty years, but Wesley expressed the hope that the Methodist revival would continue until the millennium was brought in. "We have therefore reason to hope that this revival of religion will continue, and continually increase, till the time when all Israel shall be saved and the fulness of the Gentiles shall come."[1617]

[1615]Peterson, *The Contemplative Pastor*, 26-37.

[1616]Edwards, *Some Thoughts on the Revival of Religion*, 357.

[1617]Wesley, *Letter* to Elizabeth Ritchie, 12 Feb 1779. See also *Letter* to Hester Ann Roe, 25 June 1782.

On an old English church is found this inscription, "In the year of 1653, when all things sacred in the Kingdom were either profaned or demolished, this church was built to do the best of things in the worst of time."[1618] Little did anyone know at that time that John Wesley would be born fifty years later.

Wesley expressed hope that the Methodist revival would not die. "No; I trust this is only the beginning of a far greater work — the dawn of 'the latter day glory.'" Wesley then expressed his belief that God "will carry it on in the same manner as he has begun." Thus, he expected the "latter day glory" to arrive gradually as the gospel was preached and all classes of people would be converted and enter the kingdom of God. He described this as "the grand Pentecost" fully come.[1619] Wesley preached,

> Some people say, when my head is laid, all this work will come to nothing. So it might, if it were the work of man. But it is not the work of man: it is the work of God; and it will spread more and more till the knowledge of the Lord shall cover the earth as the waters cover the sea.[1620]

The Puritans also grasped this hope. The term Puritan was coined in the 1560s. Iain Murray described the Puritan hope:

> Christians in their successive generations are but one agency in the hands of God, and for the Puritan, with his long-term view, it concerned him little whether he was called to sow or to reap; what mattered was that the

---

[1618]"The Chapel of the Holy Trinity at Staunton Harold."

[1619]Wesley, "General Spread of the Gospel," Sermon #63, ¶ 16-20; 25-27. See also "On Laying the Foundation of the New Chapel," Sermon #112, 2.6-7, and Wesley, *BE Works*, 11:276-277

[1620]*Letter* from Joseph Entwisle to James Wood, 20 Nov 1838. Entwisle, *Memoir of the Rev. Joseph Entwisle*, 537.

final outcome is certain. So persecution could be faced; or the appalling darkness of entirely non-Christian nations. For the men of this noble school neither promising circumstances nor immediate success were necessary to uphold their morale in the day of battle.[1621]

The same Spirit which was poured out at the beginning of the last days (Acts 2:17) will also be poured out frequently (Acts 3:19) and climactically at the end of the age. We do not anticipate a "Laodicean Age." Instead, we watch for a latter day rain of the Spirit (Hos 6:3; Joel 2:23).

While J. Edwin Orr emphasized preaching and praying, Richard Lovelace articulated the theology of Jonathan Edwards that there is a place for reform in revival.[1622] Bloesch wrote, "The church today needs both revival and reform, but one cannot happen without the other."[1623] David Wells concluded,

We need reformation rather than revival. The habits of the modern world, now so ubiquitous in the evangelical world, need to be put to death, not given new life. They need to be rooted out, not simply papered over with fresh religious enthusiasm.[1624]

My prayer is that this *Systematic Theology* might be an instrument in that reformation and revival.

[1621]Murray, *The Puritan Hope*, 90, 235.

[1622]Shaw, *Global Awakening*, 207.

[1623]Bloesch, *The Last Things*, 264-265.

[1624]Wells, *No Place for Truth*, 301.

GLOSSARY OF TERMS

ADVENT is based on a Latin word meaning *to come* or *arrive*. However, since God comes often — in judgment, in salvation, in revival, and in death, the first and second advent refer specifically to the two physical, literal, visible appearings of Jesus Christ.

AFFUSION — the method of baptism where water is poured on the head of the person being baptized. The word *affusion* comes from the Latin *affusio*, meaning *to pour on*. Thus, it symbolizes the outpouring of the Holy Spirit as described in Romans 5:5.

AMILLENNIALISM understands that the thousand-year reign of Revelation 20:1-6 describes that period of time between Christ's first and second advents.

ANNIHILATION. A heretical teaching that the fire of hell consumes rather than punishes.

ANTHROPOMORPHISM. This word is comprised of two Greek words, *anthropos* means mankind and *morphe* means form. The term describes a picture of God in human form. In contrast to a *theophany*, these are figures of speech when God is described as having wings or hands, even though he is a spirit.

ANTICHRIST. This term occurs five times: 1 John 2:18, 22; 4:3 (twice), and 2 John 7. Adam Clarke defined the term as any person, thing, doctrine, system of religion, or polity which is opposed to Christ and the spread of the gospel.

ANTINOMIANISM. *Nomos* is the Greek word for *law*. The prefix *anti* means *against*. To be *against the law* is to teach that under the gospel dispensation the moral law is of no use or obligation because faith alone is necessary to salvation.

APOCRYPHA. Fourteen additional books between the Old and New Testaments added by the Roman Catholic Church in AD 1546. They were never accepted by the Jews into their canon of Scripture nor by Protestants.

APOLOGETICS. The defense of, or making a case for, the Christian faith. 1 Peter 3:15 tells us that Christian believers should be able humbly and respectfully to defend their hope in Christ to anyone who might ask. Such a defense may be pre-evangelism. It also strengthens and confirms the faith of believers.

APOSTASY. This word describes a departure from the faith.

A PRIORI. A type of logic which arrives at knowledge prior to sense experience or observed facts. It moves from cause to effect.

A POSTERIORI. A type of logic which arrives at knowledge only after sense experience. It moves from effect to cause.

ARMAGEDDON. This word occurs only at Revelation 16:16. It is interpreted either as a spiritual conflict between Satan and the kingdom of God or an end-time battle in which Russia attacks Israel.

ARMINIAN. In contrast to Calvinism, Jacob Arminius taught a conditional election (God chooses all whom he foreknows will trust in him for that salvation), a universal atonement (Jesus made provision for every person to be saved), preliminary grace (the Holy Spirit will lead every person to salvation unless they resist him), and conditional perseverance (we are only saved so long as we continue to trust and obey).

THE AWAKENED STATE. The preliminary ministry of the Holy Spirit convicts the sinner of his sin, his lack of righteousness, and the impending judgment. No longer asleep to his true spiritual state, the awakened sinner can do nothing to save himself but is enabled through divine grace to repent and believe.

CALVINISM. Based on the theology of John Calvin, a sixteenth century reformer who taught a logical chain of doctrines beginning with **total depravity**—the doctrine that Adam's original act of sin so affected the human race that mankind is born with a bias toward sin. Sin has so permeated our total personality that there is nothing in man that has not been infected by the power of sin. Wesleyans do not disagree with Calvinists at this point. However, Calvin also taught **unconditional election** — the doctrine that God has predestined those he will save. **Limited atonement** asserts that Christ only atoned for the sins of those God predestined to be saved. **Irresistible grace** teaches that those God has chosen and for whom Christ died will experience an irresistible call by the Holy Spirit. It is impossible that these will be lost since God has decreed their salvation. They will **persevere** and will be eternally secure.

CANON. This word describes a rule or measure. Te *canonical books* are those sixty-six writings which measure up to the standard of apostolic authority. The canon is complete.

CATHOLIC. This word means *universal* and describes the universal church. Protestants affirm that the church is *catholic*. However, the term *Roman Catholic* refers to a denomination with headquarters in Rome.

CHARISMATIC. The Greek word for gift, *charisma*, describes the gifts of the Holy Spirit. The modern charismatic movement began in 1960 with an emphasis on one gift — the gift of tongues, which was introduced into mainline denominations. Rob Staples explained that Wesleyans believe in the gifts of the Spirit. "Thus we, too, are charis-matics. But we are charismatics *who do not speak in unknown tongues.*"[1625]

CESSATIONISM. The belief that miracles ceased after the early church era. This position is held by many, but not all, Calvinists.

CHRISTIAN PERFECTION. While absolute perfection is an attribute of God alone, Christ commands his disciples to be perfect (Matt 5:48). This perfection is a relative perfection, a perfection imputed to believers when they love God completely and love their neighbor as themselves.

COMPATIBILISTIC FREEDOM OF THE WILL. The Calvinist position that man's freedom is compatible with God's determin-ism. Thus, while man is free to act according to his own choices, since he is totally depraved he will always choose to sin. Sin is therefore his only choice.

CONDITIONAL IMMORTALITY. A heretical belief that only the righteous are raised to eternal life. Sinners sleep in the grave as their "eternal punishment." This view is closely aligned to *annihilation*.

CONGREGATIONALISM. This form of church government is based on the autonomy of the local congregation. Any associa-tion of local congregations is voluntary and cannot legislate policy for the local congregation.

[1625]Staples, "Rose is a Rose," 25.

CONNECTIONAL. The autonomy of the local congregation must be balanced by the concept of inter-dependence and connection. Connectionalism implies a level of the church beyond the local congregation.

DEDUCTIVE REASONING moves from the general to the particular, relying on abstract logic.

DEISM teaches that God is transcendent and does not intervene in human affairs. Thus, they would deny the concept of particular or meticulous providence. Deism rejects the possibility of miracles. This view was popular in the eighteenth century. It fits with the modern concept of theistic evolution.

DICHOTOMY. The view that mankind is composed of two parts — physical and spiritual. Thus, we are embodied spirits.

DISPENSATIONALISM is a recent type of premillennialism which emphasizes a distinction between Israel and the church based upon the belief that covenants are unconditional. They believe the kingdom is future and contingent upon the return of Christ. This interpretation began with John Darby in 1830 and was popularized in America by the *Scofield Reference Bible*.

DUALISM. A pagan worldview that puts evil or Satan on an equal footing with God.

EFFECTUAL CALLING. Those who advocate limited atonement must make an artificial distinction between the general call, the proclamation of the free offer of grace, and the effectual call, which regenerates only the elect.

EPISCOPAL. Based on the Greek word *episkopos*, which means overseer or bishop, an episcopal form of government implies a level of leadership above the local pastor.

ESCHATOLOGY is based on the Greek word *eschatos*, which means *last things*. Eschatology includes such fundamental doctrines as the second coming of Christ, the resurrection and judgment, heaven and hell. Eschatology is God's plan for the establishment and victory of his church.

EX NIHILO. This Latin phrase describes creation from nothing. Either God or matter must be eternal. Christianity teaches that God is eternal and spoke the cosmos into existence through divine decree.

FILIOQUE. This Latin word means *and the Son*. It describes a double procession of the Holy Spirit from the Father *and the Son*. This became controversial when the Western church added this phrase to the Nicene Creed. Yet John 15:26 seems to teach this double procession.

FUNDAMENTALISM is the concept that there is an irreducible minimum statement of Christian doctrine and that these doctrines should be defended. The great ecumenical creeds of the Christian church set forth fundamental Christian doctrine. Wesley spoke of some of these doctrines as "those grand, fundamental doctrines, original sin, justification by faith, the new birth, inward and outward holiness." While we affirm personal Christian experience, we also affirm the historic Christian creeds which state the Christian faith objectively.

FUTURIST. This position holds that everything after Revelation 1-3 will take place after the church has been raptured. Thus, everything between chapters 4-20 will occur in seven years, although only those who hold to a pretribulation rapture place it at 4:1. The futurist position is arrived at by inserting a gap between Daniel's 69th and 70th weeks.

GENERAL REVELATION or natural revelation. It describes truth discovered outside the Bible, including creation and nature, history, the constitution of mankind — especially reason, and common grace.

GNOSTIC. *Gnosticism* comes from the Greek word *gnosis* meaning knowledge, insight, or science. It teaches salvation through knowledge. The basic error of gnosticism was a dualism of matter, which was evil, and spirit, which was good. This was the first pagan philosophy that the early church had to combat.

HADES. The Hebrew word *sheol* corresponds to the Greek word *hades*. Both words refer in general to the grave, but they can be used more specifically of hell.

HERMENEUTICS. The task of *hermeneutics* is to determine the meaning of the biblical text. While words can be taken out of context and twisted to mean anything, the most objective interpretation of Scripture is to consider the historical context and the accepted meaning of words. This method is described as the grammatical-historical hermeneutic.

HISTORICAL. This approach to the book of Revelation sees the book unfolding across church history from the time of the apostles to the end of the world. The fulfillment of Revelation is thus in process. Protestants have historically seen the Roman Church, under the pope, becoming apostate and persecuting the true church, as the theme.

HYPOSTASIS means substance. Thus, the *hypostatic union* refers to the two natures of Christ — fully God and fully man combined in one person.

IMPASSIBILITY. Stoic philosophy taught that God does not have any emotions. Yet God has revealed in Scripture that he is relational and loving. He is not remote or detached. He is a person and not simply a philosophical concept.

IMPARTED RIGHTEOUSNESS. The infusion of a new nature when we are born again is the positive side of salvation. Forgiveness is the non-imputation of our sins to our account. Both come together. God does not impute to us what he does not also impart to us.

IMPUTED RIGHTEOUSNESS. When we trust in the atoning work of Christ, God no longer imputes our sins to our account. Thus, we are forgiven. However, the Bible does not teach that God imputes the righteousness of Christ to our accounts in lieu of any personal holiness.

INCARNATION. When the second person of the godhead took on a human body, he became *incarnate*. This word is based on the Latin word meaning *in flesh*.

INDUCTIVE REASONING moves from specific observations to a general conclusion. This process is also called the scientific method. Inductive reasoning is usually *a posteriori*.

INERRANCY. The Word of God is trustworthy because God cannot err. The ministry of the Holy Spirit in the process of inspiration was to ensure that the human authors accurately recorded God's revelation.

INSPIRATION. According to 2 Timothy 3:16, all Scripture is inspired. The Greek word *theopneustos* means God-breathed. This process of inspiration describes the supernatural influence of the Holy Spirit, ensuring that the human author was restrained from error and guided to write the words of God.

INTERMEDIATE STATE. The period of time between our physical death and the general resurrection at the last day. The soul remains in a constant state of either bliss or torment during this time, contrary to the false doctrine of soul sleep.

JUSTIFICATION. This word describes the forgiveness of sin which occurs when we trust in Christ alone. Our sins are no longer imputed against us through the merits of Christ's atonement.

KINGDOM of GOD or **KINGDOM of HEAVEN** refers to the rule of God over his people. A kingdom is the realm, and the people of the realm, over which a king exercises authority. The kingdom of God exists wherever the will of God is done. We enter the kingdom of God through the new birth (John 3:5). This kingdom expands as more people are born again. Thus, it is both a present reality and a future hope.

LAPSARIAN VIEWS. Calvinism has speculated on the chronological order of God's decrees regarding election. The Bible does not address the issue of an order of God's decrees. This is nothing more than speculative theology.

LAST DAYS. The period of time between the first and second advent of Christ.

LEGALISM is an attempt to earn salvation through works or to make oneself holy through extra-biblical rules and standards.

LIBERALISM or *modernism* refers to the worldview which began with the French Enlightenment period and ended with the fall of communism. Liberalism demanded a closed system in which all phenomena had to be explained within the parameters of natural causes.

LIBERTARIAN FREEDOM OF THE WILL. In contrast to compatibilistic freedom, this position states that God confers upon us the freedom of contrary choice. Thus, our actions are foreknown, but not predestined by God. This is the Arminian position.

LIBERATION THEOLOGY. A political movement which interprets the teaching of the Bible in terms of deliverance from unjust economics, political and social conditions. It began as a movement within the Roman Catholic Church in Latin America in the 1950s-1960s. The term was coined in 1971 by Gustavo Gutiérrez, a Peruvian priest.

LITURGY. The form which is followed in public worship. Those who claim not to be liturgical tend to follow the same rut, even though it is not planned or written.

MATERIALIST. This view of mankind holds that we are merely physical. This view is found in Marxism, which teaches that our identity is found in our physical labor. It is also found in behaviorism, which teaches that man is merely a machine to be programmed.

MEANS of GRACE. The divinely ordained channels through which God's grace is received.

MILLENNIUM. This term is based on the Latin word for *thousand*. The Greek word used in Revelation 20:1-6 to refer to a period of a thousand years is *chilia*. The Latin term for a thousand-year period is *millennium*. Differing interpretations of this passage have produced differing millennial views. Historically the terms *millenarians*, *chiliasts*, and *adventists* have all referred to premillennialists.

Premillennialists teach that this millennial period of time begins with the return of Christ. Postmillennialists believe Christ returns *after* this period of time. Amillennialists believe this period of time marks the time between Christ's first and second coming.

MONERGISM means that only one person is working, in contrast to *synergism*. Calvinism teaches that since man is unable to do anything to save himself, God must first regenerate him and then he will repent and believe *after* he is born again.

MYSTICISM is an emphasis on subjective personal experience rather than the objective Word of God. Mysticism becomes dangerous when it leads people to arrive at doctrinal conclusions which are based on their own revelation and which contradict the revelation of the Scriptures.

ONTOLOGICAL. This term refers to the nature or essence of being or existence. It is a branch of philosophy which deals with metaphysics. It is based on the Greek word *ontos* which means *being*. In contrast, epistemology, another branch of philosophy, deals with how we procure knowledge.

ORDO SALUTIS. The order of the salvation process.

ORIGINAL GUILT. While we share the effects of the fall, this phrase deals with whether the human race incurs the guilt of Adam's fall. Arminius rejected original guilt. Wesley taught that original guilt was cancelled as an unconditional benefit of the atonement.

ORIGINAL SIN. This term describes the corrupt nature that mankind inherited due to Adam's original act of sin. Pelagianism and liberalism reject this doctrine, affirming instead the basic goodness of mankind.

PANENTHEISM is a belief system which posits that God personally exists, interpenetrates every part of nature, and timelessly extends beyond it. *Panentheism* differs from *pantheism*, which holds that God is not a distinct being but is synonymous with the universe. *Panentheism* is the attempt to apply Alfred North Whitehead's process philosophy to the nature of God.

PATRISTICS is the study of the writings of the church fathers of the first five centuries, especially Athanasius, Basil, Gregory of Nazianzen, John Chrysostom, Ambrose, Augustine, Jerome and Gregory the Great — the eight doctors of the early Church.

PELAGIAN. Pelagius was a late fourth century theologian who taught that Adam was created spiritually neutral and that Adam's sin injured only himself. Each person enters the world without inherited depravity and can choose either good or evil. Salvation is based upon human choice and not divine grace. Man has the ability to fulfill all that God requires. Pelagianism was formally condemned as a heresy by the General Council of Ephesus in AD 431.

PENAL. The word refers to the punishment for breaking the law. It is employed in the doctrine of the atonement to describe the necessity for satisfaction of the law of God. Penal substitution means that Christ was punished for our sins.

PLENARY INSPIRATION. The term *plenary* means that Scripture is fully inspired — not simply the sections which speak to us.

POSTMILLENNIALISM teaches the kingdom was established at Christ's first advent, but its full influence has not yet been realized. It is both a present reality and a future hope. The kingdom is extended through the preaching of the gospel and the saving work of the Holy Spirit. Christ physically returns after this period, however long, to raise the dead and judge the world.

PREMILLENNIALISM teaches that Christ must physically return and set up his kingdom before the millennium can begin. Dispensationalism is a more recent variety of premillennialism. Historic premillennialism does not make the radical distinction between Israel and the church, as dispensationalists do. However, premillennialists do not believe the millennium will begin until

Christ physically returns. They believe the millennium will be a time when Jesus Christ sits on a throne in Jerusalem and rules this world for a thousand years.

PRESBYTERIAN. The Greek word *presbuteros* means elder. Thus, a presbyterian form of church government is elder rule. A presbyterian government differs from an episcopal government since the elders are elected. A group of elders is called a *session*. Members of the session from several local presbyterian congregations comprise the *presbytery*.

PRETERIST is from the Latin word *praeteritus*, meaning past or gone by. In biblical interpretation it means that most of what was symbolized in the book of Revelation took place in the first century after Christ's first coming.

PREVENIENT is from two Latin words, *prae*—before and *venire*—to come. Preventing or prevenient grace, as used by Wesley, means the grace of God which precedes or comes before human action. He understood that the grace of God enables a sinner to repent and believe. In more modern language the equivalent term would be *preliminary*.

PROGRESSIVE REVELATION means that God's revelation came incrementally, building upon what had previously been disclosed. The culmination of his revelation came in the incarnation of Jesus Christ, as Hebrews 1:1-2 explains.

PROTESTANT. John Wycliffe first coined this term with his book *Protestatio* in 1378 in protest of abuses within Roman Catholicism. The Protestant Reformation spanned the fourteenth to seventeenth centuries. While October 31, 1517, the day Martin Luther posted his Ninety-Five Theses, is often considered the birth of the Reformation, Wycliffe is properly called "the morning star of the Reformation."

PROVIDENCE. This word describes the wisdom and power which God continually exercises in his preservation and government of the world.

QUADRILATERAL. Properly understood, this term describes the primacy of scriptural authority, complemented by tradition, reason, and experience. The term was coined by Albert Outler in 1964 and has since often been distorted to imply that there are four equal sources of authority. Liberalism has tended to shop for the source that they think best supports their opinions.

RAPTURE. 1 Thessalonians 4:17 is the only place where *harpazo* is used to describe a catching away or snatching which denotes a positive and corporate action. The Vulgate translation here used the Latin term *rapio*, from which rapture comes. Dispensationalists, however, make the "rapture" a coming of Christ separate from his second advent.

REVELATION. Our knowledge of God is based on his self-disclosure. While philosophy is mankind's attempt to discover truth, *revelation* means that God took the initiative to make himself known. His revelation initially took the form of direct communication, then his revelation through Jesus Christ, and finally the inspiration of the Holy Spirit.

SACERDOTAL. The belief that salvation comes primarily through the sacraments administered by the church. This implies a corporate view of salvation.

SACRAMENTS. A sacrament is a symbolic ritual which was instituted by Christ and is commanded for his church to observe. Both baptism and the Lord's Supper meet the criteria of a sacrament. They serve as signs and seals of the covenant and are a means of grace. They are more than ordinances, but they are less than salvific.

SACRAMENTALISM exalts the sacraments to the point that faith for salvation is placed in the proper observance of ritual. While the sacraments are a means of grace, participating in baptism or the Lord's Supper does not automatically result in conversion.

SANCTIFICATION The Hebrew word *qadosh* describes the state of consecration that existed when a person or object was set apart or separated for holy use. In the NT *hagiasmos* does not refer primarily to a ritual act, but to a moral condition. When the word *sanctification* is found in Scripture it usually refers to initial sanctification unless qualified by another word such as *entire* or *wholly*.

SCRIPTURE or **SCRIPTURES**. The term *Scripture* refers to the body of sixty-six books which were inspired by the Holy Spirt and contain God's revelation to mankind. When used in the plural, *Scriptures* refer to the sixty-six books.

SEMI-PELAGIAN. This position accepts the doctrine of original sin, but believes that mankind inherently has the power to repent and believe without preliminary grace.

SEMI-AUGUSTINIAN. This position holds that man has no ability to save himself. Therefore, God must initiate the process and man can be saved only when the Holy Spirit provides saving faith. However, unlike the full Augustinian position which is also Calvinism, this position rejects monergism. This is the true Wesleyan-Arminian position, which Augustine also held before his debates with Pelagius.

SEPTUAGINT. The Greek translation of the OT done around the third century BC. Tradition claims that it was requested by the Egyptian ruler Ptolemy II for the Jewish community in Egypt, and the work was done by seventy Jewish scholars. Thus, the word *septuagint* means seventy and so the translation is often abbreviated as *LXX*.

SINFUL NATURE. The tendency toward sin which we inherited from Adam. This amounts to a depravity which affects every facet of our personhood and renders us completely unable to save ourselves. However, it should not be understood as a substance which can be eradicated. The Bible does not refer to "carnality" as an entity. Rather, this sinful nature is a twist, a distortion, and inward bent that puts our will above God's will.

SOLIFIDIANISM. The danger of an overemphasis on faith can lead to a mere intellectual assent which produces no conversion or a one-time decision which produces no fruit.

SOTERIOLOGY. The Greek word for salvation is *soteria*. Thus, the doctrines of salvation are referred to as soteriology.

SPECIAL REVELATION. This term refers to the Holy Scriptures, in contrast to general or natural revelation.

SYNERGISM. This concept means that man is enabled to respond and work with the Holy Spirit due to preliminary grace. Therefore, although we are dead in sin we are enabled to cooperate, fulfilling the demands to repent and believe, as we are empowered by the Holy Spirit.

THEODICY. The attempt to uphold and vindicate God's complete goodness in the face of evil. This word is composed of the Greek word for *God - theos* and the word for *justice - dike*.
THEOPHANY. A visible manifestation or epiphany of God to human beings. This word is based on the Greek word for *God - theos* and the word for *phainein - to show*.

THEOSIS literally means *becoming god* or *deification*. This term can refer to the pantheistic identification between God and humanity or a participation, through grace, in the divine life, as described in 2 Peter 1:4. Thus, it can mean either union, in which humanity literally becomes divine, or communion, in which humanity becomes *like* God.

TOTAL DEPRAVITY. As the result of man's original sin through Adam, we inherit a sinful nature which renders us completely unable to save ourselves. Our depravity is total since it affects our entire being — our intellect, our emotions, and our will.

TRIBULATION. Matthew 24:21 speaks of a period of "great tribulation." Preterists take this to be a first-century event; futurists think it refers to a future event, based upon a gap in Daniel's seventy weeks. Revelation speaks of 42 months and 1260 days in 11:2-3 and "time, times and half a time" in 12:14, but never of a seven-year tribulation. Assuming this tribulation is future, premillennialists differ over whether the rapture of the church comes at the beginning (pretribulation), middle (midtribulation), pre-wrath, end (posttribulation) or partial.

TRICHOTOMY. This view of mankind attempts to divide the soul and spirit. This division of soul and spirit, along with the human body, comprise three parts.

WITNESS of the SPIRIT. The direct assurance of the Holy Spirit to the believer that he is forgiven and accepted by God. This direct assurance is corroborated by the indirect witness of a good conscience.

ZIONISM. The movement for the return of the Jewish people to their ancient homeland. This idea was first articulated by Theodor Herzl in 1896. It was advanced through the Balfour Declaration in 1917, and implemented in 1948 when the state of Israel was founded. Some Christians have embraced Zionism, based on the assumption that the land of Palestine was unconditionally promised to them forever. Such assumptions are found within dispensationalism.

www.ingramcontent.com/pod-product-compliance
Lightning Source LLC
Chambersburg PA
CBHW050326270326
41926CB00016B/3336